INTRODUCTION TO
POLICING

To Officer Richard Williams,

One of the finest law men

I have ever known.

Gero

I would like to dedicate my efforts on this book to my father,
Louis F. Scaramella, M.D. and the memory of my dear mother, Nina M. Scaramella,
née Lenti. But for their unyielding love, support, and emphasis on the importance of a good
education, my direction in life may very well have gone astray. I would also like to dedicate
this work to my wife, Robin., Thank you for your love, patience, understanding, and support.
Finally, much of my work on this book is dedicated to the memory of the late Officer Philip
Handzel, a true legend of the Chicago Police Department.

—Gene L. Scaramella

For Pete—a real pistol!

—Steven M. Cox

To my parents, William H. and Toby McCamey, who sacrificed so much;
my wife Jody, for her love and support; and Troy and Diana Eeten for providing
the best grandchildren ever—Trace and Macy!

—William P. McCamey

INTRODUCTION TO
POLICING

Gene L. Scaramella

Ellis University

Steven M. Cox

Western Illinois University

William P. McCamey

Western Illinois University

Los Angeles | London | New Delhi
Singapore | Washington DC

For information:

SAGE Publications, Inc.
2455 Teller Road
Thousand Oaks, California 91320
E-mail: order@sagepub.com

SAGE Publications Ltd.
1 Oliver's Yard
55 City Road,
London EC1Y 1SP
United Kingdom

SAGE Publications India Pvt. Ltd.
B 1/I 1 Mohan Cooperative Industrial Area
Mathura Road, New Delhi 110 044
India

SAGE Publications Asia-Pacific Pte. Ltd.
33 Pekin Street #02-01
Far East Square
Singapore 048763

Printed in the United States of America

Library of Congress Cataloging-in-Publication Data

Scaramella, Gene L.
    Introduction to policing / Gene Scaramella, Steven M. Cox, William P. McCamey.
        p. cm.
    Completely reorganized and updated version of: Contemporary municipal policing / William P. McCamey, Gene L. Scaramella, Steven M. Cox. c2003.
    Includes bibliographical references and index.
    ISBN 978-1-4129-7530-8 (pbk.)
    1. Police—United States. 2. Community policing—United States. I. Cox, Steven M. II. McCamey, William. III. McCamey, William. Contemporary municipal policing. IV. Title.

HV8139.S32 2011
363.20973—dc22   2010029243

This book is printed on acid-free paper.

10   11   12   13   14   10   9   8   7   6   5   4   3   2   1

Acquisitions Editor:	Jerry Westby
Associate Editor:	Ashley Conlon
Assistant Editor:	Eve Oettinger
Editorial Assistant:	Erim Sarbuland
Production Editor:	Brittany Bauhaus
Permissions Editor:	Karen Ehrmann
Copy Editor:	Jenifer Dill
Typesetter:	C&M Digitals (P) Ltd.
Proofreader:	Eleni-Maria Georgiou
Indexer:	Diggs Publication Services, Inc.
Cover Designer:	Candice Harman
Marketing Manager:	Erica Deluca

Brief Contents

Detailed Contents

Preface

Police in the United States operate in a climate of constant change. One of the more recent and significant changes that U.S. police officials must come to terms with is the global nature of many of the problems they now face. The political, economic, and social conditions that exist throughout the world play an increasingly complex role in the organizational and functional dynamics of the police community. Police executives must think and plan globally in a spirit of interagency cooperation more now than at any point in history.

As we continue into the second decade of the 21st century, we expect police officers to continue to perform traditional tasks related to law enforcement and order maintenance and, at the same time, to become problem solvers, community organizers, and terrorism preventers. In addition, more than ever before, we expect them to perform these diverse tasks by exercising discretion wisely and within an ethical framework. As police intervene in our daily lives, many of us are suspicious of their motives and uneasy in their presence. On one hand, we recognize their role in an orderly society; on the other hand, we would prefer that they intervene in our lives only if and when we need them. It is our belief that much of the current criticism of and dissatisfaction among the police results from confusion over the appropriate role of the police and the misleading and sometimes unreasonable expectations that arise as a result of that confusion.

More than 175 years ago, Sir Robert Peel developed and promoted a model for policing that has been periodically ignored and emphasized. Many of the basic tenets of that model have been resurrected in the form of community policing and its most recent evolutions. We have come to realize, once again, that a basic requirement for effective, efficient, civil policing is a meaningful partnership between the police and other citizens. Only when such a partnership exists can the police perform their tasks as problem solvers, service providers, and occasional law enforcers because only then will the public provide the support and resources necessary for the successful performance of these tasks. This partnership must be based on open, two-way communication between the police and other citizens in the joint venture of order maintenance and law enforcement.

Although we discuss a variety of topics separately in this text, it is important to recognize that they are all interrelated and must be considered as part of the network of policing. Stresses and strains in any one area will have repercussions in others, and the relationships between the various parts must be considered if policing is to make sense.

Finally, it is important to note that the terms *policing* and *law enforcement* are not synonymous. The latter constitutes only a small, though critical, part of the former. The basic task of the police in any society is not law enforcement, but problem solving (sometimes referred to as *order maintenance*), which may or may not include, in any given encounter, law enforcement. What follows is our attempt, based on our research, collective observations and interactions, and personal experiences to acquaint readers with the complex and dynamic field of policing.

❖ The Organization

This text provides readers with an examination of an extensive list of topics that range from recruitment, selection, training, education, and operational constructs of policing to strategies based on cutting edge research and practice. In addition, we focus on promoting ethical and professional practices, operating effectively within a multicultural society, expanding the use of and reliance on technology, and preventing and investigating complex forms of criminal behavior. We also discuss transnational, organized, and white collar crime and the formation of efficient and productive partnerships with the private security industry in considerable detail. Our intent is to provide readers with academically sound and contemporary research and theory tempered by our real life experiences in law enforcement.

This book consists of 15 chapters that provide readers with thought provoking and contemporary issues that underscore today's challenging world of policing. The text begins with a discussion of past and current policing strategies in Chapter 1, which provides context for the issues discussed in subsequent chapters. Then, Chapters 2, 3, and 4 focus on the human dynamics that affect policing, such as recruitment, selection and promotion of police officers, training and education, and the subcultural influences that often determine individual and group decision making. Chapters 5, 6, and 7 provide an examination of institutional and organizational structures and processes pertaining to the law, of various styles or forms of police practice, and of administrative and leadership issues. Then, Chapters 8, 9, 10, and 11 address social, political, and economic forces affecting the field, such as ethics and accountability, forms of misconduct, the changing population in terms of racial and ethnic diversity, relations with and perceptions of police by the citizenries they serve, and various strategies that address these social issues, such as community-based policing, intelligence-led policing, and various other policing strategies. The book concludes with Chapters 12, 13, 14, and 15, which deal with recent factors affecting the field of policing, including issues such as the rapid expansion of technology, the impact of global issues such as terrorism and other forms of transnational crime, the increasing role of the private security industry on police functions, and predictions concerning changes that might be in store for the field of policing in the years to come.

❖ Key Features of the Text

Each chapter contains a variety of thought-provoking exercises and highlights, along with other supplemental materials. These unique features include the following:

Around the World. This feature highlights relevant topics in an international context to afford readers the opportunity to consider, from a worldwide perspective, what might otherwise be viewed as problems unique to U.S. police agencies. Resources for further exploration are also provided.

You Decide. This feature presents students with realistic dilemmas that might be encountered during a career in policing. Students are encouraged to consider possible solutions to these dilemmas using information from the text, other sources, or personal experiences. This feature should help promote spirited classroom discussions.

Case in Point. This feature includes real life examples from newspaper articles and other similar publications to emphasize one or more of the major issues associated with each chapter.

Police Stories. This feature brings in our personal experiences in the field of policing, and we share with students actual incidents from the past in the hope of providing meaningful learning experiences. Students might consider what they would do under similar circumstances.

In addition to these features, each chapter also includes a set of learning objectives, key terms and phrases, 8 to 10 discussion questions based on those learning objectives, and three to five Internet exercises.

We hope that these key features will make this text even more useful as you develop a deeper understanding of the complex and dynamic field of policing.

❖ Ancillaries

Additional ancillary materials further support and enhance the learning goals of *Introduction to Policing.* These ancillary materials include the following:

Instructor Teaching Site: www.sagepub.com/scaramella

This password protected instructor site offers instructors a variety of resources that supplement the book material, including:

- An **electronic test bank**, available to PCs and Macs through Diploma software, offers a diverse set of test questions and answers to aid instructors in assessing students' progress and understanding. The software allows for test creation and customization and each chapter includes multiple choice, true/false, short-answer and essay questions. The test bank is also available in Microsoft Word.
- **PowerPoint presentations** designed to assist with lecture and review, highlighting essential content, features, and artwork from the book.
- **Lecture notes** have been provided for each chapter that can be used to structure daily lesson plans.

- **Sample Course Syllabi**—for semester, quarter, and online classes—provide suggested models for instructors to use when creating the syllabi for their courses.
- **Informative websites** provide your students with another source of enrichment material related to each chapter's content.

Student Study Site: www.sagepub.com/scaramella

This open-access student study site provides a variety of additional resources to build on students' understanding of the book content and extend their learning beyond the classroom. The site includes:

- **Self quizzes** with 10-15 multiple-choice and true/false questions for every chapter allow students to independently assess their progress in learning course material.
- **E-Flashcards** reinforce student understanding and learning of key terms and concepts that are outlined in the book.
- **Video Clips** of the authors recounting stories from when they were policemen.
- **Podcasts and Audio Clips:** Each chapter includes links to podcasts, which cover important topics and are designed to supplement key points within the text.
- Carefully selected, web-based **video link** resources feature relevant content for use in independent and classroom-based exploration of key topics.
- **Web resources** provide links to relevant websites for further research on important chapter topics.
- A "**Learning from SAGE Journal Articles**" feature provides access to recent, relevant full-text articles from SAGE's leading research journals. Each article supports and expands on the concepts presented in the chapter. Discussion questions are also provided to focus and guide student interpretation.

❖ Acknowledgments

Thanks to Professors Richard Ward, Paul Ilsley, Michael Hazlett, John Wade, Matthew Lippman, David Harpool, Bob Fischer, Giri Raj Gupta, Denny Bliss, Terry Campbell, Sandy Yeh, Bill Lin, Jennifer Allen, John Conrad, John Song, Stan Cunningham, and Don Bytner for their friendship, guidance, encouragement, and contributions to the book. Thanks also to the many police officers who shared their experiences with us over the years, including O. J. Clark, Jerry Bratcher, Mark Fleischhauer, Brian Howerton, Jerry Friend, Bill Hedeen, Bob Elliott, Donna Cox, Michael Holub, Dwight Baird, John Harris, William Lansdowne, Michael Ruth, Anthony Abbate, Timothy Bolger, and Richard Williams. And thanks to Judges John D. Tourtelot, Edward R. Danner, and Thomas J. Homer.

Finally, we offer a huge debt of gratitude to Jerry Westby, Elise Caffee, and Nichole O'Grady of Sage Publications for making this book become a reality. We apologize for any gray hairs we may have caused each of you.

The authors and SAGE gratefully acknowledge the contributions of the following reviewers:

Earl Ballou, *Palo Alto College*

Lorenzo Boyd, *Fayetteville State University*

Obie Clayton, *Morehouse College*

Jennifer Estis-Sumerel, *Itawamba Community College–Tupelo*

Arthur Haydn, *Kentucky State University*

Daniel Howard, *Rutgers University*

Richard Kania, *Jacksonville State University*

Connie Koski, *University of Nebraska at Omaha*

Douglas Larkins, *Arkansas State University–Beebe*

Thomas O'Connor, *Austin Peay State University*

Jeffrey Rush, *Austin Peay State University*

Rupendra Simlot, *Richard Stockton College*

As always, your comments and concerns are welcomed.

—G.L.S
GScaramella@ellis.edu

—W.P.M
W-McCamey@wiu.edu

—S.M.C
sm-cox1@wiu.edu

Policing in America

CHAPTER LEARNING OBJECTIVES

- Describe the difficulty associated with attempting to make generalizations about the police and the functions they perform.
- Highlight the evolution of American police organizations.
- Identify some of the problematic issues currently encountered by police agencies.
- Compare and contrast the problems faced by police working in democratic societies versus those working in non-democratic societies.
- Identify and elaborate on the pros and cons of the effects of politics on the American police.
- Evaluate at least three recent policing strategies in terms of their effectiveness.
- Describe to what extent the public influences policing strategies and offer some examples to support your claim.

Every day, tens of thousands of American citizens don uniforms, pin on badges and name tags, and strap on equipment belts that may carry a firearm, extra ammunition, handcuffs, pepper spray, Taser, and baton. These citizens assemble at distinctively marked locations and disperse from these locations carrying radios and cell phones in clearly marked and equipped vehicles designed to make them easily identifiable. They go forth as police officers to spend their tours of duty providing services, maintaining order, and occasionally enforcing the law in large metropolitan, suburban, and rural areas as well as on college campuses, on the borders between the United States and other countries, in airports and harbors, and in dozens of other settings.

❖ Pʜᴏᴛᴏ **1.1a & 1.1b**   The evolution of policing through the years is remarkable.

At the same time, thousands of other American citizens conceal their badges and firearms under street or business attire and assemble at distinctively marked locations, both in and out of the United States, to work on current investigations through the use of phones and computers or to disperse from these locations in unmarked vehicles to conduct surveillance and interviews and make arrests.

Still other Americans attempt to conceal their identities as police officers, seldom visit the aforementioned distinctive locations, and attempt to pass themselves off as members of groups engaged in criminal activities in order to obtain information that will lead to arrests.

Tens of thousands of other American citizens don uniforms more or less similar to those of the police, pin on badges similar but not identical to those of police officers, arm themselves with firearms, pepper spray, Tasers, and handcuffs and proceed in marked vehicles to work in gated communities, shopping malls, industrial areas, and a wide variety of other locations to provide security for people and property. As is the case with public police personnel, these security personnel differ greatly in terms of training, education, and competency.

Simultaneously, thousands of other Americans go to work in police agencies of all types and sizes as non sworn technicians, communications personnel, administrative assistants, and in dozens of other capacities.

American police personnel are employed at the international, national, state, county, and municipal levels. Based on data provided by the Federal Bureau of Investigation (FBI) for the year 2004, over 800,000 sworn police personnel were employed at the federal, state, and local (city, county, suburban) levels throughout the United States in almost 18,000 agencies (Bureau of Justice Statistics, 2007). Table 1.1 shows the distribution of public police personnel by type of agency. Overall, there were 3.6 sworn police officers per 1,000 citizens in the United States. These officers worked in agencies ranging in size from 35,000 (New York City) to agencies with only one sworn officer (more than 20 in the state of New York alone). Some agencies have no full-time sworn personnel but hire a number of part-time officers or contract with outside agencies to provide their police services. Many agencies have and utilize modern technological equipment, while others lack such equipment. Some officers are well

Table 1.1 Law Enforcement Statistics

Type of agency	Number of agencies	Number of full-time sworn officers	
Total		836,787	
All State and local	17,876	731,903	
Local police	12,766	446,974	
Sheriff	3,067	175,018	
Primary State	49	58,190	
Special jurisdiction	1,481	49,398	
Constable/Marshal	513	2,323	
Federal*		104,884	

Source: Bureau of Justice Statistics (2007)

Note: Special jurisdiction category includes both state-level and local-level agencies. Consolidated police-sheriffs are included under local police category. Agency counts exclude those operating on a part-time basis.

*Nonmilitary federal officers authorized to carry firearms and make arrests.

trained, others receive very little training. Some intervene in the daily lives of their fellow citizens routinely, others do not. Some are held in high regard by their fellow citizens, others are not.

Estimates of private security and contract personnel indicate that between 11,000 and 15,000 companies employ at least 1.2 million private security personnel (Gamiz, 2010). These security personnel work in a number of different occupations ranging from private security or contract guards to executive protection to private eyes to industrial security to contract employees for the military. They are hired to protect against fire, theft, vandalism, terrorism, and illegal activity and to enforce laws on their employers' property. The private security industry is considered one of the fastest growing industries in the nation, with an expected growth rate of 17% by 2016 (Gamiz, 2010). We will have much more to say about private or contract security in Chapter 14.

In the following chapters, we discuss important issues common to municipal, county, state, and federal police officers. Issues concerning international and private police are also examined. Let's begin by examining the idea and origins of public police and their functions in a democratic society.

❖ The Concept of Police

Every society needs citizens who serve as mediators and arbitrators to settle disputes among its members. The term *police* is derived from the Greek words *polis* and *politeuein*, which refer to being a citizen who participates in the affairs of a city or state. There is no better way of describing the role of the contemporary police officer—he or she is a citizen who is actively involved in the affairs of a city or state. (*State* here may refer to the federal level as well as to a specific state, as in *affairs of state*.)

In all modern societies, if mediation and arbitration fail, specially designated citizens (police officers in the general sense of the word) are appointed to apprehend those who appear to have violated the rights of others and to bring them before other specially designated citizens (prosecutors, judges) who have authority to sanction undesirable behavior. The conflicting demands of various groups must all be accommodated (at least to the point of being heard) in a democratic society, and they virtually guarantee that not all parties can be satisfied at the same time. (For an example, see You Decide 1.1.) Bittner (1974) argued that the police alone in civilian society can impose, and in some circumstances coerce, solutions upon citizens when problematic or emergency situations arise (such as making arrests on the one hand and providing services for the physically or mentally ill on the other).

YOU DECIDE 1.1

In the United States, both the desire to protect individual rights and the need to insure an orderly society are apparent. In order to help accomplish the latter, police officers frequently intervene in the daily affairs of private citizens (when enforcing traffic laws or dealing with domestic violence, for example). Yet many, if not most, Americans would prefer that the government not interfere in the regulation of their daily activities (though they may be perfectly willing to have the police intervene in the daily activities of others). Police intervention in areas that citizens generally regard as private generates suspicion and hostility toward the police. Yet with increasing concerns over terrorism, criminality, and violence, citizens demand that the police address these concerns but otherwise leave them to their own pursuits. This often places individual police officers in difficult positions—both intervention and lack of intervention may lead to public criticism. Based on this analysis,

1. Do you think this dilemma can be resolved in a democratic society?
   1a. If not, are there things the police can do to alleviate hostility toward them?
   1b. If so, how can the dilemma be resolved?

2. What effect, if any, would the dilemma have on you if you were considering policing as a career?

Further, in America, many citizens have been and remain opposed to the idea of a centralized police force because they fear that such a force might become an instrument of government repression. In this respect, the police simply followed the lead of other government entities that were also decentralized (at the levels of state, county, and municipality, for example) for the same reason—fear of repression by a strong, centralized government with no local representation. The desire to protect individual rights is strong, yet the need to insure some degree of order in society is also apparent. In a democratic nation, we expect the police to operate in terms of our defining principles, which include equal treatment, respect for individual liberty, and accountability, among others.

In order to maintain order and enforce the law, police must be granted the right to intervene in the daily affairs of private citizens. Regulation of morals, enforcement of traffic laws, mediation of domestic disputes, dealing with juveniles, and other activities engaged in by the police require such intervention. Yet many early settlers in America came precisely because they did not want government intervention in and regulation of their daily activities. Predictably, then, police intervention in areas that citizens generally regard as private generates suspicion and hostility toward the police. Nonetheless, with increasing demands for public order come increasing intolerance of criminality, violence, and riotous behavior. Citizens want the police to address their concerns and to solve the problems they bring to the attention of the police, but otherwise to leave them to their own pursuits (Toch & Grant, 1991, p. 3).

Those responsible for policing society, then, occupy inherently problematic positions. A brief overview of the history of American policing may help us understand the origins and consequences of some of the issues encountered by police officers in a democratic society. In order to understand why the police encounter some of these issues, however, we should first note that the terms *police officer* and *law enforcement officer* are sometimes viewed as interchangeable. In fact, the term law enforcement officer describes very little of what police officers do. The police in the United States are primarily providers of services. Among the services they provide are law enforcement, order maintenance, and crime prevention. As Davis (1978) noted, the police "are members of the public who are paid to give full-time attention to duties which are incumbent upon every citizen, in the interests of community welfare and existence" (p. 7). However, large segments of the public prefer to leave some or all of these duties to the police—especially the duty of law enforcement. Further, police activities in the area of law enforcement tend to be far more exciting and thus are far more likely to be reported than are service activities. As a result, we often evaluate the police on their success in this area rather than on the more frequent activities of order maintenance and service. In short, the police provide far more than law enforcement to the communities they serve and devote a relatively small portion of their time to law enforcement activities.

❖ History of American Policing: An Overview

Police in America have provided and continue to provide an extremely wide range of services, many of which, as we shall see, have little to do with crime or law enforcement. Each police department exists in its own context. Policing in a large metropolitan area may be considerably different from policing in a small rural community in terms of the frequency of certain types of activities and the degree of specialization within the department, though the types of services provided are basically the same. Similarly, policing at the local, state, and federal levels share some underlying functions, but each addresses unique issues as well. Further, within any given police agency, each officer has considerable discretion with respect to the way in which he or she provides services. The diversity in American police organizations makes them unique and is often confusing to foreign visitors familiar with more centralized police services. Historical analysis will reveal the roots of many current issues in policing, such as corruption, brutality, discretion, professionalism, and inefficiency, and help clarify the nature of police operations in the United States.

Early History of Policing

To understand the complexities and variations in policing today, it is useful to revisit the historical traditions that led to contemporary police operations. The origins of policing date back to ancient empires around the world. The Greeks, Romans, Egyptians, Spartans, Israelis, Chinese, and members of other civilizations throughout medieval times to the present have all had forms of policing to enforce laws and maintain order. While policing has international historical roots, in the United States most of these roots can be traced to England. Lee (1971) noted the following:

> Our English police system . . . rests on foundations designed with the full approval of the people . . . and has been slowly molded by the careful hand of experience, developing as a rule along the line of least resistance, now in advance of the general intelligence of the country, now lagging far behind, but always in the long run adjusting itself to the popular temper, always consistent with local self government. . . ."

While Lee was speaking of the development of the police in England, everything he says can be applied to policing in the United States as well, especially, perhaps, because the origins of American policing rest in England. (p. xxvii)

English settlers (about 90% of all early settlers) in America brought with them a *night watch system* that required able-bodied males to donate their time to help protect the cities. As was the case in England, those who could afford to do so often hired others to serve their tours, and those who served were not particularly effective. During this time period, citizens often resolved disputes among themselves. Such resolution involved intergenerational blood feuds, eye-gouging, gunfights, and duels (Miller, 2000). As cities grew larger and more heterogeneous, voluntary citizen participation in law enforcement and order maintenance became increasingly less effective, and something was needed to replace it. In 1749, residents of Philadelphia convinced legislators to pass a law creating the position of warden. Each warden was authorized to hire as many watchmen as needed, the powers of the watchmen were increased, and they were paid from taxes. Others cities soon adopted similar plans (Johnson, 1981, p. 7). The wardens served warrants and acted as detectives, often recovering stolen items in cooperation with the thieves themselves (Miller, 2000). They also patrolled the streets, but they were not widely respected. In fact, as Walker (1999) indicates, "Colonial law enforcement was inefficient, corrupt, and subject to political interference" (p. 22).

By the 1800s, with the rapid growth of cities, crime and mob violence had become problems in both British and American cities. In response, **Sir Robert Peel**, who was then Home Secretary in London, developed municipal policing. Peel believed that the police should be organized along military lines, under government control. He also thought police officers should be men of quiet demeanor and good appearance and should be familiar with the neighborhoods in which they were to police. In addition, he supported a territorial strategy of policing in which officers would walk prescribed beats in order to prevent and deal with crime. Peel and **Patrick Colquhoun** (Superintending Magistrate of the Thames River Police, a forerunner of the Metropolitan police, and author of works on metropolitan policing) put many of these principles into practice in establishing the London Metropolitan Police. By 1870, Peel's territorial strategy, at least, had spread to every major city in America (Lane, 1992, pp. 6–7; Barlow, 2000, p. 166).

In the United States in the early to middle 1800s, day watch systems were established (Philadelphia–1833; Boston–1838; New York–1844; San Francisco–1850; Los Angeles–1851) in America. By the 1850s, day and night watch systems were consolidated to provide 24-hour protection to city dwellers (Berg, 1992, p. 31; Barlow, 2000, pp. 165–166).

By the middle of the 19th century, the main structural elements of American municipal policing had emerged. Watch and ward systems had been replaced, in the cities at least, by centralized, government supported police agencies whose tasks included crime prevention, provision of a wide variety of services to the public, enforcement of morality, and the apprehension of criminals. A large force of uniformed police walked regular beats, had the power to arrest without a warrant, and began to carry revolvers in the late 1850s (Miller, 2000). The concept of preventative policing now included maintenance of order functions such as searching for missing children, mediating quarrels, and helping at fire scenes. Both municipal police and county sheriffs performed these tasks, and over time, these agencies were supplemented by the development of state and federal agencies (Sweatman & Cross, 1989, p. 12).

The Political Era

Although they adopted a good many practices from their British counterparts, American police lacked the central authority of the crown to establish a legitimate mandate for their actions. Small departments acted independently within their jurisdictions. Large departments were divided into precincts that often operated more as small individual departments than as branches of the same organization (Kelling & Moore, 1988, p. 3). Colonists feared government intervention into their daily lives and thus disliked the idea of a centralized police force. Police officers represented the local political party in power rather than the legal system (Conser & Russell, 2000, p. 167; Roberg & Kuykendall, 1993, p. 59).

As a result of the political heterogeneity, officers were often required to enforce unpopular laws in immigrant ethnic neighborhoods and, because of their intimacy with the neighborhoods, were vulnerable to bribes for lax enforcement or non-enforcement (Conser & Russell, 2000, p. 168; Kelling & Moore, 1988, p.4). In addition, the police found themselves in frequent conflict with rioters, union workers and their management counterparts, looters, and others. As a result of such conflicts, the view that the police could remain impartial in administering the law was called into question.

Expectations that the police would be disinterested public servants ran afoul of the realities of urban social and political life. Heterogeneity made it more difficult to determine what behavior was acceptable and what was unacceptable. Moreover, urban diversity encouraged a political life based upon racial and ethnic cleavages as well as clashes of economic interests. Democratic control of police assured that heterogeneous cities would have constant conflicts over police organization and shifts of emphasis depending upon which groups controlled the political machinery at any one time. (Richardson, 1974, pp. 33–34)

Thus, in some cities, such as New York, political corruption and manipulation were built into policing. New York police officers in the 1830s were hired and fired by elected officials who expected those they hired to support them politically and fired those who did not. "The late nineteenth century policeman had a difficult job. He had to maintain order, cope with vice and crime, provide service to people in trouble, and keep his nose clean politically" (Richardson, 1974, p. 47). The police became involved in party politics, including granting immunity from arrest to those in power (Conser & Russell, 2000, p. 168; Lane, 1992, p.12). Corruption and extortion became traditions in many departments, and discipline and professional pride were largely absent from many departments. Police spent most of their time providing services to local supporters, maintaining a reasonable level of social order necessary for the city and local businesses to operate smoothly, and seeking out every opportunity available to them to make money (Barlow & Barlow, 2000).

According to Johnson (1981), America's brand of local self-government gave both citizens and professional politicians considerable influence in policing.

The need to respond to the diverse, often conflicting demands of various constituencies has given American policing a unique character which effects its efficiency as well as its reputation. However one views the police today, it is essential to understand how the theory and practice of politics influenced the nature, successes, and problems of law enforcement. (p. i)

Some attempts to address corruption and related issues were made beginning in the late 1800s (e.g., the **Pendleton Act,** which extended civil service protection to first federal and later state and local employees), but old traditions and perceptions died hard—and in some cases, not at all. One example of such traditions is the **sheriff,** who remains a political figure charged with police duties. The term *sheriff* stems from 12th century England and is a contraction of the term *shire reeve,* which referred to an official appointed by the king with the responsibility for keeping the peace and collecting taxes throughout a shire or county. Today in the United States, the sheriff is still typically an elected official and the chief law enforcement officer in the county in which he or she serves.

Another example of tradition is the ownership and use of firearms by Americans, whether for legitimate or illegitimate purposes. As a result of this tradition, and of the not infrequent killing of unarmed officers by armed offenders, many American police officers purchased and carried their own firearms by the middle of the 19th century. Though there were many critics of an armed police force, the reality was that Americans, unlike their British counterparts, believed that every citizen had the right to own firearms, thus making guns a part of American culture. By the 1840s, firearms were frequently used by one citizen against another, and police officers could never be sure when a disorderly citizen might have a gun (Johnson, 1981, pp. 29–30). Still, the officer was expected to intervene in order to keep disputes between a small number of people over relatively minor issues from growing into something more serious. Eventually, the public accepted an armed police because there appeared to be no other alternative (Johnson, 1981, pp. 29–30).

Throughout most of the 19th and into the 20th century, the basic qualification for becoming a police officer was a political connection, rather than a demonstrated ability (Barlow, 2000, p. 167; Roberg & Kuykendall, 1993, pp. 61-66). Men who had no education, but had criminal records and health problems, were hired as police officers (Walker, 1999). Training was practically nonexistent, with most new officers being handed equipment and an assignment and told to "hit the streets." Officers were expected to handle whatever problems they encountered while patrolling their beats, not simply to enforce the law. The lack of strong central administration, the influence of politicians, and the neighborhood ties between the police and the people ensured a partisan process of policing (Langworthy & Travis, 1999). The degree of decentralization facilitated fragmented police services, and the lack of a central command led to inconsistency, confusion, and eventually a call for reform. "For the patrolman, unless he was exceptionally stubborn or a notoriously slow learner, the moral was clear: if you want to get along, go along" (Richardson, 1974, p. 57). The police were a part of the political machinery; and politicians were seldom interested in impartial justice. The police became a mechanism that permitted politicians to solidify their power by controlling political adversaries and assisting friends and allies (Gaines, Kappeler, & Vaughn, 1999). Arrests were of little importance; the primary mission of the police was to provide services to citizens and garner votes for politicians. The police provided a range of services, including babysitting at the police station, helping people find employment, feeding the homeless, and basic medical care. The recruitment of neighborhood residents as police coupled with the level of decentralization of police services ensured that the police reflected community values in their law enforcement and order-maintenance decisions (Langworthy & Travis, 1999). However, with no accountability for either the politicians or the police, corruption, graft, and bribery reached a new level. Not infrequently, police promotions and assignments were auctioned to the highest bidder and illegal operations, including gambling halls and brothels, made monthly contributions to police officers. While some improvements resulted from reform efforts, political motivations continued to plague the selection of both officers and chiefs. "Too many chiefs were simply fifty-five-year-old patrolmen" (Richardson, 1974, p. 70).

This tradition continued into the 20th century and is, indeed, still deep-rooted in policing. The hiring and firing of police chiefs accompanying changes in the political leadership of communities continues today, as do attempts on behalf of politicians to influence the daily activity of police officers, chiefs, and sheriffs (Barlow, 2000, p. 167; Jackson, 2000). Such attempts to control the police raise an interesting issue. In a democratic society, how are the police to be controlled? How do we hold the police accountable and insure that they are responsive to the concerns of the citizens they serve? "The suggestion that police agencies be directly supervised by elected municipal executives conjures up the image of police administrators beholden to various interests—including criminal elements—on whose continued support the elected mayor, their boss, may depend . . . is this not one of the costs of operating under our system of government" (Goldstein, 1977, pp. 151–152)? We depend on elected representatives to convey our needs and desires to the institutions over which they preside.

Thus, in our society, politics and policing are inevitably interwoven, and while we must be constantly alert to potential problems that result from this relationship, this is both necessary and desirable in a democratic society.

The Reform Era

Serious attempts to professionalize the police began to materialize in the late 1800s and early 1900s. Police professionalization was recognized as an important issue by August Vollmer, Chief of Police in Berkeley, CA from 1905 to 1932 and father of modern police management systems, at least as early as 1909. In part because of the depression, policing became more attractive to young men who in better times might have sought other employment, thus making it possible to recruit and select qualified police officers. August Vollmer, Arthur Neiderhoffer, William Parker, and O.W. Wilson, among others, promoted professionalism and higher education for police officers that, coupled with the impact of various reform movements, began to show positive results. The goal of police reform was to centralize police administration, improve the quality of police personnel, and destroy the power of the political bosses (Langworthy & Travis, 1999). Reformers rapidly infused science into policing through improved record keeping, fingerprinting, serology, and criminal investigation. Training academies in which these and other subjects were taught became more common, and promotion and selection based on merit (often through the use of civil service testing) was emphasized.

As reformers attempted to define policing as a profession, the service role of the police changed into more of a crime-fighting role. The passage of the 18th Amendment in 1920 and the onset of the Great Depression in 1929 placed the police under a new public mandate for crime control and public safety (Lyman, 1999). As a result, police no longer provided the wide range of service activities, including assisting the homeless, babysitting, and helping people locate employment. Reformers began to centralize command and control and to remove the politicians from the police department (Walker, 1999). In addition, reformers adopted military customs and created specialized units, including vice, juvenile, and traffic divisions. However, the historical development of large bureaucratically organized police departments can in part be attributed to a larger movement by government to obtain legitimacy for their agencies by adopting the rational-legal formal structure that placed more emphasis on impersonal rules, laws, and discipline (Barlow & Barlow, 2000). The **reform movement** involved radical reorganization, including strong centralized administrative bureaucracy, highly specialized units, and substantial increases in the number of officers. Concern about the police reached a national level with the appointment by President Hoover of the Wickersham Commission (in 1931). The Commission was formed to investigate rising crime rates, and it directed police away from the service role, challenging them to become law enforcers and to reduce the crime rate. The onset of World War II and the Korean War made recruitment of well qualified officers more difficult during the 1940s and 1950s respectively, and the riots and civil disorders of the late 1960s and early 1970s made policing less attractive to some. During this period, observers of the police, and sometimes the police themselves, seemed to equate technological advances and improved administration with professionalism.

While important technological advances did occur (e.g., the use of patrol cars, telephones, telegraph, and radios), changes in standards, development of ethical codes, education and training provided by those outside policing, and other indicators of professionalism were largely lacking. To be sure, some important changes had occurred. Reformers had identified inappropriate political involvement as a major problem in American policing. Civil service successfully removed some of the patronage and ward influences on police officers. Law and professionalism were established as the bases of police legitimacy. Under these circumstances, policing became a legal and technical matter left to the discretion of professional police executives. "Political influence of any kind on a police department came to be seen as not merely a failure of police leadership but as corruption in policing" (Kelling & Moore, 1988, p. 5).

Policing in the 1960s and 1970s

The 1960s proved to be one of the most challenging eras in American history for the police. The crime rate per 100,000 persons doubled, the civil rights movement began, and anti-war sentiment and urban riots brought police to the center of the maelstrom (Dunham & Alpert, 1997). Furthermore, the United States Supreme Court

❖ **Photo 1.2** Officers must show restraint even when their personal beliefs differ with those of the citizenries that they serve. Of course, as illustrated above, not all officers agree with that philosophy.

placed historic restrictions on police behaviors in *Chimel v. California* (1969), *Terry v. Ohio* (1968), *Spinelli v. United States* (1969), *Escobedo v. Illinois* (1964), *Katz v. United States* (1967), and *Miranda v. Arizona* (1966). At the same time, the social disorder of this period produced fear among the public because it appeared that family, church, and the police were losing their grip on society (Barlow & Barlow, 2000). One result of this fear was that legislators began to pass laws that provided substantial resources to police agencies. In the 1960s and into the 1970s, there was a rapid development of two- and four-year college degree programs in law enforcement and an increased emphasis on training. These changes were in large part due to the 1967 report of the President's Commission on Law Enforcement and Administration of Justice, which was in part responsible for Congress passing the Omnibus Crime Control and Safe Streets Act of 1968. This act established the **Law Enforcement Assistance Administration (LEAA)** and provided a billion dollars each year to improve and strengthen criminal justice agencies. With funding available, social scientists began to test the traditional methods of police deployment, employee selection, and training and to question the appearance of racial discrimination in arrests and the use of deadly force (Dunham & Alpert, 1997; Green, 2003). Federal and state funding was available to police officers seeking to further their educations, and potential police officers began to see some advantage in taking at least some college-level courses. Although there were vast differences in the quality of college programs, they did create a pool of relatively well qualified applicants for both supervisory and entry-level positions. These developments, coupled with improvements in police training, salaries and benefits, and equipment helped to create a more professional image of the police. At the same time, however, police came under increasing scrutiny as a result of their roles in the urban disorders of the late 1960s and early 1970s. In addition, there were consistent increases in crime, despite the movement toward a more professional police.

The initial reaction of the police to the failure to control crime and disorder was to increase professionalism and militarization (Barlow & Barlow, 2000). Challenges to both authority and procedure were common, and criticism from the outside continued into the 1980s. The police were seen as partially responsible for continued high crime rates and civil unrest, and the number of complaints and civil actions brought against the police sky-rocketed. As America entered the 1990s, Bouza (1990) noted:

> It is becoming ever clearer that underlying social and economic conditions are spawning crime and that society's unwillingness to do anything meaningful about them has really sealed the fate of the police effort to cope with the symptoms. Society wants to fight crime with more cops, tougher judges, and bigger jails, not through such scorned 'liberal' schemes as social welfare programs. . . . Police executives believe that today's unattended problems, concentrated in our urban centers, will only get worse, eventually resulting in riots and heightened violence. (pp. 270–271)

There is clearly a discrepancy between what the public assumes the police can accomplish (based on media presentations, etc.) and what the police can actually accomplish. While the expectation may be that *more* police will solve the problems referred to by Bouza, the reality is that no increase in the numbers of police officers, in and of itself, will produce the desired result. The discrepancy is highly problematic and impacts not only police administrators' decisions concerning operations, but also the type of personnel who apply for police positions and the type of preparation for the job they receive. At the same time, collective bargaining and unionization in police departments have changed the complexion of relationships between police administrators and rank and file officers considerably. While police unions have undoubtedly helped improve police salaries and working conditions, they remain controversial because of their emphasis on seniority and perceived opposition to reform.

A noteworthy development in policing occurred in 1979. In response to repeated calls for police professionalism, the **Commission on Accreditation for Law Enforcement Agencies** was established. The Commission was formed through the efforts of the International Chiefs of Police Association, the National Organization of Black Law Enforcement Executives, the National Sheriffs Association, and the Police Executive Research Forum. The Commission became operational in 1983 and has been accepting applications for accreditation, conducting evaluations based on specific standards for law enforcement agencies, and granting accreditation since that time. By 2000, over 400 agencies had been accredited, with another 500 or so awaiting accreditation. In fact, many agencies originally accredited have now been through the reaccreditation process.

The amount and quality of research on the police improved drastically beginning in the 1960s. The 1967 **Presidential Commission on Law Enforcement and the Administration of Justice**, the **National Advisory Commission on Civil Disorders** in the same year, and the 1973 **National Advisory Commission on Criminal Justice Standards and Goals** represented major efforts to better understand styles of policing, police community relations, and police selection and training (Alpert & Dunham, 1997). Many other private and government funded research projects contributed to our knowledge in these and other areas relating to the police. Yet today, municipal police reflect 180 years of conflict and attempts at reform. Most chiefs continue to be selected against a political backdrop, which may be good or bad for the agency, as we have seen. There has been some consolidation and standardization of services, but not a great deal. The police appear to have become more concerned about social responsibility, but they still have difficulties interacting with some segments of society. Diversity remains the key characteristic of municipal police, and local control the key to such diversity. Progress in policing has been made on many fronts. Progressive police chiefs, concerned academics, and other involved citizens have helped push the boundaries of traditional policing and shared their thoughts and findings at both national and international levels by publishing, teaching or training, and promoting exchange programs. Research on and by the police has increased dramatically in the past several years. As Petersilia (1993) pointed out: ". . . police leaders have been under considerable pressure to manage personnel and operations as efficiently as possible. This pressure may help explain why police administrators have apparently been even more willing than leadership in other criminal justice areas to question traditional assumptions and methods, to entertain the conclusions of research, and to test research recommendations" (p. 220). Conser and Russell (2000) concluded, "Essentially, what the [police] literature describes about the policing role in the United States is that it is unsettled, subject to ongoing societal change, and continually evolving" (p. 197).

POLICE STORIES

As indicated throughout the chapter, the police have gone through many reforms or changes regarding their organization and practice, but one common denominator has stood the test of time—that being *tradition*. While tradition does have its place in any organization, it can sometimes be carried too far. For example, upon being sworn in by the Chicago Police Department (CPD), each officer is issued the following equipment: badge, hat, shield, photo identification card, plastic whistle (for traffic control), wooden baton, riot helmet, and a brass "call box" key. All other equipment must be purchased at the individual officer's expense.

Twice per year the department conducts a full uniform inspection, during which time officers must present all of their equipment. Failure to do so could, and often did, end with disciplinary action taken by the department. So twice per year, thousands of police officers would scurry around in an attempt to get all of their uniforms, weapons, and other equipment ready for inspection.

It should be noted that the last point in time when there were actually call boxes being used was back to the 1960s. Regardless, the brass call box key was an official part of the uniform. "Tradition is why we do this," would be the response from the police bosses when asked about this particular requirement.

An equally absurd practice pertained to the use of the "CO" book by command staff personnel. The CO book was the watch commander's bible for roll call sessions. These books were actually the old style, leather bound ledger books normally used by accountants. When information worthy of mention came across the teletype machine (yes, I did say teletype machine), those messages would literally be cut with scissors and pasted (using glue) onto the pages of the CO book so that the watch commander could keep the troops informed. This was going on into the 1990s, when computer technology was readily available.

That is tradition taken a bit too far. I still have my call box key, though, and I'm still on the hunt for one that may have been overlooked. Who knows, if I ever find one, it may have a half-dog of some great, aged whiskey inside.

The Community Policing/Problem Solving Era (1980–2000)

The 1980s saw numerous technological advances in policing. Increased use of computers enabled departments to institute crime analysis programs to track criminal occurrences, analyze their common factors, make predictions concerning crime trends, and develop strategies to apprehend offenders (Green, 2003). In addition, a variety of records management systems were developed to store and retrieve information and computer-aided dispatch and 911 systems were created. Together, these advances enabled communications personnel to receive calls for service, determine and dispatch the closest police officer, and provide the officer with available information while proceeding to answer the call. As the use of computers and wireless communications grew, mobile data terminals entered the picture and allowed officers to immediately access information that the communication center had received (Green, 2003).

Police administrators in the second half of the century attempted to maximize the use of technology, increase specialization, provide better training, and expand educational opportunities in an attempt to development a more professional image of the police. However, as they turned to a more professional model of policing, they created some unanticipated problems, including increasing the gap between officers and the other citizens they served. One obvious example of this was the use of patrol officers who policed the streets in vehicles that served as offices on wheels. This effectively isolated the officers from members of the public who often didn't know the identities of the officers patrolling their neighborhoods. While recognizing the need for speed and mobility provided by the use of patrol cars, many citizens preferred to have identifiable officers walking the beat. Research on foot patrol suggested that it contributed to city life, reduced fear among citizens, increased citizen satisfaction with the police, improved police attitudes toward citizens, and increased the morale and job satisfaction of police officers (Kelling & Moore, 1988, p. 10). **Community relations programs,** developed in the 1960s, were an initial experiment in what was to become a revolution in policing. "Speaking at community centers and in schools was one of the first attempts to improve community relations. These programs eventually expanded to include neighborhood storefront offices, ride-along programs, fear-reduction programs, police academies for citizens, cultural diversity training, police-community athletic programs, and **Drug Abuse Resistance Education (DARE)**." (bold added, Barlow & Barlow, 2000, p. 43).

By the early 1980s, a gradual movement away from the crime-fighting model and toward a **community-policing** model occurred. Police administrators and interested observers recognized that in their pursuit of professionalism through enhanced technology, specialization, and paramilitary organization, the police had lost touch with the citizenry they were sworn to serve and protect (Lyman, 1999). By the mid 1980s, it was clear that the police by themselves were unable to deal with increasing crime and violence. Recognizing that only with public cooperation could their performance in the areas of crime control and order maintenance improve, progressive police administrators turned to community-oriented or community-based policing as a possible solution to their problems. In fact, this move represented a return to the principles of policing originally specified by Sir Robert Peel as he sought to develop a metropolitan police force in London in the 1820s.

As the community policing model gained momentum in the 1980s and 1990s, another policing strategy known as *problem-oriented policing* began to attract increased attention. This approach to policing emphasized the interrelationships among what might otherwise appear to be disparate events. For example, in one major city, for any given year, 60% of the calls for police assistance originated from 10% of the households calling the police (Pierce et al., 1987). Rather than dealing with all of these calls as separate incidents to be handled before clearing the calls and going on to other calls, problem-oriented policing focused attention on the underlying difficulties that create patterns of incidents (Goldstein, 1979). It allows officers to take a holistic approach, working with other citizens and other agency representatives to find more permanent solutions to a variety of police problems.

Both community-oriented and problem-oriented policing emphasize the importance of the police-community relationship and the fact that police work consists in large measure of order maintenance through the use of negotiations among the police and other citizens. Sherman (1978), for example, concluded that all police education programs should emphasize the consideration of value choices and ethical dilemmas in policing and should "include comprehensive treatment of the most commonly performed police work, which falls outside of the criminal justice system" (p. 4).

❖ Recent Policing Strategies

As the review of the history of policing indicates, policing is dynamic (constantly changing). Based upon analysis of the effectiveness of past police practices, numerous contemporary strategies have emerged. While these will be discussed in some detail in Chapter 11, a brief mention of some of these strategies seems appropriate here.

Areal Policing

One strategy introduced more than two decades ago has received recent attention. This strategy is referred to as **areal policing** and is discussed in detail by Skolnick and Bayley (1986), among others. "If professional policing can be called a 'one size fits all' model of policing, community policing might be called a 'one size fits one,' meaning that police work needs to be adapted to the needs of identifiable constituencies at areal levels smaller than an entire jurisdiction." Crank and Giacomazzi (2007) found "significant variations in perceptions of crime and disorder, in perceptions of safety, in social cohesion, and in attitudes toward deputies and to the sheriff's office. Findings suggested the importance of local policy through the tailoring of services to local needs" (p. 108). The suggested tailoring of police services to areas within police jurisdictions may have particular application in an era in which some neighborhoods may contain facilities that could become targets for terrorists and therefore require concentrated allocation of police resources while other nearby neighborhoods may require fewer police resources. Similarly, police strategies for intervening in high crime neighborhoods may be inappropriate or misperceived by residents of nearby neighborhoods.

Reassurance Policing

Reassurance policing focuses on the **signal crimes** concept, and using a formal method for identifying signals, this approach has developed into what amounts to a citizen-focused problem-solving style of policing.

Signal crimes and signal disorders are acts that breach either the criminal law or situated conventions of social order and in the process function as warning signals about the presence of a risk to security to people. Signals of this kind are important because they are crucial to how individuals and groups symbolically encode and decode their environments and are interpreted as indicators about the distribution of risks and threats across social space. In so doing, signals shape how people think, feel, or act in relation to their security. (Innes, 2005)

Intelligence-Led or Intelligence-Based Policing

Intelligence-led or ***intelligence-based policing*** is a policing model that originated in Britain and focuses on risk assessment and risk management. The approach involves identifying risks or patterns associated with groups, individuals, and locations in order to predict when and where crime is likely to occur. Many agencies now conduct crime analyses on a regular basis, thus identifying reported crime patterns. An effective records management system allows front-line officers to easily obtain this information on a timely basis prior to or while responding to a call. This may assist officers in proactively identifying and anticipating problems likely to be encountered rather than reacting to them at the scene. The approach has gained momentum globally following the September 11 terrorist attacks on the United States (Gottstein, 2008).

❖ **Photo 1.3**   Today, police have found that crime mapping and other such technology-based methodologies have a significant impact on the prevention and effective investigation of crime.

During the last three decades, "the police began to reconsider their fundamental mission, the nature of the core strategies of policing, and the character of their relationships with the communities that they serve" (Weisburd & Braga, 2006). In spite of numerous innovative programs initiated in recent years, the evidence related to police performance associated with these innovations on crime reduction and community satisfaction with their implementation is limited (Braga & Weisburd, 2007).

☞ CASE IN POINT 1.1

In March, 2009, the Peoria Police department launched a crime-mapping program known as "CrimeView Community." The program, developed by The Omega Group, enables Web users to check crime trends for 90 day periods in user-designated areas of the city. Such programs are already in use in about 40 states.

It is believed that the program will help the public make educated decisions about crime in the areas in which they live, work, go to school, and shop. When users log on to CrimeView in Peoria, they will be able to search by location within the city by 16 different types of crimes. The website is scheduled to be updated daily.

Source: From "Tool Tracks City Crime," by G. Childs, 2009, *Journal Star,* A1, A8.

Terrorism-Oriented Policing

Events that occurred on September 11, 2001, led to new duties and strategies for police at all levels in the United States. Now, in contrast to much of the history of policing, the people in our cities and towns want to trust the government and the police, as agents of government, to protect them from criminals both domestic and foreign. "Terrorism and homeland security are not the only important issues facing the police agencies in the twenty-first century, but they are such serious concerns that it is necessary to contemplate whether existing police strategies are still up to the job" (Roberg, Novak, & Cordner, 2005, p. 566). What might be termed *terrorism-oriented policing* requires changes at all levels of policing. Most of these changes add new duties to those already assumed by the police and raise a number of questions. Can existing police resources be stretched to incorporate new challenges? Should police officers be specialists or generalists? If the former, how many and what new specializations are required? If the latter, can we train generalists to protect us from international terrorist conspiracies and, at the same time, from traditional crimes as well as rapidly changing, technologically sophisticated crimes? Can we continue to pursue the transparency in police relationships with the public suggested by community- and problem-oriented policing? If not, will a return to more traditional policing better protect us? Are we willing to allow further erosion of our civil liberties in the name of national security? These and other questions remain to be answered as we move into the second decade of the 21st century, and we will address them as we proceed throughout this text.

At the same time that new strategies and challenges in policing have emerged, new expectations have evolved. Some of these expectations are based upon erroneous images of the police painted by television and movies. For example, several television dramas portray crime scene investigators pursuing and arresting suspects based on the evidence they collect. In reality, most crime scene technicians do little other than process crime scenes. Other television shows portray police officers being involved in foot and auto pursuits throughout their tours of duty. While these things do sometimes happen, they are far less frequent and dramatic than the shows typically suggest. New expectations are also a result of the terrorist activities previously mentioned and the increasingly international nature of criminal conspiracies. Add these new expectations to the traditional concerns of the police and it is apparent that meeting all expectations will be a challenge indeed. Further complicating the ability to meet such expectations is the fact that police agencies at different levels are confronted with similar but not identical problems due to the diversity of services provided.

❖ Diversity in Police Services

As previously noted, police in America have provided and continue to provide an extremely wide range of services, many of which, as we shall see, have little to do with crime or law enforcement. At the federal level, the United States Marshals were the first to be established (in 1789) for the purpose of enforcing directives of the federal courts. The United States Secret Service was founded in 1865 as a branch of the U.S. Treasury Department. It was originally created to combat the counterfeiting of U.S. currency—a serious problem at the time. Later, in 1901, following the assassination of President William McKinley, the Secret Service was tasked with its second mission: the protection of the president. Today, the Secret Service's mission is two-fold: (1) protection of the president, vice president, and others; and (2) investigations into crimes against the financial infrastructure of the United States.

Numerous other federal agencies exercise police powers, and while each agency has a set of specific duties, there is a good deal of overlap and duplication among them. Four of these agencies are depicted in Figure 1.1.

Other federal agencies employing law enforcement officers include the following: Amtrak, the U.S. Supreme Court, the Environmental Protection Agency (EPA), and the Library of Congress.

Federal agencies employ more than 103,000 full-time sworn personnel (Bureau of Justice Statistics, 2007). They do not, for the most part, engage in those activities normally provided by local and county police. Relatively few federal officers, usually referred to as *agents,* are uniformed, and their primary duties involve investigation and control of federal crimes, such as bank robberies, illegal immigration, and interstate crimes. They are also responsible for protecting federal property and federal officials. Federal agencies also provide training and logistical support for state and local police.

At the same time that local and federal police agencies were going through numerous changes, and as the number of highways increased, state police agencies took on the responsibility for traffic enforcement on these thoroughfares, particularly in areas outside corporate limits of cities and towns. Eventually a bifurcation occurred, with some agencies focusing almost exclusively on traffic control (highway patrol departments)

Figure 1.1 Federal Agencies and Responsibilities

Agency	Responsibilities
Drug Enforcement Administration (DEA)	Enforcement of federal drug laws
Federal Bureau of Investigation (FBI)	Investigation of violations of federal criminal law in a variety of areas (e.g., civil rights, terrorism, organized crime, and white-collar crime)
Immigration and Customs Enforcement (ICE)	Enforcement of immigration and customs laws
Bureau of Alcohol, Tobacco, and Firearms (ATF)	Reduction of the criminal use of firearms and explosives; the collection of alcohol, tobacco, and firearms taxes; and the enforcement of federal alcohol, tobacco, and firearms laws

and others maintaining more general enforcement powers (state police investigation departments) (Roberg, Novak, & Cordner, 2005, pp. 56–59). Typically, the state police are empowered to provide law enforcement service anywhere in the state, while highway patrols have limited authority based on type of offense, jurisdiction, or assignment to specific duties.

All states except Hawaii have some type of state police agency. In addition to their basic tasks, many of these agencies provide statewide communications or computer systems, assist in crime-scene analysis and multijurisdictional investigations, provide training for other police agencies, and collect, analyze, and disseminate information on crime patterns in the state. In addition, many state police agencies have expanded their services to include aircraft support, underwater search and rescue, and K-9 assistance. State police agencies may also be responsible for state park security (park police or rangers), security of state property and state officials, and regulation of liquor and gambling related activities. The 49 state law enforcement agencies employed about 58,000 sworn police officers in 2004 (Bureau of Justice Statistics, 2007). It should be clear that given the diversity and breadth of police services in the United States, there is a great deal of jurisdictional overlap. Thus, for example, a college student may be subject to the jurisdiction of the campus police, the city police, the county police, the state police, and a variety of federal police agencies all at the same time. In point of fact, which of these agencies is likely to become involved depends upon the type and location of the offense in question and the existence of formal and informal agreements among the agencies. While each agency has some unique qualities, they all face many of the same issues as well.

❖ Current Issues in Policing

History has shown us that policing has evolved and adapted over time as the result of attempts to meet the needs of society. Since the beginning of this century, the world has become a global village where the possibility exists to travel literally anywhere within a matter of hours. So too has the ability to communicate become instantaneous. In simpler times, police personnel could be recruited from almost any walk of life because the nature of crime did not generally require great technical expertise. In this century, however, effective policing demands that police expertise be sufficient to deter and apprehend those involved in transnational crime, those who use the most advanced technologies to prey upon their victims, those who traffic in human beings across borders, and those who threaten to spread terror and chaos across the world (see Around the World, following). All of these activities and more require direct intervention into the lives of citizens.

AROUND THE WORLD

In November, 2007, the International Policing Toward 2020 conference was held in Canberra, Australia. Participants in the conference heard from experts from around the world on emerging trends in crime, sociology, geopolitics, and science and technology and considered the implications of those trends for law enforcement.

Speakers addressed issues such as conflict provoked by resource scarcity, social dislocation, increasing criminal activity online, new forms of crime enabled by evolving technology, and managing the increasing pace of change.

Additional discussions focused on the future shape of the nation state, the globalization of crime, international cooperation among law enforcement agencies, and how international governance systems might need to adapt to detect and prevent crime which increasingly transcends national borders.

Source: From *International Policing: Toward 2020.* Available from http://www.conference.afp .gov.au

As early as 1998, Meadows predicted the following: "Policing in the twenty-first century will be a more demanding and delicate process. The police and the community will share in the crime control function. . . . The police will be given more legal freedom mandates, but will continually be held accountable for mistakes. These trends signal a need for the police to be better trained in the total crime prevention process and functions associated with community service" (p. 145). This may prove to be a difficult task because, as Roberg, Novak, and Cordner (2005) noted, "Democracy represents consensus, freedom, participation, and equality; the police represent restriction and the imposition of authority of government on the individual. That is why the police in a democracy are often confronted with hostility, opposition, and criticism no matter how effective or fair they may be" (p. 8).

What are some of the issues with which the police must deal in the 21st century? A partial list appears in Figure 1.2.

In the following chapters, we discuss these and other issues confronting the police, such as changing laws, increased accountability, ethical decision making, transnational and other specialized forms of crime, technological advancements, organizational dynamics, new scientific and investigative methodologies, increased standards for education and training, stress and coping mechanisms, and community relations.

Figure 1.2 Contemporary Police Issues

New strategies in policing
Concerns with continuing education and training
Recruitment and selection of officers
Police accountability
Exercise of discretion
Ethical issues
Police misconduct
Policing in a multicultural society
Police officer stress
Changing technology and cyber crime
Globalization, terrorism, immigration, and homeland security
Privatization

❖ Chapter Summary

The number of agencies and the countless duties they are required to perform make it difficult to form any generalizations about the nature of police work. As service providers and law enforcers, police find themselves responding to a wide variety of societal needs, and these needs may vary from community to community.

The manner in which organized and professional police agencies operate today has been influenced greatly by their historical development, spanning a time period of nearly 200 years. Police officers of the early days had little to no training and there were no formal education requirements. There was considerable political influence on police officers, some of which was unprofessional at best, including unethical and unlawful acts at the behest of the politicians who controlled them. While politics still play an important role in policing, the extent of that role has diminished somewhat.

Policing has evolved over the years, and today the field of policing has become much more professional in nature, particularly with respect to training and formal education requirements. The police, however, are unlikely to be able to meet the expectations of all citizens in any given community. The nature of democracy and the freedoms that citizens enjoy present the police with difficult and sometimes conflicting demands. Some in society want a strict law-and-order approach, while others prefer a more flexible approach to solving community problems. Numerous policing strategies have been implemented and tested over the years in an attempt to satisfy the goals of various segments of the American public. Inattention to the will of diverse minorities has often been the basis of strained police-community relations.

Some of the newest policing strategies based on the tenets of community- and problem-oriented policing and in response to various global issues that now effect local police operations seem to show at least a degree of success. Strategies such as areal, reassurance, intelligence-based, and terrorism-oriented policing are but a few. The increasing complexities of policing, coupled with the technology-based nature of the world in which we live and work, demand vigilant, cooperative, and proactive forms of policing in order to effectively address a wide variety of issues.

❖ Key Terms

police

night watch system

Sir Robert Peel

Patrick Colquhoun

Pendleton Act

sheriff

Reform movement (Reform Era)

Law Enforcement Assistance Administration (LEAA)

Commission on Accreditation for Law Enforcement Agencies

Presidential Commission on Law Enforcement and the Administration of Justice (1967)

National Advisory Commission on Civil Disorders (1967)

National Advisory Commission on Criminal Justice Standards and Goals (1973)

community relations programs

Drug Abuse Resistance Education (DARE)

community policing

problem-oriented policing

areal policing

reassurance policing

signal crimes

intelligence-led or intelligence-based policing

terrorism-oriented policing

❖ Discussion Questions

1. Why is it so difficult to discuss and generalize about the police in the United States?

2. Briefly discuss the evolution of American police and the problems they currently confront.

3. How, in the conduct of human interaction, did the need for a police arise?

4. What problems confronting the police are inherent in democratic societies?

5. What are the positive and negative effects of the interaction between politics and the police in our society?

6. Discuss some of the most recent policing strategies and indicate whether or not you think they will prove effective.

❖ Internet Exercises

1. Using your favorite search engine, go online and see what you can find out about the history of policing. What two or three websites did you find most interesting? What kinds of information did these websites contain?

2. Go to the Internet and search for information about your local police department. What kinds of information did you find? How recent was the information? If you fail to locate your local police agency, broaden your search to the nearest city (county, state) agency and respond to the same questions.

Recruitment and Selection of Police Officers

❖ PHOTO 2.1   A group of new officers from the police academy, at graduation day.

Every police department is faced with the necessity of recruiting and selecting personnel to fill the complex role discussed in the preceding chapter. Personnel must be recruited and selected to fill positions at three different levels: the entry level, the supervisory level, and the chief's level. Current evidence indicates that police officer applicant numbers are increasing, a reversal from recent years when police agencies struggled to find qualified recruits (Johnson, 2009). Most agree the increase is based on the downturn in the economy and the employee reduction in corporate organizations. And police chiefs expect those that were victims of corporate reductions to be well suited for public safety positions since many have experience in the workforce, were a part of a team, and are more mature about the world of work (Johnson, 2009). Because recruitment and selection are critical to the success of any agency, and virtually all promotions in police agencies are internal, it is imperative that police administrators attract qualified applicants. This is particularly true with respect to women and minorities, an issue that is addressed in detail in Chapter 10. As we begin this chapter, several questions come to mind: Is there a group of traits that characterize the ideal police officer? Have these traits been identified? Can this group of traits be developed in recruits?

❖ The Importance of Recruitment and Selection

The importance of productive recruitment and selection procedures cannot be overemphasized, regardless of the level involved. Poor recruitment and selection procedures result in hiring or promoting personnel who cannot or will not communicate effectively with diverse populations, exercise discretion properly, or perform the multitude of functions required of the police. Table 2.1 presents a list of the traits necessary to be an effective police officer:

Table 2.1 Traits and Principles of an Effective Police Officer	
Trustworthiness	Readiness to lend assistance
Honesty	Ability to compromise for greater good
Leadership	Ability to challenge unlawful orders or authority
Confidentiality	Obedience to lawful and reasonable orders
Accept responsibility for self and others	Perspective
Accept criticism	Intolerance of corruption
Accept extra responsibility without compensation	Teamwork
Analyzes situation, does not jump to conclusions	Rejection of unearned personal praise

Source: From "Sixteen Traits Recruiters are Looking For," by P. Patti, 2009, *Police Link: The Nation's Law Enforcement Community.* Available online at http://www.policelink.com/benefits/articles/7602

Recognizing the need for candidates with such traits, most departments expend considerable time and money in the process. The extent to which such recruitment efforts are successful largely determines the effectiveness and efficiency of any department.

Many argue police departments are recruiting and selecting a new breed of police officer. Police agencies are addressing issues related to retiring baby-boomer officers while experiencing the addition of Generation X and Y police officers. "There are differences between the old (traditional) police officer and the new, based on the experiences of the individuals of the **Baby-Boomer generation** and those of **Generation X and Y**" (McCafferty, 2003, p. 79). While generation gaps are not new, they are much more complex today than those previously experienced (Sanders & Stefaniak, 2008). For example, many police officers who lived in the Baby-Boomer Generation had been in the military and were used to discipline and a hierarchy of authority. They had the ability to cope with stress in the crucible of military training and service and fit readily into the paramilitary structure that defined police organizations (McCafferty, 2003). However, according to McCafferty (2003) the Generation X and Y recruits have been exposed to modern liberalism, the passage of affirmative-action laws, drug use, increased civil disobedience, and the breakdown of both the family and authority. These differences often create conflicts in values between generations or between the veteran baby-boomer officers and the Generation X and Y police officers. Notwithstanding these differences, Hubbard, Cromwell, and Sgro (2004) believed future generations could have a very positive role in police organizations.

> The exciting news is that Generation Y behaviors and career choices are driven first and foremost by their quest for opportunities to play important roles in meaningful work that helps others. This is perhaps the most socially conscious generation since the 1960s and they are exhibiting strong signs of altruism already. (p. 44)

Of course these differences should be considered in light of the fact that Generation X is now well established in the workforce (40%) compared to Baby-Boomer employees (45%) and Generation X employees are moving into positions of power and control (Eckberg, 2008). In other words, in many departments Generation X police officers are now supervising baby-boomer officers. This has resulted in several perceptional differences related to management style and organization success. For example, according to Marston (2007), since WWII each generation has made two assumptions about the younger generation entering the workforce.

1. Senior generations assume that younger generations will measure "success" using the same criteria.

2. Senior generations believe that younger workers should "pay their dues" following the same paths to achieve the same levels of success. (Marston, 2007, as quoted in Sanders, 2008, p. 4)

However, most agree that new police officers are different and do not measure success in the same terms as previous generations, nor do they believe in paying their dues (Sanders & Stefaniak, 2008).

Raines (2002) identified the following generational differences: They have a different work ethic, have been influenced by the digital media, regard the threat of terrorism as a fact of life, and live in a global community that is constantly connected. Furthermore, Lundborn (2002) concluded that Generation Y employees are confident, idealistic, eager, and passionate about their quality of life. Sanders and Stefaniak (2008) reported that Generation Y police personnel "who might value their lifestyle and personal time or commitments over work obligations and/or upward mobility" (p. 5) have the potential to pose a conflict for police organizations. Today's police organizations never close and often require personnel to continue to serve beyond the end of a shift or to be called in from off-duty to the scene of an emergency and to replace missing personnel. Israelsen-Hartley (2008) described the new generation of police officers' desires as "to be efficient, get the job done and get on to the next part of their lives" (p. 1), but often this attitude clashes with police work, which does not follow an 8:00 to 4:30 schedule.

Beck and Wade (2004) argued that a systematically different way of working exists between Baby Boomers and Generation Y employees and is attributable to maturing with video games (Sanders & Stefaniak, 2008). Harrison (2007), a retired police chief, believes the traits associated with video games will have a positive effect on policing and will allow those agencies that recruit and retain these new generation officers to thrive. Specifically, he cited the following characteristics associated with Generation Y police applicants:

• Work in teams
• Perform work of significance
• Have flexibility in their daily environment
• Engage in activities consistent with heroism (Harrison, 2007, p. 5)

The strong tradition of service by the police to the community could be a powerful motivator for the new generation of police officers. "Many police agencies, through the evolution of community policing, are seeking a new type of candidate to keep pace with their broadening responsibilities and the expansion of community partnerships" (Schapiro, 2008, p.1). Schapiro (2008) believed it is important that police agencies market law enforcement as an "exciting profession that offers adventure and a spirit of service" (p. 2). Realizing many police agencies have been slow to recognize the changes that accompany today's police applicant, Delord (2006) believes the new generation of police officers needs to feel they will be included in decision-making, be recognized for their achievements, and will work for an organization with high moral values.

❖ The Process of Recruitment and Selection

It must be pointed out that recruiting and selecting officers and chiefs and promoting supervisors is, in many cases, done in large part by those outside of policing. That is, police and fire commissioners, personnel departments, or civil service board members often determine who will be eligible for hiring and promotion, and assessment teams, city managers, mayors, and council members typically determine who will fill the position of chief. To be sure, in the former case, police officials may select officers from among those on the eligibility list and, in the case of promotions, have a good deal of input—as we shall see later. Still, much of the recruitment and selection of police personnel is done by civilians with varying degrees of input from police administrators.

It is important to note that recruitment and selection are ongoing processes that recur throughout the career of an officer. Once selected for an entry-level position by a specific department, the officer is likely to be involved in selection procedures involving appointment to different assignments (detective, juvenile officer, crime technician, patrol officer, etc.), to different ranks (via promotional examinations), to different schools or training programs, and so on. For some, the process ends with their selection as chief; for others, the process continues as they seek the position of chief in other agencies; and for some, the process begins and ends at the rank of patrol officer.

Nonetheless, even for the latter, the process is repeated over and over throughout their careers, even though they may choose not to participate directly. That is, some officers make a conscious choice to remain patrol officers and to not seek opportunities for training. These officers, too, are important in understanding the recruitment and selection process involved in promotions because they may become perceived as outside of the pool of candidates to be recruited for such advancement or training. In addition, those who are selected for such assignments must be prepared to deal with career patrol persons, just as these patrol persons must be prepared to deal with those promoted. An examination of the various requirements and strategies employed in the recruitment process reveals some of the difficulties involved in selecting personnel who will both fill the official vacancy and meet the situation-specific needs of various departments. However, before we turn our attention to recruitment and selection at the various levels, we need to understand the legal context in which such processes occur.

Equal Employment Opportunity and Affirmative Action

For most of our history, American employers, both public and private, have felt relatively free to hire and promote employees according to whatever criteria they established and, similarly, to exclude from employment and promotion those they deemed, for whatever reason, to be unfit. This was true even though the U.S. Constitution, in the First, Fifth, and Fourteenth Amendments, prohibits deprivation of employment rights without due process of law. Further, the Civil Rights Acts of 1866, 1870, and 1871 (based on the Thirteenth and Fourteenth Amendments) prohibited racial discrimination in hiring and placement as well as deprivation of equal employment rights under the cover of state law (Bell, 2004).

Still, it wasn't until 1964 and the passage of the Civil Rights Act of that year, and specifically Title VII of the act, that many employers began to take equal employment rights seriously. It should be noted that the main motivation of employment discrimination laws is to prevent employers from treating applicants and employees adversely on the basis of several characteristics that in many cases were determined at birth or involve characteristics individuals should not be asked to change. "Title VII of the Civil Rights Act of 1964 protects individuals against employment discrimination on the basis of race and color as well as national origin, sex and religion" (Find Law, 2002, p. 1). Furthermore, "discrimination on the basis of an **immutable characteristic** associated with race, such as skin color, hair texture or certain facial features violated Title VII, even though not all members of the race share the same characteristic (Find Law, 2002, p. 1). In addition, the Office of Personnel Management has interpreted the prohibition of discrimination based on conduct to include discrimination based on sexual orientation. In fact, certain personnel actions cannot be based on attributes or conduct that does not adversely affect employee performance, such as marital status and political affiliation (Equal Employment Opportunity Commission [EEOC], 2009). The Equal Employment Opportunity Act (EEOA) established a commission (EEOC) to investigate complaints of discrimination. Following these changes in federal law, states also began passing such laws in the form of fair employment statutes (Bell, 2004).

In general terms, these laws hold that **discrimination** occurs when requirements for hiring and promotion are not bona fide (i.e., they are not actually related to the job) and when a **disparate impact** occurs to members of a minority group. A disparate impact involves an employment policy or practice, although neutral on its face, that adversely impacts a person or group (U. S. Department of Commerce, 2010). Federal legislation requires that all employers with more than 15 employees refrain from policies and procedures that discriminate against specified categories of individuals (EEOC, 2009). The burden of demonstrating that requirements are job-related falls on the employer, while the burden of showing a disparate impact falls on the complainant. For an employer to be successfully sued in this regard, both conditions must be met. That is, it is possible to have job requirements that have a disparate impact but are nonetheless valid. For example, if it could be demonstrated that police officers routinely have to remove accident victims from vehicles in order to avoid the possibility of further injury due to fire or explosion and if this job requirement also eliminated from policing women or other categories of applicants, the requirement would not be discriminatory under the law. If, however, these actions are seldom if ever required of police officers, the requirement would be discriminatory. We will have more to say about such requirements later in this chapter, but it is important to understand here the context within which charges of discrimination are filed and decided.

The combined impact of equal employment opportunity laws and executive orders eventually came to be realized by government agencies, among them the police. Prior to the early 1970s, most police departments employed predominantly white men, a practice that came to be the focus of numerous legal challenges. These challenges came in the form of both court actions and complaints to the EEOC alleging discrimination on the part of employers.

During the same period, the concept of **affirmative action** gained prominence. Affirmative action programs have two goals. First, they are intended to prevent discrimination in current hiring and promotional practices. Second, they may be used to help remedy past discrimination in hiring and promotion.

Equal employment opportunity and affirmative action programs may be implemented in a number of different ways. First, some employers voluntarily establish affirmative action programs because they recognize the importance of hiring without regard to race, creed, or ethnicity. Second, some employers implement such programs when threatened with legal action based on alleged discrimination. Third, some employers fight charges of discrimination in the courts and are found to be in violation. When this occurs, such employers are in danger of losing federal financial support and agree to develop and implement affirmative action programs in order to prevent this loss of federal monies. This typically occurs through the use of a **consent decree** in which the employer agrees to strive to achieve some sort of balance in terms of race or ethnicity and gender in the workforce. In other cases, the courts impose plans and time tables on employers and can impose severe sanctions in the form of fines if the goals of the plans are not met within the specified time period.

The use of consent decrees has led to a good deal of confusion and widespread ill feelings on behalf of employers and white, male employees. On one hand, the EEOA prohibits discrimination based on race, creed, religion, sex, or national origin and states that employers will not be forced to hire less well qualified employees over more well qualified employees. On the other hand, quotas have been used as a remedy as part of a consent decree or out of court settlement in discrimination law suits (Pincus, 2003). In most cases, there must be a compelling state interest to justify a quota, which is often only applied when no other policy is likely to work (Pincus, 2003).

The most recent decision by the United States Supreme Court concerning the issue of quotas was *Ricci v. DeStefano,* in which the Court found that employment law only rarely permits quotas to remedy racial imbalance (Thernstrom, 2009). The case involved 58 white, 23 African American, and 19 Hispanic firefighters that tested to determine eligibility for promotion to captain and lieutenant. The city of New Haven civil service board refused to certify the results, denying promotions to those who had earned them. The results of the test generated a disparate impact since the African

American and Hispanic applicants did worse than the white candidates for the open positions (Epstein, 2009). The Court said that New Haven civil service board violated Title VII of the 1964 Civil Rights Act. Burns (2009) believes *Ricci v. DeStefano* indicates that employers should carefully evaluate the likelihood that a test or any method of selection may have disproportionate adverse effects on certain groups, whether a less discriminatory method of testing or selection is available, and how accurately the test or method of selection will be in correctly selecting those employees who are "best able to perform the required duties and responsibilities of the relevant job" (p. 3). This is particularly important for police agencies that require applicants to perform a variety of testing procedures prior to appointment as a police officer.

For years, a number of police administrators complained that they had been forced to hire minority employees who did not meet the standards they had established to improve police services, and thousands of white, male applicants for police positions complained that, although they are better qualified than minority candidates in terms of test results, the latter were hired or promoted. Both of these complaints are, in individual instances, justified, but they must be viewed in light of the goals of affirmative action—especially the goal of remedying past discrimination.

In essence, white men applying for police positions or promotions in some areas have suffered the same fate their African American and Hispanic counterparts suffered over the past three centuries in American society. The shift from discriminatory employment practices in policing, as well as in many other areas, has been slow and sometimes painful, yet it is necessary in order to maximize the number of qualified applicants and to make police agencies representative of the communities they serve. As Cox and Fitzgerald (1996) noted, the police will not be viewed as understanding community problems unless they have members who can view them from the community's perspective.

Many agencies have made and are making deliberate attempts to hire and promote minority group members for the obvious advantages that result. The following list illustrates that in either case, certain requirements must be met to avoid charges of discrimination in employment.

- Requirements must be valid
- Requirements must be reliable
- Testing must be consistent
- Testing must accurately reflect the job
- Rating errors and bias must be monitored (Billikopf, 2006)

While several federal laws exist that prohibit discrimination in any aspect of employment, three are of particular interest to police agencies. We have previously mentioned Title VII of the Civil Rights Act of 1964 and will discuss additional aspects of this law. In addition, we will also review the Americans with Disabilities Act (ADA) and the Age Discrimination Act and how these laws apply to police organizations.

Title VII of the Civil Rights Act of 1964

Title VII prohibits job discrimination based on the specific characteristics of a person that are determined at birth and other characteristics applicants should not be expected to alter (race, gender, age, national origin, disability, religion). Besides these characteristics, a number of employer practices can also become violations of Title VII. For example, it is illegal to discriminate against an individual because of their birthplace, ancestry, culture, or linguistic characteristics common to a specific ethnic group (EEOC, 2009). In addition, requiring that employees speak only English on the job may violate Title VII unless the organization shows that the requirement is necessary to conduct business. While police departments require English, many have also established minimum competency levels for Spanish.

With respect to religion under Title VII, employers are required to reasonably accommodate the religious beliefs of an employee or prospective employee, unless doing so would impose an undue hardship on the organization (EEOC, 2009). For example, in *Fraternal Order of Police Newark Lodge #2 v. City of Newark*, the federal appeals court held that the police department "could not enforce a no beard policy on two Muslim police officers who initiated an exemption request on religious grounds" (Ruiz & Hummer, 2007, p. 111).

Title VII also involves a number of broad prohibitions concerning sex discrimination. Agencies must ensure that pregnant applicants and employees are afforded the full protection of the law, policies, and practices with respect to evaluating applicants for positions within the department (District of Columbia, 2008).

Age Discrimination in Employment Act (ADEA)

The ADEA provides for a broad ban concerning age discrimination. An age limit may only be specified in the rare circumstance where age has been proven to be a **bona fide occupational qualification** (BFOQ) (EEOC, 2009). A bona fide occupational qualification is a requirement that is necessary to the normal operation of an organization. As an example, Elk Grove Village, IL (2008) only hired police officers that at the time of application were between 21 and 35 years of age, or up to 40 years of age if the applicant was already certified as a full-time police officer. In most cases, police agencies are allowed to restrict the age of applicants if they pass the two step test for analyzing BFOQs that pertain to certain age groups. In other words, "an employer must show that there is either (1) a substantial basis for believing that all or nearly all the employees above a certain age lack the qualifications for the position in question; or (2) that reliance on an age classification is necessary because it is highly impractical for the employer to insure by individual testing that its employees will have the necessary qualifications for the job" (Rhodes, 2002, p. 1). In most cases, the approach involved in restricting the age for police applicants or setting a mandatory retirement age requires the employer to "show a relationship, usually empirical, between age and increased risk to public safety; age and physical ability, agility or decline; or age and risk of personal injury or trauma" (Landy & Salas, 2005, pp. 266–267).

The Americans With Disabilities Act

The Americans with Disabilities Act (ADA) was enacted in 1990. A discussion of the ADA is in order because there is little doubt that many police agencies could be involved in litigation as a result of the act.

The ADA makes it illegal to discriminate against persons with certain categories of disabilities, limits blanket exclusions, and requires that the selection process deal with individuals on a case-by-case basis. To be protected under the ADA, the individual must have a disability or impairment (physical or mental), or must have a record of such disability, or must be regarded as having such a disability, and must be otherwise qualified for the position in question. *Qualified Individual with a Disability* means that the applicant must be able to perform the essential elements of the job with or without reasonable accommodation. *Reasonable accommodation* refers to new construction, modifying existing facilities, work schedules, or equipment, as long as such modification does not cause the agency undue hardship (significant expense or difficulty). In most cases, the ADA applies to persons who have impairments, and these must substantially limit major life activities such as seeing, hearing, speaking, walking, breathing, performing manual tasks, learning, caring for oneself, and working (U.S. Equal Employment Opportunity Commission, 2002). A person with epilepsy, paralysis, HIV infection, AIDS, or a substantial learning disability is covered, but an individual with a minor, nonchronic condition of short duration such as a sprain, broken arm, or the H1N1 flu would not be covered. Examples of accommodation include building ramps to provide access to buildings or work sites, designating parking spaces for those with disabilities, installing elevators, and redesigning work stations and restrooms.

The ADA divides the employment process into three phases: the application/interview phase, the postconditional offer stage, and the working stage (Colbridge, 2001). During the first phase, the ADA limits inquiries to nondisability qualifications of applicants. Employers may not ask about prior drug addiction, for example, because that is covered under ADA. They may ask about current illegal drug use because that is not covered under ADA. Similarly, applicants may be asked how they would perform job-related functions, as long as all applicants are asked the same question. "Applicants indicating they would need reasonable accommodation to perform job-related tasks must be provided such accommodation unless doing so would create an undue hardship for the employer" (Colbridge, 2001, p. 25).

The psychological examination may be viewed as part of the medical examination if it is used to uncover recognized mental disorders and, therefore, violates the ADA because the ADA protects those with mental impairments who are otherwise job-qualified. In such cases, the psychological test, like the medical examination, should be delayed until after an employment offer is made. "Psychological tests dealing with honesty, tastes, or habits of the applicant are not considered medical examinations" (Colbridge, 2001, p. 26) and may be used at the application/interview stage.

Once a conditional offer of employment has been made, employers may ask about disabilities in order to determine whether reasonable accommodation is necessary and feasible. If it is necessary and reasonable, such accommodation must generally be provided. Medical examinations also may be required during the postconditional phase, and again, reasonable accommodation for disabilities must be provided (Colbridge, 2001). In most cases, police departments can administer tests that measure an applicant's ability to perform job-related tasks or physical fitness tests before any job offer is made (U.S. Department of Justice, 2006). These tests are not considered to be medical exams, but any test that screens out a police applicant with disabilities must be job-related and consistent with business necessity. Also, it is not a violation of the ADA to ask a police applicant to provide a certification from a medical doctor that he or she can safely perform the physical agility test. Following employment, the ADA requires that disability-related inquiries be made only if they are job related, and reasonable accommodation is again required.

The EEOC is charged with enforcing the ADA. If the Commission determines that discrimination does not exist, the claim is dismissed (although the complainant still has the right to sue the employer). When the Commission determines that there is reasonable cause to believe discrimination has occurred, it will seek a negotiated settlement or bring a civil action against the employer (Colbridge, 2000).

Let us now turn our attention to the entry-level requirements that have been established for police officers and the recruitment and selection process at this level.

❖ Entry-Level Recruitment and Selection

According to Alpert and Dunham (1997), "It is difficult to emphasize sufficiently the importance of recruitment, selection and training. After all, a police agency is no better than those who perform the day-to-day tasks. Police work is a labor-intensive service industry, in which roughly 85 percent of the agencies' budgets are devoted to these personnel costs . . . the most significant investment police departments make is in the recruiting, selection and training of their personnel" (p. 40).

One important personnel cost for any organization is that associated with attracting qualified applicants to fill vacancies. This is certainly true in policing, which, as indicated previously, is labor-intensive. The costs of recruitment begin with the advertising process and, hopefully, end with the successful completion of the probationary period. In other words, the objective of the recruitment process is to select potential police officers who can not only meet entry level requirements, but also successfully complete training academy requirements and the probationary period. While recruit qualifications vary tremendously in different departments, some general requirements and concerns can be discussed.

The objective in advertising is to attract from the total pool of potential applicants for police work those, and only those, who are both qualified and seriously interested in policing. The more applicants attracted who do not meet both of these requirements, the more expensive the recruiting process. Let us assume, hypothetically, that the cost of processing one police recruit from application to placement on the eligibility list is $1,000. Suppose the agency attracts 50 applicants for one available vacancy. And suppose that 40 of the 50 applicants pass all the tests given in the early stages of the selection process. When the agency conducts background investigations of those who have successfully completed the tests, however, it is discovered that 10 of the applicants have prior felony convictions. In essence, the municipality has wasted the money spent on hiring these individuals because, in most jurisdictions, they could not be hired as police officers regardless of their performance on the tests. Again, suppose that 10 more applicants have no interest in police work once they discover something about its nature and would not accept a police position if it were offered. The time and money spent on these individuals is also wasted. Now there are 30 applicants remaining, but the agency has only one vacancy. As you can see, the cost of recruiting the one individual who is selected is quite high.

To some extent, these difficulties are inherent in the recruitment/selection process, and to some extent they may be offset by the establishment of an eligibility list (if there are other vacancies within a relatively short period of time). That is, those involved in the hiring process probably cannot determine at the outset who will and will not decide to accept the position if it is offered, and if several of the people who qualify are hired, the costs may be reduced. Costs also may be reduced, however, by developing an advertising campaign that clearly states the requirements of the position and that, to the extent possible, accurately describes the duties to be performed. Thus, a statement that those with prior felony convictions need not apply might be part of the advertisement. While this does not guarantee that such persons will not apply, it at least indicates to them that they have no chance of being hired if discovered and probably prevents many with prior convictions from applying. The point is that the more accurately the qualities sought are described, the less likely it is that large numbers of unqualified people will apply, thus helping to keep recruiting costs as low as possible. At the same time, however, advertisements must be designed to attract as many qualified applicants as possible. This includes not only describing the benefits associated with the available position, but also indicating that the police department is an equal opportunity employer and women and minorities are invited to apply. Including these statements is especially necessary in police recruitment because police departments, for reasons detailed previously, have traditionally been viewed by both minorities and women as basically white, male domains. Advertising campaigns must take this fact into account, and advertisements should be placed in magazines and on Internet sites likely to be read by women and minorities as well as in the more traditional professional journals and newspapers.

Further recruiting efforts may be directed at college campuses, high schools, and minority neighborhoods. Conducting orientation sessions that provide a realistic picture of police work in the department in question for applicants is another valuable tool in "selecting out" those who find they have no interest in such work. Many police departments utilize the Internet to advertise vacancies, and some allow application over the Internet. Those seeking jobs as police officers can also use the Web to learn how to take entry-level tests (Brandon & Lippman, 2000). Although those responsible for recruiting police personnel have made strides in these areas in recent years, there is still much to be done. The bottom line is that if those charged with hiring police officers want to have representative police departments in order to provide the best services available to the communities served, they must attract the best qualified candidates.

When the application deadline indicated in the advertisements has been reached, the applications that have been filed must be analyzed. The better the application form, the easier the analysis. The form might request information on prior experience in policing, prior criminal convictions, educational background, reasons for the interest in police work, prior drug and alcohol use, and other information considered pertinent by specific departments. It should also provide some indication of the applicant's writing ability. Some departments have found that charging a nominal fee for the application eliminates some applicants who might simply be testing the waters, and detailed application forms that request specific information probably also eliminate some who are using narcotics, some who have prior felony convictions, and so on. The more of these applicants eliminated at this stage, the less costly the recruiting process. However, in today's tight market, charging an application fee, especially when not all agencies do so, may not be in the department's best interests.

As we have stated, standards of selection for police officers were virtually nonexistent in the early days of American policing. When standards did begin to emerge, they often required little more than allegiance to a particular politician or political party.

The past two decades have seen an increase in the concern with establishing minimum entry-level requirements for police officers, and only in the past several years has what has been called the ***Multiple-Hurdle Procedure*** become common (Decicco, 2000). The term refers to a battery of tests or hurdles that must be successfully completed before the recruit can become a police officer. In the following sections, we critically analyze each of these tests, which may be generally divided into the following categories:

1. Status tests

2. Physical tests

3. Mental tests

4. Tests of morality

5. Tests of ability to communicate

It should be pointed out that the different types of tests sometimes overlap, but we discuss each independently.

Status Tests

Status tests have to do with areas such as citizenship, possession of or ability to obtain a driver's license, residency, service in the military, educational level, and age. Police officers are required to be citizens in most cases, though some court challenges to this requirement are being made. Is citizenship a bona fide job requirement? Can one who is a citizen perform police functions better than one who is, for example, a permanent resident who has passed a test covering the U.S. and state constitutions? As an example, in order to become an FBI Police Officer you must be a U.S. citizen or a citizen of the Northern Mariana Islands (Federal Bureau of Investigation, 2009). And in order to serve as a Los Angeles Police Officer a candidate is required to be a U.S. citizen or a permanent resident alien who, in accordance with the requirement of the U.S. Citizenship and Immigration Service, is eligible and has applied for citizenship (Los Angeles Police Department, 2009). These requirements are consistent with The Immigration and Reform Control Act, which requires employers to assure that employees hired are legally authorized to work in the United States (EEOC, 2009). The requirement that the applicant has or be able to obtain a driver's license seems likely to be upheld for obvious reasons. Some municipalities and states require that newly hired personnel be residents, or be willing to become residents, of the jurisdiction involved. "This requirement, too, has been and continues to be subject to court battles, and a majority of jurisdictions have modified the requirement" (Gaines & Kappeler, 2008, p. 110). Many suburban police departments, for example, simply require that officers live no more than 20 or 30 minutes from their place of duty.

Questions concerning prior military service arise because bonus points (veterans' preference points) may be added to the test scores of applicants if they have such prior service, thus affecting the final eligibility list. As an example, the Philadelphia Police Department (2009) will add 10 points to the raw score of a veteran's entrance examination and waive the residency requirement that requires one year of residency prior to appointment as a police officer. Most departments have minimum educational standards, typically possession of a high school diploma or its equivalent, that must be met by applicants, and these standards have been upheld by the courts.

Finally, the vast majority of departments require that applicants be adults (the age of majority) at the time of employment and not be more than 36 to 40 years of age at the time of initial employment in policing. The minimum age requirement makes sense in terms of maturity and meeting statutory requirements for entering certain types of establishments. The upper age limit has been called into question as a result of the Age Discrimination Act of 1990, which prohibits age discrimination with respect to those over age 40. As an example, Memphis (TN) Police Department's minimum age for applicants is 21 years of age, however there is no maximum age limit (Memphis Police, 2009). Whether the applicant meets the status requirements can be determined largely from the application form.

Physical Tests

Physical tests include physical agility tests, height-weight proportionate tests, vision tests, and medical examinations.

Physical Agility Tests

Physical agility tests are used by about 80% of police agencies to determine whether applicants are agile enough, in good enough condition, strong enough, and have enough endurance to perform police work (Decicco, 2000). These tests must be job-related, and many have fallen by the wayside as the result of court challenges. Tests of coordination and actual agility can typically be shown to be job-related, whereas tests based on sheer strength are more difficult to validate. Many departments at one time required that applicants be able to complete a specified number of pull-ups or push-ups in a specified time period. It is difficult to justify such tests on the basis of job-relatedness, however. How often does a police officer have to do pull-ups in the performance of his duty? A more realistic test is the wall test in which the applicant must clear a wall of a certain height. One can at least envision the possibility of this type of activity in the performance of police duties.

As we previously discussed, all testing of police applicants should be valid, reliable, consistent, and should accurately reflect the required duties of today's police officer. However, when police agencies conduct research to validate physical agility testing protocol they usually employ job analysis techniques that suffer from validity problems (Lonsway, 2004). "Research that documents what an officer does on the job does not tell us anything about whether the officer should have done it, what happens when the officer decides not to do it, and whether it could have been done with the assistance of another officer (Lonsway, 2004, p. 6).

Many police departments require applicants to complete a **simulation** or **work sample test**. These tests involve "measuring job skills by using samples of behavior under realistic job-like conditions" (Landy & Conte, 2009, p. 151). Police officer applicants often complete these tests, which involve pushing a police vehicle a required distance, firing an unloaded firearm a certain number of times, or searching a mock crime scene. However, in some cases these types of tests have been found deficient due to lack of adequate job analysis, lack of relationship between the job and test performance, and the arbitrary nature of the cutoff score (Med-Tox Health Services, 2009). Nonetheless, if properly constructed, these types of tests can be valuable in the screening of police applicants.

Currently in police applicant testing, those standards that prove to be job related and consistent with a business necessity and that represent the least discriminatory alternative to selection are likely to be upheld by courts (Lonsway, 2004).

Height-Weight Proportionate Tests

Height-weight proportionate tests have replaced traditional height requirements, which eliminated most women and many minority group members from policing. Such tests make sense in the context of police work and the previously discussed agility requirements. As originally employed, these tests seemed largely superfluous because few departments required that proportionate height and weight be maintained after initial employment, but many, if not most, departments now test for proportionate height and weight on a regular basis. As an example, the New York State Police Recruitment Center (2009) provides a chart of height and weight requirements by gender, and those who do not fall within the acceptable limits must submit to a fat content test using a skin caliper.

Vision Requirements

Vision requirements vary greatly among departments and are the subject of controversy. When such requirements are for uncorrected vision, they are especially controversial. Most departments have established corrected vision requirements that may be justified on the basis of driving ability, ability to identify license plates or persons, or weapons qualification (Holden & Gammeltoft, 1991). In a related study, Good, Maisel, and Kriska (1998) concluded that police must be able to perform two essential tasks when visually incapacitated: identifying a weapon in a typical room and finding spectacles that have been dislodged. They showed that a noticeable performance decrement begins to appear at 20/125 level of acuity. Many of these earlier studies are used to justify the current vision requirements for police applicants. Even though technology has provided a variety of alternatives for vision correction not mentioned in earlier studies, many police departments have adapted their current hiring requirements. For example, San Diego Police Department (2009) addresses corrective measures such as eyeglasses, hard contact lenses (semi-soft, semi-rigid, semi-permeable, gas permeable), soft contact lenses, orthokeratology, radial keratotomy, or similar procedures. In many cases applicants must sign an agreement to wear the lenses or glasses at all times while on duty and in some cases must wait up to one year following certain visual correction procedures before submitting to a department medical examination. Many are concerned that the visual acuity requirements are implemented at time of hire but only enforced in the most extreme cases. As we know, many people suffer from visual acuity changes with age, and some police officers with more than 20 years of service may experience a reduction in uncorrected vision. Currently, few departments address these issues and enforce vision requirements for police applicants, even though new recruits and officers with over 20 years of service perform the same duties involving weapons, driving, and identifying license plates.

Medical Examinations

The medical examination is a critical part of the testing process from the point of view of the department. This is so because an officer who becomes disabled as a result of injury or illness is often eligible for life-long disability payments. To detect conditions that may lead to such illnesses or injuries, virtually all police agencies require a medical examination, which is intended to detect problems of the heart, back, legs, and feet, among others. These conditions may be aggravated by police work, and the department would prefer to eliminate from consideration applicants with such problems. Due consideration must be given to the requirements of the Americans with Disabilities Act, which states that an employer may only ask about an applicant's disability or administer a medical examination after the employer has made a job offer. In most cases, police departments make the job offer conditional upon passing the medical exam.

Mental Tests

Mental tests may be divided into two categories: (1) those designed to measure intelligence, knowledge, or aptitude; and (2) those designed to evaluate psychological fitness.

Tests of Intelligence, Knowledge, or Aptitude

Written tests are used by a majority of police agencies. The paper-and-pencil and computerized versions come in a variety of forms and are intended to measure a variety of things. To be of value, the tests must deal with job-related issues and must have predictive value; that is, they should be able to predict whether an applicant has the ability to perform police work well. The International Public Management Association for Human Resources (IPMA) is a common resource for entry level police tests and supports the tests by criterion-related validity studies and psychometric analysis. IPMA (2009) assesses critical abilities of entry level police applicants related to the following areas:

- Ability to learn and apply police information
- Ability to observe and remember details
- Ability to follow directions
- Ability to use judgment and logic

These written tests have historically eliminated most minority group members. Millions of dollars have been spent in attempts to develop "culture fair" tests to avoid this bias, but with, at best, only moderate success (Winters, 1992). And perhaps for lack of a better screening device, the vast majority of departments continue to use written tests in spite of their obvious inadequacies. In most departments where such tests are used, they are scored on a point system, and the score obtained becomes a part of the overall point total used to determine the eligibility list. Differences of 1 or 2 points might, therefore, make the difference between hiring one applicant and another, even though differences of 5 to 10 points probably indicate little difference between candidates. Although a score of 70 is often established as the cutoff point for passing, this score may be raised or lowered, depending on the candidate pool—indicating that there is nothing magical about the score itself. The very fact that there are many different tests and forms of tests available implies that there is no consensus about a best test or best form.

While there are some difficulties involved in conducting the research necessary to evaluate written entry-level tests, such research is essential if we are to develop a test with predictive power. Such research would require that a department hire applicants regardless of their scores on the test (including those who failed), keep the test results secret from those who evaluate the officers' performance over a period of time (preferably at least 18 months to two years), and then compare performance evaluations over the time period with initial test scores. If those who scored high on the written test were also the best performers on the job, the validity of the test would be demonstrated, all other factors being equal (which they seldom are). Although the research required is relatively simple, questions of liability exist for a department choosing to participate in such research. What happens, for instance, if an applicant who failed the test is hired and performs so badly that someone is injured or killed as a result? In addition, the time period involved is quite long, and many agencies and test constructors are unwilling to wait the required time to obtain meaningful results.

Still, most police agencies continue to use written entry-level tests as screening devices in spite of their obvious shortcomings. Despite the intensive effort to improve written tests, there is little convincing evidence that test scores can predict what officer performance will be over any extensive period of time. Bartol and Bartol (2008) argue that screening of applicants for police positions should go beyond simply using standardized intelligence tests. They believe what is needed is a multi-assessment procedure that involves standardized tests plus other measures and screening procedures. In the next section, we will discuss the call to evaluate emotional stability and personality characteristics of police applicants.

Some agencies are considering the use of integrity tests, which, unlike the cognitive ability tests, are designed to predict the same counterproductive work behaviors (drug usage, theft, etc.) screened by psychological evaluation and polygraph tests (Tawney, 2008). If administered early in the selection process, an integrity test could remove applicants likely to fail a polygraph test or psychological testing, thus saving the agency the costs of administering these two tests.

Psychological Tests

Psychological tests present even more difficulties than written tests of intelligence, aptitude, or knowledge. Psychological tests have increasingly been used to test police applicants, and the President's Commission in 1967 recommended they be used by all police departments to determine emotional stability (Meier, Farmer, & Maxwell, 1987). In spite of the many weaknesses discussed here, psychological tests continue to be employed both because of the liability that may result from hiring police officers without the use of such tests and because many police administrators believe that they at least screen out those applicants who are clearly suffering from emotional disorders. Cochrane, Teft, and Vandecreek (2003) suggested that 90% of police departments require psychological evaluation of applicants. The most frequently used personality measures were the Minnesota Multiphasic Personality Inventory—Revised (71.6%), the California Psychological Inventory (24.5%), the Sixteen Personality Factor (18.7 %), and the Inwald Personality Inventory (11.6%) (Cochrane et al., 2003).

The task of predicting psychological stability—for short time periods, let alone the career of a police officer—is a formidable one. This is especially true because the psychological characteristics of the ideal police officer have not been, and perhaps cannot be, identified. The diversity in American policing discussed in the first chapter of this book, in combination with the complexity of the police role, makes obtaining a consensus about the characteristics of the ideal officer highly unlikely. According to Bartol and Bartol (2008), policing draws a wide spectrum of personalities, most of which do a commendable job of policing across a wide range of tasks and responsibilities. Consequently, they believe attempts to discover a particular type of personality best suited for policing are unlikely to be productive.

Benner (1989) discussed the extent to which psychological tests can select out police applicants who are either unstable or unsuitable (or both) and concluded, "It matters little that the field of psychology is only marginally capable of predicting 'bad' officer candidates. Psychologists and psychiatrists are expected, not only, to screen out the 'bad' but be able to screen in the 'good.' Unfortunately, consensus definitions of 'good' or 'suitable' have not been developed either among the professionals or members of the lay public" (p. 83).

Pendergrass (1987) indicated that psychological tests can make a contribution to the selection process but should not "replace other methods nor are the results of psychological assessment without error in prediction of success of candidates . . . selection based entirely upon psychological testing is likely to eliminate a number of good candidates and retain some poor candidates in error" (p. 29).

While the literature on psychological testing of police recruits is confusing, at best, it appears certain that such testing, unless used to supplement the other procedures discussed here, is of limited value. In other words, "although many different assessment techniques and personality inventories are used in the screening, selection, and promotion of law enforcement officers, it is usually not known whether many of these testing procedures are valid predictors of effective on-the-job law enforcement performance" (Bartol & Bartol, 2008, p. 49). "Still, there is a question as to whether psychological testing done only at the time of application can ever be an accurate predictor of police officer behavior, because psychological problems may result from serving as a police officer even though they may not have existed at the time of hiring" (Alpert & Dunham, 1997, p. 55).

Tests of Morality

Tests of morality include background investigations, drug tests, and polygraph examinations. We refer to these requirements as tests of morality because they are used to evaluate the moral character of police applicants. Certainly drug testing also constitutes a physical test, but it is typically the use of drugs rather than the impact of the drugs on the physical well-being of the applicant that is of primary concern.

Background Investigations

Background investigations are used by almost all police agencies, but the extent and intensiveness of these investigations vary considerably. In some cases, listed references are simply checked by phone, while in other cases, a good deal of time and money are expended to verify the character of the applicant. In cases of the latter type, the investigation normally includes the types of information listed in Table 2.2, which are often public records created by government agencies. However, it is important to note that school records, credit reports, medical records, and military service records are often confidential and require written consent of the applicant (Find Law, 2008).

Table 2.2 Information Included in a Background Check			
Driving records	Vehicle registration	Credit records	Criminal records
Social Security number	Education records	Court records	Workers' compensation
Bankruptcy	Character references	Neighbor interviews	Medical records
Property ownership	Military records	State licensing records	Drug test records
Past employers	Personal references	Incarceration records	Sex offender lists

Source: From "Employment Background Checks: A Jobseeker's Guide," by Privacy Rights Clearinghouse, 2009, p. 2. Available online at: http://www.privacyrights.org/fs/fs16-bck.htm

In short, a major purpose of the background investigation is to determine the honesty of the applicant as reflected by the information she provided on the application form and in subsequent communications with those in charge of recruiting and selecting. Departments tend to place an emphasis on the background investigation because an intensive background check can help to ensure departments hire only the most qualified applicants and also can indicate an individual's competency, motivation, and personal ethics (Decicco, 2000, p.2). Background investigations may exclude, or highlight for further inquiry, applicants who have prior felony convictions or who are currently wanted; those with a history of serious employment, family, or financial problems; those who have been dishonorably discharged from the military; and those who have failed to tell the truth during the application process. In addition, prior and current use of alcohol or other drugs is typically explored in the context of making reference contacts. The rationale for excluding or further investigating applicants with problems in these areas is relatively clear. It makes little sense to hire as a police officer an individual who has serious drug-related problems; in virtually all jurisdictions, those with prior felony convictions are excluded from policing by statute. Those with histories of domestic violence or bankruptcy also present problems because they may be corruptible or prone to the use of force in their positions as police officers. In short, the background investigation represents an attempt to select into policing only those with what is defined as good moral character. (See Case In Point 2.1 involving a state background investigation.)

☞ CASE IN POINT 2.1

Ten new police officers were sworn in to the East St. Louis Police Department, and at the Ceremony, the Mayor proclaimed to everyone in the room, "You are safe as anybody now, in this city, in this room." However, documents obtained by Post-Dispatch revealed that two of the new appointed police officers had prior criminal histories. Furthermore, one of the officers at the time of swearing in had a valid outstanding arrest warrant for domestic battery.

The records for the police officers included "arrests for misdemeanors, extensive traffic citations and multiple bankruptcies." The City admitted they expedited the process to attempt to place as many officers as possible in the next police training academy class. The City relied on its own investigation instead of waiting for the Illinois State Police background checks. Most agree that criminal behavior is one of the most important parts of the background check.

Source: From "Checkered Pasts in East St. Louis Police Recruits Included Criminals' Rushed Investigation. City, Desperate for Officers, Didn't Wait for State Background Check," by A. Leventis, 2008, *St. Louis Post-Dispatch*. Available online at: http://infoweb.newsbank.com

---

Drug Tests

The possession, manufacture, distribution, and sale of illegal drugs are all serious problems in our society, and applicants for police work are not immune to these problems. However, in the past decade, many police departments have modified their zero tolerance policy that disqualified all applicants who had previously used any type of drug. As Baxley (2000) indicated, due to increasing difficulties in recruiting, there is a "growing tendency to tolerate some history of drug use or criminal activity by recruit candidates. . . . Many agencies now take into consideration the type and amount of drugs used, the length of time since the last use, and the nature of the offense. Those who have merely 'experimented during high school or college' are often allowed to join the force" (p. 371). As an example, Santa Rosa Police Department (2009) considers the following factors when there is evidence of past abuse of controlled substances: patterns of use, how the drug was obtained, type of drug used, circumstances of the start of the drug use, and discontinuance and nature of treatment and prognosis. Evidence of the modification of prior zero tolerance drug use requirements for police applicants is presented in Table 2.3.

Although the issue of drug testing, usually accomplished through urinalysis, has led to a great deal of litigation, it appears that when such testing is done according to a schedule (as opposed to random testing) and when it is done in a reasonable fashion and on reasonable grounds, the courts will allow the testing as it relates to policing. This appears to be so because of police departments' interests in protecting the safety of the public and other employees. The possibility of a drug-impaired police

Table 2.3	Illegal Drug Use Guidelines	
Substance	**Minimum years since last use**	**Maximum number of times used**
Marijuana	3	50
Hash/Hash oil	3	20
Amphetamine	5	5
Cocaine (powder)	5	5

Source: From "Illegal Drug Use Guideline," by the Santa Rosa Police Department, 2007. Available online from http://cisanta-rosa.ca.us/doclib/Documents/Drug_Standard.pdf

officer injuring a colleague or another person as the result of a vehicle accident, firearm discharge, or use of excessive force clearly exists. Thus, drug testing is likely to become even more prevalent among police agencies than it is now because the legal requirements for such testing are more clearly elaborated by court decisions and revisions of statutes.

Another drug use issue addressed by many police departments involves the restriction of the use of anabolic steroids by police applicants. Humphrey et al. (2008) indicated that anabolic steroids appeal to police officers who desire a tactical edge or an intimidating appearance to improve their performance. Currently, testing for performance-enhancing substances presents a myriad of challenges and is not as straightforward as discovering heroin in an applicant drug screen (Humphrey et al., 2008).

Polygraph Examinations

❖ PHOTO **2.2** A police applicant undergoes a polygraph examination as part of the selection process for being hired as a police officer.

Polygraph examinations are employed by many police agencies in the United States, although changes in federal legislation have already greatly restricted their use in the private sector and may eventually have the same impact on the public sector. Currently, a police agency can conduct a polygraph before a conditional offer of employment but must avoid asking any prohibited disability-related inquires in administering the pre-offer exam (U. S. Department of Justice, 2006).

The rationale behind the use of the polygraph for recruitment and selection appears to be twofold. First, the results of the examination are used as one indicator of the honesty of the job applicant. Second, the results are used to eliminate applicants whose responses are not acceptable to the police agency in question, regardless of the honesty of the applicant. As an example, during the polygraph exam, police applicants are often questioned about a variety of prior experiences (see Table 2.4).

Either or both of these purposes for the exam may be justified, but there is, and always has been, considerable controversy over the accuracy of polygraph tests, which raises the issue of rejecting some qualified applicants while accepting others who are deceitful (Decicco, 2000). Numerous Internet sites offer advice on how to beat the polygraph using deliberate attempts to alter the data, often caused by physiological changes with body movements (Gordon, 2008). In response to this type of information, the polygraph profession has added a fourth parameter, which involves monitoring body movements associated with countermeasures. This change is in addition to the three basic physiological functions monitored today: blood volume and pressure, respiration, and sweating (Gordon, 2008). Currently, research is exploring a new generation of lie detection technology through the use of functional magnetic resonance imaging, electroencephalography, near-infrared light, and other technology that permits access to brain function (Wolpe, Foster, & Langleben, 2005). The problem with polygraph tests is not with the machine, which simply measures heart rate, rate of breathing, and **galvanic skin response** (changes in electrical resistance in the skin) over time. The interpretation of the results and the way in which the test is administered depend on the polygrapher. The training, skills, and competence of polygraphers vary widely, and the conditions (anxiety and nervousness on behalf of applicants) under which employment and promotional polygraph interviews are conducted are less than ideal for ensuring accurate results.

Table 2.4   Polygraph Examination Areas

- Accuracy of information provided on the written applications and documents
- Honesty, integrity, and reliability of the applicant
- Criminal history, either previously detected or undetected
- Traffic history, either previously detected or undetected
- Involvement with illicit drugs

Source: From "Police Officer Exam Process," by the Arlington, Virginia Police Department, 2009. Available online from http://www.arlingtonva.us

Tests of Ability to Communicate

As indicated earlier, many of the recruitment and selection procedures used with respect to the police overlap. This interdependence of procedures is perhaps best illustrated by tests of ability to communicate. Properly conceived, these tests include the application form and the written tests taken by applicants and the oral interview typically required of potential police officers. Because we have already discussed the application and written tests, we concentrate here on the oral interview or *oral board,* as it is often called. Let us simply note that it is both possible and desirable to evaluate the written communications skills of applicants by requiring them to write a job history or autobiographical statement as a part of the application form because a large measure of police work involves writing reports that require accuracy and comprehensiveness. While a misspelled word or two is probably no cause for concern, serious defects in the ability to communicate in writing indicate, at the very minimum, the need for some remedial work in this area.

The Oral Board

Oral interviews of police applicants are used by most agencies. These interviews, or boards, are typically conducted by members of the fire and police or civil service commission or by the personnel department in larger police agencies, often in conjunction with representatives of the police agency. In some cases, the latter actually participate in the interview, while in others, they simply observe. The number of interviewers varies, but three to five is typical.

POLICE STORIES

Most police hiring processes involve numerous activities. For example, the specific elements of the physical agility test are no secret and allow a police applicant to prepare for the test either through running, lifting weights, or engaging in other forms of exercise. In addition, in most cases applicants have taken multiple choice tests in school and are prepared to challenge a department's written exam. However, as a Merit Commissioner for a Sheriff's Department, I have observed many applicants encounter problems at the oral board interview. The oral interview is stressful, and many applicants are eliminated from the hiring process based on their performance.

To be successful at the oral board, I tell students to dress professionally, leave cell phones in the car, and arrive early to locate the building, designated parking, and the specific room. I encourage them, upon entering the interview room, to introduce themselves to members of the board by shaking hands.

(Continued)

(Continued)

I indicate to students that there may well be questions concerning ethics, such as those related to arresting off duty police officers or city officials that have openly committed criminal acts. I tell them I hope they will respond by indicating they would do the right thing and that I'm sure they know what the "right thing" involves.

I believe applicants should know as much as possible about the department to which they are applying. At the conclusion of the interview, board members will often ask if the interviewee has any questions. Questions concerning the department and the community might be appropriate, but questions such as "What is the starting salary?" are generally unnecessary since this information is readily available on most police department's websites.

Police applicants can expect questions from the board about background, future goals, and current police issues in the form of hypothetical scenarios. Finally, the board might conclude the interview by asking "Why should we hire you over all the other applicants?" This is the applicant's chance to hit a home run and convince the board that he or she is one of the top applicants immediately before they begin the process of calculating final scores. I also tell students to remember that the more oral board interviews they participate in by applying at various departments, the more comfortable they will become with the process.

The expressed purpose of the oral board is to select a suitable applicant to fill the existing police vacancy. There is often, however, a second goal in these interviews: that of selecting a certain kind of person to fill the vacancy. In addition to demonstrating the skills necessary to fill the formal organizational position, the applicant's loyalty to the department, trustworthiness with respect to other police officers, and, although legally and formally forbidden, their race, gender, and general presentation of self may be considered (Cox & Fitzgerald, 1996). While it is undoubtedly true that efforts to reduce the amount of subjectivity in oral interviews have been made in the form of standardized questions and independent evaluation by the raters, it is equally true that the way we look (dress, skin color, gender, etc.) and act (eye contact, handshake, degree of self-confidence expressed) affects our daily interactions and, despite attempts to minimize the impact of these variables on the scoring of the interview, also affect the interviewers (Falkenberg, Gaines, & Cox, 1990). Having served on oral boards periodically over the past 25 years, it is the authors' definite impression from conversations with other board members that factors that are expressly forbidden from consideration, in terms of equal employment opportunity guidelines, for example, do affect the judgment of interviewers in subtle, if not obvious, ways.

The interview format varies a good deal. In most cases, general questions about the applicant's background, experiences, education, prior training, and interest in police work in general and in the specific department in question are asked. These may be followed by a series of questions to test the applicant's knowledge of some legal, moral, and ethical issues related to police work. For example, the applicant may be asked how she would respond to the apparent corruption of another officer, what response would be appropriate if a traffic violator turned out to be the mayor, or how much force is justified in a certain type of incident. Some of the typical performance dimensions addressed in a police applicant oral board interview are included in Table 2.5.

Questions may be asked slowly, with follow-up questions, or they may be asked in such a fashion that they create stress for the interviewee (see, e.g., Holloway, 2000). The responses to the questions are evaluated by each of the raters independently and, should major differences in evaluation occur, may be discussed among the raters in an attempt to reach some consensus about the applicant's worthiness. The final scores for the oral board are then added to the scores from the other portions of the testing procedure to establish an eligibility list from which the chief of police or personnel department may select candidates to fill existing and future vacancies.

There is a definite irony here that needs to be pointed out. Although the selection process today is conducted under the guise of objectivity—including having the written tests sent elsewhere for scoring, scoring by identification numbers as opposed to names, rating interviewees independently, and calculating scores to the nearest point (or in some cases, tenth of a point)—when the process is completed, the final rank order based on the complex scoring system may be ignored by the chief or personnel department. That is, the applicant who scored third highest overall may be selected to fill the vacancy instead of the applicant who scored highest. Although there is perhaps nothing wrong with giving the chief some input at this stage of the selection process, it calls into question the value of all the apparent objectivity surrounding the process, particularly during the promotion process, to which we shall soon turn our attention.

In the past, many police recruits have come from families with a history of involvement in policing or from military backgrounds (Baxley, 2000). This is perhaps less true today than at any time in the recent past. Recruits are most likely to be interested in a good salary and a good benefits package. They also may assess the state of

Table 2.5   Police Applicant Performance Dimensions
• Problem solving
• Judgment and reasoning
• Decision making
• Team work orientation
• Interpersonal skills
• Oral communications and presentation skills
• Honesty and integrity
• Self-motivation and initiative
• Stress tolerance and composure

Source: From *Master the Police Officer Examination,* by F. M. Rafilson and T. DeAngelis, 2008, Georgetown, CT: ARCO Publishing.

departmental technology, opportunities for advancement, and equipment available before making a career choice. And such choices are increasingly made with the assistance of the Internet. Thus, police agencies must be attuned to the goals of potential recruits in order to establish recruitment practices that meet the needs of recruits.

The recruitment and selection process does not end with the establishment of the eligibility list. Rather, it continues as those selected for hiring go to the training academy, as they return to the department to serve their probationary period, and as they proceed through their careers in policing. See Around the World for an example of a selection process for the New Zealand Police.

AROUND THE WORLD

New Zealand Police Selection Process Requirements

- 18 years of age at time of graduation from the Royal New Zealand Police College
- No upper maximum age
- Tests assess abstract, numerical, verbal reasoning
- Psychological profiling
- Physical appraisal test
- Physical competency test (running, press-ups, jump, squeeze test)
- Formal interview
- Reference checks
- Medical examination
- Must pass swimming test
- Uncorrected/corrected vision requirements
- Any drunk driving charge will exclude the applicant

Source: From "Frequently Asked Questions," by the New Zealand Police, 2009. Available online at http://www.newcops.co.nz

---

❖ Supervisory Recruitment and Selection

As indicated earlier, the recruitment and selection process does not end with initial employment but continues as some individuals are promoted to supervisory positions and special assignments. If it is important to select prospective police officers carefully, it is equally important to promote carefully to ensure that those who supervise new recruits are well prepared to do so. As Baxley (2000) indicated,

> Too often we promote persons to supervisory positions on the basis of their longevity with the department. A long-term employee does not always make a good supervisor. . . . Well-trained supervisors who make good decisions earn the respect of both their troops and their community. They also create an environment where the troops enjoy working—and happy troops are a department's best recruiting tool. (p. 371)

The same equal employment and affirmative action rules discussed previously apply when selecting and recruiting police supervisors, including chiefs. The vast majority of police supervisors are promoted from within the ranks of the department (with the exception of police chiefs, about whom we shall have more to say in the following section) because lateral entry is the exception rather than the rule in American policing.

As Bouza (1990) noted, there are two ways of shaping supervisory talent: formal education and on-the-job training. For the latter to produce a highly skilled supervisor, a wide variety of experiences should be included (a variety of different assignments). Because the police culture largely downplays the importance of theories of management and liberal arts education, on-the-job training is critical. However, it often fails to provide the necessary breadth of training because the skills of the up-and-coming officer may be so valuable to the chief that he comes to rely almost totally on that officer for certain kinds of information or input. Thus, the about-to-be-promoted may remain in the same positions for most of their prepromotional careers. This narrow focus makes it difficult for those promoted to understand the broader police picture and leads to scorn on behalf of line officers. Further, the testing procedure itself is almost always suspect from the perspective of both those applying for advancement and those who will be affected by having new supervisors. Basically, observers tend to believe that it is who you know rather than what you know that leads to promotion.

Advertisements typically consist of position vacancy announcements posted within the police agency. Outside advertisement, although it may sometimes occur, is greatly limited (e.g., to other agencies that employ city workers).

Because most police departments retain paramilitary structures, promotional opportunities exist at the level of the field supervisor (typically at the rank of sergeant), shift or watch commander (typically at the rank of lieutenant or commander), division commander (typically with the rank of captain or above), and for a host of specializations in larger departments (juvenile, burglary, fraud, vice, and so on). As is the case at the entry level, the vacancy announcements should clearly state the qualifications for the positions and indicate how interested parties may go about applying. Individuals applying for these positions are required to pass status tests similar to those discussed for entry-level employees, with the additional stipulation that they have served a specified number of years in policing or at the level immediately below the one for which they are applying. In other words, to become a lieutenant, an officer would have to meet the basic status requirements of the department and, in addition, might be required to have served three years at the rank of sergeant.

Typically, physical tests are not employed in the selection of supervisors. The assumption may be that they have already passed such tests as the department requires or that the position to which they aspire does not require the same degree of physical agility required of line officers. Neither of these assumptions is entirely justified, however, and some measures of physical fitness appear to be appropriate. At a minimum, a thorough medical examination should be required.

As we will discuss in the next section, assessment centers are now an important part of most police promotional processes. While the assessment center is costly to develop and implement, its record of validity and legal defensibility has justified its increased use (Love & DeArmond, 2007).

Assessment Centers

❖ **Photo 2.3** Today, many police agencies use sophisticated processes to select personnel, particularly with those seeking promotion to the supervisory ranks.

The **assessment center** had its origins in the 1920s and was used by the military in World War II. The concept was furthered in the 1950s in private industry (Cosner & Baumgart, 2000). An assessment center is not a specific location but a formal process that involves a series of exercises designed to test how well a candidate would perform in a job using task simulations and role players to replicate real, on-the-job situations (Executive Office for Administration and Finance, 2009). As O'Leary (1989) indicated, prior to the 1970s, many police departments promoted people because they had "influential contacts, or did well in objective paper-and-pencil tests, or impressed a civil-service board made up of a variety of people from law-enforcement in neighboring departments, state highway patrol, private-sector managers, and perhaps representatives of the local department of human resources" (p. 28). Such promotions often resulted in ineffective supervisors because the interviewers had an inaccurate picture of the duties and responsibilities accompanying the position. The interview, as a predictive tool, proved to be only marginally effective. Paper-and-pencil tests also turned out to be poor indicators of supervisory performance.

To use the assessment center, there must first be a comprehensive, accurate job description of the position advertised. Second, a group of trained observers, usually three to five, must observe the candidates for the position as they go through a number of job-related activities. "By using a multiple-exercise process, candidates who often do not perform well in one exercise, such as an interview, may do very well in another exercise, such as an analysis and presentation exercise" (McLaurin, 2005, p. 2). This results in a more objective process in which the assessors rate the applicants individually on each of the tasks assigned over a one- or two-day period. Examples of multiple exercises employed in a typical assessment center include the following:

- In-basket exercises: measures the person's administrative and decision-making abilities through day to day administrative activities.
- Written problem-solving: tests the candidate's ability to perceive a problem and gather sufficient data to document a solution.
- Group discussion: involves an exercise where candidates are involved in a timed group discussion in which they attempt to reach a joint solution to one or more problems.
- Oral presentation: candidates present ideas or tasks to the group with or without prior preparation.
- Counseling session: an exercise with an interview simulation that involves assessment of the following abilities: "motivate work performance, correct misbehavior, provide key information, direct actions towards an appropriate solution, develop an effective working relation, demonstrate flexibility, analyze problems and demonstrate effective oral communication." (Ohio Association of Chiefs of Police, 2001, p.1)

In some cases, the applicants' performances are videotaped and may be reviewed by the assessors at their convenience. Polygraph, drug, and psychological tests, as well as an updated background investigation also may be required for promotion. Tests of ability to communicate are incorporated into the assessment center when it is employed, or they may be evaluated by an oral board in a fashion similar to that discussed for entry-level personnel. Candidates are interviewed by the assessors using a standardized format that provides latitude for assessors to raise questions concerning issues brought to light by the various exercises in which the candidates have engaged. In most assessment centers, the assessors evaluate candidates based on the following dimensions: "oral communications, command presence, technical and professional knowledge, decision making, judgment, planning and organization, work perspective, and problem analysis" (McLaurin, 2005, p. 3).

Finally, the assessors, usually under the direction of a team leader, meet to discuss their scores for and impressions of the applicants. Each assessor must be prepared to defend his scores, and discrepant scores often become topics of heated debate. In the ideal case, differences can be resolved through discussion, and the applicants are then listed in order of the assessors' preferences. Final selection is accomplished by the personnel department, police chief, city manager, mayor, or council, or some combination of these.

As previously mentioned, while the costs of the assessment center are high, success in predicting good performance has been equally high, and when measured against the costs of making a bad appointment, the costs are less imposing than they might seem. Many police departments use assessment centers not only to determine who should be hired for top-ranking positions, but also as a promotional process and a way to identify strengths and weaknesses of an agency and its employees

(McLaurin, 2005). In most cases, assessment center participants can identify their shortcomings and learn from the assessment process how to improve their own job performance and the training deficiencies of the individual as well as the organization (Hale, 2005). An assessment center can also have a positive effect on morale if the assessment center is viewed as an objective, reliable, and fair process in which the most qualified person is promoted.

Evaluations based on past performance are also frequently used when considering applicants for promotion. The usefulness of these measures remains to be established because they are typically based on behaviors relevant to the current position of the applicant that may or may not be related to the position for which she or he is applying. That is, excellent performance as a street officer may be totally unrelated to performance as a supervisor. Nonetheless, in many departments, these evaluations account for 20% to 30% of the total score considered for promotion.

❖ Recruitment and Selection of Police Chiefs

The skills required of a police chief are, in many instances, significantly different from those required of new recruits or lower ranking supervisors. The chief not only maintains general control over the department, he or she is also its representative in dealing with other municipal agencies, other police agencies, and elected officials. In some very small departments, the police chief must perform patrol and investigative functions and has few supervisory responsibilities. In police agencies with more than four or five employees, however, administrative and supervisory responsibilities become more important than street work.

Advertising for police chiefs is generally done through professional police publications as well as through the use of Internet sites, area newspapers, and bulletins. Recruitment for the position of chief may involve going outside the department, staying within the department, or a combination of the two (Kroecker, 2000). Thus, lateral entry, while seldom a possibility at other police ranks, is possible at the level of chief. This was confirmed by Piotrowski (2007), who found that in Illinois municipalities between 5,000 and 11,000 residents, approximately 36% of the chiefs were hired from outside the agency.

The status requirements discussed with respect to other supervisory personnel typically apply, the level and extent of police experience required varies across communities. Hiring is done primarily by the mayor, city manager, or city council (Piotrowski, 2007). As is the case with other supervisory personnel, written tests related to administrative and supervisory tasks are often employed, and in addition, attempts may be made to assess the extent to which the candidates view themselves as part of a management team. Education and training requirements also vary considerably, ranging from high school graduation and basic police training to possession of a master's degree and attendance at one of the more prestigious police management schools (such as the FBI Academy or the Southern Police Institute).

While many chiefs are hired based on interviews with officials of city government, performance on written tests, and background investigations, more and more are being processed through assessment centers designed to test their administrative skills.

The vast majority of police chiefs come from the police ranks, and hiring those without prior police experience, though it does occasionally occur, is the exception. Unlike other police personnel, chiefs are seldom required to attend training academies after being hired, although the political and public relations skills required to be successful indicate the need for further training in many, if not most, cases.

While some improvement has occurred in this area, promotion to the rank of chief from within undoubtedly contributes to continuing resistance to change in many police agencies. Some chiefs are basically contract chiefs, serving for a specified period of time with periodic reviews. Others are essentially given tenure when hired, though most all serve at the pleasure of the head of city government and the council, and job security is often a major concern (Frankel, 1992). When the chief reports directly to the mayor or council, political considerations are often extremely important. The city manager form of government provides some insulation from direct political ties and—from the perspective of promoting a professional, somewhat apolitical department—is probably superior.

❖ Chapter Summary

The recruitment and selection of entry level police officers, supervisors, and chiefs of police is critical to the success of police agencies. It is important that these processes be performed within the requirements established by the Equal Employment Opportunity Act, Title VII, the Americans with Disabilities Act, and the Age Discrimination in Employment Act. The selection process for entry-level police officers involves many steps to ensure only qualified applicants who are seriously interested in a career in policing are selected for the training academy.

These decisions are not easy, and the processes used to make these judgments can be quite expensive. Careful, thorough, and lawful hiring and promotion of qualified personnel should reduce the number of lawsuits, increase performance by personnel, and improve the overall professionalization of the agency. (See You Decide 2.1.)

Many factors influence recruitment and promotional practices, such as the use of valid and reliable test instruments and related materials, thorough background investigations, physical and psychological fitness tests, potential leadership capabilities assessments of applicants, and the implementation of proper performance evaluation techniques.

Police administrators must realize that with the passage of time, new demands are consistently being added to the list of police duties, and as such, new policies and shifts in philosophy regarding crime control and the overall functions and priorities of law enforcement agencies require the organization to be flexible. One significant issue that is germane to this organizational flexibility is the fact that there are three different generations working in police agencies: the baby boomers, who occupy the majority of high ranking positions, and Generation X and Y officers. The motivations and actions of officers from each of these generations are quite different from one another, and while challenging, departments must find ways of effectively supervising and accommodating the legitimate needs of officers. Not doing so can result in poor morale, high turnover, and low overall performance, which tends to stymie the growth and development of any organization.

Finally, special attention must be given to the considerations used in the hiring of police chiefs. Should the chief be promoted from within the existing ranks or selected from outside the department? What minimum criteria should be used regarding the background of applicants with respect to formal education, past administrative accomplishments, specialized training, and leadership ability?

Conducting careful and legitimate recruitment, selection, and promotional practices is required in today's society.

YOU DECIDE 2.1

The U.S. District Court of Connecticut decided a case in which a police applicant was denied the opportunity to become a police officer based on a score on the written examination. One part of the testing process for police officer required the applicant to take the "Wonderlic Personnel Test and Scholastic Level Exam. Wonderlic's User's Manual suggests a range of 20 to 27 for consideration as a patrol officer, and the City of New London followed that recommendation."

The plaintiff in this case scored a 33 on the test, which was deemed to be too high for consideration as police officer. "Subsequent to notification of his ineligibility for the position of police officer due to his high test score," a suit was filed against the City of New London.

The Court concluded that the City "followed Wonderlic's recommendation as well as reasonably relying on professional literature that concluded, 'hiring overqualified applicants leads to dissatisfaction and turnover,' they did not violate the Equal Protection Clauses."

1. Should police applicants be denied employment based on a high score on a written examination?

2. Do you believe written examinations can accurately predict an applicant's ability to perform the duties of a patrol officer? Explain.

Source: Reproduced from the Journal of Applied Testing Technology © 1999–2010, Association of Test Publishers™.

❖ Key Terms

Baby Boomer Generation

Generation X

Generation Y

immutable characteristics

discrimination

affirmative action

consent decree

bona fide occupational qualification

qualified individual
  with a disability

reasonable accommodation

Multiple Hurdle Procedure

status test

simulation of work sample test

galvanic skin response

assessment center

❖ Discussion Questions

1. Why are the costs of recruitment of police personnel so high? How can such costs reasonably be reduced?

2. Can you locate any websites dealing with police recruitment? What are they, and what kinds of information do they contain? Do any allow you to apply online?

3. Why is recruitment of qualified personnel so important to police agencies?

4. Discuss some of the changes in the selection of police officers that have occurred as a result of equal employment opportunity laws and affirmative action programs. What are some of the positive and negative consequences of EEOC and affirmative action programs?

5. List and discuss the five basic types of police officer selection requirements. How do such requirements apply to promotions?

6. What is an assessment center, why are such centers increasingly being used, and what, if any, disadvantages do they have?

7. What are the backgrounds of most police chiefs, and what implications do these backgrounds have for policing as a profession?

8. How do the provisions of the Americans with Disabilities Act affect the police?

❖ Internet Exercises

1. Select one of the tests administered to police officer applicants discussed in the chapter (drug test, physical agility, polygraph, etc.). Go to the Internet and locate information about this test. How is the test administered? What method is used for scoring the test and interpreting the results? Is the test you selected a valid measure of a critical task performed by today's police officers?

2. Locate an advertisement for a police chief that discusses the selection requirements. How is the selection process for chiefs of police different from the process for the selection of police officers? Based on the advertisement, what knowledge, skills, and abilities should today's police chief possess?

Police Training and Education

❖ Pʜᴏᴛᴏs **3.1a & 3.1b** Police work clearly requires a combination of effective, relevant training as well as completion of higher education coursework.

❖ Introduction

The extent and nature of police training and education have been controversial since at least 1908, when August Vollmer began formal training for police officers and advocated for a baccalaureate degree as a requirement for entry level police officers in the Berkeley, California Police Department. Although the two issues are intimately interrelated, they are distinct, and we address them separately in this chapter.

One of the most frequently debated issues concerns the nature of the distinction between training and education. While there is clearly a good deal of overlap, **training** may be regarded as the provision of basic skills necessary to do the job, and **education** may be viewed as providing familiarity with the concepts and principles underlying the training. From this perspective, training is more concrete and practical, and education more abstract and theoretical. The discussion that follows is based on these distinctions, though the reader should note that there is no absolute agreement concerning the distinctions made. Baro and Burlingame (1999), for example, argued that a good deal of contemporary police training (e.g., cultural diversity, communications, and interpersonal skills) is based on scholarly theory and research; thus, the lines between education and training are sometimes blurred. Many also believe that the training and education of police should not be viewed or researched as disparate or discrete issues but rather should be viewed as complimentary forces that create a synergy to improve both police practice and the level of professionalism in the field. As Giannoni (2002) noted ". . . higher education serves to elevate the quality of [police] training. Educators and trainers are needed to build a bridge over the chasm that currently separates higher-education and university criminal-justice programs [from] police training." (p. 37).

❖ Police Training

Policing is a difficult and complex career. The police officer is called on to play psychiatrist, doctor, lawyer, judge, jury, priest, counselor, fighter, and dogcatcher. The training requirements to become a police officer, then, are quite complex. According to Nowicki (1990a), "Police officers must be experts in interpersonal communications, possess intimate knowledge of counseling and crisis intervention strategies, and be able to defuse potentially volatile domestic disturbances. Yet the time allotted to these topics in my police academy is a paltry seven hours total. . . . Police officers . . . can and do make decisions to arrest and restrict a person's freedom, and the power of life and death is literally at their fingertips, but on the average they receive less than one-quarter of the training required to give someone a haircut." (1990a, p. 4).

Since 1989, however, both the duration and variety of topics covered in police training centers throughout the United States have increased, although there are significant differences across state boundaries. Police administrators and the governmental bodies they represent spend millions of dollars on training personnel. There is no longer any debate that initial, basic training for police officers is mandatory, both to improve their performance and as protection against any liability that may result from failure to train (Phillips, 1987). "Inadequate or inappropriate training can lead to poor decision making, too much or too little self-confidence, and inaccurate assessments of situations" (Graves, 1991, p. 62). But, how much training should be done? Who should do it? What should the content of the training be? What form should it take? How can training best be used to benefit officers and the citizens they serve? How effective is the training received? Answers to these questions are not always easy to come by, but they are essential if our goal is to develop highly trained, competent police officers.

How Much Training Is Enough?

Simply put, police officers can never have enough training, and training is, therefore, a career-long commitment. This observation is based on the assumption that the world is constantly changing and that police officers and other professionals must constantly respond to that changing world. This *inservice training,* as it is referred to in police circles, is also known as *continuing professional education,* and engagement in this form of learning is one of the cornerstones of professionalism. So much is happening in the world at such a rapid pace that no one of us can possibly keep up with all the changes in technology and theory. Only proper training and education (as we shall see later in this chapter) can keep police officers current. This is indicated by the increase in the use of computers for communication, forensics, crime analysis, and so on. The need for training pervades all levels of policing, including that of police chief. Unfortunately, police administrators sometimes fail to take advantage of training opportunities as a result of busy schedules, lack of interest, or the mistaken belief that they already know all there is to know. A frequently heard comment from patrol officers in training sessions is, "I wish the chief could hear this." A police administrator who wants a well-trained department must send the message that training is important in a variety of ways, including by his or her own at least occasional attendance at training sessions.

Before proceeding to an in-depth analysis of the many issues surrounding training and education, it is important to note here that a number of states now mandate training both at the entry level and on a continuing basis. Peace Officer Standards and Training commissions now operate in all states, prescribing and supervising training for police officers.

❖ Types of Training

Basic Recruit Training

Most new police recruits attend police training institutes or academies. Such training is referred to as *basic* or *recruit training* and comprises (roughly in order of the amount of time spent on each) patrol techniques and criminal investigation, force and weaponry, legal issues, administration, communications, criminal justice systems, and human relations. "A 1986 survey of state and municipal police agencies (in cities with at least 50,000 population) indicated that the mean (average) length of basic training was 13.5 weeks, or 541.5 hours" (Sapp, 1986, p. 6). As of 2000, the lowest number of training academy hours mandated was 320; the highest number of mandated hours was 1,118; and the mean number of training hours required of entry-level recruits was 516 (Magers & Klein, 2002, p. 108). While this nearly 100% increase in the amount of training looks extremely promising at a glance, what must be emphasized is that in almost none of these academies does the amount of time spent on human or community relations and ethical decision making exceed 10%—even though the vast majority of a police officer's time is spent in encounters and duties that require skills in these areas. The paradox in the current state of police training is that the majority of training is designed to teach police officers what they will be doing during a small percentage of their on-duty time" (Birzer, 1999, p. 17). This must change if police officers are to perform their duties competently and ethically in the journey along the continuum of professionalization. Birzer (1999) and others felt that as policing evolved to become more community-oriented, academies would include more than the mechanical aspects of policing in their curriculums. Unfortunately, many never did, and now that community policing initiatives are no longer funded to the same extent they were during the late 1990s and early 2000s, the topical areas covered remain dominated by the concrete and practical approach mentioned previously. Thus, for example, the Bureau of Justice Statistics (BJS) (2009) reported the following. (It should be noted that unlike the data cited in the above studies, this report examined police recruits attending all state, local, municipal, and college campus-based training academies, regardless of population.)

- As of the end of 2006, there were 648 police training facilities offering basic recruit training.
- Basic training programs averaged 19 weeks in length.
- Topics with the most instruction included firearms, self-defense, health and fitness, patrol procedures, investigations, emergency vehicle operations, criminal law, and basic first aid.

- Of the approximately 57,000 police recruits who entered the basic training program in 2005, 86%, or 49,000, graduated from the academy.
- Academies with a predominately non-stress, or academic, orientation (89%) had a higher completion rate than academies with a predominately stress, or paramilitary, orientation (80%).

Field Training

Although the information provided in basic training academies is crucial, there is often a considerable gap between what is taught and what actually occurs on the streets. In a very real sense, academy training is simply a preparatory step for on-the-job or field training. The first opportunity to practice what the recruit has been taught comes during the first year or two of service, often referred to as the ***probationary period***. Normally new officers are, or should be, involved in field training under the supervision of field training officers (FTOs) who have been selected and trained to direct, evaluate, and correct the performance of recruits immediately after their basic academy training. Such programs have become widespread since their inception in San Jose, California, in the early 1970s. They provide daily evaluation of recruits' performance by two or more FTOs, as well as weekly or monthly evaluations by other supervisory personnel. The programs are typically divided into introductory, training, and evaluation phases and are, on average, approximately 180 hours in duration (Hickman, 2005). If the recruit successfully completes these phases, she or he becomes a full-fledged police officer at the end of the probationary period. If remedial training is required, it is provided. If remedial training fails to produce the desired results, FTO evaluations may serve as a basis for terminating undesirable or ineffective personnel. Herein lies much of the problem because when FTOs and supervisory personnel determine or recommend that a recruit be terminated for unsatisfactory performance, many police executives remain reluctant to terminate the individual(s) in question due to the significant costs associated with the hiring process. This economic short-sightedness, however, generally ends up costing the agency much more through the years, in terms of civil liability and strained community relations, than the cost of training. It seems to make sense, then, that when the need arises, probationary officers who do not satisfy the demands placed on them by their field training be terminated.

POLICE STORIES

Soon after graduating from college and majoring in Criminal Justice, it seemed like I applied to every police department in the Chicagoland area. The Chicago Police Department, which was really where I wanted to work, was not hiring at the time so I began applying at numerous suburban police agencies. It wasn't too long before I was hired by one of those agencies. For a suburban agency, it was a fairly large department with more than 100 officers.

(Continued)

(Continued)

Upon successful completion of my initial police academy training, it was time to hit the streets. I vividly recall the day I was introduced to my FTO—and many of the activities that soon followed. One Saturday, while working the day shift, I recall my FTO telling me that the day shift was for shopping . . . hardware items, clothing, or anything else one might be in need of. After visiting several stores with my FTO, I noticed that he either received goods or services for free or at a significant discount. When I inquired about this he told me, "Hey . . . we're the police and we're like crime . . . we don't pay . . . for nothin'!"

I wish I could say that I did not engage in those practices during my time on the job, but I did. After all, all the other cops were doing the same thing—even the supervisors. That's how I justified my actions, but I did not realize at the time that the forces of the police subculture were taking hold. This "group think" mentality, another characteristic of the subculture of policing, also influenced my decision to ignore any wrongdoing committed by my fellow officers. My justification was that "Hey, I'm not my brother's keeper." In retrospect, I was foolish to adopt that point of view. Due to my position as a police officer, my inaction made me just as liable as the cops who committed the misconduct in my presence.

Reflecting on this even more, there was no academy training on ethics or related issues at the time, though I have my doubts if such training would have made me act any differently—especially since the time period to which I refer was some 30 years ago.

The reasons for recruit failure are not always directly attributable to the shortcomings of the new officer. One example is a case involving the South San Francisco, California, Police Department (SSFPD) in 2002. It was during that year that the chief became concerned about the 50% failure rate of recruits in the FTO program. He had been to a conference that addressed the importance of acknowledging and responding to various adult learning styles in the training and education environment, so he set up a series of meetings with training personnel and professors from a local university. A review of their FTO program showed no deference to the fact that adults learn in different ways and concluded that this may have caused confusion among the recruits (Massoni, 2009, p. 1). Key actions that led to the modification of the SSFPD's FTO program included the following:

- A more detailed understanding of adult learning principles and different learning styles, provided by the local professoriate.
- Recognition of generational differences in culture between FTOs and recruits, since during the time period in question the FTOs were baby boomers and the recruits were both Generation Xers (born between 1965–1980) and Millennials (or Generation Yers, born between 1981 and 1999);
- Proper assessment of preferred learning styles among recruits
- Commensurate changes to the program (Massoni, 2009, pp. 2–3)

The most significant program changes instituted as a result of this effort were as follows:

- Inclusion of approaches, taking audio, visual, and kinesthetic preferences into account.
- Customizing training by facilitation through the integration of preferred learning styles, whenever possible or feasible.
- Engagement of recruits in more dialogue so that the new information can be related to their past experiences.
- Reinforcement of learning by having recruits verbalize their understanding of what they have just learned (Massoni, 2009, pp. 3–4).

As the author concluded, "This rather simple solution to a rather complex problem has resulted in a greater success rate among recruits . . . and required minimal initial expense" (Massoni, 2009, p. 5).

This issue aside, formalized field training programs make it easier for both the FTOs and the recruits to assess progress. Since each recruit has two or more FTOs during the course of the training, the possibility of personality conflicts or bias leading to unfair judgments is reduced (McCambell, 1986). As Nowicki (1990b) indicated, "FTOs are no longer macho types, although certain physical and survival skills remain important. Good FTOs teach their trainees how to recognize and deal effectively with problems in ways other than the use of physical force. Trained FTOs know that an officer's verbalizations should be used to avoid problems rather than create them" (p. 34). This claim is bolstered by Johnson's (1998) work, titled "Citizen Complaints: What the Police Should Know." He found that in the municipal agencies included in his study, more than 50% of all citizen complaints against police pertained to officers' verbiage and demeanor—perhaps an indication that increased training in the area of human relations and communication skills is desperately needed.

POLICE STORIES

After working five years for the suburban police agency, my dreams came true. The Chicago Police Department began hiring again so I applied, did well on the written exam, and was soon hired. After my academy training, my first assignment was in the patrol division on the midnight shift. The district station to which I was assigned was old and decrepit, built in the late 1800s. Roll call was on the second floor of the building, and the room was quite small. Seating was limited and was reserved for veteran officers; since I was a rookie, I stood in the back of the room with the other rookies.

The watch commander entered, walked up to the podium in the front of the room, and began reading the beat assignments aloud. A moment or two after he started, an elderly officer, who was seated in the front row, fell out of his chair to the floor. As we (the rookies) began moving to the front to aid the veteran,

(Continued)

(Continued)

the room broke out in laughter. We were told to return to our positions and then heard the watch commander tell another officer to see "that his partner got home safely." The officer who fell out of his chair was drunk and had passed out. What struck me later was that there was barely a break in the routine of the roll call proceeding. It was as if nothing unusual had occurred.

After roll call, I was introduced to my field training officer and my first night on the streets of Chicago began. Between a few relatively routine assignments, my FTO directed me to certain locations. He told me to wait in the car because he "had to go see someone for a minute" and that he would be right back. What I soon discovered was that he was entering different taverns and having a few drinks at each establishment. Being on probationary status (as all rookies are out of the academy), I realized the serious nature of my FTO's actions. If he were caught, I would be the one immediately terminated—while he would only face the consequences of an internal and seldom enforced rule violation. Despite these serious circumstances, I did nothing about it except pray that his actions and my deliberate indifference to those actions were not discovered.

In retrospect, I was once more influenced by the subculture, the desire to "get along" and "go along." I was lucky . . . these transgressions were never discovered or reported. But I did learn an important lesson. Though the police subculture was certainly alive and well in the suburban agency where I had previously worked, it had already climbed to a whole new level in the big city.

While the FTO program remains in wide use today, The Police Training Officer (PTO) program is designed to be an enhancement to the FTO program (Pitts, Glensor, & Peak, 2007). The popularity of these programs is increasing, which indicates that officers enter the field with problem solving skills rarely seen at the early stages of their career. According to Pitts, Glensor, and Peak (2007), the PTO program involves two primary training areas: substantive topics and core competencies. Those topics and competencies are included in Table 3.1.

Pitts et al. (2007) concluded that the PTO-trained officers may possess greater leadership potential and an enhanced ability to develop partnerships with local communities.

Pitts et al. (2007) may well be correct that the change in emphasis resulting from the community policing movement calls for a different type of field training. Walker (2005) indicated that a new model, the **Reno Model,** focuses more on instructing trainees in the use of problem-solving techniques than does the San Jose Model (more traditional in nature), which was in use for decades before the onset of the

Table 3.1 Police Training Officer Substantive Topics and Core Competencies

Substantive Topics	Core Competencies
Nonemergency incident response	Police vehicle operations
Emergency incidence response	Conflict resolution
Patrol activities	Use of force
Criminal investigation	Local procedures, policies, and laws
	Report writing
	Leadership
	Problem-solving skills
	Community specific problems
	Cultural diversity
	Legal authority
	Individual rights
	Officer safety
	Communication skills
	Ethics
	Lifestyle stressors

Source: From "Police Training Officer (PTO) Program: A Contemporary Approach to Postacademy Recruit Training," by S. Pitts, R. Glensor and K. Peak, 2007, *The Police Chief, 74*(8), pp. 34–40.

community policing era. PTOs use an adult learning technique referred to as *problem-based learning* (Walker, 2005). This approach encourages trainees to define the problems they encounter on the job, determine the resources needed to solve the problem, construct a solution to the problem, and begin implementing the solution. In addition, the Reno Model focuses on substantive topics (such as patrol procedures or domestic violence responses) and core competencies (the knowledge, skills, and abilities needed to perform as a patrol officer), such as those listed in Table 3.1, which are addressed by the trainers. Trainers keep a daily journal of the activities engaged in by the trainee and then act as coaches to help improve trainee performance (Walker, 2005). The developers of this alternative field-training model believe it will help prepare officers to function in a community policing environment. The actual effectiveness of the approach remains to be seen, but it does indicate the willingness of police professionals to question prevailing techniques and experiment with new ones.

☞ **CASE IN POINT 3.1**

Testimonials Regarding the Reno Model of Police Training

Greenwood Village (CO) Police Department

Our organization also instituted the tenants of a "Learning Organization" which also helped impact the necessity to transition our hiring and training system. With a great deal of research, our organization chose the Reno PTO program for several reasons. First, the PTO program met our needs for building the foundations of problem solving and community policing. Secondly, it provided a framework for adult learning and increased the overall training experience. Finally, the Reno PTO program is flexible and allowed the Greenwood Village Police Department to develop the training program around our agency-specific needs. Additionally, Jerry Hoover and his staff have been available to us for any need. We have implemented the Reno PTO program and have reaped significant rewards in the skills and ability level of officers released to solo patrol. The PTO program has exceeded our expectations in terms of quality training.

—Sergeant Joe Harvey

Carol Stream (IL) Police Department

Since its inception, we have had the opportunity to train several officers under the model. I am very pleased with the model. It allows our training officers to concentrate more on teaching the necessary skills to trainees as opposed to concentrating on evaluating their performance. The model also provides an excellent foundation for problem-based policing. These officers have an excellent grasp on problem solving and are better problem solvers because of the model. Some of our Police Training Officers have commented that one reason they like the Reno Model is that it allows them to focus more on mentoring, coaching, and teaching the trainee instead of evaluating them. I would highly recommend the Reno Model to any police executive that wishes to move their department field training program toward today's style of policing.

—Sergeant Kevin Orr

Rapid City (SD) Police Department

The Reno Post Academy Training Program prepares our officers for a successful career, whereas, our former training program prepared them for the job. The training program inspires critical thinking, problem solving, and relationship skills which produces a mature officer with a better sense of community. The demands on law enforcement today are greater than it has ever been.

New officers need a high degree of emotional intelligence, and the ability to multi-task to achieve success, the Reno Post Academy Training Program will give them that foundation. The (Hoover Group of Reno) training staff is committed to the professional development of law enforcement officers. They not only provided training to our staff, but, they continue to provide support for our program.

—Lieutenant Peter Ragnone

Source: Reprinted with permission from The Hoover Group of Reno.

"Agency trainers are the men and women who are tasked with the responsibility to see that officers are safe and that they perform their duties within acceptable standards," said Harvey Hedden, deputy executive director of the International Law Enforcement Educators and Trainers Association (**ILEETA**). "Trainers need to do all they can to see that all officers receive the best training possible." (Nowicki, 2008, p. 32)

ILEETA, the International Law Enforcement Educators and Trainers Association, is a professional organization dedicated to serving the professional needs of its members. ILEETA publishes three periodicals, periodically e-mails the *ILEETA e-Bulletin;* publishes an annual issue of *The ILEETA Chronicle;* and presents an annual international training conference and exposition (International Law Enforcement Educators and Trainers Association [ILEETA], 2009).

POLICE STORIES

I recall another incident with my FTO from the Chicago Police Department. We were on patrol working the midnight shift and it was getting close to quitting time, about 6:00 a.m. We received a radio call of a purse snatching in progress. I immediately began proceeding to that location as quickly and as covertly as I could. My FTO then reached down and activated the lights and siren. I asked him "what the *$#^ he was doing . . . the offender would hear us coming. He then responded, "Exactly, I'm not working overtime, I have things to do." As it turns out, the offender was gone upon our arrival.

Once again, I did not protest. . . . I just continued to go along and get along. But that incident sickened me. While there was no guarantee we would have caught the offender, here was a veteran officer with his young, rookie counterpart who had purposely been negligent in doing what they were hired to do. Fortunately, I survived all of the risks and transgressions my FTO had exposed both of us to.

(Continued)

(Continued)

Being rid of that FTO and eventually completing my probationary period were happy times in my life. I was finally able to find a suitable partner and did not have to worry about the antics perpetrated by my former FTO and others like him. This did not mitigate the effects of the subculture, but what it did eventually do was give my regular partner and me more latitude regarding our own actions or the use of our own and more responsible discretionary authority.

One thing I can say though, today, if faced with the same circumstances, I would not have tolerated my FTO's actions. I would have acted as his "watchdog," which I now know would have resulted in him asking for a different recruit to train. One more thing, my former FTO was terminated by the department about five or six years later as a result of a pattern of misconduct charges. I was a happy man that day too!

❖ **Photo 3.2** Training officers mentor, observe, and evaluate probationary officers.

Inservice Training

Also referred to as *continuing professional education* (CPE), most police personnel receive periodic inservice training that is provided either by department personnel or by training consultants hired by the department or by regional or local training boards. Most law enforcement agencies require their officers to complete inservice training in order to maintain competency. From management's perspective, inservice training raises efficiency and effectiveness and may be an important factor in work motivation (Rainey, 2003). Further, inadequate training could be a basis for liability under Section 1983 actions (del Carmen & Walker, 2000). The U.S. Supreme Court, in deciding the case of *City of Canton v. Harris* (1989), noted that inadequate police training may constitute a jurisdictional liability ". . . if the failure to train amounts to deliberate indifference to the rights of persons with whom the police come into contact and the deficiency in the training program is closely related to the injury suffered" (del Carmen & Walker, 2000, p. 262).

While most departments offer occasional inservice training, many conduct it on a hit-and-miss basis, with no real plan or program in mind. Further, it is sometimes viewed as a necessary evil by both those conducting it and those being trained—rather than as a valuable means of keeping current in the field. Perhaps Ilsley and Young (1997) described this dilemma in police training best:

> Education and training can transform the current police culture into one that values inter-departmental communication . . . community involvement, and the power of learning. Paramount in any organizational transformation is the role continuing education and training will play. Continuing criminal justice education will not be transformative until some basic issues are addressed. For one thing, there is no reason why training cannot be more relevant and interesting, as opposed to dry and even punitive. There is every reason for continuing professional criminal justice education to be cutting edge, high interest, and even enjoyable. But first there must be a stronger reason to attend other than orders. As for new skills necessary for effective policing as we enter the 21st century, they are numerous. New equipment, procedures, and operations top the list of new things to learn. Computers will play a much bigger part than they do now. We should see an increase in simulation training, competency-based education and performance-based training, as a result of such things. (pp. 5–6)

Source: Reprinted with permission.

The question is, Does participation in CPE activities keep one current in the field? An even more appropriate question is, Do police personnel in this country participate in these activities? If they do, are they forced into participating? Would they participate if they were not forced to? Answering these questions requires an analysis of the literature pertaining to professional education. The purpose and benefits of CPE and whether participation should be mandatory for professionals took center stage in the relevant literature for nearly two decades, from the mid- or late-1970s to the early 1990s. During the past three decades, there has been a growing concern by consumer groups, various governmental agencies, and professional regulatory boards regarding the competency of practitioners in many of the professions. Dramatic advances in technology and the accompanying information explosion have caused many to question whether initial licensure or certification ensures competency throughout the span of one's career (Rockhill, 1983).

In response to this public concern, either through direct government regulation of licensure laws or through indirect regulation via employer and professional organization membership requirements, the vast majority of professions across the United States require professionals to participate in a prescribed amount of educational activities to maintain their licenses (Rockhill, 1983). For example, in Illinois, the Department of Financial and Professional Regulation (IDFPR) is responsible for the licensing, testing, and certification of more than 219 different types of licenses, encompassing nearly 100 different industries. The mandate of the IDFPR is to ". . . serve, safeguard and promote the health, safety and welfare of the public by ensuring that licensure qualifications and standards for professional practice are properly evaluated, applied and enforced" (IDFPR, 2009).

The categories of covered professions span a wide range of workgroups, from physicians and pharmacists to barbers and roofers. Noticeably absent from this rather lengthy list of professions that require participation in CPE activities as a condition of re-licensure is the field of policing. As cited in Scaramella's (1997) review of the literature, researchers point to a variety of benefits associated with a policy of mandatory continuing education (MCE), including the following:

- MCE serves to either eliminate the laggards from the ranks of the profession or revive their interest in learning. (Phillips, 1987)
- By virtue of its very existence, the quantity and quality of programs tends to increase. (Frye, 1990)
- Participation in MCE is viewed as being more acceptable to professionals than periodic re-examination for license renewal. (Rockhill, 1983)
- It protects the public from those who are unwilling to keep up with current developments in their field, thus increasing public confidence. (Maple, 1987)

It must be emphasized at this point that among the previously mentioned professions and their related literature, participation in MCE is no longer an issue; rather, it has become accepted practice.

Unfortunately, the field of policing has not incorporated this educational philosophy into its practice. For the most part, participation in CPE endeavors is left entirely up to individuals and their respective agencies. Even the minuscule amount of inservice training that is mandated for American police officers normally pertains to areas associated with civil liability, such as the use of firearms, physical force, the handling of hazardous materials, and high-speed vehicle pursuits. Moreover, because liability is almost always directed toward employers, such training efforts are usually only offered because of court orders or malpractice insurance requirements. Thus, as Schwartz and Yonkers (1991) pointed out, "Unlike many other American professions, or unlike policing in some other countries, such as Germany, there are often no continuing education requirements for American police officers" (p. 50).

In addition, most of the other inservice training efforts seem to have fallen victim to many of the early criticisms of MCE in other professions. For example, research is rarely used to identify training needs and to link new knowledge and skills with practice. Perhaps more providers of police inservice training should follow the British philosophy, in which "teaching methods include facilitated learning in small groups to encourage depth of understanding; didactic teaching is usually reserved for those occasions when the principal aim is to impart knowledge" (Bunyard, 1991, p. 13).

One shortcoming of police training is that there is not enough emphasis placed on the skills needed to deliver training effectively. Golden and Seehafer (2009) pointed to the trainer's need to establish a three-dimensional delivery environment. First, the instructor must have the requisite knowledge to deliver accurate topical information. Second, the trainer must possess the facilitation skills needed to deliver information effectively. Third, the trainer must have the ability to accurately assess trainee retention (p. 21). The researchers offered additional tips for the presentation of a positive training experience, including the following:

- Accommodation of the three broad categories of learners, visual, auditory, and kinesthetic, by combining techniques designed to capture all three audiences.
- Technical considerations such as knowing the average skill level of attendees ahead of time and planning accordingly. This also includes having more than a fundamental understanding of modern audio-visual equipment and being prepared should the equipment fail for some reason.

- Utilization of real life or job related applications to emphasize and clearly demonstrate the benefits of the training at hand. When feasible, a hands-on approach for the learners is a wise choice as well, especially when demonstrating how to use technical equipment (Golden & Seehafer, pp. 22–23).

A related issue not addressed directly by these authors pertains to education requirements for police trainers. According to Hickman (2005), only about two thirds of all the police training facilities had an educational requirement for trainers. Of those, the most frequent requirement was a high school diploma or GED and the least frequent requirement was a baccalaureate degree (p. 3). (Later in this chapter we discuss the many issues surrounding higher education and the police.)

Other shortcomings associated with inservice training pertain to geographic availability and cost. In response to this dilemma, some states have developed mobile training units responsible for planning and providing training within specified geographic areas on a regular basis. These units frequently arrange training at different locales within their territories to make it easier for police personnel from rural areas and small towns to attend. Unfortunately, budgetary cutbacks and, in some instances, union contracts have made it increasingly difficult for departments to release personnel to attend such training.

Other attempts to offset the high costs associated with training have been implemented and actually show promise in this regard. A good example is the Public Safety Council Consortium of Lake County, Indiana. The Consortium is composed of 22 agencies from northwest Indiana that have pooled their money to provide training opportunities for their personnel. The many advantages to such an operation include the following:

- It is centrally located.
- The center operates on a year-round basis.
- The curriculum covers a wide array of contemporary topics.
- It keeps the cost down to a minimum—only $50 per year per officer.
- It allows personnel from smaller departments the opportunity to attend training activities they might not otherwise be able to experience.
- The instruction is facilitated by professional educators, normally drawn from the ranks of regional universities. (Marsh & Grosskopf, 1991)

A similar and equally promising inservice training innovation was developed by the Columbus, Ohio, Police Department and has been appropriately named the Entrepreneurial Training Program. As stated by its program administrator, "The idea is simple: Instead of always sending officers to training seminars in other cities, the program brings trainers to Columbus for some of those sessions. Then other law enforcement agencies are invited to attend for a fee. The money saved in transportation coupled with money brought in through fees helps the program nearly pay for itself" (Narciso, 2001, p. 2B).

A similar innovation was developed by the Suffolk County, New York, Police Department. In addition to keeping training costs down, their new training program for more than 500 Detective Division personnel addressed more logistical impediments to inservice training efforts, such as maintaining full coverage of work schedules, days off, overtime, and funding to facilitate the training sessions. As Kiley (1998) concluded from his work on inservice training for detectives,

> Using experts within the department as instructors, coordinating efforts among all levels of supervision, and incorporating flexibility into the planning of the program, the department succeeded in developing a training program that keeps its detectives on the job and its overtime budget minimally affected. Other law enforcement agencies may benefit from implementing such an in-service . . . course. (p. 18)

In an era of increased fiscal accountability, police executives are well advised to follow the lead of their counterparts from Indiana, Ohio, and New York.

Most recently, however, the type of police training showing the most promise for reaching large numbers of officers and for keeping associated costs down to a minimum and affordable expense is online training. Online education initially gained popularity approximately 10 years ago and has been going full steam ahead since then. Improved technology has produced sophisticated yet user friendly online delivery platforms that make student to teacher interaction as robust as that of a traditional training or education environment. These training sessions and courses can be delivered using both synchronous and asynchronous instructional strategies. Audiovisual capabilities and document viewing and sharing capabilities offer training possibilities limited only by the imagination.

An additional example of alternative methods being used for police training involves the Use of Force Training Simulator (UFTS), which employs computer-generated images (CGI) and speech technology that enables variability in characters and scenarios as well as character and scenario responses to user commands and conversation (National Law Enforcement and Corrections Technology Center [NLECTC], 2008). The computer-generated images allow the police trainer to incorporate an array of features such as character ethnicity, voice, gender, mood, and compliance, in addition to weather and time of day. The speech recognition capability of the UFTS enables the police trainee to converse with CGI characters, and the nature and the tone of the conversation from the trainee influences the character and scenario responses (NLECTC, 2008). In other words, the officer can attempt to gain suspect compliance by employing a weapon or less-lethal force; on the other hand, the officer could cause the suspect's level of resistance to the officer's commands to escalate.

Many law enforcement agencies have since availed themselves of this new and interactive form of training from a distance. Perhaps the leader of the pack in this regard is the program started and sponsored by a partnership between the Minnesota Chiefs of Police Association, the Minnesota Sheriff's Association, and the League of Minnesota Cities Insurance Trust, known as Police Accredited Training Online (PATROL Minnesota, 2009). Dozens of training courses are now offered asynchronously online and are available to any law enforcement agency in the state for a nominal fee of $85 per officer per year. As many as 12 different training courses can be taken by each officer in a given year. The topics are varied and run the gamut from domestic violence and traffic accident investigations to legal updates and communication skills.

While online training in not suitable for all police training needs, the majority of the topics are and it is anticipated that more agencies will turn to this readily accessible and affordable form of training as an effective means of making training available to a much larger audience. With advances in information and telecommunication technology, distance learning has become increasingly feasible. (See the Around the World section that follows for an example.) According to Nelson's (1998) study of criminal justice education, distance learning has almost the same effectiveness as classroom instruction in terms of student achievement. After reviewing many distance learning studies, Barry and Runyan (1995) found that this educational approach could be at least as effective as traditional models. Connors (1998) found that when distance learning employs technology and teaching methods appropriately, effectiveness is equivalent to traditional education. "Since it is a more cost-effective method than traditional classroom education, governments and institutional administrators are increasingly supporting this method. Also, distance learning can reach a wider range of audiences" (Jang, 2005, p. 3).

AROUND THE WORLD

The Interpol Anti-Corruption Academy

Our global landscape is characterized by ever-changing social, political, and economic conditions, all of which affect the operations of police agencies throughout the world. When these factors are coupled with the technological advances we, as a society, have made during the past decade, we are indeed living in a borderless world.

These complex problems require complex solutions. One international effort that was launched in 2009 and sponsored by Interpol was the creation of an anti-corruption academy, located in Austria. As cited on the website (http://www.interpol.int/public/corruption/academy/Copie%20de%20default.asp), their focus is as follows: "Internationally recognized scholars, practitioners and prominent academics will be engaged by the Academy to ensure that it becomes the most innovative global provider of anti-corruption education, training, investigative assistance, and research. Furthermore, especially to meet the need in developing countries to undertake more complex investigations, the Academy will become a forum to express and exchange innovative ideas to confront the most vexing problems facing the global law enforcement community."

After familiarization with the Academy and its operations, please visit the home page of Interpol, the sponsor of the Academy. "INTERPOL is the world's largest international police organization, with 187 member countries. Created in 1923, it facilitates cross-border police co-operation, and supports and assists all organizations, authorities and services whose mission is to prevent or combat international crime." http://www.interpol.int/default.asp

Jang (2005) studied some 47 law enforcement agencies (40 municipal departments, six sheriff's offices, and the Texas Department of Public Safety). Results from the study showed that 60% of the agencies studied had a written policy regarding inservice training. Jang asked respondents to choose five priority inservice training courses. As might be expected based on our previous discussion, among 44 possible training courses, firearms training received the highest priority, followed by defensive tactics, use of force, arrest, search and seizure, and emergency vehicle driving (Jang, 2005). Respondents were also asked whether they had any future plans to contract with distance learning providers for officer training. Eighty-seven percent of the agencies indicated they had no plans for distance learning inservice training, even though 81% had Internet-ready computer facilities. Ninety-four reported that their agency's officers would choose traditional training methods if the same course was offered through both traditional and distance learning methods. Finally, the survey asked about the perception of the effectiveness of online inservice training. Sixty-eight percent responded that online training is inferior to traditional training. Only 28% agreed that online training had the same effectiveness as its traditional classroom counterpart (Jang, 2005). Thus, even though research indicates that the effectiveness of distance learning is not different from traditional education, the perception of the police personnel in this study was basically negative.

Other Types of Training

Selected police personnel have the opportunity to participate in longer term, more intensive training offered by a variety of training institutes around the country. Among the more popular of these training groups are the Northwestern Center for Public Safety, the Southern Police Institute, and the FBI National Academy, all of which offer courses lasting a week to several months. Courses offered by these institutions cover topics ranging from traffic investigation to executive management. California's Law Enforcement Command College began operation in 1984 with the mission of preparing "law enforcement leaders of today for the challenges of the future" (California Commission on Peace Officer Standards, 2009). The program focuses on the following:

- Leadership principles needed to influence the future direction of the organization.
- Strategies to identify emerging issues and provide a proactive response.
- Skills and knowledge necessary to anticipate and prepare for the future.
- Methods and benefits of sharing information.
- Use of stakeholders in problem solving.

The primary goal of the Command College is to provide an enhanced leadership course with a futures perspective to prepare the law enforcement leaders of today to lead into the future. The program has an emphasis on adult learning theories, placing accountability and responsibility on the student (California Commission on Peace Officer Standards and Training, 2009).

The International Association of Chiefs of Police offers management training and self-help programs to police administrators and officers nationwide. "Operation

Bootstrap," begun in 1985, "covers such subjects as effective supervision, conflict resolution, group problem-solving, and stress management. . . . Currently, more than a thousand departments have signed on for the program, and the only cost to the department is a nominal administration fee" (Office of Justice Programs, 2007). Strong support has been expressed by those who have attended the programs.

To be sure, in some instances, these longer training courses are offered to senior-level personnel as a reward for longevity rather than to personnel who are in positions in which they could make active use of the information provided. In addition, much of the information provided during these courses remains locked in the minds of those who attend rather than being disseminated to others in the department through inservice training sessions. Still, a good deal of the information obtained from such courses has practical application.

All training is, or should be, interrelated. Those with specialty skills need to update these skills on a continuing basis and can share these skills with others through inservice training. This sharing will be effective, however, only when it includes supervisory personnel who may otherwise find the concepts disseminated difficult to understand and may continue to operate using outdated information. Again, the commitment to training must come from the top, along with the recognition that training is one of the few forms of recognition available to police personnel. Merit-based selection for a specialized training course conducted at the department's expense is a rewarding experience, as is recognition of an officer's ability to train others. Without such recognition, training may be viewed in an unfavorable light.

Training and Police Leaders

None of the subjects dealt with in training programs are static. Each one is constantly changing, and what we knew to be true yesterday may turn out to be myth tomorrow (Bracey, 1990a). One way of determining the value police supervisors attach to training is to examine the extent to which they subject themselves to it.

Historically, many police supervisors (including chiefs) avoided training and rationalized their absences by pointing out the demands on their time in terms of meetings, planning, administrative chores, and bureaucratic requirements. In reality, the absence of police supervisors from training sessions may have more to do with other factors. Why should those at the top sacrifice their time and energy to attend training when those still striving for such positions may benefit more? Bracey (1990b) believes it is unhealthy for the functioning or morale of an organization if the people at the top cannot communicate in an informed and sophisticated manner about concepts and ideas suggested, as a result of their education and training, by those who work for them. It is clearly frustrating to return from a period of training and education with an idea that seems ideal for implementation in one's own organization, only to be misunderstood or ignored by supervisors.

Last, but not least, some police executives like to operate as if they were omniscient, with no need for additional information. Related to this may be doubts about how well he will perform in the classroom. What if he appears ill-informed before classmates, including subordinates? What if his contributions to the training session are not appreciated or well received? What if his performance is exceeded by that of other, lower-ranking trainees? While these concerns are real, they are worth risking in order to demonstrate that training is not a frill or simply a superficial symbol of the progressive nature of the organization, but rather a valued, ongoing part of that organization.

Training Effectiveness

The effects of training are relatively easy to determine but are infrequently properly assessed by police agencies. Does training provide useful information? Did those attending understand the material presented? The answers to these questions lie in a simple evaluation process that is too often neglected because of the assumption that the information provided is understandable and absorbed. The only way to assess the value of training is to conduct routine evaluations. Ideally, such evaluations would include a pretest of attendees' knowledge of the material to be presented and a posttest of such knowledge. While these basic evaluation efforts may suffice for some programs, one of the major problems criminal justice training programs have encountered through the years is their lack of emphasis on evaluation with respect to the relevance and applicability of training. Many other professions utilize sophisticated evaluation techniques to assess program effectiveness and relevancy. Similarly, most professions emphasize research that attempts to link training to job performance (Bumgarner, 2001; Holmes, Cole, & Hicks, 1992). Does training change the way employees do their job? Is the change in the direction desired by employers?

Vendors of police training are still analyzing program effectiveness by evaluating participants' attitudes only *after* instruction is completed. Research concerning CPE activities and their impact on relevancy, competency, and improved job performance suggests that evaluation efforts should concentrate on techniques such as practice audits and complex task analyses if a positive relationship between participation in CPE activities and professional competency is to be achieved (Phillips, 1987).

In his seminal research, Phillips (1987) offered insight as to why some training programs are more effective than others in producing positive changes in job performance. He analyzed eight studies that produced positive changes in performance by physicians after participation in CPE activities. There were five elements that were common to all of the studies:

1. *Specified audience:* All of the participants expressed a desire to learn something.

2. *Identified learning needs:* All participants could identify a learning need and a gap between present and optimal performance.

3. *Clear goals and objectives:* It was clear to everyone involved what was to be learned.

4. *Relevant learning methods and emphasis on participation:* Learning was participative in nature, occurred in familiar surroundings, and involved small group discussions.

5. *Systematic effort to evaluate:* In other words, assessment and evaluation procedures began the day the programs were developed, course development was based on clear definitions of learning needs, and a variety of evaluation techniques were employed.

Purposes of Training

A basic purpose of training is to keep police personnel up to date with respect to important changes in the profession. Police training should identify, instill, and help develop the key competencies that enable officers to do their jobs (Bumgarner, 2001, p. 34). In a larger sense, however, the purposes of training depend on the way in which the role of the police is defined. In the 1960s and 1970s, crime fighting and law enforcement were emphasized, and to some extent, many officers still view these aspects of the police role as the most important part of police work. As a result, training courses dealing with survival techniques, patrol techniques, criminal investigation, use of force, and the law are among the most popular courses. It is typically easy to recruit officers for courses dealing with these issues. Vodde (2009, p.1) believes today's police training, not withstanding incremental changes, continues to reflect the influence of the Reform Era in policing. "This era was characterized by employing traditional, prescriptive, pedagogical, and militaristic methodology." He further asserted that "not only is this form of training contrary to the needs and interests of a rapidly, ever-changing and sophisticated constituency, but it undermines the actualization of skills and competencies required of today's police."

During the past decade, we have come to recognize that while law enforcement and crime fighting are critical parts of the police role, they are not the most important in terms of time spent or citizen satisfaction. As is commonly understood, police personnel spend the majority of their time negotiating settlements between spouses or lovers and between neighbors and providing other services that have little or nothing to do with law enforcement. As buffers between aggrieved parties, police personnel need to develop skills in this area. Successful intervention into the daily lives of citizens requires such skills, as well as cooperation on the part of the non-police citizens involved. Increasingly, then, communications skills (both verbal and nonverbal) and human, community, and minority relations skills are emerging as among the most important assets of a competent, effective police officer.

A look at basic training curriculums indicates that little emphasis is placed on these skills in the on-the-job setting. Recent research regarding this issue shows mixed results. While approximately 80% of police academies offer recruits at least some form of training in community-policing-related subjects, the amount of time spent on those and other like issues pales in comparison to the more traditional subjects, such as firearms training, physical fitness, and the like (Hickman, 2005). Yet communicating with others in the process of negotiating is what police officers do most often. Some police officers have excellent skills in these areas, but others have practically none. The importance of these skills is most clearly illustrated by focusing on those officers who lack them. Such officers are unlikely to get cooperation from diverse segments of the public, either because they alienate other citizens by assuming an authority figure stance as a defense for their poor communications skills or because they cannot express clearly and convincingly what they want or need the public to do. They receive little input from the public about crime or their own performances. They routinely enforce the law in an attempt to maintain order when their more skilled colleagues could have maintained order without resorting to arrest. They become unnecessarily involved in physical encounters (Pritchett, 1993; Reiss, 1971).

They create numerous and constant headaches for their superiors or, if they are supervisors, for those who work for them.

Training in communications, human relations, minority relations, analysis of encounters, and negotiating is available, but while more popular than a decade or two ago, such training is often not well attended unless officers are required to be present. Typically, officers who are forced to attend such training fail to see the benefits that may accrue. Such benefits are present, of course, whether a crime is being investigated (interviewing and interrogation skills), whether a police action is being questioned by the public (public relations), whether orders or directives are involved (departmental policies cannot be successfully implemented unless they are understood), or whether evaluations or promotions are involved (both require clear communication between those being evaluated or promoted and those doing the evaluating or promoting).

Such skills also are at a premium when the police are trying to educate the public, whether about a crime prevention program, new police policies, proper complaint procedures, or other issues. Such training is increasingly being recognized as a major aspect of the police role. And not least important, communications skills are critical when the police are training their own (Overton & Black, 1994; Pritchett, 1993).

One of the major purposes of police training, then, is—or should be—to make better communicators of the public servants responsible for maintaining order (Means, 2008). Courses dealing with both verbal and nonverbal communications should be required of all police personnel. It is also possible, however, to improve communications skills regardless of the specific content of the training. Any topic that requires feedback from the participants can be presented in an organized fashion and can help participants learn to express themselves more clearly and become better listeners. Police officers who are trained to express themselves clearly and to be good listeners are likely to be better at both order maintenance and law enforcement. This need should be abundantly clear based in part on Johnson's (1998) research, cited earlier in this chapter, which determined that slightly more than 50% of all citizen complaints against police pertained to officers' spoken words and body language.

Who Should Conduct Police Training?

Based on the information contained in the preceding discussion, it is clear that police trainers may, and do, come from diverse backgrounds. Certainly, police officers themselves may be trainers when they have both information to share and the skills to present the information. Let us be clear that these are two separate, equally important requirements. It does little good to use an expert in any area as a trainer unless she has good communications skills. Similarly, it does little good to have an expert communicator present useless (out-of-date or irrelevant) information. Both extremes are found in the arena of police training. When an inservice or retired officer meets both requirements of a trainer, she often has a significant advantage over other trainers—provided the material presented requires an understanding of the police world. While others may have such understanding, the fact that the trainer is, or has been, a police officer often heightens her credibility among police personnel.

It is essential, however, that police training also be conducted by those outside the profession, for two very good reasons. First, many of the skills required of trainers and educators are not frequently found among police officers. Skills needed to set up and run a computer software package, skills required to analyze interaction patterns, and skills necessary to prevent infection resulting from communicable diseases are only a few examples. Hickman (2005) found that only 26% of police academies required police trainers to have some sort of certification as a trainer. Second, relying only on those within the profession for training typically leads to a myopic world view, which serves to isolate members from the rest of society—and the police can ill afford further isolation. So who should train the police? Those meeting the previously outlined requirements, regardless of the area of their expertise, can serve as trainers. Trainers may include police officers, physicians, computer experts, self-defense experts, college professors, members of minority groups, and business leaders, to name just a few. In general, the broader the spectrum of qualified trainers and the greater the exposure to different skills, the better (Bumgarner, 2001; Marsh & Grosskopf, 1991).

Nowicki (2006) identified eight qualities of effective law enforcement trainers. These include humility, honesty, dedication, passion, preparedness, inspiration, purposefulness, and style. To be sure, those who have a passion for training and the subject matter at hand, are well-prepared to train, whose style is conducive to interaction with students, and who appear to be willing to learn as well as train are well-suited to the task.

It has been suggested that police training must attain a positive identity within the police community and that this is difficult to accomplish because police training has few easily measurable results. The impact of training is often measured in terms of the numbers of hours or programs attended annually, but what happens when the number of hours or programs is cut? There is typically no measurable effect because training does not often result in clearly measurable end products. Thus, training is relatively easy to cut in times of budgetary shortfalls. For training to gain and maintain a degree of importance, it must be shown that resources expended for training lead to positive results for both the police and the community they serve. There is perhaps no better topic than communication skills to demonstrate the cost effectiveness of a training program.

While advances in training techniques have been made in the past decade, many questions remain to be answered, and the impact of training on the job has yet to be clarified. However, adopting a policy of mandatory participation in CPE activities; focusing more training on the less traditional aspects of policing, to include human relations training, communication skills, community policing strategies, ethical decision making, and the responsible exercise of discretionary authority; encouraging executives to lead by example and assume an active role in the training process; searching for innovative methods for the provision of training opportunities; and facilitation of training not only by content experts, but also by experienced and knowledgeable educators would go a long way toward improving this critical aspect of policing.

There is no doubt that the field of policing has advanced along the continuum of professionalization during the past few decades. However, if the law enforcement community wishes to be perceived as professional, they must demonstrate many of the same characteristics that are used to distinguish members of a profession from those of an occupation. Regardless of the approach utilized in making such a distinction, the common denominator among all of them is a demonstrated ability to keep abreast of current trends in one's field through participation in CPE activities. It is no secret that the issues of safe practice, the technological revolution, and public accountability are some of the underlying reasons that it is important that professionals consistently update their knowledge and skills. The history of MCE has shown us that when professional groups refuse to maintain their level of competence in a responsible and professional manner, government intervention is inevitable. Imposition of increased education and training standards from within policing is critical. Only when the police begin to perceive participation in CPE activities as a natural extension of the preprofessional process will they achieve the desired goal of continuing professional competency. Law enforcement agencies face a dilemma. While they confront new burdens, such as computer crimes, identity theft, other domestic problems, the threat of terrorism, and the need for homeland defense, resources are not growing as rapidly as the demand for police services. Many agencies have actually seen a drop in funding, and training often represents one of the first budget items cut because many administrators see education as addressing the future and use the analogy "fire prevention is great, but not when the house already is on fire" (Nelson, 2006, p. 14).

❖ Police Education

One of the most popular proposals for improving the quality of policing in the United States has focused on better educated officers. The idea that a college-educated police officer would be a better police officer spawned a federal program (LEAA) that provided millions of dollars annually in support of such education, a dramatic increase in the numbers of college programs related to policing, and an increase in the number of police officers with at least some college education (Polk & Armstrong, 2001). The debate over the importance of police education continues, federal funding for such education has diminished considerably, new federal programs are being proposed, and there are continuing concerns over the content and quality of police education.

Many of the current concerns surrounding police education result from our inability or unwillingness to decide exactly what we want the police to be and do in our society. It is extremely difficult to develop courses and curricula for the police under these circumstances. Some believe that liberal arts courses provide the best background for police officers in a multiethnic, multicultural society; others are convinced that specialized courses in criminal justice are preferable; while still others question the value of college education for police officers. In spite of these continuing concerns, the number of programs in criminal justice and related areas increased dramatically in the 1970s. Broderick (1987) noted, for example, that criminal justice education grew rapidly in the early 1970s, so that by 1976 there were 699 colleges and universities offering 1,245 degree programs, ranging from the associate to the doctorate: "Many of these programs, however, were of poor quality, consisting of 'war stories' and technical and vocational training" (pp. 217–218). Data collected in 1985 indicated that many in academia still perceived criminal justice education as being basically technical or vocational training, often taught by faculty without proper credentials. While this may have been the case during the past couple of decades, there seems to be a glimmer of hope now. The training or applied nature of many criminal justice degree programs that brought so much criticism from others in academia seems to be changing. In sharp contrast to Farrell and Koch's (1995) sentiment that such degree programs were the "epitome of anti-intellectualism and the death of humanism" (pp. 53–54), many feel or believe that criminal justice education has flourished intellectually and broadened its scope. Most contemporary programs attempt to achieve a more structured balance between the academic and applied needs of their students (Carlan & Byxbe, 2000).

In response to the aforementioned concerns, the U.S. Department of Justice (1999) created the Office of the Police Corps and Law Enforcement Education.

> The Police Corps was designed to address violent crime by helping police and sheriffs' departments increase the number of officers with advanced education and training assigned to community patrol. The program offered competitive college scholarships for students who agreed to work in a state or local police force for at least four years. Students accepted into the Police Corps received up to $3,500 a year to cover the expenses of study toward a bachelor's or graduate degree. (Office of Justice Programs, 2004)

The goal of the program was to weave a college education with state-of-the-art police training to produce highly qualified personnel who are able to confront the demands and intricacies of 21st century policing. Highlights of the program were as follows:

- Participants must possess the necessary mental and physical capabilities and emotional characteristics to be an effective law enforcement officer, be of good character, and demonstrate sincere motivation and dedication to law enforcement and public service.
- Participants may receive up to $3,750 per academic year, with a maximum per student total of $15,000.
- The student's service commitment must follow receipt of the baccalaureate degree or precede commencement of graduate studies funded by the Police Corps.
- A police agency whose size has declined by more than 5 percent since June 21, 1989; or which has members who have been laid off but not retired cannot participate in the Police Corps program (Oregon State Police, 2007).

However, funding for the program has currently been eliminated, and the Police Corps is no longer awarding scholarships or providing training.

Types of Police Education

Assuming that higher education for police officers is desirable, what type of education provides the best background? One survey of police departments serving cities with populations of 50,000 or more found that about half of all police executives who responded prefer to hire officers who have majored in criminal justice (Carter & Sapp, 1992). A similar number indicated no preference in college degrees or majors. Those who preferred criminal justice majors did so because of the graduates' knowledge of policing and criminal justice, while those stating no preference indicated they preferred a broader education to prepare officers to deal with a wide variety of situations, including those not dealing with law enforcement.

The same study indicated a general perception among police executives that colleges and universities do not have curriculums that meet the contemporary needs of law enforcement agencies. While the respondents found that criminal justice graduates were very knowledgeable about the criminal justice system and policing in general, they were often "narrow in ideology" and lacked the broader understanding of divergent cultures and social issues confronting the police. These executives do not want colleges and universities to teach police skills; they seek graduates who can integrate the duties of a police officer with an understanding of democratic values (Sapp, Carter, & Stephens, 1989). The consensus is that liberal arts curriculums should be part and parcel of college and university criminal justice programs. Many respondents noted that a quality education is needed, particularly in the area of communications skills. Other areas perceived as requiring greater attention included critical thinking, decision making, research, the ability to integrate concepts, and understanding diverse cultures. Finally, the police executives indicated there is a lack of communication between colleges and universities and police agencies, with less than 25% indicating they were regularly consulted by these institutions and more than a fourth indicating they were never consulted about issues of common interest. The authors of the study concluded, "The results of this national study suggest that colleges and universities should be developing policies, changing and modifying curricula, and focusing on providing the educational background needed by students and society. Criminal justice educators must introspectively give detailed attention to curricula to ensure that today's curricula fit today's needs in law enforcement and other areas of the criminal justice system" (Sapp, Carter, & Stephens, 1989, p. 5).

YOU DECIDE 3.1

You have just been appointed the chief of police of the Middletown Police Department (MPD). Middletown is a city of about 200,000 and has 260 sworn officers on their police force.

During the past several years the MPD has been plagued with a significant increase in reported crime, citizen complaints against police, and poor morale on the part of their officers. Members of the community and the local media are beginning to voice grave concerns with the ability of the MPD to effectively respond to the needs of the community.

The Middletown city manager told you that the primary reason she hired you was because of your reputation as a progressive police administrator. She has given you the green light, so to speak, along with the needed resources to improve the department on as many fronts as needed.

One of the first issues you must attend to is to prepare for the next police exam. Your new department has 8 immediate openings for entry level police officers and it is anticipated that it will have 20 to 30 additional vacancies in the next 2 years.

Your administrative assistant asks you to prepare an announcement for the exam, along with all of the qualifications, so that these ads can be published in a timely fashion. The last ad in this regard, and all of the ads prior to that, posted the following requirements:

21 to 35 years of age

High School or GED equivalent

U.S. citizen

Pass written exam

Pass background investigation

Pass medical exam

In light of the information covered in this chapter, write an ad with the qualifications you believe are necessary in this situation. Justify each of your listed qualifications and discuss your reasoning with your colleagues.

Carlan (2007) attempted to assess the value that police officers with criminal justice degrees place on their personal educational experiences, while comparing those perceptions with officers educated in other academic disciplines. Based on a survey of 1,114 police officers, Carlan concluded that officers with criminal justice degrees reported that the degree substantially improved their knowledge and abilities on a wide range of areas, from the criminal justice system to conceptual and managerial skills. Interestingly, responses did not differ significantly from officers educated in non-criminal justice academic disciplines. Thus, it appears that police officers with college degrees, at least in this study, found the degrees to be useful, regardless of the academic specialty in question.

The criminal justice profession has responded to many of the concerns and recommendations voiced by law enforcement executives. The Academy of Criminal Justice Sciences (ACJS) is the largest professional organization in the world dedicated to the advancement of knowledge in the criminal justice profession. As stated on their website, "The Academy of Criminal Justice Sciences is an international association established in 1963 to foster professional and scholarly activities in the field of criminal justice. ACJS promotes criminal justice education, research, and policy analysis within the discipline of criminal justice for both educators and practitioners" (ACJS, 2009).

One of their many added features is that they offer curriculum guidelines and recommendations for colleges and universities seeking to offer degree programs in criminal justice, inclusive of associate, baccalaureate, masters, and doctoral programs. The recommended curricula for these criminal justice programs were developed via numerous working groups consisting of law enforcement executives, university professors, and many other actors within the criminal justice community. The ACJS also offers voluntary certification to those colleges and universities electing to have their criminal justice programs designated as such (ACJS, 2009).

Police Educational Requirements

In the survey conducted by Sapp, Carter, and Stephens for the Police Executive Research Forum, only about 14% of the responding agencies reported requiring any college at all, and less than 1% required a bachelor's degree. Yet almost two thirds of these agencies had some form of educational incentive program. In part, this apparent discrepancy appears to be due to a belief among agency officials that higher education requirements could be effectively challenged in the courts or in contract negotiations. This belief is based on concerns about possible discrimination against minorities and the difficulty in demonstrating that higher education is a bona fide job requirement for police personnel (Carter & Sapp, 1992; Sapp, Carter, & Stephens, 1988).

As a result, it appears that while many departments do in fact give preference to recruits with college educations, few are willing to make college education a formal requirement. This conclusion is supported by the fact that the mean educational level of police officers, as determined by this survey of over 250,000 officers, is 13.6 years, compared with 12.4 years in 1967. The authors conclude that in light of the fact that some departments do require college education as a condition of initial employment and the willingness of the courts to uphold college education as a requirement in at least some cases, it is possible to establish a "defensible college education entrance requirement for employment" (and, for that matter, for promotion) in law enforcement (Carter & Sapp, 1992, p. 11). This would require developing a policy outlining the rationale for the requirement by individual police agencies desiring to implement educational requirements. Travis (1995) noted the following:

> We have come a long way from the commissions of nearly thirty years ago, when the issue was relatively simple—whether it made sense to require a college degree of police officers. Unquestionably, that issue is now resolved, but requiring a college education does not begin to meet the larger educational challenge the policing profession faces—how to prepare everyone in the department, from line officer to highest executive, to exercise an increasing degree of discretion in an increasingly complex world.

Facts in support of such a rationale are available, though they may be more qualitative than quantitative. In the case of *Davis v. City of Dallas,* the United States Supreme Court allowed the Dallas Police Department's requirement of 45 semester-hours of college coursework for entry-level officers to stand (*Davis v. City of Dallas,* 1986). Other police departments, such as those in San Jose, California, and Lakewood, Colorado, have had longstanding entry-level educational requirements as well; and numerous other court decisions support educational requirements for the police (Scott, 1986). According to Stevens' (1999) work, titled "College Educated Officers: Do They Provide Better Police Service?" it is estimated that "10 percent of all police agencies mandate college degreed candidates and 7% mandate community college degrees."

College Education and Police Performance

According to Swanson, Territo, and Taylor (1998, pp. 211–212), it has been argued by some that police work, especially at the local level, does not require a formal education beyond high school because such tasks as directing traffic, writing parking tickets, conducting permit inspections, and performing clerical tasks do not require higher education. In addition, it has been suggested that a highly intelligent and well-educated person would soon become bored with these mundane and repetitive tasks and either resign or remain and become either an ineffective member of the force or a malcontent. Others have argued that the complex role of policing a multiethnic, culturally diverse society requires nothing less than a college degree as a condition of initial employment for police officers (Carter & Sapp, 1992; National Advisory Commission on Criminal Justice Standards and Goals, 1973).

In a review of the evidence on the relationship between higher education and police performance, Hayeslip (1989, p. 49) highlighted the assumed benefits of college education for police officers: greater motivation, more ability to utilize innovative techniques, clearer thinking, better understanding of the occupation or profession, and so on. Based on the studies reviewed, Hayeslip concluded that education and police performance are consistently related, though the relationship is moderate.

Sherman and Blumberg (1981) found no consistent relationship between educational level and police use of deadly force. Daniels (1982), examining the relationship between educational level and absenteeism among police personnel, found that employees without college degrees missed more than three times as many work days through unscheduled absences as those with a four-year degree.

Griffin (1980) found an inverse relationship between educational levels of patrol officers and performance ratings, but a significant relationship between educational levels and what he refers to as job achievement. Meagher (1983) examined police officer educational levels and differences in delivery of services and concluded that college graduates were more likely to explain the nature of complaints to offenders, talk with people to establish rapport, analyze and compare incidents for similarity of modus operandi, recruit confidential informants, and verify reliability and credibility of witnesses than were officers with some college or high school education. However, Meagher was unwilling to attribute these performance differences solely to educational differences.

Other studies of the relationship between higher education and police performance have found that those officers with the best performance evaluations also had significantly higher education (Baeher, Furcon, & Froemel, 1968), that college-educated police officers are less authoritarian than those without college educations (Smith, Locke, & Walker, 1968), and that those with at least some college education had fewer civilian complaints and less sick time than those without such education (Cohen & Chaiken, 1972).

A study conducted by Cox and Moore (1992) found police higher education to correlate positively with a number of variables, including more effective communication skills, better problem-solving and analytical abilities, an increase in public perception of police competence, fewer citizen complaints regarding verbal and physical abuse, and fewer disciplinary actions taken against college-educated police officers. Michals and Higgins (1997), in their examination of higher education level and performance ratings of campus police officers from 16 different campuses, indicated a significant relationship between college education and supervisor performance ratings on report writing proficiency, communication skills, and overall performance.

Worden (1990) concluded that college education was weakly related to some police officer attitudes and unrelated to others. He found that officers' performance in police–citizen encounters, as measured by citizen evaluations, was "largely unrelated to officers' educational backgrounds" (p. 587).

Kappeler, Sapp, and Carter (1992) concluded that while officers with four-year degrees generated at least as many violations of departmental policy as those with two-year degrees, the former perform better than the latter in the areas of courtesy and citizen complaints.

In a study conducted by Cunningham (2006), a positive correlation between college educated officers and fewer disciplinary issues was discovered. The researchers examined the disciplinary actions taken by Florida Criminal Justice State and Training Commission (CJSTC) over a five year period, from 1997 to 2002. The CJSTC handles disciplinary cases that can lead to loss of the police officer's certification. The results were clear: Those officers with higher education levels than the state's minimum requirement of a high school diploma or GED equivalent had significantly lower levels of discipline. Of the officers disciplined, 58% had a high school diploma and were responsible for 75% of all the disciplinary actions taken. Officers with associate degrees, 16% of the total, were responsible for 12% of the disciplinary actions. Officers with baccalaureate degrees, 24% of the total, were responsible for 11% of the total disciplinary actions. Finally, with respect to certification revocations, 77% of those losses were attributable to the high school group.

Other studies that examined the relationship between higher education and police performance seem to be positive in nature. Polk and Armstrong (2001) examined the effects of higher education on the career paths of Texas law enforcement officers. They found that higher education reduced the time required for movement in rank and assignment to specialized positions and was positively correlated to promotion into supervisory and administrative posts. The implications are that higher education will enhance an officer's probability of rising to the top regardless of whether the agency requires a college degree as a precondition of employment.

In an era of community policing, many police executives expect college-educated officers to be both more open-minded and more humanitarian in nature. Carlan and Byxbe (2000) set out to link education with an increased humanistic philosophy.

Students from three southern colleges read vignettes and sentenced a murder defendant and an automobile theft defendant to a term of imprisonment. Three hypotheses were tested. First, it was expected that police-oriented criminal justice majors would not issue more severe sentences. Second, it was anticipated that greater exposure to college from the freshman to the senior years would be accompanied by less severe sentences. Third, sentencing would be independent of social characteristics. The results provided little evidence supporting a more authoritarian and more punitive stereotype of criminal justice majors interested in pursuing police careers.

According to the Police Association for College Education (PACE), a professional organization dedicated to the professionalization of law enforcement, higher education is beneficial for a number of reasons (Stevens, 1999):

- It develops a broader base of information for decision making.
- It provides additional years and experiences for increasing maturity.
- It inculcates responsibility in the individual through course requirements and achievements.
- It permits an individual to learn more about the history of the United States and the democratic process. (p. 37)

Wilson (1999) attempted to measure the relationship between educational attainment of police prior to their date of hire and its effect on the frequency of citizen complaints. The following is a summary of the research: A ten year period of citizen complaint data from the files of 500 working police officers was retrieved and correlated with officer demographic variables of gender, age, years employed, ethnicity, and level of post-secondary education. An analysis of these data produced statistics illustrating the relationship of the variables to the frequency of citizens' complaints. The main finding of this study was that certain levels of college education appeared to relate favorably to the receipt of fewer citizens' complaints. The results of Wilson's research seem to corroborate an earlier and often cited study conducted by Johnson (1998) on citizen complaints. He, too, found that college-educated officers had a significantly lower rate of citizen complaints directed toward them.

Aamodt and Flink (2001) examined the performance on examinations of more than 300 cadets in a police academy in Virginia. Cadets with associate degrees performed better than cadets with high school diplomas; cadets with baccalaureate degrees scored better than those with associate degrees; and those with master's degrees performed better than those with baccalaureate degrees. It appears that, among the study group at least, higher education and the ability to absorb new information and demonstrate knowledge of that information covary as least with respect to performance on examinations.

Higher Education and the Police: A Continuing Controversy

The controversy surrounding the need for higher education for police personnel continues in spite of the fact that virtually every national commission on the police over the past half-century has recommended such education. (See Table 3.2 for a summary of such studies and reports). One basic argument against college education for the police is that there is insufficient empirical evidence to indicate that such education is necessary for performing the police function. This argument is countered by recognizing the fact that there is scant evidence to indicate that college education is necessary for performing any occupation, but considerable evidence that such education may improve the performance of those in the occupation (Scott, 1986).

Responding to criticism about the lack of empirical evidence on the relationship between higher education and police performance, Bostrom (2005) attempted to determine whether a link between education levels of officers and good work habits existed. The study examined data from the records of 452 police officers of the St. Paul, Minnesota Police Department covering a 3-year period of time. The variables of age, gender, ethnicity, years of experience, years of education beyond high school, and type

Table 3.2   Studies of Police Officers With College Degrees.

Author	Title	Year	Findings/Recommendations
President's Commission	Task Force Report	1967	BS for entry level police. Needed to address complex social problems.
Rand Corporation (Cohen & Chaiken)	Police Background Characteristics . . .	1972	Strong correlation between level of education and citizen complaints.
U.S. National Institute of Mental Health	Functions of the Police in a Modern Society	1972	Recommended a Master's degree for entry level police.
American Bar Association (Goldstein & Krantz)	The Urban Police Function	1973	Traits such as those provided by higher education (i.e., intellectual curiosity, ability to synthesize information, etc.) are needed by police.
Finckenauer	Higher Education & Police Discretion	1975	Police recruits with a college education were more likely than those without to use discretion in a much more community-minded fashion.
Sanderson	Police Officers: Relationship of College Education to Job Performance	1977	The author shows strong correlation between college education and performance (i.e., lower absenteeism rate, fewer complaints, promoted more frequently).
Carter, Stephens, & Sapp	Effect of Higher Education on Police Liability . . .	1989	Police officers with college degrees received significantly less citizen complaints. A policy of a college degree was recommended to reduce agency liability.
Kappalar, Allen, Sapp, & Carter	Police Officer Higher Education, Citizen Complaints, and Department Rule Violations	1992	Police officers with college degrees received significantly fewer citizen complaints than those officers without college degrees.
Tyre & Braunstein	Higher Education & Ethical Policing	1992	The authors concluded that officers with higher levels of education tended to select more ethical courses of action than their counterparts without a college degree.
Committee on Integrity: Report to Mayor Daley	Final Report: Volume 1: Corruption	1997	The report recommended an entrance requirement of a baccalaureate degree for police officers to mitigate corrupt police practices.

Author	Title	Year	Findings/Recommendations
Wilson	Post-Secondary Education of the Police Officer and its Effect on the Frequency of Citizen Complaints	1999	The research showed that officers with college degrees received fewer citizen complaints than those officers without a college degree.
Fullerton	Higher Education as a Prerequisite to Employment as a Law Enforcement Officer	2002	Fullerton summarized several research projects between 1967 and 1992 that addressed the issue of higher education and the police. Throughout the studies, several traits were associated more with college educated officers, such as fewer citizen complaints, less authoritarian, better decision making, and many others.
Aamodt	Research in Law Enforcement Selection	2004	From a review of more than 300 studies related to police officer selection policies, officers with a college education received better performance evaluations, received fewer citizen complaints, had less absenteeism, and tended to use less force than the officers without college degrees.

Source: Reprinted with permission from Police Association for College Education (PACE).

of college degree were cross-tabulated against indicators of work habits (i.e., commendations, vehicle traffic crashes, sick time usage, and number of times disciplined). The following highlights of the study provide some interesting data:

- Type of college degree was the most significant factor. Officers with a bachelor of arts degree used less sick time, were involved in fewer traffic crashes, were disciplined less often, and received the most commendations of any group. This held true when controlling for the other variables as well.
- When officers holding bachelor of science degrees were added to those with bachelor of arts degrees, the mean of this combined group fell below the mean with regard to the number of commendations and above the mean with respect to accidents, sick time usage, and discipline.
- Bostrom (2005) offered the following explanation for the surprising results:

  The reason that the officers with bachelor of arts degrees did well in this study could be related to the type of course work required to earn a bachelor of arts degree. For example, a bachelor of arts degree emphasizes problem-solving from a variety of viewpoints, develops understanding of how perceptions influence behavior, increases a person's comfort level with ambiguity, and assumes that the things going on in the world are fluid and interrelated.

While these results are limited to the St. Paul Police Department, further inquiry into this phenomenon seems to be in order.

Education and the knowledge acquired in the process of pursuing a degree are of paramount importance to the police as order maintainers and negotiators. That is, as indicated throughout this book, the police role has changed and is changing. Scott (1986) recognized this fact more than two decades ago:

> Police must have the ability to understand human problems in their community and they must be trained to identify and understand a variety of social, economic, and developmental ills for which they must be able to refer, recommend, or involve themselves in an effort to seek the best available solution. College education does appear to develop and enhance these abilities and skills. (p. 26)

Scott concluded that entry-level requirements for police officers should include a four-year degree requirement and that police officers already in the field should avail themselves of opportunities to pursue bachelor's degrees. This is the same conclusion reached by the National Advisory Commission on Higher Education for the Police some years ago.

Recently, Landahl (2009) noted that studies by Roberg and Bonn (2004) support the fact that college educated officers are more sensitive to community relations, more understanding of human behavior, and hold higher ethical and service standards than their peers.

❖ PHOTO 3.3 The ability to communicate with citizens of all ages, ethnicities, and educational levels is critical for police officers.

Commitment to education, like commitment to training, should be career-long for police personnel. For officers who already have college degrees, as well as for those without such degrees, continuing education courses can be challenging, motivating, and worthwhile. (See the discussion in the previous section on training.) Such courses also are beneficial for officers who do not wish to pursue a college degree. However, the benefits of continuing education for police officers are not limited to course content. It has been our observation over the past 30 years that a good deal of benefit accrues from having police officers and other students share the same classroom, coming to know each other as individuals and hearing one another's perspectives on a variety of issues. This is perhaps particularly true when the class is diverse with respect to age, race and ethnicity, gender, size of hometown, and cultural background.

Departmental incentives for becoming involved in continuing education indicate to officers that their efforts are appreciated. Such incentives may include tuition reimbursement, time off to attend classes (or allowing officers to attend class while on duty in an "on-call" status), reimbursement for the cost of books, and so on. In many departments that provide these incentives, enhanced chances for promotion also exist. As is the case with training, commitment to education and continuing education must come from the top (Carter & Sapp, 1992).

The debate over the proper extent and nature of police training and education continues. An increasing body of legal evidence is accumulating and indicates that failure to train may lead to serious financial consequences for police agencies, agents, and municipalities alike. Further, there appears to be increasing legal support for higher education of police officers. Coupled with the fact that the perceived role of the police has changed dramatically in recent years, these indicators would appear to support increasingly higher standards for police training and education. The transition to police officers with higher education has not, however, been smooth or easy.

Though only a small proportion of police agencies now require college education for initial employment or promotion, informal discussions with police executives indicate that such education is of considerable importance and that increased education requirements are inevitable. A promising report in this regard, sponsored by the Bureau of Justice Statistics and conducted by Liming and Wolf (2008), is that by 2016 it is projected that 52% of police officers in this country will possess at least an associate degree and that 33% will hold a baccalaureate degree or higher upon entrance to the field.

The police themselves tend to ascribe advantages to higher education. Bruns' (2005) study used self-report surveys to poll the opinions of nearly 400 patrol officers regarding the perceived benefits of higher education in policing. The vast majority of respondents (82%) believed at least some higher education requirement to be necessary in today's policing environment. Ironically though, while nearly 90% of the officers surveyed had some college education, 22% of them also reported that their respective agencies were not supportive of their educational pursuits. Moreover, 65% of the officers polled reported that their agencies had no formal policies linking higher education to promotion.

Moreover, in a study of police chief performance and leadership styles, Krimmel and Lindenmuth (2001) surveyed 205 city managers in Pennsylvania and asked them to rate ". . . the performance and leadership attributes of the police chief working under their direct supervision." (p. 469) Chiefs with college educations were rated significantly higher than their high school graduate counterparts on 35 of 45 performance indicators. Perhaps the most significant finding in this study was that "those police chiefs with poor ratings were identified as those without college credit. Education was the only significant predictor of police chiefs being rated as bad or poor." (p. 481)

Mayo (2006), speaking of the intellectual liberation many college graduates feel to several hundred police chiefs at an international conference, drove his point home when he said "The culture of a police department that successfully requires college degrees for officers differs from that of a department that does not. The former creates a culture of responsibility, the latter, of obedience."

It is obvious that the increasingly complex nature of crime and of requests for police services and the laws regulating activities in these areas support the need for better educated and trained police. To reach these goals, colleges and universities, as well as police training institutes and academies, must continually revise and update curriculums while maintaining high standards. Vocational training for police officers is necessary, but it should not be confused with education. The two types of programs can and must coexist; and improved cooperation between proponents of each can only lead to more qualified police officers. As Carter and Sapp (1992) noted, law enforcement agencies no longer can fail to recognize the changes that are taking place in policing. These changes include an increase in the educational level of citizens and the number of police programs based on increased police–citizen interactions. These two developments require review of law enforcement educational policies. Carter and Sapp are convinced that "the question is not whether college education is necessary for police officers, but how much and how soon?" (p. 14). Perhaps Landahl (2009) put it best:

> The age of valid excuses for not pursuing higher education as a law enforcement officer has passed. The men and women in uniform who are near the end of their careers had very few options for earning their degrees. They made the sacrifices, drove to [classes] each week, adjusted their schedules or took time off to get to class, dragged themselves to libraries to do research, and suffered through the marathon to earn a degree. Modern technology has not diminished the effort necessary or time commitment, but has provided extreme flexibility in when and how you put in the time to earn a degree. Options for courses in distance education format and the availability of electronic library resources provide the ultimate flexibility in pursuing higher education. (p. 26)

❖ Chapter Summary

The underlying issues regarding police training, in all of its forms, and education have always assumed an aura of controversy. Questions such as the following continually arise: How much initial and continuing training is actually needed? What should be the minimum level of formal education required of police officers? Are training and higher education related to work performance? Who should conduct the education and training, academicians or police officers?

Other issues involving training and education are intimately related to organizational and individual civil liability issues. Agencies must be prepared to demonstrate to the courts that their officers have received proper training, such as in firearm proficiency, the use of force, Constitutional issues germane to policing (i.e., search and seizure requirements, excessive use of force, and so forth). The courts have also ruled that police agencies must be able to demonstrate that they utilize sound supervisory practices and that they do not retain personnel in a way that could be construed as negligent.

One form of training stressed in this chapter is of extreme importance: officers' initial field training received after successful completion of academy or basic training. The selection of the right officers to be field trainers is critical because those individuals have tremendous influence on the subsequent behavior of the rookies they train. As such, these officers should be men and women committed to professional policing and the mission of their respective organizations. Appointment to these positions due to seniority in the department is an unwise policy and should be avoided.

The latter part of the chapter dealt with formal education. There have been numerous studies conducted through the years that concluded that officers with higher levels of education tended to be more professional, received fewer citizen complaints, possessed more tolerance for diversity, possessed better oral and written communication skills, and seemed better suited for community-oriented policing strategies than their high school graduate counterparts. Still, there are those who maintain that it's the street experience rather than the higher education that makes or breaks an officer. Most authorities, however, maintain that higher education is a definite advantage to the individual officers, their respective agencies, and to the profession.

❖ Key Terms

training	International Law Enforcement Educators and Trainers Association (ILEETA)
education	
inservice training	Use of Force Training Simulator (UFTS)
recruit training	Police Accredited Training Online
field training	Office of the Police Corps and Law Enforcement Education
probationary period	
Police Training Officer (PTO) program	Academy of Criminal Justice Sciences (ACJS)
Reno Model	Police Association for College Education (PACE)

❖ Discussion Questions

1. Why is recurrent training so important to police personnel? What are some of the possible consequences of failure to train?

2. What kinds of topics should be included in police training? Who should conduct the training?

3. How would you go about evaluating the effectiveness of a police training program? Why is evaluation so important?

4. What is the relationship between education and training? Can one replace the other? Why or why not?

5. Discuss the arguments for and against college education for police officers.

6. What are some of the weaknesses of existing college programs in criminal justice and law enforcement noted by police executives in recent surveys? How might these weaknesses be corrected?

7. Is there legal justification for requiring some college for entry-level police officers? What are the legal issues involved with this requirement?

8. Has the relationship between college education and improved police performance been thoroughly documented? What needs to be done to further examine this relationship?

❖ Internet Exercises

1. Use the Web to locate the home page of the Police Association for College Education (PACE). Acquaint yourself with the various reports and data sets located and and take a position regarding the benefit of higher education standards in the field of policing.

2. Use the Web to locate the home pages of at least five different local police agencies. Find information pertaining to their entry-level requirements and compare and contrast those agencies to find any significant differences. Take a stand regarding which one(s) you feel is the best.

3. Regarding criminal justice curricula in higher education, go to the home page of the Academy of Criminal Justice Standards (ACJS) and peruse the sections relevant to what they refer to as their "curriculum standards." Do you agree with their recommendations? Why or why not?

4. Find the home page of a journal called the FBI Law Enforcement Bulletin. Examine applicable journals from the issues generated during the past couple of years and identify the FBI's, as well as other federal law enforcement agencies, views or stance on the importance of higher education for those working in law enforcement.

5. Proceed to the website that hosts the International Association of Chiefs of Police (IACP) and try to determine their stance or recommendations regarding higher education and inservice training in the field of policing.

The Police Culture

CHAPTER LEARNING OBJECTIVES

- Describe the various ways in which the police subculture conflicts with the official norms and values of policing.
- Compare and contrast the various forms of an organization's culture.
- Identify and elaborate on variables that influence police officers' acceptance of the subculture.
- Describe the positive aspects of the police subculture.
- Identify the sources of *police stress*.
- Highlight the various strategies that both organizations and individual officers can implement to mitigate the negative effects of job-related stress.
- Describe the ways that the police subculture and stress are related.
- Identify and provide examples of the ways in which community policing can both increase and decrease stress levels among police officers.
- Describe the characteristics associated with the phenomenon of police *burnout*.

In Chapter 4, we focus on organizational and administrative aspects of policing, on the formal structure and the impact of police leaders. While these formal considerations are crucial to an understanding of the police role, there are two other contributing factors that must be considered in our attempt to understand policing as an occupation: the police subculture and the pressures and stresses of police work. Police administrators and the law specify the broad parameters within which officers operate,

❖ **PHOTO 4.1**   This patrol officer is attempting to explain to members of his department's administrative committee on traffic safety why the traffic accident he was involved in was unavoidable.

but the police subculture tells them how to go about their tasks, how hard to work, what kinds of relationships to have with their fellow officers and other categories of people with whom they interact, and how they should feel about police administrators, judges, laws, and the requirements and restrictions they impose.

Combined, the effects of formal pressures and the pressures generated by the police subculture often lead police officers to experience a great deal of stress in their occupational, social, and family lives—resulting in cynicism, burnout, and retirement, as well as a host of physical and emotional ailments. Further, many officers, at least initially, fail to recognize the extent to which the police subculture and their chosen occupation affect the way in which they view and act toward others.

According to Inciardi (1990), police officers develop resources to deal with the isolation from the community that results from the job and the police socialization process. These police subcultural attributes include "protective, supportive, and shared attitudes, values, understandings and views of the world," which result in a ***blue wall of silence*** (p. 227), or closed police society. Furthermore, this process of socialization or the creation of a blue fraternity begins at the police academy, but as with most forms of occupation socialization, it is an ongoing process throughout the police officer's career.

These factors interact and are reinforced by other officers, eventually leading to the development of attitudes, behaviors, beliefs, and perceptions that reflect the dominant beliefs of almost all police officers. Ultimately, police officers cope with their organizational environment by taking a "lay low" or "cover your ass" attitude and adopting a crime-fighter or law enforcement orientation (Paoline, Myers, & Worden, 2000, p. 578). They quickly discover that when they are recognized, it is usually for a mistake or a violation, rather than for an achievement or effective policing, and they learn that hard work entails the risk of exposure and sanction. "Some believe that the professionalization of the police (i.e., removing politics from policing, scientific advances, and anti-police misconduct strategies) has been the catalyst for this isolation and the strengthening of the us-versus-them attitude associated with the police culture" (Paoline, Myers, & Worden, 2000, p. 579). Thus, the police culture is often viewed negatively, and the blue wall of silence has resulted in police officers not being held accountable for misconduct (Frye, 2006). However, it is important we realize that an organizational culture can have many positive effects and can actually reduce anxiety and uncertainty in human relationships and communicate the ideology that defines what the organization is all about (Champoux, 2006). Most agree that the organizational culture of a police department affects the behavior of the officers. Thus, the establishment of a professional, moral, ethical culture in a police organization can control, prevent, and punish misconduct and corruption. Of course the establishment of this type of culture relies in part on the organization's hiring, retention, promotion practices, leadership, and socialization process for new police officers.

❖ The Police Subculture

According to the seminal work of William Westley (1970), the **police subculture** is a crucial concept in the explanation of police behavior and attitudes. The subculture, in his view, characterizes the public as hostile, not to be trusted, and potentially violent; this outlook requires secrecy, mutual support, and unity on the part of the police. Manning (1977) suggested that the inherent uncertainty of police work, combined with the need for information control, leads to police teamwork, which in turn generates collective ties and mutual dependency. Traditional characterizations of the police culture have focused on describing the shared values, attitudes, and norms created within the occupational and organizational environments of policing (Paoline, 2004, p. 205). However, some research has begun to investigate the assumptions associated with a single police culture. Paoline (2004) proposed the existence of different attitudinal subgroups of police officers. For example, although some groups of police officers represent many of the negative attitudes of the traditional culture, others often possess attitudes that would be considered polar opposites. In other words, as police departments have become more heterogeneous, a single cohesive police culture could be expected to give way to a more fragmented occupational group (Paoline, 2003). This expectation is supported by the representation of racial minorities, females, and college-educated personnel who bring to policing different outlooks and attributes based on past experiences that may affect the way in which police collectively interpret the world around them (Paoline, Myers, & Worden, 2000).

We must emphasize that the presence of an organizational culture in policing is not unique. Almost all organizations have a form of culture associated with the values, beliefs, and norms that are unique to the occupation and even to the individual organization. In most cases, police officers are influenced by formal organizational structures and expressed organizational values and also by informal values, beliefs, norms, rituals, and expectations of other police officers that are passed along through the organizational culture (Adcox, 2000, p. 20). For example, a new police officer learns at the academy the laws and formal rules required before initiating a traffic stop on a motor vehicle. However, beyond these formalities, new officers quickly learn the importance of tone of voice, posture, and initial approach to a hysterical, threatening, or often apologetic driver. Veteran police officers in many cases have refined through many years of traffic stops a ritual or standard approach and accompanying explanation for almost all drivers.

POLICE STORIES

During your lifetime, it is likely you will be stopped by the police while driving a vehicle. Every driver is different, and even off-duty police officers admit they are sometimes nervous when a police car follows their vehicle. I have observed drivers watching a marked police vehicle in the rearview mirror almost collide with the vehicle in front of them. Other drivers upon observing the police, attempt to quickly fasten their seatbelt and often either run off the road or swerve into the approaching lane of traffic.

Often, drivers stopped by the police are nervous, angry, or remorseful. Some honestly admit their violations, while others lie to the police. I was taught to decide whether to write a ticket before you approach the vehicle and not let the emotions or statements of the driver influence the decision to arrest or issue a verbal warning. While this advice has merit, it is often not reality.

I stopped a person for driving 29 mph through a busy park that was posted 20 mph. Given the number of persons present watching whether I was going to ticket the driver and the fact that the driver had exceeded the speed limit by 9 mph, I decided to issue a speeding ticket before I exited the vehicle. However, as I completed the traffic stop, the driver quickly exited the vehicle and began running back toward my police car. At this point it became evident that the driver had not placed the car in park, but in reverse. The vehicle barely missed seriously injuring the driver and sustained major damage after crashing into a large tree. Needless to say, I completed an accident report and decided to not arrest the driver for speeding.

For a variety of reasons, a police officer may decide not to enforce the law. The exercise of discretion involving individual choice and judgment by police officers is a normal, necessary, and desirable part of policing.

Champoux (2006, pp. 70–91) discovered different but related forms of organizational culture: artifacts, values, and basic assumptions. The **artifacts** are the most visible parts of the organizational culture and include sounds, architecture, smells, behavior, attire, language, products, and ceremonies. Police culture is in part transmitted and defined by certain artifacts. For example, police recruits quickly learn police jargon, how to address superiors, how to communicate on the radio, a writing style for police reports, and a host of other behaviors unique to policing.

Another form of police artifact is the patrol officer's uniform, which is a symbol of law and order and allows members of society to readily identify a police officer. Some departments have researched the use of blazers or a more casual form of dress to encourage police–community interactions and avoid the paramilitary style of uniform. However, today, almost all police departments have uniformed patrol divisions patrolling in squad cars.

The second form of organizational culture involves the values embedded in the organization. Champoux (2006, pp. 70–91) indicated that the in-use values are the most important because they guide the behavior of the organization. For example, new police officers often complete months of training on the street with an Field Training Officer. We cannot overemphasize the role of an FTO, especially in conveying the values of respect, integrity, honesty, and fairness to a new police officer. However, in policing, as in many occupations, conflicts often exist between values. For example, Pollock (2008, p. 291) concluded that if a police officer feels isolated from the community, her loyalty is to other police officers and not to the community. The following hypothetical scenarios ask you to consider the concept of loyalty in the police culture.

YOU DECIDE 4.1

1. You are on patrol and discover one of your fellow officers asleep in their squad car. What action would you take? Why?

   a. Wake them

   b. Wake them and tell them their behavior is unacceptable

   c. Notify your supervisor

   d. Take no action

   e. You would take another action (Explain)

2. During routine patrol at approximately 3:00 a.m. you observe a vehicle driving erratically. There is no traffic present and you stop the vehicle, conduct field sobriety tests, and believe the driver is intoxicated above the legal limit of .08 BAC. At this point, the driver shows you identification that he or she is a state police officer who resides in your village.

What action would you take? Why?

   a. Immediately place the driver under arrest for driving under the influence

   b. Notify your supervisor

   c. Allow the driver to call someone on their cell phone to take them home

   d. Allow them to lock the vehicle and take them home in the squad car

   e. You would take another action (Explain)

The third and final form of organizational culture involves the basic assumptions of the organization. According to Champoux (2006, pp. 70–91), veteran employees of an organization are not consciously aware of the basic assumptions that guide the organization's behaviors. These assumptions develop over the history of the organization and include many aspects of human behavior, human relationships in the organization, and relationships with the organization's external environment. In most cases the assumptions are unconscious and are often difficult for veteran police officers to describe to new police officers. Often police officers comprehend these assumptions by observing the behaviors of other police officers in a variety of different situations. For example, Nelson and Quick (2006) described the presence of certain **organizational assumptions** or deeply held beliefs that guide behaviors and communicate to members of the organization how to perceive and think about things. Gaines, Kappeler, and Vaughn (2008, pp. 327–330) described the presence of a police **ethos** (fundamental spirit of a culture). They identified three concepts of the utmost importance in policing: bravery, autonomy, and the ethos of secrecy. Crank (2004) defined *secrecy* as follows:

> A cultural product, formed by an environmental context that holds in high regard issues of democratic process and police lawfulness, and that seeks to punish its cops for errors they make. Secrecy is a set of working tenets that loosely couple the police to accountability, that allow them to do their work and cover their ass so that they can continue to do the work they have to do without interfering oversight. (p. 278)

Evidence of secrecy is clearly articulated in postulates which say, "Watch out for your partner first and then the rest of the guys working," "Don't give up another cop," "Don't get involved in anything in another cop's sector," "If you get caught off base, don't implicate anybody else" (Reuss-Ianni, 1983, pp. 14–16).

Many police officers view themselves as teammates linked together by portable radios and cell phones, part of a team that is no stronger than its weakest member. As members of the team, they feel a good deal of pressure to live up to the expectations of other team members and support the practice of secrecy. Among the attitudes and values identified as characteristics of a police culture are adhering to a code of silence, with grave consequences for violating it, and maintaining loyalty to other officers above all else.

The police subculture, or blue fraternity or brotherhood, consists of the informal rules and regulations, tactics, and folklore passed from one generation of police officers to another. It is both a result and a cause of police isolation from the larger society and of police solidarity. Its influence begins early in the new officer's career when he is told by more experienced officers that the "training given in police academies is irrelevant to 'real' police work" (Bayley & Bittner, 1989, p. 87).

What is relevant, recruits are told, is the experience of senior officers who know the ropes or know how to get around things. Recruits are often told by officers with considerable experience to forget what they learned in the academy and in college and to start learning real police work. Among the first lessons learned are that police officers share secrets among themselves; that these secrets, especially when they deal with activities that are questionable in terms of ethics, legality, and departmental policy, are not to be divulged to others; and that administrators cannot often be trusted. This emphasis on the police occupational subculture results in many officers regarding themselves as members of a "blue minority" (Cox & Fitzgerald, 1996; Skolnick & Fyfe, 1993).

In many cases, police officers tend to socialize with other officers (not unlike members of other occupational groups) and come to realize (unlike members of many other occupational groups) that their identities as police officers sometimes make them socially unacceptable, even when off-duty. That is, in some circles at least, there is a kind of stigma attached to those who are perceived as being "too close" to police officers; and police officers themselves are sometimes suspicious of the motives of non-police who become too friendly. In other words, the dangers associated with policing, which we will discuss in the next section, often prompt officers to distance themselves from the chief source of danger—other citizens (Terrill, Paoline, & Manning, 2003, p. 5). The authority provided to police officers also separates them from other citizens. Thus, police officers who are socially isolated from the public, and rely on each other for support and protection from a dangerous and hostile work setting, are said to develop a "we versus them" attitude toward the public and a strong sense of loyalty toward other officers (Terrill et al., 2003, p. 5).

While everyone agrees police work is dangerous, Cullen, Link, Travis, and Lemming (1983) identified a paradox of policing concerning the perception of danger and the actual danger encountered by police. In many instances it was not the actual danger that resulted in fear but the potential for danger that was constantly present (Crank, 2004, p. 158). Cullen et al. (1983) concluded that the fear of danger by police was both functional and dysfunctional. The very real hazards of police work require that police be alert to the risks of the job. However, the constant concern over danger can contribute to increased levels of stress and burnout, which we will discuss later in this chapter.

When officers divide the world into we-versus-them, the former consists of other police officers; the latter encompasses almost everybody else. To be sure, members of other occupational groups also develop their own subcultures and worldviews, but often not to the same extent as the police (Skolnick, 1966). In his classic text, Skolnick (1966) noted, "Set apart from the conventional world, the policeman experiences an exceptionally strong tendency to find his social identity within his occupational milieu" (p. 52). Postulates indicative of the we-versus-them view include the following (Reuss-Ianni, 1983):

- Don't tell anybody else more than they have to know; it could be bad for you, and it could be bad for them.
- Don't trust a new guy until you have checked him out.
- Don't give them (police administrators) too much activity.
- Keep out of the way of any boss from outside your precinct.
- Know your bosses.
- Don't do the bosses' work for them.
- Don't trust bosses to look out for your interests.
- Don't talk too much or too little.
- Protect your ass. (pp. 14–16)

Skolnick (1966) indicated that factors inherent in police work contribute to this tendency. Among these factors are danger, authority, and the need to appear efficient.

Danger, Authority, and Efficiency

Although police work is not the most dangerous occupation, danger is always a possibility. Who knows when the traffic stop at midday will lead to an armed attack on the police officer involved? Who can predict which angry spouse involved in a domestic dispute will batter a police officer (or for that matter, whether both spouses will)? Who knows when a sniper firing from a rooftop will direct his shots at the windshield of a patrol car? Under what circumstances will a mentally disordered person turn on an officer attempting to assist? Will drivers approaching an intersection heed the flashing lights and siren of an officer's car? Does the fleeing youthful burglar have a firearm under his shirt? Danger is always a possibility in policing, and it is highly unpredictable except in certain types of situations. (See the Case In Point that follows.) "The potential to become the victim of a violent encounter, the need for backup from other officers, and the legitimate use of violence to accomplish the police mandate all contribute to a subculture that stresses bravery, which is ultimately related to the perceived and actual dangers of policing" (Gaines, Kappeler, & Vaughn, 2008, p. 327). In fact, because of the unpredictable nature of danger in policing, police officers are trained to be suspicious of most, if not all, other citizens they encounter. Police are encouraged to treat other citizens they encounter as *symbolic assailants,* to approach them in certain ways, to notify the dispatcher of their whereabouts when making a stop, to wait for additional officers or backup to arrive before proceeding in potentially dangerous cases, and so on (Barker, Hunter, & Rush, 1994; Skolnick, 1966). Even though violence occurs in a low percentage of police–civilian interactions, "the highly unpredictable and potentially dangerous persons, who cannot be dependably identified in advance, conditions officers to treat each individual with suspicion and caution" (Johnson, Todd, & Subramanian, 2005, p. 4). Examples of symbolic assailants include two men walking in a quiet residential neighborhood at 3 a.m. or a police officer receiving the description of a person approaching a subway station carrying a "suspicious package." In other words, police officers create in their mind an image of what they perceive to be the behaviors of a threatening person. This image is based on training, past experiences, and sharing of war stories by veteran officers, and this image is ever changing depending upon the perceived threat to the safety of the officer and the community.

☞ CASE IN POINT 4.1

Officer Joe Brown recently graduated from the police academy after 21 years in the Marine Corps. In an interview he discussed his perception of the dangers of being a police officer. "We are all warriors in this job, and every day when we are out on the streets, the possibility exists that we might not come home at night."

Another graduate Brian Perris believes police officers cannot take anything for granted. "Nothing is routine in this job, and you must keep these incidents (three officers were killed at a domestic violence call and four were fatally shot while working on computers in a coffee shop) in the back of your mind."

Perris has never doubted his career switch to policing. "This is what I want, and I think I can make a difference." Similar thoughts were echoed by Trooper Stanford Webb who says he does not "soft-peddle" to potential police officer candidates. "I don't paint a rosy, perfect picture. It is dangerous, and you might have to take someone's life or have your life taken. But the world today is dangerous in general."

Source: "Police Rookies, Recruits Believe Doing Job Trumps Danger," by J. K. Greenwood, 2009. *Pittsburgh Tribune-Review* (PA). Record number 657574. Available from http://infoweb .newsbank.com

During everyday contacts with the public, police officers believe they can minimize the potential danger they will confront, as well as properly display their coercive authority, by always being prepared—or "one-up"—on the public (Rubinstein, 1973; Sykes & Brent, 1980). Van Maanen (1978) explored this attempt to identify people with whom police must interact and identified three types: "suspicious persons," "assholes," and "know-nothings." Suspicious persons include those persons who are most likely about to commit or might have already committed an offense. The assholes include those individuals who disrespect the police and do not accept the police definition of the situation. These individuals often receive some form of *street justice* or "a physical attack designed to rectify what police take as a personal insult" (p. 310). The know-nothings are the typical citizens who interact with the police when they request service.

Academy instructors teach police officers to assess others with whom they are involved in terms of their ability to physically handle these individuals if it becomes necessary and to be aware that, in most instances, their encounters with other citizens will be perceived as creating trouble for those citizens. They teach them that they work in an alien environment in which everyone knows who they are, while they lack such information about most of the people with whom they interact (Rubinstein, 1973).

In addition, of course, as representatives of government, police officers are told they have specific authority to intervene in a wide array of situations. They are equipped with a Taser, firearm, handcuffs, a portable radio, backup officers, and a uniform to be sure that their image as authority figures is complete and unmistakable. And they are told that when dealing with a dispute in progress, their definition of the situation must prevail, that they must take charge of the situation. Police are taught that, as a part of their role, they must give orders, exercise control over law enforcement and order maintenance situations, place restraints on certain freedoms, enforce unpopular laws and ones they do not agree with, conduct searches, make arrests, and perform a number of other duties (Alpert & Dunham, 1997, p. 109).

❖ PHOTO 4.2   The officer above bears the authoritarian tools of his trade.

What is not routinely stated to police officers, but what they learn very quickly on the streets, is that other citizens, not infrequently, resent their intervention. And other citizens, when treated suspiciously by the police, may react with hostility, resentment, contempt, and occasionally, physical violence. Nor are police officers routinely taught that certain segments of the population hate them or hold them in contempt simply because they wear the badge and uniform. If members of these groups challenge the authority of the police, the police will, based on their training, often resort to threats of force or the use of force to impose their authority, which often escalates the level of danger in the encounters. On those relatively rare occasions in which the challenge to authority is prolonged or vicious, danger may become the foremost concern of all parties involved, and the capacity to use force, including deadly force in appropriate circumstances, becomes paramount (Bittner, 1970). Under the circumstances, the need for police solidarity and the feelings of isolation and alienation from other citizens become apparent. Alpert and Dunham (1997, pp. 112–113) suggested that police unity bolsters officer self-esteem and confidence, which enables the police to tolerate the isolation from society and the hostility and public disapproval.

At the same time, Skolnick (1966) argued, we expect the police to be efficient, and the police themselves are concerned with at least giving the appearance of efficiency, if not the substance, because performance evaluations and promotions often depend on at least the former. Concerns with efficiency and the resulting pressures they produce have increased dramatically with the computerization of the police world and other technological advances. Simultaneously, taxpayers have begun to demand greater accountability for the costs involved in policing and the addition of well-educated (and therefore more costly) police personnel. The resulting "do more with less" philosophy has led many police executives to emphasize even more the importance of efficient performance. According to Carey (1994), "Citizens expect professional police behavior, respectful treatment, maintenance of human dignity, responsiveness, and a high value on human life. In addition, these increasingly sophisticated taxpayers also insist that the police achieve maximum effectiveness and efficiency in the use of their tax dollars" (p. 24).

However, in some cases, the police subculture has established standards of acceptable performance for officers and resists raising these standards. Officers whose performance exceeds these standards are often considered *rate-busters* and threats to those adhering to traditional expectations. For example, fueling the patrol car, in some departments, is an operation for which the officer is expected by the subculture to allot 20 to 30 minutes. Because the operation may actually take less than 5 minutes, administrators concerned about accountability, totaling the amount of time lost in this operation for, say, 10 cars, recognize they are losing two to three hours of patrol time if they fail to take action to modify the fueling procedure. At the same time, however, officers concerned about accountability who wish to patrol an additional 15 to 20 minutes and fuel the car in less time make those officers adhering to the 20 to 30 minute standard look bad, and they are under considerable pressure to conform to the established standard. Similar expectations and conflicts exist with respect to the number of drunk drivers who can be processed in a shift, the number of felonies that may be processed, the number of subpoenas that may be served, or the number of prisoners who may be transported. Officers must make choices as to whose expectations are to be met and sometimes operate in a no-win situation, in which meeting one set of expectations automatically violates the other, leaving the officer under some stress no matter how she operates.

Sparrow, Moore, and Kennedy (1992) argued that the police subculture creates a set of truths, according to which officers are expected to live. Note that there is some basis in fact for each of these subcultural truths and that each makes integrating the police and the citizens they serve more difficult.

- The police are the only real crime fighters.
- No one understands the nature of police work but fellow officers.
- Loyalty to colleagues counts more than anything else.
- It is impossible to win the war on crime without bending the rules.
- Other citizens are unsupportive and make unreasonable demands.
- Patrol work is only for those who are not smart enough to get out of it. (p. 51)

As discussed in previous chapters, society has witnessed major changes in the concept of police in the past decades. Accordingly, the police culture has experienced change. For example, Paoline, Myers, and Worden (2000, p. 581) believed that the adoption of and experimentation with community policing may have altered both the occupational and organizational environments of policing, and within these environments, the stresses and strains experienced by police officers. They cited the greater attention to officers' efforts to reduce disorder, solve problems, and build rapport with the public that could modify the us-versus-them outlook. Some similar issues related to the police culture are also found in other countries (see Around the World).

AROUND THE WORLD

The impact of conflict on police culture was explored in the three African states of Uganda, Rwanda, and Sierra Leone. Baker (2007) found the following common patterns:

Cooperation of the public is vital in providing intelligence to the police, keeping law and order, and in implementing anti-crime strategies.

Divergences exist between cultures of command, middle management, and lower ranks.

All three governments embraced the "community policing" and "sector policing" approach but in "none has it taken hold seriously, mainly due to suspicion among the middle and lower ranks."

A major change in the police culture may occur "when the state police realize that they do not have a monopoly on policing and never will—when they learn to work in security networks with the other agencies."

Source: From Conflict and African Police Culture: The Cases of Uganda, Rwanda, Sierra Leone, by B. Baker, 2007. In M. O'Neil, M. Marks, and N. Singh, (Eds.), *Police Occupational Culture: New Debates and Directions*, Oxford: Elsevier Science. Available online at: http://www.ssrnetwork.net

---

❖ The Police Personality: Myth or Reality?

Some have suggested that the impact of police work and the police subculture itself lead to the development of a distinctive police personality. Berg (1999, p. 297) concluded that the police personality was a combination of characteristics and behaviors that are commonly used to stereotype the police. Often, these characteristics included a "desire to be in control of the situation, assertions, cynicism, authoritarian attitude, a wish to be aloof from citizens, an increased solidarity with other police officers and a tendency to be physically aggressive" (Berg, 1999, p. 297). How does such a personality develop? Is it a predispositional model of personality, or does it develop from the work itself (an organizational socialization model) (Twersky-Glasner, 2005, p. 56)? Some believe policing attracts individuals who possess a certain type of personality, while others propose that the exposure to violence, corruption, and danger creates an elusive personality.

Over the years, the literature on the police has characterized them as more authoritarian and prejudiced than other occupational groups. Authoritarian personalities tend to be conservative, rigid, punitive, and inflexible, and they tend to emphasize authority and rules (Adorno, Frenkel-Brunswik, Levinson, & Sanford, 1950). Prejudice (in this case, unfavorable attitudes toward a group or individual not based on experience or fact) appears to be more common among those with authoritarian traits. Prejudiced individuals tend to develop and adhere to stereotypes based on race, ethnicity, occupational group, and other factors. Police actions based on such stereotypes are discriminatory and clearly inappropriate in a democratic society. Because these stereotypes and prejudices are attitudes and cannot be directly observed, they are difficult, if not impossible, to eliminate among police officers—as well as among the general public. Discriminatory actions, however, are observable, and steps to prevent such actions can and must be taken. The extent to which prejudices and stereotypes translate into discriminatory action remains an empirical question, though there is no doubt that it does sometimes happen.

It may be argued that these characterizations are based in part on the previous history of the police. As we noted in Chapter 1, the 1960s was a time of civil unrest and of protests against the police amid accusations of police brutality. However, most agree recent changes in policing have likely had a significant impact on the characterization of the police personality and culture. These changes include a more diverse police organization through the attraction of women and minorities, more educated police officers, and technical sophistication (Siegel, 2009, p. 280). In addition, because of the changes in the police role, departments began seeking officers with the personalities and characteristics that were consistent with quality-of-life issues and problem-solving expertise (Carter & Radelet, 1999, p. 183). One of the main reasons for the changes in today's police culture may be the implementation of community policing, which has dissolved some of the barriers between the police and the community (Dantzker, 2005, p. 279). **Cynicism** is another feature of the police officer's working personality that is addressed by students of the police. As defined by Niederhoffer (1967, p. 96), cynicism involves losses of faith in people, of enthusiasm for police work, and of pride and integrity. Niederhoffer and others (Regoli & Poole, 1978) found that cynicism peaked in the 7th to 10th year of police service, and the latter noted that the level of cynicism varied with the organizational style of the department and the type of department (urban or rural). Similar findings were proposed by Gould (2000), who concluded that "although most individuals entering police work are idealistic, service-oriented and outgoing, by about the fifth year in the profession some officers tend to develop attitudes that are cynical, defensive, alienated, authoritarian, and often racist" (p. 41). However, Niederhoffer's classic 1967 study found that cynicism set in shortly after graduation from the police academy. What causes these changes in a police officer's personality that would result in these types of attitudes?

According to Graves (1996), this is related to the "reality of the streets, particularly in large cities that have high crime rates and more anonymity—which shocks the new officers, causing them to lose faith in others and only trust other police officers" (p. 17). In another study, cynicism was found to vary inversely with rank and preferred assignment (day shift) and in a curvilinear fashion with the police officer's length of service (Dorsey & Giacopassi, 1987, pp. 1–16). This curvilinear relationship between tenure and cynicism was later replicated by Hickman, Piquero and Piquero (2004). However some argue that the changes in a police officer's personality are the result of a socialization process. This process results in rank and file police officers who begin to view their administrators as dangerous outsiders to the patrol subculture and somewhat personally and professionally threatening (Kappeler, Sluder, & Alpert, 1998). This tension between police officers and police administrators is primarily due to the discrepancy between what patrol officers are commanded to do and what they can realistically be expected to accomplish (Bennett & Schmitt, 2002, p. 494). Gould (2000) also found that race and gender influenced cynicism and that white female police officers were the least affected group and black females were the most affected group. In addition, black male officers were apparently more affected by their exposure to policing compared with white male officers. Thus, Gould (2000) concluded that the race of the officer followed by the gender of the officer influence the strength of the effect.

Niederhoffer (1967) defined four stages that lead to police cynicism:

- Stage One—Pseudo Cynicism: New recruits are idealistic, their desire is to "help people."
- Stage Two—Romantic Cynicism: Involves the first five years of police work; these officers are the most vulnerable to cynicism.
- Stage Three—Aggressive Cynicism: Failures and frustrations, resentment, and hostility are obvious and prevalent at the tenth-year mark.
- Stage Four—Resigned Cynicism: Detachment, passiveness, an acceptance of the flaws of the system. (p. 95)

Within different police subcultures, cynicism is thought to involve different issues, including the public, the police administration, the courts, training and education, dedication to duty, and police solidarity (Bouza, 1990). Alpert and Dunham (1997) concluded, "There is some evidence for the existence of a police working personality. Most of the evidence points to the influence of socialization and experiences after becoming a police officer as the main source of the unique traits" (p. 112). Broderick (1987, pp. 22–115) believed there were four working personalities of police: enforcers, idealists, realists, and optimists. Enforcers emphasize the law enforcement function, while idealists focus on individual rights. Realists place little emphasis on social order and individual rights. Optimists view policing as an opportunity to help people (Broderick, 1987). Each of these working personalities involves a different level of cynicism. For example, the Enforcer is a crime fighter rather than a problem solver and becomes easily frustrated with the criminal justice system, the public, and others.

In contrast, Terry (1989) reviewed numerous studies that found essentially no differences between police officers and those in other occupations with respect to either authoritarianism or prejudice, and studies that have found police officers to be intelligent, emotionally stable, and service oriented. Carpenter and Raza (1987) reported that police applicants differ from the general population in several positive ways: "They are more psychologically healthy than the normative population, as they are generally less depressed and anxious, and more assertive and interested in making and maintaining social contacts" (p. 16). Terry (1989) conceded that while some of the research on police personalities does appear to distinguish certain traits, no one has been able to "disentangle the effects of a person's socioeconomic background from the demands that police work and its subculture places upon individual officers" (p. 550). Johnson (2007, p. v) agreed and concluded that the study of police cynicism reached its zenith in the 1980s, but it has slowed in the present day, leaving many questions unresolved. In other words the research does not support the existence of a single dominant personality type among police officers. Yarmey (1990) stated, "There is no evidence for such a thing as a typical police personality showing a cluster of traits that is constant across time and space" (p. 42).

❖ Stresses and Strains of Police Work

Previously, we discussed the formal police organization and the police subculture, both of which contribute to the stress levels experienced by police. The effects of formal pressure from police organizations and pressures generated by the police subculture often lead police to experience a great deal of stress in their occupational, social, and family lives, resulting in cynicism, burnout, and retirement on the job, as well as a host of physical and emotional ailments. We also know that those police officers who reported higher levels of stress reported more acts of deviance. Correspondingly, as the stress levels of police officers were reduced through reassignment from high stress duties, the reported deviance decreased (Arter, 2008).

The Personal Costs of Police Work

In spite of the fact that there does not appear to be a cluster of personality traits that distinguish police officers from other occupational groups, there is no doubt that the nature of police work and the subculture in which it occurs creates difficulties for officers, their families, and friends. The need to perform under stress is a concern in many professions; policing is probably not as stressful as some other occupations. However, according to Adams (2007, p. 473), stress is one of the most common of all occupational hazards for police and can be extremely debilitating, leading to early onset of stress-related illness. Of course, the cost associated with a stressful event is a function of how each individual perceives the event (Waters & Ussery, 2007, p. 3). In other words, what may be viewed as very threatening to one police officer may be perceived as simply an exciting challenge by another police officer who experienced the same event. Since many individuals are capable of venting their feelings and discharging their emotions, they do not suffer as much from stressful events (Waters & Ussery, 2007).

According to Nelson and Quick (2006), stress is one of the most creatively ambiguous words in the English language. For most people, stress has a negative perception and is something to be avoided. However, stress is a great asset in managing legitimate emergencies and achieving peak performance. Champoux (2006) proposed that "a person experiences **stress** when an event in their environment presents a constraint, an opportunity, or an excessive physical or psychological demand" (p. 380). Nelson and Quick (2006, pp. 217–221) used four approaches to define stress. These approaches, which emphasize demands or sources of stress in organizations, include task demands, role demands, interpersonal demands, and physical demands.

Task Demands

Task demands or the lack of task demands can impose high stress levels on police. Quantitative input overload is a result of too many demands for the time allotted, while qualitative input overload is the result of complexity and limited time (Whisenand, 2001, p. 206). These two types of input overload are known as *hyperstress.* Quantitative overload occurs when police officers experience stacking of calls or when more calls are being received than can be answered. Emergency calls are prioritized by 911 systems, but minor theft cases, criminal damage to property cases, trespassing violations, and other nonemergency calls are answered in the order in which they are received. In other words, an officer on a busy shift might respond to 25 calls for service, with little time for patrol or personal breaks. Obviously, with this number of calls, the quality of the police interaction with the public can suffer. However, investigators assigned a large number of cases more readily experience quality overload. Each case must follow case management criteria and may include interviews, interrogations, evidence collection, search warrants, and numerous reports. The number of cases assigned by supervisors and the pressure generated by prosecutors to complete an investigation affect the quality of investigation and the extent of overload experienced by individual officers.

Whisenand (2001, p. 206) found that low levels of mental and physical activity cause *hypostress,* which is the result of quantitative and qualitative input underloads. Police officers who work a third shift with no calls experience high levels of boredom when the only activity is random patrol and personal breaks. Furthermore, as we have discussed in previous chapters, answering service call requests, one of the primary roles of a police officer, is often seen by officers as routine, mundane, and at times boring.

Role Demands

Role demands develop two types of role stress in the work environment: role conflict and role ambiguity (Nelson & Quick, 2006, pp. 217–221). **Role conflict** is a result of the inconsistent or incompatible expectations communicated to the person. A role conflict can occur when society's expectations of police behavior conflict with certain police principles, beliefs, and behaviors. For example, for many decades, society has condemned the use and sale of illegal drugs. However, the police are limited in their ability to successfully reduce drug abuse. Thus, Crank (2004) concluded the following:

> Cops must avoid the harsh glare of the external observation which would reveal (1) that they were frequently in violation of the law, and (2) that they were doing exactly what the public wanted them to do, generating arrests for drugs the only way they can—fabricating evidence, dropsy, lying on the witness stand, entrapment, in a word, by being more criminally sophisticated than the criminals. (p. 298)

Thus, the perceptions of society and the actual behaviors of police performing undercover drug enforcement can generate high levels of stress, especially for police who must become a part of the drug culture, appear in court as a professional police officer, and still maintain relationships with spouses, children, and other family members.

Role Ambiguity

Role ambiguity is the confusion a person experiences related to the expectations of others (Nelson & Quick, 2006, pp. 217–221). For example, according to Manning (1977), the police are seen by the public as "alertly ready to respond to citizen demands, as crime-fighters, as an efficient, bureaucratic, highly organized force that keeps society from falling into chaos" (p. 100). However, as we have seen in other chapters, this is an exaggeration of actual police work. Manning concluded that "most police work resembles any other kind of work: it is boring, tiresome, sometimes dirty, sometimes technically demanding, but it is rarely dangerous" (p. 100). And to add to the role confusion, the public has demanded an even higher level of the crime fighting activities which are grossly exaggerated in books, movies, electronic games and television shows.

Interpersonal Demands

Abrasive personalities, sexual harassment, and the leadership style in the organization are interpersonal demands for people at work (Nelson & Quick, 2006, pp. 217–221). Even with general support by the public, police typically encounter individuals with abrasive personalities. According to Alpert and Dunham (1997, p. 105), many citizens feel the police are just a little above the evil they fight or believe that the police are against them and misuse their right to use force to uphold the law. The police often perceive an extreme negative evaluation by citizens, leading to increased levels of occupational stress.

In most cases, besides the on-duty demands on police officers there are also off-duty requirements that affect the stress levels of officers and their families. For example, language similar to the following can be found in most police department policy manuals: "A police officer's character and conduct while off-duty must be exemplary, and maintain a position of respect in the community" (University of Oklahoma Police, 2008). To an extent, police are never off-duty, which generates high levels of stress in police officers and their family.

Leadership styles are another interpersonal demand that can create stress in the work environment. Management styles play an important role in work environment stress levels. Lind and Otte (2006) found significant differences in employee stress levels among management styles. Furthermore, when management styles were included as a predictor variable, the styles were one of the primary predictors of stress in employees. This is especially true in police organizations that are characteristically authoritarian but attract college-educated personnel. Roberg, Crank, and Kuykendall (2000, p. 414) concluded that college-educated police would be less willing to work in, and be less satisfied with, authoritarian departments and managerial practices.

Physical Demands

Extreme environments, strenuous activities, and hazardous substances create physical demands for people in the work place (Nelson & Quick, 2006). While once believed to be a very high-stress occupation, more recent research suggests that policing may not be as stressful as originally believed (Roberg, Crank, & Kuykendall, 2000, p. 466). This change may be in part due to different hiring processes, stress-reduction training classes, and individual characteristics of the officers. However, police, on a regular basis, are exposed to situations rarely experienced by other members of society. Death, extreme physical abuse, and fear of the unknown have significant affects on the physical and mental health of police. Stevens (1999, pp. 1–5) found that the top five stress producers for police officers are child abuse, the killing of an innocent person, conflict with regulations, domestic violence, and killing or hurting a fellow police officer. Johnson (2010), in a more recent study, confirmed that the largest stressor for police involved crime and incidents against children. For example, a police officer responding to a trouble call finds that the father has shot his two young children, his wife, and then himself. The public will read only a short abstract about this tragedy in the newspaper, but the image of the young child gripping her doll just before being shot in the head with a shotgun by her father will remain with the officer forever.

❖ Forms of Police Stress

According to Zhao, He, and Lovrich (2002), the central attention of research on police stress has focused on the violent nature of the work and the organization structures found in almost all police agencies. For example, Garcia, Nesbary, and Gu (2004) found that the top-ranked stressor was concern for fellow police officers being injured or killed. However, Zhao, He, and Lovrich (2002) concluded that other research failed to demonstrate a clear association between the dangers of police work and the level of stress experienced among officers. With respect to the dangers of police work, a report by the Los Angeles Times ("California Sees," 2009) indicated the number of police officers killed in the line of duty in 2009 was one of the lowest in 50 years.

Research concerning stressors in policing tends to view police organizational structures and various management practices as one of the primary sources of stress (Zhao, He, & Lovrich, 2002). For example, Golembiewski and Kim (1991) concluded that the quasi-military nature associated with police organizations often breeds alienation among street officers, who are required to utilize high levels of discretion while being tightly controlled by supervisors and administrative rules. Additional **stressors** identified by Garcia, Nesbary, and Gu (2004) included public criticism, family demands, career stages, and working the late shift. To this list we might add excessive paperwork, red tape, lack of participation in decision making, and competition for promotion, among others. One study found new and more severe sources of stress for police: increased scrutiny and criticism from the media and the public and anxiety and loss of morale as a result of layoffs and reduced salary raises (National Institute of Justice, 2000). The National Institute of Justice concluded that even positive changes, such as the movement to community policing, have caused increased levels of stress for many officers. Today, the increasing response to or the threat of terrorism is also a police stressor (Dowling, Moynihan, Genet, & Lewis, 2006).

Peak (2009) divided stressors experienced by police into the following five major categories:

- Stressors originating within the organization: Poor supervision, absence of career development opportunities, inadequate reward system, offensive policies, and paperwork (pp. 377–378)
- Stressors external to the organization: Absence of career development (not able to transfer to another department), jurisdictional isolation, seemingly ineffective corrections system, courts, distorted press accounts, derogatory remarks, and adverse government actions (pp. 378–379)
- Stressors connected with the performance of police duties: Role conflict, adverse work schedules, fear and danger, sense of uselessness, and absence of closure (pp. 379–380)
- Stressors particular to the individual officer: Feeling overcome by fear and danger, pressures to conform (p. 380)
- Effects of critical incidents (p. 381)

In addition, Carter and Radelet (1999) devised a typology of seven police stressors that selectively interact with a police officer's job activities, decision making, and organizational life:

- Life-threatening stressors (ever-present potential of injury or death)
- Social isolation stressors (cynicism, isolation, and alienation from the community; prejudice and discrimination)
- Organizational stressors (administrative philosophy, changing policies and procedures, morale, job satisfaction, misdirected performance measures)
- Functional stressors (role conflict, use of discretion, and legal mandates)
- Personal stressors (police officer's off-duty life, including family, illness, problems with children, marital stresses, and financial constraints)
- Physiological stressors (fatigue, medical conditions, and shift-work effects)
- Psychological stressors (possibly activated by all of the above and the exposure to repulsive situations). (p. 292)

An additional classification of police stress was proposed by Waters and Ussery (2007), which involved three primary types of stress:

- Explosive: crimes in progress, natural disasters and terrorist attacks such as September 11, 2001. In most cases police suppress their reactions and emotion to fulfill their role as a police officer. However, the effects of exposure to explosive levels of stress can be long-term and result in posttraumatic stress syndrome.
- Implosive: internal conflicts and inability to solve all problems the police encounter over the course of their career.
- Corrosive: daily tensions that erode the confidence and wear away at the individual's hardiness and resiliency. In many cases these authors believe police officers fail to engage in self protective behaviors and police departments trivialize the negative consequences of police work. "The implication is that only the weak suffer from stress related symptoms." (p. 172).

The National Institute of Justice (NIJ) (2000, p. 19) concluded that today's police are experiencing new levels of stress based on a perceived increase in public scrutiny, adverse publicity, and a perceived decline in police camaraderie. Fear of contracting air- and blood-borne diseases (TB, HIV, hepatitis), the focus on cultural diversity and political correctness, and the transition to community policing have also increased stress levels, according to the Institute. Furthermore, these newly perceived stressors have serious emotional and physical effects on police. The NIJ concluded that the consequences of stress reported by police include cynicism, suspicion, and emotional detachment from everyday life. In addition, stress leads to reduced efficiency, increased absenteeism, and early retirement, as well as excessive aggressiveness, alcoholism, and other substance abuse. Marital and family problems (extramarital affairs, divorce, domestic violence) and posttraumatic stress disorders are yet other products of stress.

Stages of Stress

All occupations involve stress, but stress need not always be harmful. In fact, moderate stress appears to be positively related to productivity. Elimination of all stress is neither possible nor desirable. However, the effects of prolonged high levels of stress are clearly dysfunctional, producing both debilitating psychological and physical symptoms. In part, the damage caused by stress occurs because of the **general adaptation syndrome** identified by Selye (1974). In the first stage of this syndrome, the body prepares to fight stress by releasing hormones that lead to an increase in respiration and heartbeat. In the second stage, the body attempts to resist the stressor and repair any damage that has occurred. If the stress continues long enough and cannot be successfully met through flight or fight, the third stage, exhaustion, occurs. Repeated exposures to stressors that cannot be eliminated or modified by the organism eventually lead to stage three.

Often, a police officer's career is divided into significant phases, according to the development of stress at various periods of his career. "These stages include the initial phase, which involves academy training; the middle phase, which deals with years of working various assignments and promotions; and the final stage, which examines the time immediately preceding retirement and the subsequent return to civilian life" (Flynn, 1997, p. 1). Police officers experience such stressors repeatedly in the performance of their duties as well as during off-duty time (carrying an off-duty weapon).

According to Violanti and Marshall (1983), four transitory stages exist in a police officer's career:

- Alarm Stage (0–5 years). Stress increases as the officers adjust to new experiences, including death, an authoritarian style of management, and the dangers of policing. The officer quickly learns that the academy training, education classes, and television do not truly reflect the street environment.
- Disenchantment Stage (6–13 years). Stress levels continue to increase in this stage as the officer realizes that crimes do not have easy resolutions and that many of the problems they encounter do not have a resolution.
- Personalization Stage (14–19 years). During this stage, there is a substantial decrease in the stress levels experienced by police officers. In all sizes of department, the officer has become somewhat comfortable with the job and has seen almost every type of call.
- Introspection Stage (20 years and over). Stress continues to decrease during this stage. Police officers are concerned about retirement and personal issues and are very secure in their job. If the officers experience frustration, they can retire at any time. (p. 3)

Source: Reprinted from Violanti, J. M., & Marshall, J. R., "The police stress process" in *Journal of Police Science and Administration, 11,* 389–394.

From this study, it is apparent that stress-reduction training should be provided early in a police officer's career. The National Institute of Justice (2000) reported that this can be performed during the initial training period because police recruits are a "captive audience" (p. 22) and because the information may remain with them throughout their entire police career. However, others believe that recruit training is not the most effective time or approach because most academy attendees are not experienced enough to recognize the stresses of the job. They believe the optimal time to reach a new police officer is after she has worked the street for six to eight months.

Burnout

The inability to find a way to relieve stress may lead to **burnout**, which is characterized by emotional exhaustion and cynicism. Individuals unable to cope with stressors reflected in psychological, behavioral, and physical symptoms are said to manifest burnout (Johnson, Todd, & Subramanian, 2005, p. 6). Repeated exposure to high levels of stress results in emotional exhaustion. Depersonalization of relationships follows emotional exhaustion as a coping response. Police suffering from these stages view victims and complainants as case numbers—and with little empathy or individual attention. An additional contributor to burnout is the fact that police often suppress their emotions. This begins when new recruits observe police academy instructors, field training officers, and veteran officers, and they learn or are told directly to control and hide their emotions, particularly when they are in public view (Johnson et al., 2005). This control is referred to as displaying a "court room face" or a face with no emotion.

The final stage of burnout involves reduced personal accomplishment, in which the officer loses interest in the job, performance declines, and motivation is lacking. It is important that police administrators understand the implications of burnout because research has revealed that elevated levels of stress and associated burnout in police officers can decrease job performance (Goodman, 1990). Scaramella, Shannon, and Giannoni (2005) reported that the benefits of higher education and critical reflection by police on their career showed great promise for alleviation or mitigation of the symptoms of burnout.

More (1998) argued that the onset of burnout occurs through five stages:

- Honeymoon, enthusiasm phase. New police officers are excited, ready to help people, and want to save the world from crime. If a coping mechanism is not in place, these officers move to the next stage.
- Stagnation stage. Police in this stage expend less energy, new challenges have disappeared, and police work becomes boring and routine.
- Frustration stage. Police exhibit anger and resentment, and begin to withdraw from the job.
- Apathy stage. Officers become obsessed with the frustrations of the work environment.
- Hitting the wall/intervention. Burnout becomes entwined with alcoholism, drug abuse, heart disease, and mental illness. (pp. 248–249)

As noted, officers experiencing such stress sometimes turn to alcohol or other drugs, physical aggression, and even suicide in attempting to alleviate it. The literature has theorized that police officers consume more alcohol than the general population (Lindsay, Taylor, & Shelley, 2008). The authors indicated that most believe the consumption of alcohol by police is related to stress or social camaraderie issues. However, Lindsay et al. (2008) found that most of the officers surveyed reported drinking levels equivalent to those reported by the general population. Furthermore, they asserted that the generally accepted notion that an alcohol problem exists "seems to be a classic example of Quinney's (1970) famous distinction between reality and social reality—between what is true and what is merely thought to be true" (p. 596). It can also be argued that stress symptoms experienced by police officers influence other members of the family. We will discuss the effect of stress and burnout on police families in the next section.

Perhaps an example of the incidents occurring in the first few hours of a police offi-cer's tour of duty will help clarify the stressors to which officers are routinely subjected. Shortly after reporting "in service," the officer receives a call that another officer requires immediate assistance. The officer responding to the call for help turns on red lights and siren and drives as rapidly as possibly to reach a colleague. On the way, he prepares for the possibility of a physical struggle or armed resistance, and the physical changes described are taking place. The officer is tense and excited, but also frightened. The fear experienced may have to do with anticipation about what will happen when he arrives at the scene, but it also has to do with what other drivers, noting the red lights and siren—or failing to note them—will do. Will they yield at intersections? Will they pull off to the right? Will they pull to the left? Will they stop in the middle of the street? Will they slow down or speed up? What will happen if the officer is involved in an accident?

Arriving at the scene, the officer finds the situation under control, a suspect in cus-tody, and the colleague uninjured. As the officer gets back into the patrol car, another call comes from the dispatcher. This call involves an accident with serious injuries. The officer proceeds to the scene (with the same set of concerns about arriving safely). As the first emergency officer to arrive, he finds that several people have been seriously injured and an infant killed. After the accident has been handled, the officer gets into the police vehicle and is told to come to the station to meet with the chief. His concerns on the way are somewhat different but perhaps equally stressful. For the next several hours and, in some cities, for the next several days, weeks, and years, these scenarios are repeated. The ups and downs of police work take their toll, and the officer experiences repeated stress, anxiety, and perhaps burnout.

The literature on police stress is extensive and suggests that the interaction of per-sonality and situational factors often determines the amount and type of stress experi-enced by the individual. In some cases this could lead to suicide, and according to psychologist Audrey Honig, suicide rates for police officers (at least 18 per 100,000) are higher than the general population (as discussed in Ritter, 2007, p. 3A). Similar beliefs are held by psychologist Elizabeth Dansie, who believes many police suicides in the past were ruled as accidents and that the statistics are much higher than records indicate due to the shame factor (as discussed in Ritter, 2007). In another recent study, Chambers (2008) discovered that police officers were at least 8 times more likely to die from suicide than from accidental death. Crosby and Sacks (2002) suggested that suicide ideation, planning a suicide, and attempts to commit suicide were more likely to occur when indi-viduals were exposed to the suicide of another person. In most cases police are one of the first responders at the scene of a suicide and are required to perform an investigation. Thus, police officers have a much higher exposure to the act of suicide compared to the general population. However, Gaines, Kappeler, and Vaughn (2008, pp. 345–346) claimed that comparing suicide rates of the general public and police may be deceptive since drastic differences often exist between the two groups. These differences include male domination in policing, all are over 21 years of age, have access to firearms, and most police officers work in urban areas. Further, they concluded that besides the stress of police work, other factors contribute to police suicides. Among these are abuse of alcohol and drugs, involvement in deviance and corruption, depression, and working in a male-dominated organization. Family and economic problems, alienation, and cyni-cism associated with the police culture; role conflict; and physical and mental health problems are other contributing problems (Gaines, Kappeler, & Vaughn, 2008, p. 346).

Stress and Police Families

Yet other studies have focused on the effects of police work on the police family. For example, Picanol (2009) reported that a police officer's level of emotional exhaustion was related to the level of job satisfaction, depersonalization, and marital distress. Furthermore, Prabhu and Turner (2000) concluded that domestic violence committed by police officers against their intimate partners occurred at the same rate when compared to the general population. However, apart from the fact that most families will not air dirty laundry, domestic violence by police officers was often not detected due to the officer's strong adherence to a code of secrecy, commitment to camaraderie, and resistance to external intrusion (Klein, 2000). Similarly, Johnson et al. (2005) argued that individuals who marry a police officer marry into the police family and are expected to follow the values and norms of the subculture.

Family-related stress has the potential to adversely affect the job performance of employees. Police officers not experiencing job stress can be adversely affected by problems in the home environment. Several sources of stress commonly cited by police officers' spouses are as follows:

- Shift work and overtime
- Concern over the spouse's cynicism, need to feel in control in the home
- Inability or unwillingness to express feelings
- Fear that officer will be hurt or killed in the line of duty
- Police officer's excessively high expectations of their children
- Avoidance, teasing or harassment of the officer's children by other children because the parent is a police officer
- Presence of a weapon in the residence
- Perception the police officer prefers to spend time with other officers rather than with the family
- Perception the officer is paranoid, excessively vigilant and overprotective
- Problems in helping the officer cope with work-related problems
- Critical incidents or officer's injury or death on the job (Borum & Philpot, 1993, pp. 122–135).

One of the greatest risks is that police "become so inflated, narcissistic, and self-involved that they chance alienating their real families by over investing their time and energy in the work family, which all too frequently turns out to be fickle and unsupportive" (Kirschman, 2000, p. 247).

In 1985, Blumberg and Niederhoffer, in discussing the police family, stated:

> The police profession is a jealous mistress, intruding in intimate family relationships, disrupting the rhythms of married life. The danger of police work arouses fears for the safety of loved ones. The revolving schedule of a patrol officer's "around-the-clock" tours of duty complicates family logistics. . . . Although wives adapt to the pressures of the occupation on family life, they, nevertheless, gripe about the injustices and inconsistencies. They resent the "secret society" nature of police work that obstructs free-flowing communication between spouses. Paradoxically, although they are treated as aliens in the police world, their family lifestyle is scrutinized by a curious public. (p. 371)

❖ Police Shootings and Critical Incidents As a Source of Stress

On average, one law enforcement officer dies in the line of duty in the United States every 53 hours, and since the first known line-of-duty death in 1792, approximately 19,000 U.S. law enforcement officers have been killed (National Law Enforcement Officers Memorial Fund [NLEOMF], 2009a, 2009b). In 2009, the number of police officer deaths declined by 6%, the fewest line-of-duty deaths since 1959. The National Law Enforcement Officers Memorial Fund (NLEOMF) (2009a) attributed this decline to a reduction in traffic-related deaths. However, they also found that the number of firearms-related fatalities of police officers increased compared to 2008. Contributing to the increase in police shootings was the fact that several officers were killed in groups: four officers each in Lakeland, Colorado and Oakland, California and three officers in Pittsburgh ("Numbers," 2009).

It is important to note that even with an increase of police firearm fatalities in 2009, the number of officers killed is still lower than all but three years for the past five decades (NLEOMF, 2009, p. 2). The factors that likely influenced these results include the use of body armor or bullet-proof vests, better communications, increased training, better police practices, and improved medical care. The majority of police fatal shootings involved the officer responding to domestic disturbance calls.

In any case, the stress of actually being involved in a shooting, whether as shooter or victim, is very real. In many cases, prior research argued that officers involved in a shooting experienced **Post-Traumatic Stress Disorder**. Symptoms associated with this emotional disturbance included numbing of emotions, insomnia, nightmares, aggression, depression, fear, and obsessive behaviors (Dumont, 1999). However, recent research from the National Institute of Justice (2006) found that few police officers involved in shooting incidents suffer long-term negative emotional or physical effects. In fact, "following about one-third of the shootings, officers reported feelings of elation that included joy at being alive, residual excitement after a life-threatening situation, and satisfaction of pride in proving their ability to use deadly force appropriately" (NIJ, 2006, p. 3). Thus, according to the NIJ report, these findings call into question the appropriateness of training that stresses the emotions of guilt and depression that accompany a police shooting. Training that focuses on responses by police officers that occur infrequently could be seen as misleading and even counterproductive in some cases.

Most research involving police stress has involved police shootings. More recently, however, the research has expanded to include stress induced by critical incidents. A critical incident is an event that has a stressful impact sufficient enough to overwhelm the usually effective coping skill of an individual (Kulbarsh, 2007, p.1). Critical incidents involve very powerful events, and almost every police officer will experience a marked reaction during and after a critical incident event. Examples of critical incidents include officer-involved shootings, hostage standoffs, a mass suicide, an infant at the bottom of a pool, a family trapped in a burning vehicle, school shootings, and natural disasters (Kulbarsh, 2007). Additional examples of critical incident hazards include terrorist bombings, exposure to toxic chemicals, and biological or

❖ **Photo 4.3**   The photo shows the aftermath of the off-duty officer who took his own life using his service weapon, the most serious consequence of police burnout.

radiation hazards (Paton, 2006). The importance of a Critical Incident Stress Debriefing Team to address such occurrences was reported by the San Jose Police Department (Benner, 1994). For example, during 1972 and 1987, when the Team did not exist, 52 police officers were involved in shootings and 17 left the department. However, according to Benner, after creation of the Team, 122 officers were involved in shootings and none left the department. Obviously, a number of limitations exist that could have affected the outcomes of this comparison, such as training and individual differences among officers.

❖ Attempts to Combat Police Stress

Recognition of the fact that police work can exact a high toll in personal costs has led to numerous attempts to identify and deal with such stress. Many of the factors identified as related to police stress have been discussed previously. This section examines the attempts to lessen the impact of these factors, keeping in mind our earlier statement that stress cannot be entirely eliminated and, unless it is prolonged and severe, serves some useful function. There is no exact formula for stress reduction. Individuals differ markedly in the events they define as stressful, in the ways they react to pressure, and in techniques for dealing with stressful events that will be successful (Ellison, 2004).

Torres and Maggard (2003 pp. 1–7) summarized various managerial attempts to address police stress. These attempts are made to help police officers better manage the stresses they encounter.

1. Provide employee assistance programs, including services to officers and families.

2. Orientation programs for the new officer's transition into the police culture.

3. Pre-academy programs that emphasize physical conditioning.

4. Teach coping mechanisms related to crime, death, boredom.

The Los Angeles County Sheriff's Department is an example of an agency that has developed an organizational consultant program designed to provide police supervisors with the tools needed to recognize and remedy police officer stress (Higginbotham, 2000, pp. 1–3). The program takes a proactive approach to stress and trains supervisors in prevention and early intervention. The Sheriff's Department's program teaches police supervisors how to deal with difficult people, how to manage police stress, and strategies for counseling police officers. Another example for dealing with stress is the Spousal Academy. The Collier County, Florida, Sheriff's Office offers training to spouses and other domestic partners of deputies and recruits who are enrolled in the regular training academy (NIJ, 2000, p. 21). The program includes an introduction to law enforcement work and discussions concerning the effect policing will have on family lives. In addition, spouses discuss the structure of the department, stress management, and conflict resolution techniques.

The movement toward community policing also may be important in the reduction of stress among police officers. If a good deal of the stress officers experience results from constant contact with the criminal elements in the community, and from constantly working in an environment in which the police are regarded as causing trouble for other citizens, then increasing contact with law-abiding citizens under positive circumstances should help alleviate stress. To some extent, this gain may be offset by the additional problem-solving responsibilities placed on community policing officers, but if the administration accepts risks and occasional failures as part of the growing process in community-oriented policing, this stress, too, can be reduced.

Dealing With Stress in Police Organizations

In summary, it is clear that policing can be a stressful occupation. Whether it is more stressful than other occupations is debatable, but the point is that efforts should and can be made to reduce stress in the interests of the officer, the department, the officer's family, and the public. Police officers often either fail to recognize the signs of stress or fail to seek help when they do recognize the symptoms. This may be due, in part, to the influence of the police subculture, which holds that "real" police officers can handle their own problems and do not need the help of "shrinks," employee assistance programs, clergy, or other outsiders (Bouza, 1990).

To the extent that stress results from discrepancies between the official expectations of police administrators and the unofficial expectations of the police subculture, these discrepancies need to be confronted. Because both official and subcultural expectations will continue to play roles in policing, efforts must be made to reduce existing differences between the two. To the extent that stress is created and sustained by administrative policies that frustrate and befuddle officers, revisions need to be made. As an example, according to Gershon, Barocas, Canton, Li, and Vlahov (2009) "progressive police departments actively implement innovative strategies (e.g., providing peer counselors, encouraging officers and couples to enter confidential counseling, making structural administrative changes, adding diversity programs, changing hiring and training practices, adding critical incident programs, etc.) to help minimize the risk of work stress among police" (p. 286).

❖ Chapter Summary

All organizations have cultures and subcultures that to some extent influence the behavior of employees. Many of these cultures and subcultures are consistent with legitimate goals and serve as a positive influence on the operations of these organizations. However, the police culture can involve police adhering to a code of silence and extreme loyalty to other police officers.

Additional influence of the police culture often involves feelings of isolation from the communities that they serve and a mistrust of supervisory ranks. Perhaps the most powerful influence cited is the one pertaining to the desire to be accepted by the group. Unfortunately, one of the ways in which this aspiration is met is by turning a blind eye to the misdeeds of their colleagues. This aspect of the subculture has a powerful and long-lasting effect on organizational attempts to mitigate incidents of misconduct by police officers.

Stress is another factor affecting police officers, the sources of which are both real and perceived. The isolation feature or the us-versus-them attitudes are key examples of stressors. Policing involves numerous stressors, both individual and organizational in nature.

How officers deal with these various stressors is more important. Many police officers cope with stress well by performing daily fitness routines and maintaining their commitment to the legitimate goals of the law enforcement profession. Officers that exhibit responses to stress associated with the negative aspects of the police subculture are much more likely than their counterparts to fall victim to a phenomenon referred to as police burnout. Burnout, in a general sense, is characterized by emotional exhaustion and cynicism.

In order to combat the negative influences of the police subculture and the subsequent forms of stress, police administrators must be vigilant in their efforts to identify behaviors exhibited by officers.

❖ Key Terms

blue wall of silence	predispositional model
police subculture	organizational socialization model
artifacts	prejudice
organizational assumption	cynicism
ethos	stress
symbolic assailants	hyperstress
police personality	hypostress

role conflict   burnout

role ambiguity   Post-Traumatic Stress Disorder

general adaptation syndrome   critical incident

❖ Discussion Questions

1. What is the police subculture, and in what ways does it conflict with the official mandates of police work?

2. What are the forms of organizational culture? Give an example of each form.

3. Why is it so difficult for police officers to avoid getting caught up in the subculture? Give specific examples.

4. Is subculture affiliation unique to the police? If not, should we be concerned about participation in and support of a subculture? If so, why?

5. Is policing a stressful occupation? Why and in what ways?

6. What are some of the major sources of police stress? How might some of these stresses be alleviated? Can they be eliminated?

7. What are the relationships among police stress, alcohol use, suicide, and family disruption?

8. How are police stress and the police subculture interrelated?

9. Discuss the ways in which community policing may help to reduce police stress. Can community policing also increase stress levels among officers? Explain.

❖ Internet Exercises

1. Go to the Internet and search for information about *suicide-by-police*. Is this a recent phenomenon, and how often does it occur? How does involvement in a suicide-by-police affect the officer, the family, the police department?

2. Most agree that police officers experience high levels of stress. Using your favorite search engine, go online and search for information on the effects of chronic stress and cardiovascular disease in police officers. How can police officers improve their cardiovascular health? Should police departments require all applicants to complete a cardiac stress test?

5

Law, Court Decisions, and the Police

CHAPTER LEARNING OBJECTIVES

- Differentiate between civil and criminal law.
- Identify and elaborate on the various influences the Constitution and court decisions have on police discretion.
- Identify the proper role of police when their personal beliefs conflict greatly with lawful actions of the public.
- Describe the potential impact the most recent U.S. Supreme Court ruling on the Second Amendment may have on police practice.
- Identify at least three factors that may influence police officers to manufacture probable cause to justify their actions.
- Describe the evolution of the Miranda case from the initial decision in the 1960s to the present and provide examples of circumstances when the Miranda warning is and is not required.
- Define the legal doctrines associated with the due process clause of the Bill of Rights and identify which specific amendments apply to these doctrines.
- Identify the effects of the war on terrorism on due process rights.
- Provide examples of organizational practices that can be adopted to mitigate the potential for wrongdoing regarding the expansion of police powers.

❖ **Photo 5.1** Is justice really blind as it applies to the criminal justice system?

In Chapter 8, we discuss the ways in which discretion, ethics, and accountability influence (or fail to influence) police activity. The parameters of police activity are also governed by federal and state constitutions, municipal ordinances, and court decisions. Both the substance and procedures enacted into criminal law (and all other law as well) must be consistent with the federal constitution and with the constitution of the state in which the law is enacted. "American criminal law is mostly statutory, with courts interpreting the meaning of penal codes as necessary" (Garland, 2009, p. 35). *Criminal law* is that body of law established to maintain peace and order, and its basic purpose is to protect society from the injurious acts of individuals. *Civil law* defines and determines the rights of individuals to protect their persons and property. There is considerable overlap between the two basic types of law, and police officers are involved with enforcing not only criminal, but also some forms of civil law. In fact, an act causing injury to a person or damage to property may be both a civil wrong, referred to as a *tort,* and a crime (Cox & McCamey, 2008). In the remainder of this chapter, we explore some of the legal requirements impacting the police.

If laws were written in perfectly clear language, contained no contradictions or ambiguities, simply involved applying the principles stated in laws to particular situations, and if all officers were thoroughly familiar with all laws, deciding whether or not a particular law had been violated would be a simple and straightforward task for the officer (Cox & McCamey, 2008). Under these circumstances, the need for police discretion would be minimal. Unfortunately, these conditions, taken either singly or in combination, are seldom met. The law in the United States is a huge, complex, sometimes contradictory, and constantly changing collection of prescriptive and proscriptive rules. The fact that professionally trained legal experts make their living arguing over different interpretations of the law gives some indication of the ambiguities and complexities involved in applying the law. Most police officers are not, and for that matter do not need to be, lawyers—but a familiarity with the basics of law is required if officers are to discharge their responsibilities appropriately. Since even the best police training programs provide limited information on the law, most of the police officer's understanding of the law is achieved indirectly. Through the informal instruction and advice offered by colleagues and supervisors, inservice training programs, cramming for promotional exams, self-initiated reading, day-to-day work experiences, and experiences in the courtroom, however, police officers quickly acquire what might be called a "working knowledge" of the law. This working knowledge constitutes the law as it functions in the day-to-day activities of police officers. It is this work-generated interpretation of the law, which might or might not correspond with the interpretations of lawyers and judicial officials, that guides officers as they carry out their duties (Cox & McCamey, 2008).

The law explicitly grants some discretionary powers to police officers and creates a framework within which other discretionary judgments may legitimately be made. It is one measure of the importance of discretion in police work that these are among the first items that become incorporated into the officer's working knowledge of the law. The officer understands, for example, that certain leeway is permitted in determining whether or not probable cause for a search is present (though legislation and court rulings have increased the confusion surrounding the legal latitude granted the officer in these matters). It is also common knowledge among officers that the overlap that frequently exists among laws gives police officers the opportunity to pick and choose which laws, if any, will be cited once a suspect is apprehended. Thus, the officer can choose to "throw the book" at a suspect by citing violations of several laws or can charge the suspect with a more or less serious offense than circumstances might warrant. In a variety of ways, then, the law, as interpreted and understood by the police officer, creates the framework within which, and sometimes around which, police discretion is exercised (Conser & Russell, 2000; Cox, 1996; Cox & McCamey, 2008).

Determining whether or not a law has been broken is a technical judgment, dependent on the officer's knowledge of the law and capacity to apply the general principles embodied in the law to the particular events that have occurred. However difficult this judgment may be (and it is difficult in many instances), it is a decision that merely sets the stage for a far more consequential one—deciding whether or not to take official action. If the police officer decides not to arrest, the remainder of the legal machinery in the criminal justice network does not normally come into play (Cox & McCamey, 2008). The police officer, to be sure, is not alone in making legal decisions. It is the responsibility of the prosecutor (state's attorney, district attorney, attorney general) in a given jurisdiction to advise the police in matters pertaining to law and to help them prepare cases for trial. Cooperation between the prosecutor's office and the police department is essential to both so that the police can follow legal procedures that help the prosecutor obtain convictions.

In the remainder of this chapter, we will examine some of the constitutional amendments and related legal concepts that govern police behavior. Specifically, we will examine the relationship of the First, Second, Fourth, Fifth, Sixth, and Fourteenth Amendments and related court decisions to police conduct. This is not to imply that none of the other amendments have a bearing on police conduct. Please keep in mind that this is not a law or criminal procedure text, so only the general outlines of the implications of the amendments will be presented here.

❖ The First Amendment

The first ten amendments to the Constitution are known collectively as the Bill of Rights. The **First Amendment** states that Congress shall make no law prohibiting free exercise of religion or abridging the rights of free speech and peaceful assembly, and the police are frequently involved in protecting these rights. With respect to the rights of freedom to assemble and free speech, the police, whether or not they agree with protestors' causes or statements, may be called upon to protect them from those who disagree with them. In fact, it is not uncommon for the police to be caught between parties in conflict, both verbal and physical in such situations, nor is it uncommon for members of both parties in the conflict to direct their hostilities toward the police. Not infrequently, the Ku Klux Klan marches in cities where their views are unwelcome to the majority of residents. The police attempt to prevent violence between the parties involved. Political protests and demonstration often find the police risking their lives to protect the lives and property of those subject to the protest as well as the lives of the protestors. Religious activities have also been a focus of police attention following the events of the 9/11 terrorists attacks. For example, when unpleasantness arises between Muslims and those of other religious persuasions, mosques as well as individual members of the faith may be threatened, or Muslims may threaten those who hold other religious beliefs. In such cases, the police may be called upon to maintain order or protect lives and property.

In other cases, where protestors fail to follow approved procedures and become destructive or violent, or both, the police are called upon to use force to arrest those responsible. At the same time, the police may be involved in undercover operations in which officers infiltrate groups with histories of violence and destruction in order to prevent outbursts during protests through advanced knowledge of events that are likely to occur. Police must ensure, though, that these undercover infiltrations of protests are used to collect only criminal intelligence. What follows is a case in point: During the civil unrest of the late 1960s, the Chicago Police Department (CPD) was sued civilly due to the actions of members of their Intelligence Unit. The case was adjudicated some 15 years later by virtue of a consent degree between the plaintiffs (Alliance to End Repression and the American Civil Liberties Union) and the CPD. The allegations were that many of the CPD's covert intelligence operations during that time period were not focused on criminal wrongdoing; rather their intent was to gather information for local and national politicians to use to gain advantages over their opponents. Because of this case and the ensuing consent decree, the official policy of the CPD was that investigations directed at First Amendment conduct were prohibited unless express written permission for said conduct was granted and monitored by the Superintendent of Police. Legal abuses from the past continued to hamper legitimate law enforcement efforts until 2004, when the city of Chicago asked the court to relax the investigative restrictions on their police department, citing changes in case law and judicial philosophy. The court found in favor of the city of Chicago (*Alliance to End Repression et al., v. City of Chicago*, 2004).

In other circumstances, the police may be present at athletic events, holiday parades, and concerts in order to control pedestrian and vehicular traffic and to deter unruly participants from engaging in activities that would disrupt the enjoyment of those in attendance. For example, consider the case in which the American Civil Liberties Union contended that Pittsburg Police too frequently issued citations for swearing, making obscene gestures, and other acts deemed disrespectful ("Pittsburgh Police Trial," 2009). The case concerned a man who was arrested for disorderly conduct for flipping his middle finger. In 2006 he made the gesture to another driver, and he made the same gesture when he heard someone yelling at him. The person yelling at him was a police officer. A federal judge ruled that the person should not have been arrested because he was engaging in constitutionally protected expression ("Pittsburgh Police Trial," 2009).

Similarly, the police may become involved in dealing with those whose speech goes beyond the limits of First Amendment protections. They may, for instance, arrest an individual whose verbalizations constitute a clear and present danger to others (the classic example being the individual who cries "fire" in a crowded venue when no fire exists, causing panic and perhaps serious injury to some in the crowd). Hate speech, fighting words (i.e., words that, by their very nature, inflict injury or incite violent conduct), and obscenities may also lead to police intervention, though the boundaries that must be crossed for this response to occur are often unclear. The use of the Internet and related technologies has raised additional issues with respect to freedom of speech. The sharing of child pornography via the Internet, for example, has been ruled beyond the protection of the First Amendment. Other uses of the Internet to intimidate, harass, or humiliate targets may also be beyond such protection, though the law is not yet well established in this area (see You Decide 5.1).

YOU DECIDE 5.1

A perpetrator uses the Internet to humiliate another person by describing her as physically and mentally unattractive. The perpetrator sends hostile and hurtful comments that have supposedly been written by the target's peers over the Internet on a continuing and frequent basis. Ultimately, the target commits suicide, leaving a note indicating she could no longer deal with the hurt to which she was being subjected. Should the perpetrator's actions be protected by the First Amendment? Why or why not?

❖ The Second Amendment

While the Second Amendment does not deal with due process, it is nonetheless important to the police for a variety of reasons. The **Second Amendment** deals with the right to bear arms and has been the source of considerable litigation. This amendment is of concern to the police not because it spells out appropriate police procedures, as do some of the other amendments discussed in this chapter, but because its interpretation determines to some extent the number of citizens who have access to and permission to carry weapons and the circumstances under which this can occur legally. The right to carry concealed weapons has received a good deal of attention in the last few years, with law enforcement officials coming down on both sides of the argument. (See the Case in Point that follows.) In addition, attempts by states and municipalities to control licensing, ownership, and carrying of guns have come under scrutiny. Gun control statutes typically impose licensing and registration requirements on gun owners and specify who may and may not own a gun (e.g., convicted felons and those with histories of mental illness may be prohibited from gun ownership) and the circumstances under which it may be carried either openly or concealed. Such statutes further impose requirements on gun dealers by specifying the type of weapons and ammunition they may sell and the waiting period required for delivery of the weapon (Garland, 2009). At the same time, 48 of the 50 states now allow some form of concealed carry of firearms. The controversy over concealed carry continues, with advocates insisting it will help prevent some violent crimes and opponents arguing it will increase injuries and deaths. As indicated in the following Case in Point, police personnel are divided as to the consequences and desirability of concealed carry.

☞ CASE IN POINT 5.1

Police say concealed-carry law would deter criminals

Some local police chiefs and other police personnel in the Peoria, IL area indicated that putting fear into the minds of criminals on the streets is one of the best arguments for allowing concealed carry. "If you're not sure if a guy has a gun, you may not try to do some things to him that you might otherwise try to get away with," said Peoria police Officer Troy Skaggs, president of the Peoria Police Benevolent Union. "It's the fear of the unknown." Further, the Illinois Sheriffs' Association passed a resolution supporting a concealed-carry law in Illinois, with several conditions in place.

According to Peoria Police Chief Steven Settingsgaard who, along with 250 worldwide law-enforcement executives, recently spent 10 weeks at the FBI's National Academy, "Everyone I spoke to was in favor of concealed carry."

Source: "Police Say Concealed Carry Law Would Deter Criminals," by R. Ori, 2009. Available from http://www.pjstar.com/news/x1730895291/Police-say-concealed-carry-law-would-deter-criminals.

Concealed weapons bill meets objections on campus

Opposition to a concealed weapons bill comes from the Missouri University Police Department and two organizations it belongs to—the International Association of Campus Law Enforcement Administrators and the Missouri Association of Campus Law Enforcement.

The bill is opposed because it might expose campus police officers to heightened danger. For instance, if an officer were to respond to a situation in which a Good Samaritan was trying to stop a criminal and both parties were armed, how would the officer know which is which? In such cases, innocent people might be injured or killed. If alcohol played a role in the confrontation, the danger for all concerned would be even greater and parties and events where alcohol is involved are common on college campuses.

Source: "Concealed Weapons Bill Meets Objections on Campus," by N. Winters and R. Barros, 2009. Available from http://www.columbiamissourian.com/stories/2009/04/22/concealed-weapons-bill-met-objections-campus/

In 2008, in the case of *D.C. v. Heller,* the Supreme Court struck down one of the nation's strictest gun-control laws when the majority ruled that individuals have the right to own firearms, meaning that it was unconstitutional for local officials to prohibit the vast majority of Washington, D.C., residents from owning handguns. Prior to the decision in *Heller,* gun control advocates had made the case that only organized militias were protected by the Second Amendment. This ruling applied only to the District of Columbia, and other cities have continued to ban handgun ownership. In 2010, the Supreme Court agreed to hear a case that has a definite bearing on these cities. In the case of *McDonald v. Chicago,* residents of that city who want handguns for protection in their homes asked the Court to extend its 2008 decision in support of gun rights in Washington, D.C., to state and local laws ("Court Looks," 2010). The Supreme Court ruled that the personal right to keep and bear arms applies not only to the the federal government, but to state and local government, as well. Since the Court decided to extend the decision, police personnel will likely encounter an increasing number of handguns when they enter households and make stops. Whether or not an extension of the decision will result in an increased number of incidents involving the police, handguns, and shots fired remains to be seen.

❖ The Fourth Amendment

The **Fourth Amendment** prohibits unreasonable searches and seizures of persons, houses, papers, and effects and requires that probable cause be demonstrated prior to the issuing of warrants. A **search** occurs "when an expectation of privacy that society is prepared to consider reasonable is infringed. A **seizure** of property occurs when there is some meaningful interference with an individual's possessory interests in that property" (*United States v. Jacobsen,* 1984). With reference to police searches and seizures, in practical terms, the former refers to the fact that a police officer invades the privacy of an individual to seek evidence of a weapon, crime, or contraband, and the latter refers to the confiscation of that weapon, evidence, contraband, or the person suspected of committing the crime in question. In other words, both property and persons may be seized under appropriate circumstances. In order to comprehend the impact of this amendment, the police must be conversant with the underlying concepts of probable cause and reasonableness. This takes vigilance because the Fourth Amendment is probably the most fluid regarding changes in case law as to the requirements that must be met in order to search persons, properties, and automobiles. Many of these changes are noted throughout the chapter.

Probable Cause and Reasonableness

The notion of **probable cause** is derived from the Fourth Amendment to the United States Constitution, which says, in part, "The right of the people to be secure in their persons, houses, papers, and effects, against unreasonable searches and seizures, shall not be violated, and no warrants shall issue, but upon probable cause. . . ." Understanding the concept is important to police officers in the process of stopping and questioning citizens, making arrests, and conducting searches. In regard to effecting an arrest, in *Brinegar v. United States* (1949), the United States Supreme Court found that probable cause exists when facts and circumstances within a police officer's knowledge, which are based upon reasonably trustworthy information, are

❖ **Photo 5.2** Police officer using forcible entry to execute a search warrant.

sufficient to warrant a person of reasonable caution to believe that an offense has been or is being committed by the person being arrested. It is important to note that the decision recognizes two different ways in which the officer may come into possession of information related to probable cause. First, the officer may observe conduct that leads to the conclusion that an offense is being or has been committed. Second, someone else may observe such conduct and then relay information concerning the conduct to the officer. In the latter case, the officer must reasonably believe that the information provided is being provided by someone who, in the present circumstances, is likely to be reliable.

A further attempt to clarify the standard of probable cause was made by the Court, in *Illinois v. Gates* (1983). In this decision, the Court noted that the standard for probable cause is a "practical, nontechnical conception" dealing with probabilities based upon "factual and practical considerations of everyday life on which reasonable and prudent men, not legal technicians, act." These decisions, of course, raise the issue as to what is reasonable. **Reasonableness** generally refers to what a reasonable person, in similar circumstances, based upon similar information, might conclude. For example, arresting someone who happens to be in the general area in which an offense may have been committed, and with no other evidence that the individual in question may be the perpetrator, may well be unreasonable. The individual could be a witness, a nearby resident, a passerby, or even a victim. Arresting that same individual in the area in which an offense was reported and who matched several of the characteristics of the offender (height, gender, race, and clothing) reported by a witness would be reasonable, and this arrest would almost certainly meet the probable cause standard even if the individual arrested turned out not to be the perpetrator. It appears that the courts have determined that reasonableness is not a single standard but may vary from case to case. Taking official action must be balanced against the expectation of privacy guaranteed by the Fourth Amendment (*Illinois v. Rodriquez,* 1990). Further, it is important that the officer taking action based upon probable cause or reasonable suspicion be able to articulate the facts that led to the action. While simple suspicion is generally insufficient to meet the standard of probable cause, **reasonable suspicion,** based on objective facts and logical conclusions given a specific set of circumstances, may be used as the basis for stopping and frisking suspicious individuals.

The notions of probable cause and reasonable suspicion are important in virtually all aspects of the policing process. In order to obtain a search warrant, for example, the requesting officer must demonstrate to the issuing judge that it is reasonable to expect to find the items identified at the location specified. Similarly, prior to making a traffic stop, an officer must be able to articulate the reasons for the stop—exceeding the speed limit, equipment problems, weaving back and forth across traffic lanes, and so on. (Exceptions may exist with respect to "safety checks," in which every vehicle is stopped and examined, but these vary considerably by locale.) An important point to keep in mind is that the reasonable suspicion or probable cause must have preceded the stop or arrest and cannot be based on the evidence found after the stop or arrest. Failure to act in terms of probable cause typically results in evidence collected during an unreasonable stop or search being excluded at the time of the trial. Recognizing the importance of probable cause as a basis for official action, police officers sometimes create probable cause after the fact in order to use the fruits of their wrongful stops and searches (see Chapter 9).

There are a number of exceptions to the requirements imposed by the Fourth Amendment based upon a series of court decisions. While we cannot go into detail with respect to all these exemptions, a few illustrations should suffice to indicate the scope of the amendment as currently interpreted.

Searches and Seizures With a Warrant

While a warrant is the preferred means of justifying searches and seizures, the circumstances involved in police encounters with other citizens often preclude obtaining a warrant. For example, when a police officer makes a traffic stop and discovers contraband or evidence of a crime or when an officer comes upon the scene of a crime in progress in which a weapon has been or may be involved, there may be no time to obtain a warrant. Further, if an officer pursues a suspected drug dealer into a building and the suspect runs into a restroom, there is reason to believe the suspect may destroy evidence if immediate action is not taken. Nonetheless, where possible and practical, a **warrant** is preferred because it requires the officer to demonstrate to an independent third party (magistrate or judge) the probable cause or reasonable suspicion upon which her anticipated action is predicated. A search warrant, for instance, is an order in writing, issued by a judicial authority, which commands the officer requesting it to search for certain types of property in certain locations and to bring the fruits of that search before the judicial authority in question. An arrest warrant is an order to take a certain person into custody and bring him before the judicial authority (Ferdico, 2002, p. 160).

POLICE STORIES

My regular partner and I, both younger officers assigned to a busy district in the Chicago Police Department, were assigned to a permanent beat. That particular beat was characterized by a high minority population, a high unemployment rate, and a serious problem with street crime, primarily as a result of the heavy presence of street gangs.

(Continued)

(Continued)

It did not take long to figure out that when we observed young, white males driving by the "hot spots" (where drug dealing occurred) of the district, most of the time they were buying drugs from street gang members. Thus, when we observed this phenomenon, we sat in covert position and watched. When we witnessed a drug sale, we waited a few moments and then stopped the car driven by the young, white males in question away from where the incident occurred. We then got the occupants out of the car (passengers included, if applicable), searched them and the inside of the car, and if they had drugs in their possession, placed them under arrest. I recall one particular incident. We were at the station filling out the paperwork and, of course, had to include our probable cause for stopping the car and for searching the driver and the car. I recall asking my partner in a jovial manner why we stopped the car. He replied, "The guy didn't use his turn signal when he turned off of the side street." Regarding the search I said "and he gave us permission to search his car, how about that!" Thus, that's how the story was documented with respect to these types of arrests.

Were our actions improper? Sure they were, but we justified our actions by knowing that we had done a good job for the community and the department by removing some drugs from the street. After all, we were in pursuit of a "noble cause," and we weren't going to let silly court rulings stand in our way. The bad guys don't play by the rules, so why should we? Besides, the majority of our arrestees were used later by tactical unit officers to help build a case against the dealers that sold them the drugs. We even received honorable mentions by the department on several occasions.

In retrospect, an "ends justifies the means" approach is not a good idea for obvious reasons. For example, what if one of our cases went to trial rather than being pled out by the prosecutor? We would have had to take the stand and commit perjury. (Thankfully we never had one of those cases go to trial.) Faced with similar circumstances today, I would play by the rules for fear of potential consequences and for the sake of professionalism.

Police Stops

A police officer may stop and briefly detain (or with a warrant, arrest) a person if the officer can articulate facts that generate reasonable suspicion, based upon the totality of circumstances as perceived by the officer, that criminal activity has occurred (Ferdico, 2002). **Totality of circumstances** requires that an officer have a "particularized and objective basis for suspecting that a particular person" is or has been involved in criminal activity. The totality of circumstances ("the whole picture") includes "various objective observations, information from police reports, if such are available, and consideration of modes or patterns of operation of certain kinds of law-breakers" from which the "officer draws inferences and makes deductions" concerning the probability that the party in question is involved in criminal conduct (*United States v. Cortez,* 1981). Further, as noted, the officer must be able to provide reasons that justify the stop is above and beyond mere suspicion. After making such a stop, a police officer can briefly detain the person, ask questions, and check identification because the "law enforcement interests at stake in these circumstances outweigh the individual's interest to be free of a stop and detention that is no more extensive than permissible in the investigation of imminent or ongoing crime (*United States v. Hensley,* 1985). Such stops, often referred to as *Terry Stops,* must be discontinued in light of evidence that demonstrates the officer's initial interpretation of the circumstances was incorrect (*State v. Garland,* 1984; *Terry v. Ohio,* 1968). The *Terry* case for which such stops are named involved an experienced police officer observing Terry engaged in behavior that indicated to the officer that Terry was likely "casing" a store in order to commit a robbery. Upon stopping and questioning the suspect, the officer concluded that Terry might be armed. A pat down search led to the discovery of a firearm. The Supreme Court determined that the temporary stop did not violate the Fourth Amendment and that such stops are permissible based on reasonable suspicion.

Thus, if the officer making a stop reasonably believes that the person stopped may constitute a threat (e.g., may be armed and dangerous), she may frisk the suspect. The frisk must be initially limited to a pat down of the suspect's outer clothing and may become more extensive only if the officer detects something that may be a weapon. Absent the discovery of an object that may be a weapon, no further search of the suspect is permissible at this point. If a suspicious object is discovered during the pat down, the officer may reach into the suspect's pockets or clothing for the sole purpose of seizing the weapon. However, any contraband (e.g., illegal drugs) found during the search for a weapon may be confiscated and used as evidence in a criminal trial related to the initial stop.

In *Michigan v. Long* (1983), the Supreme Court extended the range of a search for weapons to include the passenger compartment of the car driven by a suspect if the police have reasonable suspicion (e.g., see a weapon in plain view when approaching the car) that the driver is a dangerous person. The **plain view doctrine** holds that if a police officer sees an incriminating object in plain view during a legitimate stop, he may seize the object.

There are literally dozens of exceptions and specifications to stop and frisk rules. Discussion of these particulars is beyond the scope of this text but may be found in any text on criminal procedure (see, for example, Ferdico, 2002) or through a search of cases related to stop and frisk on the Internet.

Police Searches Incident to Arrest

Discussing searches incident to arrest requires an understanding of what constitutes an arrest. In general terms, an **arrest** occurs when an individual authorized to take a person into custody detains that person with the intention of making an arrest and when the person being arrested understands that the intention of the person making the arrest is detaining him for that purpose. The arrest may be affected with or without a warrant, though the latter is preferable when possible.

The basic law governing searches incident to arrest can be found in *Chimel v. California* (1969). In order to justify a full search, the suspect must be taken into custody by the officer and that search must be conducted by the arresting officer. Further, the search must be conducted at the time of or shortly after the arrest in order to be legal. In addition, generally speaking, the officer may use the degree of force necessary to protect himself and others or to prevent the flight of the suspect or the destruction of evidence. In general, the arresting officer may search the arrestee for weapons or evidence and may extend into any area under the direct or immediate control of the arrestee at the time of the arrest. The search may be extended to companions of the arrestee if the officer reasonably believes that these companions may present a threat or may destroy evidence (*United States v. Simmons*, 1977).

The U. S. Supreme Court recently decided *Arizona v. Gant* (2009), which addressed the circumstances related to the search of a vehicle incident to the arrest of an occupant. Gant was arrested for driving with a suspended license, handcuffed, and locked in a patrol car before police officers searched the passenger compartment of his vehicle and found cocaine and a firearm. The Court held that police may search the passenger compartment of a vehicle incident to a recent occupant's arrest only if it is reasonable to believe the arrestee might access the vehicle at the time of the search or that the vehicle contains evidence of the offense of arrest (*Arizona v. Gant*, 2009). In some arrests for traffic violations, there is reasonable basis to believe that the vehicle contains relevant evidence (Federal Law Enforcement Training Center [FLETC], 2009). However, in other cases, such as arrests for possession of controlled substances, the basis of the arrest will supply acceptable rationale for searching the arrestee's passenger compartment and any containers inside. Some might suggest that *Arizona v. Gant* encourages unsafe police practices such as leaving the arrestees unsecured to justify a search incident to arrest. However, according to Federal Law Enforcement Training Center (FLETC) (2009), Justice Scalia addressed this issue in *Thornton v. U.S.* (2004). He stated "if an officer leaves a suspect unrestrained nearby just to manufacture authority to search, one could argue that the search is unreasonable precisely because the dangerous conditions justifying it existed only by the virtue of the officer's failure to follow sensible procedures."

Consent Searches

Another type of search frequently conducted by the police requires neither probable cause nor a warrant. A *consent search* occurs when an individual voluntarily waives her Fourth Amendment rights and allows a police officer to search her person, belongings, vehicle, or home. An example of a consent search might involve a traffic stop during which the officer asks the driver of the stopped vehicle if he would mind opening the trunk of the vehicle. Many individuals comply with the request either because they have nothing to hide from the police or because they are uncertain of the consequences if they refuse the request.

The courts have made it clear that consent searches must be voluntary; that no coercion, either implicit or explicit, may be used; that no deception or misrepresentation be used; and that the consent be clearly stated (either orally, by gesture, or in writing) (*Schneckloth v. Bustamonte*, 1973; *United States v. Gonzalez-Basulto*, 1990).

Limits on the scope and object of the search have also been imposed by the courts. Finally, in *State v. Lewis* (1992) and other cases, it has been held that the consenting party may revoke his consent at any time after the search has begun.

This section briefly summarized some of the procedures and court decisions related to the Fourth Amendment. There are numerous other exceptions and procedures related to the amendment, and readers are encouraged to seek additional information in criminal law texts and court decisions.

❖ The Fifth Amendment

The **Fifth Amendment** provides that no citizen is to be tried for a capital or "otherwise infamous crime without a presentment or indictment" by a grand jury (exception here is that the grand jury clause does not protect those serving in the armed forces, whether during wartime or peacetime), or may be subject to trial for the same offense twice, or compelled to incriminate himself, or be deprived of life, liberty, or property without due process of law. This is a far-reaching amendment, but for our purposes here (since due process will be discussed in relation to the Fourteenth Amendment), the right against self-incrimination is of particular importance since it often relates directly to police encounters with suspects. Initially, the **privilege against self-incrimination** seems straightforward. It implies that no person can be compelled to incriminate herself—that the suspect need not answer questions or disclose information that would support her own conviction. The courts have ruled that the privilege refers to testimonial communications and does not prevent compelled appearances in lineups or photo lineups, handwriting samples, fingerprints, or blood-alcohol tests (among other things) (Ferdico, 2002, p. 18). It is interesting to note that while compulsory appearances in lineups do not constitute constitutional violations for persons in custody, evidence collected by the Innocence Project shows that roughly 75% of wrongful convictions found through subsequent DNA analysis involved some form of mistaken eyewitness identification (Johnson, 2009). As a result, several states and some major police agencies are changing their policies concerning photo and in-person lineups (Johnson, 2009).

The impact of the privilege against self-incrimination on police actions is considerable since it is related to statements, admissions, and confessions given to police officers. The courts have ruled that all three of the above must be given voluntarily and with knowledge on behalf of the suspect that he has the right to remain silent or request the presence of an attorney (note that the Sixth Amendment also guarantees the right to counsel) once police interrogation commences. Involuntary confessions are considered to be both unreliable and a violation of due process when based upon police coercion. This is true even though the statement, admission, or confession itself may actually be reliable. Thus, the Supreme Court held in *Townsend v. Sain* (1963) that "any questioning by police officers which in fact produces a confession which is not the product of free intellect renders that confession inadmissible."

A key question for the police concerns the point at which questions asked during an investigation become an interrogation. In *Escobedo v. Illinois* (1964), the Court held that when "the investigation is no longer a general inquiry into an unsolved crime but has begun to focus on a particular suspect" and "the suspect has been taken into police custody, the police carry out a process of interrogation. . . ." Then, in *Miranda v. Arizona* (1966), the Court indicated that when a person is taken into custody or otherwise deprived of his freedom by the police and is subjected to questioning, the privilege against self-incrimination is jeopardized. At this point, procedural safeguards must be employed to protect that privilege. This decision resulted in the now famous warning the police give prior to interrogating suspects: "You have the right to remain silent; anything you say can be used against you in a court of law; you have the right to the presence of an attorney; if you cannot afford an attorney, one will be appointed for you." The suspect is then typically asked whether she understands these rights and whether she wishes to continue talking to the police. If the suspect asks for an attorney at this point in the process, or at any other point, the interrogation is to stop until an attorney is present. In *Berghuis v. Thompkins* (2010), the Supreme Court elaborated on *Miranda,* indicating that suspects must explicitly tell police they want to remain silent (rather than simply remain silent) to invoke Miranda protections during criminal interrogations (Zash, 2010). Failure to inform suspects of their rights under *Miranda* likely means that any statement, admission, or confession obtained is inadmissible at the time of trial. Currently, the Obama administration is contemplating legislation to initiate changes in *Miranda* in order to expand the ability of authorities to question international terrorists (Ferrechio, 2010).

Not all statements, admission, or confessions are invalidated by failure to provide the *Miranda* warning. Statements voluntarily made prior to the beginning of any interrogation and not in response to police questioning may be admissible. Similarly, information obtained in the process of routine questioning (e.g., in the booking process) are not generally protected by *Miranda.* Questions spontaneously asked by the police in regard to an emergency or related to public safety, or impulsively asked, are not typically held to be interrogation (Ferdico, 2002, p. 483). Further, it should be noted that *Miranda* applies only to custodial interrogation conducted by the police. Thus, statements, admissions, and confessions made to private citizens are likely to be admissible in court.

Finally, questions often arise concerning whether a suspect knowingly and voluntarily waived his rights under *Miranda.* To help insure that this is the case, the police often request a written waiver and may provide the necessary warnings in more than one language. The general rule of thumb for police officers is that it is better to be safe than sorry. Thus, the *Miranda* warning may be given when it is not needed simply to insure that it has been given should questions arise concerning the privilege against self-incrimination.

❖ The Fourteenth Amendment

The **Fourteenth Amendment** is often referred to as the **due process** amendment because it provides that no state can deprive any person of life, liberty, or property without due process of law. Currently, the rights guaranteed by the First, Fourth, and Sixth Amendments, along with parts of the Fifth and Eighth Amendments, have been applied to the states (Ferdico, 2002, p. 9; Garland, 2009, pp. 17–18; Reid, 2009, pp. 12–14). As it relates to the police specifically, due process requires that evidence of a crime be presented in court, both testimonial and physical, be obtained according to the rules discussed previously. In addition, the **equal protection clause** of the Fourteenth Amendment applies to the police in that it prevents both the federal government and all states from denying the protection of the law to any group of persons by making arbitrary, unreasonable distinctions based on race, religion, gender, and national origin (Reid, 2009). Thus, this Amendment is the basis for a good deal of the civil rights legislation we have seen in the past 50 years. For example, we discuss the problems of biased enforcement and racial profiling by the police, both of which are clearly prohibited by the equal protection clause, in Chapter 8.

Due process has become a cornerstone of the American legal system, and it is sometimes problematic for the police because of the requirements it establishes for many police activities, including arrest, interrogation, collection of evidence through searches and seizures, as well as many other activities. Briefly stated, it would be much easier for the police to operate under a crime control than a due process model. The *crime control model* allows for the arrest of individuals who are known to be factually guilty of committing a crime. The *due process model* requires that evidence of guilt presented in court be obtained according to legal guidelines. The due process model relies on equal treatment of all accused persons and imposes a variety of restraints on the actions of the police. For instance, the police might receive a tip from an anonymous caller who states that a specific individual living in a specific college dorm room is distributing illegal drugs from that location. Using the crime control model, the police break down the door to the room, find the drugs, arrest and charge the offender, and use the drugs as evidence in the ensuing trial. Under the due process model, the police must demonstrate that the tip came from a reliable informant, obtain a proper search warrant, and maintain a proper chain of evidence or the drugs will be inadmissible as evidence in court and the defendant will be acquitted. That is, even though the defendant was factually guilty of distributing illegal drugs, he is not legally guilty because the procedures established to safeguard the rights of citizens were violated in this case. While the emphasis on technicalities related to due process shifts with changes in political administrations, public opinion, and the judiciary, the underlying right to due process remains. This may be frustrating to the police who often view due process requirements as obstacles to successful enforcement of the law. Still, most officers would probably agree that if they were the focus of an investigation, they would prefer the due process model.

Let us now turn our attention to the consequences of police failure to adhere to due process requirements.

❖ The Exclusionary Rule

The *exclusionary rule* is a judicially imposed requirement that any evidence obtained by the police using methods that violate an individual's constitutional rights be excluded in a criminal prosecution against that individual. Note that the wrong done by the police must involve constitutional questions for the exclusionary rule to apply. The rule was first expounded in *Weeks v. United States* (1914) and applied only to federal law enforcement officers. In *Wolf v. Colorado* (1949), the Supreme Court held that the rule applied to the states as part of the due process clause, discussed in the section of this book on the Fourteenth Amendment. Then, in the case of *Mapp v. Ohio* (1961), the Court mandated enforcement of the rule by the states.

Interestingly, the exclusionary rule was specifically designed to prevent police misconduct and applies to both police officers and those acting as their agents. Thus, if a police officer, without probable cause or a warrant, indicates to a private citizen that she might assist the police by searching the purse of a third party, any evidence obtained would be subject to the exclusionary rule. If the same woman searched the same purse on her own initiative, however, the fruits of the search might well be admissible in court proceedings.

The exclusionary rule applies to evidence obtained directly as the result of constitutional violations and also to evidence found indirectly as a result of the violation under what is referred to as the *fruit of the poisonous tree doctrine*. For example, if the police conduct an illegal search and discover stolen property in the home of a suspect and, at the same time, discover evidence that a second suspect was involved in the crime, neither the stolen property nor the name of the second suspect are admissible in court. As you might expect, based upon an earlier discussion in this chapter, there are a number of exceptions to the exclusionary rule. Among these are what is known as the good faith doctrine, the inevitable discovery doctrine, and the independent source doctrine.

The *good faith doctrine* deals with searches conducted with a warrant, and it states that when a police officer acting in good faith obtains a warrant, conducts a search, and seizes evidence, that evidence will not be excluded from court proceedings even if the warrant is later invalidated (*United States v. Leon,* 1984). Describing a recent decision (2009) by the U. S. Supreme Court, a headline in the *New York Times* declared that the court was a "step closer to repeal" of the exclusionary rule (Savage, 2009). The case in point, *Herring v. United States,* involved a police investigator who had several run-ins with Mr. Herring. When the police officer saw Herring, he requested a warrant check, and a neighboring county reported there was a warrant for his arrest. Acting on this information, the police officer stopped Herring's vehicle and located methamphetamine in his pocket and a handgun under the seat (Savage, 2009). Approximately 10 minutes later, the police officer learned that a mistake had occurred and the warrant had been withdrawn five months earlier. The U.S. Supreme Court held that when police mistakes that lead to an unlawful search are the result of isolated negligence attenuated from the search, rather than systematic error or reckless disregard of constitutional requirements, the exclusionary rule does not apply (*Herring v. United States,* 2009).

The *inevitable discovery doctrine* allows the admission of illegally obtained evidence if it would have been discovered lawfully in the "normal course of events" anyway (*Murray v. United States,* 1988). The normal course of events, for instance, might include routine police procedures or testimonial evidence from a witness. Finally, the *independent source doctrine* holds that illegally obtained evidence may be admitted if it was also obtained through an independent source not tainted by police misconduct.

In summary, the exclusionary rule indicates the extent to which the courts have gone in attempting to guarantee constitutional rights by preventing police misconduct. It appears that the courts are not convinced that the police can or will adhere to all procedural requirements without judicial oversight.

❖ Police Use of Force

As we begin the discussion of police use of force, we once again caution the reader that the material presented here is a brief summary of relevant issues and is in no way intended to provide comprehensive coverage of all the legal issues related to the use of force. Again, we refer the reader to a text on criminal law and procedure for a more complete discussion of the issues.

From time to time in the performance of their duties, the police must resort to the use of force to either prevent criminal activity or apprehend criminals. Under common law, police officers could use less-than-lethal force to arrest a felon and, as a last resort, deadly force to arrest a fleeing felon. **Less-than-lethal force** refers to force used by the officer that is not likely to result in serious bodily harm or death, whereas **lethal or deadly force** may result in great bodily harm or death. Examples of less-than-lethal force include launchable and hand-deployable chemical agents, kinetic energy or impact munitions, and electronic control devices (Tasers), among others (Dowe, 2009). In some cases, use of less-than-lethal force has resulted in death or serious injury to suspects. Recently, **TASERs** (electroshock weapons that use electrical current to disrupt voluntary control of muscles) have come under increasing scrutiny in this regard; the American Civil Liberties Union (ACLU) indicated in 2009 that it submitted a petition to the Supreme Court to hear a case on the constitutionality of excessive force related to police use of Tasers (Senter, 2009).

Over time, the maximum penalty for various felonies has been reduced from death to imprisonment. While under common law, police officers would have been permitted to use deadly force against criminals who committed such felonies, the current maximum punishment upon conviction would be imprisonment. It made no sense to allow the police to continue to use deadly force in cases where a conviction in court could not result in capital punishment. Thus, police officers today are not empowered to use deadly force against unarmed or otherwise nondangerous offenders.

Generally speaking, police officers are authorized to use reasonable force (recall our earlier discussion of the criteria for reasonableness) to make arrests, to prevent escapes, and to protect themselves and others from harm (Ferdico, 2002, pp. 130–131; Skelton, 1998, p. 349). The Supreme Court language in *Tennessee V. Garner* (1985) best describes the current situation: "A police officer may not seize an unarmed, nondangerous suspect by shooting him dead" but "where the officer has probable cause to believe that the suspect poses a threat of serious physical harm, either to the officer or to others, it is not constitutionally unreasonable to prevent escape by using deadly force." When determining probable cause in such cases, officers typically consider a series of factors, including the suspect's motivation to harm or escape, their propensity for violence, current state of mind, combat experience (in cases where this is known), possession of a weapon, and the location in which the encounter occurs (Means & Seidel, 2009).

In addition to using force to affect an arrest or prevent an escape, police officers may be confronted with the need to use force to enter a dwelling or a vehicle. Typically a warrant is required for such entry, but in **exigent circumstances,** the officer may enter without a warrant. Such circumstances may exist when the police are in hot pursuit of a fleeing felon, when there is a danger of imminent destruction of evidence, when a suspect is escaping, or when there is imminent danger to the officer or others. Where the officer has legal authority to enter a dwelling, she should first knock on the door, announce her purpose, identity herself as a police officer, and demand entry. If the demand to enter is refused or met with silence, the officer may enter after waiting a reasonable (usually quite short) period of time. And in *Wilson v. Arkansas* (1995), the Supreme Court recognized that announcing the presence of a police officer and waiting outside for a response is unreasonable in certain cases. Some instances in which the requirements to knock, announce, and wait may be waived include those in which the safety of the officer or others is at stake, where the procedure may allow the offender to escape, and where knocking and announcing might allow the suspect to destroy evidence.

One additional example of an issue relating to the use of deadly force is that of high speed police pursuit. In such pursuits, the police vehicle itself may become deadly for either innocent bystanders or those being pursued (to say nothing of the pursuing police officers). A recent Supreme Court decision shed some light on the current pursuit situation. In *Scott v. Harris* (2007), the Court concluded the following:

> We are loath to lay down a rule requiring the police to allow fleeing suspects to get away whenever they drive so recklessly that they put other people's lives in danger. It is obvious the perverse incentives such a rule would create. . . . A police officer's attempt to terminate a dangerous high-speed car chase that threatens the lives of innocent bystanders does not violate the 4th Amendment, even when it places the fleeing motorist at risk of serious injury or death.

A major concern of police officers everywhere, as well as of police administrators whose forces span out across the city 24 hours a day, is with **liability** for their actions. Under 42 U.S.C. § 1983: US Code - Section 1983 (Civil Action for Deprivation of Rights), suits may be brought against both officers and their supervisors (as well as the branch of government they represent in some cases) for failure to train officers properly and for developing unconstitutional policies and practices. These fears seem well founded since some estimates of the monetary cost of such suits range as high as $780 billion annually (Kappeler, 2001)—even though most suits are eventually decided in favor of the officer. If the alleged violations by the officer are criminal in nature, action may be taken by prosecutors in addition to the civil action that may be taken in state and federal courts. Thus, the family of an individual killed by a police officer may allege wrongful death and file civil suits in both state and federal courts to collect damages. If a prosecutor has cause to believe that the death resulted from inappropriate behavior on the part of the officer, she may file criminal charges as well. Defenses commonly employed against such actions include the good faith doctrine and the reasonable belief that probable cause existed as discussed elsewhere in this chapter.

The decision concerning use of force, particularly deadly force, is one of the most critical a police officer is required to make. Such decisions are typically made in a matter of seconds, but they have consequences that may last a lifetime.

❖ The Patriot Act, Homeland Security, and Terrorism

Prior to September 11, 2001, very few discussions of police behavior focused on their role in preventing terrorism and apprehending terrorists. Now, terrorism is one of the critical issues of our time for police officers at all levels. According to the Code of Federal Regulations, "**terrorism** consists of the unlawful use of force or threat of force against persons or property to intimidate or coerce a government, a civilian population, or any part thereof in furtherance of political or social objectives" (FBI, 2006, p. 1). Most terrorists claim not to be criminals, but rather freedom (religion, ideology, special interest) fighters—but almost all terrorist acts violate criminal laws (Fischer, Halibozek, & Green, 2008).

Law enforcement officials around the world have reported a significant increase in the range and scope of international terrorist activity over the past several years. We are frequently warned that the danger from terrorists has not passed and that we cannot afford to let down our guard against further such actions. Further, we are reminded of the danger every time we travel by air or enter a public building as a result of the visible police presence. And of course, with the continued danger of terrorism comes the continued temptation to dilute our constitutional ideals concerning the right to privacy and searches and seizures (note the scanners at airports, coupled with pat down searches and seizures of bottles of liquid containing more than a few ounces). Similarly, many public buildings, including courthouses and schools, have metal detectors through which employees and visitors alike must pass upon entry. Clearly the events of 9/11 have caused Americans to reconsider their approach to national and local security issues.

The passage of the Patriot Act in October, 2001 and the Homeland Security Act (HSA) in November, 2002 have raised legal issues that could impact the lives of every American. The intent of the Patriot Act, when it was passed in 2001 as an immediate response to the 9/11 attacks, was to provide federal law enforcement officers with better means to defend against terrorists. Key points included the expansion of surveillance activities, tighter prohibitions on money laundering, and increased information sharing. Section 216 of the act, for example, made the Internet subject to surveillance. Section 351 created directives to financial institutions that increased auditing and reporting requirements (American Civil Liberties Union, 2005).

Through the **Homeland Security Act** and the **Patriot Act**, the United States government focuses on several terrorism prevention strategies and tactics. Among these are developing public safety programs to protect vulnerable targets and locations, enhancing community participation in "terrorist watch" programs, improving intelligence by increasing the cooperation between law enforcement agencies worldwide, improving training for security forces by developing realistic antiterrorist action scenarios and organizing regular exercises for security forces and citizenry, and fostering coordination between security forces and communities on the basis of model local, state, and federal plans for responding to terrorist attacks (Devanney & Devanney, 2003).

The FBI Joint Terrorism Task Force (JTTF) effort, first established in 1980, involves multiple law enforcement agencies working together to increase dialogue, improve relationships, and maximize information sharing (Barker & Fowler, 2008). JTTFs have proven successful in thwarting numerous terrorist plots in the United States and in providing an effective venue for local officers to assist in the mission of national security. The FBI benefits from having officers assigned to JTTFs in that its efforts in counter-terrorism are enhanced by cooperation of state and local police officers with street-level experience and knowledge of local jurisdictions. Police departments also benefit from having an officer assigned to a JTTF since these officers may undergo extensive specialized training and gain investigative experience in managing complex investigations (Barker & Fowler, 2008).

The significance of attacks by terrorists throughout the world cannot be minimized, but it is also important to consider the possibility of overreaction. Tension has been created by the need to monitor people entering the country as well as those already here. Government agencies are asking for unprecedented access to personal information. At the same time, however, the right to privacy requires that steps are taken to protect personal information. Some argue that parts of the Patriot Act take away checks on law enforcement and threaten the very rights and freedoms that we are struggling to protect. For example, without a warrant and without probable cause, the FBI now has the power to access private medical records, library records, and student records, and it can prevent anyone from telling those being investigated that it has been done. The constitutionality of many of these acts is questionable. Police officers, especially, need to know both the scope and the potential hazards of these federal statutes (American Civil Liberties Union, 2005).

Some limited conclusions about the impact of the Patriot Act and the HSA on state and local police can be drawn. First, the ways in which state and local law enforcement personnel continue to assist in the effort to prevent terrorist attacks are multifaceted and critical. Perhaps contrary to popular belief, police officers encounter known and suspected terrorists in both urban and rural areas. With the growth of the joint terrorism task force concept and enhanced information sharing techniques, obtaining and analyzing information is considerably improved. With these new tools at their disposal, state and local law enforcement authorities will continue to play an important role in preventing future terrorism (McCormack, 2009).

While it is clear that everyone intends local police be early responders, many of the details about how training, coordination, and funding will be provided remain unclear. Communications between federal and local police have improved, but there is a great deal yet to accomplish. For example, what do the various alert stages (amber, orange, or red) mean to local police in terms of how they should react, what they should look for, and what kinds of information they should provide to the public? What types of intelligence do federal authorities expect from state and local police concerning terrorism (Sheehan, Everly, & Langlieb, 2004)? Will constitutional guarantees be diminished in the attempt to prevent and apprehend terrorists? Among those guarantees that may be in danger, according to some observers, are the very amendments we discussed in this chapter (the First protecting free speech, the Fourth protecting privacy, the Fifth protecting the right against self incrimination, and the Fourteenth guaranteeing due process). Are compromises involving constitutional rights really necessary to help keep America safe from terrorists?

❖ Photo **5.3**   The U.S. Patriot Act at work. Besides routine checks on passengers using basic screening procedures, the Act gives law enforcement personnel the authority to conduct further, more intrusive screening procedures, such as complete searches of the person, use of explosive screening devices, and searches using dogs trained to detect the presence of drugs, explosive materials, and other contraband.

❖ Chapter Summary

As we conclude this chapter, keep in mind that it is impossible to cover in depth the wide variety of rules and regulations governing police behavior in the United States. In addition to the issues discussed here, the police are also subject to hundreds of state, county, and municipal rules and regulations and to departmental policy as well. We have attempted to highlight some of the more important laws and court decisions in order to indicate the extent of the legal parameters surrounding police activities and the subsequent impact these statutory and judicial decisions have on police policies and procedures.

Local police, as well as law enforcement personnel at all levels, enjoy a tremendous amount of discretionary authority regarding their daily practice. For the most part, enforcement of the law, methods used to obtain information, conduct involving interaction with citizens, and the majority of other police actions are accomplished using a wide range of discretionary authority. The public enjoys protection from any unlawful police practices in the form of civil and criminal laws that exist at both the state and federal levels.

Added protections are provided by judges at all levels of government through case law. Case law has a major impact on a variety of police actions and administrative policies. Issues such as search and seizure, use of force, interrogation methods, and other related constitutional concerns are often the focus of court decisions issued within a constitutional framework. In addition, case law applicable to the use of deadly force, high speed vehicle pursuits, negligent training and supervision, negligent retention of personnel, and investigative methodologies using profiling are examples of the court's impact on police policy. It is also important to note that when these court-imposed dictates are ignored and violated, individual officers oftentimes expose themselves to criminal and civil liability, and their respective agencies can be held civilly liable, which may result in court awards of millions of dollars.

More recent concerns involve the impact of the increasingly global nature of crime. The effects of the U.S. Patriot Act and similar laws have broadened the scope of police power and policies and have raised additional constitutional questions concerning police behavior, which may take years to resolve in the courts. It is interesting to compare the limitations on police conduct in the United States with those from other countries.

❖ Key Terms

criminal law	privilege against self-incrimination
civil law	Fourteenth Amendment
First Amendment	equal protection clause
Second Amendment	crime control model
Fourth Amendment	due process model
search	fruit of the poisonous tree doctrine
seizure	good faith doctrine
probable cause	inevitable discovery doctrine
reasonableness	independent source doctrine
reasonable suspicion	less-than-lethal force
warrant	lethal or deadly force
totality of circumstances	Taser
plain view doctrine	exigent circumstances
arrest	liability
consent search	terrorism
Fifth Amendment	Homeland Security Act and the Patriot Act

❖ Discussion Questions

1. What are some distinctions between criminal and civil law?

2. Why is it important to understand the role of police discretion when discussing constitutional law and court decisions?

3. What is the proper role of a police officer assigned to work at a protest involving hundreds of people when the officer vehemently disagrees with the protestors?

4. What are some of the possible consequences for police officers as a result of the most recent Supreme Court ruling concerning the Second Amendment?

5. Why do some police officers invent probable cause for a stop they made without such cause?

6. Is it usually preferable for a police officer to make an arrest or conduct a search with or without a warrant? Provide examples to support your answer.

7. When in doubt, should a police officer administer the Miranda warning to a suspect or not? Why or why not?

8. Does the exclusionary rule deal only with the Fourteenth Amendment? If not, what other amendments are involved?

9. What is the purpose of the due process clause? How is the concept of fruits of the poisoned tree related to the due process clause?

10. What is the recognized role of local police officers in the war on terror? What are some resources that are available to the police to help them in their counter-terrorism efforts?

❖ Internet Exercises

1. Go to the Internet and type in the key words *Muehler et al. v. Mena,* 125 S. Ct. 1495, (U. S. Sup. Ct., No. 03–1423, March 22, 2005). In this case, the police obtained a search warrant to search a house for deadly weapons and evidence of gang activity. The plaintiff in this case was an occupant of a house the police wanted to search. During their search of the plaintiff's house, the police placed her in handcuffs and sat her down to wait. While the police conducted their search, a police officer and an INS agent questioned the plaintiff about her immigration status. At the conclusion of their search (about 2 or 3 hours later), the plaintiff was released from custody.

   In your opinion, based upon the material discussed in this chapter, were the plaintiff's constitutional rights violated when she was placed in handcuffs during the search of the house she occupied? Why or why not?

2. Type the key words *Groh v. Ramirez,* 540 U. S. 551, (U. S. Sup., No. 02–0811, February 24, 2004) into your search engine. In this case, an ATF agent decided to raid a Montana ranch to look for weapons, explosives, and records. He completed a detailed affidavit in support of a request for a search warrant that explained exactly what the feds would be looking for. Unfortunately, the agent failed to include within the warrant itself any explanation of what they would be looking for. The warrant stated where they wanted to search but it did not even mention what they would be looking for. In addition, the warrant did not mention the affidavit and clearly did not incorporate it by reference. For some reason, the Federal Magistrate signed the warrant and it was executed.

   In your opinion, based on the material discussed in this chapter, were the defendant's Fourth Amendment rights violated by the execution of this warrant? Why or why not?

Police Work

Operations and Functions

CHAPTER LEARNING OBJECTIVES

- Identify the tasks most frequently performed by municipal police officers.
- Explain why the way in which police view their role determines the nature of the functions they perform.
- Identify various duties and responsibilities associated with an investigation unit.
- Describe various ways in which the adoption of community policing strategies has influenced investigative units.
- Identify the typical functions performed by a forensic science unit within a law enforcement agency.
- Compare and contrast the policing styles espoused by both Wilson and Broderick.
- Highlight the most common methods used to both compute the number of police personnel required and determine the appropriate method for the assignment of personnel.
- Explain why or why not the current methods used to deploy manpower are consistent with the seminal Kansas City preventive patrol experiment and other similar research results.
- Distinguish between hard and soft performance measures used in performance evaluations.
- Explain how the relationship between the local police and the local media can either enhance or retard police–community relations.
- Identify the various strategies police agencies can adopt to foster a positive working relationship with the local media.

❖ Photo **6.1** An officer performing a frequent police function, a "routine" traffic stop.

As we have noted, the functions of the American police are extremely diverse, as is the manner in which the functions are performed. American officers are expected to police public manners and morals, prevent crime through territorial patrol, apprehend criminals, recover stolen property, bring an end to domestic disputes, and accomplish dozens of additional tasks. As we saw in Chapter 5, police performance in these and other areas is generally governed by the federal Constitution, related statutes, and court decisions, which outline the powers, duties, and limitations of police officers. Municipal charters and ordinances further govern operations at the municipal level. The following is an example of the unique powers granted by state statutes to police officers.

The *Illinois Compiled Statutes* (Illinois General Assembly, 2010) describes police officers as "conservators of the peace" with powers to (1) arrest or cause to be arrested, with or without process, all persons who break the peace or are found violating any municipal ordinance or any criminal law of the state; (2) commit arrested persons in custody overnight or on Sunday in any safe place, or until they can be brought before a proper court. (65 ILCS 11-1-2)

What authority does your state provide to police officers?

Other states, of course, have similar statutes that serve to indicate some of the specific functions of the police (e.g., serving warrants, detaining persons), as well as some of the general ones (e.g., keeping the peace). In addition, the Bill of Rights and civil rights legislation restrict police behavior by establishing, defining, and guaranteeing certain freedoms for all American citizens (see Chapter 5). Basically, this means that police powers and actions cannot conflict with the rights of the individual to freedom of speech, religion, press, assembly, and security from unreasonable searches and seizures.

❖ Basic Police Functions

Frequently, newspapers, news magazine, and "reality" police programs on television show police officers reaching for their guns as they burst through the doors of an apartment in a housing project. In the background is a police car with flashing red lights. A less dramatic scene shows a policewoman talking to a grateful mother whose lost child was returned. Which of these illustrations most accurately describes the police role? How frequently do the events depicted by these illustrations occur? What percentage of police activity is violent and dangerous? Have police activities changed since the terrorist attacks on September 11, 2001 or since the devastation of hurricane Katrina, which struck New Orleans in 2005? What do police officers really do?

The answer to the question, "What do police officers really do?" is that they spend a good deal of their time on routine matters, including coffee breaks, meals, taking reports, running errands, and attending court. Traffic, social service, police-initiated events, and crimes against property account for most of the rest of a patrol officer's time. Only a small percentage of the officer's time is spent on serious crime.

A study of patrol officers' responsibilities in large municipal police departments revealed the following rankings of tasks by frequency:

- Patrol
- Traffic enforcement
- Community relations
- Criminal investigation
- Warrant service and property control
- Narcotics investigation
- Identification
- Civil process
- Vice investigation
- Dispatching
- Bail/court officer and other duties (Michigan Commission on Law Enforcement Standards, 2006).

The Michigan Commission on Law Enforcement Standards (2006) also noted that the number of crimes associated with technology, such as identity theft, have dramatically expanded the responsibilities of police over the past decade.

The way the police view their role helps to determine the nature of the functions they perform and, as we shall see, the manner in which they organize to perform these functions. Thus, it is apparent that any list of police functions must be arbitrary and incomplete, but the following police functions are common in many agencies:

- Preservation of public peace
- Protection of the rights of persons and property
- Prevention of crime
- Detection and arrest of offenders against the law
- Enforcement and prevention of violations of state laws and city ordinances
- Service of processes and notices in civil and criminal proceedings (Honolulu Police, 2009)

Order Maintenance

Arriving at a formal definition of the role of the police, one that is universally accepted, is difficult. Most authorities recognize the existence of a law enforcement role and an order maintenance component of policing. For example, Greene (2006) proposed that in maintaining order the police engage in an activity that is both necessary and controversial at the same time. It is necessary because the community dislikes disorder and controversial because the police often use some form of force. A somewhat similar definition was proposed by Jurkanin, Hoover, Dowling, and Ahmad (2001), who believed that the phrase *order maintenance* should be described as "temporal order maintenance" (p. 45). The concept of temporal order maintenance involves the police maintaining the status quo or, in other words, keeping society stable and functioning by acceptable rules by using interventions with short-term effects. They believed this concept had three strategic objectives: public service/public safety, conflict management, and law enforcement. In prior research, Brooks (2001) recognized that the distinction between law enforcement and order maintenance for certain activities (such as a domestic violence arrest) was not clear. Jurkanin et al. (2001, p. 46) proposed that the on-scene objectives of the police and their preferred intervention techniques were best represented as a continuum of responses, not as separate categories. For example, a theft involving acquaintances is often conflict management, while a lost child, which appears to be a public service/public safety problem, may evolve into a law enforcement issue (e.g., kidnapping, rape, or murder). Hence, the police often respond to a given situation with an assumed on-scene objective and with a preferred intervention technique, but both very often change as further information is obtained (Jurkanin et al., 2001, p. 47). In other words, clear, mutually exclusive categories of police intervention techniques do not exist. At best, a "continuum of objectives and techniques are intermingled, although patterns of association certainly are definable" (Jurkanin et al., 2001, p. 47).

While most agree it is difficult to succinctly define **order maintenance**, it typically involves calls for service, such as suspicious person complaints, intoxicated persons, loud music calls, and a variety of other complaints. Such complaints are described by Kelling and Wilson (1982) in their research on "broken windows." A major premise of **broken windows theory** is that neighborhood social disorder causes a decline of overall conditions in a neighborhood and leads to more and more violent criminal activity (Golub, Johnson, Taylor, & Eterno, 2003). To prevent serious criminal activity, police focus on order maintenance or disorder issues, many of which do not directly involve criminal behaviors. Brook (2006) argued "according to broken windows theory, fighting the minor indicators of neighborhood decay and disorder—broken windows, graffiti, even litter—helps prevent major crimes." As we previously mentioned, most police organizations adopted this theory and began some form of broken windows policing or order maintenance and disorder enforcement in the 1980s.

Others have questioned the theory, arguing that broken windows policing has resulted in "mass stop-and-frisks, mass suspicionless searches of housing projects, prohibitions against loitering with known gang members, and aggressive, even repeated arrests of minor misdemeanants" (Taslitz, 2006, p. 271). Still others have questioned the effectiveness of the broken windows theory in light of an increase in some reported crime rates. (See Case In Point 6.1 for a discussion of the challenges to broken windows theory.)

☞ CASE IN POINT 6.1

Levitt and Dubner in *Freakonomics* "present a controversial theory claiming that the legalization of abortion in the 1970s was the biggest factor in the crime drop of the 1990s. According to this hypothesis, the decline in the birth of unwanted, often poor and fatherless children in the '70s, led to the decline in the number of juvenile delinquents in the '80s and hardened criminals in the '90s."

Harcourt and Ludwig attributed the rise and fall of reported crime to crack cocaine instead of broken windows policing. As this drug became more available in the '90s the price dropped, fewer people risked their lives for the income resulting in a reduction in the incidents of violent crime.

Harcourt and Ludwig also studied the movement of public housing occupants "from inner-city projects to safer, more orderly neighborhoods. Contrary to what broken windows would suggest, there was no decrease in criminality among relocated public housing tenants." The reported crime rates in the safer, orderly neighborhood were no different from the rates in the high disorder neighborhoods.

Source: "The Cracks in 'Broken Windows,'" by D. Brook, 2006, *The Boston Globe*, p. A1.

Another example of order maintenance by the police results from the fact that they often assume sole responsibility for dealing with mentally ill persons whose behavior warrants some form of intervention. Research has shown that the frequency of contact between police and persons with mental illness has increased significantly in the decades since deinstitutionalization (Lamb, Weinberger, & DeCuir, 2002). Similarly, public inebriates also often become the responsibility of the police because limited bed space and selective admission practices at detoxification centers hinder police attempts to find shelter and care for those who are drunk in public. At the same time, of course, the use of jails to house public inebriates is deemed inappropriate, placing further restrictions on the alternatives available to the police. The police also are frequently called to remove the homeless from streets and parks because these persons have a negative impact on businesses, create an appearance of community neglect, and are often a danger to themselves (especially in cold weather). But what options are available to the police? Shelter facilities have limited space, and many refuse to admit those who are mentally ill or alcoholic. Thus, finding a suitable alternative for the homeless often becomes a difficult task for the police.

Investigations and Forensic Science

Another important function of the police is the investigation of crimes, complaints, and calls for service. Almost all calls to the police involve some type of investigation.

The investigation unit is responsible for obtaining and processing evidence and effecting arrest. Bayley (1998) concluded that "about 15% of police personnel are assigned to it, much smaller than the 60% assigned to patrol" (p. 71). Levinson (2002) reported similar percentages from a national study of detective work that concluded investigators account for 16% of police agency personnel. The duties and responsibilities associated with an investigation unit include, but are not limited to, the following:

- Determine whether a crime was committed
- Search the crime scene
- Photograph and sketch the crime scene
- Collect and process physical evidence
- Interview victims and witnesses
- Interrogate suspects
- Maintain field notes and write preliminary, follow-up, and supplemental arrest reports
- Maintain surveillance of suspects and known criminals
- Recover stolen property
- Arrest suspects
- Prepare criminal cases for court
- Testify (Palmiotto, 2004).

Previous research by the Rand Corporation and the Police Executive Forum examined the efficiency of the criminal investigation process. The Rand Study concluded that a substantial amount of an investigator's time is spent in nonproductive work and that investigators' expertise has little impact on the solving of cases. Furthermore, this study concluded that more than half of all serious crimes received no more than superficial attention from investigators and that half of all investigators could be eliminated without negatively influencing the crime clearance rate (Gilbert, 2001, 2009; Greenwood, 1979). Many argue that the actions of patrol officers are extremely important if a criminal investigation is to be successful. Often, the single most important determinant of whether a case will be solved is the information a victim provides to the responding patrol officer (Greenwood & Petersilia, 1975). If information that uniquely identifies a perpetrator is not available when the crime is reported to the police, the perpetrator is often not identified (Greenwood & Petersilia, 1975).

Police investigate all types of incidents, from simple vandalism to homicide. Many criminal investigative divisions have established cybercrime units because of the popularity and potential for criminal violations on the Internet. Some of these violations include online sexual predation, distribution of online child pornography, and computer frauds and thefts by computer. Police investigators often assist the FBI in operations related to the FBI's National Security Priorities (FBI, 2009). These include the following:

- Counterterrorism
- Counterintelligence
- Cybercrime
- Public corruption
- Civil rights
- Organized crime
- White-collar crime
- Major theft or violent crime

The adoption of a community policing philosophy by many police departments has also influenced investigative unit functions. Many departments reexamined the traditional method of permitting only specialists to conduct criminal investigations and have now trained patrol officers as generalists, permitting them to conduct follow-up investigations. In this form of investigation, there is little consideration as to the type of crime committed. The community receives immediate police service since the investigation is no longer forwarded to an investigations unit. This increases the continuity of the investigation and allows the responding officer, in many cases, to advance the investigation from the initial report through all of the steps in the process until the time of trial.

Even with the changes we have discussed, "police work as we know it has remained relatively unchanged over the passage of time; responding to calls for service, investigating crime, and dealing with victims and offenders, for example, have been constant" (Fantino, 2007, p. 1). However, the police have experienced major changes in the application of forensic science techniques to the increasing complexity of criminal investigations. Caddy and Cobb (2004) defined *forensic science* as any branch of science used in the resolution of legal disputes. As an example, the West Virginia State Police Forensic Laboratory (2009) provided the following forensic science examinations and functions:

- Analysis and identification of controlled substances
- Analysis of urine and blood specimens
- Identification of paint, glass, building materials, ignitable liquids, and gunshot residues
- Analysis of biological materials
- Analysis, comparison, evaluation, and verification of friction ridge skin impressions
- Analysis of tool marks, firearm comparisons, and obliterated marks
- Analysis of questioned documents and footwear and tire tread impressions

What has been the effect of these rather dramatic changes in techniques employed by the police in criminal investigations? Some believe these advancements have resulted in a *CSI effect,* where unrealistic portrayals of the science have translated to equally unrealistic expectations from not only the public but also other professions that operate within the justice system who believe in magic (Fantino, 2007). Consider this example of the **CSI effect**. "I once heard a juror complain that the prosecution had not done a thorough job because 'they didn't even dust the grass lawn for fingerprints'" (Shelton, 2008, p. 2). However, one study of randomly summoned jurors revealed that "although the CSI viewers had higher expectations for scientific evidence than non-CSI viewers, these expectations had little, if any, effect on the respondents' propensity to convict (Shelton, 2008, p. 4).

A recent study by Roman and colleagues (2009) revealed the positive impacts of DNA analysis on criminal investigations. They concluded that when conventional investigative techniques were used, a suspect was identified 12% of the time, compared with 31% of the cases using DNA evidence. Additional findings of this recent study include the following:

- Property crime cases that involve the processing of DNA have twice as many suspects identified, arrested, and accepted for prosecution compared with traditional investigations.
- DNA is approximately five times as likely to result in the identification of a suspect compared with fingerprints. (Roman et al., 2009).

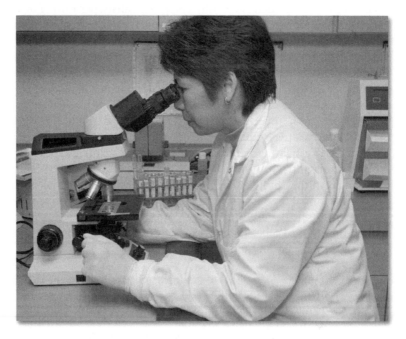

❖ **Photo 6.2** A forensic examiner from the crime lab at work using a comparison microscope on evidence retrieved from a crime scene.

Police functions are performed through the processes of arrest and detention, investigation, and police–community relations programs. To help ensure that these processes are carried out successfully, the police must recruit, select, train, educate, evaluate, and promote officers capable of facing ever increasing challenges. Some of the near-future challenges to law enforcement include "local and transnational criminals engaging in more elaborate schemes, the increased movement of money through sophisticated local and international communications systems, and the migration of criminal enterprises to terrorist related activities" (Fantino, 2007, p. 3).

AROUND THE WORLD

Transnational organized crimes present a number of challenges to law enforcement agencies. Three major approaches have been created to address the problem of transnational organized crime.

Task Forces: A number of law enforcement agencies have joined a multijurisdictional task force that combines resources. "For example, Operation Trifecta, a 19-month transnational investigation led by the U.S. Drug Enforcement Administration, involved 9 Federal agencies and 67 State and local law enforcement agencies from 8 states" (p. 1).

Heightened Awareness: Transnational organized crime is often present on streets patrolled by local police. Local police should be aware of overseas contacts, the involvement of foreign nationals, certain false documents, and large amounts of cash.

Improved Communications: Local police need to be aware that satellite phones, Web-based transactions, and e-mail facilitate transnational organized crime. They must understand what action to take when they encounter cell phones, computers, and various other electronic devices. Transnational organized crime criminals can easily communicate across international boundaries.

Source: Effectively Combating Transnational Organized Crime, by J. O. Finckenauer, 2007. National Institute of Justice. Retrieved from http://www.ojp.usdoj.gov/nij/topics/crime/transnational-organized-crime/effective-practices.htm

Even though the selection and training procedures employed by the police result in the hiring of officers capable of addressing these challenges, there is tremendous variation in the manner in which officers perform their tasks—even on the same shift, in the same division, and in the same department. As we have seen in previous chapters, the exercise of discretion by police officers plays an important role in their encounters with other citizens. So, too, does the manner in which the police organize to perform their tasks.

❖ Styles of Policing

James Q. Wilson (1968) identified three relatively distinct types of policing. The first type, referred to as the *watchman style,* involves police organizations in which the principal function is order maintenance rather than law enforcement in cases that do not involve serious crime. The police use the law more as a means of maintaining order than of regulating conduct and judge the seriousness of infractions less by what the law says about them than by their immediate and personal consequences. In other words, circumstances of person and situation are taken into account. Police officers are encouraged to follow the path of least resistance in carrying out their daily duties. "Little stuff" is to be ignored, but officers are to be "tough" when serious matters arise. This style of policing often occurs in departments with low-level educational requirements (high school education or less), relatively low wages, little formal training, considerable on-the-job training, and few formal policies. Such departments have few specialized personnel; thus, departmental transfers are rare. Officers are encouraged to take personal differences into account both when enforcing the law and when addressing citizens. Other than in serious cases, who the citizen is, is as important as what she has done (Wilson, 1968, pp. 140–171).

The second style of policing is the *legalistic style.* In such police organizations, officers are encouraged to handle commonplace situations as if they were matters of law enforcement as opposed to order maintenance. Traffic tickets are frequently issued, juveniles are often detained and arrested, misdemeanor arrests are common, and the police take action against illicit enterprises on a regular basis. Patrol officers are under pressure to "produce" arrests and tickets and are expected to simply "do their jobs," as defined by an administration that views a high volume of traffic and other stops as simply a means of discovering more serious crimes and enhancing revenues. Technical efficiency is highly valued, and promotions are based on such efficiency. Middle-class officers with high school educations are recruited, and a professional image (new buildings and equipment) is viewed as important. The law is used to punish those perceived as deserving of punishment. Orders are issued by supervisory personnel and are followed, regardless of whether officers deem them appropriate (Wilson, 1968, pp. 172–199).

The third policing style is the *service style.* Service style police officers intervene frequently but not formally, take seriously all requests for service, and frequently find alternatives to arrest and other formal sanctions. Officers are encouraged to be consumer-oriented and to produce a product that meets community needs. Officers are expected to be neat, courteous, and professional. Authority is less centralized, and community relations and public education are viewed as important aspects of policing. College education is valued, salaries are reasonably good, and specialized expertise is encouraged (Wilson, 1968).

An additional description of police operational styles was proposed by John Broderick (1977). He focused on individual officers rather than entire police organizations and proposed that there were four officer personality types. *Enforcers* are concerned with the enforcement of laws versus protection of individual rights. *Idealists* place value on the individual rights of all citizens. *Realists* focus on neither enforcement of laws nor the protection of individual rights, and *optimists* are more service-oriented and value individual rights (Broderick, 1977; Dempsey & Forst, 2009).

While most police organizations have characteristics of all three or four styles of policing, tendencies to emphasize one style over the others are often easily discernible. In fact, particular communities sometimes become known for their emphasis on a specific style of policing. ("Don't speed in that town; they ticket everybody"; "The town lives off income from traffic citations"; or "You can get anything you want in that town as long as you don't rock the boat.") While many watchman and legalistic departments exist, service-style organizations appear to represent the current trend in policing. Given the popularity of community policing and cooperation between the police and other citizens in maintaining order and enforcing the law, this trend is not surprising. An emphasis on community policing and problem solving have required police administrators to reexamine the abilities of available personnel to accomplish these initiatives.

We should also point out that while research supports the belief that police officers have certain general styles that influence their behaviors, the consensus on styles dissipates when other issues are examined (Greene, 2006). These factors involve personal characteristics (age, gender, education, and so on); situational characteristics (demeanor of the parties involved, seriousness of the offense); environmental characteristics (amount of perceived crime in the neighborhood, social disorganization); and organizational characteristics (department style, shift assignment, management support) (Brooks, 1997; Roberg, Novak, & Cordner, 2005; as discussed in Greene, 2006). Thus, while the styles developed by Wilson and Broderick assist us in comprehending the attitudes and beliefs of police, it is important to note that many factors influence the individual styles exhibited by police officers. Furthermore, a police officer's style could change during his career, following the assignment to a special unit such as narcotics, or even upon assignment to a different patrol shift.

❖ Patrol Strength and Allocation

Police administrators must not only consider the abilities of the officers they supervise, but also the number of officers assigned to various tasks. There is no exact standard for determining the required number of officers, but there is an expectation that police administrators can justify staffing levels. For example, determining the number and assignment of patrol officers is critical not only internally (to meet staffing needs) but also externally when considering the impact of numbers on the type of police service that can be provided to the community (Anderson, 2008). Thus, two cities with very similar populations may have different numbers of patrol officers on the same shift. Population is one factor that helps to determine the number of police officers needed to answer service requests. Additional factors to be considered include the types of service provided (bomb disposal, underwater recovery, school-crossing services, search and rescue), whether the department has a community policing plan, available resources, and other variables. It should be noted that beginning in 2008, many police department's budgets were reduced and some small departments experienced difficulty in maintaining continuous patrol coverage. In some of these areas that lacked patrol coverage, other police agencies, such as a county sheriff's department or the state police, provided patrol and responded to calls. In the following sections, we examine the methods used to determine the number of police officers needed for patrol and the allocation or the assignment of patrol officers.

Before discussing the process of determining the required number of patrol officers and their allocation, we must determine the desired outcomes of patrol. Alpert and Dunham (1997, p. 166) stated that patrol can be divided into three related outcomes. First, the presence of patrol officers may frighten offenders away or influence them not to commit violations until the police leave the area. There is sufficient evidence to conclude that these actions do not actually prevent crime, but rather simply displace or move the criminal activity to other locations that may lack sufficient police patrols. Second, patrol provides police an opportunity to determine the probabilities of criminal behavior and, through preventive strategies, to reduce or eliminate those probabilities (Alpert & Dunham, 1997). Finally, Alpert and Dunham found that patrol provides police the opportunity to respond or react to calls for assistance in a timely manner. A similar conclusion was reached in a later study by Moore, Thacher, Dodge, and Moore (2002), who confirmed that police patrol staffing has three performance measures: crime reduction, visibility, and political accountability, which must be considered when attempting to determine how to achieve desirable results. They argue that no single component of policing will suffice as a clear measure of the outcomes of patrol and regard other factors, such as community support and cooperation, as important in assessing the desired outcomes.

POLICE STORIES

Patrol is defined as moving about an area and observing or inspecting. When I first began to patrol, one of the most important requirements besides responding quickly to all dispatched calls was to achieve approximately 100 miles on the vehicle's odometer per shift. This was a method used to motivate patrol officers to avoid parking the vehicle and spending an excessive amount of time in the police station, at fast food restaurants, or at the officer's residence.

I realized that patrolling for most of 8 hours did have an impact on some persons. In some cases, those that were thinking about committing an illegal act exited the area. In some cases, the mere presence of the police vehicle resulted in voluntary compliance by individuals thinking about committing a crime. I was also initially surprised at the number of people who wave at all police officers who drive a police car. Many of these individuals do feel an increased sense of security because of the presence of a police vehicle in their neighborhood, mall parking lot, or public park, especially at night.

Today, the evaluation of police personnel involves much more than simply answering dispatched calls and recording 100 miles on the vehicle's odometer by the end of the shift. In fact, in some cases the required 100 miles was easy to achieve by driving the police car back and forth to a rural area or to a nearby city in a very short interval of time.

There are a variety of ways to determine the appropriate number of police personnel for any given jurisdiction (e.g., intuitively, comparatively, and by workload) (Roberg, Kuykendall, & Novak, 2002). Roberg et al. (2002) concluded that the ***intuitive approach*** involves little more than an educated guess and is often based on tradition (personnel numbers from previous years). However, this approach is in part based on the number of crimes cleared or the total number of arrests. In other words, many administrators demand more police officers be hired as crime rates increase. However, Bayley (1994) concluded that differences in crime rates should not be attributed to variations in the number of police. He found that since World War II, increases in the number of police have closely paralleled increases in crime rates. Communities hire more police when crime rates rise, but this is a desperate game of catch-up that has no effect on the rate of increase in crime (Bayley, 1994).

The ***comparative approach*** involves comparing one or more cities using the ratio of police officers per one thousand population units; if the comparison city has a higher ratio of police to population, it is assumed that an increase in personnel is justified to at least the level of the comparison city (Roberg et al., 2002). For example, on average, in 2004 the number of full-time sworn police personnel in the United States declined from 252 (in 2000) to 249 per 100,000 residents (Reaves, 2007). In other words, there were approximately 2.49 sworn police personnel per 1000 residents in 2004. The exclusive use of this method to compute police personnel needs is not recommended. Communities possess unique characteristics concerning the size of the area served, miles of roads to be covered, crime rate, number of juveniles, economic strength, employment rates, unique problems of a growing elderly population, and special tourist attractions, which could have a substantial impact on the number of personnel required to respond to requests for police service. Currently, there is no universal number that accurately reflects the police personnel needs of all jurisdictions.

The final approach, ***workload analysis***, requires an elaborate information system, standards of expected performance, well-defined community expectations, and the prioritization of police activities (Roberg et al., 2002). The workload analysis of patrol often involves the following (Cordner & Sheehan, 1999):

- Documenting the total amount of patrol workload that occurs
- Determining the time it takes to handle that workload
- Translating the workload data into the number of patrol officers required to handle it
- Determining how many patrol officers are needed at different times of the day (allocation)
- Determining how many patrol officers are needed on different days of the week (scheduling)
- Determining how best to assign patrol officers to geographic areas (deployment) (p. 442)

The actual computation of patrol workload is also complicated by the issue of uncommitted time. For example, Famega, Frank, and Mazerolle (2005) reported that over three quarters of a police officers' shift involves uncommitted time and that only 6% of unassigned time is directed by police supervisors, dispatchers, other officers, or citizens. These figures are based upon statistical averages and are not reflective of behavior in any one organization. Officers at various times and in various locations may respond to one call after another and have numerous service-oriented calls waiting to be answered. It might be suggested that more proactive policing is possible based upon the statistics available, but there has been little research concerning uncommitted patrol. During a typical shift, police officers may enjoy substantial amounts of unassigned or uncommitted time, during which they may self-initiate a wide range of tasks at their own discretion (Famega et al., 2005). However, self-initiation by patrol officers is often based on the individual officer's motivation and can be influenced by perceptions of the desired style of policing discussed earlier. Webster (1970) found that police are not monitored in conducting self-initiated activities as they are in responding to calls for service via completion of reports.

Only a few studies have developed workload approaches to patrol staffing, such as the Patrol Allocation Methodology (1975) by the Rand Institute and the Patrol Allocation Model (1993) by The Center for Public Safety at Northwestern University. One of the more current models is the **Allocation Model for Police Patrol** (AMPP) developed by Justex Systems, Inc. The AMPP is designed to provide an estimate, based on a reported call load, of the number of patrol officers required to maintain a specified level of deterrent patrol, visibility, response time, and immediate availability for emergency response (Waco Police Association, 2008). More specifically, this patrol staffing model has four primary performance objectives for patrol: visibility of the patrol officer, ability to respond to Priority One calls, response time to Priority Two calls, and the availability of patrol officers for a Priority One call. Even though many workload analysis models have been demonstrated to be methodologically sound, few jurisdictions use these devices to compute patrol staffing. Most administrators cite the cost, complexity of the formula, and extensive data collection as the reasons for not using a workload formula.

Once the police administrator has used the intuitive, comparative, or workload approach to compute the number of police personnel required, he or she must determine the appropriate method for the assignment of personnel. The unique problems found in all communities prohibit the equal assignment of personnel across all shifts, districts, beats, or zones. The effective assignment of personnel involves a variety of factors, some of which are unique to different jurisdictions and are ever changing as new problems develop and others are resolved. For example, some of the factors Adams (2007, pp. 38–39) recommends administrators consider in the deployment of police personnel include:

- Resident population and character of the community
- Nature of the area
- Number and types of crimes and arrests
- Times and locations of crimes and traffic collisions
- Prioritized concerns and fears expressed by citizens
- Locations and numbers of frequent incident spots
- Disproportionate distribution of the population
- Socioeconomic factors
- Size and shape of the jurisdiction and proximity to other cities
- Geography and topography
- Parks and recreation facilities
- Locations and nature of attractive nuisances
- Age ratios of the population

As geographic information systems (GIS) and other computer systems improved, *operational analysis*—the analysis of internal operations as a method of allocating patrol resources more effectively—began to achieve higher status in the literature (Bruce, 2009). According to Bruce (2009), the creation of even basic workload statistics for patrol can create a number of questions:

- Should officer-initiated activities be calculated as a part of the service total?
- What about directed patrols and selective enforcement?
- If an incident occurred in a different area than the one the call came from, toward which area should it be counted?

☞ CASE IN POINT 6.2

Ultimately, for any allocation of assignment of patrol officers, the administrator must decide how to most effectively and efficiently accomplish the functions of patrol. However, Greene (2006) stated that the design and implementation of an allocation model for police is only the initial step in the effective deployment of police personnel. He found that any allocation of officer plan must be followed by an ongoing workload assessment plan. This is especially important for patrol officers since workloads fluctuate and it would be possible to overstaff one area while understaffing another. In other words, as with the initial allocation models, it is imperative that police administrators continually assess the following factors related to the nature and number of tasks and their complexity, location, and time required for completion:

- Number of incidents handled by patrol during a specified time
- Average time required to handle the incident
- Calculation of the average time available for handling incidents
- Time lost due to days off, holidays (Illinois Police Accreditation Coalition, 2009)

The intent of the various **deployment models**, such as the police district, zone, or area, is for police work to be channeled through dispatch so that the closest police car is assigned to calls. However, Douglass (2009) believed the fixed-grid form of deployment that is used by most police agencies is unworkable in practice. For example, "You leave your district to answer a call in another district; while you are gone, another officer from another district is sent to answer a call in your assigned area. And so it begins, one call leading to another until, shortly, no officers are close to their assignments." (p. 6) Thus, in response to the traditional district model, some departments have begun the creation of a model that allows supervisors to deploy patrol officers to hot spot areas. According to Douglass (2009), these deployments (a transition from a dispatch model to an incident-command model using hot-spot technology) experience ongoing change, and a patrol officer could be assigned to any number of deployments throughout a given shift. Douglass (2009) believed the paradigm has shifted and that an increasing number of police organizations are turning to geographic analysis and advanced technology to make decisions about how to best utilize police resources to address problems as they develop. For example, Roberg, Novak, and Cordner (2009) reported the use of computerized crime mapping to determine the best locations in which to concentrate police patrol activities.

> Data obtained through a department's computer-aided-dispatch (CAD) and records-management systems (which store and maintain calls for service, records of incidents, and arrests) are matched with addresses and other geographic information such as beats, and districts; maps can then be computer generated for a geographic area to be overlaid with specific information. (as quoted in Rich, 1996, p. 200)

❖ Types of Patrol

Police use a variety of techniques to complete the tasks associated with patrol. Often, these variations depend on the size and individual needs of the local jurisdiction. The Law Enforcement Management and Administrative Statistics (LEMAS) report (Reaves & Hickman, 2004) noted a substantial increase in the number of departments routinely using foot and bicycle patrols in comparison with statistics in previous LEMAS reports.

Foot patrol was the original form of patrol. While many agencies report that they routinely use foot patrol, a number employ this strategy for special occasions, such as festivals, concerts, sporting events, and parades. Foot patrol works extremely well where there are large concentrations of people on foot, such as in shopping malls, multiple-family residential villages, parks, beaches, recreational and amusement areas, and any other area where patrol officers on foot are in a one-on-one situation with other people who are also on foot (Adams, 2007, p. 164). Levinson (2002) noted the importance of foot patrol officers interacting with the community and concluded that it is not simply the existence of foot patrol that improves police–community relations, but the actions of the officer.

Significant research studies on the evaluation of foot patrol were conducted in Newark, New Jersey, and Flint, Michigan. In Newark, foot patrol officers were assigned patrol beats in one of eight neighborhoods (Pelfrey, 2000). The results of these studies suggested that increased foot patrol by police officers was not associated with reduced levels of crime, but it was noticed by citizens and appeared to reduce fear of crime and increase public satisfaction with the police (Moore, 1992). Wilson and Kelling (1999, p. 154) concluded from the Newark study that citizens felt more secure and had a more favorable opinion of the police compared with those residing in other areas. Directed foot patrol (assigning the officer to a specific area) is the most popular form of foot patrol and is utilized in areas that allow the police to interact easily with large numbers of people. Another form of foot patrol involves the "Park, Walk, and Talk" initiative, in which "officers are required to get out of their patrol cars and conduct 30-minute foot patrols at least twice a shift" (Young, 2000, p. 315). This form of foot patrol is not directed at a specific area or crime problem. The intent of this program is to encourage communication between the police and the residents of the areas they patrol. Some communities also are using trained volunteers to walk neighborhood streets, parks, and schools to deter crime and report incidents and problems (Office of Neighborhood Involvement, 2009).

Bicycle patrol is popular in many departments. Bicycles have the advantage of low cost compared with automobiles, but bicycle patrols do require additional training and special equipment. The benefits of bicycle patrols include the following: Officers are accessible to the public; officers can silently approach a situation on specially designed bicycles; much more area can be covered compared with foot patrol; and bicycles can travel where automobiles are unable to patrol (Metro Nashville Police Department, 2000). In a recent study by Menton (2008), bicycle patrols reported more than double the number of contacts as automobile patrols. The results were 10.5 people contacted per hour from cars compared with 22.8 people per hour from bicycles.

Another form of patrol involves air support units consisting of fixed-wing aircraft and helicopters. Air support units often assist ground units with fleeing felons, high-speed pursuits, missing person searches, drug suppression activities, and general crime prevention. While there is little question about its effectiveness, air support is by far the most expensive type of police patrol. However, studies claim that helicopters have 15 times the surveillance capacity of a ground unit and that one helicopter can be as effective as 23 ground officers in terms of observation ability (Denver Police Department, 2000).

Mounted patrols are popular in larger departments with unique patrol requirements, including parks and lakefronts. Mounted patrols are involved in crime prevention, community interaction, and crowd control. The Chicago Police Department (1998b) estimated that one mounted police officer has the effect of 10 to 20 police officers on foot. However, with the addition of bicycles, more foot patrols, and all-terrain vehicles (ATVs), the number of mounted patrol units has been declining.

❖ Patrol Innovations

Although the patrol division involves the largest number of personnel in a police department, little research into the effectiveness of this division was completed until 1960. Prior to this, patrol officers provided a wide range of services, dealing with almost any problem presented to them, with minimal accountability to administrators, the public, or the courts. Parks, Mastrofski, Dejong, and Gray (1999) described the duties of patrol as "**911 policing.**" This involves allocation of resources in a case-by-case fashion (incident-driven basis) as citizens demand them (reactively). According to Parks et al. (1999), "Under 911 policing, departments have invested in increasingly sophisticated systems to receive citizens' calls for service, to locate calls spatially, and to designate a patrol unit for rapid response" (p. 484). However, the concept of 911 policing has been somewhat modified by the adoption of community policing. As we discuss in Chapter 11, community policing involves the reorientation of police patrol to increase citizen interaction and, to a great extent, turns traditional police practices upside down.

Various reform efforts and tensions between the police and citizens led to the examination of several aspects of policing, including patrol. As an example, the **Kansas City preventive patrol experiment** was one of the most comprehensive assessments of the effectiveness of random police patrol. The experiment analyzed variations in the level of routine preventive patrol within Kansas City. In the reactive beats, routine preventive patrol was eliminated and police officers responded only to calls for service. In the control beats, routine preventive patrol was maintained at its usual level. In the proactive beats, routine preventive patrol was intensified by two to three times its usual level through the assignment of additional patrol cars and the frequent presence of cars from the reactive beats. The experiment concluded that decreasing or increasing routine preventive patrol in the areas tested had no measurable influence on crime, citizen fear of crime, community attitudes toward the police on the delivery of patrol services, police response time, or traffic accidents (Kelling, Pate, Dieckman, & Brown, 1974).

The results of the Kansas City study had minimal effect on the primary strategy of police. Today, almost 40 years since the Kansas City experiment in 1972, random, mobile, uniformed patrol is still the primary strategy used by police. Bayley (1998) concluded that the Kansas City preventive patrol research results "are generally accepted as being true; its research strategy is considered to be seriously flawed; it has never been replicated; it has not lessened appreciably the reliance of the police on random patrolling; but it has encouraged a rethinking of police purposes and methods" (p. 27). In other words, the implications of the Kansas City study were that personnel normally allocated to preventive patrol could be assigned to more productive crime control strategies. For example, the Police Foundation (2009) stated the results indicated that police deployment strategies could be based on targeted crime prevention and service goals rather than on routine preventive patrol.

Crank (1998) argued that the phrase ***random preventive patrol*** is self-contradictory and without meaning. He suggested that random preventive patrol permits many opportunities for proactive activity on the part of individual officers. Random preventive patrol is a way of doing police work that allows police officers to control their territories. As Crank stated, "Officers have the discretion to do what they want where they want it, guided by the cultural stipulation that they must control what goes on in their territory" (p. 46). However, Engel (2003) confirmed that police supervisory styles influence patrol officer behavior in the community. Patrol officers who were managed by an active supervisor were more likely to be proactive in their policing activities and to spend more time per shift engaged in problem solving and community-oriented activities. Let's briefly examine what police do while on random preventive patrol.

An early study by Greene and Klockars (1991) concluded that police spend 26% of their work time on criminal matters, 9% on order maintenance assignments, 4% on service-related functions, 11% on traffic matters, 2% on medical assistance, and 12% on administrative matters. Using the data from this study, Dempsey (1999) found that when the percentage of time involved in unavailable, administrative, and clear time is excluded from the data, the data indicate that the police spend approximately 50% of their time on criminal matters, 16% on order maintenance, 8% on service, 21% on traffic, and 4% on medical assistance. Thus, he concluded that 47% of a police officer's time was not spent on actual assignments. This is a reasonable amount of uncommitted time because most service organizations in reality have limited numbers of contacts with their clients. An interesting attempt to specify the desired amount of time police officers spend engaged in specific tasks is presented by the Longmont, Colorado, Police Department. According to their Staffing Study (Longmont Police Department, 2006),

> There is some agreement among community policing departments that a patrol officer's day should be divided between reactive, coactive and proactive policing. Though no nationally recognized standard exists, the Longmont Police Department strives for a benchmark where patrol officers, on a routine and daily schedule, spend at least 60 percent of an average day handling calls for service and report writing (reactive), 30 percent conducting proactive and coactive patrol, and 10 percent dedicated to administrative duties, such as briefing, court appearances, meal breaks, meetings, etc. Note that this time breakdown does not include training time. Training time is recognized as a necessary addition to every officer's on-duty obligation, however it is not an everyday event. When training is provided, it will reduce the percentage of time spent in the other three areas for that particular day or week. (p. 5)

The results of these studies challenge police to examine their patrol operations and to develop alternative strategies for random mobile patrol. The police have responded by developing a number of new strategies:

Directed Patrol, which involves specifying a set of desired outcomes toward which personnel, groups, or the organization should work.

Hot Spot Policing, which involves focusing on geographic areas with clusters of criminal offenses occurring within a specified interval of time.

Differential Response Policing, in which the police prioritize calls and responses based upon their seriousness.

Saturation Patrol and Crackdowns, which includes adding officers to designated areas to increase visibility and targeting certain types of crime respectively.

Third Party Policing, in which the police encourage or coerce personnel from other agencies to take some responsibility for crime prevention.

Evidence-Based Policing, in which police administrators use the best available research results to create policy and regulations and to conduct training.

Intelligence-Led Policing, which is informant and surveillance based with respect to recidivists and serious crime offenders and provides a central crime intelligence mechanism to facilitate objective decision making.

Situational Crime Prevention, which involves reducing crime by reducing crime opportunities and increasing risk to the offenders.

Pulling Levers Policing, which involves selecting a particular type of crime, convening an interagency work group, conducting research to identify offenders and patterns, and developing a response to halt or reduce crimes of the specific type.

CompStat, which provides police agencies with preliminary crime statistics used for tactical planning and officer deployment.

Each of these new strategies is discussed in detail in Chapter 11.

❖ Evaluation of Police Performance

Evaluation of performance and the measurement of employee performance are closely related to the delivery of services by an organization. According to Cordner and Scarborough (2007), "Without such measurement devices, we will not know when the organization needs improvement; we will not know what aspects of the organization need improvement the most; and, following the implementation of changes, we will not know whether improvements have been achieved" (p. 345). However, any evaluation of performance can have an effect on employees and can strongly influence their completion of daily activities. For example, if the number of bicycle tickets written is an important part of the department's evaluation instrument, many police officers will seek to increase the number of bicycle citations they issue. Depending on the perceived weight or importance of the evaluation, some officers will ignore other citations and focus only on bicycle violations. Cordner and Scarborough (2007) found that "performance criteria originally selected because of the ease of their measurement may become, in effect, the goals of the police department and the objectives of its individual officers" (p. 350). However, if properly administered, this form of evaluation will permit advancement of organizational objectives and accomplishment of certain career goals. The administrator would have to continually assess the evaluation criteria and ensure that the evaluation process is fair for all police personnel. For example, an officer assigned to the "power shift," from 8 p.m. to 4 a.m., would be less likely to encounter as many bicycle violations as would a day-shift officer.

Shane (2007) reported two types of **performance measures**: hard and soft. A *hard measure* is expressed numerically (quantitative) and is rather easy to formulate: the number, rate, percent, or ratio of something. He also described a *soft measure* as an intangible attribute or characteristic that is usually expressed in terms of degree of excellence, desirability, attitude, or perception (qualitative) and is often output or outcome based: for example, citizen satisfaction with police or citizen's perceived levels of fear.

As discussed in previous sections, the role of modern police is often difficult to define using terms that permit easy measurement and evaluation. It is difficult to apply quantifiable measures to many of the tasks performed by the police. Police have consistently used a set of conventional indicators of police performance that involve the counting of certain desirable law enforcement activities: the number of field reports submitted, number of tickets written, number of referrals made to other agencies, and number of arrests or number of felony arrests (LaGrange, 1998, p. 365). However, the number of arrests and reports only represents the quantitative measures of police performance. According to Roberg and colleagues (2002, p. 166), because it was more difficult to assess the qualitative measures of policing (order maintenance, community service, and problem solving), the law enforcement activities became the most important, prestigious, and rewarded. And besides only representing a portion of the role of the police, quantitative measures are subject to misinterpretation. As Dantzker (1999) concluded, "Reporting a low crime rate may not actually indicate that the police department is doing a great job, only that crime reporting is low" (p. 251). Dantzker further suggested, "One could argue that citizens do not report crimes to police agencies they do not trust or they believe to be ineffective, while they report crimes when they believe that the local police agency is honest, responsive, and effective" (p. 251).

In other words, according to this logic, crime rate measures could be an inverse measure of police performance.

It is important to note that a substantial part of most police departments' mission statements focus on quality of life, professionalism, respect, and public safety. Thibault, Lynch, and McBride (2001) found that qualitative measures of police performance could be accomplished through "community leadership meetings and discussions with questionnaires, focus groups from the community where the services were delivered, and community attitude surveys" (p. 57). Thus, most agree that there is no one measure of police performance that accurately describes today's police. For example, in 2006 the Los Angeles Police Department was assessed on the following performance dimensions:

- Crime reduction
- Compliance with federal consent decree
- Deployment strength
- Diversity in hiring and promotion
- Homeland security and disaster preparedness
- Anti-gang policies
- Fiscal management (McGreevy, 2006)

Similarly, Shane (2007) modified a multidimensional performance system created by Moore et al. (2002), which included critical dimensions that attempted to capture the services provided by the police to the public.

- Reducing crime and criminal victimization
- Holding offenders accountable
- Reducing fear, blight and enhancing personal safety
- Guaranteeing safety in public and quasi-public places
- Using financial resources fairly, efficiently and effectively
- Using force fairly, efficiently and effectively
- Satisfying customer demands and achieving legitimacy with those policed (p. 35)

The value of measuring police performance subjectively became apparent during the 1980s, when researchers discovered that public perceptions had behavioral consequences that affected the quality of life (Bayley, 1994, p. 98). For example, fear of crime can produce sickness and cause absenteeism and truancy; suspicion of the police reduces the willingness of people to provide essential information to the police, thereby decreasing the chances that crimes will be solved; fear of victimization can raise distrust among neighbors, undermining the ability of communities to undertake cooperative crime-prevention action; and the fear of crime may contribute to the decline of neighborhoods as people stop maintaining their property, avoid local businesses and places of recreation, and move to safer, more desirable communities (Bayley, 1994; Wilson & Kelling, 1999).

As with almost any service organization, the measurement of quantitative and even qualitative tasks performed by the police is a challenge because few consistent work tasks exist. For example, how many cases should a juvenile officer handle in a month? How many traffic tickets should a traffic officer write per month? How many drug arrests should a narcotics officer complete per month? The evaluation of police personnel may be even more challenging with the implementation of community policing. For example, how does a supervisor rate an officer who is no longer making arrests because there is not as great a need? How do you quantify interaction with citizens that simply garner good will? We will discuss the evaluation of police performance since the inception of community policing in Chapter 11.

❖ Police and the Media

No discussion of police operations would be complete without considering the media. The media play a very important role in shaping the public's attitudes and images of the police and the relations between the police and the community. According to the National Institute of Justice (2009), "episodes where police engage in excessive use of force have been well publicized in the media. Television shows regularly portray excessive use of force. Widespread media attention to these events unfortunately conveys the impression that rates of use of force, or excessive use of force, are much higher than what actually occurs" (p. 1). And as Walker (2008) stated,

> The myth of the crime fighter endures for many reasons. The entertainment media play a major role in popularizing it. Movies and television police shows feature crime-related stories because they offer drama, fast-paced action, and violence.... The news media are equally guilty of overemphasizing police crime fighting. ... A serious crime is a newsworthy event. There is a victim who engages our sympathies, a story, and then an arrest that offers dramatic visuals of a suspect in custody. A typical night's work for a patrol officer, by way of contrast, does not offer much in the way of dramatic news. (pp. 4–6)

For most people not directly involved in crime events, the images and impressions of the participants in police encounters, of the issues involved, and of police procedures are shaped by the media. Because press, radio, and television to some degree select the events, the people, and the issues to be covered, and because these are the principal sources of information about what is happening in a community or in the nation as a whole, the media are recognized as very powerful forces. They reach large numbers of people on a regular, frequent, and continuing basis, and no police department can long maintain a favorable image without their support (Cox & Fitzgerald, 1996, p. 65).

The media affect and sometimes determine police community relations. As an example, Miller, Davis, Henderson, Markovic, and Ortiz (2004) concluded that "police officers and their supervisors know that news coverage about a citizen's negative encounter with the police, particularly coverage that erupts to the level of a public scandal, can quickly destroy their efforts to nurture a positive relationship with the public" (p. 5). An excellent example of the power of the media was the attention given to racial profiling by the police. Hundreds if not thousands of newspaper articles, Internet sites, and interviews on television have built a library of anecdotal information concerning police persecution of minority (racial and ethnic) drivers. Yet at least one observer challenged this anecdotal information, claiming that if crime statistics implicate disproportionate rates of crime among minorities, overrepresentation of minorities in traffic stops is to be expected, whether or not race and ethnicity are overriding factors. According to MacDonald (2001), one way to make sure that nasty confrontations with the facts about crime don't happen again is to stop publishing those facts. "New Jersey State Police no longer distribute a typical felony-offender profile to their officers because such profiles may contribute, in the attorney general's words, to 'inappropriate stereotypes' about criminals. Never mind that in law enforcement, with its deadly risk, more information is always better than less" (p. 25).

The media and the police have experienced major changes due to "three separate but intersecting phenomena: the introduction of community policing, the evolving economics of the media industry, and the explosion of communications and information technology" (Braunstein, 2007, p. 1). The demands for transparency in police organizations in light of increasing public scrutiny and the shift to community policing gave added significance to the role of the media in relation to law enforcement (Braunstein, 2007). Furthermore, in the past, reporters often developed police stories and printed the results in a newspaper or released the information on local radio or television stations. However, today with satellite, cable, and Internet breaking news, the media involves an ever growing number of diverse information outlets. For example, according to Braunstein (2007), a video of an alleged incident of police brutality can be captured on a cell phone and released on the Internet moments after the activity occurs. And in many cases, videos such as these can be viewed by a large segment of the population before the police chief is even aware of the incident.

It may be useful to distinguish between two different functions of the media in their coverage of police–community conflicts. On one hand, when covering the police in action, the media have a responsibility to the community they serve: to observe with as much objectivity and to report with as much neutrality as possible. To fulfill this responsibility, the media actively seek to discover what is going on and why and then to inform their readers, viewers, and listeners about their observations. In this aspect of their role, the media may provide background information, including providing an opportunity for those involved to explain their positions, air their

❖ **Photo 6.3** The department's media spokesperson debriefs reporters on a recent, critical incident.

views, and account for their behavior. It is essential that the police are aware of this aspect of the media's role. When appropriate, a department spokesperson should be available to furnish information about the role, obligations, and conduct of the police in the situations being discussed. On the other hand, those involved in disputes with the police, being fully aware of the power of the media to shape public opinion, may view reporters as forces to be manipulated to their own ends. In this phase, the media become the objects of other people's actions. In certain cases, groups deliberately stage events in order to attract the attention of the press or television cameras. In some of these instances, calculated attempts are made to provoke extreme, inappropriate responses from the police in order to undermine their reputation and authority. In this way, groups may seek to engage the sympathy of media audiences for themselves and for the cause they espouse. When the police are deceived by such provocations and respond by using excessive force, these reactions seriously impair police–community relations. In addition, there is the physical harm inflicted on those who are objects of such treatment. Pictures of uniformed officers wielding Tasers on crouched or prone civilians are vivid in the memories of many American citizens. It is precisely when the temptation is greatest for the police officer to retaliate in a very personal, violent way that it is essential to respond with the minimum necessary force. This is characteristic of a well-trained and disciplined professional police officer.

The police should regard difficult situations as valuable opportunities to demonstrate their ability to keep their cool and to function well under stressful conditions. They should take advantage of such opportunities to display the professional care and skill with which they discharge their obligations. Thus, they can keep the public informed about police behavior during such events. This has not always, of course, been the case, and the relationship between the media and the police has often been antagonistic. To avoid embarrassment to the department, police officials are sometimes reluctant to have certain matters reported to the general public. This reluctance may conflict with media representatives' responsibilities to keep the public informed. On numerous occasions, police resist dissemination of information that threatens investigations, creates a level of fear, or endangers the public (Greene, 2006). But as "police organizations moved from a paramilitary organizational structure toward a more open community service orientation, they began to understand the value of the media as an important resource" (Greene, 2006, p. 778).

Of course the media, too, may make the relationship more difficult by reporting inappropriate information gleaned from questionable sources within or without the department. And the media can be fickle. What is news one day is not the next day, and editorial opinion often fluctuates. For example, for 18 months in 1999 and 2000, the New York media waged war on the New York Police Department (NYPD), characterizing its members as racist and brutal. Then, when the Puerto Rican Day Parade in June 2000 deteriorated into a situation in which dozens of women were fondled, stripped, and robbed, the New York media opportunistically chastised the NYPD for being too soft on crime and unassertive. MacDonald (2000) argued that the media's prior campaign was in part to blame for the police failure to take aggressive action and that the media's response to the attacks on women showed the partisan nature of media coverage.

Former commissioner of the London Police Department, Sir Robert Mark (1977) put it in these terms:

> We had always adhered to the principle 'Tell them [the media] only what you must.' After consultation with most of the principle editors in London, we reversed this to 'Withhold only what you must' and we delegated to station level the authority to disclose matters of fact not subject to judicial privacy or policies within the sphere of the home office. (pp. 50–51)

Playing things too close to the vest only exacerbates images of secrecy and self-protection among police personnel (Cox & Fitzgerald, 1996, p. 67). The media can and should be viewed as police allies, rather than as critics of policing. The primary goal of the media is to observe life conditions and objectively report these events to the public. The positive influence of the media is often overlooked by the police because of the perceived adversarial nature of their relationship. Media attention is a powerful tool, and a continuing relationship with media representatives (e.g., phone calls, personal visits) will establish a pattern of repeated coverage. Not all coverage will be completely sympathetic to the police cause, but establishing a solid professional relationship will create a foundation of honesty and mutual respect (Scaramella & Newman, 1999).

Media Relations Programs

That the media quickly pick up on any negative behavior on behalf of the police is widely known. Corruption, brutality, discrimination, and other forms of misconduct are frequently lead topics on television, radio, and Internet news as well as in the headlines of newspapers. Prime time television shows also frequently develop plots based on such negative behavior shortly after the behavior is revealed to the public. Staszak (2001) stated, "The overwhelming search for news should warn law enforcement that the media will get their story one way or another" (p. 11). Convincing the media to cover routine or positive encounters between the police and other citizens in order to provide balanced coverage is the task before the police. To accomplish this task, police administrators need to develop and implement media relations programs. For most police administrators, police–media relations are the most important aspect of the police department's community outreach program (Greene, 2006).

A **media relations policy** based on the public's right to know about the workings of government agencies (with certain important exceptions) and the media's obligation to keep the public informed is important to every police agency. Although various state laws and departmental policies restrict the release of certain information by the police (e.g., information concerning ongoing or anticipated investigations), police personnel should be willing to explain why such information is withheld. The goal of police departments is to develop a cooperative relationship with the media in which information may be provided that does not hamper police operations or violate constitutional rights.

Some police agencies appoint a **public information officer** (PIO) to represent the agency in all contacts with the media. This officer typically reports directly to the chief and is responsible for informing and educating the public on matters of public safety. The chief of police also is typically available to address issues of mutual concern, to release information concerning the department, and to provide news releases concerning major crimes and investigations. Funneling all information through these two individuals is done to avoid the confusion that sometimes results from having several different individuals provide information. With the explosion of different types of media discussed earlier, PIOs are finding the release of information to the public to be more challenging. According to Braunstein (2007), newspaper websites are among the most popular news sites and are fairly easy for police information officers to access.

During a typical shift, a police officer encounters numerous routine, repetitive events that are not newsworthy. However, "the odd call about an alligator in a swimming pool, the vulture that flew into a resident's open living room window, or the deeds of the community's unsung hero are the stories that the media really want" (Morley & Jacobson, 2007, p. 3). A PIO should consider distributing accounts of these incidents to build a relationship with the media and to illustrate the problem-oriented policing principles that are in place at the department.

One context in which the media are especially significant is in their treatment of encounters between the police and protestors. Heavy media coverage can help transform a neighborhood disturbance or protest into a citywide or national phenomenon and, in the process, escalate a local neighborhood issue into a citywide crisis. Decisions by media executives not to cover or to discontinue coverage of a demonstration severely restrict the extent to which others may become aware of or involved in the event, and they raise serious questions about the proper role of the press in society.

In the final analysis, in spite of accusations of bias in coverage and the potential for abusing the public's trust, the presence of the media in the various arenas of community conflict appears to be in the best interests of both the police and the public. Besides functioning as reporters of community events, the fact that media observers are present, that they have the ability to communicate their observations quickly to many others, tends to discourage extreme behavior in all parties to a conflict in most circumstances. Furthermore, in a democracy, exposure to public scrutiny is a salutary experience for all-powerful forces, including the police.

❖ Chapter Summary

The responsibilities of police have expanded over the last decade. The operations and functions of a police agency are varied and depend largely on factors such as the size of the populations they serve and the organizational structure they utilize to perform their functions. As a result, most police administrators now assess the number and allocation of police personnel on a continuing basis. The duties of police officers range from animal complaint calls and thefts of bicycles to burglary and murder investigations.

The purpose and effects of patrol techniques have been challenged from time to time. Patrol techniques prior to the community policing era focused on rapid response time to calls for service and the deterrent effect on crime of marked police cars randomly patrolling the community. Key studies such as the Kansas City Preventive Patrol experiment identified significant flaws associated with this strategy. Today, police utilize a variety of strategies, including directed patrol, hot spot policing, differential response, saturation patrol and crackdowns, and CompStat. Evaluation of these strategies has shown mixed results.

The evaluation of police performance and media relations are important issues. Performance evaluation criteria should be consistent with the mission and goals of the organization. Finally, it is important that police agencies maintain positive relationships with the media.

YOU DECIDE 6.1

In Peoria, IL arrested prostitutes and their clients names and faces are posted on the city's web site. The Peoria Police Department is planning to launch a new web site with names and photographs of individuals "arrested at drug houses during police raids."

The police hope the publicity on the web site will curb prostitution, drug users and dealers by "embarrassing offenders and discouraging others from committing these crimes."

This issue has developed some controversy since some believe the practice of displaying photographs and personal information about prostitutes and drug users and dealers will provide publicity to the offenders and could cause "undue harm."

1. Should police be allowed to post names and photographs on web site of persons arrested for victimless crimes?

2. What should be done if the person arrested for prostitution is eventually found not guilty?

3. Do you believe the website posting of names and photographs of those arrested for prostitution on prevents crime? Explain.

Source: "Drug Raid Offenders May Get on the Web-Peoria Police Department Expected to Launch Web Site Displaying Names and Faces," by F. Radosevich, 2008, *The Peoria Journal Star,* p. A1.

❖ Key Terms

order maintenance

broken windows theory

forensic science

CSI Effect

watchman style

legalistic style

service style

enforcer

idealist

realists

optimists

intuitive approach

comparative approach

workload analysis

Allocation Model
for Police Personnel

deployment models

foot patrol

bicycle patrol

911 policing

Kansas City
preventative patrol experiment

random preventative patrol

performance measures

media relations policy

public information officer

❖ Discussion Questions

1. Discuss the functions of today's police.

2. Describe the investigative function of today's police.

3. Describe Wilson's three styles of policing.

4. What are the expected outcomes of police patrol?

5. Is random police patrol an effective technique?

6. Describe the methods for determining the appropriate number of police personnel. Discuss the strengths and weaknesses of each method.

7. Discuss the factors used in the allocation of police personnel.

8. Describe the various forms of police patrol.

9. Compare and contrast the relationship between the strategies of directed patrol, differential response, and saturation patrol and crackdowns.

10. How can we best evaluate police performance?

11. Why are police media relations so important to the police? The public?

❖ Internet Exercises

1. Go to the Internet and locate a media policy for a police department. What types and forms of information can be released to the media? Who is in charge of releasing this information?

2. Select one of the police innovations discussed in the chapter (hot spots, directed patrol, third party policing, etc.). Go to the Internet and find information about this innovation. How is this innovation evaluated? What has been its effectiveness in relation to crime prevention or crime reduction?

Police Organization and Administration

An Overview

CHAPTER LEARNING OBJECTIVES

- Identify various tasks that must be performed by organizational administrators.
- Identify the variables that influence the organizational structure of a police agency.
- Describe the principles that influence "pyramid" organizations.
- Differentiate between line and staff personnel.
- Highlight at least three examples of both the operational and administrative functions of organizational divisions.
- Identify advantages and disadvantages associated with both the bureaucratic or paramilitary design.
- Expound on the factors most likely to influence organizational models in the future.
- Expound on the factors that are crucial in determining the criteria for promotion to leadership positions.
- Identify the pros and cons of collective bargaining in police organizations.
- Explain why policing is or is not considered to be a profession.
- Describe the purported advantages of accreditation in the field of policing.

In order to perform the functions discussed in Chapter 1, the police have developed a variety of organizational structures. Organizations are among the more rational, efficient forms of grouping people, they have existed in one form or another for centuries, and the best of them are both effective and efficient. Effective organizations accomplish their goals, while efficient organizations make optimum use of resources.

One way of looking at **organizations** is to view them as arenas in which tasks are performed. The dynamic nature of organizations can easily be seen in a comparison with a sports arena in which the major focus of attention is on the playing field, in which people are constantly changing positions (entering and leaving), in which some spectators and participants are happy while others are unhappy, and in which a large number of secondary activities are occurring at any given time (concession stand sales, souvenir sales, business conversations, etc.). All of these activities in the arena (organization) require planning, organizing, staffing, directing, and controlling, and these activities are performed in varying degrees by personnel occupying positions at different levels within the organization. Such is the case with police organizations.

Early in the 20th century, police management adopted practices suggested by Luther Gulick's (1937) research, which indicated that seven tasks must be performed by organization administrators. The acronym **POSDCoRB** stands for these tasks, which include the following:

- **P**lanning—a broad outline of what the organization needs to accomplish
- **O**rganizing—establishment of a formal structure for the purpose of accomplishing the organization's mission
- **S**taffing—the personnel functions, including recruitment, selection, and training of employees
- **D**irecting—the decision-making process involving the development of rules, policies, and procedures
- **Co**ordinating—a process of ensuring that groups work together toward a common mission
- **R**eporting—record keeping and communication process
- **B**udgeting—fiscal planning and management of organization resources

Planning and organizing typically involve more consideration by upper level managers, while managers at lower levels likely spend more time directing and coordinating everyday activities. In terms of police organizations, for example, the chief of police and his or her immediate staff are likely to be involved in budgeting and policy making, while shift and field supervisors are more concerned with day-to-day operations (directing and controlling personnel). Nonetheless, personnel at all ranks in an organization perform all of these functions from time to time. In other words, a police sergeant and police captain both engage in some level of planning, but the captain typically performs more planning, and plans on a different scale, than the sergeant (Schroeder & Lombardo, 2004). The chief of a small police agency must perform all the tasks associated with planning, coordinating, reporting, and directly supervising employees. Recognizing these facts, we can analyze organizations in terms of the tasks (functions) they perform, keeping in mind that organizations are in a constant state of change brought about by both internal (e.g., number, quality, dedication of personnel) and external (e.g., legal, political, financial) factors.

❖ Organizational Structures

The types of functions police officers perform depend to a considerable extent on the type of organization in which they are employed and the position they occupy within the organization. The organizational structures of police departments vary considerably depending on the style of policing involved, the size of the community and the police force, the resources available, and so on, and these variables are, of course, interdependent. Organizational structures range from the small, single-person department in which the chief of police performs all functions related to policing to those involving thousands of police personnel and dozens of specializations. The largest police departments exhibit staggering variety in the way they are organized. Some have 4 or 5 rank levels, whereas others have 10 to 12 different ranks (Maguire, 2003). In addition, certain police departments operate from one headquarters, whereas others have many different substations and storefront stations. The way in which these organizations are structured helps to determine productivity, the manner in which goals are achieved, and the influence of individual variations on the organization. Police organizations exist in certain contexts— they possess different histories and traditions, exist in variety of sizes, and approach policing in many different ways (Maguire, 2003, p. 5). Recognizing the uniqueness of police organizations makes the study of these organizations both interesting and challenging.

❖ Police Hierarchy and the Pyramid

Through the years, police leaders have explored a variety of organizational structures, but most police organizations are accurately described as **hierarchies**. Most hierarchical organizational charts resemble pyramids, as illustrated in Figure 7.1, with numerous employees at the bottom of the pyramid and few management personnel at the top. There are three important characteristics of a pyramid structure. First, a pyramid organization is based on the principle of **unity of command**, which specifies that every member of the organization, except the CEO (Chief Executive Officer), should have a single immediate superior (Sawada, 2008). Thus, patrol officers in a police agency are typically responsible to a field supervisor (e.g., a sergeant), the field supervisor is typically responsible to a shift administrator (e.g., lieutenant), who is responsible to a division commander, and so on.

The second characteristic of a pyramid organization is **rank structure**. This rank structure, or chain of command, identifies who communicates with and gives orders to whom and clearly and precisely identifies lines of authority (Regoli & Hewitt, 2007). The complexity of the chain of command and the number of ranks depends in part on the size of the police department. Small departments tend to have fewer ranks and oftentimes operate informally, but they still have a chain of command. In almost all cases, the chain of command and rank structure in a police department is indicated by different colors of uniforms or caps, different brass accessories, or different types of striping on the uniforms.

The chain of command of a police organization may be confusing because it often involves multiple hierarchies, such as an authority hierarchy and a status hierarchy (King, 2005, p. 98.). For example, a police commander with 15 years of experience holds a higher rank in the department than a shift sergeant with 25 years of experience. However, in the seniority hierarchy, the sergeant occupies a higher position than the police commander.

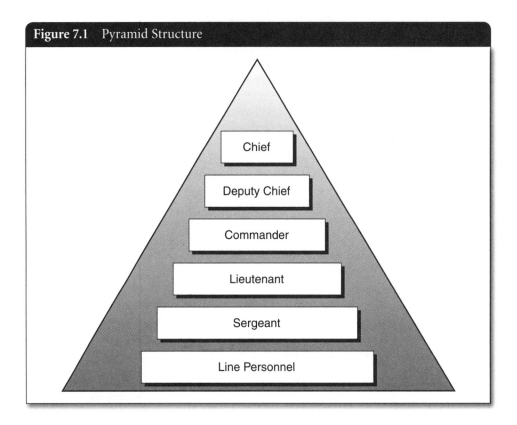

Figure 7.1 Pyramid Structure

The final important characteristic of a pyramid structure is the **span of control,** or the ratio of supervisors to subordinates. The span of control differs from one rank layer in the hierarchy to the next, and the ratio of supervisors to police officers is usually smaller near the top of the departmental hierarchy compared to the bottom (King, 2005).

Pyramid organizational structures tend to suffer from a variety of communications problems. Communications that travel up and down the hierarchy may be distorted or lost. In order to overcome some of these communication problems in emergency situations, police executives developed **Incident Command Systems** (ICS) to achieve effective coordination of police personnel, insure appropriate allocation of resources, and allow emergency responders to adopt an integrated organizational structure equal to the demands of any single incident or multiple incidents without being hindered by jurisdictional boundaries (U.S. Department of Labor, 2009).

Organizations with numerous levels of administration, present a number of problems to personnel. Top administrators communicate explicit orders and directives downward, but there are few provisions for upward communications from lower ranks or for communications outside the organization. Note that the pyramid structure in Figure 7.1 concerns the police department only and does not show that the department is accountable to a mayor, city manager or commissioner, and the community.

AROUND THE WORLD

Part of the development of Iraqi police and Iraqi police departments focused on infrastructure and organizational effectiveness, which is very important to the long-term evolvement of the police force. The United States police transition team trained new recruits on police operations and integration into the community. Trainers realized these organizations could not be developed in a vacuum, but must work closely with the entire Iraqi security structure.

The coalition also initiated an aggressive recruitment initiative to place more police officers on the streets of Baghdad. In many cases this involved recruiting the police officers from their own communities to avoid cultural clashes.

In order to overcome the prior problems of corruption, the coalition encouraged the involvement of community leaders to identify the needs of the community. Iraqi citizens now seek assistance or make complaints at the police department, and many are assisting the local Iraqi police.

Source: "Coalition Focuses on Iraqi Police Infrastructure, Organization," by S. Moore, 2007, *American Forces Press Service*. Retrieved from http://www.defenselink.mil/news/newsarticle .aspx?id=48345

The base of the police hierarchy or pyramid consists of those who do the actual police work in the organization: **line personnel**, such as patrol officers and investigators. In most organizations, positions in the hierarchy dictate the level of responsibility of the person occupying the rank. Thus, chief executives have greater responsibility than middle managers, who have greater responsibility than lower level employees. However, in policing, the status of police officers is inversely proportional to their responsibilities (Bayley, 1994, p. 72). In other words, police officers on the street have more policing responsibilities than administrators but occupy lower ranking positions.

The Paramilitary Structure

Early police organizations developed a close relationship with the public and were focused on resolving problems. The police organizational structure during this time (prior to 1900) was very informal, and the police were characterized by a lack of accountability, training, and supervision. With the power and authority accorded the police, accusations of graft, corruption, abuse of authority, and other violations were perhaps inevitable—especially since local politicians controlled, promoted, and hired the police. Police administrators needed to distance officers from the public in an effort to minimize corruption and also wanted to achieve increasing levels of efficiency in their operations (Jones, 2008). Thus, during the professional era (1950–1980) an emphasis was placed on centralization and control of the police. The resulting organizational structure resembled that of the military because of its focus on accountability and rigidity in structure (Kerilikowske, 2004). One result was unyielding top-down structures that employed strict control measures in an attempt to more closely monitor line officers (Jones, 2008). Under the paramilitary model, police agencies focused on enforcing the law and fighting crime rather than attempting to solve community and citizen problems. The intent of the structure was to improve the efficiency of operations, provide fast responses to emergency situations, use "retrospective criminal investigation to achieve organizational objectives" (Engelson, 1999, p. 64), and to attempt to ensure the fair and impartial enforcement of the law. As a result of the focus on centralized control, accountability, and rigidity, the classical principles of management through a paramilitary structure became rooted in policing. The typical characteristics associated with this paramilitary model include the following:

- Central command structure
- Rigid differences among ranks
- Terminology similar to that of the military
- Frequent use of commands and orders
- Strong enforcement of rules, regulations, and discipline
- Discouragement of individual creativity
- Resistance of system to change (LaGrange, 1998, p. 318)

As noted previously, these organizational structures often fail to promote communication horizontally and from the bottom up, and they frequently fail to encourage employee commitment through participation. In fact, Roberg, Novak, and Cordner (2009, p. 100) noted that the nature of the police role is quite different from the expectations associated with the paramilitary design. They discovered that strict rules and orders are rarely required due to the nature of the work and the fact that police are on the street out of view of supervisors. Furthermore, "if the job is to be performed properly, a great amount of initiative and discretion are required" (p.100). To be sure, there are times in policing and in the military when a highly centralized, authoritarian command structure is an advantage. There is little time to call a committee meeting to decide what to do when riotous protesters are threatening the police station or when police officers respond to a 911 armed robbery in progress call. But as officers become increasingly well educated and trained, the demand for explanations of, and participation in, decision making in less trying circumstances increases as well. Partially as a response to the inflexibility of the paramilitary organizational structure, informal arrangements often arise among various divisions and individuals, which speed up organizational procedures or impede such procedures. Thus, a police lieutenant who desires to change the activities of his or her shift personnel may not go to the patrol commander, who would then have to approach the assistant chief, who would finally seek the chief's approval. Instead, the lieutenant might see the chief after duty or even discuss the issue with an alderman to gain support. Similarly, individual patrol officers and detectives may meet informally to discuss a case and share intelligence information that their immediate supervisor may not wish to share as a result of internal rivalries (Cox & McCamey, 2008, p. 156). It is important that we consider the formal and the informal arrangements that characterize all police agencies.

Many police organizations have adopted the paramilitary model in highly specialized police units, called **police paramilitary units** or PPUs (Roberg, Crank, & Kuykendall, 2000, p. 118). PPUs include such units as SWAT (special weapons and tactics), SRTs (special response teams), and ERUs (emergency response units). Well before September 11, 2001, police departments were adopting and adapting military tactics in patrol operations and in their response to and management of crime (Hodgson & Orban, 2005, p. 7) In the aftermath of Al Qaeda's attack, paramilitary policing increased faster than at any other time in history (Muzzatti, 2005). However, most police work is not of this nature. In fact, many are concerned that a terrorist-oriented mission will accelerate the militarization of police, rather than bring the police closer to the community (Mastrofski, 2006, p. 64). There is minimal research into the effects of the paramilitary model on police operations; however, Peak (1997, 2008) found that the quasi-military organizational structure places restrictions on personal freedoms, is characterized by communications blockages, and demonstrates a lack of flexibility and a narrowness of job descriptions. The authoritarian paramilitary command structure was inadequate in the latter parts of the 20th century and has become even more problematic when applied to the 21st century demands and expectations of a community (Hodgson & Orban, 2005). It is not surprising then, that there are currently a number of different designs for police departments. We begin by examining three of them: functional design, place design, and time design.

Functional Design

A **functional organizational design** involves the creation of positions and departments on the basis of specialized activities (Hellriegel & Slocum, 2008). The functional design is one of the most widely used methods of organizing police agencies and involves identifying and consolidating common tasks (functions) and areas of work. The functional method of organizing is based on a consideration of the tasks performed by all police departments, but it recognizes differences based on size. In large departments, it can be efficient and cost effective to establish a specific unit for a specific task. For example, in a very large department, the operations function could be divided into patrol, traffic, burglary, narcotics, juvenile, vice, and many other specialized areas. One advantage to this type of organization is that responsibility and accountability for the completion of work is clearly understood by employees assigned to each unit. A disadvantage is that the functional method fosters a limited point of view in which employees often lose sight of the functions of the organization as a whole (Hellriegel & Slocum, 2011). In addition, the functional organization design has minimal application to small police departments, in which officers are expected to possess multiple skills and broad knowledge concerning the police role. For example, in one incident, a small-town officer may be handling a traffic problem, in the next, a juvenile issue, and then the officer may be called on to handle a major burglary, which requires crime scene search skills (Turner, 2000, p. 50).

Realizing that no one officer can readily accumulate all the sophisticated skills associated with all of the functions performed by police officers, numerous small departments have developed alternatives. Many agencies have begun to contract for specialized services with other law enforcement agencies, created mutual aid agreements, or consolidated services in regional crime laboratories (Turner, 2000, p. 50).

Departments with a sufficient number of personnel tend to organize by function by creating at least two divisions with distinct, if somewhat overlapping, responsibilities. These divisions are Operations and Administrative/Staff Services. Each of these typically includes several subdivisions, and as the number of subdivisions grows, problems with coordinating the functions of the various subdivisions arise.

❖ Operations Division

The **operations division** is usually the largest division, in terms of number of personnel and other resources, and it typically consists of patrol officers and investigators.

Patrol

Patrol operations have long been regarded as the backbone of the police organization. Patrol is typically the largest division in a police department, with as many as 6 of every 10 officers assigned to patrol duties (Stevens, 2008, p. 140). However, the proportion of police officers responding to 911 calls ranges from 6 in 10 among departments serving 100,000 or more residents and to about 9 in 10 in police departments serving less than 100,000 residents. The patrol division is responsible for providing continuous police service and some degree of visibility. In the past, patrol operations were assumed to deter crime, and many police administrators still believe that patrol serves a deterrent function and enhances citizen satisfaction. In spite of the fact that a number of patrol studies suggest that routine patrol does not perform either of these functions (Kelling Pate, Dieckman, & Brown, 1974; Lavery, 2008; Skolnick & Bayley, 1986; Toch & Grant, 1991), many police administrators continue to operate as if it did. Lavery (2008) put it like this:

> As a police officer if you get into your cruiser after roll-call and then drive out toward your pre-assigned patrol district to roam the streets looking for trouble and waiting for a service call then you are wrong. Additionally, I would argue, you are wasting your time, and the taxpayers' hard earned money, by driving in circles burning fuel. You are, as a protector of your community, ineffective. Actually, if you sat on-station during your entire tour, and never entered your patrol car until receiving a call, then really you are more effective than working the 'preventative patrol' function, because at least you are saving money on gas and vehicle wear-and-tear. Why am I saying this? Law enforcement research has been telling police executives this same information for years (in some cases over three decades), but your boss is not listening. (p. 1)

An increasing number of police administrators, recognizing that routine patrol may not pay good dividends, are experimenting with other types of patrol (discussed in Chapters 6 and 11) This is not to say that patrol officers have no impact on other citizens. Patrol officers respond to calls for service in their zones, beats, or districts, and they patrol the streets in their assigned areas when they are not responding to calls or completing the reports that inevitably accompany calls for service. The majority of patrol work is reactive, although patrol officers do occasionally come upon a crime in progress. They also often use patrol to initiate contact based on traffic violations, and patrol officers are generally responsible for securing crime scenes and conducting preliminary investigations as first responders.

Once a crime scene has been secured, patrol officers often turn further responsibilities over to the investigative or detective division, although in some departments, patrol officers maintain responsibility for such investigations. In addition to their involvement in crime control, patrol officers are also responsible, in smaller departments, for traffic control and investigating traffic accidents. Larger departments are likely to have separate traffic and accident investigation units within the operations division. In some departments, watercraft, aircraft, bicycle, and canine-assisted patrols are employed, and in others, civilian volunteers are used to patrol specific areas under the supervision of police officers.

☞ CASE IN POINT 7.1

The Peoria, IL Police Department deployed refurbished Brinks trucks or nuisance property surveillance vehicles in response to citizen complaints from blighted areas. The vehicles have been named "Armadillo".

The specially designed truck is parked in specific locations and is intended to annoy residents that disturb neighbors. It is outfitted with vedio cameras to record outside activity, an impenetrable exterior, tires filled with foam and locks and guards over headlights, gas tank and the hood.

The truck visits properties that have been deemed a "chronic-problem" because of various quality-of-life violations and could be located anywhere in the city.

Source: Fark, L. (2009, January 20). City will deploy 'Armadillo 2' this summer. . . . *Journal star*, B2.

Investigations

The investigations bureau is a subdivision of the operations division and is basically responsible for obtaining and processing evidence and making arrests based on such evidence. The evidence involved may be tangible (physical evidence collected at a crime scene or at the residence of a suspect) or intangible (accounts from witnesses or informants). While this division is often regarded as the "glamour division" because it is thought to involve "real" police work, the evidence indicates that investigators are not particularly likely to solve crimes unless a witness steps forward to identify the offender (Greenwood, Chaiken, & Petersilia, 1977).

Nonetheless, investigators spend a good deal of time sketching crime scenes; locating, interviewing and interrogating suspects and witnesses; and sifting through records and reports. Crime scene investigators are involved in photographing, collecting and analyzing fingerprints, and processing other materials that may contain leads relevant to specific crimes. Once evidence has been obtained, investigators are responsible for establishing a custody chain that governs storage, transmission, and protection of the evidence. Case preparation and testifying in court are additional responsibilities of investigators, who are also responsible for conducting undercover operations and developing informants (though many patrol officers also have informants), often in connection with investigations related to vice or drugs.

POLICE STORIES

Research has revealed that criminal investigators spend much of their time testifying in court at preliminary hearings, trials, and evidentiary hearings. Most investigators prepare for testifying in their first case by observing other investigators testify or by participating in role-playing exercises.

Investigators are told to visit the courtroom where the trial or hearing will occur to become familiar with the location of the clerk, judge, court reporter,

(Continued)

(Continued)

jury, prosecutor, and most important, the location from which they will testify. In other words, first impressions are very important when the investigator initially enters the court room and answers "I Do" to the oath.

The first case in which I testified involved a reckless homicide that resulted from a serious vehicle accident. Other investigators told me about maintaining eye contact with the jury, sitting erect, and trying not to look nervous. One piece of advice they emphasized was to always pause before giving an answer. In other words, don't blurt something out you might have to retract later, don't let the defense attorney try to trick you, and collect your thoughts before you respond to a question from the prosecutor or defense attorney.

On the day of the trial, I entered the court room, took my seat, and made eye contact with the jury. At this point, I felt this was not going to be as terrible as I had imagined. The assistant state's attorney asked me to "state my name and spell my last name." I took a long pause and clearly stated my name. He next asked me "What agency do you work for?" I took another rather long pause and responded, but noted some stress, odd facial expression, and look of frustration at this point by the prosecutor. Needless to say, after I got past these two questions, the remainder of the testimony in the case went well.

Juvenile or youth officers are frequently found in the investigations bureau as well. Among these officers are specialists in gang intelligence, physical and sexual abuse of children, and crime prevention among youth. Others specialize as school liaisons or resource officers and serve as counselors, facilitators, and coordinators for youth and as representatives of other service agencies and schools. Included in this latter category are DARE (Drug Abuse Resistance Education) officers who teach in the school system. In an increasing number of states, youth officers must be specially trained or certified because they deal with laws relating to juvenile or family court acts, which are often considerably different from criminal statutes in terms of procedural requirements.

❖ Administrative or Staff Services Division

The other division commonly found in a police department is the **administrative division** or **staff services division**. Primary functions of this division include record keeping, communication, research and planning, training and education, and often logistics. While many of these functions are performed by sworn officers, there is a trend toward the employment of civilian personnel to perform a majority of the staff services tasks. The administrative services division may include several subdivisions (Thibault, Lynch, & McBride, 2007):

- Personnel
- Research and planning
- Budgeting
- Data collection/crime analysis/computer section

- Training
- Counseling services
- Maintenance
- Communications/records
- Civilian employees
- Legal advisors
- Internal affairs

Personnel employed in this division are often specialists, as you can see from the preceding list. They are not typically in the chain of command, although the rank structure in the division may be the same as in other divisions. These staff personnel provide information and advice to the chief and other supervisors concerning a wide variety of topics and process the mass of information that is characteristic of police organizations.

A typical functional design organizational chart for a small police department would look something like the one shown in Figure 7.2. In larger police organizations, the number of specializations within each division increases, leading to an organizational structure such as the one shown in Figure 7.3. In departments of the size and complexity illustrated in Figure 7.3, officers may not even know all the officers who work on their shifts or in their divisions. Further, only designated officers may be permitted to handle cases in their specialization. That is, an officer working in burglary may not handle a robbery or some other type of theft. Officers may become so specialized that they handle only one particular type of crime (e.g., computer theft). Patrol personnel may be limited by departmental policy as to their involvement in investigations, in part because they lack the specialized training required to handle certain types of investigations.

As indicated in the organizational charts shown in Figures 7.2 and 7.3, police departments employ both sworn and nonsworn (civilian) personnel. One of the major trends accompanying community policing in the past decade has been to increase the number of civilians employed. In fact, the proportion of civilians working in police agencies reached a high of 30% in 2004 (Kostelac, 2006). Civilianization has allowed police agencies to offload routine tasks from sworn police officers, fill new specialist positions such as computer technicians, and staff community policing programs, including community coordinators, domestic violence specialists, or crime prevention planners (National Institute of Justice, 2000). There are two motivations behind the addition of civilian employees to organizations traditionally staffed by sworn police personnel. The first one is financial. Civilians are paid less, have less generous retirement plans, need less equipment, and are subject to less mandatory training than sworn police personnel (Stenberg & Austin, 2007). The other motivation is to increase the diversity of police agencies. "Employment of women, minorities, older citizens, and persons with disabilities is often more logical in civilian positions than in sworn positions" (Stenberg & Austin, 2007, p. 334).

Place Design

Place design involves establishing an organization's primary units geographically while retaining significant aspects of functional design (Hellriegel & Slocum, 2008). For example, patrol divisions are responsible for all geographic areas within the limits of the municipality. The city is typically divided into beats, zones, districts, or areas, with each having coverage on 8-, 10-, or 12-hour shifts. Patrol officers perform their

Figure 7.2 Oswego Police Department

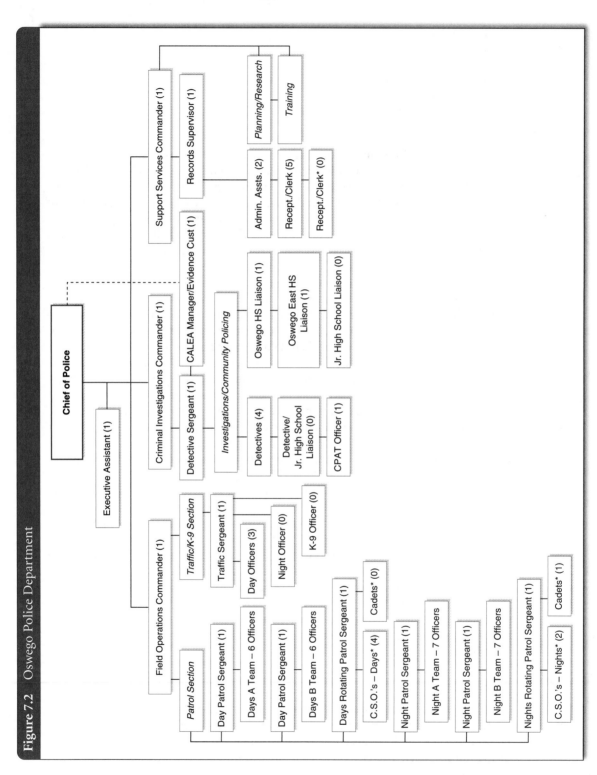

Source: Courtesy of the Oswego Police Department.

Figure 7.3 San Diego Police Department

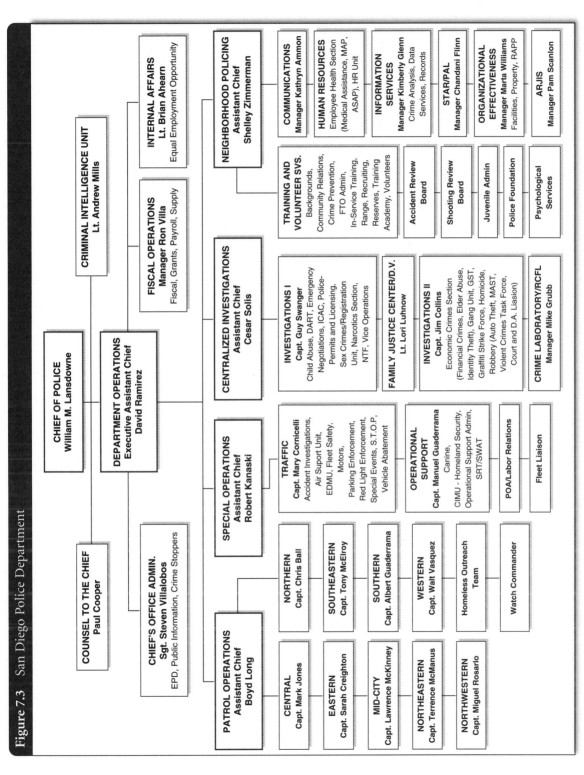

Source: Courtesy of the San Diego Police Department.

basic functions within the assigned geographic areas, but they sometimes leave the beat to assist officers in other beats. In large cities, beats may be combined to form sectors, which are administered by a sergeant or a lieutenant, or both. In the largest cities, sectors may be combined to form precincts. Precinct houses are distributed geographically, and each may be viewed, to some extent, as a separate department with ties to central headquarters. For example, the New York Police Department has 34,500 police officers, distributed among 76 police precincts, plus additional officers assigned to transit districts and housing services areas (NYPD, 2010). As with the functional design, the place design can increase coordination problems, depending on the number and location of beats, zones, districts, areas, sectors, or precincts.

Time Design

The final organization design found in police agencies involves organization by time. The patrol division may be divided into three watches, tours, or shifts to provide 24-hour coverage. The day shift often operates from 8 a.m. to 4 p.m., the afternoon or evening shift from 4 p.m. to midnight, and the night shift from midnight until 8 a.m. Some departments employ power shifts, which typically involve assigning additional personnel to cover part of the evening and part of the night shift (e.g., adding additional personnel who work from 8 p.m. until 4 a.m.).

While officers have traditionally been assigned to 8-hour shifts five days per week, with two days off, some departments schedule officers for 10-hour shifts. However, a 24-hour period requires three 10-hours shifts, creating significant overlap between the shifts (Tucker, Jordan, & Deliums, 2007, p. 3). Depending on conditions, some overlap can be useful, but much of the overlap is wasted. Other agencies divide the 24-hour required coverage into 12-hour shifts and thus require only two shifts rather than the typical three shifts. The 12-hour shift schedule results in an 84-hour schedule over a two week period, increasing the number of hours worked by police officers by 104 per year while at the same time providing an extra 26 days off (Tucker, Jordan, & Deliums, 2007, p. 4). Tucker, Jordan, and Deliums (2007, p. 4) argued that adding these additional hours means additional police officers on the street. However, Bayley (1994, p. 52) believed that in order to increase the street presence of police by one additional officer, it would be necessary to hire as many as ten additional police officers. He concluded that only "60% to 70% of all police are assigned to patrol," leaving approximately 17.5% on the street at any given moment, due to the need to cover shifts. Furthermore, Bayley (1994, p. 53) found that sick days, leave, training, administrative tasks, and numerous other activities further reduced the number of patrol officers on the street.

Future Organizational Designs

Based on limitations in the previous designs and the need for an organizational structure to be able to adapt to a changing environment, many police agencies are experimenting with more decentralized structures. The adoption of a community policing philosophy by police agencies was the catalyst for organizational change that decentralized structures and decreased formalization in police organizations (Jones, 2008, p. 4). As a result, police organizations modified the traditional paramilitary style of policing. Police agencies that adopted the community policing model became more decentralized and began to share decision making with patrol officers at lower levels of the hierarchy. Much of the literature related to community policing also called for flatter organizations, or police departments with few ranks, but this change became problematic for departments with collective bargaining contracts and was viewed as an issue that could create morale and motivation problems. Last, community policing encouraged the development of police officers as generalists to serve the diverse needs and different problems in a community instead of focusing only on crime control.

If the traits of the paramilitary model were ever conducive to effective policing, they are considerably less so with the transition to better educated, better trained officers. While some police chiefs reflect on the "good old days" when officers simply did what they were told by an officer of superior rank and seldom questioned the orders and directives they received, most realize that current conditions require officers who can think on their feet; question, understand, and explain the rationale for the directives they follow; and exercise discretion wisely. Proactive police work in contemporary society calls for organizations that achieve the following:

1. Support the exercise of initiative and discretion at all levels.

2. Exert control through the use of guidance and techniques, coaching, and counseling.

3. Are characterized by communications that flow both vertically and horizontally in both directions.

4. Use positive reinforcement as opposed to punishment to motivate personnel.

5. Promote flexibility in operations.

6. Are more decentralized.

7. Encourage decision making at the lowest possible level.

8. Emphasize participative management.

9. View change as an indicator of organizational health.

10. Develop and distribute guidelines delineating organizational expectations and evaluate personnel in terms of these guidelines (Cox & Fitzgerald, 1996; Skolnick & Bayley, 1986; Sparrow, Moore, & Kennedy, 1990; Toch & Grant, 1991).

Today, policing requires innovative organizational designs. Of course, as previously discussed, the application of these organizational design characteristics cannot be generalized to every situation. In police work, certain emergency situations demand an immediate response that can best be achieved by adhering to the paramilitary model. When such situations arise, there is often little or no time for debate. Nonetheless, debriefings following such situations afford the opportunity for input from all parties involved, and lessons that may lead to a more effective response in future similar incidents are often learned. For example, as we will discuss, CompStat has altered some aspects of the organizational structure of many departments by delegating decision making and authority to police commanders or middle managers. In the past, authority and decision making was reserved only for upper level managers or those at the top of the hierarchy.

Another example of a challenge to the traditional organization designs is the matrix structure. A **matrix structure** is based on multiple support systems and authority relationships whereby some employees report to two superiors rather than one—a clear violation of the principle of chain of command adhered to in the paramilitary structure (Hellriegel & Slocum, 2008). The formation of a drug task force is an example of a matrix organization. The drug task force has a supervisor who directs task force operations, but officers assigned to the task force (selected based on their expertise and their ability to contribute to the group) may still be required to report to the supervisors of the units or departments from which they were selected. This can cause confusion for the officers involved and can also lead to hard feelings between the supervisor of the task force and the supervisor of the unit or department. Nonetheless, because a task force assignment is often temporary, the personnel involved eventually return to their regular duties and regular supervisors after a specific length of time or after the task force has completed its goal.

Let's summarize the evolution of organizational structures in police organizations. If you recall, during the earliest political spoils era, police were generalists who maintained close contact with the citizens they served as well as with politicians (Chriss, 2007). As we discussed, the police and the public developed a close relationship, and the police were involved in providing medical care and child care, and in assisting people with all types of problems. During the professional era, police operated as specialists in crime control and distanced themselves from citizens and political influence under the paramilitary model in an attempt to eradicate the corruption and patronage abuses endemic to the previous era (Chriss, 2007). Crime continued to increase, and community policing research called for police to once again become generalists involved in solving problems and providing service to the community. Of course, the role of generalist in policing today must be developed based on changes in society and in the community. We will discuss community policing and other contemporary policing strategies in greater detail in Chapter 11.

What is the future of the police organizational structure? What role will terrorism, homeland security, and performance-based policing have in the development of future police organizational models? Jones (2008) concluded that "instituting performance-based policing models will create an attraction back to command and control organizations models that emphasize efficiency and routine work technology, rather than innovative policing methods (pp. 6–7)." And with the shift of funding from community policing toward homeland security, Lee (2007) believed police are more likely to revert to a traditional law enforcement model. Please stay tuned on the Sage website, where we will continue to explore the changes in policing organizations as they evolve.

Police Organizations in Context

It is important to note that police organizations do not exist in a vacuum, nor are police functions determined totally or even largely by the police themselves. The police always operate in a political arena under public scrutiny (though a good many try to minimize such scrutiny). The municipal police chief heads the police department, but he or she is responsible to a city manager, mayor, police commissioner, and city council. In many instances, in which city government regards the separate public service agencies as consumer oriented, chief executive officers are viewed as part of a cooperative team, with responsibilities to one another as well. Thus, the chief of police may request new equipment monies one year but defer to the fire chief the next. Further, in the vast majority of police agencies, hiring, disciplining (beyond a limited amount), termination, award of benefits, and so on, are governed not by the police chief, but by fire and police commissions or civil service merit boards. This description applies with changes in titles to county, state, and federal officers as well.

As is the case with all organizations, police departments exist in environments from which they draw resources and in which they provide services. The extent to which these resources are allocated and the manner and type of services provided are largely controlled by external sources. Finally, police departments are only one component of the criminal justice network that sets parameters within which the police must operate. The courts, for example, have indicated clearly that they are willing to intervene in police practices ranging from search and seizure, to interrogation, to hiring and promotion.

❖ Change in Police Organizations

The way in which an organization deals with change tells us a great deal about its effectiveness and efficiency. As indicated earlier, change is a given in all organizations. Personnel retire, resign, and are injured, recruited, and promoted. Resources fluctuate with the state of the economy and the political power of the organization. Realistically, police personnel must be willing to accept change as a normal part of their occupational world, and police supervisors must be prepared to administer change. Change, whether in personnel, legal requirements, technology, distribution and types of crime, or requests for service, is a challenge. Change is often resisted because we have become comfortable with the status quo. When sudden or drastic change imposed from above occurs, reactions are likely to be negative. For example, the move from a traditional reactive style of policing to community policing resulted in several challenges. Still, change can be accomplished if employees are involved in the decision-making process, are knowledgeable about the consequences of the change, and feel as though a need has been fulfilled by the change (Robbins, 2005). Similarly, when change occurs in organizations that are flexible, encourage initiative, and allow for the exercise of discretion in implementing change, the results can be favorable. The tendency among police personnel to resist change results from the fact that they operate in a reactive, paramilitary setting for the most part. As Gaines, Southerland, and Angell (1991) noted,

> Innovation is stifled in the traditional organization; members of traditional organizations tend to resist changes which challenge the old ways of operating. . . . Members of traditional organizations are also exposed to a conflicting set of expectations—one moment they must make on-the-spot life-and-death decisions, and the next they are treated like children who are not permitted to decide which uniform to wear when the weather changes. (p. 106)

As police administrators adopt less rigid, less hierarchical structures and encourage more participation on the part of personnel at all levels, the police will come to act and think in terms of change rather than to react to change as if it were a crisis.

❖ Police Leadership

The quality of leadership in police organizations varies greatly. Some organizations carefully select entry-level personnel, carefully evaluate their potential for promotion, promote based on merit, and prepare those who are to be promoted by sending them to appropriate training or educational programs. Other organizations do none of these things. Many, perhaps most, political leaders have a difficult time deciding what types of police leaders or supervisors they want. Should leadership positions be offered to personnel with exceptional communication and supervisory skills? Should positions be offered only to personnel with extensive street experience? Are policing skills or management skills more important? Answers to these questions are crucial in determining the criteria for promotion or selection to leadership positions. The issue is further complicated by the fact that, at the level of the chief at least, an understanding of city politics and the ability to cooperate as an agency representative with respect to other public service agencies sometimes conflict with expectations of agency personnel.

Field supervisors, typically holding the rank of sergeant, are selected based on years of experience (a minimum of two to three may be required in order to test for the position), performance evaluations based on patrol or investigative work, written examinations, and oral interviews. Unfortunately, neither years of service nor performance in investigative or patrol functions necessarily indicates ability to succeed as a supervisor. Mistakes made in promotions at this level are likely to be perpetuated because those promoted to the rank of shift supervisor (typically lieutenants) are generally selected from a pool of sergeants with a specified minimum level of experience. Similarly, division commanders (captains) are selected from the ranks of shift commanders based on the criteria mentioned previously. Lateral entry at any of these levels is rare, although exempt rank positions, particularly at the upper ranks, are becoming more popular. Exempt rank personnel serve at the pleasure of the chief, although they may have continued employment rights (civil service rank) if demoted from their exempt positions. Individuals occupying exempt rank positions are not always well received by other police personnel because they have jumped rank and because they sometimes come from outside of the ranks of the police.

Police Chiefs

Those occupying the position of police chief run the gamut from "good old boys" who have worked their way through the ranks of the department to become chief to those who are highly skilled, trained, or educated professional managers. While the most prevalent path to chief is the insider path, outsiders with police experience and advanced education are increasingly in demand in progressive agencies.

Most police chiefs have very little job security and are beholden to politicians for their tenure in office and must respond to external pressure (Maguire, 2003). Chiefs, in many cases, serve at the pleasure of the city council, mayor, or city manager (at state and federal levels they also serve at the pleasure of political bodies). Without job security, the ability of a chief to implement broad changes in the department is in question. Maguire indicated that the average tenure of municipal police chiefs is slightly more than 5 years, which is longer than reported in earlier research. The position of chief of police in major cities and small towns is a virtual revolving door that results in numerous expenses for local agencies, according to Rainguet and Dodge (2001) who found that health concerns, stress, politics, and personnel issues were related to the short tenures of chiefs.

❖ Police Unions, Professionalism, and Accreditation

Police Unions and Collective Bargaining

Unionization and collective bargaining in police agencies have received a good deal of attention over the past three decades, although the history of police labor disputes dates back to the 1800s. Generally speaking, public-sector unionization in the past lagged behind that of the private sector by at least 25 to 30 years. There were several reasons for this slow development in the public sector. First, the government had legal mechanisms with which to squelch labor movements that were not available to the private sector (Holden, 2000). Second, public opinion opposed strikes by police and firefighters, whose duties were to protect people and property. Thus, unionization of police personnel did not become an issue of major importance until the 1960s and 1970s, at which time the increasing complexity of policing was recognized and police officers demanded compensation commensurate with the task and more comparable to that of the private sector (Sapp, 1985). Today, the membership trend has reversed, and "more public sector workers in 2009 belonged to a union than private sector employees, despite there being 5 times more wage and salary workers in the private sector" (Bureau of Labor Statistics [BLS], 2010, p. 1). Unlike many other governmental occupations, there currently is no national police officer union. Although there is national recognition of the Fraternal Order of Police, Police Benevolent Associations, and Police Officers' Associations, there is no one organization recognized as the leader (Dantzker, 2005).

The unionization of police employees proceeded slowly for several reasons. Among the more important was public and legislative reaction to the Boston police strike in 1919, following which, looting, robberies, and general disorder occurred until the state guard was called in to reestablish order. Some 1,100 police officers were fired by Governor Calvin Coolidge and never regained their jobs. Some observers felt that the "impact of the Boston disaster was sufficient to force unionization of police personnel into dormancy for the next 50 years" (Thibault, Lynch, & McBride, 2007, p. 440). The perceived vulnerability of communities to criminal activities during work stoppages has resulted in a generalized rejection of police strikes by the public. Many police officers share this public rejection of any police work stoppage and view collective action as self-defeating because it may result in hostility on the part of the public, the police chief, or others in positions of power.

Most states and local governments bargain collectively with police officers. Although such negotiations affect a substantial portion of state and local budgets, they are often hidden from the public (Reitz, 2007). **Collective bargaining** consists of negotiations between an employer and a group of employees to determine the conditions of employment (Cornell University Law School, 2009). In most cases, such negotiations involve professional representatives for the state or local government and the police officers and have a goal of agreeing on wages and benefits for the police officers involved. In order to secure union representatives, police employees petition state labor boards for recognition of exclusive bargaining agents. A petition of this type is typically followed by an election, in which it is determined whether the majority of employees want union representation and, if so, which union. Those eligible to vote in police organizations differ from jurisdiction to jurisdiction but generally include those with a mutuality of job interests. Thus, rank-and-file employees are likely to be members of one union, but supervisors at different levels may belong to another union or may have separate unions of their own. Regardless of the specific union involved, it appears that police officers have joined unions in increasing numbers for numerous reasons, particularly the monetary benefits, which include salary, overtime, and fringe benefits. Little research has explored the effectiveness of collective bargaining in obtaining benefits for police officers. However, Wilson, Zhao, Ren, and Briggs (2006) concluded that large police organizations that engaged in collective bargaining offered higher minimum wages to officers during the time period of the research.

Among the major concerns of police unions in negotiating with management are salary, insurance, vacation and sick days, pensions, longevity pay, compensatory time or pay, hiring standards, assignment policies, discipline and grievance procedures, promotions, layoffs, productivity, and the procedural rights of officers. In other words, negotiations cover the entire range of working conditions, not simply the economic factors. Further, many union and management conflicts result from different perceptions of **management rights**, such as management's belief that they have the right to determine the level of and the manner in which activities are conducted, managed, and administered. Such rights often include the exclusive right to determine the mission of the department, "set standards of service," determine procedures and standards for selection and promotion, "direct employees, take disciplinary action, relieve employees from duty due to economic reasons or for cause, maintain efficiency of government operations, take all necessary action to carry out the mission in emergencies, and exercise complete control and discretion over its organization and the technology of performing work" (City of Santa Barbara, 2009, p. 5). The use of force, including the use of deadly force, is another concern for police officers and agencies. Some states, such as Illinois, prohibit collective bargaining related to the circumstances in which a police officer is permitted to use force (Sherk, 2008).

If negotiations fail to lead to an agreement, the possibility of a work stoppage exists in unionized police departments. As indicated previously, police strikes are, for the most part, prohibited by law, but police officers occasionally use **job actions** involving "blue flu," work slowdowns, or work speedups. The blue flu may from time to time affect large numbers of police officers working for the same department at the same time, creating difficulties in providing police coverage. Speedups involve writing considerably more citations than are normally written so that the public complains to the chief or city council members, who will presumably pay more attention to the desires of the officers as a result.

Traditionally, the public has been strongly opposed to the use of work stoppages by the police, and the courts have generally been willing to issue injunctions to bring them to a halt in a relatively short time. Further, many police managers, recognizing the possibility of work stoppages, have prepared contingency plans to guarantee the continuation of police services. When implemented, these plans have generally shown that a community can survive without its regular police force, and such plans have cut short police strikes, concluding them without meeting union demands.

Collective bargaining often involves an adversarial relationship between the union and management. Management offers certain incentives for the coming contract period. The union presents management with a list of the demands of its members. Management responds by stating either that it will meet those demands or that it cannot meet them. The demands of the union are supported by evidence gathered for that purpose; the response of management is typically explained using evidence gathered for that purpose. Bargaining sessions are then scheduled to attempt to convince the opposing side of the validity of the arguments presented or to reach a compromise acceptable to both parties. "Despite the fact that policing is a public-sector organization, that police unions are suppose to be quasiprofessional organizations, and that there is a prohibition against the ultimate job action (a strike), nevertheless relations frequently degenerate" (Hoover, Dowling, & Blair, 2006, p. xix). However, today many police managers and police union representatives strive to create a cooperative atmosphere during negotiations. In spite of the stereotypical perception that management and labor are constantly at odds, chiefs and union leaders surveyed agreed that their working relationship with their counterpart was for the most part positive and pleasant (Hoover et. al., 2006). In this study, 80% of police chiefs and 63% of union leaders described their working conditions as either collaborative and fully engaged or at least cooperative and friendly.

❖ **Photo 7.1** This photo depicts an arbitration hearing between collective bargaining unit representatives and members of the agency's administration.

Bargaining (negotiating) is often accomplished in good faith by representatives of both sides in an attempt to reach a reasonable solution in a reasonable period of time. The powers of the two parties are articulated in a labor relations or public employment relations act, as are the rights of the two parties, the procedures to be followed, and the scope of the negotiations. An **impasse** results when negotiations, properly conducted in terms of the applicable regulations, fail to lead to an acceptable compromise. Procedures for resolving the impasse are also found in labor relations law. Such procedures typically involve mediation or fact finding and, if these approaches fail, some form of arbitration (e.g., voluntary, binding, final offer).

As a result of an impasse or stalemate between the union and management, either side can claim an **unfair labor practice (ULP)**. A ULP (also known as an *IP* or *improper labor practice*) occurs when management does one or more of the following:

1. Interferes with, restrains, or coerces employees in regard to forming or joining a labor union.

2. Dominates or interferes with the formation or administration of a labor union.

3. Discriminates against employees for the purpose of encouraging or discouraging membership or activity in the union.

4. Refuses to negotiate in good faith with the recognized or state-certified representatives of the employee union.

5. Assigns work performed by union employees to nonunion employees. (Thibault, Lynch, & McBride, 2007, p. 452)

The final product of collective bargaining negotiations is a contract that covers specific areas of employer–employee relations and that binds both parties legally and morally to abide by its provisions during a specified time period.

What factors were responsible for the growing interest in police unions? First and, in many ways, most important was the problem of unenlightened managers. Because many police leaders came up through the ranks of paramilitary organizations, they learned how to issue orders and to expect that such orders be obeyed, often without question. Some learned the importance of listening to subordinates and explaining the reasons for orders issued, but many did not. Some felt their orders should be followed because they occupied leadership positions, rather than because their arguments made sense or because they were good leaders. Some felt that policing was a unique enterprise and that the principles and procedures that worked in other types of organizations did not apply in theirs. Others were less concerned about the well-being of their officers than about the trappings of professionalism, in the form of new technologies and hardware. Some simply became so far removed from the streets and those who policed them that their perceptions of the requirements of the occupation or profession were no longer realistic. Still others apparently felt that fraternizing with subordinates diminished their authority or importance. And to some extent, these problems continue to plague police managers and those they supervise. To the extent that such problems continue, they create environments in which union organizers are likely to be successful.

There are a number of other reasons for the increasing unionization of police personnel. In the 1960s and 1970s, union representatives began to recognize that further organizing in the private sector was likely to become increasingly difficult because of saturation and increasingly enlightened management. They realized the tremendous potential for growth in the expanding public sector and began to explore this new market. Coupled with police dissatisfaction with wages, working conditions, and level of public support, these changes resulted in a wave of union activities in police agencies. Further, the police had seen the results of well-organized, concerted action among other groups. The protests of the 1960s and early 1970s often resulted in grievances being redressed or at least looked into. If such actions could succeed elsewhere, why not among police officers?

Police managers and union members frequently compromise, with the results being beneficial to both sides. Nonetheless, police managers and union negotiators often "differ in their perceptions of their respective willingness to confer on citizen complaints, scheduling of police officers, communication channels, relations with political entities other than the city/county, and the response to racial profiling" (Delord et al., 2006, p. 96).

Police Professionalism

Police professionalism was a focal point for police reformers during much of the 20th century. However, ambiguity concerning the police role seriously hampered efforts to professionalize the police because deciding on the proper role of the police was a necessary precursor to outlining and assessing steps towards professionalism. In addition, police professionalism means different things in different places and at different times, making consensus about the requirements for a professional police force difficult to achieve. Finally, it is important to note that professionalism may refer to police organizations or to police officers, or both. Some police administrators refer to tangible improvements such as computers, the latest weaponry or communications, or advances in crime lab equipment as signs of professionalism. In fact, a department may have all of these tangible indicators but still be unprofessional if officers fail to meet the requirements of professionals discussed in this section. That is, the assumption that changes of this sort will automatically increase professionalism among officers is not necessarily valid. Professionalism involves belonging to a profession and behaving in a way that is consistent with professional standards. According to Carter and Wilson (2006) "A profession is an occupation that requires extensive training and the study and mastery of specialized knowledge" (p. 1). Furthermore, a **profession** usually requires some form of accreditation, certification, or licensing and has a code of ethics which holds members accountable.

As police agencies became more bureaucratic, relied more on civil services rules and regulations, and became more unionized, officer discretion tended to be more restricted. That is, officer autonomy was increasingly curtailed—yet autonomy is highly valued by most professionals. The distinguishing feature of professional work is the freedom to make decisions according to professional norms of conduct without having to temper every decision by bureaucratic constraint (Caplow, 1983).

Characteristics of a profession include the following (Barker, Hunter, & Rush, 1994; Roberg & Kuykendall, 1993; Swanson, Territo, & Taylor, 2001, 2007):

1. A body of professional literature

2. Research

3. A code of ethics

4. Membership in professional associations

5. Dedication to self-improvement

6. The existence of a unique, identifiable academic field of knowledge attainable through higher education

To what extent do the police currently meet the requirements of a profession? With respect to the first two criteria, there clearly is a growing body of professional literature on the police. Journals such as *Police Quarterly* and *Policing: An International Journal of Police Strategies and Management* contain reports of police research (the second criterion). Periodicals such as *Police Chief,* the *FBI Law Enforcement Bulletin,* and a rapidly expanding number of government reports and texts on the police contribute additional information on police operations, organizations, and programs. In addition, there are literally hundreds of master's theses and doctoral dissertations concerning the police. Much of the information contained in these publications has been collected using legitimate research techniques, and the body of literature based on police research has expanded dramatically in recent years as grant monies from a variety of sources have become available.

The International Association of Chiefs of Police developed and later modified a code of ethics (conduct) for police. It is difficult to determine the extent to which police officers are familiar with these documents, but our observations indicate that many officers know a code exists but are unfamiliar with its contents.

There are a number of professional police associations, mostly for chief executive officers. Organizations such as the Fraternal Order of the Police are oriented toward rank-and-file officers as well, but they have typically served more as either social organizations or, more recently, as collective-bargaining agents. Associations for staff personnel and field supervisors have traditionally been far less common, making creating and sharing a professional body of knowledge among those occupying such positions difficult. In recent years, there has been some expansion of professional organizations among police planners, investigators, and those assigned to the accreditation process.

The evidence is mixed when it comes to dedication to self-improvement. There are currently no national minimum standards for either departments or police personnel. Many states do not even mandate training on a recurring basis after completion of the basic-training program. Concurrently, among more progressive police personnel, there is an increasing interest in establishing police officer standards and in accreditation.

A unique, identifiable field of study in police science has emerged. As we have seen, there are hundreds of college-level academic programs in policing and criminal justice. The quality of these programs varies tremendously, but generally speaking, they seem to have improved over the past decade. While there is no consensus on precisely what topics are to be included in these programs, there is enough agreement to argue that the field is unique and identifiable in general terms at least. Further, an increasing number of officers are earning both undergraduate and graduate degrees in police science, law enforcement, and criminal justice programs. These achievements notwithstanding, police professionalism remains an elusive goal for a variety of reasons. Dedication to the attainment of professional standards exists among some police executives, is given lip service by some others, and is totally lacking among some. A key determinant of such dedication appears to be the background, particularly the educational level, of police personnel. The professionalization of policing through higher education is not a new challenge to policing but was a topic of discussion as far back as the 1930s. Even though later presidential commissions recommended a higher education requirement, police have failed to keep pace with many other professions that help people. Friedmann (2006) concluded, "the professions of nursing and health, teaching and education, social work and psychology have a basic entry-level requirement of varied college degrees in the social services field, and as such, are recognized as professions" (p. 1). By far the most common education requirement in policing is still a high school education. In fact, some departments that required a four-year college degree recently eased their hiring requirements and began accepting applicants with two years of college or three years of service in the military (Johnson, 2006). Even though some departments offer higher salaries to those with a four-year degree, many are not able to find enough applicants to fill the positions they have open, especially in large departments that have on-going vacancies. However, according to Friedmann (2006), we need to realize that the education requirements set now will determine how police officers and policing are going to look 50 or 100 years from now.

Another factor involved in the pursuit of professionalism is resistance on behalf of both rank-and-file and middle-management personnel. To the extent that these personnel view their jobs as blue-collar shift work involving little need for advanced education, dedication to self-improvement may be minimized. To some extent, of course, this view is encouraged by both the paramilitary nature of police organizations and the police subculture, which often regards police work as piecework—a certain number of moving citations, nonmoving citations, responses to service requests, and arrests equals a good day's work. To be fair, some police administrations encourage this view as well. Finally, unionization of police officers may inhibit progress toward professionalism. This relationship is complex and deserves a closer look.

Police Unions and Professionalism

As we stated earlier, professionalism in policing faces several challenges, and one involves the relationship between unionized officers and police administrators. Collective bargaining typically results in highly formalized rules indicating the rights and obligations of both parties. The formal nature of such rules makes it difficult to bend them, even though both parties may be willing to cooperate. In clarifying the relationships between police administrators and line officers in a union contract, negotiators may go overboard and tie the hands of one or both sides when it comes to the exercise of discretion. For example, a contract that limits the amount of overtime an officer may be required to work may prevent an officer who is willing to work, and is needed on a particular shift, from working.

There is little doubt that the protection offered by unions in terms of salaries, working conditions, and governance is required in some police organizations. In such organizations, administrative personnel appear to be more concerned about productivity than people, and the rights of employees need to be protected. Unfortunately, some employees are unwilling or unable to contribute their fair share to the organization but are protected by unions. And the principle of rewards based on merit is most often compromised in the process of unionization, so that those who perform best can be rewarded no more than those who perform at minimum levels.

It has been argued that unions promote mediocrity by requiring only minimal performance levels and by failing to allow rewards for those who exceed these levels. Those who are self-motivated, dedicated, and interested in advancing their careers and the organization are not encouraged to do so, and those who contribute little to the organization are protected. In addition, unions tend to take on lives of their own, and union leaders sometimes represent their own interests, or those of the larger union, rather than those of the officers immediately involved. Union representatives may come to see these positions as more important than their positions as police officers, and police administrators may come to view union representatives as adversaries rather than employees. Unions and management need not be adversaries. Both can work toward the betterment of the organization and its employees; this sometimes happens in the case of the police. More frequently, however, unions and managers do see each other as adversaries and, even though compromises may be worked out, come to distrust one another. Thus, in some departments, there are different unions representing different groups, based on rank or race or some other factor (e.g., the National Organization of Black Law Enforcement Officers or the National Latino Police Officers' Association). This differentiation may create divisiveness within a department, so that middle-management personnel turn to their unions to promote their welfare, field supervisors turn to their union, whites to theirs, blacks to theirs, and so on. Professional standards are very likely to get caught in the shuffle.

While it is our observation that unions and professionalization, as we have discussed them here, are basically incompatible, unions in policing are here to stay. This being the case, it behooves police administrators to become, or to hire, good negotiators and to negotiate, to the extent possible, contracts that are compatible with professional growth. Hoover et al. (2006), argued that "efforts labeled as Community Policing, as well as those labeled CompStat, require new roles, scheduling flexibility, assignment changes, and above all, commitment and cooperation by all parties" (p. xix). Contracts that provide reimbursement for improving one's education are good examples, as are those that require open, honest evaluations and disciplinary proceedings. Contracts that are viewed in terms of victories or losses are seldom of these types. Contracts that are viewed as representing legitimate efforts on behalf of both parties to improve the organization and the welfare of those employed may achieve this goal. An alternative is the concept of shared leadership or participative management which seeks to promote the interests of both employees and the organization without the need for third-party intervention.

Accreditation

Through the combined efforts of the International Association of Chiefs of Police, the National Organization for Black Law Enforcement Executives, the National

Sheriff's Association, and the Police Executive Research Forum, the Commission on Accreditation for Law Enforcement Agencies (CALEA) was established in 1979. The foundation of **accreditation**, a significant professional achievement, lies in the development of standards containing a clear statement of professional objectives (Bureau of Justice Assistance [BJA], 2004, p. 157). Participating law enforcement agencies conduct a self-analysis to determine how existing operations can be adapted to meet the objectives developed by CALEA. When the procedures are in place, a team of trained assessors verifies that the application standards have been successfully implemented, resulting in accreditation for the agency (BJA, 2004).

The Commission developed a voluntary accreditation process through which law enforcement agencies at the state, county, and municipal levels were evaluated in terms of more than 900 standards. The current edition of the process includes 462 standards that cover nine law enforcement subjects:

1. Roles, responsibilities, and relationships

2. Organization, management, and administration

3. Personnel structure

4. Personnel process

5. Operations

6. Operational support

7. Traffic operations

8. Detainee and court-related activities

9. Auxiliary and technical services (CALEA Online, 2009)

These standards are intended to help police agencies do the following:

1. Strengthen crime prevention and control capabilities

2. Formalize essential management procedures

3. Establish fair and nondiscriminatory personnel practices

4. Improve service delivery

5. Solidify interagency cooperation and coordination

6. Boost citizen and staff confidence in the agency (CALEA Online, 2009)

To become accredited, the agency first files an application and receives materials designed to allow agency personnel to conduct a self-evaluation of the agency's current status with respect to applicable standards. Once the self-evaluation is completed, the agency may either determine that it is not yet ready for accreditation and work toward that goal or they may request an on-site assessment. In the latter case, the Commission appoints a team of impartial assessors who conduct an on-site assessment. These assessors author a formal report on their findings, and the Commission on Accreditation renders a decision (BJA, 2004). Costs vary, depending on the size of the agency involved. Internal preparation costs are relatively high because it often takes a year to 18 months for the designated coordinator to prepare for the assessment. To remain accredited, agencies must remain in compliance with applicable standards, and a number of agencies are currently involved in that process. It should be noted that many states have police accrediting organizations and many police departments have attained accreditation at the state level.

Several unanticipated consequences of the accreditation process have emerged. A number of states have formed coalitions to assist police agencies in the process of accreditation, thereby improving interagency cooperation. Some departments report decreased insurance costs as a result of accreditation. The most often cited advantages of the CALEA Accreditation Process include the following:

- Develops a comprehensive set of written directives.
- Provides the necessary reports and analyses to make informed management decisions.
- Requires a preparedness program to address natural and human-made critical incidents.
- Improves the agencies' relationship with the community.
- Strengthens an agencies' accountability.
- Can limit liability and risk exposure. (CALEA Online, 2009)

Individuals who serve as assessors are constantly updated with respect to the latest developments in policing and can share their experiences with others in the field, thereby promoting both dedication to and attainment of professionalism.

While professionalism has proved an elusive goal for the police, and while there are still pockets of resistance to meeting the requirements of a profession, a growing number of police personnel appear to be committed to that goal. Enlightened police administrators and unions should participate as partners in the search for professionalism.

❖ Chapter Summary

The organization structures implemented in policing today vary depending on the style of policing adopted, size of the community, and resources available to the agency. Furthermore, organizational structure is often influenced by size of the organization, tradition, function, degree of professionalism, receptiveness to change, and style of leadership. Whether or not an agency is unionized may also play a role in determining organizational structure. Finally, the size of the organization depends on the surrounding environment; whether the police agency is a municipal, county, state, or federal organization; and on political and economic considerations.

Consistently, most police organizations have implemented a form of hierarchical structure that involves the principles of unity of command, rank, structure, and span of control. Police agencies utilize three organizational designs: functional, place, and time. However, many departments have implemented and experimented with more decentralized organizational structures. This was in part based on adoption of community oriented policing, which called for flatter organizations, fewer ranks, and the development of police officers as generalists.

Unionization and collective bargaining in policing date back to the 1800s. Major concerns of police unions in negotiations with management include issues of salary, insurance, vacation and sick days, pension, longevity, compensation time, discipline, and grievance procedures. However, departments retain certain management rights that involve the right to determine the mission of the police department, standard of service, and procedures for selection and promotion. In most cases, if negotiations fail between the police union and management, strikes are prohibited by law. Resolution of an impasse between the union and police management usually involves a form of mediation, fact finding, or arbitration.

Police professionalism means different things in different places and at different times, making a consensus about the requirement for a professional police organization challenging. Most believe a profession requires some form of accreditation, certification, or licensure and has a code of ethics that applies to all members. Some movement toward professionalization in policing occurred in 1979 when the Commission on Accreditation for Law Enforcement Agencies (CALEA) was established. CALEA involves the development of standards for police agencies that contain clear statements of professional objectives.

YOU DECIDE 7.1

"In the late 1950's and 1960's an unusual employee-driven process took root in America as fatigued shift workers convinced management that major scheduling changes were needed." This shift adjustment was embraced by police officers who in the past worked their entire career assigned to an 8 hour patrol shift. According to Jacques (2010) work schedules are very important to the police since they have a greater impact on the personal and job life of a police officer than any other nonlife-threatening variable. Related to this are the generational differences associated with Generation Y police officers and the concerns that police leaders have related to quality of life for their officers. In other words, the better the perceived quality of life by police officers, the more likely the department will not experience the loss of quality, trained officers.

Source: "A Fresh Look at 12-Hour Shifts," by E. Jacques, 2010, Police Officers Association of Michigan. Available from: http://www.poam.net/main/journal/fresh-look-at-12-hour-shifts.html

1. What are the effects of a 12-hour shift on a police officer and her family?

2. How would a 12-hour patrol shift affect your productivity as a police officer?

❖ Key Terms

organizations	line personnel
POSDCORB	police paramilitary unit
hierarchies	functional organization design
unity of command	operations division
rank structure	administrative and staff services division
span of control	place design
Incident Command System	time design

matrix structure   impasse

collective bargaining   unfair labor practice

management rights   profession

job action   accreditation

❖ Discussion Questions

1. Describe the current state of police organizations.

2. What are the relationships among police discretion, police organization, and police functions?

3. Describe the traditional police organizational structure. Discuss its strengths and weaknesses.

4. Compare and contrast the advantages of small (fewer than 10 personnel) and large police agencies from the perspective of the public, the officers involved, and the chief executive officer.

5. Compare and contrast the function, place, and time organizational designs.

6. Discuss the context in which police organizations operate and the importance of the environment to the police.

7. Assess the current state of police leadership in your community, using whatever sources are available (interviews with police supervisors, the media, etc.).

8. Discuss some of the factors that have made the police search for professionalism so difficult.

9. What are the characteristics of a profession? To what extent are these characteristics currently found among police personnel?

10. Why were police unions so slow to emerge? What are some of the reasons for the rapid increase in the number of police unions in the past two decades?

11. Are police unions and police professionalism compatible? Why or why not?

12. What are the relationships between police professionalism and accreditation? What is the rationale behind police accreditation?

13. Are the police currently professionals? If not, will they become professionals?

❖ Internet Exercises

Go to the Internet and search for information about a police department.

1. Does the department provide information or a chart describing the agency's organizational structure?

2. What forms of organizational design do they use? Explain how they are organized by function, place, and time.

Discretion, Ethics, and Accountability in Policing

CHAPTER LEARNING OBJECTIVES

- Define *police discretion* and comment on the importance of the use of discretionary authority by police.

- Describe the interrelatedness of the police subculture and the use of discretion by police.

- Highlight additional factors not related to the police subculture that can affect the use of discretion by police.

- Identify both the positive and negative consequences associated with the use of discretionary authority by police.

- Discuss the ramifications of the following: the abolition of the use of discretion by police; organizational control over the use of discretion by line officers; non-use of discretion by the police and its effect of the court system.

- Describe the effects of the use of discretion by police and the practice of any form of profiling (racial, etc.).

- Identify and elaborate on the tenets of the Police Code of Ethics as espoused by the International Association of Chiefs of Police.

(Continued)

(Continued)

- Define the term *ethics* and discuss its importance in the field of policing.
- Identify and describe various organizational strategies that can be used to mitigate unethical police conduct.
- Describe the relationship between personal and organizational accountability and ethical decision making.
- Provide examples of common obstacles to police accountability.

❖ **Photo 8.1**   Featured in the photo is a controversial practice referred to as roadblocks or checkpoints to conduct random safety checks on motorists. Many have questioned if these checkpoints really are random in nature.

❖ Introduction

Due to the multiple roles the police are expected to perform, along with the myriad of external and internal influences that tend to shape police policy and public expectations, a good deal of discretionary authority is required. Fulfilling the police mission in a competent and responsible fashion requires a sustained organizational and individual commitment to the underlying tenets of ethics, accountability, and professionalism.

If the police are to be perceived as professionals, they must exercise discretion wisely in light of ethical considerations while remaining accountable to the public they are sworn to serve. In this chapter, we discuss the following:

1. The exercise of discretion and the factors influencing discretionary decisions

2. The importance of ethics in policing

3. The notion of accountability in public service

4. The interrelationships among discretion, ethics, and accountability as they relate to professionalism

It is appropriate to consider discretion, ethics, and accountability together because of the complex interrelationships among the three. As we shall see, discretion is a necessary and desirable part of policing and involves selecting among several possible courses of action. Only some of these possible courses of action are ethical, and eliminating or reducing the number of unethical options is a continuing pursuit of ethical police administrators. Wise exercise of discretion by police officers demands ethical choices. Further, whether or not the police make wise choices among available alternatives, they are accountable to the public for their actions.

❖ Police Discretion

Police **discretion** can be defined simply as "the exercise of individual choice or judgment concerning possible courses of action" (Cox & McCamey, 2008, p. 34). Whether defined in this fashion or as Nickels (2007) defined it—"in terms of perceived job autonomy with a division into two discrete global constructs, one as organizational and the other as operational" (p. 575)—the consequences of the use of unethical or otherwise improper discretionary authority by police can have devastating outcomes. These consequences range from poor morale and civil liability issues to public mistrust of the police.

According to Nickels (2007), operationally, discretion amounts to the perceived ability to choose when, how, and in what order to complete assigned work. Nickels concluded that "if discretion is to be spoken of as a real and variable aspect of policing that is believed to influence police behavior, then it needs to be defined in such a way that it lends it to direct observation and to quantification" (p. 577).

Discretion is a normal, desirable, and unavoidable part of policing that exists at all levels within a police agency and at all levels of policing. Administrative discretion involves decisions to selectively enforce laws and establish role priorities. Supervisory discretion involves decisions by supervisors to allocate resources in specific ways at specific times in response to specific requests for services.

Discretionary behavior is required because the code of criminal law, to say nothing of departmental policies, is expressed in terms that often make a clear interpretation of the writer's intentions difficult. In addition, police resources are limited; the police cannot be everywhere at once. Further, policing, like many other occupations, consists of a number of specializations, and not all departments have the specialized personnel to investigate all types of crime or provide all types of services. Finally, the police are well aware that the other components of the criminal justice network also have limited resources (court time, jail cells, etc.).

While police officers are not, in the strictest sense of the words, judges or jurors, they must and do perform the functions of both on certain occasions. That is, they must decide what the facts are in any given encounter, what the law has to say with respect to the encounter, and how best to bring the encounter to a successful conclusion. They also consider extenuating and mitigating factors because each individual wants to provide his or her own account of the circumstances leading up to the encounter.

"The extent to which police officers are encouraged to exercise discretion varies from department to department, from shift to shift, and among divisions within the same department, but the exercise of discretion is routine in all police agencies" (Reiss, 1992, p. 74). This is true because, as mentioned, the police simply cannot enforce all the laws all of the time or perform all of the services demanded at the same time. "Thus, both law enforcement and policing are selective processes in which some laws are enforced and some services are provided most of the time, while others are not. The determination of which, and when, services are provided rests to some extent with police administrators, the general public, prosecutors, judges, and other politicians, but police officers do not typically operate under immediate, direct supervision. Therefore, they are relatively free to determine their own actions at any given time. Their decisions are typically influenced by the following factors (Cox, 1996):

1. The law

2. Departmental policy

3. Political expectations

4. The situation or setting

5. The occupational culture in which they operate" (p. 47)

Clearly, the exercise of discretion is necessary for effective policing. Problems arise, though, when the public perceives discretion as being applied in a discriminatory or biased fashion. For many years, minority group members, particularly African Americans, and many criminal justice scholars have been pointing to the disproportionate number of minority group members who enter the criminal justice system—from the point of arrest through the point of incarceration. While some empirical studies do lend support to such concerns, others do not. What is clear, though, is that concerns of this nature consistently appear in the press. One example of this is *racial profiling* (one type of **biased enforcement**), which may be defined as the targeting of minority group members by police for traffic or other law enforcement practices.

Law enforcement practices that turned the spotlight on racial profiling and that evoked a huge public outcry in this regard occurred in the states of New Jersey and Maryland in 1998, when members of the New Jersey and Maryland State Police were formally accused of stopping black motorists on their states' respective highways for no reason other than race (Barovick, 1998). Empirical evidence resulting from data collection efforts regarding traffic stops, detention and investigation, and arrests of black drivers on those states' highways paints an alarming picture. In New Jersey, researchers wanted to ascertain whether state troopers stopped, ticketed, or arrested black motorists at rates significantly higher than other racial and ethnic groups. To determine this, the researchers measured the rate at which blacks were being stopped, ticketed, or arrested (Harris, 1999).

The results of the data collection efforts in New Jersey were direct and disturbing. Based on analysis of the approximately 42,000 cars involved in the study, the following conclusions were drawn:

- There was little or no difference concerning the frequency and type of traffic violations committed by black and white motorists.
- Approximately 73% of the motorists stopped and arrested were black, but only about 13% of the vehicles involved in stops had a black driver or passenger.
- Blacks drove or occupied only about 13% of the vehicles in question, but accounted for 35% of the total number of traffic stops.

Results from a similar study in Maryland yielded remarkably similar results. In this case, 6000 vehicles were included in the data collection, and as in the New Jersey study, the purpose was to discover whether Maryland state troopers were stopping, issuing citations, searching, or arresting predominately minority-group motorists. The following quotation summarized the Maryland results in clear fashion:

> Blacks and whites drove no differently; the percentage of blacks and whites violating the traffic code were virtually undistinguishable. More importantly . . . analysis found that although 17.5% of the population violating the traffic code on the road . . . studied was black, more than 72% of those stopped and searched were black. In more than 80% of the cases, the person stopped and searched was a member of some racial minority. (Harris, 1999, p. 277)

Since the coverage of these incidents, dozens, perhaps hundreds, of law enforcement agencies have come under scrutiny for similar biased-enforcement practices, opening the floodgates, so to speak, for civil and criminal civil rights litigation and prompting legislatures from all levels of government to sponsor and adopt laws designed to eradicate this form of malfeasance by police. Complaints from the minority community were not limited to those voiced by African Americans, but included complaints from other racial and ethnic groups as well. Following the events of 9/11, profiling of Middle Easterners was a major focus of attention by the media. Further, complaints of biased enforcement are not limited to traffic related operations, but to stops and searches conducted on the streets and at airports, arrests, and to verbal harassment. The complaints from the minority citizenry were so numerous that the American Civil Liberties Union (ACLU) posted an online complaint form and questionnaire on the World Wide Web in an effort to compile statistical data to bolster an plea to various units of government for support in eliminating these law enforcement practices. Currently, each state and the federal government have adopted laws requiring the collection and reporting of data pertaining to traffic stops (i.e., ticket issues, driver or occupant(s) searches, etc.).

A point that needs to be emphasized is that public perceptions of biased enforcement are not limited to the minority communities in this country. The Gallup organization conducted numerous national polls addressing these issues. The following is a synopsis of the public opinion polls resulting from Gallup's efforts:

• When racial profiling is operationalized as "police officers stop motorists of certain racial or ethnic groups because the officers believe that these groups are more likely than others to commit certain types of crimes" (Newport, 1999), 59% of the adults surveyed, regardless of race or ethnicity, believe this practice to be widespread. In addition, 81% of the respondents disapprove of this practice.

• When broken down by race, more than 4 out of 10 African Americans believe they have been stopped by the police because of their race. Moreover, of those who claim to have been stopped because of their race, 6 out of 10 say they have been stopped three or more times. It should also be noted that the responses varied significantly by age and gender within the African American community: ". . . it is black men, and especially young black men, aged 18 [to] 34, who are most likely to report having been stopped because of their race" (Newport, 1999).

• When respondents were asked to give their opinions of both their local and state police, among whites there is barely a difference, with 85% giving favorable opinions of their local police and 87% giving favorable opinions of their state police. Newport (1999) stated that blacks have a less favorable opinion of both, with 58% having a favorable opinion of their local police, and 64% of state troopers. Once again, age was a significant factor. More than 50% of young black men, aged 18 to 34, had unfavorable opinions of both groups of police. Unfavorable opinions of the police from the respondents in the 35 to 49 age group dropped to 36%.

• When respondents were asked if they felt they were treated unfairly during interactions with their local and state police, race, age, and gender seemed to account for the most pronounced differences. For whites, the number of those who reported being treated unfairly was small: 7% for local police and 4% for state police. Black respondents reported quite differently: 27% for local police and 17% for state police. When age was factored in, 53% of young black men, aged 18 to 34, reported being treated unfairly by local police, and 29% reported being treated unfairly by state police (Newport, 1999).

Delattre (2002) strongly advised police executives to be willing to justify their policies, procedures, and actions to the public or any other source of inquiry. Reluctance to conform to public demand arouses suspicion of wrongdoing and acts as a barrier to the trust and confidence of the public in the police that are absolutely essential if the police are to operate effectively. As Delattre (1996) pointed out:

> When authority, power, and discretion are granted to public officials . . . rational people presume that they will not use more than they need for their legitimate purposes, because rational people would never grant more authority or discretion to abridge liberty or use force than they believed necessary. The presumption is not of guilt but of official respect for restraint. Citizens expect public officials to justify their use of authority or power when questions arise. (p. 63)

Controlling Discretion and Encouraging Ethical Behavior

According to Manning (1978), the police occupational **subculture** emphasizes the following assumptions:

1. People are not to be trusted and are potentially dangerous.
2. Personal experience is a better action guide than abstract rules.
3. Officers must make the public respect them.
4. Everyone hates a cop.
5. The legal system is untrustworthy; police officers make the best decisions about innocence or guilt.
6. People must be controlled or they will break laws.
7. Police officers must appear respectable and be effective.
8. Police officers can most accurately identify crime and criminals.
9. The basic jobs of the police are to prevent crime and enforce laws.
10. More severe punishment will deter crime. (pp. 11–12)

The consequences of these assumptions, if carried over to the realm of police discretion, might (and in fact quite often do) lead to the following behaviors on behalf of police officers:

1. Ignoring abstract rules and principles (including laws)
2. Resorting to the threat or use of force to make the public show respect for police officers
3. Displaying paranoid behavior
4. Using street justice
5. Preferring efficiency over effectiveness
6. Regarding nonenforcement tasks as less than real police work
7. Adding charges when making arrests in order to try to ensure that some punishment or more severe punishment will result

The police subculture, important though it is, is not the only determinant of police discretion, and street level officers are not the only police personnel who exercise such discretion. Among other important considerations in the exercise of discretion are the law, the seriousness of the offense in question, departmental policy, personal characteristics of those involved in a given encounter, the safety of the officer involved, pressure from victims, disagreement with the law, available alternatives, and the visibility of the decision (Gaines, Kappeler, & Vaughn, 1994, pp. 195–202; Schmalleger, 2008, pp. 138–140).

Further, the education, training, and length of service of the officer and the wishes of the complainant have been shown to affect decisions rendered by police officers

(Brooks, 1993). A department involved in community policing may provide more education and training in the exercise of discretion and more encouragement to use discretion than a more traditional department. Still, the department's policy will have differential impact on officers with different lengths of service and various levels of education who may be assigned to diverse neighborhoods.

Failure to recognize and communicate the importance of discretion at all levels in policing may lead to a pretense of full enforcement and equal treatment in similar conditions, when the reality is selective enforcement and unequal treatment. Thus, a necessary first step in dealing with discretion is to recognize its existence and importance. Once we admit that discretion exists in police work, we can talk about its proper and improper uses, we can stop attempting to deceive the public, and we can provide training with respect to the appropriate uses of discretion.

For example, we agree that a driver who is exceeding the speed limit by three or four miles per hour should not be subject to arrest. We might thus establish a tolerance limit of five miles per hour and instruct officers that those driving over the speed limit, but within the tolerance, need not be arrested. While this does not guarantee absolute control over officers' behavior (they could, for example, still cite a driver for driving two or three miles per hour over the speed limit), it does let them know that it is permissible to ignore or warn those who are only marginally speeding (Langworthy & Travis, 1994, pp. 294–295).

Similarly, we might agree that an officer who decides to render service or enforce the law based solely on the gender, race, or physical appearance of the other citizen involved is exercising discretion inappropriately (based on personal characteristics). Supervisors could then discourage such behavior and explain why decisions based solely on personal characteristics of subjects are unacceptable. In effect, we would be enhancing the value of police discretion by providing the officer with appropriate education and training.

Because the police are a public service agency, honesty and accountability to the public are particularly important. Admitting that selective (discretionary) enforcement does occur and that not all police officers respond in the same way to similar situations (already "open secrets") are steps in the right direction. Although a comprehensive set of guidelines for the exercise of police discretion may not be possible, improvement of current guidelines is clearly possible. Such clarification will not only assist the community in understanding police actions, but it also might remove some of the confusion among police officers themselves as to how much and what types of discretion are available to and expected of them. Simply telling an officer to exercise his discretion, in the traditional police world, is likely to have little effect because there are other indicators that innovation is seldom rewarded and mistakes seldom go unpunished.

A typical response to controlling police discretion is the use of negative sanctions to prevent or correct discretionary behavior. A number of side effects are likely to accompany the punitive approach: temporary rather than permanent change, inappropriate emotional behavior, inflexibility, possible changes in desirable behavior, and fear or distrust of those administering the negative sanctions. Further, the stigma accompanying punishment may have negative effects on self-esteem and status as well, which may lead to anger and hostility in those punished. Still, Klockars, Ivkovic, and Haberfeld (2004), in their study of more than 3,000 police officers in some 30 agencies across the United States, found that one of the factors determining whether or not police officers would report misconduct of fellow officers was the way in which such violations were punished by the department in question. It may be that the more severe the punishment administered for unethical or illegal conduct, the more serious the violation is perceived to be by officers. Thus, although punishment in and of itself is unlikely to end unethical conduct, it may have some positive as well as negative connotations.

A better approach to controlling discretion may involve the use of incentives to promote voluntary compliance with policies concerning discretion. Such incentives include officer participation in policy formulation, establishment of specialized units to deal with specific tasks, positive disciplinary practices (aimed at correcting the aberrant behavior without humiliating the officer involved), and more and better training with respect to the exercise of discretion and the social and historical context, which requires the police to be accountable to several audiences (public, administration, colleagues) for their behavior. Similarly, training and education dealing with police ethics may provide the foundation for making appropriate discretionary decisions in a variety of different situations (Brooks, 1993; Gaines, Kappeler, & Vaughn, 1994).

There are a number of other steps police administrators can take in mitigating instances of unethical and illegal discretionary behavior and in improving organizational and individual decision making.

Commitment to the Importance of Ethical Decision Making

Leaders set the tone for the entire organization; therefore, without a strong commitment that stresses the importance of **ethical decision making** by the chief executive officer and her entire command staff, instances of unethical and perhaps illegal practices are sure to follow. O'Malley (1997) noted the following:

> The importance of upper-level management in determining a department's ethics and overall quality cannot be overstated. A common thread in most widespread police corruption cases is an absence of oversight from above. A recent examination of multi-officer corruption cases uncovered an unwillingness by police executives to acknowledge corruption and found, in some cases, a 'willful blindness' to unethical behavior. (p. 22)

Zuidema and Duff (2009) recommended that law enforcement executives with a commitment to ethical behavior encourage ethical behavior in the following ways:

1. By incorporating the ideals of ethics and integrity into their organization's mission statement.

2. By making the focus of ethical decision making part of the organization's formal functions. One example given was that before the commencement of any departmental or unit meeting, members would stand and recite the Law Enforcement Code of Ethics.

3. By emphasizing ethical behavior as part of the agency's organizational philosophy.

4. By implementing zero tolerance policies for unethical behavior or decision making. (pp. 8–9)

Police administrators can also mandate the study of ethical decision making in their inservice training and bring pressure to bear on state training directors to stress this activity at the recruit level as well. In addition, those responsible for directing training practices should revisit their curriculum designs and ensure that the training is delivered or facilitated by experienced educators and trainers who understand and emphasize the importance of ethical considerations and discretionary activities. All policies governing individual and collective police behavior should be consistent with the ideals of justice and morality.

POLICE STORIES

One midnight shift roll call experience really stuck with me through the years. While the shift (about 30 police officers and two or three sergeants) was in the roll call room waiting for the watch commander to begin the proceedings, a lieutenant entered the room and alerted us to the fact that the "street deputy" was in the building and would be coming with our watch commander shortly to address the troops. (The street deputy was a member of the command structure who represented the Superintendent of Police during off hours, from 6:00 p.m. until 8:00 a.m. the following morning and on weekends. All members of the command staff would rotate on a daily basis to fill that position.)

As our watch commander and the street deputy entered the room, we all rose to attention. The deputy immediately said, "Sit down and relax, this is a friendly visit." He went on to give us a warning of sorts. He said, "The 'G' (FBI) is on to you. It's no longer acceptable to steal money from the 'Pollocks' (Polish immigrants) on Milwaukee Avenue. Guys from three districts are hitting that area and it's getting out of hand." The deputy then left the room and we concluded our regular roll call session.

After a few of hours on patrol, my partner and I met with a couple of other younger officers for a cup of coffee. One of those guys said, "Let me get this straight. The representative of our Superintendent came to address a group of police officers to tell them that it's not okay to steal money from 'Pollocks' anymore." We all had a pretty good laugh over that absurd incident.

Upon further reflection, it really made me aware that malfeasance by individual officers was and is not strictly the result of the few-rotten-apples explanation that many police chiefs had claimed (and still do to this very day regarding acts of misconduct by police). Sadly, it's more consistent with the corrupt-leadership-structures explanation espoused by Delattre (2002) and several of his contemporaries. In this particular case, everyone knew what was happening to the Polish immigrants but no genuine actions to remedy the situation were ever taken by the department. About 15 years after this infamous roll call session, several officers were indicted and pled guilty to felony theft charges as a result of a sting operation involving thefts from and robberies of Polish immigrants. The sting was headed by the FBI and assisted by the CPD's Internal Affairs Division. Most of the officers involved received terms of probation and the loss of their pensions as a result of plea negotiations. It should also be noted that two of the officers involved in this scandal were in the room during that fateful roll call session years earlier.

In addition, we all knew who these "police bandits" were and what they were doing. If faced with those circumstances today, we could have put an end to that by overtly following those officers while on patrol. I believe this would have sent a strong signal to those officers that their misconduct would not be tolerated, tacitly or otherwise.

Improved Hiring Practices

Presently, most state, county, and municipal law enforcement agencies utilize the services of merit boards or boards of police and fire commissioners, comprised chiefly of civilians from the community at large, to oversee their hiring and promotional practices. Normally mandated either by state statute or county or local ordinance, this practice guarantees that the communities these agencies serve have at least some input with respect to their law enforcement personnel. While this process may be good in theory, practically speaking, these boards and commissions may not be effective in selecting and hiring the most ethical candidates for policing. Members of these boards and commissions are often political appointees and in many cases have little or no experience in the field of policing or in the area of human resource development. Perhaps it is time to change the composition of boards so that those in the community who have expertise in one or both of these areas are included. It may be that policing can benefit from the experiences of the private business sector, whose hiring and promotional practices are quite different and, by most accounts, more effective. For example, private-sector practices differ in the following ways:

- Place less emphasis on outdated and at times prejudicial physical agility and power tests
- Increase reliance on in-depth oral interviews conducted by experienced and knowledgeable professionals within the field
- Increase minimum education requirements for those seeking admission or promotion (Perhaps it is time for the minimum requirement of a baccalaureate degree to be implemented, at least for those desiring promotion within police ranks.)
- Utilize appropriate and complex task analyses for the position sought
- Use appropriate testing procedures to evaluate effective written and oral communication skills (from our perspective, the single most important set of skills to bring to the job)
- Conduct extremely thorough background investigations

These recommendations should significantly increase the probability that those selected will fulfill the requirements of the agency in question and the field of policing.

This, in turn, should increase the level of professional policing and mitigate or decrease the incidence of unethical conduct.

Elimination of Quotas

Most administrators, when asked whether officer performance is, in large part, based on ticket and arrest activity, would answer that there are no quotas in their respective agencies. Rather, they would most likely point to performance standards, which tend to identify acceptable ticket and arrest activity of department members, using measures of central tendency, such as means and medians. Regardless of what they are called, whether *quotas* or *performance standards*, officers' performance evaluations are based almost entirely on the number of tickets and arrests. What must be emphasized is that, in many cases, this may cause some officers to engage in biased enforcement practices in order to meet agency expectations. We can recall an instance when a police officer told us that near the end of the month, more stops of vehicles driven by male Hispanics in certain areas of the city occur because of the assumption that they are poor and often operate ill-equipped vehicles. Multiple citations can be issued, thus allowing the department ticket quota or standard to be met.

POLICE STORIES

District personnel (patrol division) in the Chicago Police Department had quotas or minimum standards of performance to meet, but those standards were quite easy to satisfy (e.g., moving violations, parking tickets, answering radio calls in a timely fashion, and other similar patrol officer functions). Personnel from specialized units, on the other hand, such as district tactical units, gang crimes, narcotics, and others, were held to much higher quotas or minimum performance standards, and they were based almost entirely on the number of arrests each period (28 day cycles). Also, personnel assigned to these units, unlike members of the patrol division, were not protected by the union with respect to transfers made by the department. Thus, officers in these specialized units could be transferred out of the units literally by the stroke of a commander's pen. If officers wanted to stay in these units, they had to consistently meet their arrest quotas.

If you worked in the patrol division, it did not take long to learn when the work period (28 days) was coming to an end because an onslaught of gang crimes and tactical unit personnel would race to our routine radio calls to make an arrest before the beat officers. I recall one incident in particular. My partner and I received a call of a domestic disturbance, which unfortunately was a common occurrence, and there were two gang crimes unit cars (four officers) already on the scene upon our arrival. As we exited our car, we observed an elderly male in handcuffs being escorted by the gang crimes officers from the house. I remember one of those officers smiling and telling us, "He's a 'gangster disciple,' what a coincidence." (The gangster disciples are a large street gang operating in Chicago and many other cities). The significance of this event is that on the police department's case report there is a box to be checked if the offender listed on the report was a gang member. Gang member or not, which in this case I highly doubted, the man they had arrested for battery was identified as a gang member on the reports. I can't even hazard a guess as to how many times similar incidents would occur toward the end of a work day cycle.

The moral of this story is that because of the pressure exerted on these officers, they often falsified their police reports to meet arrest quotas. While minimum arrest quota policies are not a justification for wrongdoing on the part of individual police officers, the real culprit in cases like this is implementation of poor performance evaluation standards by the command structure of the police department. Sadly, to this day, my former colleagues from the department tell me things have not changed much in this regard.

Zero-tolerance arrest policies also are notorious for increasing the probability of biased enforcement practices. These policies are normally reserved for "high crime" areas, usually found in geographic areas of low socioeconomic status and high minority population. When narcotics, gang crime, and vice enforcement are conducted in this fashion, allegations of unethical and otherwise inappropriate police behavior, justified or not, are sure to follow. Such policies should be routinely evaluated to determine whether they are having the desired impact and whether they lead to biased rather than evidence-based enforcement.

Intolerance of Malfeasance

Rather than focus on zero-tolerance arrest policies, some police administrators adopted zero-tolerance policies concerning inappropriate conduct by department members. As stated earlier in this chapter, the vast majority of our nation's police officers perform their duties ethically, professionally, and competently. The small minority of officers who engage in unethical and criminal activities damage the reputation of the entire field of policing. The sad truth of the matter is that most honest, hard-working officers know these miscreants. Moreover, these unprofessional officers are known by command staff as well. The problem here is often the reluctance of otherwise ethical officers to report the wrongdoings of their colleagues. A National Institute of Justice (NIJ) study (2005), designed to promote integrity in the police profession, involved surveying officers and administrators from 30 police agencies and focused on the following issues:

- Whether or not agency members know the rules
- The degree of individual and organizational support for those rules
- Member familiarization with disciplinary actions associated with violations of rules and policies
- Perception of the fairness of the disciplinary measures
- Member willingness to report misconduct (pp. 1–2)

As stated in the executive summary of the report, "An agency's culture of integrity, as defined by clearly understood and implemented policies and rules, may be more important in shaping the ethics of police officers than hiring the 'right' people (NIJ, 2005, p. i).

The data also indicated that officers learn quickly how various acts of misconduct will be treated by observing their organization's ability to identify unethical conduct and discipline errant officers. "If unwritten policy conflicts with written policy, the resulting confusion undermines an agency's overall integrity-enhancing efforts" (NIJ, 2005, p. i). The report also offered recommendations for encouraging officers to come forward to report acts of misconduct by their co-workers. They included the following (pp. 7–8):

1. Making it clear that officers and supervisors who do not report misconduct will be disciplined

2. Terminating any department member caught lying during an internal investigation pertaining to member misconduct

3. Issuing rewards, in anonymous fashion, to officers who do report misconduct

4. Allowing for anonymous or confidential reporting

5. Regularly rotating supervisors and officers between shifts, districts or precincts, and other units of assignment

In-Car Video Cameras

Many police departments have adopted policies that require placement of video cameras, capable of recording sight and sound, inside their vehicles. Use of this technology could potentially help insure the safety of both officers and those citizens they encounter in the performance of their duties. In addition, they provide a more or less permanent record of events captured during such encounters should allegations of misconduct be made by any of the parties involved. The cameras, which activate from the beginning to the end of an officer's shift, can be shut on and off only by supervisory personnel. All tapes are collected and maintained for review, if the need arises. Because the videotape is always rolling during a shift, many officers claim that this makes them better officers, more professional and more than ever willing to abide by department policy.

In 2000, the Cook County Sheriff's Police Department (CCSPD) (Cook is the county in which the city of Chicago is located) placed video cameras in a number of their squad cars as a test program to evaluate the usefulness of what was then a relatively new phenomenon. The responses from both line and staff personnel were overwhelmingly positive (Keoun, 2000).

Advocates of the cameras, which in recent years have been adopted by police departments across the nation, say they provide officers with additional evidence to convict traffic offenders, especially in drunken-driving cases. But the cameras are also touted as a way of protecting officers against false complaints of brutality and racial profiling. Motorists benefit from the camera because officers are less likely to

❖ PHOTO 8.2 In-car audio-visual technology allows officers to not only be videotaped interacting with subjects they encounter, such as during traffic stops, but small portable microphones record verbal communications as well.

misbehave during traffic stops if they know they are being taped. As one CCSPD officer put it, "With the video camera, it makes you a better officer because you know you're being videotaped. . . . I would never want to work without a camera. If I had to, I'd feel it was a disadvantage" (Keoun, 2000).

Based on numerous similar accounts, police agencies throughout the country have adopted these cameras for the benefit of both the public and their officers. The advantages in terms of improved community relations and increased professionalism far outweigh any conceivable disadvantages.

Responsible and Proactive Data Collection Efforts

As previously stated, legislative acts and judicial orders are forcing many law enforcement agencies to collect data regarding the race or ethnicity of all motorists and passengers who are stopped by police on our nation's roadways. The methodologies established for collecting these data do not always paint an accurate picture due to a number of factors. The lack of accurate baseline demographics from which to compare agency statistics is a significant limitation. This has created a genuine conundrum for many police executives. Are stops in areas with disproportionate minority populations to be regarded as racial profiling? Should officers be warned against stopping minority group members in circumstances in which they would ordinarily make stops even when they are violating the law? In cases where race or ethnicity is unclear, should officers ask the subject for his or her race or ethnicity? Doesn't asking for such information emphasize the issues of race and ethnicity, thereby making it appear to be a major concern of the officer?

In 1991, long before the term racial profiling was coined, the Bloomingdale Illinois Police Department (BPD) decided to examine and monitor the racial makeup of all motorists ticketed that year by first establishing a minority roadway population on their city's major thoroughfares, collecting the racial composition of all motorists ticketed, and comparing the statistics for abnormalities. Examine the highlights from their analyses:

- Of the thousands of traffic tickets issued during that time period (1991–1992), black drivers accounted for 9% of the tickets issued, the town having a 6.5% minority population.
- There were three officers who were writing 40% or more of their tickets to black motorists, a clear indicator that those individuals were targeting certain drivers. The officers in question were then counseled, sent to sensitivity training, and afterward closely monitored by supervisory personnel. Those corrective actions appeared to solve the problem.
- The BPD attributed these biased enforcement practices to their former use of ticket quotas. That policy of performance evaluation was quickly abandoned by the agency (Higgins, 2000).

As stated by a BPD commander, "The problem officers let the work go to the end of the month, and they've got to catch up. Who catches the brunt of the enforcement effort? It's the people who can't afford the good car—people who are on the lower socioeconomic rung. . . . They're easier targets . . ." (Higgins, 2000, p. 2D5).

The members of the BPD who initiated this study are to be commended for their professionalism and proactive policing style. Among a host of allegations of racial profiling recently directed at agencies in close proximity to their borders, the BPD received none. More importantly, they developed sound, empirical data to analyze allegations of biased enforcement practices. According to David Harris, a law professor and noted expert in the area of racial profiling, "This early foray into monitoring the racial breakdown of ticketed drivers is impressive. . . . My hat is off to them. . . . It's very unusual. For 1991, it's stunningly unusual" (Higgins, 2000, p. 2D5).

Though efforts such as these may, upon initial consideration, seem too costly to implement, the potential for increased community relations and the mitigation of legal liability when accusations concerning biased enforcement arise may far outweigh implementation costs. Numerous agencies have adopted this strategy in order to be prepared to deal with allegations of racial profiling, to examine internal practices to insure that such behavior does not occur, and to take remedial steps when required. These agencies indicate clearly to all officers that discretionary activity based solely on the personal characteristics of citizens is inappropriate.

Positive Media Relations

As indicated in Chapter 6, in our present age of technology, the media, both print and broadcast, have the ability to transmit news stories throughout the world in a matter of seconds. For a variety of reasons, police–media relations in this country have not always been positive. Many police officials, line and staff personnel alike, tend to shun media representatives whenever possible, withholding information on newsworthy events even when disclosure of information could not possibly harm anyone or compromise a criminal investigation. When actions like this occur, the information garnered for the news story is often provided by questionable sources and frequently leads to inaccurate depictions of the incidents in question. Transparency with respect to police operations, when possible (e.g., when such transparency does not jeopardize ongoing investigations), even if it involves disclosure of unethical conduct or poor discretionary choices on the part of the police, may result in more balanced coverage and more focus on the positive contributions of the police.

In summary, in order to perform their role competently and effectively, the police must maintain a high degree of discretionary authority. Such authority must be exercised ethically and responsibly if public trust is to be established and maintained. Without public trust, the journey toward professionalism in policing will be long and arduous.

The implications of discretionary authority are both clear and considerable. Police agencies must focus on hiring men and women of excellent character. Police executives must both lead by example and be intolerant of acts of unethical conduct and ill-considered discretionary decisions by their personnel. Policies that emphasize the importance of an ethical foundation for the exercise of discretion are critical in this regard.

❖ Ethics in Policing

Before proceeding to an analysis of ethics and its related principles, a working definition of the term is needed. While there are many different bases for the study of ethics, for our purposes, *ethics* may best be described as "the study of right and wrong, duty, responsibility, and personal character . . . [we] should regard all of these concepts . . . as having an implicit modifier—'moral'—attached to them. Ethics is concerned with moral duty, what is morally right and wrong. . . " (Close & Meier, 1995, p. 3). Or as Delattre (2002) put it, ethical conduct involves "doing the right thing in the right way at the right time for the right reasons" (p. 6).

From an early age, most parents teach their children to tell the truth, not to steal, and not to cheat. And yet by the time they take college classes, the vast majority of criminal justice students indicate that they would not turn in a classmate who lied, cheated, or stole (Cox, 2002). A significant proportion indicate at this stage that, upon becoming police officers, they would not turn in a fellow police officer who lied, cheated, or stole (Scaramella, Rodriguez, & Allen, 2009). Where did the message that it is acceptable to let others do these things without taking action originate? How did doing the right thing become the wrong thing to do?

More than 30 years ago, the **Knapp Commission** discovered that the majority of New York City police officers did not aggressively seek out opportunities to engage in unethical conduct (Knapp Commission, 1972). These officers, referred to by the Commission as *grass eaters,* chose not to get involved in such conduct, but refused to turn in fellow officers who did—thus, in effect, condoning unethical acts. This reluctance to report wrongdoing is now generally referred to as *nonfeasance* in the literature (Delattre, 2002). Are we creating generations of grass eaters outside as well as inside policing? Do we unwittingly teach youth in general, and police recruits specifically, to condone unethical conduct?

In many cases, the answer appears to be yes. Although we teach our children not to lie, steal, or cheat, many of us also teach them not to get involved when others lie, steal, or cheat. "It's not your business, stay out of it!" "Don't get involved!" "You just worry about yourself, not about other people." These and other similar pieces of advice may indeed lead youth to become grass eaters who simply turn away from lying, cheating, and stealing. They learn very early that "ratting" on another individual is unacceptable behavior in many settings, perhaps as bad as being directly involved in unethical conduct. Of course, the police subculture often builds on exactly this consideration. Loyalty to the group (other officers) is held out as a virtue, even when it means engaging in unethical conduct (covering, making excuses, telling "white lies") to protect unethical individuals (involved, for example, in perjury or theft from victims or crime scenes). Yet police officers are required by the **Code of Conduct** (see Table 8.1), as well as by federal law (Civil Rights Act, Title 42 United States Code section 1983), not to condone such behavior.

Research has shown that some police agency policies allow or encourage officers to accept precisely those gratuities, favors, subscriptions, and gifts that the Code of Conduct prohibits (Dorn, 2001). Other policies prohibit accepting such favors but are ignored in practice, sending the message that it is acceptable to violate policy in at least some instances (Klockars, Ivkovic, & Haberfeld, 2004). Where do such violations stop? We know of no policies that allow or encourage perjury, theft, or brutality, so all such acts are clearly recognized as violations of policies as well as of the Code of Conduct and the law. However, there is a small portion of the literature that asserts that the blanket prohibition of small gratuities is not wise in light of the community policing era. Del Pozo (2005), for example, contended that while "... police gratuities remain problematic ... to accord with both the philosophy of community policing and the tightly-held sensibilities of many police officers, the acceptance of gratuities of de minimis value be permitted provided the officers are thoroughly and effectively trained in the potential hazards of accepting them" (p. 25). This may be true, but the **slippery slope** may be a subcultural force too strong to reckon with and may thus lead to additional questionable or unethical acts.

In some cases, policy issues are reflective of administrators who are not committed to ethical conduct. According to Trautman (2002),

> After researching thousands of incidents of serious misconduct, the single most damaging category of misconduct in law enforcement is administrators intentionally ignoring obvious ethical problems. There is nothing as negative as a chief, sheriff, director or superintendent knowing his department has ethical problems and intentionally looking the other way, trying to make it to retirement. (p. 118)

Some administrators model unethical conduct on a regular basis, allowing officers to rationalize that their misconduct is no worse than the administrator's. Putting all the

Table 8.1   Law Enforcement Code of Conduct

Police Code of Conduct

All law enforcement officers must be fully aware of the ethical responsibilities of their position and must strive constantly to live up to the highest possible standards of professional policing. The International Association of Chiefs of Police believes it important that police officers have clear advice and counsel available to assist them in performing their duties consistent with these standards and has adopted the following ethical mandates as guidelines to meet these ends.

Primary Responsibilities of a Police Officer

A police officer acts as an official representative of government who is required and trusted to work within the law. The officer's powers and duties are conferred by statute. The fundamental duties of a police officer include serving the community, safeguarding lives and property, protecting the innocent, keeping the peace, and ensuring the rights of all to liberty, equality, and justice.

Performance of the Duties of a Police Officer

A police officer shall perform all duties impartially, without favor or affection or ill will and without regard to status, sex, race, religion, political belief, or aspiration. All citizens will be treated equally with courtesy, consideration, and dignity. Officers will never allow personal feelings, animosities, or friendships to influence official conduct. Laws will be enforced appropriately and courteously and, in carrying out their responsibilities, officers will strive to obtain maximum cooperation from the public. They will conduct themselves in appearance and deportment in such a manner as to inspire confidence and respect for the position of the public trust they hold.

Discretion

A police officer will use responsibly the discretion vested in his position and exercise it within the law. The principle of reasonableness will guide the officer's determinations, and the officer will consider all surrounding circumstances in determining whether any legal action shall be taken. Consistent and wise use of discretion, based on professional policing competence, will do much to preserve good relationships and retain the confidence of the public. There can be difficulty in choosing between conflicting courses of action. It is important to remember that a timely word of advice rather than arrest—which may be correct in appropriate circumstances—can be a more effective means of achieving a desired end.

Use of Force

A police officer will never employ unnecessary force or violence and will use only such force in the discharge of duty as is reasonable in all circumstances. The use of force should be used only with the greatest restraint and only after discussion, negotiation and persuasion have been found to be inappropriate or ineffective. While the use of force is occasionally unavoidable, every police officer will refrain from unnecessary infliction of pain or suffering and will never engage in cruel, degrading or inhumane treatment of any person.

(Continued)

Table 8.1 (Continued)

Confidentiality

Whatever a police officer sees, hears, or learns of that is of a confidential nature will be kept secret unless the performance of duty or legal provision requires otherwise.

Members of the public have a right to security and privacy, and information obtained about them must not be improperly divulged.

Integrity

A police officer will not engage in acts of corruption or bribery, nor will an officer condone such acts by other police officers. The public demands that the integrity of police officers be above reproach. Police officers must, therefore, avoid any conduct that might compromise integrity and thus undercut the public confidence in a law enforcement agency. Officers will refuse to accept any gifts, presents, subscriptions, favors, gratuities, or promises that could be interpreted as seeking to cause the officer to refrain from performing official responsibilities honestly and within the law. Police officers must not receive private or special advantage from their official status. Respect from the public cannot be bought; it can only be earned and cultivated.

Cooperation With Other Police Officers and Agencies

Police officers will cooperate with all legally authorized agencies and their representatives in the pursuit of justice. An officer or agency may be one among many organizations that may provide law enforcement services to a jurisdiction. It is imperative that a police officer assists colleagues fully and completely with respect and consideration at all times.

Personal–Professional Capabilities

Police officers will be responsible for their own standard of professional performance and will take every reasonable opportunity to enhance and improve their level of knowledge and competence. Through study and experience, a police officer can acquire the high level of knowledge and competence that is essential for the efficient and effective performance of duty. The acquisition of knowledge is a never-ending process of personal and professional development that should be pursued constantly.

Private Life

Police officers will behave in a manner that does not bring discredit to their agencies or themselves. A police officer's character and conduct while off duty must always be exemplary, thus maintaining a position of respect in the community in which he or she lives and serves. The officer's personal behavior must be beyond reproach.

Source: From *Police Code of Conduct,* by the International Association of Chiefs of Police, 2005, p. iv. Available from http://shr.elpasoco.com/NR/rdonlyres/7A3D02A5-E92B-4055-AF7E-90D92A3DF6D3/0/code_of_conduct.pdf. Reprinted with permission.

blame for unethical conduct on administrators, however, may encourage individual officers who engage in such conduct to attempt to escape responsibility for their actions.

In a recent study that examined frontline supervisors' perceptions of police integrity, the supervisors reported reluctance to act on the misconduct of their subordinates because of the perceived unethical practices of high ranking supervisors in their organization. The authors of the study posited the following question, ". . . though supervisors may believe in the need for reform, will they act on those beliefs when they do not believe their own supervisors are legitimately committed to improvement" (Schafer & Martinelli, 2008)? Unfortunately, the answer is, more than likely, no.

It must be stated clearly at this point that we firmly believe that the vast majority of police officers in the United States perform their duties honestly, ethically, and professionally. Still, a small minority of officers tarnish policing by engaging in inappropriate behavior. Unfortunately, these select few do a tremendous amount of damage to the reputation of policing and place the field in the uncomfortable position of having to constantly convince the public that acts of police malfeasance are not widespread. Far too often, those who do the right thing by telling the truth and exposing corruption and brutality are the victims of vicious attacks from within their ranks. Expose unethical conduct and you risk your life. Do the right thing and you become a pariah. Confronting unethical conduct under these circumstances requires bravery above and beyond the call of duty, and many officers would simply prefer to keep their distance.

The maintenance of ethical standards within the field of policing is important for several reasons, all of which are obvious and none of which can be taken lightly. First and foremost, the police are public servants, agents of the government sworn to uphold the laws of the land. As such, they must be role models for all of society, on and off the job. When police officers violate the public trust by engaging in unethical behavior, illegal or otherwise, the trust and confidence between themselves and the public they serve is shaken. Furthermore, and perhaps even more devastating, when the bond between the public and police is severed, the ideals of the entire criminal justice system may be called into question. As stated by FBI Director Mueller (2006), "Public corruption is the betrayal of the public's sacred trust. It erodes public confidence and undermines the strength of our democracy. Unchecked, it threatens our government and our way of life." More specifically, one high ranking official from the FBI recently stated, "The oath taken by the men and women of law enforcement to uphold the law is not an idle one. Corruption cases involving a police officer erode the public trust and thereby complicate and impede the efforts being made by the law enforcement community at all levels." (U.S. Department of Justice, 2007)

☞ CASE IN POINT 8.1

Two public safety officers were placed on paid administrative leave Monday pending an investigation into recordings in which they made vulgar sexual remarks about female co-workers and crime victims, City Manager John Smithson said during a news conference here.

Police Maj. Walt Floyd and police Lt. Don Repec will remain on paid leave until the investigation is complete. Smithson said he does not know how long the investigation will take.

(Continued)

(Continued)

Floyd had been the department's interim director. Smithson said police Capt. Rick Buddelmeyer now will be interim director.

Mayor Marilyn Hatley said she was "dismayed, disgusted and sickened at the content and graphic descriptions" of the comments, which were secretly recorded by former police Lt. Randy Fisher.

"I am appalled by this behavior," Hatley said. "I am appalled it took place while these officers were on duty. We do not excuse this behavior."

Smithson and Hatley also blamed Fisher, who was forced to resign in November, for failing to bring the recordings to their attention. The city learned of the conversations after The Sun News reported on them Sunday. Fisher has provided copies of the recordings he made to The Sun News.

"I'm also disappointed and disturbed that Mr. Randy Fisher, a former lieutenant with the Public Safety Department in North Myrtle Beach, would allow these things to happen while he idly sat by," Hatley said. "Mr. Fisher recorded these conversations and failed to bring these comments or issues to light. By his failure to do so, he has lost all credibility in the eyes of the council."

Fisher could not be reached for comment on Monday.

The recordings show Fisher repeatedly complained to Floyd—his supervisor—about what he termed improper and unethical behavior within the public safety department. Fisher also expressed concerns to Steve Thomas, the assistant city manager, and told Thomas in a letter that he had recorded conversations to back up his claims. Fisher told The Sun News no city official ever acted on his complaints until after the issues were publicized in The Sun News.

Smithson said Fisher should have been more specific about his complaints.

"He should have been more explicit about what he felt he needed to tell us," Smithson said. "He could have come to my office, laid the recordings on the counter and said, 'I have something you need to listen to.'"

Hatley said it was Fisher's responsibility to bring the information to Smithson.

"We as a council are here today to tell you we do not condone or appreciate Mr. Fisher's failure to act," she said.

Mike Ragusa, a Barefoot Resort resident who has been critical of city leaders, said Hatley's comments about Fisher "are typical of the way the city tries to attack anyone who points out problems."

Fisher was forced to resign after Thomas accused him of giving confidential information about an April wildfire to Ragusa. Fisher, who is Ragusa's friend, has said he did not provide any confidential information.

On one of the recordings, Floyd can be heard disagreeing with Fisher and police Lt. Don Repec about whether criminal sexual conduct charges should be brought against a 17-year-old male who was accused of having sex with his 14-year-old girlfriend. The male had been charged with committing a lewd act on a minor, but Fisher and Repec wanted to ask a judge to upgrade the charges to the more serious violation, according to the recording.

Floyd states on the recording that the lieutenants "don't need to charge that boy."

Floyd then asks the lieutenants if they ever had sex at that age.

"Damn if I wouldn't have screwed her when I was that young," Floyd said on the recording.

On another recording, Floyd and the two lieutenants are discussing a female co-worker. Repec said on the recording he thinks the co-worker is a prude and the type of person "that'll turn the lights off and get under the covers before she'll have sex."

"Don't you know you won't cut the lights off," Floyd said on the recording. "If I can't see it, I don't want it."

Floyd then makes several sexual comments referring to the co-worker.

On another recording, Repec and Floyd are talking about the number of criminal domestic violence cases that have been reported.

"All these criminal domestic violences in here, can the victim advocate start enrolling people in, some of these women, in obedience school so they don't have all these problems with their men," Repec said on the recording.

"We probably need to," Floyd said on the recording, in response to Repec's repeated request to enroll the victims in obedience school.

The recorded statements have prompted the executive director of a statewide group that advocates for domestic violence victims to call for an expanded investigation of the department by the State Law Enforcement Division.

SLED already has been asked to investigate allegations that William Bailey, the city's former public safety director, covered up a criminal domestic violence investigation because it involved the daughter of a top political supporter of Mayor Marilyn Hatley.

Vicki Bourus, executive director of the S.C. Coalition Against Domestic Violence and Sexual Assault, and Smithson asked SLED to investigate those allegations earlier this month. Smithson said a SLED officer visited city hall last week but the agency has not said whether an investigation is imminent.

Bailey was demoted to lieutenant last week because he admitted he lied to Smithson about the circumstances surrounding the theft of his city-issued police handgun. Smithson's investigation into that issue took four weeks.

Ethics in policing are also important because true ethical practice encapsulates a host of intimately related characteristics that are the essence of **professionalism**, an end state that most law enforcement practitioners seek to achieve. Professional police officers are those who have the following qualities:

1. Possess excellent personal character

2. Understand the concepts of justice, temperance, and truthfulness

3. Respect laws, policies, and credos consistent with democratic ideals

4. Remain accountable to both their organizations and their respective communities

5. Possess a commitment to higher education and continuous learning throughout their careers

6. Remain intolerant of misconduct within their ranks. (Delattre, 2002)

To encourage ethical conduct, police agencies must recruit, select, hire, and promote individuals of excellent character, and they must demonstrate a sustained commitment to professionalism. In addition, they should emphasize ethics in recruitment, selection, and hiring practices. Stephens (2006) cited a statement made by former President Theodore Roosevelt, the topic of which is perfectly aligned to the importance of ethics and good character. "No man can lead a public career really worth leading, no man can act with rugged independence in serious crises, nor strike at great abuses, nor afford to make powerful and unscrupulous foes, if he is himself vulnerable to his private character" (p. 222).

In addition, criminal justice curricula in higher education institutions should incorporate and emphasize the study of ethics. In an attempt to ascertain whether four-year public institutions, which offer baccalaureate degrees programs in criminal justice, incorporate a course or courses in the study of ethics as a part of their core curriculum, Scaramella (2001) examined six public universities in the state of Illinois. Unfortunately, none of the six mandated a class in the study of ethics as a component of its core curriculum at the time of the study, and only one of the six currently mandates such a course.

Using a survey instrument, Scaramella (2001) also attempted to assess the ethical attitudes of students who were enrolled in criminal justice classes (see Tables 8.1–6). This instrument included scenarios that described common police encounters along with a corresponding scale of potential responses from which students could select. The responses ranged from ethical on one end of the scale to criminal behavior on the other end. The individual scenarios included a wide range of misconduct: on-duty consumption of alcohol, acceptance of gratuities, use of excessive force, verbal abuse, acceptance of kickbacks, perjury, theft, and nonfeasance. Since the initial study, three additional studies using the same survey instrument, methodologies, and data analyses have been conducted. Two of the studies (Scaramella, 2001; Scaramella et al., 2009) had similar student survey populations, and the remaining two (Allen, Mhlanga, & Khan, 2006; Turano, 2001) had similar police officer survey populations. A comparison of responses from the four samples showed similar results with some notable exceptions. Student respondents were nearly twice as likely as their police officer counterparts to respond ethically when dealing with an off-duty police officer stopped for driving while intoxicated. Similar responses (student respondents reporting significantly more ethically than police officer respondents) were observed with ethical dilemmas pertaining to theft by a police officer at the scene of a burglary, the use of excessive force by co-workers, witnessing supervisory misconduct, and stopping an off-duty police officer for a serious traffic offense.

Perhaps the most alarming result, however, was that in each of the studies, an average of 26% of the student respondents reported a willingness to perjure themselves to keep themselves or co-workers out of trouble or for ensuring the conviction of someone they knew to be guilty, with the latter response being the most prevalent. Conversely, approximately 3% of police officer and other criminal justice professional respondents reported a willingness to perjure themselves for the same reasons.

Data from the variable pertaining to the theft of cash during the execution of a search warrant showed that approximately 25% of respondents from each study indicated that they would neither interfere with the theft nor report the misconduct of their co-workers to a supervisor. (Refer to Appendix A to view the actual data.)

It appears that what many have called nonfeasance, or a police officer's reluctance to report the wrongdoing of a co-worker(s), is responsible for the majority of unethical responses given in each study. These findings are consistent with mainstream research in the study of ethics in policing.

❖ **Photo 8.3**   Testifying truthfully in court is an ethical obligation of every police officer.

POLICE STORIES

One night my partner and I were working the midnight shift patrol duty on the streets of Chicago. We were assigned a radio call of an active burglar alarm at a gas station. When we arrived at the gas station, we noticed that the glass to the front door had been smashed and that (an) unknown offender(s) had entered the premises and pried open the cash register drawer. After a thorough search of the premises for any offender(s) with negative results, we asked the dispatcher to contact the owner and a board-up service. While waiting for the owner to arrive, we sat in our patrol car and began the paperwork. Our sector sergeant then pulled into our location, exited his vehicle, waved hello, walked over the broken glass, and entered the premises. A moment later he came out of the gas station, again walked over the broken glass, waved goodbye (while holding several packages of cigarettes from the gas station in his hand), got into his car, and drove off.

Needless to say, we were more than a bit perplexed at what we had just witnessed. I recall asking my partner if he just "saw what I just saw," and he replied, "I didn't see nothing." Neither of us took any action whatsoever, official or unofficial.

Why didn't we report our sergeant or talk about what we had just seen? Our decision was the result of that aspect of the police subculture that maintains that cops don't rat on other cops. Because of the influence of our subculture, we witnessed a crime committed not just by a fellow officer, but by our direct supervisor, and did nothing about it.

As a law enforcement officer, you may run across incidents where the police subculture affects your actions, and you will need to decide how you will respond. If faced with similar circumstances today, I would tell the sergeant that what he was doing was making me uncomfortable, note him being on the scene in the report, and leave it at that.

Can this reluctance to report wrongdoings of officers by other officers be changed? If so, how? First, criminal justice educators can place more emphasis on the study of ethics in college curricula. Second, police officials can require ongoing inservice training in ethical decision making for their officers. Third, psychological testing and applicant background investigations can focus more on eliminating applicants who have demonstrated unethical behavior. These actions may ultimately prove to be ineffective, however, if the police subculture continues to reinforce nonfeasance as an indicator of group loyalty. It should be remembered based on our discussion in Chapter 4 that group loyalty is deeply imbedded in the tradition of the police subculture in the United States.

Many students aspiring to join the ranks of law enforcement engage in illegal and unethical activities during their teens and early twenties (illegal drug use, petty theft, etc.), prior to applying for a job in the field. Due to applicant background investigations, drug screenings, and other checks, these students have effectively disqualified themselves from service in the law enforcement profession before applying for police officer positions. Stephens (2006), addressing this issue, reminded us that we must hold ourselves accountable for our past indiscretions, even if they occurred prior to application for employment. In a speech given to criminal justice college students, Stephens (2006) said that he intended to deliver ". . . a wake-up call, a gentle reminder that for every decision one makes, one may later be held accountable." (p. 23) Further, for those who desire a career in law enforcement, decisions made in the past may not remain in the past but are likely to be revealed through investigation and are likely to have consequences.

Racial Profiling

In the past decade or so, the police have been under attack by the media for allegedly biased enforcement practices, or what journalists and other public watchdog groups refer to as *biased enforcement* or *racial profiling*. **Racial profiling** is a component of biased enforcement involving the practice of disproportionately targeting minority group members for various law enforcement initiatives (i.e., selective traffic enforcement, narcotics interdiction efforts, etc.). While allegations of racial profiling initially dealt largely with traffic stops of blacks, expanded police concern with terrorists, along with increased police presence in airports, have led to allegations of ethnic and religious profiling involving Middle Easterners. At the same time, illegal immigration from Mexico, which once affected primarily border cities and western states, has grown to be a national problem (Pendergraph, 2008). In fact, by the end of 2007, more than 100 police agencies in 15 states had completed or enrolled in federal programs discussing methods for identifying undocumented immigrants during routine law enforcement activities. "The five-week course includes instruction on civil rights and immigration laws, prohibitions on racial profiling, cross-cultural issues and treaty obligations that require officers to notify foreign consulates about arrests for violent crimes such as homicide in death-penalty states" (Anonymous, 2007, p. 1). When and where racial profiling or biased enforcement occurs, it constitutes a violation of law since race, ethnicity, gender, and age do not constitute probable cause for making a stop. Such behavior also constitutes an ethical violation since using any of these personal characteristics as the sole basis for police action is wrong. Further, such stops, when they occur, also violate departmental policy.

Allegations of racial profiling, true or not, have brought about increased judicial, legislative, and public concern and legislatures in each state and at the federal level have enacted laws requiring mandatory data collection regarding the police activities cited. As a result, most police departments have developed written directives or policies to establish procedures for officers in their relations with traffic violators. Such policies may provide that officers should strive to make stops educational and leave the violator with the impression that the officer has performed a necessary task in a professional and friendly manner. They also specify that officers not stop, detain, search, or arrest any traffic violator based solely on the person's race, ethnicity, age, gender, or disability unless they are seeking an individual with one or more of those identified attributes (e.g., officers may consider a person's apparent age or race when investigating a violation when the age or race of a suspected perpetrator is known).

Currently, when making a traffic stop, officers are often required to complete a Traffic Stop Form that requires the following information:

If a warning or citation was issued, the violation charged or warning provided

Whether an arrest was made as a result of either the stop or the search

The race or ethnicity and gender of the person stopped

If an arrest was made, the crime charged

The location of the stop

Further, officers are directed to treat every person with courtesy and respect and to provide their name, serial or badge number, and reason for the vehicle stop to the person stopped. Whenever a person complains that an officer has engaged in practices prohibited by this directive, the officer is directed to notify his or her supervisor. If possible, a supervisor may respond to the stop location when advised that a person is making a complaint alleging profiling or other improper conduct and, after discussion with the person, provide the complainant with a Citizen Complaint Form if the matter is not resolved. The complainant is to be provided guidance in completing and filing the complaint form. Departments then periodically review the statistical information collected from the Traffic Stop Form to determine compliance. If the review reveals a pattern of discrimination, an investigation will be conducted to determine whether or not officers routinely stop members of minority groups for violations of vehicle laws as a pretext for investigating other violations of criminal law. Officers found to have engaged in race-based traffic stops then receive appropriate counseling and training.

❖ Police Accountability

In a democratic society, all public servants are ultimately accountable to the public through the political process. Presidents, governors, county and municipal administrators, and the legislative bodies with which they work are responsible for overseeing the efforts of public servants, including the police. Various segments of the public, through the election process, make their desires known to these overseers who must balance these desires with legal considerations. We had more to say about the law and its impact on the police in Chapter 5. In this section, we address accountability to the public and those elected to represent them.

Because the powers granted the police are considerable, citizens are likely to be vigilant in monitoring police actions and aware of their right to demand that the police account for their behavior. Requirements that the police issue periodic reports concerning their activities are one indicator of such vigilance, as is the increasing demand for transparency in policing. Both of these considerations make it likely that members of the media will insure that police activities are continually visible to the public (with the exception of ongoing operations that might be jeopardized by disclosure).

As Walker (2005) noted, police accountability has two dimensions.

> The first of these is agency accountability for services the agency is expected to provide—in the case of the police things such as crime control, order maintenance, openness to citizen complaints, and a variety of other services. The second dimension refers to the accountability of individual officers—their treatment of individuals, their use of force, the fairness they demonstrate or fail to demonstrate to individuals regardless of social status or personal characteristics, and so on. (p. 7)

Over the years, the police have attempted to demonstrate accountability by becoming more professional, using internal affairs units, improving citizen complaint procedures, and **early intervention programs** that focus on identifying officers whose behavior is problematic, intervening to correct the problem behavior, and following up with those who have received intervention (Lersch, Bazley, & Mieczkowski, 2006). While all of these agency attempts to insure accountability are worthwhile, as Bills, Ching-Chung, Heringer, and Mankin (2009) noted, police officers themselves have an obligation to demand peer-to-peer accountability when they believe professional transgressions have been committed. As we have noted elsewhere in this chapter, this is a desirable, difficult to achieve, goal.

Involvement in community policing (COP) is seen by some police administrators as a step in the right direction with respect to accountability. Formation of genuine partnerships between the police and the citizens they serve, and the increased visibility of police operations accompanying these partnerships, might serve to bridge the gap between the police and the public. The establishment of ride-along programs, citizen police academies, and neighborhood watch groups enable the public to become more knowledgeable about actual police operations while, hopefully, promoting improved relationships between officers and those residing in the neighborhoods they patrol. While the emphasis on community policing has waned in recent years, there is at least some reason to believe that some of the core elements of COP have been incorporated into many police departments.

Outside the police agencies, society has attempted to hold the police accountable through litigation, improved hiring practices, and the formation of citizen oversight groups. Many of these attempts focus on holding the police legally and ethically responsible for their actions by establishing limits on discretionary conduct, and many involve increased reporting related to police performance. Success in these attempts has been limited by the failure to adopt uniform standards of accountability, by failure to maintain those standards that are established, and by lack of supervisory oversight.

In the long run, it is essential that the police respond to public demands for accountability in order to establish public trust. When such accountability exists, the public can judge for itself how successful the police are in exercising discretion wisely and in conducting themselves ethically.

❖ Professionalism and the Police

As we noted in Chapter 3, professionalism was a focal point for police reformers during much of the 20th century. Ethics is one of the cornerstones of professionalism, as indicated by the fact that many professions have adopted codes of ethics. A special code of ethics or conduct is required for the police because of two special ethical problems confronting police officers. First, the police are entitled to use coercive force. Second, they are entitled to lie to and otherwise deceive others in the course of their duties (e.g., while conducting undercover operations or interrogating suspects). Further, special standards of conduct appear to be necessary in policing because police officers, over the years, have engaged in activities that have offended the moral sensibilities of a good number of people. Finally, the need for special ethical standards arises whenever certain types of conduct are not subject to control by other means, usually when practitioners exercise considerable discretion and when those affected must trust them to be ethical. As noted throughout this book, this is clearly the case with the police.

Yet a code of ethics is not the only requirement for a profession. The professional is also typically accountable to a group of peers for the decisions he or she makes (e.g., the American Medical Society and the American Bar Association). Professionals are also required, in most cases, to attain at least a minimum level of education and training related to the field in which they practice. And professionals typically have a considerable degree of discretion or autonomy in career-related decision making.

YOU DECIDE 8.1

You are the chief of police of Middletown, U.S.A., whose emblem shown on police shirt patches and displayed on marked police cars says "Professionalism, Honesty, and Bravery." Your agency has a new police exam approaching for those aspiring to join the ranks of the department. You also have a few openings for supervisors, one for the rank of sergeant and two for the rank of lieutenant, which in many cases is a promotion to a command position. Based on the material presented in this chapter regarding professionalism and on much of the information found in Chapter 3 "Police Training and Education," develop a policy regarding formal and continuing education requirements for all three ranks: entry level officers, sergeants, and lieutenants. Be as specific as possible.

Some would argue that policing has attained at least a degree of professionalization, particularly in the past 15 to 20 years. Many law enforcement agencies across the country have raised their minimum education and basic recruit training requirements for entry level as well as supervisory positions. Although these accomplishments are important in the eyes of many police administrators and criminal justice scholars, unethical conduct consistently emerges as the major obstacle to further professionalization. Ricciardi and Rabin (2000), for example, noted in their 10-year analysis of corruption within the ranks of the Los Angeles Police Department that one of the major culprits was lack of training relevant to ethics and to racial or cultural diversity issues. To see how these issues affect policing in other countries, see the following Around the World.

AROUND THE WORLD

"The bodies in charge of public safety in Mexico do not fully guarantee the individual and legal safety of citizens, nor a harmonious coexistence among the members of society" (p. 3).

"Mexican law enforcement agencies were originally designed as instruments of political control, authorized to make use of force outside of formal controls. In exchange for carrying out this task of control, police forces were granted a broad margin of impunity that allowed for the consolidation of informal systems of relative self-government within the forces" (p. 9).

Unfortunately, there is a collective feeling of lack of safety and impunity in the country. The increase in organized crime and drug trafficking, as well as the lack of coordination between the higher ranks of law enforcement and the bodies in charge of safety, have generated corruption and inefficiency problems which have undermined the police forces' response capacity. (p. 3)

In Mexico City, complaints "...received by the Human Rights Commission of the Federal District (*Comisión de Derechos Humanos del Distrito Federal:* CDHDF) from October, 2001 to July, 2005, totaled 25,257 [and] complaints advanced by complainants were related to the improper exercise of public service, arbitrary arrests, injuries, forceful disappearance, torture and summary executions" (p. 2).

It appears that ". . . police accountability, understood to be an internal and external control system of the evaluation of results and of learning, is not among the priorities of the most relevant political actors and civil society, nor is it, of course, among that of the police forces themselves" (p. 12).

"Problems inherent to the police forces are related to the poor training and precarious economic conditions of officers, as well as to the extortion suffered by officers at the hands of their superiors, deficient equipment and the negative image of officers held by the general public" (p. 4).

There is a clear expectation among Mexican citizens of being able to corrupt the police. Almost two thirds of a sample of Mexican citizens interviewed believed that "they can bribe a police officer in order to avoid arrest" (p. 13). To date, no poll has found that a majority of respondents trust the police.

Source: From *Approaches to the Mexico City Police Force and Its Makeup,* from the International Conference on Police Accountability and the Quality of Oversight: Global Trends in National Context. Available from http://www.altus.org/pdf/m_mlk_en.pdf.

Arnold's (1997) in-depth analysis of police ethics training in Illinois found the following:

- Less than 1% of police academy training focuses on ethical and moral decision making.
- As a topic of continuing professional education or inservice training, ethics and moral decision making are seldom offered.
- There is very little consistency in training programs with respect to instructor qualifications, instructional philosophy and methodology, and course content.
- Training in ethics at the inservice level is sporadic at best and normally has little support from police executives.
- Data also demonstrate that there is little to no agreement among police executives, regional training directors, and police academy training directors concerning what constitutes police ethics.

Arnold's (1997) conclusions seem to indicate a need for significant changes in the areas of training curricula, organizational and executive-level commitment, instructional philosophies, and instructor qualifications, topics that were discussed in more detail in Chapter 3.

Other research focusing on issues pertaining to police integrity espouse similar recommendations (i.e., the need for increased emphasis on the study of ethics and its related principles), both at the recruit and inservice level (U.S. Department of Justice, 2001; U.S. General Accounting Office, 1998). More specifically, the Department of Justice report recommends that basic and inservice training curriculums be expanded to include and stress the importance of subjects such as ethical decision making; responsible use of discretionary authority; racial, ethnic, and cultural diversity; and the development of effective interpersonal communication skills. The National Law Enforcement Policy Center, an arm of the International Association of Chiefs of Police, recently stated the following in a policy paper:

> . . . most popular literature and movie depictions of police work deal extensively with the moral and ethical dilemmas that officers face on the job . . . proper ethics training for police officers is as vital as any other instruction that officers receive . . . and [this] training needs to be emphasized not only at the beginning of an officer's career, but also throughout his or her service. (Law Enforcement Employment Bulletin, 2008)

❖ Chapter Summary

The use of discretion by police is a necessity in the world of policing for obvious reasons. The problem, though, is that the exercise of this broad power is not always underscored by responsible and ethical decision making, and it is our old friend, the police subculture, that has a tremendous influence on the use of discretion. For example, oftentimes discretion regarding the enforcement of certain crimes is not applied equally to all segments of the community. When this perception takes hold, real or imagined, an erosion of trust between those segments of the community and the police is bound to occur and will more than likely lead to strained police–community relations.

One of the most significant issues in the recent past is what the press dubbed racial profiling, or the targeting of minorities and other certain classes by police for no other reason than race, ethnicity, and perhaps social class. Because of the vast media coverage of this topic, as well as related research projects, there was a further erosion of trust between the public and the police, particularly among minority populations. This was not the only cost as Congress and state legislatures in the nation created laws requiring mandatory data collection by police agencies regarding police encounters with citizens pertaining to detention, search and seizure, and arrests or other legal sanctions. The economic cost for the implementation of these new policies came at great expense to individual agencies.

The latter part of this chapter examined the importance of ethics in policing. Unethical conduct by police ranges from violations of department rules and regulations to more serious issues such as unlawful searches and seizures, the use of excessive force, covering up for the malfeasance of fellow officers, and more.

Police officers are held to a higher ethical standard than most other citizens because of the oath they took when they entered the field of policing. Honesty, integrity, responsibility, accountability, and professionalism (on and off duty) are the underlying tenets of that oath. When fiduciary responsibilities are breached by officers, the consequences can be damaging not only to the individual officers, but to their respective agencies and the communities they serve, the most serious of which is a loss of faith or trust by those communities.

There are many reasons why unethical practices by some police officers continue, and chief among them are the negative influences of the police subculture, lack of strict accountability on the part of all police officers, ineffective supervisory practices, and weak or ineffective leadership structures.

In sum, ethical practice is a requisite for professional status, and if the field of policing is to progress further along the path to professionalization, all parties concerned must commit themselves to achieving this end. Whether the police are able to attain this end depends, in large part, on the responsible and accountable exercise of discretionary authority.

❖ Key Terms

police discretion	nonfeasance
racial profiling	mandatory data collection
police subculture	Knapp Commission
police ethics	grass eaters
biased-enforcement	Police Code of Conduct or Ethics
quotas	slippery slope
zero-tolerance arrest policies	professionalism
malfeasance	early intervention programs

❖ Discussion Questions

1. What is police discretion? How extensive is its use?

2. Why is the police subculture important in understanding discretion?

3. What are some possible negative consequences of the exercise of discretion? What are some positive consequences?

4. What factors besides the police subculture affect the exercise of police discretion?

5. Can we eliminate the exercise of police discretion? Should we eliminate it? How might we gain better control over it?

6. Discuss racial profiling as an example of poor discretionary decision making.

7. Discuss the evolution of the police code of ethics or conduct. Why are ethics especially important for the police?

8. List and discuss strategies that may be undertaken to improve the current state ethical decision making.

9. Why is police accountability important and how can it best be promoted?

10. What are some of the obstacles to police accountability?

❖ Internet Exercises

1. Using the key words "international police accountability," locate and discuss information concerning attempts to establish police accountability in at least one foreign country other than Mexico.

2. Use the Internet to locate the code of ethics or code of conduct for a police agency in your area. How does this code compare to the code established by the International Association of Chiefs of Police? In your opinion, is the code enforceable?

3. On the Internet, locate information concerning racial profiling or biased enforcement in your city, county, or state. Does it appear that racial profiling or biased enforcement is a problem in your area? Describe information that supports your conclusion.

❖ Appendix A

Table 8.1 illustrates that there is statistical significance and moderate strength of association, the null hypothesis is rejected. Of the responding students, 49.6% answered they would place the DUI officer under arrest. Police officers choosing arrest as a viable option totaled 5.7%. Notifying a supervisor was the second most popular response, totaling 20.8% of the police officers and 16.3% of student respondents. Responses in the "other" category included driving the officer home or arranging other methods of transportation, calling a relative or friend to pick the officer up, and

Table 8.1	Off-Duty Police Officer Stopped for DUI				
Crosstab					
			respondent id		
			student	police officer	Total
off duty officer dui	place driver under arrest for DUI	Count	70	11	81
		% within respondent id	49.6%	5.7%	24.3%
	issue a verbal or written warning	Count	19	6	25
		% within respondent id	13.5%	3.1%	7.5%
	notify a supervisor	Count	23	40	63
		% within respondent id	16.3%	20.8%	18.9%
	take no action	Count	3	9	12
		% within respondent id	2.1%	4.7%	3.6%
	other	Count	26	126	152
		% within respondent id	18.4%	65.6%	45.6%
Total		Count	141	192	333
		% within respondent id	100.0%	100.0%	100.0%

Source: From Scaramella, G., Rodriguez, R. & Allen, J. (2010).

Note: N=333. M=2. Chi-square=118.071, df=4. C=.595, p<.05

combining one or more of the listed options along with notifying the officer's department. The results do not support the research hypothesis.

Table 8.2 depicts that there is statistical significance and moderate strength of association, the null hypothesis is rejected. Of the responding police officers, 60.9% indicated they would notify a supervisor. None of the surveyed officers indicated they would take merchandise, and 6.8% of police would voice disapproval and take no further action. Surveyed students responded that 41.1% would notify a supervisor and 26.2% would voice disapproval and take no further action. In addition, 1.4% of students responded that they would take merchandise themselves. Responses in the "other" category included warning the officers to return the merchandise or that the incident would be reported. The results support the research hypothesis.

As shown in Table 8.3, both the students and police officers chose the ethically appropriate course of action regarding dealing with an officer using excessive force. There is no statistical significance, therefore the null hypothesis would be accepted.

Table 8.2   Theft From a Burglary Scene

Crosstab

			respondent id		Total
			student	police officer	
theft from scene of burglary fellow officer	place co-worker under arrest	Count	21	4	25
		% within respondent id	14.9%	2.1%	7.5%
	tell co-worker you disapprove & take no further action	Count	37	13	50
		% within respondent id	26.2%	6.8%	15.0%
	notify a supervisor	Count	58	117	175
		% within respondent id	41.1%	60.9%	52.6%
	help yourself to some merchandise	Count	2		2
		% within respondent id	1.4%		.6%
	other	Count	23	58	81
		% within respondent id	16.3%	30.2%	24.3%
Total		Count	141	192	333
		% within respondent id	100.0%	100.0%	100.0%

Source: From Scaramella, G., Rodriguez, R. & Allen, J. (2010).

Note: N=333. M=2. Chi-square=53.540, df=4. C=.401, p<.05

Table 8.3   Excessive Force

Crosstab

			respondent id		Total
			student	police officer	
fellow officer excessive use of force	place co-worker under arrest	Count	5	1	6
		% within respondent id	3.6%	.5%	1.8%
	tell co-worker you disapprove/take no action	Count	52	57	109
		% within respondent id	37.1%	29.5%	32.7%
	notify a supervisor	Count	54	90	144
		% within respondent id	38.6%	46.6%	43.2%

			respondent id		
			student	police officer	Total
	take no official action	Count	18	24	42
		% within respondent id	12.9%	12.4%	12.6%
	other	Count	11	21	32
		% within respondent id	7.9%	10.9%	9.6%
Total		Count	140	193	333
		% within respondent id	100.0%	100.0%	100.0%

Source: From Scaramella, G., Rodriguez, R. & Allen, J. (2010).

Note: N=333. M=2. Chi-Square=7.636, df=4. C=.151, p>.05 ns

As Table 8.4 shows, there is statistical significance and moderate strength of association; the null hypothesis is rejected. Of responding students, 34.5% would issue a citation, compared with 2.6% of police. However, 76.2% of police answered unethically, and would take no official action, compared with 50.4% of students. Additionally, 4.3% of students would notify a supervisor,

Table 8.4 Off-Duty Officer Stopped for Serious Traffic Violation

Crosstab					
			respondent id		
			student	police officer	Total
off duty officer traffic violation	issue the citation	Count	48	5	53
		% within respondent id	34.5%	2.6%	16.0%
	take no official action	Count	70	147	217
		% within respondent id	50.4%	76.2%	65.4%
	notify supervisor	Count	6	6	12
		% within respondent id	4.3%	3.1%	3.6%
	other	Count	15	35	50
		% within respondent id	10.8%	18.1%	15.1%
Total		Count	139	193	332
		% within respondent id	100.0%	100.0%	100.0%

Source: From Scaramella, G., Rodriguez, R. & Allen, J. (2010).

Note: N=332. M=3. Chi-Square=63.095, df=3. C=.436, p<.05

compared with 3.1% of police officers. Responses in the "other" category included issuing a warning to the officer, notifying a supervisor, notifying the officer's department, and deciding on a course of action depending on the offending officer's attitude. The results do not support the research hypothesis.

Table 8.5 depicts the results as statistically significant, and there is moderate strength of association; the null hypothesis is rejected. Of responding police officers, 95.3% indicated they would never perjure themselves. However, 2.6% responded they would commit perjury to prevent themselves from scrutiny or to ensure conviction of a defendant they knew to be guilty. In addition, 25.4% of responding students indicated they would commit perjury, while 71.7% indicated they would never commit perjury. Responses in the "other" category included statements that the criminal justice system is unfair, that defendants lie regularly, and that perjury would never be committed deliberately. The results support the research hypothesis.

Table 8.6 illustrates that there is statistical significance and moderate strength of association; the null hypothesis is rejected. Of the responding officers, 80.6% responded they would either notify a supervisor (39%) or not participate in the theft of the money and not take any official action (41%). In addition, 87.1% of students responded in the same manner as police. Of surveyed officers, 39.2% would notify a supervisor, compared to 27.7% of the students. However, 5.8% of students reported they would take a portion of the money, while none of the police officers

Table 8.5	Perjury				
Crosstab					
			respondent id		
			student	police officer	Total
willing to commit perjury	prevent self or other officer from scrutiny	Count	12	2	14
		% within respondent id	8.7%	1.0%	4.2%
	ensure conviction of defendant you knew was guilty	Count	23	3	26
		% within respondent id	16.7%	1.6%	7.9%
	would never perjur yourself	Count	99	184	283
		% within respondent id	71.7%	95.3%	85.5%
	other	Count	4	4	8
		% within respondent id	2.9%	2.1%	2.4%
Total		Count	138	193	331
		% within respondent id	100.0%	100.0%	100.0%

Source: From Scaramella, G., Rodriguez, R. & Allen, J. (2010).

Note: N=331. M=4. Chi-Square=40.024, df=3. C=.348, p<.05

Table 8.6 Theft of Cash During Execution of Search Warrant					
Crosstab					
			respondent id		
			student	police officer	**Total**
inventory of seized drug money	will not participate in theft of money	Count % within respondent id	74 54.0%	75 41.4%	149 46.9%
	take a portion of the money	Count % within respondent id	8 5.8%		8 2.5%
	notify a supervisor	Count % within respondent id	38 27.7%	71 39.2%	109 34.3%
	take no action	Count % within respondent id	9 6.6%	2 1.1%	11 3.5%
	other	Count % within respondent id	8 5.8%	33 18.2%	41 12.9%
Total		Count % within respondent id	137 100.0%	181 100.0%	318 100.0%

Source: From Scaramella, G., Rodriguez, R. & Allen, J. (2010).

Note: N=318. M= 17. Chi-Square=32.225, df=4. C=.318, p<.05

responded in that manner. In addition, 6.6% of students indicated they would take no official action, compared to 1.1% of the police officers. The response most frequently submitted in the "other" category was to tell the offending officers that if they persisted, the incident would be reported. The results support the research hypotheses.

Police
Misconduct

❖ **Photo 9.1**   Some symbols of the various and potential forms of police misconduct.

❖ Introduction

Police misconduct is a complicated topic with a long and convoluted history in the United States. Misconduct may be broadly divided into two categories—corruption and physical or emotional abuse—and may be either organizational or individual in nature. Each of these categories includes numerous subcategories, which often overlap, and are violations of the ethical standards of police officers. As pointed out in earlier chapters, in a general sense, *ethics* refers to the moral obligation of humans to act in ways that are good and proper. Applied specifically to police officers, ethical conduct is especially important because of the authority granted officers and because of the difficulty of overseeing the daily behavior of police officers on the street.

> Police possess at least two capacities whose use raises special ethical problems. Police are entitled to use coercive force and to lie and deceive people in the course of their work. Moreover, as sociologist Egon Bittner reminds us, while "few of us are constantly mindful of the saying, He that is without sin among you, let him cast the first stone, only the police are explicitly required to forget it." (Klockars, 1989, p. 427)

In addition, of course, police performance has traditionally been subject to a good deal of moral controversy, partly because officers deal with moral issues on a regular basis and partly because their behavior has sometimes offended the moral sensitivities of others. Finally, the police engage in discretionary behavior regularly, and other citizens must place a good deal of trust in police conduct with little in the way of assurances that that conduct is subject to adequate control (Klockars, 1989). Many ethical violations by the police fall under the general heading of conduct unbecoming a police officer and are investigated by other police officers. In light of the potential for police misconduct resulting from the periodic need to coerce or deceive the public, there is clearly a need for more attention to **police ethics** than is commonly paid.

In our present era of community policing, law enforcement executives, government officials, community groups, and academicians all advocate policing strategies that include partnerships with the public in the control and suppression of crime, thus providing for an overall improvement in the quality of life. Such strategies, sound though they are, require an atmosphere of trust and confidence between the citizenry and those who have been sworn to serve and protect them—the police. Unfortunately, various acts of misconduct by a minority of police officers occur all too frequently, serving to create an aura of suspicion, mistrust, and uncertainty between the police and the public they serve. When allegations of corruption arise and are confirmed, effective policing strategies are severely inhibited.

This issue of misconduct in the field of policing is the focus of this chapter, and we provide a brief historical analysis of police conduct; identify various forms, causes, and consequences of police corruption; and offer recommendations for an improved response to this serious problem.

❖ Police Corruption

One need only briefly examine daily media accounts to realize the breadth of corrupt and unethical law enforcement practices. Consider the recent news items listed in Tables 9.1a and 9.1b. Unfortunately, accounts of police misconduct are not hard to find. The examples in Table 9.1a were located after only a cursory search of a news service database. Even more alarming for police executives is that these particular acts of misconduct pertain to allegations of criminal conduct, and criminal offenses perpetrated by police officers represent only a small percentage of the activities routinely classified as police misconduct. Before examining the various forms of police misconduct, a few words regarding this phenomenon are in order.

Table 9.1a Examples of Police Misconduct: United States			
Author(s)	Title	Year	Summary of Misconduct
Strunsky, S. Associated Press	"Two More Officers Charged in Newark Police Corruption Case."	2004	At least four indictments of officers charging the sale of narcotics and shaking down drug dealers for money and drugs.
Associated Press	"Fourth Defendant Sentenced in Memphis Police Corruption Case."	2006	Sting operation. Cases involved taking money to protect drug dealers, burglary, and transporting prostitutes to remote casinos.

(Continued)

Table 9.1a (Continued)

Author(s)	Title	Year	Summary of Misconduct
Associated Press	"Topeka Police Corruption Story."	2006	Case involved two officers accused of stealing thousands of dollars intended for undercover drug buys.
Associated Press	"Chicago Police Dept. not Doing Enough to Stop Corruption."	2006	Chicago officials were accused of a "practice of indifference to corruption . . . making officers who engage in misconduct feel protected."
Tram, M. Associated Press	"More Arrests as Chicago Police Corruption Investigation Widens; 3 Officers Charged."	2006	Officers accused of shaking down drug dealers, home invasion, and armed violence. Earlier in the same year, four other officers from the same Gang Crimes Unit were charged with robbery, kidnapping, and making false arrests.
Melia, M. Associated Press Worldstream	"Police in Puerto Rico Rocked by Scandals."	2007	Ten officers were accused of planting drugs on people and making false arrests. This indictment came amid several police scandals with more than 50 federal indictments of police officers the previous year. The protection of drug dealers was the most common offense regarding those cases.

Table 9.1b Examples of Police Misconduct: International

Author(s)	Title	Year	Summary of Misconduct
Japan Economic Newswire	"Japan Urged to do More to Tackle Police Corruption."	2005	Series of scandals involving the theft of public funds . . . monies intended to pay informants.
Pogatchnik, S. Associated Press Worldstream	"Ireland to Crack Down on Police Corruption After Judge Catalogs Abuses."	2006	Judicial reports cited the planting of evidence to frame people for murder and other crimes. Panel also describes the Donegal Division of the National Police as having a weak and corrupt management structure that encourages corrupt practices.
Gibb, F., O'Neill, S., & Ball, J. *The Times* (London)	"Police Misconduct Costs Forces & Pounds."	2007	Police forces in the Ulster and Cleveland areas have paid out more than 44 million pounds to victims of police misconduct, including wrongful arrest, abuses of human rights, assaults, and malicious prosecutions.
Canberra Times	"Corruption Mars Victoria Police."	2007	Police brass resigned amid allegations of leaking confidential information on a murder case. Government calls for independent watchdog groups similar to those operating in three other provinces.

Author(s)	Title	Year	Summary of Misconduct
Xinhua News Service	"Mexican President Promises to Fight Police Corruption."	2008	With confidence in the country's police at an all time low, President Calderon vows to fight police corruption. Many officers are accused of having connections with criminal gangs who routinely engage in crimes such as kidnapping, extortion, and murder.
Slack, James *Daily Mail* (London) ——— *Anonymous.* Police Department Disciplinary Bulletin.	"Cops and Robbers; Police With Convictions for Theft, Assault and Dishonesty Allowed to Stay in Their Jobs." ——— "Big Police Scandal in Small Town"	2008 ——— Feb 2009	Police officers with convictions for weapons offenses, fraud, violent assaults, possession of marijuana, disorderly conduct, and theft were allowed to stay in their posts. Most of these crimes occurred while the officers were on duty. Officials are concerned that testimony given by these officers will not be given any credibility in the courts and may very well erode public confidence even more. ——— The Massachusetts Department of Public Health suspended the license of Hamilton's police-run ambulance service after an investigation revealed that a majority of the town's officers—including the chief—participated in a scheme to falsify emergency medical technician training and certification records. The successful scheme enabled them to continue to run the ambulance service—and receive thousands of dollars in bonus pay as officer-EMTs—despite the apparent failure to keep up with mandatory continuing education and refresher training designed to protect the public.

❖ The Background of Police Corruption

The history of the American municipal police is replete with examples and discussions concerning corruption. Reform movements have been initiated periodically to reduce or eliminate corruption but have largely failed to achieve their goals. The reform movement of the middle 1800s attempted to remove blatant, undesirable political influence from policing. The civil service reforms of the late 1800s sought the same goal, and though there were some successes, they were bitterly opposed and circumvented by those wishing to retain undue influence over the police (Johnson, 1981;

Richardson, 1974; Trojanowicz, 1992). According to Bracey (1989, p. 175), in 1894 the **Lexow Commission,** an investigative group appointed by a coalition of concerned citizens and good government groups, closed its hearings into police corruption and ineffectiveness in New York City. It reported that corruption was systematic and pervasive, a condition that it attributed in large part to malfeasance, misfeasance, and nonfeasance in the higher ranks. The next 15 years saw similar investigations and findings in almost every major American city.

Reforms in the early and middle 1900s emphasized the importance of professionalism as a means of reducing corruption of all types, and reform-oriented chiefs were appointed in many cities across the nation. Yet the problem of corruption resurfaced, sometimes in departments previously marred, other times in departments previously untouched by scandal. Lacayo (1993) reported, "For cops as for anyone else, money works like an acid on integrity. Bribes from bootleggers made the 1920s a golden era for crooked police. Gambling syndicates in the 1950s were protected by a payoff system more elaborate than the Internal Revenue Service" (p. 43), In 1971, Frank Serpico brought to light police corruption in New York City, and the **Knapp Commission** investigation that followed uncovered widespread corruption among officers of all ranks. According to Lacayo (1993), "In the 1980s Philadelphia saw more than 30 officers convicted of taking part in a scheme to extort money from [drug] dealers" (p. 43). A major corruption scandal "hit Miami in the mid-1980s, when about 10% of the city's police were either jailed, fired, or disciplined in connection with a scheme in which officers robbed and sometimes killed cocaine smugglers on the Miami River, then resold the drugs"(Lacayo, 1993, p. 44). As Cooksey (1991) stated, "The Los Angeles County Sheriff's Department discharges approximately 20 officers a year, primarily as the result of misconduct" (p. 7). In 1993, 22 years after Serpico's disclosures in the same department, Michael Dowd and 15 to 20 other New York City police officers led "a parade of dirty cops who dealt drugs and beat innocent people [that] has shocked the city during seven days of corruption hearings" (Frankel, 1993b, p. 3A). A 1998 report by the Government Accounting Office cited drug-related police corruption in Atlanta, Chicago, Cleveland, Detroit, Los Angeles, Miami, New Orleans, New York, Philadelphia, Savanna, and Washington, DC. In 2009, four former members of an elite Chicago police unit admitted to breaking into homes and stealing money and to stopping Hispanic drivers, taking their keys, illegally searching their homes, and dividing any money they found ("4 Chicago Officers", 2009). And also in 2009, 15 police officers in Illinois were charged with conspiracy to possess and distribute cocaine and heroin in drug dealing operations that played out in parking lots at suburban [Chicago] shopping centers and hotels (Anonymous, 2009b). Some departments were built on corrupt foundations, with politicians requiring payments for positions, while others gave police positions away in return for political favors. Allegations of corruption still occur on a regular basis in many large departments, as noted. Our observations in recent years indicate that corruption of authority remains widespread in small- and medium-sized (less than 500 sworn personnel) departments as well. Several of the other forms of corruption also have been noted in smaller departments.

Corruption occurs when a police officer acts in a manner that places his personal gain ahead of duty, resulting in the violation of police procedures, criminal law, or both (Lynch, 1989). According to Barker and Carter (1986), "Corrupt acts contain three elements: (1) They are forbidden by some law, rule, regulation, or ethical standard; (2) they involve the misuse of the officer's position; and (3) they involve some actual or expected material reward or gain" (pp. 3–4). It must be emphasized though that measuring police corruption is a difficult, if not impossible, task. As Ivkovic (2003) indicated, there are several factors to consider.

- What exactly is corruption? How is it operationalized by researchers?
- There is currently no official source of data on corruption, such as those provided by the Uniform Crime Report and National Crime Victimization Report for most other crimes.
- If it cannot be measured, how can it be determined if anticorruption strategies are working?
- Actual crimes that are indicative of corruption, such as bribery, are not labeled as such.
- Distinguishing between the various types of police can be a difficult task as well. Police officers from the state, county, local, campus, and even federal levels have many times been grouped together by researchers, oftentimes skewing their analyses.
- Data is hard to come by. Without public statistics researchers are generally left to the mercy of police administrators, who often are reluctant to share this type of information for fear of negative consequences from the press, local politicians, and the community.

Police corruption is best viewed not as the aberrant behavior of individual officers, but as group behavior guided by contradictory sets of norms. It involves a number of specific patterns that can be analyzed in terms of several dimensions, including the acts and actors involved, the norms violated, the extent of peer group support, the degree of organization, and the police department's reaction. It is difficult to estimate the proportion of police officers directly involved in police corruption, but it is probably small. Still, the actual number of police officers involved nationwide is significant, and these officers attract a good deal of negative attention when their acts of corruption are made public. And while most police officers are not directly involved in corrupt activities, large numbers do condone such activities by their failure to speak out or take action against them. These are the officers, referred to as *grass eaters* by the Knapp Commission, who passively accept the presence of corruption as a part of the police world (Knapp Commission, 1973). *Meat eaters* are those officers, typically far fewer in number, who actively seek out the opportunity for corrupt activities. Recognition that those officers who actively seek out corrupt activities are relatively few has led many police administrators to espouse the "rotten apple" theory, which holds that while there are a few corrupt officers in policing, most officers are unaffected by corruption.

In fact, it is virtually impossible for a single corrupt officer to survive (other than in a one-person department). In other words, most forms of corruption require some degree of organizational support, at least in the sense that others within the organization turn their heads and refuse to confront the corrupt officer. This failure to take action against corrupt officers, even on the part of other officers who clearly dislike such activities, may be due in part to the police subculture.

Some time ago, Stoddard (1968) discussed the informal code of silence that exists among police officers with respect to a variety of types of deviant behavior. He and others (Bouza, 1990; Frankel, 1993a; Klockars, Ivkovich, Harver, & Haberfeld, 2000; Weisburd & Greenspan, 2000) have indicated that such deviance is an "open secret" within the fraternity, but its existence is denied to those outside the group. Frankel (1993a,) reported that, for Bernie Cawley, a New York police officer, it was "nothing to lie to grand juries, to steal drugs, weapons, and money, and to protect other cops doing the same thing" (p. 1A). His fellow officer, Michael Dowd, testified, "Cops don't want to turn in other cops. Cops don't want to be a rat" (Frankel, 1993a, p. 3A). According to Johnson (2007), Alex Busansky, who formerly prosecuted police cases in the Civil Rights Division of the Justice Department, "says the code of silence and lack of physical evidence hampers many investigations. Without the cooperation of witnesses— often other police officers—the cases are reduced to allegations and denials." This was the case when a Milwaukee jury failed to convict three police officers on battery charges for a beating in which a suspect was kicked in the head and stabbed in both ears. Such cases are frequently plagued by problems such as a lack of strong physical evidence and the **code of silence** adopted by some officers who refuse to testify against others in their ranks. (For a further discussion of the code of silence, see Chapter 8.)

In some departments, officers who are "straight" are regarded as stupid or as failing to take advantage of the benefits of corrupt activities that have come to be defined as inherent in the job. When an officer does decide to take action against corrupt colleagues, the fraternity may react violently and is very likely to ostracize the officer who violated the code or broke faith with those in the subculture.

Police corruption has been recognized as a problem in this country for at least 100 years, and various reform movements and departmental programs to reduce or eliminate corruption have been attempted, as we shall see shortly. Given these initiatives, why does police corruption remain problematic? The answer seems to lie, at least in part, in the relationship between the police and the larger society. It has been said that police are a reflection of the society or community they serve, and this is nowhere more true than with respect to police corruption. Simply put, a large percentage of corrupt practices by police could be stopped quickly if we wanted to eliminate them. If other citizens stopped offering bribes, free services, and other gratuities, and started reporting all police attempts to benefit in unauthorized fashion from their positions, as was recommended by the Knapp Commission in 1972, it would be very difficult for corrupt police officers to survive unscathed.

To some extent, it appears that we want our police to be corrupt, or at least corruptible. It gives us something to talk and write about, it provides us with a sense that the police are not morally superior to others, and it perhaps gives some of us a feeling of power over those who are recognized as having a good deal of power. Do we want our police to be totally honest and trustworthy? Or would we prefer to believe that they would overlook at least minor violations as a result of the favors we have provided them? Are we satisfied regarding the police as morally superior because they routinely turn down opportunities to earn thousands of dollars by accepting payoffs from drug dealers, gunrunners, pimps, and those involved with other illegal activities? If the police do in fact adhere to high ethical standards, and if they are, after all, basically citizens like ourselves, and if we would be tempted by opportunities to earn large sums of money by simply failing to enforce the law, are we less ethical, less moral? Or are we, too, convinced that corruption is inherent in the police role and that there is little we could do about it even if we wanted to?

Seron, Pereira, and Kovath (2004) believed the public has more to do with police corruption than one would think. These researchers described acts of misconduct by police resulting from various social phenomena, some of which stemmed from legal guidelines and some of which flowed from mitigating factors or circumstances. Citizen respondents were asked to rate the seriousness of a variety of hypothetical police–citizen encounters. Respondents used both the legal and extralegal circumstances described in the scenarios to rate the level of seriousness. From a legal standpoint, the use of excessive force and offensive language directed at citizens by police bore high ratings. When viewed from the extralegal perspective though, the ratings were significantly reduced when confrontational demeanors on the part of citizens were introduced to the scenarios. The study concluded the following:

> Citizens expect officers to behave professionally, or by the book, but with a recognition that "street-level" discretion has a place in an officer's toolkit. . . . [This] is also demonstrated by findings for the dimension abuse of authority: Abuse or threatening behavior by officers [was] not a significant predictor of serious police misconduct. (Seron et al., 2004, p. 665)

Unfortunately, when the "officers toolkit" is added to the list of citizen actions, perceptions, and contradictions regarding how police should and should not act, the ethical conundrums faced by police in their daily duties become even more clouded.

Two publicized commissions were formed to investigate police corruption and offer recommendations for change, the first of which was the **Christopher Commission**. Created by former Los Angeles Mayor Tom Bradley in 1991 in response to several high-profile media accounts of various acts of misconduct by LAPD members, the Commission specifically addressed structure and operation, recruitment and training practices, internal disciplinary procedures, and citizen review and oversight issues (Human Rights Watch, 1998). Headed by attorney and former U.S. Secretary of State Warren Christopher, the final report, titled "The Christopher Commission Report," painted a disturbing, but all too familiar, picture of the LAPD for both the public and the police. Key findings of the report included the following:

- A small, but significant, number of police officers systematically engaged in acts involving excessive force.
- Police administrators clearly knew who these problem officers were but took little or no preventive measures to address the problem.
- A new policy needed to be adopted that would hold both individual officers and command staff personnel strictly accountable for future acts of malfeasance (Christopher Commission, 1991; Human Rights Watch, 1998).

Whether the LAPD adopted any of these recommendations stemming from the Christopher Commission Report is subject to debate. Many remain skeptical that any fundamental changes occurred within the LAPD.

For many of the same reasons cited by Los Angeles public officials and enraged citizen groups, former Mayor Rudolph Giuliani of New York City formed a special commission to investigate allegations of corruption within the ranks of the NYPD. Officially formed in 1994 and commonly referred to as the **Mollen Commission**, headed by retired New York State Supreme Court Justice Milton Mollen, the charge of the Commission was to investigate allegations of misconduct, analyze the effectiveness of anticorruption mechanisms within the department, and offer recommendations for improvement. Key findings and recommendations included the following:

- Much of the corruption was closely tied to the illegal drug market and the use of excessive force.
- Many of the corrupt acts were perpetrated by police officers acting in concert with one another, sometimes with as many as 15 conspiring officers.
- Corruption occurred primarily in crime-ridden precincts, populated predominantly by minority group members.
- The leadership structure of the Department demonstrated no sense of commitment to rooting out corrupt practices.
- There existed a strong police subculture that frowned on honest officers reporting the wrongdoings of corrupt coworkers.
- The internal mechanisms responsible for uncovering and investigating misconduct were ineffective and, in many instances, focused on the whistle-blowers rather than the perpetrators.
- There existed a department-wide belief that the identification of corruption would cause the Department administrators to retaliate for bringing discredit on the NYPD.
- A recommendation was made to create a permanent, external panel to monitor internal anticorruption measures and conduct investigations (Tran, 1994; Treaster, 1994).

It appears that the mayor and police administrators have yet to adopt the recommendations of the Mollen Commission and strongly object to oversight outside the control of the NYPD. This reluctance may be, in part, responsible for the continued allegations of misconduct plaguing the NYPD. Nearly 15 years after the Mollen Commission findings and recommendations were released, the Executive Director of the New York Civil Liberties Union recently stated the following:

Under his [Commissioner Raymond Kelly] watch the discipline of officers guilty of misconduct has deteriorated dramatically, and many misconduct cases have been closed without any action whatsoever. . . . The police department has sabotaged independent scrutiny of officer practices, creating an atmosphere in which even the most egregious misconduct goes unpunished—unless, of course, a YouTube video puts the lie to the official truth. (Lieberman, 2008)

Clearly, a brief comparison of the major findings and recommendations of both the Christopher and Mollen Commissions reveals many more similarities than differences: the inability of these two agencies to police themselves, a reluctance to proactively and seriously confront this issue or encourage independent oversight, subcultures that discourage honest police officers from reporting coworker misconduct, and leadership structures that do not actively promote and support anticorruption measures. Moreover, the recommendations offered by these and other similar commissions were never followed with any degree of seriousness. (See Table 9.2 for some examples.)

While the aforementioned reports focused on two of our nation's largest police departments, the critical issues that formed the core of both investigations seem to ring true, albeit in differing magnitude, for all size departments and in all regions of the country.

Table 9.2 Historical Attempts at Investigating Police Corruption

Name of Commission	Year of report	Conclusions	Recommendations
Lexow Commission (Cox & McCamey, 2008; "Defense," 1895)	1894	Corruption was pervasive and systematic in the NYPD, largely due to malfeasance, misfeasance, and nonfeasance in the higher ranks. Political corruption from the infamous Tammany Hall played a significant role as well.	Appointment of honest and capable police magistrates; appointment of honest, efficient, and responsible police administrators; passage of the "Police Magistrates Bill."
Wickersham Commission (American Law and Legal Information Law Library, 2009).	1932	Their report was titled "Lawlessness in Law Enforcement." Findings included widespread nationwide use of brutality by police, bribery, entrapment, evidence tampering, intimidation and coercion of witnesses, unlawful wiretapping, and collusion with organized criminal gangs.	Widespread reforms not just in policing but in the entire CJ system. Need for more professional police departments higher qualifications for the job of a police officer, and insulation of the police from political influences.
Knapp Commission (Knapp Commission Report on Police Corruption, 1973).	1972	Started as a result of police whistleblowers. Widespread corruption in the NYPD; identification of two types of corrupt officers, grass eaters and meat eaters; and citizens' willingness to bribe police for preferential treatment perpetuates corruption.	Increased supervisor accountability for actions of subordinates, creation of internal affairs units in all units of the department, improved screening and increased qualifications for all ranks, and undercover informants to be assigned to all units in the agency.
Fitzgerald Commission (Fitzgerald, 1989).	1989	Rampant corruption in the state of Queensland, Australia. Deep-seated corrupt practices found throughout the Queensland Police Department. The activities included bribery, protection of and kickbacks from vice operations, evidence tampering, excessive use of force, and perjury.	Improved professionalism, increases hiring and promotional standards, creation of watchdog groups, limit terms of police executives to mitigate political influence, and a change in culture.

(Continued)

Table 9.2 (Continued)			
Name of Commission	Year of report	Conclusions	Recommendations
Christopher Commission (Human Rights Watch, 1998).	1991	Corrupt LAPD police culture that tolerated various acts of misconduct, a relatively small group (44) of officers responsible for a significant portion of malfeasance (group received no discipline) committed during the "CRASH" years), planting evidence, brutality, and perjury.	Improved selection and training criteria, implementation of community-oriented policing strategies, and more supervisor accountability for the actions of subordinates.
Mollen Commission (Treaster, 1994).	1994	Significant amount of corruption tied to the drug markets, weak leadership structure with no commitment to uncovering corrupt practices, strong police subculture encouraging officers not to rat on one another, weak internal affairs unit, and many acts of corruption committed by officers acting together in small groups.	Change in leadership structure, more department-wide emphases on anticorruption measures, better trained internal affairs unit, and an external panel to oversee misconduct investigations.

YOU DECIDE 9.1

Based on the corrupt practices cited in the news articles noted in Tables 9.1a and 9.1b and the malfeasance identified and investigated by the various commissions noted in Table 9.2, were there any common denominators? If so, what were they? Were there any major differences? If so, what were they?

In addition to the recommendations offered by these commissions to the agencies in question to mitigate the frequency of police misconduct, would you add any others? Which ones would you add? Why? How would you enforce your recommendations?

Discuss your findings with your classmates.

❖ Types of Misconduct

Because of their vast legal and discretionary power and authority, and the multiple roles that they perform and assume in a democratic society, police officers consistently find themselves in the midst of a wide range of ethical dilemmas. The structural and functional opportunities for all forms of misconduct are unfortunately omnipresent in the everyday world of policing. While few would argue with the assertion that the vast majority of the men and women who serve their communities do so in an exemplary fashion, it is equally true that the minority of officers who bring discredit on their departments by compromising the **Police Code of Conduct** causes severe damage to their respective agencies in the areas of public trust, department morale, and overall community relations.

Rosoff, Pontell, and Tillman (2007), in their work on police corruption and in their analyses and interpretation of earlier research by Barker and Roebuck (1974), set forth a typology that encompassed a variety of misconduct, ranging from violations of departmental rules and regulations to statutory violations of state and federal law. A brief examination of each category follows.

Corruption of Authority

The **corruption of authority** is the most widespread form of police misconduct and includes "a wide variety of unauthorized material inducements, anything from discounted underwear to free commercial sex" (Rosoff, Pontell, & Tillman, 2007, p. 448). While this acceptance of gratuities on the part of the police often violates department policy, it does not violate criminal law statutes when the gratuities are offered voluntarily. In many cases, they are viewed as coming with the job and are overlooked by police departments unless they become a matter of public concern. In other words, the acceptance of gratuities is often condoned if not approved.

The difficulty with accepting gratuities is that the officer never knows when the corruptor may expect or request special services or favors in return. This may, of course, never happen, but if it does, it places the officer who has accepted the gratuities in a difficult position, although she may certainly refuse to grant such requests. In addition, it becomes difficult to draw a line between such gratuities and other types of corrupt activities in terms of monetary value and violation of ethical standards.

Such actions also may have an effect on the police image. For example, two police officers were witnessed during lunch hour at a fast food chain. One officer was in uniform, the other in plain clothes. In front of a large number of lunch-hour customers, the person taking the orders told the uniformed officer he would receive a 50% discount on the price of his meal. This started some murmuring in the crowd. The second officer then informed the cashier that he, too, was a police officer, and entitled to a 50% discount, and he showed his badge to prove it. The cashier apologized, saying she hadn't recognized him as a police officer and assured him that he would receive his discount. Needless to say, the muttering in the crowd became rather negative, with other patrons indicating that they now understood why so many police officers visited the establishment in question.

DeLeon-Granados and Wells (1998) explored an ecological model called the "gratuity exchange principle," which predicts that the mere act of receiving a gratuity is likely to offset police patrol practices. Their research found that gratuities increased police coverage, in that establishments that offered free or discounted menu items received greater police coverage compared with similar types of establishments that did not offer gratuities to police officers. DeLeon-Granados and Wells indicated the need for further discussions of the social costs of police receiving gratuities. Others, such as Ruiz and Bono (2004), agreed and stated that the acceptance of gratuities by the police is both harmful and degrading and should be discouraged. They concluded that accepting gratuities provided an opportunity for corrupt intent, whether the intent was initially that of the giver or the receiver. Once that opportunity has been grasped, officers may find themselves on a slippery slope of compromise and opportunism. Coleman (2004) discussed five types of situations that are particularly problematic for police and suggested that in these types of situations, gratuities should always be refused:

1. When gratuities are offered because the recipient is a police officer

2. When gratuities are offered on a regular basis

3. When the value of the gratuities offered is disproportionate to the services rendered

4. When the person offering the gratuity is under the impression that certain services will be provided only if a gratuity is offered

5. When the person offering the gratuity is not authorized to do so.

The issue of police officers and gratuities continues to be debated, but the weight of evidence seems to suggest that they are best avoided when offered by commercial enterprises. Whether or not they pose a major problem when they are offered by a grateful citizen and involve nothing more than a cup of coffee and a cookie remains controversial. It is clear, however, that if a departmental policy prohibiting acceptance of any form of gratuity exists and is ignored, a bad precedent has been established.

Kickbacks

Kickbacks constitute a second type of police corruption and refer to the practice of obtaining goods, services, or money for business referrals by police officers (Rosoff, Pontell, & Tillman, 2007). Those involved in offering these quid pro quo schemes include lawyers, doctors, towing contractors, auto body shop operators, and others who reward police officers who refer customers to them. While some of the forms of misconduct in this category are not illegal per se, it is easy to cross the line between violations of department rules and regulations and illegal activities. The difficulties inherent in such activities are obvious, but in some police departments, they too are condoned unless a public issue arises as a result.

Shakedowns

The third type of misconduct involves **shakedowns** and occurs when officers take money or other valuables and personal services from offenders they have caught during the commission of a crime (Rosoff, Pontell, & Tillman, 2007). Drug dealers, prostitutes, and motorists seem to be favorite targets, though incidents like these occur when any arrestee is willing to buy his or her way out of an arrest.

Bribes

This type of malfeasance can assume many different forms. Sometimes referred to as *the fix,* it involves police officers taking no enforcement action when they are normally required to do so, usually in exchange for monetary remuneration (Rosoff, Pontell, & Tillman, 2007). Common examples include officers who, in exchange for money, will not write a motorist a ticket or officers who deliberately misdirect an investigation or perjure their court testimony to ensure a favorable outcome for the defendant (Hyatt, 2001, p. 79).

Opportunistic Theft

This form of misconduct pertains to police officers who steal money or other valuables when, for example, they are guarding a crime scene, as in the case of a burglary, or steal other such goods from unconscious, inebriated, or dead people (Rosoff, Pontell, & Tillman, 2007). Similar activity also may occur when money and other property are stolen from arrestees either prior to or during the booking process.

POLICE STORIES

I recall one incident when working on a Paddy Wagon (a truck-like police vehicle used for transporting arrestees, dead bodies, etc.) for the Chicago Police Department. My partner that day was a veteran *wagon man,* as they were called, of 35+ years. We received a call of a dead body at a residence. The deceased was an elderly gentleman (grandfather of the homeowner) who had expired while seated in an easy chair. He had a history of serious illness and the Medical Examiner's Office gave us permission to transport the deceased to the funeral home of the family's choice.

We placed the fully-dressed deceased onto a stretcher and loaded him into the back of the wagon for transport to the funeral home. Just before reaching the funeral home, my partner asked me to pull into a nearby alley. He got out and proceeded to open the rear compartment of the vehicle. I exited the vehicle to see what was happening.

My partner removed the shoes (a rather new set of oxfords) from the deceased, put those shoes on his own feet, and began pacing up and down the alley as if he was trying on a new pair of shoes in a shoe store. He indicated that the shoes fit well and that he was going to keep them. I protested, saying that the family had seen what the deceased was wearing when we took him from their home and that the shoes should not be taken. He replied "Don't worry about it, kid. They don't bury you with your shoes on, and besides, I need the shoes more than he does."

(Continued)

(Continued)

Though many find this story somewhat amusing, the reality of the situation was that I had just witnessed the commission of what researchers have coined *opportunistic theft* and took no action to prevent the theft. Because I took no action to prevent this crime or to report the wrongdoing to my supervisor, that made me as culpable as my partner due to my position as a police officer. Why did I choose that course of action? The forces of the subculture were at it again—one never rats on a fellow officer.

This incident occurred more than 20 years ago. Faced with the same circumstances today, I would not allow another police officer to do that in my presence; we would have a genuine "face to face" encounter.

Protection of Illegal Activities

Protection of illegal activities is one of the most egregious forms of misconduct, and it involves police officers taking money or other valuables in exchange for their protection of criminal activities (Rosoff, Pontell, & Tillman, 2007). The most common forms of criminal activity protected by police are narcotics trafficking, gambling, prostitution, the fencing or sale of stolen property, and chop shop or auto theft operations. Unfortunately, allegations of this type of behavior occur all too frequently. To protect the illegal behaviors, a good deal of organization is often required. It does little good for one officer to look the other way when gambling occurs if his replacement for days off and vacations or officers on other shifts fail to protect the parties involved.

☞ CASE IN POINT 9.1

Conspiracy Cops—Bad Apples or Bad Barrels?

In what is the biggest story of the week so far, New Orleans LA police Lt Michael Lohman has plead guilty to a federal obstruction charge concerning his testimony to federal agents about his role in a cover up of the Sept 4, 2005 post-huricane [sic] Katrina officer-involved shooting incident on the Danziger bridge that left 2 dead and 4 seriously injured. Lohman was not there when the shootings took place, but instead had responded afterward to direct an investigation into the incident and he found out pretty quickly that it was a "bad shoot" . . . in other words, it was an unjustified shooting incident.

The factual basis document signed by Lohman goes into detailing a rather convoluted process by which he conspired not only with the officers involved in the shooting incident, but also the officers that he had assigned to investigate the shooting incident to develop a plausible false story to justify the shooting that included planting a gun since none were found at the scene of the shooting.

The conspiracy to cover up the unjustified shooting went so far as to involve Lohman not only telling the officers to get their stories straight before being interviewed, but to also sit down with all of them to help them get their falsified stories together . . . and when that failed, he rewrote the entire report on his own to make it more convincing.

If anyone ever wondered at what extent law enforcement officers might go to concoct a cover up, the Danziger bridge incident now offers us a rare view into that depth, and it's pretty deep. At each point in the process, from the time he arrived on the Danziger bridge to the point where he finally agreed to cooperate with federal investigators and plead guilty, he knew he was building a lie to hide the murder of two people and attempted murder on several others.

The scope of this conspiracy to obstruct justice involved not [sic] only Lohman and the 7 officers involved in the incident, but also the officers that he assigned to investigate it, bringing the total number of officers involved up to at least 9, if not more. While headline-worthy not only for the history of the case, but also for the scope of the subsequent cover-up, this type of conspiracy to obstruct justice is not unique by any stretch . . . in fact, there have been several other similar cases recently:

On February 16, 2010, Stoughton, MA police officer Anthony Bickerton plead guilty to obstructing a federal investigation into corruption within the Stoughton Police Department that involved theft when Bickerton hid evidence at his home for another officer targeted by the probe. Bickerton was the third officer ensnared by this particular probe that had another officer plead guilty in January and a third turn over and cooperate with federal agents. All three had resigned abruptly late last year.

On December 15, 2009, federal authorities indicted the Shenandoah PA police chief and two of his officers for conspiracy to obstruct justice, witness tampering, and evidence tampering in a racially motivated murder case involving several local teens that the officers allegedly helped concoct stories to prevent their prosecution for the crime. Not only this, but the police chief and a fourth officer were indicted for extortion charges in a separate case. On top of this, a lawsuit was filed alleging yet another cover up where officers allegedly beat a detainee to death then hanged the man in an effort to make the beating death appear to be a suicide.

On January 21, 2010, the city of Marlow OK fired two officers and continues to investigate the chief of police on allegations that they had lied about a drug bust at trial which forced prosecutors to drop all charges in the case. Furthermore, allegations of rampant corruption within the department includes missing drug evidence, warrantless raids, motorists being robbed by officers, a cover up of an officer-involved fatality, and allegations of child molestation made by 8 minors against one officer still on active duty. The police chief has been on paid leave since late October.

(Continued)

(Continued)

On February 11, 2010, four Manhattan Beach CA police officers where placed on paid leave while investigated on allegations that they attempted to cover up a DUI hit and run accident that involved a fellow officer's vehicle. The vehicle in question caused a three car pileup and fled the scene before officers arrived. While it was later located, abandoned at a nearby gas station, officers never filed a report once they discovered it was registered to a Manhattan Beach cop.

On February 11, 2010, the town of Dolton IL was ordered to pay $110,000 in damages to a man who had been beaten and threatened with a loaded rifle pointed at his head, then was wrongfully arrested to cover for the incident when officers allegedly planted drugs on him to justify the arrest. While the victim was later cleared of all charges, the police chief was accused of purposefully withholding exculpatory evidence that would have cleared him sooner. After all was said and done, 5 officers and the police chief were implicated in the assault and subsequent attempted cover up.

Source: From "Conspiracy Cops—Bad Apples or Bad Barrels?" by D. Packman, 2010, *Injustice Everywhere.* Available from http://www.injusticeeverywhere.com/?p=1904. Reprinted with permission.

Even more disturbing than this review of unethical and criminal conduct by police officers are the results of research conducted by Barker and Wells (1982) and Annarino (1996), cited in Hyatt's (2001) work on police misconduct. They surveyed police chiefs in the southeast region of the United States in an effort to ascertain whether their respective agencies had official regulations explicitly covering the range of misconduct cited previously and their opinions regarding the type of disciplinary action these activities would warrant. The following is a brief summary of the results:

- Kickbacks: More than 50% of the chiefs indicated that they would reprimand or suspend officers involved in kickbacks.
- Opportunistic thefts: Approximately 60% of the departments had regulations pertaining to this category of malfeasance. However, only 35% of the chiefs indicated a willingness to pursue criminal charges.
- Shakedowns: Approximately 60% of the respondent departments had regulations pertaining to this activity, and only 37% of the police chief respondents considered the initiation of criminal charges.
- Bribes: Even more disturbing was that only 39% of departments had regulations governing this form of conduct, and less than 30% of the chiefs believed this activity to be serious enough to recommend criminal prosecution (Annarino, 1996; Barker & Wells, 1982; Hyatt, 2001, pp. 79–80).

The reluctance by chief executive officers to take appropriate disciplinary action against officers engaged in unethical behavior serves only to strengthen the force the police subculture exerts on so many officers. Moreover, these types of attitudes by chiefs send a very disturbing, but clear message to subordinates—that more often than not, at least with respect to this research population, the penalty for malfeasance will not be commensurate with the seriousness of the offense. In any event, this view of corruption by chiefs of police is an issue that begs more attention, both through research and professional development activities.

Although one type of corruption does not necessarily lead to another, where one finds more serious types of corruption, one is also likely to find most of the less serious types. Consider, for example, a department that condones internal payoffs. If a supervisor attained her position by paying someone for it, it becomes difficult to deal with less serious forms of corruption among those supervised because they may have knowledge of the way in which the promotion was obtained. In the long run, such a department is likely to be characterized by all other forms of corruption. In addition, services to the public are likely to be less efficient and effective than they might otherwise be because promotions are not usually based on merit, and less competent or incompetent people may become supervisors. As Richardson (1974) stated early on,

> Discipline may be especially weak since any action might lead to unpleasant publicity. If a large portion of a police department is implicated in such corrupt relations, no one can enforce the law against the police themselves. Officers outside the network of payoffs have to turn their backs on what goes on around them and deny publicly that any such activity exists. . . . Moreover, what is the effect on a young patrolman who learns that his colleagues and commanders are often more interested in profiting from the law than enforcing it? (p. 154)

Frankel (1993b), dealing with similar issues, noted the following:

> Daniel Sullivan, former head of the [NYC] department's Internal Affairs division, testified that the message from the top brass to his investigators was simple: "We shouldn't be so aggressive because the department doesn't want bad press. . . . Honest officers testified that their efforts to report and investigate corruption ran into resistance and retaliation. (p. 3A)

Walker, Spohn, and DeLone (2006) concluded that many police agencies fail to discipline officers who are guilty of misconduct. Such actions, or failure to act, send a clear message to line officers: We are not committed to ethical conduct. The resulting consequences may be disastrous.

❖ Causes and Consequences of Police Misconduct

While not specifically included in the original typology developed by Barker and Roebuck (1974), Rosoff, Pontell, and Tillman (2007), and others, there are additional categories of malfeasance that should be specifically identified, along with associated causes and consequences.

Nonfeasance

Nonfeasance in the context of policing refers to the reluctance of most police officers to report wrongdoings committed by their coworkers. Why is this so? Can the situation be changed? The code of silence (discussed earlier in this chapter as well as in Chapter 8) among police officers results in collective feelings and attitudes, as misdirected as they may be, of cynicism, isolation from the community in which the police live and work, and a sense of blind loyalty to their colleagues. Cox (1996) described the police culture as consisting of the informal rules and regulations, tactics, and folklore passed on from one generation of police officers to the next. The cycle of corruption is allowed to perpetuate because honest police officers, due to fear of retaliation from coworkers and supervisors, often hesitate to report the illegal and unethical acts of coworkers. Until this aspect of the police subculture can be significantly diminished, and honest police officers develop the courage to do the right thing, police misconduct will continue to flourish. The effects of this continued pattern of misconduct will then spread and exert even more strain on the already tenuous relationship that exists between many police departments and their respective communities.

Evidence of the problematic relationship between the police and the public they serve can be found in a Gallup News poll (Jones, 2005): "The decline in confidence [in the police] has generally occurred across demographic subgroups, as members of most key groups are less confident in the police. . . . Gallup also finds a new low in the percentage of Americans who say they have a 'great deal' of respect for the police in their area" (p. 419). A Gallup Poll taken in June 2009 found that 28% of

❖ **Photo 9.2** The aftermath of a successful narcotics raid, with the fruits of the crime showing. The seizure of large quantities of illicit drugs and cash has frequently been the downfall of many police officers.

those surveyed had a great deal of confidence in the police and another 31% had quite a lot of confidence in the police. Although the public perception of and confidence in the police undoubtedly has numerous causes, reported and suspected police corruption may well be among them.

Drug-Related Corruption

Another form of police misconduct involves **drug-related corruption**. A 1998 study by the U.S. General Accounting Office (GAO), titled "Drug-Related Police Corruption," provided insight into the systematic, narcotics-related corruption in the field of policing. The study analyzed federal drug-related investigations and prosecutions of police officers from several state and municipal police departments. Through its examination and analysis of government and academic reports and interviews with numerous federal law enforcement sources specializing in the investigation of public integrity matters, the GAO generated interesting data to be considered in the study of police corruption. The following is a summary of the major conclusions of the GAO report:

- Drug-related police corruption differs from other forms of police misconduct.
- Officers involved in this corrupt practice "were more likely to be actively involved in the commission of a variety of crimes, including stealing drugs and/or money from drug dealers, selling drugs and lying under oath about illegal searches" (p. 3).
- Power and vigilante justice were found to be additional motives for drug-related corruption.
- A recurring pattern of this form of corruption was that the misconduct involved small groups of officers who consistently conspired and helped one another commit a variety of crimes.
- The culture surrounding drug-related corruption was characterized by the all too familiar code of silence, blind loyalty to group members, and cynicism about the criminal justice system.
- Younger officers, as well as those lacking experience and at least some form of higher education, were found to be more susceptible to these corrupt practices.
- A variety of critical management and administrative issues were also associated with this form of corruption, such as lax and/or incompetent supervision; no real commitment from department brass to promote integrity; weak or ineffective investigative methodologies used to combat corruption; inadequate training, both basic and in-service, particularly in the area of ethical decision making; police brutality; and informal pressures stemming from officers' personal friendships and affiliations with neighborhood figures. (GAO, 1998, pp. 3–5)

Although the GAO report is somewhat dated, it is nonetheless a seminal piece of research regarding police corruption. Further, the conclusions drawn appear to be supported by the vast majority of news stories highlighted in Tables 9.1a and 9.1b, as well as the conclusions formed by the majority of police corruption commissions highlighted in Table 9.2. The issues pertaining to the strength of the police subculture, the support of peers in the commission of acts of misconduct, lax supervisory practices, and ineffective leadership structures seem to be key variables in the continuation of corrupt activities.

Noble Cause Corruption

As the phrase implies, **noble cause corruption** pertains to various situations in which officers circumvent the law in order to serve what they perceive to be the greater good. Perhaps Delattre (2002) described this behavior best by posing the following dilemma to both officers and administrators: "If you have a perpetrator in custody, and he has information that could save the life of an innocent victim, is it right to use extreme methods to get the information" (p. 185)? Although questions such as that posed by Delattre always generate enthusiastic debate on both sides of the issue, the answer is actually quite clear—police officers are sworn to uphold the law and should never, under any circumstances, willfully violate the rights of anyone in their custody. Those who disagree with this assertion point to the life-and-death nature of Delattre's scenario. The question that begs an answer, however, is how often do cases like this occur in the daily lives of police officers? Most would argue that they occur rarely, if ever, during an officer's career.

The debate underlying noble cause corruption, then, must focus around more commonplace activities encountered by police officers. Imagine plainclothes officers approaching an individual on the street to conduct a field interview. The person in question abruptly turns a corner, and while temporarily out of view of the officers, drops a quantity of illegal narcotics to the ground. The police then find the contraband and arrest the subject. What should the officers do? If they tell the truth, the case will most likely be dismissed in court. If they elect to fabricate their report and possibly perjure themselves in court, they have removed a dope dealer from the street. Herein lies the problem with adhering to the noble cause corruption philosophy—two wrongs never make a right, and if left unchecked, the collective behavior of officers may eventually even assume a vigilante-like mentality (Delattre, 2002).

Incidents like the one just described occur all too often, and officers and administrators who approve of this manifestation of the police subculture, even if only tacitly, run the risk of systemic corruption taking hold in their agencies. According to Harrison (1999), no matter how routine or exigent the circumstances may be, the following is true:

> When officers use unlawful means to gain a desired end, they damage the system they represent. Beyond the damage to the justice system, however, officers who engage in illegal behavior denigrate not only the uniform of the guardian but also the individual within. The eventual result to society is a loss of confidence in those charged with the protection of others, leading to a fraying of the tapestry of the culture that binds communities together. (p. 5)

❖ Physical and Emotional Abuse

Police misconduct also includes many other categories, such as perjury, emotional abuse or harassment, physical abuse, and even murder. To some extent, perjury and other forms of unauthorized deception serve as links between corruption and other forms of misconduct. What is the difference, for example, between a police officer perjuring himself in order to fix a ticket in return for payment from the defendant and one who perjures herself in order to cover up the fact that she used physical force unnecessarily against a defendant? How does one draw the line between lying to informants and drug dealers and deceiving one's superiors? Once perjury and deception gain a foothold, they tend to spread to other officers and to other types of situations until, in some cases, the entire justice system becomes a sham.

This is the case, for instance, when police officers perjure themselves in criminal cases in which the defendant is also perjuring himself, the respective attorneys know that perjury is occurring, and the judge knows that none of the parties is being completely honest. The outcomes of such cases appear to depend on who told the most believable lie, or the last lie. The overall impact is to increase the amount of suspicion and distrust of the justice system among all parties, and this is certainly not the desired end product if we wish citizens to participate in and believe in the system.

Chevigny (1969), Cray (1972), Manning (1974), Skolnick (1966), and Roberg and Kuykendall (1993) addressed the issue of police lying and all agree that the behavior, in some cases, becomes accepted as an inherent part of the job in much the same way as corruption. Adding to this, Foley's (2000) research on police perjury strongly indicated that nobody should be surprised that perjury by police officers is a significant problem since "... the courts, police agencies, and society have acknowledged, justified, and approved ..." (p. iv) of the use of lying and deception by the police. This appears to be true particularly in cases in which police misconduct has occurred and the officers involved are trying to cover up the misconduct. Police officers who stop other citizens without probable cause and harass them, and police officers who use force unnecessarily, must attempt to justify their actions or face relatively severe sanctions.

As a case in point, Foley (2000) interviewed nearly 200 NYPD officers and presented a series of vignettes representing various issues associated with police misconduct. Most of the data pertaining to perjury by the police was not surprising. For example, 77% of officers in the study "... indicated perjury would likely be committed in some of the vignettes presented" (p. 132). Examine other related highlights from Foley's (2000) research:

- The three crimes found to be most significant in affecting officers' decisions to perjure themselves were the sale of narcotics, rape, and assault.
- Officers seeking promotion were more likely to perjure themselves.
- Officers with a significant need for overtime pay were highly likely to commit perjury.
- The past performance of officers in this regard was a strong predictor of continued acts of perjury.
- The duty assignments of officers affected their likelihood to commit perjury. Uniformed officers were more than twice as likely as detectives to commit perjury.
- Officers who had been expressly warned by their supervisors on prior occasions not to perjure their testimony or lie on arrest reports were highly unlikely to engage in this form of misconduct again.

The implications from this research are important for police administrators to consider and further investigate, particularly the finding that express warnings from supervisors appeared to lead to fewer cases of perjury on behalf of the warned officers.

AROUND THE WORLD

Police Integrity Commission

New South Wales Government

The Police Integrity Commission (PIC) of New South Wales, Australia was formed due to that state's worst police corruption scandal. Visit the PIC website at http://www.pic.nsw.gov.au/ and familiarize yourself with its many features.

After you are finished acquainting yourself with the PIC website, answer the following questions and be prepared to discuss your answers with your classmates.

1. What was the name and basis of the scandal that led to the formation of PIC?

2. Have there been any scandals involving misconduct by the New South Wales Police since PIC's creation? If so, what were the allegations and what was the result of the investigation?

Do you recommend the formation of similar investigative commissions in other countries, including the United States? Why or why not?

Emotional Abuse and Psychological Harassment by Police Officers

As indicated elsewhere in this text (see Chapter 11), police officers, like those in other occupational groups, sometimes employ stereotypes and divide the world into *us* and *them,* or insiders versus outsiders. Those who are perceived as outsiders are often labeled, and occasionally these labels are used openly to refer to the members of groups so designated. The use of racial slurs is but one example of the kind of harassment under consideration. Other special categories and labels are created for those belonging to particular types of "deviants," for example, drug dealers, homosexuals, prostitutes, and protestors. The creation of special categories and the ensuing labels are not unique to the police, but as public servants who represent the authority of the government, the police are in a unique position when it comes to using the labels created.

POLICE STORIES

I recall working for a short time in one of districts of the Chicago Police Department, the geographical boundaries of which were well known by Chicago residents due to the diverse nature of its citizenry. Parts of the district housed some of the wealthiest people in Chicago, and other parts had a significant homeless population, gang activity, and a substantial number of persons living alternative sexual lifestyles. One area of the district catered to the gay lifestyle and was referred to by many as "Boy's Town." It was common practice for many officers to verbally harass gays. For example, when passing by persons on the street that officers thought to be gay, many would activate their loud speakers and utter derogatory remarks, such as "get off the street, fagot," "don't you look pretty tonight," "bet your ass*%#* is bigger than a sewer cover," as well as other similar remarks.

This was also an era when the incivility directed toward gays by some police extended to citizens from other areas of the city. In a practice known as *gay bashing,* a phrase coined by the media to describe incidents in which gay men were targeted at random by groups of thugs who would chase them down and beat them . . . sometimes very severely and for no reason other than being gay or being perceived as being gay. It was not uncommon to hear radio calls regarding this practice or for officers to sometimes witness a group of males chasing other males who were pegged as being "queer." Many of those radio calls and cries for help were either completely ignored by many officers or their response was to deliberately drive very slowly to the location.

While neither my partner nor I engaged in this form of misconduct, we knew it was happening and we knew many of the officers who frequently demeaned gays or ignored or responded slowly to incidences of gay bashing. Did I do anything about it? Sadly, I must say no. Why? It was the police subculture once again. I perceived the pressure to go along and get along as intense.

Looking back on those days makes me ashamed of myself for ignoring those injustices. Given those same set of circumstances today, I would let those officers know, in a face to face manner, that if they continued doing what they were doing in my presence I would report them. No longer would I care about getting along with ass&#$^ like that; and the more I think about it, even 20 to 30 years ago the vast majority of officers were honest and hard working. I don't think they would mind seeing those kinds of officers face the consequences of their actions.

First, the police are supposed to represent all citizens, regardless of race, creed, nationality, gender, age, political beliefs, or sexual orientation. When they use dehumanizing terms or harass others, the impression may be that because they represent government, they are expressing the attitudes of those who govern—though in fact they may simply be expressing personal dislikes, contempt, or hostility. Second, because of the fact that they represent governmental authority, they are in turn very likely to be subject to harassment, name calling, and challenges. When those being policed use dehumanizing terms, and deliberate attempts to harass or provoke the police occur, the possibility that the police will reciprocate in kind is heightened. Third, the occupational subculture legitimizes the use of labels behind squad room doors or among police officers, keeping these labels alive and meaningful. Fourth, few of those other citizens harassed or verbally abused are likely to report the abuse, which tends to reinforce the abusive behavior. Fifth, as an alternative to arrest, many of those harassed probably view the harassment as the lesser of two evils (homeless people, for instance, who are "escorted" to the city limits by police officers with a warning not to return).

Members of minority groups (both racial and behavioral), particularly in high-crime areas, report that **psychological or emotional abuse** is a routine part of their encounters with the police. And in fact, the best available evidence supports this contention. Although his study is dated, Reiss (1968) provided information concerning the incidence of police psychological mistreatment of other citizens:

> What citizens object to and call "police brutality" is really the judgment that they have not been treated with the full rights and dignity owing [sic] citizens in a democratic society. Any practice that degrades their status, that restricts their freedom, that annoys or harasses them, or that use physical force is frequently seen as unnecessary and unwarranted. More often than not, they are probably right. . . . Members of minority groups and those seen as nonconformists, for whatever reasons, are the most likely targets of status degradation. (pp. 59–60)

Hacker (1992), for example, noted that "most black Americans can recall encounters [with the police] where they were treated with discourtesy, hostility, or worse. . . . And it would appear that at least a few police officers still move in circles where no censure attaches to using the word 'nigger'" (p. 189).

According to Lurigo, Greenleaf, and Flexon (2009), complaints of harassment and disrespectful treatment were widespread among the young black and Hispanic men they interviewed. These men described repeated instances of verbal abuse by officers, including antagonistic language, name-calling, profanity, and derogatory remarks.

What constitutes police brutality is, at least in part, a matter of definition, and police definitions and those of other citizens may not always coincide. What some segments of the public see as police harassment or brutality, the police are likely to view as aggressive policing that is necessary for their survival on the streets as well as for maintaining some degree of order and crime control. Is a police officer in a high-crime area, where many residents are known to carry deadly weapons, harassing a citizen when she approaches cautiously, pats the citizen down for weapons, appears suspicious, and has another officer back her up? The answer depends, in part, on whether the person is the police officer or the person being stopped, questioned, and searched—because while the latter knows whether he is a dangerous person, the officer typically does not. Obviously, the way in which such encounters are carried out is important. Reiss (1968) and others (Lurigio, Greenleaf, & Flexon, 2009) noted that it is not always what the officer says, but how she says it that is degrading, and that whites, as well as racial or ethnic minority group members, may be victims of psychological harassment. The conclusions drawn by Reiss are supported by the findings of the National Advisory Commission on Civil Disorders (1968) and by (Lurigio, Greenleaf, & Flexon, 2009). All concluded that foremost among the complaints of minority group members about the police were the use of improper forms of address (use of terms such as *boy,* or use of a first name when a surname is appropriate) and stopping and questioning people for no apparent reason other than their race or ethnicity.

All of these findings and incidents, and others as well, imply that harassment and psychological brutality, if not actual physical brutality, continue to occur in police encounters with at least certain citizens. This is supported by the fact that repeated public opinion polls regarding the police typically indicate that the police are looked upon less favorably by minorities. For example, a CBS News/New York Times poll taken in July of 2008 asked respondents whether they felt they had ever been stopped by the police just because of race or ethnicity. Just 7% of whites responded "yes" to the question compared to 43% of blacks and 30% of Hispanics (CBS/New York Times Poll, 2008).

Excessive Use of Force

Nothing seems to grip the attention of the public more than the accounts of police officers overextending their legal authority by using **excessive force** to either effect an arrest of or to coerce information from individuals they interact with during the course of their duties. Celebrated cases such as the Rodney King incident in Los Angeles and the Abner Louima case in New York City are indelibly etched into the minds of many Americans, but are the abusive tactics in question commonplace in policing? Has police brutality reached epidemic proportions? To answer these questions and ascertain whether abuses similar in nature occur frequently and are perpetrated by a significant number of police officers requires a systematic examination of data pertaining to the overall use of force by police.

One relevant study examined citizen complaints filed against police officers in Florida, Illinois, Missouri, Pennsylvania, and Washington. Approximately 50% of all the complaints focused on the verbal conduct and overall demeanor of the officers. An additional quarter of the total complaints involved a wide variety of nonviolent, illegal conduct committed by officers on and off duty. The remaining quarter of complaints dealt with excessive force issues, once again by officers on and off duty (Johnson, 1998).

Actual complaints arising from on-duty arrest situations were responsible for less than one quarter of the complaints filed against police officers. While these numbers are significant, the author did not indicate whether these complaints were sustained or whether the officers were exonerated of wrongdoing. Either way, the data "reveals that excessive force by police officers while affecting an arrest represents a problem to address, it does not appear as widespread as the media portrays" (Johnson, 1998, p. 3).

A much more representative investigation of issues involving use of force by police was conducted by the NIJ in a 1999 study titled "Use of Force by Police: Overview of National and Local Data." According to this and other NIJ reports, only a small percentage of police–public interactions involve the use of force, with an even smaller percentage resulting in incidents of conduct that would be classified as excessive. Data

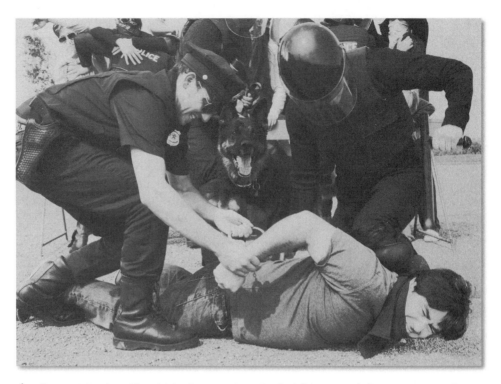

❖ **Photo 9.3** An officer(s) is shown using physical force to subdue an arrestee. Some characterize the officer's action as excessive and others claim it to be justified.

used in their analyses were gathered from a variety of sources, including police reports, citizen complaints, victimization surveys, and ethnographic methodologies. A summary of the highlights of their research follows:

- With respect to custody arrests of adults, of the 7,512 cases studied, police used physical force less than 20% of the time. In those instances, nonviolent or weaponless tactics such as grabbing were used in the majority of cases.
- Approximately 2% of the cases involved the use of weapons by police, and chemical agents such as pepper spray were used in the majority of those cases.
- Use of force by police typically occurs when a suspect is resisting arrest.
- When physical injuries do occur as a result of arrest, they are usually minor (e.g., bruises or abrasions).
- Instances of the use of force do not seem to be associated with officers' demographic characteristics, such as age, gender, and ethnicity. (This finding seems to be at odds with an earlier study in which officers who received the bulk of citizen complaints, albeit not all for excessive force, tended to be male, white, under 30 years of age, with less than five years of experience, and with little or no formal education [Johnson, 1998].)
- Use of force by police occurs more often when dealing with individuals who are under the influence of alcohol or drugs and with emotionally disturbed persons.
- A small number of police officers tend to be involved with an unusually high percentage of use-of-force incidents.

No matter how one interprets the data, the evidence seems to suggest that cases that involve severe beatings with fists, feet, and batons are not at all typical of the use of force by police. That is not to say that such cases do not exist or that police brutality is limited to use of fists or batons. Consider the case of Chicago police lieutenant Jon Burge, whose arrest capped a long-running controversy over allegations that beatings, electric shocks, and death threats were used against suspects at Burge's Area 2 violent crimes headquarters. The former high-ranking police official was arrested on charges that he lied when he denied that he and detectives under his command tortured murder suspects (Anonymous, 2008). When these cases do occur, however, data also demonstrate, as they do with many other forms of police misconduct, that excessive use of force is committed by a disproportionately small number of officers (National Institute of Justice [NIJ], 1999).

The evidence cited is consistent with a more recent NIJ sponsored research project regarding citizen contacts with the police in 2005 (Durose, Smith, & Langan, 2007). Of the 43.5 million persons who reported having face-to-face contact with police, approximately 2.3% of those individuals reported experiencing force or the threat of force by police at least once during that time period. Additional highlights were as follows:

- 55% of those respondents who reported experiencing force or threat of force, claimed that police actually used force (i.e., pushing, pointing a gun, and use of chemical sprays)
- 28% reported force being threatened by police but no force was used
- 10% reported police officers shouting or cursing at them but not applying force
- Approximately 17% of those respondents experiencing force admitted to provoking the officers by threatening them or resisting arrest

The NIJ reports also identified areas in need of further research, areas that may further assist in helping us understand the sources of and the answers to issues pertaining to bona fide incidences of excessive use of force by police. These areas include administrative policies, hiring practices, disciplinary procedures, use of technology, and the various influences of situational characteristics on the use of force.

Reiss (1971, p. 2) observed, "At law, the police in modern democracies such as the United States possess a virtual monopoly on the *legitimate* use of force over citizens." Bittner (1970) described the capacity to use force as the core of the police role. And Rubinstein (1973) discussed the police officer's body as his most important tool and the process by which he evaluates other citizens in terms of his physical ability to "handle" these other citizens if an encounter should turn nasty. That the police have the capacity to use force is indicated by the baton, mace, and sidearm they carry into every encounter, as well as by their sheer numbers in certain types of encounters. It should not be surprising, therefore, that the issue of misuse of force by the police should arise occasionally. This is perhaps especially true when we recognize that we live in a society characterized by violence. Spouse abuse, child abuse, and drug-related street violence are common occurrences in our society; and the police are routinely involved in dealing with all three.

What is clear is that the perception that such incidents occur is widespread in minority communities in cities of all sizes across the country. This perception becomes the reality for those involved, whether the perception is grounded in reality or not.

The perception creates hostility and resentment on behalf of some citizens who view themselves as particularly likely to be victims of harassment and brutality and on behalf of the police who view themselves as particularly likely to be harassed, challenged, and criticized by certain segments of the population. In spite of these misgivings on both sides, the vast majority of police encounters with other citizens occur without physical brutality on the part of either party.

Occasionally, however, suspicion, fear, resentment, and hostility escalate, resulting in physically violent encounters. In addition, of course, the police must be concerned about the possibility of violence that has nothing to do with harassment or social status but is based on felonious behavior. The possibility of physical violence always exists when the officer responds to calls involving domestic disputes, bar fights, robberies in progress, burglaries in progress, bomb threats, street protests, gunrunning, and drug trafficking, to mention just a few. In a small proportion of these cases, the result will be the use of deadly force by one or more of the parties involved.

❖ Misconduct: Management and Administrative Issues

There is perhaps no phrase or cliché more relevant than the following when directed toward command staff personnel in the context of police misconduct: The buck stops here. Since the early days of policing, and following a review of major law enforcement scandals and the reports of the various commissions that investigated the misconduct in question, one common denominator surfaced—the leadership structures of the agencies in question demonstrated no real sense of commitment to investigating and ferreting out corruption from within. As Delattre (2002) and others pointed out, with respect to police misconduct, the problem does not lie with the few "rotten apples" that many police chiefs espouse as the problem; rather, it is the result of rotten leadership structures and administrative policies that seem to avoid rather than promote strict accountability for all department members who engage in misconduct. Moreover, these structures and policies do not support sound investigative methodologies that are necessary to proactively investigate malfeasance.

Marche's (2009) research confirmed what Delattre (2002), Klockars et al. (2000), and many others have said about the inaccuracies associated with these "**rotten apples" hypotheses** and corrupt police practices. He found that the police culture, the organizational culture of many police agencies, actually fosters corruption. Marche's (2009) research also indicated that ". . . incentive structures within police agencies increase the problem of corruption . . ." (p. 463). Arrest quotas and arrest rates of officers used as a criterion to be assigned to more sought after assignments, such as Gang Crimes, vice, and so on, and even used as criteria for promotion are not good management practices.

The Mollen Commission (1995) report pointed to another potential problem in reducing misconduct—the existence of a department-wide belief that the identification of corruption would cause department administrators to retaliate for bringing adverse public attention to the agency. These retaliatory actions, were often directed toward the whistleblowers. Unfortunately, the history regarding the treatment of officers who came forward with the intent of exposing corruption is replete with instances of unpleasant and, in many cases, threatening actions bestowed on them by their superiors and coworkers.

In response to data such as these, some chiefs emphasize the harm done to community relations when misconduct becomes public. They mistakenly believe that covering up, ignoring, or simply having wrongdoers resign rather than face the disciplinary ramifications commensurate with their misdeeds, is for the greater good. Yet according to Bracey (1989), the following is true:

> Management accountability is perhaps the most important, effective and most difficult proactive tool for preventing and detecting police corruption. This is not a program or a device, but rather a thorough rethinking of the meaning of supervision and management responsibility. The driving assumption underlying accountability is that commanders are responsible for all police activity that takes place on their command. At its simplest, a policy of accountability means that commanders may not plead ignorance and surprise when corruption is discovered in their areas. (p. 176)

Bracey goes on to indicate that while the accountability approach clearly can work, it can be carried to extremes by supervisors so concerned with protecting themselves from liability that they trivialize the process.

Trojanowicz (1992) noted that supervisors can have an impact on corrupt activities, but also said the following:

> [They] must go the extra distance to ensure that the officers under their command treat people with respect and that they have not crossed the line. . . . The good news is that departments which have embraced Community Policing have taken an important step in fostering a climate where average citizens may well feel encouraged to share any such concerns or suspicions. (p. 2)

No matter how one analyzes the situation, any administrative action short of holding all members of the organization strictly accountable for their misdeeds serves only to perpetuate the problem and send a disturbing message down the organizational ladder—a message that tacitly approves of corrupt practices. Some chiefs clearly recognize that a different sort of message needs to be sent in these circumstances. Former Chicago Police Superintendent Terry Hillard, after concluding a 2-year joint Internal Affairs Division–FBI investigation into the allegations that some police officers were shaking down Polish immigrants, had the officers involved arrested at their residences, without affording them the usual custom of advance notice. As one official in the Hillard administration put it, "The superintendent wanted to treat them like any other thieves" (Main, Sadovi, & Sweeney, 2000, p. 1).

Other administrative issues that may unwittingly lead to corrupt practices are related to the various get-tough-on-crime, no-nonsense, zero-tolerance policing strategies initiated by many law enforcement executives. While their intentions may be noble, do the results of such endeavors outweigh the possible negative consequences associated with them? Such strategies are normally reserved for locales ridden with crime, generally the lower socioeconomic areas of our nation's cities. Officers who are assigned to police these areas usually work in specialized units such as gang crimes, narcotics, and vice control, and many times they are forced to work under quota-type pressure if they wish to remain assigned to those units. Consequently, the pressure to make arrests will lead to increased citizen encounters, substantially raising the possibility of an increased number of citizen complaints concerning activities that range from illegal searches and seizures to excessive force and discriminatory or biased enforcement practices. When poor or inadequate supervisory practices and the "conspiracy of silence" are added to the mix, the result can prove to be disastrous for agencies in terms of public relations and department morale.

In addition to the negative consequences associated with zero-tolerance policies, the underlying tenets of these techniques are, in many cases, diametrically opposed to the principle of community policing. The us-versus-them mentality that tends to accompany get-tough-on-crime crusades serves more to alienate the public than to reduce crime and solve other social problems through collaboration and partnership with members of the community. Moreover, it must be emphasized at this point that the majority of society that views the police most suspiciously reside in the geographic areas most likely to be targeted by these traditional, zero-tolerance policing initiatives.

There may, however, be a glimmer of hope for those police administrators who prefer get-tough-on-crime and no nonsense police tactics. Through their research, Davis, Mateu-Gelabert, and Miller (2005) attempted to explain why, at a time when crime in New York City dramatically decreased and the number of citizen complaints against police dramatically increased after implementation of a new police strategy in 1994, two police precincts in the South Bronx managed to experience a reduction in the number of citizen complaints, to below the level in 1993. They determined the answers to be related to two key variables: (1) a new department-wide policy called CPR (courtesy, professionalism, and respect) and (2) the dedication to improving community relations by the precincts' commanding officers. This latter variable was accomplished through commanding officers taking a keen interest in "repeat offender" officers, or those receiving multiple citizen complaints. It did not take long for officers to figure out that their commanders were keeping tabs on them. Davis et al. (2005) concluded by stating ". . . that the most likely explanation for the decline in citizen complaints in these two precincts was efforts made by precinct commanders to promote respectful policing and change a police culture that tolerated citizen complaints" (p. 229).

Other techniques used by management to detect corruption include the use of field associates, "turning" officers who have been found to be corrupt, and rotation of assignments. *Field associates* are those officers specially trained and sometimes recruited to obtain information on corrupt activities while performing normal police functions. This information is relayed to management without other officers knowing who the informants are, creating an atmosphere of suspicion among officers when the existence of the program is known. "Turning" involves offering leniency or immunity to corrupt officers who agree to provide information on other corrupt officers. Rotation of personnel across shifts and geographic assignments is a technique used to disrupt possible corruption by making it difficult for officers and citizens to establish permanent ties. While this may have a positive impact on corruption, it may also disrupt the flow of information between officers and citizens, negatively impact community relations, and make community-oriented policing impossible.

Another strategy that may be employed to reduce misconduct is selective recruitment. Recruiting police personnel of high moral character and providing training in ethics early in their careers appear to be steps in the right direction (Cooksey, 1991; Lynch, 1989; Meese & Ortmeier, 2003). If the department and subculture also foster an anticorruption attitude, promote on the basis of merit, and pay relatively well, the allure of corruption may be somewhat reduced. Internal affairs units and external review boards have also been used to help curb corruption by identifying and charging those involved.

It is difficult to assess the extent to which anticorruption programs have been successful. To some extent, police corruption may be related to economic conditions, but the relationship appears to be curvilinear. That is, when police and other wages are low, the temptation to accept dirty money may be great. Alternatively, as Lynch (1989) indicated

> When the wages of sin are incredibly lucrative, as they are in so many instances today, the appeal of corruption is proportionately more alluring. . . . Let me suggest to you that given the potential for misuse of police power, the wonder is that police officers, who witness crime, inhumanity and degradation every day, do not lose their sense of integrity and do not violate their oath of office more frequently. (pp. 166–167)

This holds true today with the potential for police officers to accumulate large sums of money by working with drug dealers in a variety of ways. Many officers could undoubtedly make much more by protecting drug dealers and selling drugs themselves than they could hope to make in their official capacities as police officers.

In the long run, the only way to significantly reduce police corruption is to prosecute, to the fullest extent of the law, those involved—sending a clear message to the corrupt, uncorrupt, and corruptors that such action will be taken and that the consequences may be severe. While such actions in and of themselves may have limited impact on corrupt police officers, when widely publicized they may alert the community to the fact that reform in the police department is required. Although such reform is seldom sweeping enough to keep the problem from reemerging, it is possible to achieve positive results. And at a minimum, it disrupts the corrupt activities already in progress and alerts those involved to the fact that their activities are not secret and may result in official action.

❖ Correcting and Preventing Misconduct

Klockars, Ivkovich, and Haberfeld (2005), acknowledging the fact that measuring police corruption is a difficult task, ". . . applied a new approach—rather than focusing on corruption, researchers measured the integrity of police officers and their organizations" (p. ii). This was accomplished by the application of four dimensions of organizational integrity:

- Communication of all organizational rules
- Professional investigation of and disciplinary action taken for rule violations
- Intolerance of officer silence concerning rule violations
- Managing outside influences, such as public perception and expectations of officers (p. 2)

Klockars et al. (2005) examined the responses of 3,235 police officers from 30 different agencies in multiple states to several different hypothetical scenarios involving various forms of misconduct. They developed a number of questions and recommendations related to the issue of integrity:

- Do all officers in the agency know the rules? If not, they must be taught.
- How strongly do officers support the rules? If they do not, they should be told why they should be supportive.
- Do officers know the disciplinary actions associated with breaking the rules? It is imperative that this be well known and publicized.
- Do the officers believe the disciplinary actions associated with rule violations are fair? If they do not, the chief must either modify the discipline or correct the officers' perceptions.
- How willing are officers to report misconduct of their colleagues? If they are not, the chief must establish a policy which encourages the reporting of misconduct, such as rules which call for the termination of any officer who had knowledge of misconduct and did not report them, guarantees of anonymity to officers who come forward and report misconduct, etc. (pp. 1–2)

Klockars et al. (2005) concluded that police officers evaluate the seriousness of various acts of misconduct by examining their department's efforts in proactively detecting misconduct to see if disciplinary actions commensurate with the rule violations are consistently enforced. If either rules or disciplinary actions are interpreted by officers as weak or inconsistent, efforts designed to mitigate misconduct are undermined. The following quotation captures the essence of the study: "An agency's culture of integrity, as defined by clearly understood and implemented policies and rules, may be more important in shaping the ethics of police officers than hiring the "right" people" (p. ii).

A similar study conducted on the international level by Ivkovic (2005) found that ". . . by controlling agency-related factors, police administrators may influence the level of seriousness with which police officers view police corruption." (Ivkovic, 2005, p. 546)

Ivkovic and Shelley (2008) studied many of the same issues in yet another international context, focusing on 1,055 police officers from Bosnia and the Czech Republic. The results with respect to officers' opinions about the seriousness of police malfeasance, associated disciplinary actions, and willingness to report misconduct were remarkably similar to those reported for officers in the United States. Specifically, officers from both countries had the following similarities:

1. Shared an understanding of what constitutes serious issues of misconduct

2. The infamous code of silence was observed by the majority of respondents from both countries, unless the misconduct at issue fell on the serious end of the misconduct continuum.

3. Officers from the Czech Republic were more willing to expect disciplinary action for rule violations, and officers from Bosnia felt that discipline was controlled by an informal set or rules and norms—and most felt they would not receive any discipline at all, unless the misconduct was viewed as severe.

Ivkovic and Shelley (2008) concluded that the most significant finding was that the disciplinary culture of the two countries affected the views of individual officers more than any other variable.

The complexities of our society are a challenge for today's police administrators. Effective police operations, however, become even more difficult when acts of misconduct continue to surface. As the public, legislative bodies, and judicial decisions increase the level of accountability placed on the police, law enforcement administrators must respond accordingly by eliminating corrupt practices to the best of their abilities. This is no easy task, but there are a number of recommendations that, if followed, might significantly mitigate instances of corruption.

A 2001 report issued by the U.S. Department of Justice (DOJ), titled "Principles for Promoting Police Integrity: Examples of Promising Police Practices and Policies," offers recommendations for curbing police misconduct and improving the continued professionalization of the field. The following is a summary of the various recommendations from the DOJ report.

1. *Accepting Complaints:* Many police departments have policies that require those wishing to file a complaint against a police officer to do so in person, oftentimes requiring them to submit a formal written statement. It is recommended that citizens be allowed to file a complaint using any medium of communication (e.g., e-mail, telephone, mail, or facsimile). Not to allow these options is tantamount to discouraging reports of wrongdoing.

2. *Reports of Misconduct:* This portion of the DOJ report deals with the nonfeasance issue identified earlier in the chapter. Police executives should adopt formal policies that hold officers responsible for not reporting the wrongdoings of their coworkers. In addition, the disciplinary action reserved for acts of nonfeasance should be commensurate with the serious nature of this failure to act.

3. *Avenues for Reporting Misconduct:* Departments should also have mechanisms in place that encourage and allow officers to come forward and report acts of misconduct, anonymously if necessary. Currently, the NYPD and other agencies seem to be moving in that direction, and "this policy change attempts to insure protection of officers who come forward and report other officers' misconduct and corruption" (Sykes, 1999). Many critics of such policies warn about potential Constitutional abuses and liken this practice to the treatment of confidential informants and protected witnesses. In a perfect world, police departments would not have to employ such tactics. At this point in time, however, this policy of anonymity appears to be a good starting point.

4. *Whistle-Blowing Policy:* Formal policy addressing retaliation against officers reporting misconduct should be implemented and rigorously enforced. If officers are afraid to report misconduct, the problem of corruption will continue to grow. Recent research on whistle-blowing by Rothwell and Baldwin (2006) attempted to apply ethical climate theory to various predictors of willingness to blow the whistle on misconduct. Predictor variables included size of the agency, supervisory status, length of time employed, existence of a policy manual, a policy requiring the reporting of misconduct, existence of internal affairs units, use of polygraph exams, and civilian versus police status (pp. 222–224). The results of this research were somewhat surprising in light of the fact that ethical climate theory consistently failed to predict whistle-blowing, supervisory status was the most consistent and significant predictor of whistle-blowing, and

civilian employees of these police agencies were more inclined to abide by the infamous code of silence than their sworn counterparts (pp. 237–238).

5. *Assistance From Other Arms of the CJ System:* Police administrators can turn to prosecutors and judges when they have reason to believe that an officer may have engaged in inappropriate behavior during the course of a criminal investigation or court proceeding. Incidents involving perjury and bringing false charges against a defendant to justify malfeasance are particularly heinous in this regard.

6. *Effective Investigative Methodologies:* Investigations that focus on allegations of serious misconduct, such as constitutional violations, should be conducted by a special unit or body charged only with these responsibilities. It must be emphasized that individuals working in these specialized units should be competent and experienced investigators, with access to state-of-the-art investigative aids. Most important, investigators in these units need the support and encouragement of the entire command structure of their agencies.

7. *Resolution of Misconduct Investigations:* When the evidence warrants, and officers are found to be culpable for misconduct, they should be held strictly accountable and punished accordingly. On deciding disciplinary action, police chiefs should not only look at the seriousness of the misconduct, but consider the officer's history of similar misdeeds. After resolution, the complainant should be notified, in writing, of the disposition of the case, the reasons for the decision, and the disciplinary action taken.

8. *Accountability and Effective Management:* According to the DOJ (2001), "Studies of law enforcement agencies yielded empirical data that a small number of police officers are responsible for a disproportionate amount of problematic police behavior" (p. 10). In light of this information, police departments are advised to maintain a computer database that identifies potentially problematic behavior patterns of officers. Information entered into the database should include, but not be limited to, incidents involving the use of force; number of citizen complaints, as well as commendations and honorable mentions; criminal and civil actions initiated against officers; disciplinary record; and training history. Rather than use such information solely for punitive purposes, supervisors can use it as part of an early warning program that inappropriate behavior patterns may be beginning to develop. Armed with this information, remedial actions can be taken before serious problems develop.

On a more recent note, Greene, Piquero, Hickman, and Lawton (2004) examined the personnel records of more than 2,000 Philadelphia police officers to identify characteristics most associated with disciplinary issues. More than 4,000 patrol officers were then surveyed regarding their attitudes toward police work, their department, and police misconduct. Variables pertaining to background, academy performance and attitude proved useful in predicting future problematic behavior in police officers. The strongest predictor of problematic officer behavior was departmental discipline, followed by physical abuse complaints, internal investigations, and off-duty incidents (Greene et al., 2004).

9. *Supervision and Leadership:* Supervisors should lead by example and be alert for signs of misconduct. Nothing hurts the morale of ethical employees more than seeing

supervisors either ignore the misdeeds of their subordinates or engage in inappropriate behavior themselves. If supervisory personnel are held accountable for the actions of individuals within the span of their direct control, acts of misconduct should diminish substantially.

10. *Public Information, Feedback, and Civilian Input:* Police administrators should actively seek feedback from the public regarding performance of the agency. A relatively convenient and inexpensive way to elicit this information is by the random distribution of what is commonly referred to as community satisfaction surveys. The key is to analyze the feedback provided by the public and to address negative comments when appropriate.

11. *Community Meetings:* It is suggested that regular meetings be held to disseminate all relevant information to members of the community. These meetings also give residents an opportunity to voice their concerns regarding police operations.

12. *Citizen Oversight:* With respect to the goals of community-oriented policing, it is recommended that police departments utilize some form of citizen oversight when investigating allegations of misconduct. For example, Walker (2001) concluded that citizen oversight agencies have resulted in the development of more open and accessible complaint procedures, compared to the traditional procedures used by many police departments. He concluded that many police agencies have failed to investigate complaints in a thorough and fair fashion and have failed to use hostility from citizen complaints as a learning tool. Thus, in many agencies, citizen oversight agencies have improved police accountability and resulted in positive changes in the police organization. However, many citizen oversight agencies have not been successful. Walker (2001) also found that these agencies were unable to establish independence from the police agency, suffered from leadership problems, and, in many cases, faced unrelenting police resistance. While the effectiveness of citizen oversight remains subject to debate, the inclusion of community members in this process goes a long way toward the removal of barriers that for decades have prevented the police and the communities they serve from coming together.

13. *Training:* Basic and inservice training curriculums should be expanded to both include and stress the importance of such subjects as ethical decision making; responsible use of discretionary authority; racial, ethnic, and cultural diversity; and effective interpersonal communication. It is also important that individuals who serve as academy instructors and facilitators of continuing professional education be well versed not only in the topics they are assigned to cover, but also in the basic principles of learning and instructional technology.

One last study regarding the importance of leadership is worthy of note. Leadership must start at the very top and must be done by example. Zuidema and Duff (2009) focused their research on curtailing corruption through organizational ethics and effective leadership. The central hypothesis of their study was that the level of corruption in any given agency was strongly associated with the quality of its leaders; thus, agencies should encourage the development of ethical leadership to mitigate corrupt practices. During their case study of the Lynchburg, Virginia Police Department (LPD), they discovered that agency leaders encouraged ethical behavior in a variety of ways. First, they routinely espoused the importance of ethical behavior. For example, through some creativity on the part of their officers, they decided that the letter L in Lynchburg would stand for leadership, the letter P for professionalism, and the letter D for dedication. This motto was then imprinted on coffee mugs, t-shirts, hats, the agency website, patrol cars, and brochures. These efforts sent the intended signals to both agency members and the community at large. In addition, during public ceremonies and department-wide meetings, all sworn officers were asked to stand and recite the International Association of Chiefs of Police Oath of Honor. Last, they do not tolerate unethical behavior of any kind (pp. 8–9).

LPD members also take seriously the notion that the younger officers who represent the future leaders of the department need to be groomed as such. Drawing on any and all resources available, the LPD academy developed and now offers a multitude of inservice training activities that focus on new leader development (p. 9).

Finally, to close the loop, LPD administrators constantly encourage and reward ethical practice by their officers. This too is part of their routine, and is a key ingredient in their recipe for individual and organizational success (Zuidema & Duff, 2009).

❖ Chapter Summary

The issue of misconduct is a problem that has plagued the field of policing since its inception. Even though the range of activities categorized as malfeasance occur infrequently and are committed by a relatively small number of officers, the harm caused by these actions often takes years to repair. The costs in terms of community relations, department morale, and reputation are too devastating to bear any longer. The message is clear—it is no longer acceptable for police departments to operate with impunity or without accountability. Police executives should strive to continuously advance the field of policing along a path of professionalization.

There is hope, however. There have been many recommendations made by police researchers, police executives, and governmental agencies to mitigate the frequency of the many forms of misconduct covered throughout this chapter. The International Association of Chiefs of Police and the U.S. Department of Justice have offered many sound recommendations. As Klockars et al. (2005) noted, and which encapsulates the essence of the aforementioned recommendations, "An agency's culture of integrity, as defined by clearly understood and implemented policies and rules, may be more important in shaping the ethics of police officers than hiring the "right" people" (p. ii).

Leadership lies at the foundation of this issue. Supervisory personnel must lead by example, and the examples need to start at the top. To do otherwise is tantamount to nonfeasance, thus making leaders of these agencies part of the problem rather than the solution. One theme that consistently emerges from the literature is that police misconduct tends to flourish, absent real commitment from the top rungs of the organizational ladder to put an end to corrupt policing practices.

❖ Key Terms

police ethics	grass eaters
Lexow Commission	meat eaters
Knapp Commission	police code of silence
police corruption	Christopher Commission

Mollen Commission

Police Code of Conduct

corruption of authority

kickbacks

shakedowns

bribery

opportunistic theft

protection of illegal activities

nonfeasance

noble cause corruption

emotional abuse/psychological harassment

excessive use of force

rotten apple hypothesis

field associates

❖ Discussion Questions

1. What are some of the more important ethical issues in policing? Should police recruits be taught ethics?

2. What constitutes police corruption? Can you cite examples of police corruption from your own experiences?

3. Why is corruption of authority (accepting gratuities such as free coffee, food, etc.) critical in understanding police corruption in general?

4. Does society desire or demand police who are incorruptible? Why or why not?

5. What are the relationships between internal corruption in police agencies and other forms of corruption?

6. Do circumstances involving the philosophy of "the end justifies the means" or "noble cause corruption" mitigate the serious nature of misconduct by police? Why or why not?

7. Why would a police officer perjure himself? What is the impact of such perjury on the criminal justice network and other citizens in general?

8. Is psychological brutality an important form of police misconduct? Why and in what ways?

9. What recommendations have been offered to mitigate the frequency and depth of police corruption?

10. Do you think police misconduct is as serious a problem now as it was a decade or so ago? Support your answer.

❖ Internet Exercises

1. Using the Web, locate examples of three "real life" scandals pertaining to at least three different forms of corruptions identified in the chapter.

2. Using the Web, locate what recent strategies are being used by law enforcement and other government personnel in their fight against the drug cartels of Mexico.

3. Research the term or phrase *narcoterrorism*, and define it in detail. Document at least two examples of this form of terrorism.

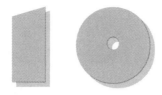

Policing in a Multicultural Setting

❖ **PHOTO 10.1** Officers should represent the racial, ethnic, and gender make-up of the citizens they serve.

As we have noted throughout this book, the police cannot be effective or efficient without public support. Without such support, they will be uninformed of most crimes, are likely to receive inadequate resources, will not be able to collect information needed to solve cases and apprehend offenders, and will be unsuccessful in recruiting quality employees. There is little doubt that, in democratic societies at least, community relations are the cornerstone of good policing. The police are, or should be, protectors of civil liberties and civil rights, as well as of life and property. If the police are to serve the community effectively and in a manner acceptable to citizens, they must demonstrate their effectiveness in these areas in order to establish a reasonable working relationship with the public.

❖ Policing in a Multicultural and Multiethnic Society

Developing such working relationships in a rapidly changing, multicultural society is difficult. According to the U.S. Census, slightly more than one third of the United States population claims minority status based on race or ethnicity, an increase of 11% from 2000 (Minckler, 2008). The U.S. population is becoming increasingly diverse, with Hispanics and Asians continuing to be the two fastest-growing minorities. Currently in four states—Hawaii, New Mexico, California, and Texas—more than 50% of the population is composed of people other than non-Hispanic whites. The foreign-born population has grown to some 37.5 million according to the Census Bureau's 2006 American Community Survey (Minckler, 2008).

In 2006, the nation's total minority population topped 100 million, or about one third of the total (Fullbright, 2007). Latinos were the fastest-growing minority group nationwide, reaching 44.2 million, up 3.4% from 2005, according to the annual estimates (Fullbright, 2007). The nation's Asian population also grew rapidly, up almost 3% between 2005 and 2006. Blacks numbered 40.2 million in 2006. If present trends continue, non-Hispanic whites will account for about 47% of the population by 2050 (Reuters, 2008).

At the same time, the elderly constitute an increasing proportion of our population, and a new type of generation gap is arising with most people over 60 being non-Hispanic whites, while most of those under 40 are not (Fullbright, 2007). In addition, gays and lesbians, the homeless, religious minorities, neo-Nazi skinheads, and refugees from the Middle East, Central and South America, and island countries all constitute significant minorities. Many of the immigrants coming to this country bring different languages, religious observances, dress, and lifestyles, and different views of the police. Some, having come from countries where the police are integrated with the military and police actions are not regulated by strong constitutional and human rights guarantees, have very negative images of the police (Barak, Flavin, & Leighton, 2001, pp. 257–259; Scott, 1993, p. 26). These changes will likely make it difficult for the police to provide adequate services and create problems related to language and cultural understanding. The changes are further complicated by the fear that terrorists from abroad may hide among the numerous immigrants to the United States, while terrorists from within continue to present very real threats. All in all, the police at all levels have their work cut out for them. O'Brien's (1978) observation some 30 years ago is perhaps even more appropriate today:

> The central position of the police in the community critically affects all sections of society. The multiple duties of the police at all times and in all areas of the community dictate that they must influence the daily life of each citizen. . . . Unfortunately, in recent times there has been a rupture of mutual trust between the police and some segments of the community. (p. 304)

❖ Police–Community Relations

Actually, as we have seen, the "rupture of mutual trust" noted by O'Brien has deep historical roots in American policing. Conflict between the police and other citizens is rooted in the basic structure of American society and the values on which it rests. The extent to which this is so can be seen in numerous discussions of police–community relations that are described, presumably unintentionally, in terms of "police encounters with citizens." Describing the relationship in this way makes it appear that the police are not, themselves, citizens and points to a dichotomy that has emerged in our society between the police and other citizens.

In many respects, the police are viewed as adversaries not only by those involved in criminal activities, but also by basically law abiding citizens who occasionally violate speed limits or drive when they have had one too many drinks or protest what they consider to be legitimate grievances without going through proper channels to obtain a permit. In fact, of course, police officers are first and foremost citizens—historically, traditionally, and legally. Yet the language we use to describe things often indicates the way in which we view them, and to some extent, many of us tend to view the police as being distinct from "citizens." While the use of such terminology may not widen the gap between the police and other citizens, it does little to close it. Police encounters with other citizens are, at base, encounters between fellow citizens.

Another point needs to be made here. When we are talking about police–community relations, we tend to think in terms of police encounters with the public. In fact, we are not dealing with one large homogeneous group called a public, but with many diverse publics. These publics are divided by factors such as geography, race, sex, age, social class, respect for law and order, and degree of law-abiding behavior (Cox & McCamey, 2008, pp. 12–13). These different publics have unique interests and concerns that separate them from one another in many ways. The police, as public servants, are to serve all these various publics, and they themselves organize in various ways to meet what they perceive to be the needs of the publics they serve. Because the expectations of members of these different publics are often dissimilar, providing effective service is often difficult, as recognized by Hennessy (1993),

> Our communities are changing quickly—often too quickly for law enforcement to keep up. Failing to understand many of these changes, and still trying to conduct business as usual, we find that the tools and rules that worked before don't work now. For many seasoned officers, their main concern is to make it through each shift and go home in one piece. This only serves to reinforce a force-oriented culture that brings officers closer to each other and further from the community they serve. (p. 48)

In addition, members of the various publics are often apathetic about issues involving the police but have very specific expectations when they, or other members of their group, require police services.

The necessity of attempting to satisfy these different, sometimes conflicting, expectations should alert us to the fact that good police–community relations are not easy to achieve. In a large, industrialized, multiethnic society, one based on values that include democratic decision making, individual freedom, and tolerance for diversity, the need for social order and the demand for freedom will inevitably lead to conflict on some occasions (Cox & Fitzgerald, 1996).

To some extent, then, conflict between the police and other citizens is inevitable and perhaps even healthy within limits. The problem, however, cannot be ignored when the conflict becomes extensive or certain groups experience differential treatment by the police. Solutions to conflicts of this type are not found easily and are not the sole responsibility of the police. Yet we cannot easily force other citizens into classes on human or public relations, even though we recognize that successful programs in either of these areas require reciprocity. Therefore, the burden of trying to improve police–community relations often rests with the police.

Police–community relations comprise both human and public relations. The concept of **human relations** refers to everything we do to, for, and with other people. Included under this concept are such things as showing respect for one another, being sensitive to the problems of others, tolerating divergent points of view, and showing respect for human dignity. **Public relations**, from the police perspective, include all of the activities in which they engage while attempting to develop or maintain a favorable public image (Cox & Fitzgerald, 1996). Let's examine each of these concepts as they relate to police encounters with other citizens.

Human Relations in Policing

With respect to police–community relations, human relations in the millions of day-to-day encounters that take place are the foundation for community relations, good or bad. It is important to recognize that these encounters between individuals do not occur in a vacuum. When we enter into encounters with others, we often know, or think we know, a good deal about them, even though we have never met them before. Thus, for example, we have preconceived notions about members of different racial, religious, age, or ethnic groups, and about police officers. These preconceived notions, or **stereotypes**, are based on prior encounters, word of mouth/rumor/gossip, and information provided by the media. These notions may be accurate or inaccurate. Whichever is the case, we act in terms of these perceptions, at least until the encounter in which we are involved gives us additional or different information on which to base our beliefs and actions (see You Decide 10.1).

YOU DECIDE 10.1

Conflict Between a Police Officer and a Harvard Professor

In July, 2009, Harvard professor Henry Louis Gates Jr. was arrested by Cambridge police Sergeant James Crowley (who is white) who was investigating a possible break-in. According to the police officer, he arrested Professor Gates (who is black) because the professor became angry after being asked for identification and proof of his address (the home he was allegedly breaking into was his own). Crowley said the professor berated him and continued to do so after being warned multiple times. The officer insisted that he was following police procedures in making the arrest and he refused to apologize as Gates requested.

Professor Gates refuted the sergeant's description of his behavior, saying he had used no racial slurs, employed no profanity, and made no threats. Gates added that he does not consider himself above the law, and that he is "profoundly grateful for all of the services performed by the police," but indicated he did not believe that standing up for his rights as a citizen should be against the law.

Charges against Professor Gates were eventually dropped and the police and Gates issued a joint statement calling the incident "regrettable and unfortunate."

(Continued)

(Continued)

The debate was fueled by President Obama in a nationally televised news conference where he said that the Cambridge police department "acted stupidly," though he acknowledged that he did not know all the facts of the Cambridge case and that Professor Gates was a friend of his.

Questions:

1. Based upon what you have read, is there any indication of racism in this encounter? If so, what indications?

2. Do you believe Sergeant Crowley should apologize to Professor Gates? Should Professor Gates apologize to Sergeant Crowley?

3. Should the President have made the comments he did given that he had no factual knowledge of the situation?

Source: Adapted from "Officer Defends Arrest of Harvard Professor," by L. Robbin, 2009, *The New York Times.* Available from http://www.nytimes.com/2009/07/24/us/24cambridge.html

Consider an encounter between a uniformed police officer and another citizen. The officer is easily identifiable because of the uniform, badge, nightstick, handcuffs, and gun; and all of these help identify her role in the encounter. The role that is, in part, defined by the tools of the trade includes the fact that the officer has authority and may use force under certain circumstances to gain compliance with her wishes. This should indicate, and for the most part appears to indicate, to other parties to the encounter that the officer's definition of the situation will be the prevailing one—that is, that the officer is in control or will gain control.

For this definition of the situation to prevail, certain obligations must be fulfilled by the other party or parties to the encounter. These include deferring to the officer's authority, treating the officer with some degree of respect, and complying with her directions. To do otherwise is to risk offending the officer, who may then resort to more drastic actions in light of what may be viewed as a challenge to her authority. Some officers are extremely sensitive to such challenges and to the perceived loss of face that accompanies them. Such officers may feel compelled to respond quickly and forcefully to maintain their control. Obviously, such a response may lead to suspicion and hostility on behalf of the other party to the encounter, and the encounter may become nasty in short order. This is especially true when the two parties to the encounter bring negative impressions of each other into the encounter, as sometimes occurs when the police and racial or ethnic minority group members interact. Such negative impressions also often exist when the police are called into a domestic violence situation in which they regard the offender with suspicion and the offender believes that police intervention into his home and into an essentially private matter is improper. This may be doubly true when there are also cultural prohibitions against involving outsiders in intimate relationships, making the officer's intervention even more problematic. Such may be the case in domestic situations involving individuals from Latin American countries or from the Middle East.

The extent to which encounters between the police and other citizens become problematic depends on a number of factors. These include the impressions brought to the encounter, the setting in which the encounter occurs (private or public, familiar or unfamiliar), the number and types of participants involved, the degree of control exercised by the participants, and what actually happens during the encounter. For example, the mere sight of a police officer puts some people on guard. They drive more slowly and more carefully; if they are involved in illegal activities, they may try to appear innocent, and they may treat other persons more civilly. For their part, police officers are trained to be suspicious of others, especially when past experience or present knowledge leads them to believe an offense may be involved. Thus, the danger and difficulty of police encounters ranges from very great, as in an encounter with a known felon in the process of committing a felony in an isolated location, with the officer and the felon being the only participants involved, to very little, as in the case of locating a missing child lost in a shopping mall where other participants are attempting to assist.

It is possible to exaggerate the difficulties involved in police encounters with other citizens. Most such encounters are civil, characterized by some degree of mutual concern, understanding, and respect (Reiss, 1968). Still, there is no denying that encounters between the police and some citizens are more likely to be problematic than others. As we have seen, police–minority encounters in our society have been particularly problematic over the past several decades, and it is to these encounters that we now turn our attention.

❖ Police–Minority Encounters

One of the most controversial areas of police–community relations in our society involves the police and racial or ethnic minority group members, particularly police interactions with blacks and Hispanics, and more recently with Middle Easterners, though members of other racial and ethnic minorities are sometimes involved as well. Our country has a long history of conflict between the police and minorities. In the 1960s, there were five years of riots involving blacks and the police, and in the 1990s a number of incidents, beginning with the highly publicized Rodney King beating by Los Angeles police officers, which again illustrated the poor relationships that exist between the police and blacks in many parts of this country. Similar problems exist in many communities with respect to Hispanics, Native Americans, and more recently Muslims, Arabs, and Middle Easterners.

A **minority group** is comprised of individuals who are accorded unequal treatment from dominant group members in the form of discrimination and who are relatively easy to identify because of their physical or cultural characteristics, which differ from those of the dominant group. According to this definition, the police themselves might well be considered members of a minority because they are often victims of discrimination, are generally easy to identify, and have, as we have seen, some distinctive cultural characteristics (masculinity, authority, use of force, cynicism, etc.). One basic difference between police officers and members of racial or ethnic minorities is that the former are voluntary members while the latter are not. Traditional beliefs in our society have long held that members of some racial and ethnic minorities are inferior to whites in some ways, even though scientific research indicates there is no basis for such beliefs. Because many police officers come from traditional backgrounds, it is not surprising to find that some agree that minority group members are inferior—especially when these officers police in areas with high crime rates that are disproportionately inhabited by members of minorities who often view the police as intruders or members of an army of occupation (Baldwin, 1962; Hacker, 1992; Weitzer & Tuch, 2008).

That members of minority groups based, for example, on race, ethnicity, or sexual orientation hold hostile views of the police should not come as a surprise. Segregation and sexual orientation laws in the United States were long enforced by the police, who treated blacks, Native Americans, gays and lesbians, and others as second-class citizens (which, in terms of existing laws, they were). Morally and ethically objectionable as these laws were, police officers were legally obligated to obey them and sometimes appeared to do so with pleasure. When the laws changed as a result of civil rights activism, some police personnel were slow to accommodate the new laws, and members of minorities, used to unequal treatment by the police, were slow to accept the fact that at least some officers had made appropriate changes. In addition, many immigrants entering the United States come from countries where the police are corrupt, brutal, unreliable, and insensitive. For members of these groups who have been subject to both prejudice and discrimination in their home countries, learning to trust the police and accept them as public servants rather than as a group of armed and dangerous thugs is not easy and takes time. In the meantime, it should not come as a shock when encounters between members of minorities and the police are less than civil.

It is important to point out the difference between **prejudice** (a feeling about a person or persons based on faulty generalizations) and **discrimination** (which involves behavior that, in its negative form, excludes all members of a certain group from some rights, opportunities, or privileges) (Schaefer, 2000). We all have prejudices that may or may not result in discrimination. Prejudice undoubtedly exists among police officers (as it does among all other occupational groups), and though we might hope that there has been a reduction in such prejudice over the past half century with changes in civil rights legislation, hiring practices of police agencies, the election of a black president, the appointment of black and Hispanic Supreme Court justices, and the appointment of numerous minorities to cabinet-level and other important governmental positions, there is little we can do to measure the existence of prejudice except to ask police officers about their feelings (Bouza, 2001; Thornton, McKinnie, & Stetz, 1999). Further, whatever these feelings may be, they are not, in and of themselves, illegal. When these feelings carry over into behavior (discrimination), however, serious problems may result for both the police and minority group members. Thus, when police officers harass or abuse individuals because they are members of a minority or treat individuals as if they are above the law because they belong to another minority, community relations and those unfairly treated both suffer. Harassment and abuse result in loss of face and human dignity as well as occasional physical injuries, and they cannot be tolerated on the part of police officers. There is little doubt that members of many minorities—racial and ethnic as well as behavioral (alcoholics, gays and lesbians, prostitutes, drug addicts, etc.)—believe that such harassment and abuse are commonly directed to members of their groups. Verbal abuse by police officers is one of the most common complaints expressed by citizens. Racial or ethnic slurs not only demean citizens but also deny them equal treatment. As a consequence, as well as for historical reasons, individuals belonging to minority groups resent and are sometimes openly hostile toward the police. They often respond by harassing and verbally abusing the police. These actions escalate the danger and hostility involved in encounters and community relations. It is essential, then, to realize that prejudice and discrimination are not limited to the police and, therefore, that the police alone cannot ensure good community relations.

It is equally important to recognize that many police officers who might not otherwise be involved in discriminatory practices fall victim to **occupational discrimination**. That is, even though an individual officer may not believe in acting in a discriminatory fashion, his colleagues may exhibit such behavior. To be perceived as a part of the subculture described earlier, the officer may emulate the behavior of his peers, thus harassing or abusing minority group members—not because he believes it is right, but because he wishes to be perceived as a member of the "in-group."

Similarly, minority group members may not believe that harassing the police is appropriate behavior, but in the presence of other members of their group, they may do so. Some blacks in the United States, for example, have several centuries of historical reasons for disliking the police, whom they see as representatives of the establishment that, they believe, made and keeps them second-class citizens. As Sykes (1978) pointed out,

> In a democratic social order, the police are expected to be fair in their enforcement of the law and accountable to those who are policed. They are not to be an alien force imposed on a community, an autonomous body ruling by coercion, or agents of a tyrannical state, but servants of society maintaining a commonly accepted body of law in evenhanded fashion. (p. 395)

However, as we have pointed out elsewhere, the police in our society have often been an alien force when dealing with blacks and other minority group members. The police traditionally enforced the laws that made blacks second-class citizens. And in contemporary society, the police expend a disproportionate amount of their resources in minority neighborhoods. Here again, conflicting points of view and the difficulty of finding solutions to police–minority relations problems are obvious. As Weaver (1992) stated, "Simply mixing culturally different people together does not resolve misunderstandings. Quite the contrary. Differences usually become more apparent and hostilities can actually increase during encounters between culturally diverse individuals" (p. 2).

While minority group members regard the numbers of police in their neighborhoods as excessive and as a form of harassment, the police argue that minority neighborhoods typically have high crime rates and therefore require police presence. Although it may be argued that police presence contributes to high crime rates (the more police, the more crimes they discover), it is equally true that the number of victims and offenders found in such neighborhoods makes it difficult for the police to respond in any other fashion. This fact, however, does not justify the use of discriminatory tactics in minority neighborhoods.

What are some of the forms of police discrimination in minority neighborhoods? As noted, the basic form of discrimination is **psychological harassment** based on the use of racial slurs and other attempts to embarrass or humiliate members of the minority group in question. Failure to use proper forms of address (e.g., use of first name rather than Mr. or Ms. and last name) has been and remains a major complaint of minority group members (Brunson & Miller, 2006; Cox, 1984; Hacker, 1992; National Advisory Commission on Civil Disorders, 1968; Thornton, McKinnie, & Stetz, 1999; Walker, Spohn, & DeLone, 1995; Weitzer & Tuch, 2008). Failure to respond rapidly to calls in ghetto or barrio areas has also been an issue, and unreasonable use of stop-and-question and stop-and-frisk tactics alarm minority group members. Further, the relatively infrequent but totally unacceptable use of excessive force on the part of the police in dealing with members of minorities (or, for that matter, the dominant group) is of major concern (Chavis & Williams, 1993; "Police Continue," 2007; Reiss, 1970; Walker, Spohn, & DeLone, 1995). Such incidents become legend in minority neighborhoods and further the negative image of the police already present as a result of historical differences between the parties.

POLICE STORIES

I clearly remember the night the importance of police discretion, the use of the words "you are under arrest," the need for physical force, and the need for good police–minority relations was brought home to me. It was a hot summer evening, and I was working as a participant observer with a medium sized municipal police department. I was riding with a young white officer, just off probation.

About 12:45 a.m., the officer received a call of a fight in progress at a bar in a largely black neighborhood. This was his first time patrolling the area, and he had indicated some apprehension about patrolling it. He responded to the call and entered the bar with a senior officer who had come from another zone as backup. All the patrons of the bar were black and the officers and I were white.

There was no indication of a fight when we entered the bar, and the bartender told the officers that the fight was over. The officer with whom I was riding decided to stay in the back of the bar for the next 10 minutes, until closing time (1 a.m.). The senior officer also stayed, though he indicated it might be just as well to patrol in the immediate area as to wait in the bar.

Then, a black man, fairly small in stature, took a swing at a much larger man. He missed (due in large part to the fact that he was drunk), but the larger man didn't, and his punch put the smaller man on the floor. The fight was over. The young officer immediately said to the winner of the fight, "You are under arrest." The senior officer immediately called for more backup. The winner said to the young officer, "Take me if you think you can." A crowd gathered round, and the altercation, at the urging of the bartender, went outside. The arrest words were repeated again and again with the same response. The young officer made no attempt to physically restrain the perpetrator, but continued to utter those magic words: "You are under arrest."

Help arrived in the form of three other officers, including the shift sergeant who immediately sized up the situation—which was becoming very tense. He told the perpetrator that he was under arrest and was going to the station one way or another. He then took out his handcuffs and clamped one cuff on the right arm of the perpetrator, who instantly swung the arm around with the dangling cuff and caught the sergeant across the forehead, which instantly began to bleed. This caused a stir in the crowd, which was becoming increasingly hostile—now making nasty comments about the officers and beginning to push officers who were simply trying to keep the crowd away from the combatants. Another officer joined the sergeant, and the second cuff was secured. Two of the officers then attempted to lead the perpetrator to a patrol car to put him in the back seat while the remaining officers tried to keep the crowd away. Getting the perpetrator into the back seat of the patrol car proved to be very difficult until three black males stepped out of the crowd and assisted the officers. They made it clear that they didn't much like the police but thought the situation was about to get out of control and that someone was likely to be seriously injured. Needless to say, we left the scene in short order.

Reflecting back on that night, numerous thoughts pop into my mind. Should the officer have stayed in the bar for the 10 minutes until closing time? Did the officer's response have anything to do with his apprehension about policing in a black neighborhood?

Would it have been better to patrol in the immediate vicinity? Would the officer have stayed in the bar had the patrons been white?

Should the words "You are under arrest" have been spoken in the circumstances? Since the police knew the brawlers by name (and address), could an arrest have been made after the bar closed? What was the effect of those magical words? Did they leave the perpetrator free to withdraw? Did they leave the police officers free to withdraw? Why were they spoken only to the winner of the fight, not to the person who started the fight? What would have been the consequences for the police if the words hadn't been spoken?

Why didn't the senior officer step in and effect the arrest? (The officer told me later that he would have assisted the young officer had he attempted to physically arrest the perpetrator, but felt it would cause the officer a great loss of face in the black community if he had taken charge of the arrest. He also told me later that all young officers go through a trial by fire, during which senior officers make judgments about whether they can count on young officers if things get physical. This has been substantiated by numerous officers in numerous departments over the years.)

(Continued)

(Continued)

Other questions arose about police–minority relations. Why were the patrons unfriendly, if not hostile toward the police? Would the presence of a black officer have made a difference? Why did some members of the crowd assist the police officer for whom they said they had little regard? Should the police have used pepper spray? Night sticks? How many weapons were present in the crowd that night? What would have happened if a weapon had been used or threatened by either members of the crowd or the police? Would the young white officer ever feel comfortable patrolling in that zone? Would he be accepted into the police fraternity given his performance?

As the years have rolled by (now some 45 years as an observer of police activity), these questions have arisen again and again, but never again with quite the same correlates of tension, foreboding, and yes, fear, as on that hot summer night.

According to Walker, Spohn, and DeLone (1995, pp. 85, 89), "Minorities are arrested, stopped and questioned and shot and killed by the police out of all proportion to their representation in the population (p. 85). . . . The police play a far more visible role in minority group neighborhoods compared with white neighborhoods. . . . An African-American or Hispanic American is much more likely than a white American to see or have personal contact with a police officer."(p. 89) Police use arrests as a strategy for resolving a variety of problems (many of which are noncriminal in nature) in the ghettos. In some instances, the probability of a black man being arrested during his lifetime approaches 90% (Barlow & Barlow, 2000, p. 94). In 2007, for example, blacks accounted for some 28% of all arrests and 39% of arrests for violent crime (FBI, 2008). In the same year, blacks were about 12% of the population in the United States.

The patrol car in the ghetto or barrio may be perceived by blacks and Latinos as police harassment, while the police may believe they are acting in the best interests of these minority groups by providing as many personnel as possible in those areas where citizens are most likely to commit or be victims of crime. Alternatively, the young black or Latino males who use the slang and dress of their subcultures may be perceived by the police as challenging their authority. Such negative stereotypes are often inaccurate, and their persistence makes sharing a definition of the situation or mutual understanding difficult, if not impossible. Similarly, young Arab Americans became a focus of police attention following the events of 9/11. A study by Henderson, Ortiz, Sugie, and Miller (2008) examined how the terrorist attacks affected relationships between the police and residents in Arab American neighborhoods. Among the difficulties noted were mutual distrust between Arab American communities and law enforcement, lack of cultural awareness among law enforcement officers, language barriers, and residents' concerns about immigration status.

Residents of some Arab American communities indicated that they feared law enforcement agencies, "especially federal ones, more than acts of hate or violence, despite an increase in hate crimes. They specifically cited immigration enforcement, surveillance, and racial profiling" (p. ii).

This is particularly alarming in light of the fact that more than 80% of hate crimes involve serious behaviors including violent crimes such as rape or other sexual assault, robbery, or assault (Harlow, 2005). Further, Fox, Nobles, and Piquero (2009) indicated that non-whites, on college campuses at least, are more likely to report being fearful of crime than whites. Thus, even though minorities may be more fearful of crime, they are often hesitant to report it to the police, whom they may fear even more.

Clearly, human relations problems involving the police and minority group members are not a thing of the past. Kane (2001) stated the following:

> One national study found that more than half of all black men report they have been victims of racial profiling by law enforcement. Overall, roughly 4 in 10 blacks and 3 in 10 Hispanics believe they have been unfairly stopped by the police simply because of their race or ethnicity (p. 3). (Also see Figure 10.1.)

Results of a study by Weitzer and Tuch (2004) indicated that African Americans and Hispanics are significantly more dissatisfied with the police than whites. Neighborhood crime conditions, direct experiences with police, and mass media representations of police were all found to impact residents' attitudes toward police. The findings thus indicate that Hispanics and African-Americans hold more critical views of police based on their disproportionate adverse experiences with police, exposure to negative media depictions of police, and residence in high-crime neighborhoods where policing practices may be contentious.

Figure 10.1 Perspectives on Police Stops by Race

"Have you ever felt you were stopped by the police just because of your race or ethnic background?"

	Yes	No	Unsure
	%	%	%
ALL	13	86	–
Whites	7	93	0
Blacks	43	57	0
Hispanics	30	69	1

Source: Adapted from CBS News/New York Times Poll. July 7–14, 2008.

Based on the survey results, the authors recommend "that police officers be required to apologize for a stop and search that yields nothing" (Weitzer & Tuch, 2004, pp. 25–26) and indicated that police officers could provide more information about reasons for stopping citizens in an attempt to improve police–minority relations.

In studying a sample of youths enrolled in public high school, Lurigio, Greenleaf, and Flexon (2009) found race to be one of the most powerful variables in explaining public attitudes toward the police. They found that in this specific sample, "both African Americans and Latinos who had been stopped and disrespected by the police were less willing to assist them and less likely to believe that the police care about their neighborhoods" (p. 38). They suggested that adverse contact between police officers and such youths might have an additive effect on juveniles' reactions to the police. The authors concluded that youth will be more inclined to cooperate with the police if they have been treated fairly and with respect. Similarly, Brunson and Miller (2006) suggested it is important to measure the impact of accumulated negative experiences in order to better understand police–minority relations.

Responses from a Gallup Poll taken in 2006, concerning the honesty and ethical standards of policemen from the perspective of different racial or ethnic groups are shown in Figure 10.2 below.

Figure 10.2	Honesty and Ethical Standards of Policemen by Race				
Race/ethnicity	Very high	High	Average	Low	Very low
%	%	%	%		
White	13	45	33	7	1
Non white	8	29	41	15	6
Black	5	18	49	18	9

Source: Adapted from *Sourcebook of Criminal Justice Statistics Online,* Available from http://www.albany.edu/sourcebook/pdf/t2212006.pdf

As you can see, significant differences continue to exist in public perceptions of the police by race/ethnicity. A 2003 study by Maxson, Hennigan, and Sloane suggested that race and ethnicity may be more important in citizens' assessments of police officer demeanor than in performance assessment and that the media had little effect on assessments of either performance or demeanor. They concluded that the police can improve public opinion by increasing informal contacts with citizens and can increase approval of their job performance by "participating in community meetings, increasing officers' visibility in neighborhoods, and talking with citizens" (p. 1), at least in what they refer to as disorderly neighborhoods.

Problems in police–minority relations are likely to persist for all of the reasons we have discussed unless something dramatic occurs. Given the current state of affairs with respect to illegal immigration and the fear of terrorism, the number of encounters between minorities and the police will likely grow, making resolution of some of

❖   **Photo 10.2**   White officers are shown frisking minority suspects.

the problematic aspects of such encounters even more important. The issue is further complicated by the fact that cooperation and trust among local, state, and federal agencies does not always exists (see Case in Point 10.1).

☞ CASE IN POINT 10.1

Some state and local police agencies have complained that under new federal rules their cooperative relationship with Immigration and Customs Enforcement (ICE) to help enforce immigration laws by checking the legal status of prisoners is proving too costly. In addition, it doesn't help their relationships with immigrants. According to Houston authorities, they probably won't join the program that allows them access to ICE databases that may be helpful in criminal investigations. To gain such access, the Houston Police Department would be required to train officers to enforce immigration laws. According to a spokesperson for Houston's mayor, if crime victims fear they will be snatched up and deported, they won't trust in the police [and presumably wouldn't report their victimizations or cooperate in other ways with the police].

(Continued)

(Continued)

At the same time, in Arizona, ICE has stripped Sheriff Joe Arpaio of immigration authority outside the jail due to allegations of racial profiling and discrimination. The sheriff says he will still conduct sweeps under state law because it is against his principles to ignore illegal immigrants who are by definition criminals.

Source: Adapted from "Some police agencies resist new immigration controls," by E. Bazar (2009, October 15), *USA TODAY*, p. 3A.

Police Public Relations

The second component of police–community relations, public relations consists of those efforts on behalf of the police to develop, maintain, and present a favorable image. While it is true that community relations programs are doomed to failure if the day-to-day human relations practices of participants are poor, publicizing the positive practices and programs of police departments can certainly affect the impression of the police in the minds of other citizens. The uniform of the officer, the symbol on the squad car, and the response of the dispatcher or receptionist at police headquarters all create an impression of the police, and they are all parts of police public relations efforts.

Police pamphlets, public-speaking engagements, department-sponsored programs, news conferences, widely advertised training in cultural diversity, and many other activities also fall within the public relations domain. Public relations involve two interdependent components. The first of these, *policy*, consists of decisions, statements, and plans made by management in an attempt to influence public opinion. The second component, *practice*, is the process of putting the policies into action (Cox & Fitzgerald, 1996; Nolte, 1979). In most police agencies, policies are formulated by the chief in consultation with her staff and those for whom the chief works (city manager, mayor, councilpersons), while putting the policies into operation is typically a task of rank-and-file officers. In earlier chapters, we discussed the importance to police personnel of good communications, and there is perhaps no better example than in the area of public relations. Ill conceived policies, policies formulated but not acted on, or formulated but not explained or understood, can hardly be expected to result in sound practice.

Similarly, policies developed without communication with those they will affect or those who will eventually be responsible for putting them into action are often of little value. Policy and practice go together. Both must be present, and some coordination between the two is necessary if either is to be valuable. It is here that many police administrators fail at implementing effective community relations programs. Some administrators recognize the importance of policy making and work hard at developing policies with appropriate input. Some recognize the importance of human relations and emphasize to every officer the importance of encounters with other citizens. Far fewer appear to recognize that policy making and practice are intimately intertwined and that policymakers and those who implement the policies must be in constant communication to allow for feedback and evaluation on a routine basis.

Such feedback and evaluation should focus on measuring and evaluating public opinion concerning the police, on developing and implementing policies to maintain favorable public opinion or to change it so that it becomes more positive, and then on reevaluating policies, practices, and opinions. Public relations is a process that is repeated over and over as conditions and opinions change. And we should emphasize once again, police public relations programs will maintain or lead to a favorable image only if they accurately reflect practices that are acceptable to the public. No amount of image building will convince citizens that they have a professional police department if the daily encounters between police and these other citizens are conducted in an unprofessional fashion. The concern with biased enforcement in the form of racial profiling serves as an excellent illustration of this point. We have discussed racial profiling as a form of biased law enforcement at some length in Chapter 8. Nonetheless, it deserves mention in the context of this chapter as well.

❖ Biased Enforcement and Racial Profiling

In recent years, the controversy over biased enforcement engaged in by some police officers reached the boiling point. In order to control this form of police misconduct, legislation has been passed in most states that requires the police both to record detailed information on the race or ethnicity of persons involved in encounters with the police and to attend sensitivity training.

As noted in Chapter 8, racial profiling by police officers occurs when officers base their actions solely on the perceived race or ethnicity of the citizens they observe. This type of racial profiling occurs in practice when officers stop citizens solely because of their skin color or other identifiable racial or ethnic characteristics. In other words, there is no legitimate probable cause for the stop. Most observers, including most police officers, would agree that this practice is unacceptable. As Jurkanin (2001) noted,

> Police are sworn to uphold the 'rule of law' in the protection of individual rights, while dutifully enforcing traffic and criminal laws for the protection of the public at large. . . . It is essential that law enforcement administrators take every necessary action to ensure zero tolerance regarding enforcement actions that are discriminatory against any segment of the population. (p. i)

Yet there are a certain number of police officers who continue to engage in such practices. The fact is, we do not know how many such officers exist. For a variety of reasons, we suspect that the proportion of officers involved in such practices is small, but all officers should be aware that taking official action based solely on race is unacceptable and is grounds for disciplinary action. Harassment of individuals short of taking official action also is unacceptable.

We all have the right to go into any neighborhood we choose, at any time of day or night, without police interference. Yet the experience of police officers often tells them that our presence in certain areas at certain times may indicate involvement in illegitimate behavior. They believe that the citizens of their communities, as well as their police supervisors, would want them to take action under such circumstances (Cox & Hazlett, 2001; Hoover, 2001).

An example of such behavior, which indicates that blacks and Hispanics are not the only potential targets of racial profiling, concerns police actions following the events of 9/11, when federal agents swept through Arab, Muslim, and South Asian neighborhoods throughout the country, snatching men from sidewalks, as well as from their homes, workplaces, and mosques (ACLU, 2004).

> It soon became clear that most, if not all, of the several thousand detainees picked up by federal agents in the immediate aftermath of 9/11 were guilty of little more than being Arab, Muslim or South Asian, and in the wrong place at the wrong time.... Of the thousands of men who were detained and questioned, not one has been publicly charged with terrorism. (ACLU, 2004, p. 5)

It is, of course, no surprise that law enforcement agents have focused on men of Middle Eastern origin since all of the terrorists involved in the 9/11 attacks were of Middle Eastern origin. However, lengthy incarceration of innocent individuals, coupled with verbal and physical abuse, did little to encourage the cooperation of the Middle Eastern community in preventing future acts of terrorism (Brown, 2004). In fact, if police authorities want the intelligence that can only be provided by members of the Middle Eastern community, they must first treat members of the community with respect while protecting their civil rights and dignity.

Police officers frequently respond to calls from the public concerning "suspicious persons." In some cases, these calls are based on observations of suspicious behavior, but in others the only thing suspicious about the person is his race. Having learned from the media that young black and Hispanic males are overrepresented in crime statistics, whites observing these males in predominantly white neighborhoods may regard them as suspicious persons. They call the police and then watch to see what happens. How, police officers say, are we supposed to respond? Not to respond may be perceived as dereliction of duty by both superiors and the public. And common sense suggests to the officer that something be done. Taking no action goes against all the training the officer has received.

Should the officer involved in situations of this type choose to stop and question the so-called suspicious person, allegations of racial profiling or discrimination may be expected. This is especially true when the stop or questioning become harassing in nature. Telling people to "move along" or to "go back to your own neighborhood" or threatening to take (unjustified) official action is very likely to result in the belief that racial factors are playing a major role. When such communication characterizes interaction with persons of one racial or ethnic group but not those of another, the allegations should be seriously considered.

As mentioned, in the rush to determine whether racial profiling exists in various communities or states, legislation mandating that officers record race and ethnicity has been introduced. The concern with confronting racial profiling where it exists is easy to understand and appropriate. Yet the legislation may have numerous unintended consequences.

First, such legislation may cause officers (including all those who do not partici-pate in racial profiling) to focus on exactly the characteristics we wish them to ignore as a basis for making stops or arrests. Such reporting clearly causes officers to focus on racial and ethnic characteristics precisely because they have to record them.

Second, the legislation may lead to a good deal of intentional misreporting. This may happen as a result of officers fearing that they have stopped or arrested too many minority group members in a given period of time and deciding not to accurately report the race or ethnicity of those they stopped or arrested, or deciding not to even report stops that do not lead to official action. In effect, officers may develop their own quota systems. On the one hand, this may lead to false reporting or motivate officers to not make stops or arrests that they would normally make because they fear being reprimanded for stopping too many persons of a particular race or ethnicity. On the other hand, data collection and analysis can be an excellent defense against allegations of biased enforcement when the analysis shows no evidence of such enforcement styles.

Racial profiling, as one form of biased enforcement, "inevitably leads to questions as to whether biased enforcement exists at the departmental level as a result of policy decisions" (Cox & Hazlett, 2001, p. 97). Police allocation of resources based on crime rates may lead to higher arrest rates for minorities who are disproportionately located in high-crime areas. If the police withdraw their resources from such areas, cries of biased enforcement in terms of lack of police services are likely to be heard (Cox & Hazlett, 2001, p. 98). In fact, some have argued that race is totally irrelevant to the police in most high-crime neighborhoods because nearly all of the residents are minorities (MacDonald, 2001).

Solving such dilemmas is difficult precisely because discrimination in law enforce-ment can occur in a variety of contexts, ranging from traffic stops to airport screening to field interrogations to provision of shabby services. A comprehensive plan involv-ing policy reform, officer training, and voluntary data collection may help in this regard (Carrick, 2000). Ultimately, however, the issue of racism must be dealt with by the larger society if biased enforcement and racial profiling are to be alleviated. As noted by the ACLU (2004):

> The practice of profiling by race, ethnicity, religion or national origin runs counter to what is arguably the core principle of American democracy: that humans are created equal, and are entitled to be treated equally by the government, irrespective of immutable character-istics like skin color, faith and ethnic or national origin. (p. 18)

❖ Citizen Complaints

An important part of the process of evaluating police–community relations consists of soliciting, evaluating, and acting on citizen complaints. Good community relations require that citizens feel free to discuss with appropriate authorities their complaints about police officers or police behavior. Systematic efforts to determine what those served by the police think of the services they receive should be an integral part of police management. Such efforts may be conducted by department personnel, by university personnel, or by private consultants and should attempt to establish a baseline of public opinion and then compare those opinions with others collected on a regular basis over time. A part of this process should include the developing and publicizing of policies related to citizen complaints. Citizens should know who to contact and what to expect when they make such contact. Further, those complaining should be kept advised of the efforts made to investigate their complaints and the final disposition of the complaint.

According to the 2003 Law Enforcement Management and Administrative Statistics (LEMAS) report, state and local law enforcement agencies with 100 or more sworn officers received more than 26,000 citizen complaints about officer use of force for the year 2002 (Hickman, 2006). This figure breaks down to rates of 33 complaints per agency or 6.6 complaints per 100 full-time sworn personnel. About 8% of use of force complaints were sustained, meaning there was sufficient evidence to justify disciplinary action against the officer(s) involved (Hickman, 2006). Keep in mind that misuse of force is among the more serious complaints filed against police officers and represents a small minority of all citizens complaints, most of which are never brought to the attention of the authorities.

Many citizens who feel they have been abused or harassed by the police do not know how to file a complaint or fear retaliation from the officer involved or her colleagues if they do complain. Public relations messages indicating the desire of police administrators to know about such complaints, coupled with prompt, fair action when such complaints are received, can only help to improve community relations. Recognizing this fact, the Denver Police Department developed a **community-police mediation program** to address the challenges of "handling complaints in a timely manner, resolving complaints in a way that provides some level of satisfaction to both officers and community members, capitalizing on the potential of the complaint process to improve police-community relations, and the unique difficulty of establishing the truth or falsity of misconduct allegations" (Clemmons & Rosenthal, 2008, p. 1).

Mediation is a voluntary process in which community members and officers sit down in a neutral and confidential setting facilitated by a professional mediator to discuss their differences. This alternative to the traditional complaint handling process provides an opportunity for each party to be heard and to consider the other's perspective about an incident. The intent is to promote mutual understanding so that similar situations can be prevented (Clemmons & Rosenthal, 2008).

While we can do a great deal to help improve the citizen complaint process, we should be aware that most citizens who have complaints about the police will probably never voice these complaints directly to the police (Homant, 1989; Walker, 2001, pp. 20–21, 53–80; Walker, Spohn, & DeLone, 2001, pp. 106–107). Similarly, we should note that some citizens who strongly support the police file complaints in the hope of helping the police improve, rather than with negative intent.

❖ Police–Media Relations

We discussed police–media relations in some detail in Chapter 6, but they play an important role in multicultural relations and should be mentioned in this context as well. Surette (1992) acknowledged, "People live today in two worlds: a real world and a media world. The first is limited by direct experience; the second is bounded only by decisions of editors and producers" (p. 81). According to Palmiotto (2000),

The mass media reinforce the same stereotypes and display unrealistic attitudes about groups that are found in school materials. The depiction of minorities in the media is most often a caricature. . . . In analyses of the depiction of minorities in print media in one Midwestern city, it was found that Native Americans and Asian Americans were virtually invisible in the local paper, whereas Hispanic Americans were somewhat more visible and African Americans were highly visible. However, the areas in which African Americans had a major presence were crime, sports, and entertainment; their visibility in business and government was low. (p. 169)

As indicated in Chapter 6, any police agency concerned about good community relations will want to develop a good working relationship with the media. Information presented on television, on the radio, or in the newspapers is a major influence on public opinion. Police administrators today typically prefer to develop open, honest relationships with representatives of the media, although this has not always been the case. In the past, police administrators often had a policy requiring officers to tell media representatives only what they had to, thus engendering mutual suspicion and distrust. The police must balance what information the public needs to know in order to protect itself against the danger of compromising an investigation or providing information useful to the offender. "Need to know" is the standard, for example, in cases where information might allow the public to take steps to protect themselves in unsolved homicide, rape, or child molestation cases with a suspect on the loose (Leinwald, 2009).

Because many citizens never have direct contact with the police, their view of the police is based on media presentations. These include, but are not limited to, documentaries, news broadcasts, interviews with police personnel and those they serve, and police produced or assisted informational programs. These presentations also include those television shows and movies that deal with police activities, many of which are highly misleading in their portrayal of violence, gun battles, and crime fighting as the major activities of the police. In such presentations, the police often appear to be violent, sadistic, corrupt, or stupid, and their work appears to consist of going from one violent situation to another. To be sure, most viewers realize that there is no direct correspondence between what appears on the screen and what happens in reality, yet it is sometimes difficult to separate fact from fiction and to correct inaccurate impressions.

The police can benefit in many ways from creating a positive public image. Cooperation and support on the part of the public can be encouraged in a number of ways. Police ride-along programs allow other citizens to observe the daily activities of the police. Open-house days allow members of the public to view the internal workings of the police department from communications through investigations to incarceration. Walk-in centers provide the opportunity for neighborhood residents to discuss whatever is on their minds with citizen-oriented police officers. School resource officer programs, drug resistance programs, and police athletic programs provide opportunities for youth to get to know police officers as individuals, and vice versa. Providing Public Information Officers (PIOs) who are available to meet with media representatives on a regular basis to provide accurate, timely information is still another beneficial strategy (Mors, 2005). These and other public relations efforts on behalf of the police can improve community relations when accompanied by positive human relations efforts.

Other Police Efforts

There are other things police administrators can do to improve the relationship between their departments and the communities they serve. We discuss the recruitment and hiring of minority officers at length later in this chapter. Clearly, the police department that represents the community it serves in terms of race and ethnicity has an initial advantage in community relations. This is perhaps particularly true when segments of the community served fail to comprehend English well or not at all. It is difficult for Hispanics, for example, to believe that a police department with no Spanish-speaking officers is concerned about their well-being. It is clearly true that mutual trust and understanding are important components in multicultural relations, and breaking language barriers is one way to help accomplish these goals. Training that familiarizes police officers with the cultural characteristics of the populations they serve is also important. Multicultural training can reduce the number of lawsuits, as well as the possibility of civil disorder.

Programs aimed at specific minorities other than those based on race or ethnicity are also important. Police efforts to prevent crime against senior citizens, to organize neighborhood watch groups, and to help youth resist drugs or gang influence are widespread. School liaison programs in which police officers are assigned to the schools for the academic year and in which the officers participating serve as counselors and sometimes confidants to youth are also valuable. Following are examples of some programs aimed at improving multicultural understanding for both police officers and citizens.

Arvada Colorado PD

In Arvada, Colorado, the police department initiated a senior liaison officer (SLO) program in which officers worked proactively with senior citizens to identify concerns and needs. The goals of the program were to meet these needs and reduce fear of crime among senior citizens (Palmiotto, 2000, pp. 299–300).

Garden Grove California PD

In order to address crime problems in an apartment complex occupied by Hispanic and Vietnamese immigrants, the Garden Grove (California) police department opened a storefront office. Research showed that the storefront office had a positive effect on both groups. Hispanics reported less fear of crime after the storefront opened and also reported improved perceptions of the police. Vietnamese residents also reported less fear of crime, and their already very positive attitudes toward the police remained positive (Torres & Vogel, 2001).

St. Paul Minnesota PD

In May of 2009, the Minnesota Department of Public Safety awarded a $250,000 grant to the St. Paul Police Department and partnering organizations (St. Paul Intervention Project and the Minnesota Chapter of the Muslim American Society of America) for an outreach program with the Muslim and Somali communities in the city.

According to Egerstrom (2009), goals for the grant included the following:

– Increase understanding among the police, the intervention project and diverse Muslim communities.

– Increase involvement of Muslim community members with police and the intervention project to improve public safety and the community environment.

– Increase immigrant understanding of the criminal justice system.

– Increase criminal justice system accountability with the immigrant Muslim communities.

– And, help increase the Muslim communities' roles in 'affecting positive change' through various ways, including reporting crimes, seeking protection and intervention from police, volunteer community policing and through battered women's advocacy and support services.

Seattle Washington PD

In the late 1980s, the Seattle Police Department (SPD) formed Precinct Advisory Councils (PACs). The goal of the councils was to have groups of citizens, who were geographically based, become more knowledgeable about law enforcement in their communities and more invested in partnering with the Department.

In the mid-1990s, police administrators observed that established precinct advisory groups were not reflective of the diverse communities in the City, and they believed it was critical to create an avenue for the Department to reach out and develop relationships with minority communities so that their diverse voices could be heard. The goal was to create more diverse advisory groups to work with SPD on challenging issues and to educate the communities about the role and function of police.

To accomplish this goal, Officer Liaisons attended advisory council meetings and spent non-enforcement time with community-based organizations. These officers addressed and attempted to resolve problems with the aid of the council and community members. They also educated the community about the SPD role, responded to crisis situations in their respective communities, and facilitated meetings regarding police and citizen interactions.

The diverse advisory councils provided an effective way to build bridges between minority communities and the police, which resulted in increased awareness, improved understanding, and open dialogue regarding a variety of issues. The goals and objectives of these cooperative groups included:

• Creating and strengthening programs and communication in order to build trust between police and minority communities.
• Increasing participation of individuals from minority communities working with SPD on public safety issues.
• Breaking down negative perceptions of law enforcement in minority communities by building relationships between individual officers and members of minority communities
• Improving officer training and education regarding cultural norms that may impact police and citizen interactions.

- Enhancing the understanding of the role of police through educational materials tailored to specific communities and translated into appropriate languages.
- Increasing ongoing dialogue between SPD and minority communities about perceptions of law enforcement in the community. (Seattle Police Department, 2009)

Clearwater Florida PD

In 1999, the Clearwater, Florida Police Department (CPD) submitted a request for approval of a grant to provide funding for crime prevention and translation programs for the Hispanic community. The request was approved and the department developed two new programs, one utilizing Spanish-speaking police officers for translation and crime prevention activities and the other contracting with an outside social service agency for a pool of translators.

In 2000, the CPD submitted another grant application for PROJECT NEXT STEP, seeking a mobile base for community policing activities: specifically, a motor vehicle equipped with an array of television, video, and computer equipment. Many of these community policing activities were to be targeted at the Hispanic community.

Next, CPD proposed a program to create a Hispanic Outreach Services Center in Clearwater's Weed and Seed area offering victim advocacy, crime prevention, and translation services. In the same year, a delegation of government officials from the state of Hidalgo, Mexico visited Clearwater to meet with city, police, and community leaders. Hidalgo is the native home to many of Clearwater's Hispanic immigrants.

Then, the CPD met with the Regional Community Policing Institute (RCPI) to discuss Clearwater's Hispanic Initiative. It was decided that a focus group consisting of Hispanic community leaders should be held in order to determine the direction the City's initiative should take to best serve the needs of the Hispanic community. This was followed by the CPD unveiling a new overtime translation program for off-duty Spanish-speaking police officers. The program funded overtime for the call-out of off-duty, bilingual officers to translate at crime, incident, and accident scenes as well as the assignment of off-duty Spanish-speaking officers to Hispanic events in Clearwater to serve as liaison officers to the Hispanic community.

In 2005, Clearwater was awarded a grant in the amount of $101,553 by the U.S. Department of Justice, Bureau of Justice Assistance for funding of operational expenses at the Hispanic Outreach Center for a two-year period (Clearwater Police Department, 2009).

❖ The Police and Public in Multicultural Relations

In spite of the fact that the police sometimes feel separate from and in conflict with other citizens, they are nevertheless members of the community in which they serve. Both groups are controlled by the same government, both pay taxes to support the police and other public service agencies, the children of both groups attend the same schools, and both share in the fate of the community. By and large, the police are recruited from, hired by, and sworn to serve this same community. Further, the functions of the police are essential to the community, but no more essential than the services provided by others. Good relations depend on emphasizing this common community membership.

To indicate their willingness to participate as partners in the community, the police need to recognize and reflect the racial and ethnic composition of that community. Active efforts to recruit qualified minorities into policing are essential in this regard, as are promotions based strictly on merit. An all-white police department in an ethnically diverse community results in the perception that the police are different in a very obvious way and raises suspicions that the police also may be different in many other, less obvious ways. A multiethnic police department will not be problem free, but it has a definite advantage in developing good community relations. Some progress is being made in this area if Gabor (2001) was correct when he concluded the following:

> For the most part, police departments across the country are becoming a reflection of the cultural makeup of the community they serve. In fact, while it may still be the exception rather than the rule, in some California police departments, minority officers are the majority, while white officers in some departments are in the minority. (p. 15)

Innovative, regular training in human and public relations skills is an important requirement for police officers, as is training in cultural diversity. Cultural diversity or awareness programs are designed to familiarize police officers with people and customs different from those to which they are accustomed. Assigning a police officer to police a ghetto or barrio without such an introduction virtually guarantees problems. Programs designed to anticipate the types of crises that might arise in the community alert officers to the possibility that they may occur while providing them with some structure and preparation.

It is important to recognize that the types of multicultural issues discussed in this chapter are not unique to America or American policing (see the following Around the World) but occur in all societies where diverse populations exist.

AROUND THE WORLD

Gangs and the French Police

Police responsible for maintaining order in France's tense immigrant-majority housing projects liken their job to a military mission. Officers report that they are engaged in urban warfare, confronted with increasingly violent crime with the killing of police officers a goal. For example, police responding to an emergency call in Épinay-sur-Seine, north of Paris, drove into a trap. Their vehicle was surrounded and they were attacked by dozens of youths wielding iron bars and knives. Though the officers escaped, one was hospitalized with a broken jaw.

The impoverished area of Seine-Saint-Denis north-east of Paris loses officers as soon as they get enough seniority to get transferred to the provinces. Those tasked with France's most dangerous districts tend to be young junior officers.

(Continued)

(Continued)

Contempt for police appears to be almost universal among young men who claim the police are racists who lack respect for blacks and Arabs, are overly aggressive, and use racial slurs when dealing with them.

Older residents express different views. They resent the rampant lawlessness and want more, not fewer, police. These residents complain that the police do not respond when they call them.

In 2002 community policing efforts based on prevention were abandoned in favor of a strict law-and-order approach. Many local officials believe this was a major mistake because beat officers were replaced by shock "anti-crime brigades" who police the suburbs mostly from outside. Members of the anti-crime brigades enter the area only for tough security missions, but residents feel less secure than under community policing. The riots reveal a divide between police and residents and things appear to be getting worse. The law is no longer enforced in many of France's deprived suburbs.

Both sides are afraid of each other and it appears the urban warfare will continue as long as the climate of fear prevails.

Source: Adapted from "Suburban Gangs Defy French Police, by H. Astier, 2006, *BBC News*. Available from http://news.bbc.co.uk/go/pr/fr/-/2/hi/europe/6096706.stm

❖ Cultural Diversity and Awareness Training

Training in cultural diversity typically focuses on improving communications skills, recognizing signs of prejudice and bias, understanding the perspectives of people of different backgrounds, and appreciating the benefits of diversity (Barlow & Barlow, 2000; Bickham & Rossett, 1993; California Commission on Peace Officer Standards and Training, 2009; Cox & Fitzgerald, 1996; Hennessy, 1993; Scott, 1993). Before being assigned to a beat, officers should receive orientation on the various groups residing in the area. Further, as police agencies become more culturally diverse, internal problems may develop, so training should address hate crimes, racial profiling, derogatory language, racial and ethnic slurs, and ethnic jokes in the context of the police organization (Barlow & Barlow, 2000; California Commission on Peace Officer Standards and Training, 2009; Scott, 1993). The development of action plans that serve diverse communities and training sessions that include active participation and establishment of a meaningful context are equally important components of diversity training (Hennessy, Hendricks, & Hendricks, 2001).

Training programs require that police administrators recognize that multicultural relations require effort on behalf of every individual officer and the police management team. The former determine the nature of human relations in daily encounters; the latter, in consultation with these officers and the various publics in the jurisdiction, determine and evaluate the policies to be implemented and their effectiveness in practice.

❖ Police Responsiveness and Accountability

Two key terms related to police success in multicultural relations are *responsiveness* and *accountability.* **Responsiveness** refers to the provision of appropriate police services promptly and competently and with appropriate referrals in cases not within police jurisdiction. This requires that police administrators recognize and convey to the public the fact that it may be impossible or inappropriate for the police to respond to all citizen requests for service. Priorities may have to be established and differential response strategies developed in order to best allocate available resources. These tasks should be accomplished in partnership with the community, and the policies and strategies resulting from this effort should be communicated clearly to residents— thus, to the extent possible, preventing potentially negative reactions. The department must make it clear that requests for service on behalf of citizens are taken seriously and dealt with accordingly.

Accountability is the second key to police efforts to establish and maintain positive relationships with all segments of the community. Police officers are employees of the community they serve. Like other employees, they are accountable to their employers for their actions. Accountability may be accomplished in a variety of ways, ranging from periodic reports to the public on police activities, to annual reports, to developing and utilizing an internal affairs unit, to cooperation in developing a civilian review board to hearing complaints concerning the police, to establishing informative websites, to developing and implementing outreach programs for diverse segments of the community.

❖ The Role of Community Members in Multicultural Relations

We have noted the fact that the police are predominantly reactive rather than proactive. That is, the community in which they operate determines, in most instances, when the police act, about what they act on, and on whom they act. Thus, the community plays, and must accept, an important role in policing. If the community does not do its part in building positive relationships, police-initiated programs cannot succeed.

To demonstrate good faith, community residents and civic action groups can develop programs to support police efforts and recognize police performance. Providing the police with information concerning matters important to the community and being willing to serve as witnesses are among the ways in which community residents can show appreciation for their police. While the police may be required to take the lead in developing community relations efforts, the public is an important part of the team necessary for such efforts to produce the desired results: Making the task of the police easier and the community a better place in which to live. It is important that members of all communities have continual, open dialogue with police officials in order to deal with specific issues. According to Walker (2001),

> Citizen oversight of the police was an established fact of life in American law enforcement by the end of the century. It existed in many large cities and was steadily spreading to smaller communities. The spread of oversight marked a momentous change since the tumultuous 1960s. Most important, citizen involvement in the complaint process was increasingly recognized as an important means for achieving police accountability. (p. 44)

As the global nature of crime and policing continues to expand, the importance of understanding and operating in multicultural and multiethnic settings becomes increasingly apparent.

❖ Women and Minorities in Policing

Over the past 40 years there have been attempts to recruit more women and minorities into policing in order to reflect the increasingly multicultural and multiethnic composition of our society. Nationwide in 2008, 11.9% of full-time law enforcement officers were females and 61.6% of full-time civilian law enforcement employees were females. Cities with populations of 10,000 to 24,999 inhabitants employed the highest percentage (92.2) of male officers, while cities with populations of 1 million and over employed the highest percentage (18.2) of full-time female officers. Cities with populations of 100,000 to 249,999 inhabitants had the highest percentage (73.7) of female civilian law enforcement employees (FBI, 2009).

In 2003, 23.6% of full-time local police officers were members of a racial or ethnic minority (Hickman & Reaves, 2006). Minority officers comprised more than a third of the total in jurisdictions over 250,000. More specifically in 2003, African Americans accounted for 11.7% of all local police officers and Hispanics or Latinos 9.1%. Other minority groups, including Asian, Pacific Islander, and American Indians, comprised 2.8% of local police (Hickman & Reeves, 2006).

Demographics in the United States are changing rapidly. Recent immigrants and refugees have tended to remain in physical and cultural isolation, leaving them vulnerable to crime victimization both from members of their own ethnic group and the larger community. Interactions with police are often characterized by misunderstanding, causing further alienation of the minority. Police agencies characterized by ethnic diversity serve the public better, especially under the community and problem-solving approaches, by providing sworn officers who can deliver effective services within their own ethnic communities as well as to the community as a whole. Hiring minority officers helps the police to overcome obstacles that might hinder effective partnerships.

In the following pages, we examine efforts to recruit women and minority group members into policing and some of the resulting issues.

❖ Women in Policing

On September 3, 1910, in the city of Los Angeles, Mrs. Alice Stebbin Wells became the first official policewoman in the United States. Her duties included supervising and enforcing laws pertaining to dance halls, skating rinks, theaters, and other public recreation areas. She lectured to various groups around the nation in the next few years about the place of women in police service, and her efforts resulted in the Chicago City Council passing an ordinance that provided for the hiring of policewomen. By 1915, Chicago employed 30 policewomen (Swan, 1988) who worked mainly with troubled youth and women victims and offenders. During World War I, policewomen were utilized to keep prostitutes away from military camps and to assist in the return of runaway women and girls (Bell, 1982, p. 113; House, 1993, p. 139). The "women's bureau" was a separate division; policewomen did not wear uniforms, nor were they armed.

They typically received less pay than their male counterparts, though their educational qualifications were considerably better (Horne, 1980, p. 30).

Very few policewomen were hired during the Great Depression, and while women were used as auxiliary police officers during World War II, this role ended when the war did. Not until the 1960s did opportunities for policewomen begin to improve. The President's Commission on Law Enforcement and the Administration of Justice (1967) found that policewomen could be an invaluable asset to modern law enforcement and recommended that their role be broadened to include patrol and investigative duties as well as administrative responsibilities. The first woman assigned to full-time field patrol was hired in Indianapolis in 1968 (McDowell, 1992).

In 1972, Congress amended Title VII of the 1964 Civil Rights Act to prohibit discrimination by both private and public employers based on the sex of the applicant. In the same time period, the Federal Bureau of Investigation and the Secret Service appointed their first female field agents. A number of cities (St. Louis, Washington, DC, and New York City) placed uniformed female officers in patrol positions and conducted studies to evaluate their performance. These studies in the 1970s led to the conclusion that policewomen perform as well as policemen, though in a somewhat different fashion.

For example, Rabe-Hemp (2008a) suggested that women were much less likely than men to utilize extreme controlling behavior, such as threats, physical restraint, search, and arrest. Still, her findings did not indicate that women were more likely than men to use supporting behaviors favored by caregivers. These findings indicate that simply assuming female officers manifest stereotypically feminine traits in policing tasks is clearly an overly simplistic conceptualization.

Other studies have found that the attitudes of policewomen and policemen are fairly similar (Koenig, 1978); that, in small towns at least, female officers experience stressors similar to those of their male counterparts, with some notable exceptions (Bartol, Bergen, & Volckens, 1992; McCarty, Zhao, & Garland, 2007); and that organizational commitment, job satisfaction, stress levels, job-related anxiety, and attitudes toward law and order do not differ significantly by gender (Fry & Greenfield, 1980; McGeorge & Wolfe, 1976). Once hired, Block and Anderson (1974) found that female and male officers responded to calls in a generally similar fashion and that citizen respect for the police was similar for the two groups.

After reviewing 33 research articles in which gender was used either as an independent or control variable, Poteyeva and Sun (2009) concluded that the gender of an officer has only a weak effect on the officer's attitudes toward community policing, the community and neighborhood residents, job satisfaction, and domestic violence. They also found limited evidence that male and female officers differ in their attitudes toward the police role and stress. In fact, Carlan and McMullan (2009) found that female police officers' "professionalism, job satisfaction, stress, and confidence levels demonstrated a condition of psychological health and do not differ significantly from those of men officers" (p. 60). Nonetheless, some male officers and administrators continue to doubt the ability of female officers to perform, particularly in violent or potentially violent situations. Master Police Officer Beth Lavin of the King County (Washington) Sheriff's Office, noted " . . . you feel like you have to go out there and fight with somebody to prove to the guys you can handle yourself and you're not one of those wimpy female officers" (Basich, 2008, p. 28).

Numerous studies have led to the same conclusion—women perform patrol functions acceptably. Only one study concluded that women were not as capable on patrol as men. This study, done in the Philadelphia Police Department, found that women do not project the image of power and strength that policemen project and that they do not conduct building searches as well. The report concluded that women failed to handle patrol duties as safely and efficiently as men. Critics noted that this is true only if the major concerns of the police have to do with appearing powerful and conducting building searches (Horne, 1980).

❖ Policewomen as Viewed by the Public, Their Supervisors, and Male Officers

Kerber, Andes, and Mittler (1977) found that citizens generally judged male and female officers as equally competent, and over three fourths of the respondents to their survey indicated that both male and female officers should be hired to improve the quality of police services. The Kerber, Andes, and Mittler study was conducted in a university community, and therefore, the results might not be representative of attitudes in other types of communities.

Although public attitudes toward policewomen have not been extensively investigated, the information that is available indicates that these attitudes are basically positive. In fact, in the St. Louis and New York studies discussed previously, female officers were regarded more favorably than their male counterparts (Balkin, 1988). In other studies, policewomen have been rated higher than policemen by the public when it came to handling domestic disputes and showing appropriate concern and sensitivity. Some studies (Bell, 1982; Breci, 1997) found that while citizens generally believed policemen were preferable in violent situations, they also generally approved of policewomen. Still, public misperceptions about women who wear uniforms, patrol the streets, and command other officers continue to exist in some places (Gold, 2000).

Studies of supervisors' attitudes toward policewomen are also scarce, and those that do exist are conflicting. The Washington, DC, study, for example, indicated predominantly negative attitudes on the part of supervisors, while studies in St. Louis and New York showed supervisors to be more positive (Balkin, 1988). One chief put it in these terms: "I could see all kinds of problems . . . jealous wives, injuries. . . . It was a headache I didn't want" (Harris, 1999, p. 18).

Policemen's opinions of their female counterparts have been more extensively documented and, as previously indicated, have often been found to be generally negative. Some policemen view policewomen as incompetent and unfit for police work, and working with female police officers does not appear to have a positive effect on such opinions (Balkin, 1988). A good deal of the skepticism among male officers is undoubtedly due to sex role socialization. Even though significant changes have occurred over the past decade with respect to integration of occupations by gender, some occupational groups have been slow to accept such changes. This is perhaps particularly true in occupations imbued with traditional conceptions of masculinity as a required trait (e.g., the police). With changes brought on by movements for equal rights for women, by hiring better educated officers, and as a result of competent performance of women in the police role, these sex role stereotypes are gradually changing. A study by Grown and Carlson (1993), for example, found that there has been a small shift toward more favorable attitudes concerning female officers; but about 20% of male officers still did not want to work with female officers on patrol. Gold (2000) stated, "Perhaps the problem is that some hard-liners persist in the argument that such changes [more female officers] represent a feminization of policing; that real policing was, and still is, the so-called masculine image of crime-fighting" (p. 160).

While some observers believe the integration of women into policing is more complete than we have suggested here, many of our former students, both male and female, who have entered the policing world lead us to believe that a substantial division still exists. Eisenberg (2007), for example, said that in Seattle, 25 years after the first female patrol officers hit the streets, women are still striving for equality. According to Carlan and McMullan (2009), policewomen continue to face significant obstacles, and some male officers sometimes promote the subordination of policewomen. They conclude, however, that the findings of their study of 89 policewomen suggest that policewomen are mentally tough and resilient and, hence, quite capable of modulating the demands of police careers.

❖ **PHOTO 10.3** It wasn't that long ago when it was commonplace to see no women working in the patrol division of most police agencies. Today, the situation has changed for the better with women increasingly joining the ranks of law enforcement agencies.

Factors Affecting the Performance of Policewomen

Not surprisingly, the greatest source of work-related stress reported by female police officers is male police officers (Basich, 2008; Carlan & McMullan, 2009; Fields, 2000; Wexler & Logan, 1983). Bartol, Bergen, and Volckens (1992) found that policewomen experienced stress as a result of working in a male-dominated occupation, but that stress did not appear to affect their job performance because supervisors evaluated male and female officers as performing the job equally well.

As Balkin (1988) pointed out, the negative attitudes of policemen toward policewomen are most often based on personal belief, not actual experience: "No research has shown that strength is related to an individual's ability to manage successfully a dangerous situation.... There are no reports in the literature of bad outcomes because a policewoman did not have enough strength or aggression" (p. 34). Others have noted that agility, a cool head, and good communications skills may be more important than strength in dangerous situations (Charles, 1982; McDowell, 1992; Rogers, 1987, as cited in Balkin, 1988). Some suggest that the presence of a policewoman may actually help to defuse a potentially violent situation (Gold, 2000; Homant & Kennedy, 1985; Martin, 1993; Sherman, 1975). In spite of all these defenses of policewomen, many male police officers continue to be highly critical of them. The presence of women in what has typically been referred to as the police *fraternity* may undermine the sense of masculine identity that accompanies that subculture.

Whatever the reason, policemen's attitudes toward policewomen have some very real consequences for both. First, policewomen are continually in the spotlight and must repeatedly prove themselves capable before they have a chance of being accepted as "real" police officers. Some perform most capably under this added strain, but others do not—and those who fail become legend among tradition-oriented male officers.

Second, because male officers often feel uncomfortable about dealing with potentially violent situations when their partners are women, they sometimes overprotect policewomen by instructing them to stay in the car, to stay on the radio, or to stay away from the altercation. Thus, policewomen are sometimes denied the opportunity to demonstrate their skills. Further, the same officers who required their female partners not to get involved may then criticize these partners to other male officers for failing to provide adequate backup. Cohen (2000) described it as follows:

> Police work requires thinking and courage. It can be a physical job, yes, but it's first and foremost a mental exercise. As big and strong as I am, I've been tossed around like a rag doll—and any idiot with a gun and a will to do so can easily shoot me dead. We survive and get the job done by using our heads. I would sooner work with a female cop with brains and guts than any male cop who's stupid or timid, regardless of the size of his biceps. (p. 3)

Third, negative attitudes toward policewomen have undoubtedly played a role in promotional processes. Taking orders from a policewoman when one has no respect for women in the occupation is a bitter pill to swallow. The ability of policewomen to perform at supervisory levels thus remains to be tested, but there is little reason to believe that, given adequate preparation, they will prove less worthy than their male counterparts.

When women enter a male-dominated workplace, there is an excellent chance that they will be viewed as "tokens," at least initially. As has been noted (Kanter, 1977; Martin, 1993), this means that they will be subjected to enhanced scrutiny, that differences between themselves and those who have traditionally filled the work role will be polarized, and that they will be stereotyped. The stress implied by token status is over and above that experienced by others occupying the same role who are not considered tokens.

Alex (1969), in discussing the stresses experienced by black police officers, used the term ***double marginality*** to refer to the fact that black officers were not fully accepted by their white coworkers and were also distrusted by other blacks. The same term may be applied to women in police work who are not fully accepted as equals by their male coworkers and who often find other women (especially male officers' wives) somewhat suspect of their motives for entering police work. Based on these considerations, we might expect that policewomen would have relatively high turnover rates, and this appears to be the case in at least some departments (Fry, 1983; Harris, 1999). Martin (1993) found that such turnover is due to discrimination on behalf of male officers, lack of equal promotional opportunities, and the constant pressure to prove themselves. As might be expected, African American policewomen are even more likely to be viewed as outsiders within their own departments. There is evidence that they are often isolated from both white women and black men (McCarty, Zhao, & Garland, 2007; Pogrebin, Dodge, & Chatman, 2000).

Sexual harassment continues to be a problem for policewomen. According to McDowell (1992) and Rabe-Hemp (2008a and b), the harassment that persists in many police agencies includes lewd jokes transmitted over police radios and sexists remarks in the halls.

Pogrebin, Dodge, and Chatman (2000) noted that patterns of sexual and racial discrimination exist regardless of race or ethnicity. In a 1995 survey of female officers in a medium-sized department, 68% of the respondents indicated they had been sexually harassed while on the job (Polisar & Milgram, 1998). Organizational efforts to stop sexual harassment seemed to have brought some improvement, but women's concern that male officers think they cannot "do the job" persists, and women's tolerance of harassing behaviors in the workplace in order to fit in may negatively affect some women (Somvadee & Morash, 2008).

In other studies, male officers were particularly critical of female officers who did perform well and who did not allow themselves to be treated in condescending fashion. These women were frequently stereotyped as bitchy, castrating, or as lesbians by male officers (Gold, 2000; Martin, 1993). Poole and Pogrebin (1988) found the following:

> After just three years on the force, only a small proportion of women officers still aspire to rise in the police organization. It is likely that these officers have recognized in a relatively short period of time that few women actually get promoted; consequently policewomen lack a variety of female role models in higher ranks whom they could realistically strive to emulate. (p. 54)

However, a more recent study by Rabe-Hemp (2008b) led to the conclusion that despite early occupational experiences of sexual harassment, discrimination, and disrespect, after long tenures, female officers do achieve acceptance in police work and that female officers are increasingly occupying higher ranks in police agencies. Still, barriers remain when it comes to women advancing through the ranks. With very few exceptions, women are virtually absent from decision-making ranks and positions of authority. Less than 1% of police chiefs in the United States are women (Mroz, 2008). Women are or have been chiefs in Detroit, San Francisco, and Washington, but most small and rural agencies do not have any women in top command positions.

Discriminating on the basis of gender when hiring or promoting police officers is illegal. Further, women are better collectors of information than their male counterparts in certain circumstances. Finally, the presence of female officers provides diverse views on policy and practice in policing and demonstrates that women can successfully perform policing tasks (Linn & Price, 1985).

Linn and Price (1985) also indicated that the policeman is often resistant to change, in part,

> . . . because so little of his world is safe and predictable. His opposition to women on patrol stems in part from his not knowing *how* to treat a woman as a peer. Should he watch his language? Offer to drive? Buy her coffee? Talk about sports? Initiate friendliness? Could he share hours of tension, or even hours of boredom, and not become too close? (p. 75)

In spite of these concerns, in some communities, policewomen have been accepted by male coworkers and the public alike. Further, there is evidence that minorities and better educated officers are more likely to accept women, and their numbers are increasing. Because women account for about 51% of the population, and because the evidence is clear that they are capable of performing a wide variety of police functions, they should be viewed as a valuable asset in the struggle to make police departments more representative of the communities they serve and, ultimately, in the battle to reintegrate police and community.

Recruiting Female Officers

Although we discussed recruitment and selection of police officers in detail in Chapter 2, the challenges involved in successful recruitment and retention of women and minorities deserve special attention. These challenges and possible remedies are discussed here with respect to women and are addressed later in this chapter as they relate to racial and ethnic minorities.

In today's economy, law enforcement agencies are facing enormous challenges recruiting qualified candidates, yet traditional strategies for recruitment frequently overlook women as a pool of qualified applicants. Gold (2000) stated the following: "That society needs more women law enforcement officers is not in question. The controversy seems to be over how long it will take to break through the barriers and achieve gender equity, and how to eliminate the barriers" (p. 159).

The National Center for Women and Policing (2001) cited a number of advantages for police agencies that hire and retain women:

Enlarging the pool of competent candidates

Reducing the likelihood of the use of excessive force by officers

Assistance in implementing community-oriented policing

Improving law enforcement's response to violence against women

Reducing the incidence of sex discrimination and sexual harassment claims

Bringing about beneficial changes in policy for all officers (selection standards, etc.). (pp. 21–27)

Recruitment efforts for women need to focus on positive images of female officers and should be conducted in places women frequent—women's centers, shopping malls, women's sporting events, and walk-in centers in minority neighborhoods—because traditional techniques have been largely unsuccessful in attracting large numbers of female applicants; thus, a focus on women-specific strategies is required (Harris, 1999). Developing websites and using female officers as recruiters are among other strategies that may be employed. Reaching out to girls in high school may be required in order to encourage women to consider policing as a possible career. Designing and employing more female-friendly equipment (e.g., uniforms designed for women rather than altered male uniforms) may help retain female officers once they have been hired. Emphasis on programs designed to accommodate work–family issues and the value of insurance and retirement programs also may help recruitment efforts, which should take advantage of all available media resources (Campbell, Christman, & Feigelson, 2000).

Attracting female applicants may be less difficult than retaining them once hired. According to Kranda (1998), "The challenge lies in retaining those highly qualified women in whom the agencies have made significant investments during the recruiting process. . . . One tool that has helped some agencies to raise their retention rates for female recruits has been the establishment of a formal mentoring process" (p. 54). Often, this process begins even before the new recruit begins her job, when a veteran officer contacts her and lets her know what to expect at the workplace. The mentor then continues to serve as an information resource and confidant. Groups such as the National Center for Women and Policing, the National Association of Women Law Enforcement Executives, and the International Association for Women Police are available to provide guidance on recruitment and retention efforts.

Still, even if a police administrator uses all of these strategies and greatly increases the number of female applicants, the applicants may not follow through with the hiring process or might leave the job after a short time if they find that there is favoritism and sexism within the work environment.

❖ Minority Police Officers

Some of the most problematic encounters involving the police occur between white police officers and minority citizens. Encounters between the police and blacks, Hispanics, Native Americans, Asians, and Middle Easterners indicate that a good deal of hostility remains as a result of racist attitudes, historical distrust, and past discrimination. Because the police are a reflection of society, it is not surprising that they sometimes have poor working relationships with minority group members. Racial tensions remain high in some parts of the United States, as indicated in the Case in Point.

☞ **CASE IN POINT 10.2**

Police Shooting Inflames Racial Tensions

National civil rights leaders and local parishioners packed a church in Rockford, IL Saturday, praying for peace and demanding justice in the Aug. 24 fatal shooting of an unarmed African American man by two white officers in the church's basement, in front of a dozen children.

Mark Anthony Barmore, who had been arrested multiple times on battery and weapons charges and spent time in prison for residential burglary, was pursued into the church by two officers who wanted to question him about an alleged domestic disturbance involving his girlfriend.

What happened next is under investigation. Barmore, 23, was shot multiple times, including in the back. Police officials previously told reporters that Barmore grabbed for an officer's gun. Rockford spokesperson Julia Scott-Valdez said the department could not comment on a pending investigation. Brown and her teenage daughter told detectives that Barmore had his hands up when police approached him.

The shooting has ignited long-simmering racial tensions in this struggling northern Illinois town, 80 miles from Chicago.

Source: Adapted from "Shooting by Police Ignites Racial Tensions in Illinois Town," by K. Lydersen, 2009, *Washington Post.* © 2009 The Washington Post. All rights reserved. Used by permission.

Black Police Officers

Alex (1969) noted some time ago that police work is attractive to blacks for the same reasons it is attractive to whites—reasonable salary, job security, and reasonable pension (Alex, 1969). And according to Moskos (2008), the following is true:

> Despite the passage of time, many of Alex's (1969) conclusions remain valid: a dislike of police in general is still present in many minority communities; despite social differences between black and white police officers, the job is seen as a basis for cooperation that over-rides race; overt appeals from suspects for racial solidarity fall on deaf ears; and African Americans are more likely to become police officers because of the benefits in a civil service job rather than wanting to be a police officer per se. (p. 60)

Police departments have a good deal to gain by hiring blacks in terms of the benefits of *protective coloration*. Black police officers can often gather information that would be extremely difficult for white officers to gather; having black police officers on the force may make charges of racial brutality against the police less likely; and federal funding is partly dependent on equal employment opportunity and affirmative action programs. The latter benefit is self-explanatory. Nonetheless, the general premise behind the effort to increase the number of black police officers involves improving police–community relations while decreasing biased police behavior (Brown & Frank, 2006).

It is also obvious that white police officers, whether undercover or not, will arouse suspicion in predominantly black groups. And with respect to police brutality toward minority groups, it is apparent that when black police officers resort to the use of force in dealing with black citizens, the issue of interracial brutality is avoided (though the issue of police brutality remains).

The best reason for hiring and promoting qualified black applicants is the fact that a tremendous amount of talent is wasted if they are excluded from police work. Because there is no evidence that white officers perform the policing function better than black officers, it is ethically and morally appropriate to hire applicants who are black. Further, integrated police departments are more representative of the public they serve, and black officers may serve as much needed role models in the community.

Problems for Black Police Officers

Blacks first served as police officers prior to the Civil War (Dulaney, 1996). Their numbers remained low until World War II, when gradual increases began. These early black officers were largely confined to black neighborhoods, and their powers of arrest did not extend to whites. In some cities, restrictions on the powers of black officers remained in place until the 1960s (Kuykendall & Burns, 1980). Leinen (1984) found that in the mid-1960s, only 22 law enforcement agencies employed blacks in positions above the level of patrol officers. A 1971 report of the Commission on Civil Rights affirmed the need to bring minority officers into law enforcement (Margolis, 1971). Litigation involving discrimination in hiring and promotion followed in the 1970s and 1980s; consent decrees frequently resulted, leading to the hiring of more minority (particularly black) officers.

Nearly a quarter of black officers are women, whereas white, Hispanic, and other (e.g., Asian American and American Indian) women comprise approximately 8%, 13%, and 11% of police officers in their racial or ethnic groups respectively (Martin & Jurik, 2006, p. 58). Martin and Jurik (2006) concluded that several factors contributed to the larger noted proportion of black women in municipal policing. First, black women often see policing as an attractive option compared to the narrow ranges of occupations that are often open to them. And they argued that black women have been leaders in the black community, and serving as a police officer "enables a black woman to wield power in the African American community and to work to alter an organization often viewed as oppressive" (p. 58).

Black police officers confront a number of problems in addition to those confronted by their white counterparts. While many black officers are assigned to police the ghettos in hopes of alleviating racial tensions, not all black citizens prefer black officers to white. Jackson and Wallach (1973) and Alex (1969, 1976) have noted that black officers sometimes have more trouble dealing with black citizens than do white officers. As mentioned previously, Alex (1969) found that black police officers suffer from double marginality resulting from the fact that they are sometimes distrusted by their white counterparts and are often viewed as traitors by other members of the black community. Black officers may be perceived as more black than blue (i.e., police oriented) by white officers and more blue than black by others in the black community.

Jacobs and Cohen (1978, p. 171) concluded that black police officers, like their white colleagues, arrest unwilling suspects, intervene in domestic squabbles, and keep order on ghetto streets. They represent the interests of order, property, and the status quo in an environment where large numbers of unemployed minority youth, among others, do not share this same commitment. Until recently, there was little research on whether an officer's race was related to arrest decisions. However, Brown and Frank (2006) reported that a police officer's race has a direct influence on arrest outcomes and that differences exist between white and black officers concerning the decision to arrest. They found that "white officers were more likely to arrest suspects than black officers, but black suspects were more likely to be arrested when the decision maker was a black officer" (p. 2).

Encounters between black officers and white citizens do not always proceed smoothly either. Black officers report being subjected to racial slurs, distrust, and out-right avoidance. Some whites are concerned about whether black officers will respond first as members of their race or as police officers when dealing with interracial situations. In some parts of the country, blacks in positions of authority are uncommon, and whites are apprehensive about being subject to such authority. In a multiracial society, these problems are perhaps inevitable to some extent, as we divide the world into *we* and *they* groups, interact with and tend to support members of the we group, and distrust members of the they groups. As long as skin color continues to be as important as, or more important than, an individual's actions, encounters between police officers and other citizens of different racial or ethnic groups are likely to remain uncomfortable, regardless of the qualifications and expertise of the officers involved.

Black police officers have typically reported that their relationships with white officers, at least while on duty, are satisfactory. They appear to be confident that white officers will back them up in emergency situations, and they indicate that they would do the same for white officers. However, "despite an outward emphasis on the unity of blue over any division between black and white, black and white police officers remain two distinct shades of blue, with distinct attitudes toward each other and the community they serve" (Moskos, 2008, p. 57). In fact, in some instances, black officers have formed their own associations in police departments, with agendas different from, and sometimes in sharp contrast to, those of white officers.

Promotions of black officers appear to be problematic in many departments. There is a general consensus that officers of all minority groups are greatly underrepresented above the patrol level (Sullivan, 1989; Williams, 1988). This may be due, in part, to **institutional discrimination** (e.g., biased testing procedures, job assignments, and educational requirements) and to the fact that federal agencies wishing to satisfy affirmative action requirements often recruit minorities from the ranks of municipal departments. The increasing number of black politicians occupying positions as mayors and chiefs of police may, over time, help alleviate the promotional dilemma.

Hispanic Police Officers

The Hispanic population in the United States has increased dramatically in the past decade. The Hispanic population was estimated at almost 50 million in 2009, up by more than 28 million over 1990 numbers, making Hispanics one of the fastest growing minorities in the United States. About 21% of Hispanic families in the United States are living below the poverty line (U.S. Census Bureau, 2006). These facts taken together indicate that police contacts with Hispanics are already frequent and are likely to increase dramatically as this minority group increases in size. These contacts are likely to be somewhat problematic because of language differences as well as the fact that, in addition to whatever immediate reason the police have for initiating contact with Hispanics, they may also be dealing with illegal immigrants—who can be deported if detected and reported to the Immigration and Customs Enforcement. Further, in one study, just under half (46%) of Hispanics had confidence that police officers would not use excessive force on suspects, and 45 percent were confident the police would treat Hispanics fairly ("Hispanics," 2009).

The rationale for recruiting Hispanic officers is much the same as for recruiting women and blacks, with the additional consideration of being bilingual and, ideally perhaps, bicultural. Because many Hispanics are not fluent in English, police officers serving in heavily Hispanic areas need to speak at least basic Spanish in order to render assistance as well as to engage in order maintenance and law enforcement functions. Further, a basic understanding of Hispanic culture is likely to make the officer who polices in Hispanic neighborhoods more comfortable with his surroundings and more understanding of the lifestyle encountered.

There is little information about Hispanic police officers, in part because their numbers have been very small until recently. In the last few years, the number of Hispanic officers—especially in large departments—has greatly increased. Some police departments, such as the Los Angeles Police Department and the Oakland, California Police Department, have experienced a 50% increase in the number of Hispanic police officers (Scoville, 2008).

Problems for Hispanic Police Officers

A study by the Pew Hispanic Center discovered that only 16% of Latino high school graduates earn four-year college degrees by age 29, compared with 37% of non-Hispanic whites and 21% of African Americans (Navarro, 2009). Similar findings were previously reported by Carter and Sapp (1991), who concluded that college education is still disproportionately inaccessible to blacks and Hispanics, raising the possibility that a college-degree requirement for entry-level officers may be discriminatory.

The language barrier, physical size requirements, the general belief that Hispanics are not highly sought after by police departments, and the belief that other occupations or professions were more highly prized by Hispanics probably account for the relatively small number of Hispanic officers in the past. With changing physical requirements, greater emphasis on unbiased, job-related tests, and affirmative action programs, opportunities for Hispanics in policing have increased. Additional problems were discovered by Navarro (2009), who noted that Hispanics face problems related to the lack of role models, practical college advice at home, inadequate school preparation, and culture barriers involving an attachment to the extended family.

What we know suggests that Hispanics seek police positions for the same reasons as officers from all other racial and ethnic groups and share basically the same problems, including the double marginality and discrimination in promotions and assignments discussed previously with respect to black police officers. In 1988, for example, a U.S. District Court judge found that hundreds of Latino agents had been victims of discrimination by the FBI. The judge found that Hispanics were often given unpleasant assignments that were rarely meted out to their white counterparts. Kennedy (1988) noted, "A frequent complaint supported by the preponderance of the evidence is that an Hispanic agent with five years of Bureau tenure who has ridden the 'Taco Circuit' may not have the experience of an Anglo on duty for two years" (p. A2). The obvious result of such discrimination can be seen in terms of promotions, which often depend on a variety of different police experiences as well as other factors.

Reasons for failure to recruit more Hispanics continue to include a history of negative stereotypes of the police in Hispanic communities, lack of interest in law enforcement careers among young Hispanics, misdirected recruitment efforts, and a lack of role models (Shusta, Levine, Harris, & Wong, 1995). According to Bartollas and Hahn (1999), the following is also true:

> Police departments across the nation have not treated minorities who wanted to become police officers well.... Hispanic/Latino American officers have been largely ignored in examinations of policing in the United States. Consequently, without the benefit of empirical studies, it is difficult to draw many conclusions about these officers as a separate group. (p. 330)

Asian Police Officers

As the Asian American population continues to increase, as crime rates in Asian American communities increase, and as Asian Americans become more organized in pursuit of equality, the need for Asian American police officers becomes apparent. While there is little information about Asian American police officers, one study of Chinese American officers has been completed (Lin, 1987). The results indicated that Chinese American police officers share many of the same problems as other minority officers. Lin concluded that Chinese American officers are well integrated into policing in New York City and that they tend to distance themselves from other Chinese Americans in some ways, much as some officers who represent other minority groups tend to distance themselves from their racial or ethnic groups. It appears, as seems to be the case with black officers as well, that Chinese American officers prefer to be viewed first and foremost as police officers, at least while on duty.

Although the highest concentrations of Asian Americans are in Hawaii and California, Asian immigrants and refugees have developed large and growing populations throughout the country (Ancheta, 2006). For example, in Palisades Park, New Jersey, almost one half of the residents are Korean American and 90% of the shops are Korean owned (Berger, 2006). Nonetheless, in most of the communities such as Palisades Park either a very small fraction or none of the police officers are Asian Americans. One of the reasons involves Asian parents who have high ambitions for their children and tell them police work is not the type of career for which they endured the upheaval of immigration (Berger, 2006). Furthermore, Asian experiences with corrupt police officers in their country have resulted in many mature Asians expecting that American police officers are also corrupt, unhelpful to citizens, and untrustworthy (Daye, 1997).

Other Asian minorities also require the attention of the police. Refugees from Vietnam, Cambodia, and Laos have formed enclaves in many urban areas, establishing subcultural pockets as their numbers increase. Numerous officers have reported difficulties communicating with, and understanding the culture of, such refugees. Korean and Japanese neighborhoods also exist in cities around the United States, and residents of these areas may also present difficulties in terms of providing (or requesting) police services. Further, Asian neighborhoods are not the crime-free areas they were once thought to be. Often, Asian gangs will target other Asians because they understand the culture (Asian American Lawyers Association of Massachusetts, 2003). The gangs know that many of the Asian families relocate to the United States from countries where the police were corrupt, ineffective, and conspired with gangs and thus fail to report crimes.

Gay and Lesbian Police Officers

Less is known about other minorities in policing, although the body of research is growing. What we know about gays and lesbians in policing suggests that successful integration of the gay population into law enforcement is yet to be achieved. As a result, most gay police officers do not openly admit their sexual orientation for fear that fellow officers will view them negatively (Belkin & McNichol, 2002; Wooditch & Ruiz, 2009). Gay officers who openly admit their sexuality frequently find themselves ostracized and the target of jokes (Jurik, Miller, & Forest, 2003) Whether a bias against gay officers emerges on the job due to unfavorable contact with the gay population or whether discrimination is based on pre-employment conceptions is unknown.

In the past, being a gay police officer was grounds for dismissal, but this type of employment discrimination is no longer officially condoned. Still, harassment of gays became such a widespread issue that some police departments were compelled to enact a zero-tolerance policy toward homophobic actions (Belkin & McNichol, 2002). In fact, gays have filed lawsuits against police departments claiming denial of employment based on their same-sex preference. (See, for example, *Childers v. Dallas Police Department*, 513 F.Supp. 134 [N.D. Tex. 1981], aff'd 669 F.2d 732 [5th Cir. 1982].)

In recent years, some metropolitan police departments, such as those in Los Angeles, New York, and Seattle, have actively recruited officers from the gay community (Belkin & McNichol, 2002). Some urban police departments have gone so far as to create gay and lesbian liaison units, staffed by openly gay officers, to provide police response to the gay community (Gay and Lesbian Liaison Unit, 2009).

❖ Recruiting and Retaining Minorities as Police Officers

The recruitment and promotion of qualified minority group members is essential for several reasons. When police agencies do not represent the communities they serve in terms of race and ethnicity, and perhaps to some extent gender as well, suspicion and distrust arise among members of both the police organization and the minority groups in question. Research has shown that interaction that occurs among those equally well qualified for the positions they occupy tends to reduce such suspicion and distrust. Further, understanding and communicating with members of different racial and ethnic groups that are characterized by different cultural or subcultural values, attitudes, and beliefs are essential for any public servant in a multicultural, multiethnic society. In addition, minority group members who become police officers may serve as living proof that it is possible to "get up and get out" for minority youngsters who need such role models. Finally, equal treatment, regardless of race, ethnicity, religion, or gender, is the foundation for a truly democratic society.

However, there may be a downside to minority recruitment. In some cases, minority group members are recruited or promoted for reasons other than ability and competency. When this occurs, members of the dominant group are adversely affected, and a backlash may be expected. Minority group members, qualified or not, are in the spotlight in many police organizations. Their behavior is critically scrutinized at every turn, and this is especially true if the standards according to which they were hired are different from those applied to dominant group members. This may make the minority group members feel as if they are on trial or have been singled out for close observation and criticism, increasing the stress under which they operate, which, in turn, may make it more difficult for them to perform well.

In some cases, as a result of the desire to correct past wrongs as quickly as possible, some personnel are hired and promoted who should not have been. When the city of Miami responded to demands from minority communities that more minorities be hired by consenting to hire 80% minorities, many minority citizens were pleased, but police administrators and many white police officers were outraged. In what some perceive as a direct result of hiring and promoting large numbers of minority group members in a relatively short (seven-year) period, some 25 Miami police officers have been arrested for crimes ranging from burglary to murder, the morale of the police is extremely low, and there is considerable talk about a need for change in city and department administration (Dorschner, 1987). Lott (2000), in a cross-sectional study of U.S. cities between 1987 and 1993, found that lowering hiring standards in order to recruit more racial and ethnic minority officers reduced the overall quality of officers hired and led to increased crime rates.

The solution to this dilemma is obvious but difficult to achieve. In simple terms, race, ethnicity, and gender should not be considerations when hiring or promoting police personnel. There is no evidence to support the belief that any of these factors determines success, or lack of success, in policing. Eliminating these factors in the hiring and promotional process means developing tests that are not inherently biased in terms of such factors, and herein lies the difficulty. Such tests are likely to be considerably different from those traditionally employed and are likely to be perceived as inferior to those taken by officers who were hired in the past. Of course, different does not necessarily imply inferior, either in testing or with respect to race, ethnicity, and gender, and we must find ways to make this point clearly and with certainty.

As is the case with recruitment efforts aimed at women, minority recruitment efforts must overcome a number of obstacles. First, of course, members of minorities must be reached, and many conventional efforts fail to do so. Use of minority publications, recruitment efforts directed at colleges and universities, and recruitment efforts aimed at recognizing and supporting high school students who have an interest in law enforcement have all shown positive results. Enlisting the aid of national organizations such as the NAACP, NOBLE (National Organization of Black Law Enforcement Executives), NAPOA (National Asian Police Officers Association), HAPCOA (Hispanic American Police Command Officers Association), IAWP (International Association of Women Police), local church leaders, and civic and local leaders who are members of minority groups also may prove beneficial. Addressing the issues confronting minorities entering policing and moving to new communities with the help of the resources mentioned is crucial. Questions concerning establishment of a comfort level at work and in the community should be addressed. If the new officer is the first black, Asian, or Hispanic officer hired by the agency, he or she is bound to have concerns about acceptance, both in the agency and in the larger community. These questions may extend to family members and their acceptance within the new community. Civic and religious leaders may help to answer some of these questions.

Recruitment teams that include women or minorities may also help in minority recruitment. Some departments have instituted incentive pay for successful recruitment (McKeever & Kranda, 2000). Other departments have found that developing citizen police academies to familiarize the public with police activities is a beneficial strategy. Community speaking engagements by officers reflecting diversity and interest in minority recruitment, development of linkages with the military, and formation of partnerships with the media are also worthwhile minority recruitment activities (McKeever & Kranda, 2000).

Until the suggested reforms in hiring and promoting become widespread, we must continue to deal with the biases of those already employed in police work. Occupational discrimination continues to occur on a regular basis in various squad rooms, locker rooms, and patrol cars. While most police officers are smart enough to understand that racial slurs to other citizens are likely to lead to disciplinary action sooner or later, many continue to use such terms among themselves and in regard to minority officers. Indeed, to be more accepted into the fraternity, some minority group members use derogatory terms to describe members of their own racial or ethnic groups, allowing white officers to rationalize their own behavior by pointing to this fact. In spite of their lack of widespread popularity, human relations and community relations courses need to be offered on a regular basis, if for no other reason than to combat occupational discrimination that too often becomes institutionalized.

❖ Chapter Summary

To sum up the current situation with respect to minority police officers, we offer the following observations. Minority officers (women excepted) have largely achieved representation commensurate with their population share and now have the same legal rights and responsibilities as other police officers. However, it appears that minority officers may still face discrimination in duty assignments and promotion. While numerous law enforcement agencies have made attempts to eliminate discrimination in hiring and promoting minority officers, this has proven to be a difficult and complex task. Minority recruits sometimes lack the skills necessary to gain access to higher education, and many do not compete well using traditional measures such as written tests. As a result of these factors, court decisions, and civil rights legislation, police entry-level and promotional requirements have sometimes been changed. Such changes have caused some to argue that police agencies are lowering their standards and recruiting unqualified minorities. These fears that hiring minorities for police work will result in a more negative image of the police, based on lower standards and performance, remain real for many white, male police officers and for some other citizens. However, it is likely that such changes will lead to better, more representative police departments, and changing standards so that they are equitable to members of both sexes and all racial and ethnic groups need not be equated with lowering standards or poor performance.

❖ Key Terms

police–community relations

human relations

public relations

stereotypes

minority group

prejudice

discrimination

occupational discrimination

psychological harassment

institutional discrimination

community–police
  mediation program

responsiveness

accountability

double marginality

protective coloration

❖ Discussion Questions

1. Discuss the historical origins of some of the current problems in police–multicultural relations.

2. What characteristics of a multiethnic, industrial, democratic society make police multicultural relations particularly problematic?

3. What is the general perception of the police as reflected in public opinion surveys? What are some of the important factors in determining these perceptions?

4. List and discuss some specific steps the police can take to help improve multicultural relations. List and discuss the same thing from the public perspective.

5. What is the impact of biased law enforcement on police–minority relations? Are the police unique in the criminal justice network when it comes to bias?

6. Why and how have women and minority group members been excluded from police work over the years?

7. Summarize the research relating to the performance of policewomen on patrol. Are you convinced that policewomen are as capable as policemen? Why or why not?

8. What are the basic advantages police departments gain when hiring members of racial or ethnic minorities?

9. What stresses do minority officers experience in addition to those experienced by white police officers?

10. What steps can be taken to address occupational discrimination and to improve understanding among police officers of different racial or ethnic groups?

❖ Internet Exercises

1. Estimate the percentages of individuals living in your home city or county who belong to various racial groups. Next, visit the website for the U.S. Census Bureau (http://www.census.gov) and access information on your hometown or county. Compare data from the percentages of different minority groups living in the location you selected based on census data with your estimates. Did you find any surprises? If so, what were they?

2. Using the key words "police and minority relations in foreign countries," locate two articles on the Internet that deal with this issue. What countries did you select? Describe the nature of police–minority relations in each of the countries you researched. How do such relations compare with police–minority relations in the United States?

Contemporary Strategies in Policing

CHAPTER LEARNING OBJECTIVES

- Discuss and provide examples of various problems associated with traditional policing methodologies.

- Compare and contrast the underlying tenets of both traditional and community-based styles of policing.

- Offer an opinion, based on research, as to which form of policing is more effective, traditional or community based.

- Identify and elaborate on the criticisms of community policing and take a stance regarding your agreement or disagreement with those criticisms.

- Compare and contrast intelligence-led policing with traditional policing methods and comment on the effectiveness of each.

- Identify the reasoning behind the development of *differential response* policing and offer an informed opinion regarding the implementation of such a strategy.

- Define *evidence-based policing* and identify reasons offered by line personnel for resisting this form of policing.

- Identify circumstances under which an Incident Command or Unified Systems police response may prove effective.

- Select the form of policing you believe to be the most effective and justify your response with empirical evidence.

❖ **Photo 11.1** The philosophy of "police omnipresence: An effective method for the prevention of crime?"

American police officers are better educated, trained, and equipped than ever before. At the same time, the scope of police duties has been expanded as a result of terrorist acts committed in the United States and around the world, technological advances in the field of policing, and a new generation of police officers with different life goals and orientations toward work. In spite of, or perhaps because of, these factors, examples of excessive force, police corruption, and inefficiency still appear frequently in the media, and the police remain unable to prevent most crimes or to apprehend most offenders. In the two decades leading up to the 21st century, policing changed from a closed, incident-driven, reactive bureaucracy to a more open, dynamic, quality-oriented partnership with the community (Stevens, 2001). Such changes are included under the general heading of community policing.

Still, as we have seen, corruption, harassment of and by some segments of society, inconsistent leadership, and inefficiency continue to tarnish the police image. Scandals involving theft, use and sale of drugs by officers, police brutality, and other serious violations are still far too common. It appears that many of the programs developed by the police in an attempt to adapt to a rapidly changing society have resulted in or continued a cycle of isolation and alienation. Specialization, for example, was viewed as one way of providing better service to the public. As a result, numerous specialized units (internal affairs, community relations, juvenile, robbery, homicide, drug, sex crimes, and traffic) were developed. In many cases, a consequence of such development has been little cross-training; an "it's not my job" attitude; tight-knit, highly secretive units; and little effective communication between patrol officers and the officers who staff these specialized units. If and when scandals arise in such units, the confidence of both the general public and noninvolved officers within the police ranks is understandably undermined. In the past decade, gangs, drugs, race, ethnicity, immigration, technological innovations, cybercrime, and increasingly violent encounters involving automatic weapons and the willingness to use them have become focal points. Increasing visibility of immigrants and a small number of terrorist incidents within the borders of our country have led to a rebirth of concern about racial and ethnic differences and the reemergence of extreme right-wing groups. Meanwhile, relationships between the police and members of racial and ethnic minorities continue to be less than civil in many cases, and downright unpleasant in some. All of the new police technology and all of the old police traditions have failed to provide solutions to these apparently different but very much related issues. As a result, there has been a search for new ways of addressing these issues and an emergence (some would argue reemergence) of community-oriented policing. In order to comprehend where we presently stand in policing, it is critical to understand where we most recently came from.

❖ Community Policing

There is a good deal of confusion about community policing, what it might be expected to accomplish, and how or why it might be expected to work where other strategies have failed. In fact, many believe community-oriented policing (COP) simply retreads shopworn elements of police community relations programs—that it is little more than a passing fad that will fade away as have many others before it (Stevens, 2001, pp. 7–8; Tafoya, 2000; Trojanowicz, 1990). This is perhaps especially true with respect to traditional police agencies that are highly resistant to change as a result of their paramilitary organizational structures, civil services regulations, and unionization (Skolnick & Bayley, 1986; Stevens, 2001, p. 11; Tafoya, 2000). In fact, some (e.g., Scrivner, 2004) have questioned whether community policing can survive in the aftermath of 9/11.

More than two decades ago, Skolnick and Bayley (1986) studied police innovation that focused on involving the public in the police mission in six American cities. They concluded that these innovative programs, designated as community-oriented policing, took a number of different forms. Still, the researchers identified a number of elements common to all of the programs. These elements included police–community reciprocity, areal decentralization of command, reorientation of patrol, and civilianization (Skolnick & Bayley, 1986, pp. 212–220). A brief discussion of each of these elements will help create a foundation for understanding community policing.

Police–community reciprocity refers to a "genuine feeling" on the part of the police that the public they serve has something to contribute to policing. Further, the police communicate this feeling to the public, learn from public input, and consider themselves accountable to the community in which they serve. The police and the public become "co-producers of crime prevention" (Skolnick & Bayley, 1986, pp. 212–213).

Areal decentralization of command refers to the establishment of substations, mini-stations, and other attempts to increase interaction between police officers and the public they serve in a particular geographic area.

Reorientation of patrol involves moving from car to foot patrol in order to increase police interaction with other citizens. This may involve permanently assigning certain officers to walking beats or having officers park their cars so they can get out and talk to residents. Positive contacts between officers and other citizens are thought to be one result of foot patrol, and crime prevention another. In a study of police officers in Philadelphia, Kane (2000) concluded, "At least among Philadelphia public housing police officers, permanent assignment was associated with a higher level of investigative activity at the street level, from which inferences about increased beat guardianship may be drawn" (p. 278).

In other words, "These findings indicate that as a result of permanent beat assignment, officers assumed greater responsibility for their beats than before this deployment was established" (p. 273). Whether such effects are long term is a question that must still be addressed because the officers in this study were observed for a period of weeks rather than months or years.

Civilianization refers to introducing civilians to an increasing number of positions with police agencies. For example, an increasing number of civilians are being employed in research and training divisions, in forensics, and as community service officers who handle many noncrime-related tasks. Skolnick and Bayley (1986) concluded that civilianization was related to successfully introducing and carrying out programs and policies related to community mobilization and crime prevention.

In reality, then, COP requires adopting both philosophical and operational changes and, to a great extent, turns traditional policing practices upside down. It is, after all, "not easy to transform blue knights into community organizers" (Skolnick & Bayley, 1986, p. 211). Trojanowicz, Kappeler, Gaines, and Bucqueroux (1998) elaborated some of the principles on which this transformation from traditional to community policing is based. First, **community-oriented policing** is a philosophy based on the belief that law-abiding citizens should have input with respect to policing, provided they are willing to participate in and support the effort. Second, community policing is an organizational strategy requiring that all police personnel (civilian and sworn) explore ways to turn the philosophy into practice. Third, police departments implementing community policing must develop Community Policing Officers (CPOs) to act as links between the police and community residents, and these CPOs must have continuous, sustained contact with law-abiding citizens. In addition, community policing implies a contract between the police and other citizens that helps overcome apathy while curbing vigilantism. Further, community policing is proactive, and it helps improve quality of life for those who are most vulnerable (e.g., the poor, elderly, homeless). Although community policing utilizes technology, it relies on human ingenuity and interaction. Finally, community policing must be fully integrated into the department in order to provide personalized police service on a decentralized basis.

Trojanowicz et al. (1998) also pointed out what community policing is not. Community policing is not a technique to be applied only to specific problems but, rather, is a new way of thinking about the police role in the community. Community policing is not the same as public relations. Community policing is not anti-technology, but it utilizes technology in a different framework. Community policing is not soft on crime, nor is it an independent program within a police department. It must involve the entire department, and it incorporates traditional policing responses. Community policing is not cosmetic. It requires substantive changes in the relationship between the police and other citizens. Community policing is not a top-down approach, nor is it simply social work renamed. It incorporates traditional policing responses. Finally, community policing is not tradition bound but requires risk taking and experimentation.

Carey (1994, p. 24) noted that community policing is not solely directed at addressing problems that cannot be addressed by traditional policing methods. Suburban and low-crime communities also can use community policing to address the specific needs and problems of their citizens. In short, the community policing philosophy recognizes that patrol officers are the government representatives best positioned to address a number of social problems, and enforcing the law is only one of several strategies the police can employ to cope with such problems (Cardarelli, McDevitt, & Baum, 1998). Long-term interaction between police officers and neighborhood residents is thought to foster the development of relationships based on mutual trust and cooperation. It also encourages the exchange of information between citizens and police officers, including mutual input concerning policing priorities and tactics for specific neighborhoods (Walters, 1993, p. 220). According to Trojanowicz and Bucqueroux (1992):

> By challenging people to work as partners in making their communities better and safer places, Community Policing produces a subtle but profound shift in the role and responsibility of the police. No longer are they the experts with all the answers, the 'thin blue line' that protects the good people from the bad—'us' versus 'them.' Community officers are part of the community, generalists who do whatever it takes to help people help themselves. (p. 1)

In COP, patrol officers become liaisons, ombudsmen, problem solvers, and mobilizers of community resources. They seek to obtain community or neighborhood cooperation to identify and resolve problems rather than simply handling incidents. They look for patterns of incidents that are indicative of problems that may best be addressed by resources other than, or in cooperation with, the police. In short, they practice problem-oriented policing (POP is discussed in the following section) as a part of the overall COP strategy.

Implementing COP, as previously noted, requires a number of concrete changes in most police organizations. Implementation requires redefining the department's role and training all officers in COP. Employees must be evaluated differently. Officers must be assigned specific patrol areas. Calls must be prioritized, and police work must be tailored to community needs.

The LEMAS Survey

The Law Enforcement Management and Administrative Statistics (LEMAS) survey assessed the community policing practices of state and local police departments in 1997 and 1999. Highlights of the LEMAS survey (Hickman & Reaves, 2001, pp. 1–11) are summarized as follows:

1. State and local police agencies had nearly 113,000 community policing officers in 1999, compared with 21,000 in 1997.

2. In 1999, 87% of local police officers were employed by a department that provided community policing training to new recruits.

3. Approximately one third of local departments, employing about 50% of all officers, actively encouraged patrol officers to engage in problem-solving projects on their patrol beats.

4. Approximately 42% of local police departments gave patrol officers responsibility for specific geographic areas or beats.

5. In 1999, 28% of local departments surveyed citizens to gather information, compared with 30% in 1997.

It appears, then, that by the beginning of the 21st century COP had made some inroads in many departments across the country. At the same time, however, the United States was undergoing major changes in diversity with respect to race, ethnicity, and culture. Brown (2004) noted that roughly 1.5 million new immigrants arrive in the United States each year, that Hispanics have displaced African Americans as the largest minority group in the United States, and that immigrants have moved away from major population centers to establish neighborhoods in more sparsely populated areas of the country. Since police work is affected by all of these changes, it is essential that changes in recruiting and hiring, as well as in familiarization with the values, norms, and customs of an increasingly diverse population, occur. And in some cases, such changes must occur in less than favorable circumstances. Research has shown, for example, that Hispanics tend to have less favorable attitudes toward the police than whites and that many immigrants don't trust the police enough to contact them for assistance (Brown, 2004, pp. 50–51). Further, following the events of 9/11, the police have concentrated their investigative efforts of certain groups (e.g., Arab males). It can be argued whether such investigations, and the interrogations and detention which sometimes result, protect the country from further terrorist attacks. It is certain, however, that these tactics lead to hostility among the target groups, whose assistance with developing intelligence concerning possible terrorists is essential. It is therefore critical that police officers treat targeted groups with respect, help insure that their liberties are not unduly trampled upon, and allow then to maintain their sense of dignity (Brown, 2004, p. 53). COP efforts that develop partnerships with diverse groups in the community represent perhaps the best way of accomplishing these goals.

Along these same lines, Kobolt and Tucker (2004) noted that policing is constantly evolving to meet changing demands and has now evolved into what might be called the **strategic management** era. These authors indicated that the evolution into strategic management was based upon the practice of computer generated crime data and a resulting convergence of police management, technology, strategy, and community involvement (Kobolt & Tucker, 2004, p 64). The authors concluded that using technology to process intelligence provided by community resources, changing the roles of police administrators from administrative to operational, and developing strategies to attack identifiable crime hot spots and patterns led not only to the era of strategic management in policing but to reductions in crime rates wherever implemented (Kobolt & Tucker, 2004, p. 68).

Oliver (2006) believed that the terrorist attacks on September 11, 2001, set in motion a new era of policing, what he called "**the era of Homeland security.**" According to Oliver (2006), police in the era of Homeland security will have to be "more familiar with information technology, intelligence gathering, processing, and disseminating, as well as technical skills not previously learned such as weapons of mass destruction (nuclear, chemical, and biological weapons), response to mass casualty events, and both anti-terrorism and counter-terrorism methods" (p. 19). The author noted that collecting intelligence was a standard aspect of local policing that disappeared in most respects during the 1960s and 1970s, largely as a result of the fear of abuse of powers by the police. Bringing back this intelligence gathering component will mean that safeguards will need to be put in place to protect against the very same reason intelligence gathering was eliminated—the abuse of authority. Undoubtedly, the risk to civil liberties still exists, and safeguards will need to be put in place to protect against such abuse. In keeping with the general theme of this text, Oliver indicated that the selection, hiring, and training of police officers under Homeland Security will increasingly need to focus on information technology; intelligence gathering, processing, and disseminating; technical skills involving weapons of mass destruction; response to mass casualty events; and both antiterrorism and counterterrorism methods. Further, communication between police administrators and line officers, lateral communication between the police and other governmental agencies, and the vertical communication between local, state, and federal agencies will be critical in this new era of policing (see Case in Point 11.1 below).

☞ CASE IN POINT 11.1

Local Police Take Wider Role Against Terrorism

While most Baltimore police officers rely on city maps to help pinpoint crime spikes and deploy the troops to tamp down violence, Lt. David Engel has a map of the world hanging in his office. Engel, who commands the police intelligence unit, works with federal agents tracking global flare-ups of terrorist activity, and members of the intelligence unit scan the Internet and question informants about potential threats. Members of his unit speak more than a dozen languages, and include experts on detecting fraudulent documents often used by terrorists. Their work is part of a national trend that has seen local police agencies becoming more involved in domestic and international intelligence, a mission that before Sept. 11, 2001, was almost the sole domain of federal agencies.

"Police departments across the country have created intelligence units, or beefed up existing ones, because of concerns that federal agencies do not have the manpower to track down tens of thousands of potential tips and leads— any one of which could prevent a terrorist attack. And to help bridge the gap between law enforcement agencies, local detectives have joined federal antiterrorism teams helping to expand the FBI's Joint Terrorism Task Forces from 35 to 66 nationally since 2001."

In Boston, Police Superintendent John Gallagher said his intelligence unit plays a crucial role in preventing a terrorist attack since officers on the beat might be the first to learn about a plot. In preparation, members of the intelligence unit keep their eyes and ears open in order to discover and act appropriately on any apparent threat of terrorist activities.

Source: Adapted from Wilber, D. (2003, September 2). "Local police take wider role against terrorism: Baltimore is among cities beefing up intelligence," *Baltimore Sun.* Available at http://www.baltimoresun.com.

❖ Problem-Oriented Policing and COP

The concept of problem-oriented policing (POP) originated in 1979 in the works of Herman Goldstein. Goldstein (1979) noted many of the difficulties discussed in the first section of this chapter and added that while many police agencies gave the appearance of being efficient, this appearance failed to translate into benefits for the communities served. He looked carefully at public expectations of the police and determined that they involved problem solving. Goldstein concluded that if the police were expected to solve problems, they could not be accurately evaluated by focusing only on crime statistics. Instead, evaluation would have to focus on the problems encountered and the effectiveness of the police response to such problems.

Problem-oriented police officers, then, need to define the problems they encounter, gather information concerning these problems (frequency, seriousness, duration, location) and develop creative solutions to them. This model of problem solving is known as the SARA model (Eck & Spelman, 1988; Goldstein, 1990; Stevens, 2001). To expand on the previous definition, this four-step approach involves *scanning* (identifying the problem in terms of time, location, and behavior), *analysis* (answering the who, what, where, when, how, and why questions), *response* (development of alternative problem-solving approaches and selection of most appropriate), and *assessment* (evaluating the response selected to determine whether it worked).

Problem-oriented policing represents a dramatic change from traditional policing, which is incident driven and in which the police typically receive a complaint or call, respond to it, and then clear the incident. Although the specific situation is addressed, the underlying conditions are not—so more calls are likely to be made, requiring further responses to similar incidents. POP regards these incidents as symptoms of underlying conditions that must be addressed to keep the incidents from proliferating (Barlow & Barlow, 2000, p. 44; Toch & Grant, 1991, p. 6). Patterns of incidents that are similar, then, represent problems that must be attended to by the police. Problems, rather than crimes, calls, or incidents, become the basic unit of police work (Toch & Grant, 1991, p. 18). Line officers become problem identifiers and solvers. Identifying and solving community problems requires input from those who live in the community, as well as from other service providers. As Cherney (2008) noted:

> Relevant to promoting innovative problem-solving is the willingness of police to engage third parties in furtherance of crime control. Harnessing such capacities is critical to POP given that many public safety problems the police have to address require some level of partnership with external agencies. One reason for this is that many factors that lead to crime have very little to do with the police directly, but instead originate in the functioning of other institutions and the capacity of actors within those settings to assert effective social control. . . . Hence, drawing upon the crime control capacities of external parties as a core aspect of problem analysis and response is essential to the effectiveness of POP in practice. (p. 631)

Thus, POP and COP share concerns with community involvement, and both focus on conditions underlying crime and disruption of order (Oliver & Bartgis, 1998; Stevens, 2001, pp. 14–15). The National Research Council concluded that while more research needs to be done on POP, it is among the most promising of police strategies (Boba, 2009).

Research on Community and Problem-Oriented Policing

Skolnick and Bayley (1986) are not the only researchers to examine community policing. Sadd and Grinc (2000) studied Innovative Neighborhood-Oriented Policing (INOP) in eight American cities. INOP is a variant of community policing based on the premise that crime and drug problems must be addressed by communities, not just by the police. Using a variety of research techniques, these authors found that it was difficult to convince police officers to accept the new roles required for community policing, partly due to poor communication from police administrators concerning these new roles. INOP officers belonged to special units and were often distrusted by officers, especially senior officers, in more traditional assignments. Other officers felt that they had little or no input into the new program and that community residents were not generally excited about being involved in INOP due to fear of retaliation from drug dealers, which was based on the fear that the police would abandon the program and leave them to suffer the consequences. Still, with proper education and training, community residents did come to report better relationships with the police, even when INOPs' effects on drugs and crime were difficult to detect. In fact, Liederbach, Fritsch, Carter, and Bannister (2008) found that community residents tended to have more positive views of community policing than did the officers involved in COP.

Jesilow, Meyer, Parsons, and Tegler (1998), using phone interviews in 1990 and again in 1992, studied the residents' opinions of Santa Ana, California, in experimental (POP) and control (no POP) neighborhoods. They found that citizen complaints about gangs, crime, and disorder in POP neighborhoods decreased over the two-year period, while such complaints remained constant or increased in control neighborhoods. Due to limitations in their research design, the authors indicated that they cannot argue definitively that POP caused the changes, but the data are certainly suggestive. The authors also cautioned about the possibility of violations of civil rights among the powerless in POP programs that address the complaints of the more affluent. Overall, they concluded, POP seems to be a good thing in that residents involved in the program seem to be happier about their neighborhoods and the police: "The research suggests that law enforcement agencies that take the time to learn and deal with their constituents' irritants and troubles will be perceived in increasingly positive terms" (p. 460).

In their review of 12 studies of community policing, Lurigo and Rosenbaum (1994) found generally encouraging results in terms of the impact of organizational changes on police officer attitudes. Results indicated generally positive effects on job satisfaction, improved relationships with coworkers and citizens, and greater expectations for citizen participation in preventing crimes.

Cardarelli, McDevitt, and Baum (1998) conducted a survey of 82 police departments in Massachusetts communities with fewer than 200,000 inhabitants to determine the community policing strategies, if any, that were employed. They concluded that deployment strategies such as bike patrol and mini-stations may represent new ways for some departments to perform their policing functions, but that most residents do little more than provide information to departments utilizing these strategies. This is also true for departments that use a combination of deployment and crime-targeted strategies. The authors found that residents were more likely to participate in the problem-identification and problem-solving processes associated with community policing when collaborative strategies such as advisory councils and citizen academies were established. They also concluded that the police will have to take the initiative for establishing such relationships, particularly in lower socioeconomic neighborhoods.

Breci (1997) surveyed a random sample of Minnesota police officers in an attempt to determine the extent to which Minnesota police agencies sponsored or offered the kinds of training necessary for line officers to develop the skills and knowledge necessary to make the transition to community policing. Fifty-two percent (801) of Breci's surveys were returned. His findings indicated that many Minnesota police agencies had not provided officers with the training or support required for a successful transition. He concluded that "without clear guidelines and leadership from the department, efforts to connect the police with the community through the line officer will have no more success than did the old police-community relations programs of the past" (p. 774). In his study of community policing, Stevens (2001) found few accounts of automatic success in the community policing arena: "In fact, in the nine agencies studied, most of them failed at both their earlier and recent attempts to implement what they thought were solid police strategies guided by idealized versions of community policing prerogatives that allegedly worked in other departments" (pp. 1–2).

Garner (2004) discussed an extension of POP he referred to as **Solution-Oriented Policing** (SOP), which focuses on the fact some community-police issues are best addressed through the development of unique approaches or thinking outside the box. Rather than focusing on apparent causes of such issues, Garner believed that root causes should be sought out and addressed through solution-oriented responses that select the best option(s) among potential solutions to problems. Officers are encouraged to seek such causes and solutions before the resulting problems grow to unmanageable size, thus using proactive as opposed to reactive strategies.

Finally, citing current evidence on COP, Boba (2009) concluded that the existing research shows that many of the strategies employed in COP (storefront offices, neighborhood watch, and community meetings) do not lead to a reduction in crime or an increase in police effectiveness. Nonetheless, the belief that the police should engage in partnerships with the community in order to solve problems is widespread.

Criticisms of Community Policing

While there is little doubt that community policing has been a major trend in American policing—according to the Bureau of Justice Statistics (1999), in 1999 nearly two thirds of county and municipal police departments with 100 or more officers had a formally written community policing plan—there are those who have raised questions about its worth. One common criticism is that many police departments embrace the rhetoric of community policing rather than the philosophy. Indeed, there are police administrators who institute foot patrol programs or establish neighborhood watch programs and claim to have initiated community policing. As Offer (1993, p. 8) noted, the considerable enthusiasm for community policing has led to its introduction as an organizational objective with little substance in many police departments. Stevens (2001) and Palmiotto (2000) indicated that this remained the case as we entered the 21st century. While these observations are certainly accurate, they are not a criticism of community policing itself, but of those who claim the title without developing the substance. As previously noted, another major criticism of COP concerns the fact that there is little empirical evidence to suggest that community policing is effective in reducing serious crime. Stevens (2001) indicated that ". . . it has yet to be reliably supported that community policing initiatives are advantageous for all communities and/or can be implemented and operated by all police agencies"(p. 5) and Boba (2009, p. 41) concurred. Indeed, available evidence seems to indicate that while people involved in community policing efforts feel more secure, crime is not significantly reduced. It may be that people who feel more secure will use the streets and other public places more frequently, thus eventually making it more difficult for criminals to ply their trades. It may also be that people who feel more secure, but are not in fact more secure, are more likely to engage in activities that make them available as victims, thus increasing the risk of crime.

The third major criticism of community policing has to do with its costs. Implementing COP may decrease the mobility and availability of the officers involved because the officers are out of their vehicles a good deal of the time and because they are involved in community organization activities and are sometimes unavailable to respond to calls. In fact, in many programs, COP officers no longer perform routine motorized patrol, and other officers must take over this duty so that it can continue. It has also been suggested that the money spent on community policing might be better spent on improving social and economic conditions (Pisani, 1992). In fairness, it must be noted that community policing is seldom touted as a money-saving approach. While it does cost money to implement any new program, there are various ways of measuring costs. Departmental budgets may have to be increased initially to support COP (Palmiotto, 2000, p. 211; Sadd & Grinc, 2000, p. 116). If the strategy succeeds in improving cooperation between the police and other citizens, however, how do we measure the savings in crimes prevented or solved as a result of this increased cooperation? Further, some departments have found that by rearranging priorities, eliminating services for nonemergency calls, and providing reporting alternatives (telephone, fax, letters) for the public, costs can be managed (Burgreen & McPherson, 1992). It appears that the federal government agrees that continued efforts in support of COP are in order. On July 28, 2009, Vice President Joe Biden announced that the Department of Justice COPS Office awarded $1 billion in Recovery Act funding through its COPS Hiring Recovery Program (CHRP) to state, local, and tribal law enforcement to create or preserve nearly 5,000 law enforcement positions (COPS, 2008).

A fourth criticism of community policing focuses on the possibility that permanent assignment of police officers who have a good deal of independence in operations enhances the possibility of corruption. This criticism is based primarily on historical accounts of corruption by police officers who walked beats, who were not subject to routine supervision, and who frightened neighborhood business persons (legitimate and illegitimate) into paying them for not enforcing the law or for protecting them from other predators. Trojanowicz and Bucqueroux (1992) argued, however, that the very nature of COP works against such corruption. That is, COP officers are known by name to everyone in the neighborhood and have every reason to believe that they cannot "cross the lined undetected" (p. 2).

Fifth, some critics argue that the time is simply not right to change from traditional policing strategies to COP. There are always crises to be faced and numerous reasons for not changing strategies. Burgreen and McPherson (1992) recognized this fact when they wrote the following:

> If we don't risk changing when the time is right, we will be forced to change when we are not prepared. If we are afraid to change because we are comfortable, we may be holding on just to prove that certainty is better than taking a risk. No one benefits in this scenario. Not the police, and certainly not the community. (p. 31)

Whether or not the time is right, numerous variations have been developed on the community policing scheme in communities across the country.

Some Examples of Community Policing Efforts

CAPS: Chicago Alternative Policing Strategy. Community policing in Chicago is known as CAPS. The program had its origins at the time of rising crime rates in the early 1990s and was in planning stages for more than a year before it was officially instituted in 1993 in 5 of the city's 25 police districts (Hartnett & Skogan, 1999). During initial phases, officers were permanently assigned to beats and trained in problem-solving techniques. Citizen committees were formed in the various neighborhoods, and police and area residents began to meet on a regular basis. Police and residents worked together to identify and prioritize problems, develop ways of addressing them, and bring community resources to bear on them. By the spring of 1998, almost 80% of the city's residents were aware of CAPS, over 60% knew about beat meetings in their neighborhoods, and about 15% had attended such meetings. Support for the program has grown among line officers.

To be sure, not all has gone smoothly with CAPS. Within the police department, CAPS challenged the business as usual mentality of officers and created initial pessimism among officers who did not care to take on noncrime problems. Development of workable performance measures and incentives has been problematic. And "there are no measures of the extent to which officers are involved in problem solving and no indicators of their success" (Hartnett & Skogan, 1999, p. 10). Still, in November of 2008 Chicago Police Superintendent Jody Weis announced a new CAPS program called CITY, or Cops Interaction Targeting Youth. CITY is an athletic program geared toward children ages 11 to 14 to help them make the transition between grades.

The *Westwood COACT (COmmunity ACTion) Mentors Program,* sponsored by the Memphis Police Department, was created to promote positive behavior among at-risk children and as a result produce better students that are eager to advance their education rather than participate in criminal activity. Calling their mentoring program LOT (Leaders of Tomorrow), officers sent out applications via neighborhood watch leaders, churches, and schools. Under the banner "Together We can

Build Positive Futures," youth participating in LOT went on field trips to historic and business sites and were involved in the 1st Annual Black History competition involving "Jeopardy" type questions to ascertain their knowledge of black history. Future plans include a trip to a credit union where they have established an account to see how a bank operates and to learn how to manage their bank account (Memphis Police Department, 2009).

Houston Area Police Agencies added a new networking component to their communication arsenal. Called Nixle, the community information service enables public entities to send information concerning Amber Alerts, advisories, and community and traffic information directly to residents by e-mail and text. The service was launched in March and is free to agencies and residents. Residents can set up an account to receive information by going to the Nixle website. The service is a way for agencies to stay connected with the community at a neighborhood level. Agencies can send alerts to a specific neighborhood or to neighborhoods within a 2-mile or 50-mile radius, depending on the circumstances.

What, then, is the current status of COP and POP? According to Liederbach et al. (2008), over the course of the last three decades, the culture of community policing has permeated the vast majority of police organizations, so much so that tactics and strategies associated with the model have become common knowledge among policing scholars, law enforcement executives, and street-level officers. By now, it appears that "everybody knows" that police organizations need to successfully engage citizens and implement collaborative strategies to solve problems in the community.

While the emphasis has shifted to a number of new policing strategies, there is little doubt that most of these new strategies have incorporated the basic principles of COP and POP. It might, in fact, be argued that the shift toward technological innovations, intelligence gathering, antiterrorist efforts, and information exchange require more cooperation from the public than has previously been the case. As we have noted, the police cannot be everywhere all the time. In order to be effective in the contemporary world of policing, they must rely more than ever upon the eyes and ears of the public for the information they need to accomplish their tasks. As we look at some of the new strategies in policing, keep in mind the role of COP and POP in the development of these strategies.

❖ Changes and Innovations in Policing Strategies

Intelligence-Led Policing

Intelligence-led policing (ILP) builds on the major developments in law enforcement in the last two decades of the 20th century, including community policing and problem-oriented policing (McGarrel & Freilich, 2007, p. 142). Many describe ILP as a conceptual framework and an "information gathering process that allows police agencies to better understand their crime problems and take a measure of resources available to be able to decide on an enforcement tactic or prevention strategy best designed to control crime" (Ratcliffe & Guidetti, 2008, p. 3). More specifically, according to these authors, Intelligence-led policing is informant and surveillance based with respect to recidivists and serious crime offenders and provides a central crime intelligence mechanism to facilitate objective decision-making (see Around the World). While many of the examples in the literature involve traditional street crimes and gun crimes, ILP assisted in the arrests following the London subway and Madrid train bombings (McGarrel & Freilich, 2007). In these cases, intelligence gatherers utilized surveillance cameras, community informants, and prison officials.

AROUND THE WORLD

Police Detain German Hooligans

Intelligence-led policing in Cologne prevented a flashpoint between German hooligans and England supporters

Swift intervention by the police prevented serious trouble between known German football hooligans and England supporters in Cologne in June of 2006. German police deployed a huge team of plain-clothed spotters around the city after intelligence that known local troublemakers were planning to confront England fans after the match against Sweden.

According to Cologne's police president, police received intelligence during the day that there were several small groups of German hooligans on their way to Cologne to attack British fans.

Eighteen people were arrested by police in the city's old town area, the scene of trouble involving British fans the previous night.

British police officers, who are working in close co-operation with the local authorities, feared that German supporters would try to provoke fights with supporters of the British team. There was praise from the British delegation for the professionalism of the German policing operation in preventing serious trouble.

Source: From "Police Praised as German Hooligans are Detained, by A. Culf, 2008, *Guardian News and Media*. Available from http://www.guardian.co.uk/football/2006/jun/22/worldcup 2006.sport5

Reed (2008) indicated that ILP is a useful strategy that can help law enforcement agencies better prepare for and prevent serious violent crime and acts of terror by taking advantage of the partnerships built through COP. From Reed's perspective, ILP can also benefit from the problem-solving process. ILP is not only consistent with COP but fits well under the COP umbrella. According to Reed, ILP adds a new dimension of community policing based on years of COP experimentation. He concluded that "policing becomes less effective and more likely to drive a wedge between law enforcement and the public when conducted outside a comprehensive COP framework." (p. 25).

❖ PHOTO 11.2   As noted in the preceding section, intelligence-led policing has proven to be quite effective in the prevention and/or successful investigations of major crime incidents, including acts of terrorism.

Situational Crime Prevention

This innovation provides a means of reducing crime by reducing crime opportunities and increasing risk to the offenders (Greene, 2006). Most agree that reducing opportunities and increasing risk center around five major strategies:

- Increasing the effort needed to commit the crime
- Increasing the risk associated with the crime
- Reducing the reward derived from the crime
- Reducing the provocation
- Removing excuses for committing the crime (Cornish and Clarke, 2003)

A decision by New York City authorities to eliminate graffiti on subway cars serves as an example of **situational crime prevention** (Vance & Trani, 2008). The City, instead of expending resources to attempt to apprehend the violators in the act of defacing the cars, decided that any subway car that was painted would not run until completely cleaned. Since graffiti artists derive great pleasure from seeing their artwork travel around New York, the new policy removed the incentive the offenders had to paint the cars (Vance & Trani, 2008). In other words, the officials determined the motivation for the criminal acts, eliminated the rewards, and focused on the opportunity for misconduct and not the individual offenders. Situational crime prevention has been successful in reducing crime rates, though many argue that these types of innovations simply displace criminals into different venues (Holt, Blevins, & Kuhns, 2008). Situational crime prevention can be tied to an approach referred to as **Crime Prevention Through Environmental Design (CPTED),** which is based on the following premise: "The proper design and effective use of the built environment can lead to a reduction in the fear of crime and incidence of crime, and to an improvement in quality of life" (National Institute of Crime Prevention, 2009). In other words, schools, banks, businesses, housing, and so on may be constructed in such a way that potential offenders are discouraged from targeting them as a result of the materials employed, the use of open spaces and lighting, the location of the buildings, and a variety of other factors.

Hot Spot Policing

Crime **hot spots** involve geographic areas with clusters of criminal offenses occurring within a specified interval of time (Institute for Pure and Applied Mathematics, 2007). Patrol officers have always known the location of problems and responded with more aggressive patrol, surveillance of the area, and other methods. However, until recently, police crime prevention strategies did not focus systematically on hot spots and failed to address the underlying conditions that often give rise to high-activity crime locations (Braga, 2008a). Often, the strategic approach to a hot spot location involves the police implementing high-visibility patrol, zero-tolerance disorder enforcement, problem-oriented policing, police crackdowns and raids, intensive enforcement of firearms laws through safety frisks during traffic stops, and other strategies (Braga, 2008a). While there is some question as to what form of hot spot enforcement is the most effective, overall the research revealed that hot spot policing can have a meaningful effect on crime without simply displacing crime to nearby areas (Weisburd & Braga, 2006).

Directed Patrol

To improve the effectiveness and efficiency of random patrol officers, many departments began to use a form of goal setting. The concept of directed patrol developed in response to the findings from a Kansas City study and was an attempt to alter the outcomes associated with random preventative patrol. **Directed patrol** involves increasing police presence in a specified area. Wilson, Hiromoto, Tita, and Riley (2004) believed that directed patrol with a general deterrence strategy would saturate a high crime area, including stops of as many people as possible for all (primarily traffic) offenses. However, directed patrol with a targeted deterrence strategy would focus patrol officers on specific behaviors, individuals, and places. "Under both strategies, perceptions of the probability of punishment for crime generally, and under targeted deterrence, of violent crime in particular, will presumably increase, thereby deterring more individuals from committing crime" (Wilson et al., 2004, p. 12). As an example, the Kansas City Police Department utilized patrol officers in patrol cars who were relieved from the responsibility of responding to calls for service. "The officers were instructed to proactively patrol the neighborhood with a special emphasis on locating and seizing illegally possessed firearms"

(McGarrel, Chermak, & Weiss, 2002, p. i). The increased traffic enforcement led to a 70% increase in seizures of illegal firearms and a 49% decrease in the gun-related crime in this area (Sherman, Shaw, & Rogan, 1995).

Differential Response Policing

Differential response policing involves rejecting the idea of dispatching each request for assistance or service in the order the call is received. Police have consistently responded to one radio call and returned to the vehicle to answer the next call. Police would resolve an assault in progress and then immediately drive to a residence to a take a report of a theft that had occurred three weeks prior. Many began to question the effectiveness and efficiency of an immediate response to every type of call received by the dispatcher. Walker (2008) stated that differential response programs classify calls by their seriousness: (1) an immediate response by a sworn officer, (2) a delayed response by a sworn officer, or (3) no police response, with reports taken over the telephone, by mail, or by having the person come to a police station in person. Some departments support their own Web page and allow the submission of certain types of information on forms that can be downloaded from the Web page or transmitted by fax or e-mail directly to the department. For example, the Sacramento Police Department (SPD) allows residents to report many crimes online through their website. Included are crimes such as financial identity theft, harassment incidents, hit and run, mail theft, theft from a vehicle, threat incidents, vandalism, and violations of restraining orders (Sacramento Police Department [SPD], 2009). The implementation of differential response strategies may increase available time for patrol, allowing police to focus on crime prevention. Police administrators sometimes utilize **community service officers** (CSOs) to enhance differential patrol strategies. CSOs are nonsworn employees who perform duties not requiring a police officer (unlock a vehicle, file insurance reports, document minor traffic accidents). CSOs are distinguished from police officers by different uniforms and patches and by different vehicles.

Saturation Patrol and Crackdowns

Saturation patrol involves adding patrol officers, thus increasing police visibility. Crackdowns involve more planning than mere saturation. *Crackdown* refers to an increase in the number of police targeted toward a specific type of law violation, such as prostitution, drugs, domestic violence, impaired drivers, and speed and seatbelt violators. The intent of these strategies is to prevent criminal activities and decrease citizen fears. When a police crackdown is tightly focused, evidence suggests that immediate crime prevention benefits are likely (Skogan & Frydl, 2004). For example, the Chicago Police Department instituted a curfew crackdown and focused police personnel in areas of high gang activity through tactical teams and foot and bicycle patrols in parks and other areas where people congregate (Sadovi, 2009).

Third Party Policing

Third party policing involves "police efforts to persuade or coerce organizations or nonoffending persons, such as public housing agencies, property owners, parents, health and building inspectors, and business owners to take some responsibility for preventing crime or reducing crime problems" (Buerger & Mazerolle, 1998, p. 301). Often, this involves a level of cooperative consultation with these parties to encourage them to take on more crime control and prevention responsibility (Mazerolle & Ransley, 2006). However, Mazerolle and Ransley (2006) reminded us that the focus of third party policing involves the use of civil, criminal, and regulatory rules and statutes to engage or force third parties into assuming crime control responsibilities. Furthermore, it is this legal basis of third party policing that defines it as a unique strategy and distinguishes it from other policing interventions such as problem-oriented policing (p. 2).

In most cases, successful third party policing strategies result in reduced crime for less money, as civil justice mechanisms usually cost less to utilize compared to criminal justice ones (Meares, 2006). Third party policing is most often utilized in drug prone areas such as parks, malls, and on designated street corners. It has also been deployed at locations such as bus stops prone to robbery, late night bars, and locations that have spray paint available to minors (Mitchell & Casey, 2007). In these types of cases, police work with third party partners to relocate or improve safety at bus stops, reduce hours at late night bars, and restrict the sale of spray paint to minors.

Evidence-Based Policing

Evidence-based policing involves a scientific method of discovery to support an informed decision making process (Stevens, 2008). Police administrators use the best available research results to create policies and regulations and to conduct training. In earlier research, Sherman (1998) noted that police practices are often untested and that in many instances we do not know whether or not these practices work. In many cases, even after research has shown that something doesn't work, we continue to do it as a result of political pressure, inertia or ignorance (Jensen, 2006, p. 1). Today, there are a number of policing practices that have been shown to effectively prevent crime. We also know that police are currently utilizing many of these innovations, but there are some that should be eliminated or modified to better suit the needs of the community. Welsh (2006) asked whether we can expect the police to use the evidence-based model. He believed, based on historical evidence, that the answer to this question is mixed. While there will always be some barriers to research-based policing, as police are asked to do more with less, research will become an even more important part of the decision making process concerning what works and what does not work in policing.

Pulling Levers Policing

Several police agencies have utilized an innovation that has its roots in problem-oriented policing. This intervention is based on the "pulling levers" deterrence strategy, which focuses attention on a small number of chronic offenders responsible for a large share of the crime problems (Braga, 2008b). More specifically, "the approach consists of selecting a particular crime problem, such as youth homicide; convening an interagency working group of law enforcement, social service, and community-based practitioners; conducting research to identify key offenders, groups, and behavior patterns; framing a response to offenders that uses a varied menu of sanctions (pulling levers)" (Braga & Weisburd, 2007, p. 6) to halt the criminal behaviors. Continual, direct communication with these offenders is an important segment of the approach. According to Braga (2008b), an impact evaluation sponsored by the U.S. Department of Justice suggested that pulling levels policing was associated with a decrease in the monthly number of gun homicides in Stockton, California.

Broken Windows Policing

Sometimes known as *zero-tolerance policing,* **broken windows policing** (also discussed in Chapter 6) is based on a theory that suggests that a reduction in minor crimes will lead to a decrease in violent ones (Sousa & Kelling, 2006; Wilson & Kelling, 1982). The approach has remained popular over the past quarter of a century, perhaps in large measure because of its alleged success in reducing crime in New York City in the 1990s. The approach suggests that order maintenance within a community (fixing broken windows before they suggest the possibility of burning down the building) can be a major factor in crime control. Further, maintenance of property suggests that residents have a stake in the neighborhood and, by extension, that they will unite to keep the neighborhood safe and in good repair. Thus, broken windows policing ties in neatly with other COP and POP efforts and, on the surface at least, seems to make sense.

Unfortunately, however, there is little solid evidence that strict police enforcement with respect to minor violations leads to a reduction in the rate of serious crime (Harcourt & Thacher, 2005; Skogan, 1992). The debate over the effectiveness of broken windows policing continues (see You Decide 11.1).

YOU DECIDE 11.1

Go to the website http://www.legalaffairs.org/webexclusive/debateclub_broken windows1005.msp and read the arguments concerning broken windows theory set forth by Harcourt and then Thacher. Which side of the debate do you feel more comfortable with and why?

CompStat

The New York Police Department's Crime Control Model (**CompStat**) is a multifaceted system used to administer police operations. The model is a comprehensive, continuous analysis of results for improvement and achievement of prescribed outcomes (McDonald, 2002, p. 7). CompStat was created to provide police agencies with preliminary crime statistics that would permit tactical planning and deployment of police resources. According to McDonald (2002, p. 8), CompStat is composed of five basic principles: specific objectives, timely and accurate intelligence, effective strategies and tactics, rapid deployment of personnel and resources, and relentless follow-up and assessment. The essence of the CompStat process is to collect, analyze, and map crime data and other essential police performance measures on a regular basis and hold police managers accountable for their performance as measured by these data (Boba, 2009; Philadelphia Police Department, 2009).

Skeptics have noted that the declines in crime in cities that adopted CompStat were part of a broader trend. In fact, Williams (2003) noted possible conflicts between CompStat and community policing. CompStat gives police command staff most of the responsibility for reducing crime, largely excludes patrol officers from the decision-making process, and focuses on crime reduction (Williams, 2003, p. vi). He also argued that community policing devolves decision making to the street, envisions police and the community as partners in problem solving, and makes officers responsible for a broad spectrum of community problems. "At stake here are two vastly different conceptions of the officer's role in modern society" (Williams, 2003, p. vi). Alternatively, Silverman (2006) viewed CompStat as "perhaps the single most important organizational innovation in policing in the latter half of the 20th century" (p. 267). Further, according to Boba (2009, p. 42), CompStat includes quality of life data (an important aspect of COP) in the production of maps and statistics to develop interactive crime prevention and reduction strategies. As with many other innovative policing strategies, the verdict is still out on CompStat.

Incident Command Systems

As indicated in Chapter 6, **Incident Command Systems** involve a "standardized on-scene incident management concept designed specifically to allow responders to adopt an integrated organizational structure equal to the complexity and demands of any single incident or multiple incidents without being hindered by jurisdictional boundaries" (National Response Team, 2000). Such systems are thought to make managing major traffic accidents, terrorist attacks, natural disasters, and hostage situations easier by clarifying the command structure so that personnel from all responding agencies know who is in charge of various functions and the overall incident and who they are to report to concerning various issues that might arise. Incident Command Systems have also been utilized by police at nonemergencies such as large concerts, parades, sporting events, and celebrations. ICS provides a common framework within which people can work together effectively when assessing the situation, developing and implementing strategies, allocating resources, and reassessing. Many incidents require skills and capacities that are beyond those found in a single organization and therefore require a network of responders from multiple agencies who do not routinely work together. The Incident Command System organizes responses around a central command. At the scene of an accident, the central command may consist of police officers with input from medical and fire personnel.

Unfortunately, an Incident Commander often attempts to oversee all of the functions and loses sight of the activities related to logistics, media, and other agencies at the scene. Thus, a key principle of the ICS (and the basis for its success when properly implemented) is that it divides functions modularly and ensures that no one person is trying to wear all the hats.

In many cases, emergency scenarios and even nonemergency events involve multiple agencies. Examples of multiple jurisdictions include the following:

- Geographic boundaries (e.g., two states)
- Government levels (local, state, federal law enforcement)
- Functional responsibilities (police, fire, emergency medical personnel) (National Response Team, 2005)

Dual Career Ladder

Because rank promotions are often directly tied to increases in pay, recognition, and responsibility, police administrators often develop alternative incentives for the traditional rank structures. A **Dual Career Ladder** (DCL) allows a police officer to advance in his current position without being promoted to a higher rank (Zanfardino, 2009). This is especially attractive to officers in small to medium sized departments that have a limited number of supervisor positions. Without the dual career ladder many of these officers feel as though they will never be promoted unless a supervisor retires and they transfer to another police department, remain in their current position and are frustrated or leave policing for a different career. The Dual Career Ladder is in part based on self-motivation and is also attractive to police officers who do not desire to perform management and supervisor functions. Many provide for a salary increase, various methods of recognition by the police department including different uniform or insignia, increased job responsibilities and special assignments. In many cases the process is a win-win for the department and the officers. For example, suppose a police officer has a special interest being certified as an accident reconstructionist. The specialized training

❖ Photo 11.3   As the opportunity of advancement though the ranks is often times limited by the size of the agency and the fact that some officers are happy in their present positions but want to receive raises commensurate with a typical promotion, some police agencies have implemented the "dual ladder" approach.

and knowledge the officer receives along with the desire to achieve benefits the department and the community. In addition, this type of extensive knowledge based training is recognized by most Dual Career Ladders (Louisiana Department of State Civil Service, 2007).

❖ Chapter Summary

Summarizing the current state of policing strategies is a daunting task, as a review of such strategies presented in this chapter indicates. One thing appears certain: Policing continues to evolve as new and different strategies are developed, implemented, and tested in light of new demands for police services. At present, it appears that the community policing and problem-oriented policing models have been incorporated by police administrators across the country, although with diverse modifications. Equally apparent are the trends toward intelligence gathering, technological innovation, and information sharing among police agencies and other governmental agencies. These trends developed in light of the increasingly global nature of concerns about national security and terrorist activities.

In light of these trends, however, we must still ask how far we have come from the traditional reactive, incident-driven model of policing that existed 50 years ago in the United States. Further, in light of considerable evidence that the traditional model of policing is both ineffective and inefficient, what evidence is there to indicate that the innovations occurring produce greater efficiency and effectiveness? Skogan and Frydl (2004) provided a partial answer: "[There is] strong evidence that the more focused and specific strategies of the police and the more they are tailored to the problems they seek to address, the more effective the police will be in controlling crime and disorder" (p. 17). This conclusion appears to lend support to the problem-oriented policing model and its derivatives, and these approaches are in many ways tied into the community policing model that calls upon the public to participate in defining and solving problems. The more intelligence provided concerning such problems, the more easily they are defined and addressed. Perhaps, then, we are making strides in the right direction. In any event, the future evolution of policing will be fascinating to behold.

❖ Key Terms

community-oriented policing

strategic management era

era of homeland security

solution-oriented policing

CAPS: Chicago Alternative Policing Strategy

Westwood COACT (COmmunity ACTion) Mentors Program

intelligence-led policing (ILP)

situational crime prevention

Crime Prevention Through Environmental Design (CPTED)

hot spots

directed patrol

differential response policing

community service officers (CSOs)

saturation patrol

crackdowns

third party policing

evidence-based policing

pulling levers policing

broken windows policing

CompStat

Incident Command Systems

dual career ladder (DCL)

❖ Discussion Questions

1. List and discuss some of the problems characterizing traditional policing. Do you believe any of the policing strategies discussed in this chapter can successfully address these problems? If so, which ones?

2. What is community policing? In your opinion, is it a better approach than traditional policing? Why or why not?

3. Discuss problem-oriented policing and its relationship with other policing strategies.

4. What are some of the criticisms of community policing? In your opinion, are these criticisms justified? Why or why not?

5. What is intelligence-led policing? Is it an improvement over more traditional policing strategies? Why or why not?

6. Discuss the rationale for the development of differential response policing. Given the current economic conditions, does differential response policing make sense?

7. What is the role of researchers in evidence-based policing? Would you expect line police officers to willingly accept the recommendations of police researchers? Why or why not?

8. Under what circumstances are Incident Command or Unified Systems most likely to prove useful? Can you give an example based on personal knowledge or experience?

9. Describe the policing strategy you feel is most appropriate in light of the contemporary global situation with respect to terrorists.

❖ Internet Exercises

1. Go to the website http://www.cops.usdoj.gov/files/RIC/Publications/e040825133-web.pdf and access the article on Hot Spot Policing ("Police Enforcement Strategies to Prevent Crime in Hot Spot Areas") available at that site. Summarize the conclusions of the researchers concerning this policing strategy. Does it appear this strategy is worth pursuing further? Why or why not?

2. Visit the website http://www.hsaj.org/?article=5.2.4. Read the article and answer the following questions based on your reading:

   a. What does the term *global metropolitan policing* mean?

   b. How do local police establish the links necessary to interact with foreign police agencies, diplomatic agencies, and private sector agencies?

   c. Why is global policing important in the pursuit of gang and organized crime?

12

Technology
and the Police

❖ PHOTO 12.1   The "eye in the sky" image portrayed is a good demonstration of the sophisticated technologies available to law enforcement and private security personnel.

Over the past several decades we have seen dazzling technological innovations that seem to occur with ever-increasing speed. To understand the nature and extent of these changes over the past century and a half, consider the following partial list of advances:

Systematic photography for criminal identification was first used in San Francisco in the late 1850s.

Police use of the telegraph began in Albany, New York, in 1877.

One year later, in 1878, the telephone was used in police precinct houses in Washington, D.C.

In 1901, Scotland Yard adopted a fingerprint classification system.

In 1923, the first police crime laboratory in the United States was established by the Los Angeles Police Department, and the teletype machine was inaugurated by the Pennsylvania State Police.

Detroit police began using the one-way radio in 1928.

Boston police began using the two-way radio in 1934.

In 1930, the prototype of the present-day polygraph was developed.

Radar was introduced to traffic law enforcement in 1948.

In 1955, the New Orleans Police Department was one of the first departments in the country to install an electronic data processing machine.

The first computer assisted dispatching system was installed in the St. Louis police department in the 1960s, and in 1966 The National Law Enforcement Telecommunications System, a message-switching facility linking all state police computers except Hawaii, was established.

The FBI inaugurated the National Crime Information Center (NCIC), the first national law enforcement computing center, in 1967. NCIC is a computerized national filing system on wanted persons and stolen vehicles, weapons, and other items of value.

The number 911 for emergencies was first used in 1968.

In the late 1960s, attempts to develop riot control technologies and use-of-force alternatives were initiated. Wooden, rubber, and plastic bullets; tranquilizer guns; electrified batons; strobe lights that caused giddiness, fainting, and nausea; and stun guns were tested. One of the few successful technologies to emerge was the TASER, which shoots tiny darts into victims, delivering a 50,000-volt shock.

During the 1970s, the large-scale computerization of U.S. police departments began. Major computer-based applications included computer assisted dispatch (CAD), management information systems, centralized call collection using three-digit phone numbers (911), and centralized integrated dispatching of police, fire, and medical services.

In 1972, the development of lightweight, flexible, and comfortable protective body armor for the police (Kevlar) took place.

In the mid-1970s, the study of night vision gear for police officers led to widespread use of the devices.

The first fingerprint reader was installed at the FBI in 1975, and in 1979, the Royal Canadian Mounted Police implemented the first actual automatic fingerprint identification system (AFIS).

In 1982, pepper spray was first developed.

In the 1990s, more than 90% of U.S. police departments serving a population of 50,000 or more were using computers for applications such as criminal investigations, budgeting, dispatch, manpower allocation, and to map and analyze crime patterns.

In 1996, the National Academy of Sciences announced that there was no longer any reason to question the reliability of DNA evidence.

Source: Adapted from *The Evolution and Development of Police Technology,* by Seaskate, Inc., 1998, National Institute of Justice.

In the years since these developments occurred, the rapid pace of change has continued (as indicated in the following sections of this chapter). The Internet has become an invaluable communication and information resource. Wireless computer and cell phone applications appear unlimited, digital technology in televisions and cameras advance at a rapid pace, global positioning systems are now standard equipment in many vehicles and on many cell phones, and all of these are linked together not only on a national level, but internationally. These dramatic changes have affected the police perhaps as much as any other institution, and often in very positive ways. However, as is the case with technological changes at the societal level, not all the changes in policing have been positive. Proper deployment of technological devices in policing, whether in the public or private sector, requires officer training, judicious discretionary behavior, and a thorough understanding of the legal and ethical issues involved. (For an interesting discussion of the impact of technology on policing, see Chan, 2001.)

All of us who use the new convenient technologies have to be concerned about their misuse as well. Internet users risk hackers obtaining their personal information and using it for illegitimate purposes. When this occurs, the police may become involved in investigating a variety of Internet crimes. This is also the case when computers are used to access child pornography, to form conspiracies to commit financial crimes, or to steal identities. Cell phones and computers may be used to facilitate terrorism, and global positioning systems can be used to locate the exact positions of police cars to facilitate crimes in locations with no police present. Increasingly, citizens are worried about the misuse of technological devices to track their every movement and invade their privacy. For example, the ability to hear and "see" through walls may be used to conduct surveillance on us in our most private moments without our knowledge or consent.

Issues involving the use of technological devices in policing are not unique to the United States, as is indicated by the Around the World feature.

AROUND THE WORLD

Police Given Spy Powers

Federal and state police in Australia can now use computer spyware to gather evidence in a broad range of investigations. The Surveillance Devices Act allows police to obtain a warrant to use software surveillance technologies, including systems that track and log keystrokes on a computer keyboard.

In addition to redefining the kinds of surveillance devices that can be used, the Surveillance Devices Act allows surveillance for offences far less serious than those allowed under previous legislation. Previously, warrants to intercept telecommunications could only be obtained to investigate offences carrying a maximum jail term of seven years or more. However, Surveillance Devices Act warrants can be obtained for offences carrying a maximum sentence of three years.

Warrants can now be obtained if an officer has reasonable grounds to suspect an offence has been or might be committed and a surveillance device is necessary to obtain evidence. Warrants can also be obtained in child recovery cases.

Critics fear police will be able to secretly install software to monitor email, online chats, word processor and spreadsheets entries and even bank personal identification numbers and passwords.

A spokesperson for the federal Attorney-General, said there were protections in the legislation, including reporting to Parliament and allowing reviews by the Ombudsman.

Source: Adapted from "Police Given Computer Spy Powers," by R. O'Neill, 2004, *The Sydney Morning Herald*. Available from http://www.smh.com.au/news/National/Police-given-computer-spy-powers/2004/12/12/1102786954590.html

In the remainder of this chapter, we discuss a number of technological changes and their impact on the police, both public and private. Keep in mind that it is impossible to describe all of the technological changes taking place in policing, so we have focused on some of the more important ones.

❖ Computers

Over four decades have passed since LEAA first began its effort to bring technology to the fight against crime. Computers, and especially wireless computers, have become an integral part of the arsenal in managing the police and in the fight against crime. Officers use computers to access a number of databases, to fill out paperwork, and to record witness statements while they're still at the scene. They can also use wireless technology to upload digital photos they've taken of crime scenes and to check license plate numbers or suspect IDs against a database of stolen cars or outstanding warrants. They can even get a suspect's criminal record and photograph on the screen in front of them, without having to relay information through a dispatcher.

Mobile Data Terminals (MDTs) in patrol vehicles have been one of the most important pieces of technology for patrol officers since the introduction of radio communications. In the Philadelphia Police Department (Philadelphia Police Department [PPD], 2010b), for example, terminals in patrol MDTs communicate with the city's main computer system using a **Computer-Aided Dispatch (CAD)** system that operates on a cellular radio frequency. In addition to receiving radio assignments using voice communication, officers are able to view assignments on the MDT screen and have car-to-car communication capability. Officers can also receive certain radio assignments by MDT, thereby keeping voice communications to a minimum and security levels high. Data communications via an MDT have several distinct advantages over voice communications (PPD, 2010b):

- Supervisors are able to review pending assignments, check the status of all patrol units, and communicate directly with any unit by using the MDT. This permits supervisors to spot potential problems and take a proactive approach to managing their resources and workload.
- Transmissions are secure, eliminating concerns about unauthorized scanning and interception of sensitive transmissions.

- MDTs increase available airtime, freeing existing voice frequencies for both officers and dispatchers when engaging in priority transmissions.
- Officers no longer have to 'standby' while other officers and dispatchers are engaged with priority transmissions. Officers have the ability to recall up-to-the-minute pertinent data, premise history, and information on radio assignments.
- Queries of wanted persons, stolen vehicles, or PCIC (Pennsylvania Crime Information Center)/NCIC (National Crime Information Center) status can be done directly by an officer in an MDT-equipped vehicle. Officers can query as many vehicles and personnel as required, whenever or wherever needed.
- Information is accessed and received faster and more efficiently. Unlike our present voice communications, all MDT-equipped vehicles can make PCIC/NCIC queries simultaneously.

Further, use of MDTs allows for the collection of time utilization statistics, which enable better time management of officers and, thus, greater efficiency. In addition, dispatch related transactions such as dispatch receipt, status updating, busy updating, and on view and traffic stop updating, as well as access to other units' statuses, to other complaints, to location information (hazards/alerts, history, contacts, etc.), optional map display, and unit history are all possible (PPD, 2010b; Paterra, 2010).

In November, 2009, the City of Paris, Texas Police Department successfully implemented the **Automatic Vehicle Location (AVL)** system, completing the integration of CAD, records, mobile, and AVL—including mapping—and many other integrated features and functional tools such as crime analysis. The AVL system provides a real-time picture of where all on-duty vehicles are located, both for dispatchers and all other mobile units using the technology. The system uses a **Global Positioning System (GPS)** unit in each vehicle that reports its position to a computer in dispatch and displays that position on a map. GPS involves a combination of hardware and software that utilizes satellite technology to provide the latitude and longitude of specific locations (Boba, 2009). This aids dispatchers when they receive a high priority call by permitting them to look at the map and determine which officer is closest to the call location. At the same time, patrol officers also see a real-time AVL map in their vehicles and can decide who is closest to the location in question (Paterra, 2010). The technology is particularly useful for remote, often rural areas that lack specific addresses, including large forest preserve areas.

An additional component associated with the AVL is the **Geographic Information System (GIS).** A GIS is a computer program that captures, analyzes, and stores spatial data. These programs make it easy to visualize and interpret geographic information and examine the effects of crime, traffic safety, home foreclosures, and urban planning to mention a few (National Institute of Justice [NIJ], 2009a). Currently, the Dallas Police Department has AVL technology in almost every patrol vehicle and has implemented a CompStat program that focuses on directing patrol to specific problem prone areas (NIJ, 2009a). Although Geographic Information Systems (GIS) are in use in approximately 63% of large police departments, researchers still know little about the location of police officers when they are not responding to calls for service (National Institute of Justice, 2009a).

In Chicago, beginning in 2005, police officers gained access to some 5 million mug shots and other computerized crime information without having to return to the station (Spielman, 2004). Wireless portable data terminals gave police officers on the street instant access to **Illinois Citizen and Law Enforcement Analysis and Reporting (I-CLEAR)**, a computerized data warehouse designed to allow them to search for suspects based on nicknames, tattoos, country of origin, vehicle make and model, and other characteristics. Files are said to contain everything from information on gang membership and a history of previous police calls at an address to crime reports, arrest warrants and citations, and vital homeland security information, including watch lists and terrorism alerts (Spielman, 2004). Police officers are able to show mug shots to crime victims while they remain at a crime scene and to enter case reports into the system from their vehicles, disposing of a good deal of paperwork. According to DuBois, Skogan, Hartnett, Bump, and Morris (2007), "I-CLEAR represents an unprecedented partnership between the Illinois State Police (ISP) and the Chicago Police Department, one that promises to position Illinois well in the regional data-sharing arena." Further assessment of the progress of the I-Clear system has shown that not all features of the system are operational, but the potential for further development is clear (DuBois et al., 2007).

Not all the effects of computerization of police agencies are positive. For example, Nunn (2001) found that "Highly computerized cities reported larger shares of employees in technical positions, spent more per capita, and reported fewer officers per capita than cities with lower computerization levels" (p. 221). Overall, however, few would argue that the costs of computerizing police agencies outweigh the benefits.

Polygraph technology is yet another area in which innovations are occurring. The **polygraph** is a device that registers involuntary physical processes such as pulse rate and perspiration and is often used in an attempt to detect whether or not a suspect is telling the truth (thus, it is often called a *lie detector*). Frequently used in both the public and private sector for purposes of hiring and promotion, polygraphs were traditionally instruments with needles scribbling lines on a single strip of scrolling paper. These analog polygraphs were used until the 1980s but have now been replaced by digital computerized equipment. The scrolling paper has been replaced with sophisticated algorithms and computer monitors. Such computerized polygraph systems allow a trained examiner to do voice and audio recordings, to read a subject's pulse, and to gauge voice responses and the usual markers through a USB port connected to a computer. Algorithms allow comparisons of the data collected from a suspect with information known to be truthful and deceptive. In theory, at least, the computerization of the polygraph makes it extremely difficult for a suspect to deceive the instrument (Chansanchai, 2008).

In yet a further advance of polygraph technology, the Pentagon issued handheld lie detectors to U.S. soldiers in Afghanistan to screen local police officers, interpreters, and allied forces for access to U.S. Military bases (Deedman, 2008). Such handheld devices are available in other settings as well. For example, portable devices utilizing voice tension technology to measure varying degrees of vibration in the voice are available. Changes in vibrations are alleged to be caused by the person being tested going from a state of calm to a state of nervousness. These devices may even be connected to cell phones and used to measure changes in vibrations at a distance (Brickhouse Security, 2010). Whether or not the results of tests using these devices will turn out to be reliable remains to be seen.

Other police agencies are also using computer programs in innovative ways. For example, the Clearwater Police Department is addressing language problems through the use of Rosetta Stone, as indicated in Case in Point 12.1.

☞ **CASE IN POINT 12.1**

**Clearwater Police Use Computer Language
Program Rosetta Stone to Enhance Communication**

It is estimated that about 18 percent of Clearwater's population is Hispanic. Since many of these Hispanics speak little or no English, Clearwater police frequently find themselves in situations where knowing Spanish can help them assist victims and investigate crimes more quickly.

To help officers better communicate with Hispanics and to foster more trust in the Hispanic community, the police department is implementing a Spanish training program using Rosetta Stone language learning software. Officers will be allowed to use the courseware three hours a week while on duty and will have access to the program anytime while off duty, making it as convenient as possible for the officers to learn Spanish.

While the program is relatively new to Clearwater, other police agencies across the country have used Rosetta Stone to help their officers learn Spanish.

Source: Excerpts from "Clearwater Police Use Computer Language Program Rosetta Stone to Enhance Communication," by L. Helfand, 2010, *St. Petersburg Times*. Available from http://www.tampabay.com/news/publicsafety/article1072347.ece

---

❖ Video Cameras: Safety and Accountability

Police use of cameras has proliferated dramatically over the past two decades. As digital technology has become increasingly available, the use of cameras to record and store evidence has become invaluable to the police. Cameras are now attached to everything from patrol cars to uniform lapels to Tasers, and they are increasingly deployed by both public and private police to assist in the surveillance of property, traffic patterns, crowds, airports and other transportation hubs, and more. Thermal imaging and infrared cameras are also used by the police during searches by both land and air. For example, indoor marijuana growing operations can be located by thermal imaging, but the U.S. Supreme Court ruled in *Kyllo v. U.S.* that police are required to obtain a search warrant before examining a private dwelling with this technology (Wilson & Spencer, 2001). The use of closed circuit television (**CCTV**) in England has been widely publicized, as has the use of "**red light cameras**" (which record stop light violations at intersections) and police in-car cameras. In the United States, systems also exist today that can photograph suspects who are vandalizing property and notify the police that the vandalism is in progress (Schultz, 2008). Talking surveillance cameras (**graffiti cameras**) also exist, which warn intruders to leave the area and that their photograph has been obtained. In the following paragraphs, some of the uses of cameras in policing are examined.

Police vehicles are increasingly being fitted with video cameras (with sound recording capability) that can record activity inside or outside the car. Such cameras record information that can later be used to determine whether or not departmental policy was followed, whether harassment of officers or those they encounter occurred, whether laws were violated, the identities of those involved in an encounter, facts about the location of a stop, and the make and license number of a vehicle stopped by the police. Evidentiary information recorded can later be used in court to prove or disprove witness statements or can be evaluated as evidence in itself.

In 2002, the International Association of Chiefs of Police (IACP) conducted research to evaluate the impact of in-car camera systems on state police and highway patrol agencies. Study results, based on surveys, focus groups, and on-site interviews, indicated that the cameras were of considerable value to the agencies deploying them in that they did the following:

- Enhanced officer safety
- Improved agency accountability
- Reduced agency liability
- Simplified incident review
- Enhanced new recruit and inservice training (post-incident use of videos)
- Improved community and media perceptions
- Strengthened police leadership
- Advanced prosecution/case resolution
- Enhanced officer performance and professionalism
- Increased homeland security
- Upgraded technology policies and procedures (IACP, 2005)

The authors of the report also found that agencies sometimes failed to view the entire camera system continuum by neglecting components such as storing, filing, and retrieving video evidence. Some agencies also failed to gather sufficient information on officer attitudes, long term equipment maintenance costs, and other policy areas (IACP, 2005; see also Maghan, O'Reilly, & Chong Ho Shon, 2002).

❖ Eavesdropping Technology

Wiretapping originated before the invention of the modern telephone, when telegraph wires were literally tapped to intercept communications. Statutes prohibiting the use of wiretaps in this regard were enacted in the 1860s, and from the 1890s until the present day it has been illegal in the United States for unauthorized persons to listen in on or record private phone conversations.

However, in 1928, the United States Supreme Court approved the practice of wiretapping by the police and other government officials, and it was not until the 1960s that the requirement that police personnel obtain a court order to listen in on private conversations (under most circumstances) came into existence. Specifically, in 1968, Congress passed the Omnibus Crime Control and Safe Streets Act of 1968, which established strict procedures for conducting interception of wire, oral, and electronic communications (Harris, 2001).

With the development and expansion of the Internet, new concerns arose. Because Internet communications are not actually verbal conversation, they were not protected by the same laws that protected traditional phone use. This became and remains a concern because government officials as well as others can view information transmitted over the Internet using sophisticated technology. In 1986, the U.S. government enacted the **Electronic Communications Privacy Act (ECPA)** wiretapping regulation that protects e-mail, pagers, and cell phone calls (Harris, 2001).

The events of September 11, 2001, as indicated throughout this text, changed things with respect to electronic eavesdropping. In October 2001, former President Bush signed legislation expanding the ability to tap telephones and track Internet usage in the hunt for terrorists. The bill, known as the USA Patriot Act, gave federal authorities much wider latitude in monitoring Internet usage and expanded the way such data is shared among different agencies. Under the **Foreign Intelligence Surveillance Act (FISA)** for example, the purpose of electronic surveillance must be to obtain intelligence in the United States on foreign powers (such as enemy agents or spies) or individuals connected to international terrorist groups. The government must show the FISA Court probable cause that the target of the surveillance is a foreign power or agent of a foreign power in order to obtain authorization to eavesdrop. However, if the Attorney General determines that an emergency exists, he or she may authorize the emergency employment of electronic surveillance before obtaining the necessary authorization from the FISA court. Having taken such emergency measures, the Attorney General must notify a judge of the court not more than 72 hours after the authorization of such surveillance.

Since the 1980s, National Security Letters (NSL), which are written demands from the FBI that compel Internet service providers, credit companies, financial institutions, and others to hand over confidential records about their customers (such as subscriber information, phone numbers, e-mail addresses, websites visited, and more), have been used to collect extensive information concerning electronic communications. The Patriot Act (discussed earlier in the text) expanded the kinds of records that could be obtained with an NSL. These letters do not require court approval. The FBI need merely assert that the information requested in the NSL is relevant to an investigation and recipients are prohibited from disclosing that they have received the NSL (Zetter, 2009).

In 2010, President Obama signed a one-year extension of some sections of the USA Patriot Act (which had previously been extended by the Bush administration) without approving any new limits on the provisions allowing the government, with permission from the FISA court, "to obtain roving wiretaps over multiple communication devices, seize suspects' records without their knowledge, and conduct surveillance of a so-called 'lone wolf,' or someone deemed suspicious but without any known ties to an organized terrorist group" (Farrell, 2010, para. 1).

In keeping with the changes occurring following 9/11, the FBI developed "a sophisticated, point-and-click surveillance system that performs instant wiretaps on almost any communications device" (Singel, 2007, p. 1). **The Digital Collection System Network (DCSNet)**, "connects FBI wiretapping rooms to switches controlled by traditional land-line operators, internet-telephony providers and cellular companies" (Singel, 2007, p. 1).

DCSNet consists of software that collects, sifts, and stores phone numbers, phone calls, and text messages.

> The system directly connects FBI wiretapping outposts around the country to a far-reaching private communications network . . . the surveillance system[s] let FBI agents play back recordings even as they are being captured (like TiVo), create master wiretap files, send digital recordings to translators, track the rough location of targets in real time using cell-tower information, and even stream intercepts outward to mobile surveillance vans. (Singel, 2007 p. 1)

As might be expected, the expansion of government powers authorized in post 9/11 legislation has caused considerable concern. Can any of us be certain that conversations we regard as private are not being monitored? Should we give up some degree of privacy in the interests of homeland security? How far should invasion of privacy go? Should we accept not only having our communications monitored but permitting full-body scans at airports? These and other questions related to technological advances and the potential for abuse by police and other government (and perhaps some private) officials are complex and not easily answered.

❖ **Photo 12.2**   DCS 3000 Network Map: "The FBI's private, encrypted backbone, DCSNet, connects 37 FBI field offices, according to some documents. Other documents suggest the network now extends to 52 field offices, including locations in Alaska and Puerto Rico. This enhanced image is based on black-and-white FBI documents."

❖ Computers and Cameras

In combination, computers and cameras have proven useful to the police. For example, in Murrysville, Pennsylvania, police vehicles are equipped with laptops that both receive live video feeds from school buildings in the district and are able to access electronic floor plans and building diagrams. According to Chief Tom Seefield, "We're trying to be pro-active and be prepared for anything that lies ahead for us. If we have an incident in the school district, such as a gunman or somebody in there trying to kidnap a child, we would be able to go on the laptops, and the cameras in each school giving us the ability to get a live video feed. . . . That gives us eyes from outside the building to help us better prepare and plan prior to entering the building" (Paterra, 2010). In police departments in Denver, Washington, DC, Ann Arbor, Michigan, and Louisville, Kentucky among others, mobile cameras read license plates of parked and moving vehicles and compare them to vehicle databases (Hughes, 2010). The system, known as **License Plate Recognition (LPR)** helps the police fight motor vehicle theft and identify unregistered cars, and it may be of use in AMBER Alert searches as well. LPRs are one version of **Automatic Number Plate Recognition (ANPR)**, which uses optical character recognition to read the license plates on vehicles. The system takes pictures of a vehicle license plate and processes the numbers and letters using the optical recognitions software against a known database (Schultz, 2008). While some are concerned about potential misuses as revenue generators and as devices to track vehicle movements for questionable purposes, the technology appears to be gaining acceptance across the country (Hughes, 2010).

Internet Protocol (IP) cameras are basically closed-circuit television (CCTV) cameras that use the Internet to transmit image data and control signals over an Ethernet link. These cameras are commonly used by the police for surveillance and are typically deployed in a network with a digital video recorder (DVR) or a network video recorder (NVR) to form a video surveillance system (NetworkCameraReviews.com, 2009). Output from multiple cameras can be monitored from remote locations and images stored securely for future use. Police applications include traffic monitoring through the use of cameras placed at appropriate intervals along roadways, in subways, or in tunnels. IP camera networks can also be used to monitor employees in cases involving theft, compliance with regulatory requirements, and in cases where employees are suspected of conspiring to commit crimes or acts of terrorism. Further, the cameras can be used to provide views of remote sites that are not easily accessible or are extremely dangerous, such as suspected terrorist training camps (Connect802, n.d.). Thus, IP applications cover the gamut of police activities, ranging from local traffic control through Homeland Security surveillance of suspects and sensitive locations. As is the case with all surveillance technology, opportunities for abuse using IP technology certainly exist.

❖ Crime Mapping and CompStat

Crime Mapping

Crime mapping has long been associated with crime analysis and is a process that uses a geographic information system to conduct spatial analyses of crime problems and other police issues. **Crime analysis** is the systematic study of crime and disorder problems to assist police in criminal apprehension, crime and disorder reduction, crime prevention, and evaluation (Boba, 2009).

Some of the earliest crime mapping involved sticking different colored pins into a wall map to indicate the location of a reported crime. The problem with wall maps is they are difficult to keep updated and accurate and can only display limited data (Boba, 2001). Another form of crime mapping involves computer maps, which are similar to wall maps since a computer is used to place a point at a specific location. As with the wall map, the computer map does not involve analysis of the specific location. The third type of crime mapping, briefly discussed earlier in this chapter, involves a GIS and is different from the pin and computer maps. The GIS "allows an analyst to view data behind the geographic features, combine various features, manipulate the data and maps, and perform statistical functions (Boba, 2001, p. 19).

For example, at the Jacksonville (FL) County Sheriff's Office, the Crime Analysis Unit cleans, classifies, and mergers data from multiple tables in the Record Management System (White & Wiles, 2009). This information is geocoded and delivered to a base map containing a variety of geographic layers. The analysts at Jackson County employ geospatial and temporal techniques to identify emerging crime patterns and at the same time analyze long term crime problems. According to White and Wiles (2009), the County uses criminal incidents, field interviews, arrests, and other data in their analysis.

Additional analysis often involves the creation of **density analysis maps,** which are commonly referred to as *hot spots* (Bair, 2009). Density analysis can reveal areas of elevated crime activity and can also be used to perform geographic profiling. The National Institute of Justice (2009b) discovered that the statistical program CrimeStat and a desktop GIS will permit police to accomplish the following tasks:

- Identify and analyze hot spots
- Plot crime incidents on a map
- View crime concentrations over a large area
- Track offender behavior over time
- Estimate a serial offender's residence
- Study routes for high-speed chases

The interest in crime mapping and analysis has not been confined to police agencies. See Case In Point 12.2 concerning the use of crime mapping services by citizens.

☞ CASE IN POINT 12.2

Americans are increasing tracking crime trends as police departments install Internet-based crime mapping services. The services obtain live feeds from police agencies and immediately post them to their Internet site.

Many crime mapping sites were developed in 2007 with the addition of Google maps. "An Internet-enabled mapping service that provides satellite images for most urban areas, Google maps gave crime mapping a cost-effective foundation. The crime mapping services were then able to focus exclusively on software that recognized addresses and build systems capable of pulling data from police records."

(Continued)

(Continued)

As an example, one property manager in Maryland checks CrimeReports.com every morning to keep watch on her apartment units and townhouses. If a crime occurs in the areas she manages, she immediately notifies civic groups and homeowners. "That helps prevent more break-ins which leads to lower maintenance costs at the properties."

Source: From "New Programs Put Crime Stats on the Map," by B. White, 2009, *The Wall Street Journal,* p. D1.

CompStat

CompStat, which stands for computer statistics, can be summarized in one statement: "collect, analyze, and map crime data and other essential police performance measures on a regular basis and hold police managers accountable for their performance as measured by these data" (PPD, 2010a, p.1). (See Case In Point 12.3 concerning the implementation of CompStat in the Philadelphia Police Department.) The philosophy behind CompStat is composed of four principles and usually involves more than only the analysis of crime data:

- Accurate and timely intelligence: Police officers need to understand when, how, where, and by whom various crimes have been committed. Often, detectives have information on suspects or crime trends and patterns but the street patrol officers who may be in contact with potential suspects have no idea concerning the information possessed by detectives, nor the need to clear a case. (San Francisco Police Department, 2010)
- Effective tactics: Once the intelligence is collected, it is important to develop comprehensive, flexible, and adaptable tactics that recognize changing trends.
- Rapid deployment of personnel and resources: The deployment of personnel to a crime or quality of life issue "must be rapid and focused."
- Relentless follow-up and assessment: Assessment and follow-up are important to ensure recurring and similar problems have been addressed. (PPD, 2010a)

☞ CASE IN POINT 12.3

CompStat meetings occur every Thursday morning for approximately three hours in the Philadelphia Police Department. Maps prepared by the Mapping Unit are projected on a screen, and District Commanders are required to discuss what the maps portray. The data presented and discussed is usually seven days old. This provides the commanders with time to "analyze the results of deployment strategies, disposition of offenders, multiple clearances, crime patterns and other relevant data to prepare for the COMPSTAT meeting."

Hot spots or areas where serious crime has occurred and quality of life problem areas are discussed at the COMPSTAT meetings. Commanders present a plan
for addressing these problems that are indicated on the maps.

"Every fourth week the meeting focuses on performance of the Department's
specialized units, including SWAT, Canine, Mounted, Aviation, Bomb Disposal,
Environmental Response, Marine, and Accident Investigation.

The Department is extending intranet access to permit daily district-level
crime mapping that will improve deployment of personnel. In other words, a
commander can get online and "create, view and print crime maps using data
layers to look at their own crime patterns on a daily basis." Commanders have
the discretion to deploy resources to the areas where they believe they will be
the most effective.

Source: Adapted From CompStat Process, by the Philadelphia Police Department, 2010a.
Available from http://www.ppdonline.org/hq_compstat.php

Is there a relationship between CompStat and community policing? Willis,
Mastrofski, and Weisburd (2003, p. vi) concluded that CompStat provides commanders with most of the responsibility for reducing crime, largely excludes patrol officers
from the decision making process, and focuses on crime reduction. However, they also
recognized that community policing transmits decision making to patrol officers on
the street and makes officers responsible for responding to community concerns. In
light of this gap between these two models, Geoghegan (2006) discovered that even
though CompStat does not necessarily involve the community, police commanders
utilizing CompStat identify problems and develop crime control and quality-of-life
strategies that involve input and cooperation from community residents.

According to Firman (2006, p. 457), CompStat involves elements of leadership,
information technology, problem solving, proactive methods for addressing crime and
incident trends, and the mobilization and allocation of resources. Individually, none
of these elements were unknown before CompStat was implemented by the New York
Police Department. However, the popularity enjoyed by CompStat is due to the combination of many management and leadership features into a package that maximizes
those elements (Firman, 2006). The importance of leadership to CompStat was
emphasized by DeLorenzi, Shane, and Amendola (2006), who discovered that when
"commanders gather and use accurate and timely intelligence, devise effective tactics,
and relentlessly follow-up on tasks, they have an opportunity to showcase and further
develop their leadership skills, abilities, competence and initiative." (p. 5)

According to Geoghegan (2006), the effectiveness of CompStat in reducing crime
has been validated through numerous statistical data since the inception of the
process. For example, as of 2003, serious crime in New York City declined for the 13th
year. However, some criticize CompStat since New York may not be representative of
other agencies and, furthermore, the United States has experienced a general decline
in reported crime (Geoghegan, 2006). Even though there has been dispersion of the

CompStat process, many agencies have not embraced it. For example, in a 2006 study conducted by the Maryland Safe Neighborhoods Initiative, only 15% of the police and sheriffs' agencies had adopted a CompStat model (University of Maryland, 2010). However, the study discovered that 43% of the departments had a person assigned to crime analysis, 64% were using hot spot policing, and 71% were conducting problem solving activities. In other words, a higher percentage of police departments possessed programs that supported CompStat than actually implemented the CompStat process (University of Maryland, 2010).

Some municipalities have developed their own computer statistic process. For example, Baltimore created the Office of CitiStat, which evaluates policies and procedures practiced by city departments that deliver services from criminal investigations to filling potholes (City of Baltimore, 2010). Baltimore analysts examine data, and city agencies participate in a presentation format that ensures accountability.

❖ Cell Phones

Since we are familiar with many of the various uses of cell phones, we will limit our discussion of them here. A **cell phone** is a portable phone that operates over a cellular network consisting of switching points and base stations and can be used to perform many functions in addition to the standard voice function. These include, among others, text messaging, e-mail, access to the Internet, gaming, Bluetooth, infrared, camera with video recorder, sending and receiving photos and videos, operation of an MP3 player, radio, and GPS. In addition, they can be used as alarms, to keep memos, to read documents, to watch streaming video, as wireless modems for personal computers, and to record conversations.

Police officers often use cell phones rather than landlines to conduct follow-up investigations with victims, witnesses, and suspects; to contact other agencies; to speak with other on-duty officers about ongoing events when they exchange sensitive information; or when they don't want to generate radio traffic so that radio channels will stay open for 911 calls. Even if officers use the radio to let other officers and supervisors know they are responding to an incident, they may contact each other via cell phone to develop a plan of action. This is sometimes done to prevent people using police scanners from hearing what they have to say (cell phone communications may also be subject to some types of scanning, but generally speaking this is more difficult than with radio communications).

Police officers also use cell phones as sources of information for investigative purposes. For instance, the law (*United States v. Finley, 2007*) allows police to search through cell phone contents of people who have been stopped for arrestable traffic offenses. In addition, police now have the ability to track cell phone callers on maps or aerial photos with a great deal of accuracy if they have the proper equipment and software (Santiago, 2009). When an emergency call comes into the dispatch center, the system locates the caller and transmits latitude and longitude to computers. Almost immediately, a map appears with a zooming function that may even allow the dispatcher to view the caller on the map. Some software has the ability to show locations on aerial photos so a dispatcher can find the nearest GPS-equipped police cars. This type of technology greatly improves the chances of finding missing persons (who have and use cell phones) (Santiago, 2009).

❖ Fingerprints, DNA, and Other Biological Identifiers

Fingerprints

Fingerprints, since they identify unique individuals, have been used for many years to identify victims, suspects, and perpetrators. They are also used to access secure facilities and equipment and to check for criminal records. Fingerprints of criminals have been routinely kept on file by the police for years, but because they had to be checked by hand for a match and because the files were often maintained locally and not shared with other agencies, they were seldom utilized to their full potential. Currently, however, prints are stored as electronic pictures on computers and are accessible to police around the world. Computers can now rapidly scan millions of files and can locate possible matches. Today, if a suspect's fingerprints are on file somewhere in the world, it is likely they can be located and the suspect identified (Worsley School, 2001).

The **Integrated Automated Fingerprint Identification System (IAFIS)** is a national fingerprint and criminal history system maintained by the FBI. "The IAFIS provides automated fingerprint search capabilities, latent searching capability, electronic image storage, and electronic exchange of fingerprints and responses, 24 hours a day, 365 days a year. As a result of submitting fingerprints electronically, agencies receive electronic responses to criminal ten-print fingerprint submissions within two hours and within 24 hours for civil fingerprint submissions" (FBI, 2008). While some local and state police agencies might dispute the speed with which requests are processed, likely none would disagree that fingerprint technology has improved dramatically.

Another development in fingerprint technology is the increasingly widespread use of **fingerprint scanners**. A fingerprint scanner system has two basic jobs—it needs to get an image of your finger, and it needs to determine whether the pattern of ridges and valleys in this image matches the pattern of ridges and valleys in prescanned images.

Most fingerprint scanners use either optical scanning or capacitance scanning to procure the image. Once the scanner processor ascertains that a clear image has been captured, it compares the print to stored data. This is done using algorithms to compare specific features of the fingerprint, known as minutiae. To get a match, the scanner system has to find a sufficient number of minutiae patterns that the two prints have in common (Harris, n.d.). The uses of fingerprint scanners in both private and public policing are numerous, with the most clear-cut advantages being the obviation of ink and paper prints and the speed with which analysis can be accomplished.

DNA

Aside from fingerprints, the most compelling use of forensic evidence might well be DNA evidence, which can be used to identify a perpetrator—even decades after the commission of a crime (Moser, 2008). **Deoxyribonucleic acid (DNA)** is one of two types of molecules that encode genetic information. While only about one tenth of a percent of DNA (about 3 million bases) differs from one person to the next, scientists can use these variable regions to generate a DNA profile of an individual, using samples from blood, bone, hair, and other body tissues and products. In criminal cases, this generally involves obtaining samples from crime-scene evidence and a suspect, extracting the DNA, and analyzing it for the presence of a set of specific DNA regions (markers) (Human Genome Project Information, 2009).

While the analysis technologies used in forensic DNA investigations are beyond the scope of this text, there is little doubt that proper collection and preservation of DNA evidence by crime scene technicians or investigators can both help convict the guilty and exonerate the innocent. According to the Innocence Project, for example, some 200 male prisoners who have served a combined total of 2,496 years have been exonerated by DNA evidence (International Biosciences, 2010). While it may be impossible to determine the number of suspects convicted as a result of DNA analysis, the number is certainly significant, and even more advanced technology appears to be on the horizon. It is predicted that DNA chip technology (in which thousands of short DNA sequences are embedded in a tiny chip) will enable much more rapid, inexpensive analyses using many more probes and raising the odds against coincidental matches (National Human Genome Research Institute, 2009).

Still other developments that may aid police officers in apprehending offenders hold promise for the future. For example, while fingerprints can be smudged or impossible to obtain on some surfaces, and while blood, tissue, semen, or saliva may not always be present in sufficient quantities for analytic purposes, each of us leaves a unique trail of bugs (in this case, hand germs or bacteria) behind as we conduct our daily activities. Some have predicted that these germs will become a valuable new tool for forensic scientists ("Hand Germs as Evidence," 2010). These bacteria are abundant, can be lifted from small areas, and remain essentially unchanged after two weeks at room temperature. According to some researchers, it may be easier to recover bacterial DNA than human DNA from touched surfaces, although they caution that additional studies are needed to confirm initial results ("Hand Germs as Evidence," 2010).

Perhaps a caution is in order here. Technological and scientific advances make it possible to collect and preserve a wide variety of types of evidence, but the probative value of such evidence varies from case to case. In an attempt to establish some degree of balance between scientific evidence collected through the use of new technologies and presented by expert witnesses in court and the knowledge and understanding of such evidence on behalf of judges and jurors, a set of rules has been established. For our purposes, the Daubert Standard as articulated in Rule 702 of the Federal Rules of Evidence (see http://www.law.cornell.edu/rules/fre/rules.htm) is particularly instructive:

> If scientific, technical, or other specialized knowledge will assist the trier of fact to understand the evidence or to determine a fact in issue, a witness qualified as an expert by knowledge, skill, or experience, training, or education, may testify thereto in the form of an opinion or otherwise, if: (1) the testimony is based upon sufficient facts or data, (2) the testimony is the product of reliable principles and methods, and (3) the witness has applied the principles and methods reliably to the facts of the case.

The subsections of Rule 702 make it clear that the police must be trained in the collection and preservation of scientific evidence and that they must use appropriate and reliable technology in such collection and preservation. Only then can expert testimony in support of the evidence be admitted and considered by judges and jurors

(*Daubert v. Merrell Dow Pharmaceuticals, Inc.*, 43 F. 3d 1311—Court of Appeals, 9th Circuit 1995; May, 2007). Other federal rules of evidence and other court decisions apply as well (e.g., *Frye v. U.S.* 293F, 1013 [1923]), but the Daubert example should suffice as a caution against the belief that police technology guarantees success in court.

There are dozens of databases, other than IAFIS and DNA databanks, containing information useful to or provided by police agencies, and many of these are also accessible to the public:

Bureau of Alcohol, Tobacco and Firearms (ATF)—with the advent of the Internet, ATF is seizing the opportunity to employ Internet subscribers in its continuing effort to combat violent crime by advertising wanted persons

Drug Enforcement Administration (DEA) Fugitives—contains information about DEA fugitives who are being tracked and are listed by Field Division, and information concerning major international fugitives and captured fugitives is also available

Federal Bureau of Investigation Crime Alerts—provides information about the Federal Bureau of Investigation's efforts to locate fugitives and missing persons

Federal Bureau of Investigation Most Wanted List—contains information about the Federal Bureau of Investigation's efforts to locate fugitives and missing persons

Federal Bureau of Investigation Most Wanted Terrorists—includes information concerning alleged terrorists who have been indicted by Federal Grand Juries in various jurisdictions in the United States for the crimes reflected on their wanted posters

Federal Bureau of Investigation National DNA Index System—these databases contain data or records (e.g., the genotypes), and data banks store the original samples taken from offenders

Immigration and Customs Enforcement (ICE) Most Wanted Fugitives—provides information on Immigration and Customs Enforcement top fugitives

Interpol Most Wanted—Interpol official site—International Criminal Police Organization (ICPO)—Rapid access to official, controlled information (Most Wanted Criminal and Fugitive Database websites, www.indexoftheweb.com/Information/WantedCriminal Databases.htm)

As is the case with most advances in police technology, maintenance of these databases is subject to criticism on the grounds of misuses and mistaken contents. Among the objections to DNA databases, for example, are the allegations that DNA typing is not a mature enough technology to avoid false matches; that extracting DNA samples invades bodily integrity; that forensic genotyping reveals intensely personal information; that offender databases and databanks might be used for purposes other than criminal justice; that DNA databanking invades the privacy of innocent relatives; and that using samples from offender databanks for genetics research violates the Nuremberg Code (Kaye, 2001). Other databases are subject to criticism on variations of these objections (e.g., that databases on sex offenders sometimes contain inaccurate information and that they punish innocent relatives by identifying them with the listed offenders).

❖ Police Use of Speed Detection Devices or Systems

Police have used a variety of detection systems to monitor vehicle speeds and issue traffic citations for violators. Use of patrol car speedometers was one of the first techniques employed and may still be used occasionally when more technologically sophisticated systems are unavailable or inoperable. Since the late 1940s, **Radio Detection and Ranging (RADAR) systems** that use remote sensors that emit electromagnetic radio waves to determine vehicle speeds have been used. These systems may be either moving (mounted in patrol cars, aircraft, etc.) or stationary to measure the speed of oncoming and, in many cases, receding traffic. Some track only one target at a time, while others can track and display two targets simultaneously. Detection ranges vary, but may range up to a mile or more (Sawicki, 2009).

Photo radar automatically detects a speeding violation and photographs or video records the driver, the vehicle, and the license plate and records vehicle speed and typically the date, time, and location (Sawicki, 2009). In addition, photo radars often connect to a computer or printer to retrieve stored data including the number and type of prior violations. In many cases, violators do not even know they have been detected and recorded until they receive a ticket and a photograph of the driver and license plate in the mail. Even though the registered owner of the vehicle may not be the driver in the photograph, he or she still receives the ticket.

Laser radars (referred to as ladars [LAser Detection And Ranging] or lidars [LIght Detection And Ranging]) were introduced in the early 1990s and use laser light instead of the radio waves that are the basis of conventional radar to determine speed (the term *laser radar* is technically inappropriate) (RadarGuns.com, 2010). As is the case with other speed detection systems, a number of rules apply to the use of lasers to detect speed. These include the following:

1. Adequate training and experience on the part of the operator

2. Certification of the device as acceptable in the jurisdiction in question

3. Verification or calibration of the detection device prior to the beginning of the operator's shift and again at the end of the shift (to ensure the unit is operating properly)

4. Proper inspection and maintenance by the manufacturer

5. Testimony of the operator indicating that the speed reading was properly obtained and was within the limits of the equipment

6. Proper identification of the targeted vehicle

7. Testimony that the detection device was properly operated and positioned at the time of the reading (Michigan State Police, 2010)

A **Visual Average Speed Computer and Recorder (VASCAR)** is yet another speed detection device. This semiautomated technique for determining the speed of a moving vehicle is used by the police to apprehend speeders in jurisdictions where RADAR or LIDAR are illegal or to prevent detection by drivers using radar detectors. A VASCAR unit couples a stopwatch with a simple computer. The operator records the moment that a vehicle passes two fixed objects that are a known distance apart and the time the target vehicle takes to travel between them to calculate speed (Traffic Safety Systems, Inc., 2010).

Finally, **the Electronic Non-Radar Device (ENRADD)** speed detection system uses infrared beams to measure a car's speed as it passes through a 3-foot-long section of road. Sensors placed on each side of the road detect when a vehicle enters the section. The first sensor starts the system's timing device; when the vehicle passes the second sensor, it stops the timer. A computer in the patrol car calculates the vehicle's speed by dividing the distance traveled by the amount of time elapsed, and a display unit indicates the resulting number for the officer (Niederberger, 2008). When using speed detection systems such as VASCAR, police officers must trigger switches that start and stop the timing device. Operator error is sometimes alleged by motorists challenging their citations in court. When using ENRADD, the vehicle triggers the switches starting and stopping the clock. The officer has no hands-on role but simply reads the display, removing this particular challenge to citations issued (Niederberger, 2008).

The key to the use of speed detection devices or systems is officer training. When properly deployed, such systems accurately detect not only speed, but also make and model of vehicle and license number. In some cases, they also provide identification of the driver of the vehicle. None of these approaches to traffic control is completely foolproof, but the technology continues to advance rapidly.

❖ Body Armor and Weapons

Humans have been wearing various forms of **body armor** for thousands of years. In the 1960s, engineers developed a unique form of soft body armor constructed from advanced woven fibers that could be sewn into vests and other soft clothing (Harris, 2008). As a result, more than 3,000 police officers' lives have been saved by body armor since the mid-1970s (National Institute of Justice, 2008a). However, it is important to note that bullet proof body armor does not exist. Today, body armor can provide protection against various type of handgun ammunition, and the armor is usually categorized and rated for different threat levels. For example, additional protection is normally employed for SWAT team operations, hostage rescues, and Special Operation Assignments in which police officers are exposed to greater threats than can be protected against with regular duty body armor (NIJ, 2008a). In some of these great-threat types of incidents, even the perpetrators wear body armor to protect themselves from police weapons.

Most agree that body armor affords police officers protection from a variety of assaults and accidents. According to Tompkins (2006), a police officer not wearing body armor is 14 times more likely to suffer a fatal injury compared to an officer wearing body armor. Unfortunately, in 2007 Zakhary discovered that only approximately 60% of police officers wear body armor. This statistic was supported in the same article by a 2002 survey by DuPont that indicated that 45% of U.S. police departments failed to mandate vest wear by policy.

Future body armor research will most likely benefit from experiments being conducted for the U.S. Army. According to Bonsor (2010), the Army hopes to develop an advanced infantry uniform that integrates nanotechnology, exoskeletons, and liquid body armor by 2020. While this exists only in concept, the basic components include the following:

- Helmet—houses a GPS receiver, radio, and wide and local area network connections
- Warrior psychological status monitoring system—layers closest to the body contain sensors that monitor heart rate, blood pressure, and hydration
- Liquid body armor—consists of a magnetorheological fluid that remains in a liquid state until a magnetic field is applied, at which time it transforms from a soft to a rigid state in thousandths of a second
- Exoskeleton—lightweight composite devices that attach to the legs and augment the strength of the person wearing the uniform

We caution the reader that various aspects of police technology presented in this chapter will likely change in the future. As we discuss in Chapters 6, 11, and 15, the innovations required for the implementation of intelligence-led-policing, predictive policing, and other new strategies will likely result in rapid development of new police technologies.

Police Weapons

Society has provided the police with the authority and obligation to enforce the law, sustain order, and ensure the safety of citizens. In order to fulfill these obligations police officers need credible means of countering threats (Jussila, 2001). Thus, according to the research by Jussila (2001), the weapons police officers use in society involve several issues—including human considerations, judicial and societal requirements, and tactical and technical possibilities. In most cases, police employ a use-of-force

❖ **PHOTO 12.3**   The non-lethal weapon shown is broadly known as a "Conducted Energy Device" and is specifically referred to as a "Personal Halting and Stimulation Response Rifle." The weapon is designed for use in crowd control and projects a laser intended to daze and temporarily blind the target.

continuum to assist officers in determining the amount of force to utilize in a specific situation. This almost always involves more force in more severe circumstances and less force in less serious circumstances. Less-than-lethal force is most often utilized when the following conditions are met:

- Lethal force is not appropriate
- Lethal force is justified but lesser force may subdue the person
- Lethal force is justified but could cause collateral effects, such as injury to innocent bystanders (National Institute of Justice, 2008b).

The following are several examples of technology that afford police officers less-than-lethal device alternatives.

- **Conducted energy device**—involves devices, such as Tasers, stun guns, or stun belts, that induce involuntary muscle contractions that temporarily incapacitate the person. These electrical devices produce an immediate effect.
- **Directed energy devices**—technology that uses radiated energy to achieve similar effects to blunt force, but with a lower probability of injury. In many cases this device stimulates nerve endings, which causes intolerable discomfort to the person but no lasting or long term effects.
- **Chemicals**—involves chemicals such as pepper spray (known as OC [oleoresin capsicum]), tear gas, and stink bombs.
- **Distraction**—temporarily incapacitates individuals while causing little harm—includes the laser dazzle, bright lights, and noise.
- **Vehicle-stopping technology**—includes devices that disrupt and stall a vehicle's electrical system and tire-deflator devices that immobilize vehicles.
- **Barriers**—nets, foams, and physical barriers.
- **Blunt force**—projectiles such as the rubber bullets used in crowd control (National Institute of Justice, 2008b).

Physical restraints involve a variety of products that are employed to physically restrain or impede the movement of an individual. We included this technology in this section since it is almost always used in conjunction with less-than-lethal devices. A net gun can discharge a large net and incapacitate people (Officer.com). The net can snare an individual in a web of indestructible nylon and immobilizes the person without physical contact. Another form of physical restraint is a surface chemical substance that makes a surface extremely slippery or extremely sticky.

Finally, research is continuing into the use of calmative agents as a less-than-lethal option for police officers. **Calmative agents** involve pharmaceuticals or sedative drugs that produce a calming or tranquil state (Lakoski, Murray, & Kenny, 2000).

Excellent examples of new technologies being tested include a handheld detector of concealed weapons that should be available in a few years and the use of acoustic (sonic or ultrasonic) weapons to confuse or incapacitate offenders. The federal government has invested in a weapons detector that emits a sonic pulse; when a knife or gun is present, the pulse is reflected back, triggering an alarm and a light. At least some researchers are convinced that findings clearly demonstrate that acoustic technology is a low-cost alternative to conventional imaging methods for concealed weapons detection (Achanta, 2006; Wild, 2003). Applications for this technology range from use by municipal police to Homeland Security officials in settings such as airports, trains, and bus terminals, to mention just a few.

Other sonic or ultrasonic research has focused on the use of weapons that can distract, harass, injure, or even kill a target using sound. At enough decibels, sound can rupture the eardrums and cause extreme pain. Such weapons have been used on some ships to prevent pirates from gaining control, indicating potential international applications of the technology (Nordland, 2008).

YOU DECIDE 12.1

Given all the technological advances in policing discussed in this chapter, it is now possible for the police to see us, listen to us, harass us with sonic devices, and follow us whenever they choose to do so. Such advances bring great benefits to police officials, but they are also all subject to abuse. In your opinion, what are the greatest threats from the use of the technological advances discussed in this chapter? Do you think potential benefits for the police outweigh potential costs to other citizens?

❖ Chapter Summary

There is perhaps no single issue that has affected the field of policing more than technological advancements. Not that long ago, officers used in-car radios to communicate with their dispatchers and facsimile machines to transmit the fingerprint cards of arrestees to the states' bureaus of identification to check for possible outstanding warrants or to learn the criminal histories of their suspects. Now, many departments equip their officers with highly sophisticated technologies that are used as a matter of routine. Some examples include compact, mobile radios that connect instantly with dispatchers; in-car video cameras to record officers' interactions with citizens; laptop computers on which officers compose their written reports, conduct driver's license checks, and receive criminal histories on suspects instantaneously; a computer screen that can scan a suspect's hand to determine a suspect's true identity by comparing the prints in question with millions of records maintained by the FBI and states' bureaus of identification; the use of cameras in public areas to record the actions of citizens caught by the camera lenses; new and improved forensic capabilities such as DNA testing; and dozens of other capabilities used in the fight against crime.

These improvements in technology, however, do not come without potentially serious legal issues—particularly with respect to incidents pertaining to the police community's fight against terrorism and the use of video cameras. Constitutional issues such as invasion of privacy and lack of probable cause have been the subject of much debate among the legal community with respect to these new technologies. The courts have yet to rule extensively on these matters, but many cases are presently in the system.

Finally, sophisticated computer technology has given law enforcement the ability to map crime and gather all of the pertinent details associated with individual acts of crime. Systems like

CompStat and CLEAR are good examples of these types of police data bases. These programs are of great assistance in the fight against crime, particularly with respect to the prevention of crime.

There is no doubt that technology will continue to play an important role in policing. As this occurs, police administrators and the courts will inevitably set limits on the use of technology to ensure that police authority is not abused.

❖ Key Terms

Mobile Data Terminals (MDTs)

Computer-Aided Dispatch (CAD)

Automatic Vehicle Location (AVL)

Global Positioning System (GPS)

Geographic Information System (GIS)

Illinois Citizen and Law Enforcement Analysis and Reporting (I-CLEAR)

polygraph

CCTV

red light cameras

graffiti cameras

Electronic Communications Privacy Act (ECPA)

Foreign Intelligence Surveillance Act (FISA)

National Security Letters (NSL)

Digital Collection System Network (DCSNet)

License Plate Recognition System (LPR)

Automatic Number Plate Recognition (ANPR)

Internet Protocol (IP) cameras

crime mapping

crime analysis

density analysis mapping

CompStat

cell phone

Integrated Automated Fingerprint Identification System (IAFIS)

fingerprint scanner

deoxyribonucleic acid (DNA)

Radio Detection and Ranging (RADAR) systems

photo radar

laser radars

Visual Average Speed Computer And Recorder (VASCAR)

Electronic Non-Radar Device (ENRADD)

body armor

conducted energy devices

directed energy devices

physical restraints

calmative agent

❖ Discussion Questions

1. Technological changes in policing may have both positive and negative consequences. Discuss some of the potentially positive consequences. What are some of the ethical considerations involved in proper utilization of technological devices in policing?

2. Considering the global nature of policing today, what are some of the advantages to having access to computers and the Internet? What are some of the dangers involved in using computers and the Internet?

3. What are some of the technological applications of mobile data terminals, geographical positioning systems, and computer aided dispatch systems in private and public policing? Are there any major disadvantages to these applications?

4. How do video cameras in police cars (and other mobile video cameras as well) help insure accountability? What is the role of such cameras in protecting officers and other citizens during police encounters? Are there any disadvantages to having mobile cameras record such encounters?

5. Why have crime mapping and associated crime analysis become so popular in policing today? Is the evidence concerning the results of crime mapping and analysis convincing to you? Why or why not?

6. If you were to note one major advantage of DNA analysis for the police, what would it be? What is the major advantage for suspects? The major disadvantage for suspects?

7. In your opinion, has the variety of speed detection devices employed by the police reduced the number of drivers who violate speed laws? Why or why not?

8. What have been the major improvements in the area of police body armor and weaponry during the past decade? Is there any downside to the use of either?

❖ Internet Exercises

1. Go to the Web address http://www.carlisle.army.mil/proteus/docs/55-policing.pdf and access the article titled "55 Trends Now Shaping the Future of Policing," which indentifies future trends in policing through 2025. Read the sections related to future police technology. How will certain technology predictions benefit some people and organizations and at the same time become a burden to others?

2. New technology has allowed the development of new forms of criminality. However, new technology has also permitted police to investigate, prevent, and suppress a variety of crimes. Go to the *Justice Technology Information Network* (http://www.justnet.org) and identify five new forms of technology that police are using today.

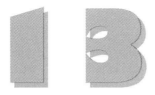

Global Issues

Implications for the Police

CHAPTER LEARNING OBJECTIVES

- Describe, in a general sense, a few of the major global issues that have affected local police operations in the United States.
- Elaborate on the various factors that have vastly expanded transnational crime.
- Identify key data collected by the United Nations with respect to transnational crime.
- Distinguish between the characteristics of a criminal organization and those of other criminal groups.
- Identify at least three common denominators of the various transnational groups listed throughout the chapter.
- Describe or list the various categories of white collar crime and identify which are considered to be transnational in nature.
- Provide commentary on the economic, social, and political costs associated with white collar crime.
- Explain and provide examples of Ralph Nader's notion of "postponed violence."
- Identify and elaborate on the global conditions that gave rise to the frequency of acts of terrorism.
- Describe the major functions of the Department of Homeland Security.
- Identify the fundamental constructs of the U.S. Patriot Act and the RICO statute.
- Provide commentary on the roles of local law enforcement with respect to terrorism.
- Identify recommendations for improved law enforcement and citizen responses to terrorism.

❖ Introduction

The police community, particularly at the state, county, and local levels, can no longer afford to ignore criminal activities once faced only by members of federal law enforcement or by the police in other countries. Continuous progress in technology, the increased mobility of persons from one country to another, significant changes in the socioeconomic conditions of the global marketplace, and modified legal agreements and changing political relationships between the United States and other countries have combined to dramatically change the way in which the police community operates.

The purpose of this chapter is to address the global issues that now significantly impact the roles and responsibilities of police in the United States. These issues include the following:

- Transnational crime
- Organized crime (though a form of transnational crime, because of the severity of this global phenomenon it will be addressed separately)
- White collar crime (though many of these crimes can be labeled as forms of organized crime as well, it will be briefly addressed separately due to its impact on police internationally)
- Terrorism (though a form of transnational crime, because of the extreme nature of this form of global crime, it will be discussed separately)
- Homeland Security and the role of the police in the national strategy to combat global threats
- Recommendations for an overall improved local law enforcement response

It is our intention to provide readers with an overview and a basic understanding of these global issues. Topics such as transnational crime, organized crime, white collar crime, and terrorism are extremely complex, and each is the subject of textbooks. We urge readers to explore these phenomena further in order to learn more about these topics.

❖ Transnational Crime

Transnational crime encompasses several specific types of criminal offenses. In its broadest sense, **transnational crime** is defined as ". . . crime that takes place across national borders . . . [that] is poorly understood but has had profound consequences for the ordering of the world system" (Sheptycki, 2007, p. 391). Criminal organizations, whose criminal operations were once confined primarily to their respective countries of origin, now operate in multiple countries throughout the world. The frequency and magnitude of the illicit activities perpetrated by these nefarious organizations are in many instances strengthened by cooperative efforts among such organizations. These alliances were essentially formed in order to capitalize on opportunities created by relatively recent political, economic, and social upheavals throughout the world, such as the **North American Free Trade Agreement (NAFTA)**, the breakdown of the former Soviet Union, **Perestroika**, and the transition to a unified monetary system in most of Europe. Consequently, their abilities to expand their criminal operations were increased dramatically.

The first meaningful international effort to investigate the prevalence of transnational crime was conducted by the United Nations in what was referred to as the *Fourth Annual United Nations Survey on Crime Trends and the Operations of Criminal Justice Systems* (United Nations Crime Prevention and Criminal Justice Division, 2009). In addition to questions pertaining to crime rates and other traditional data on crime, an additional survey was included that was designed to elicit member countries' perceptions of the crime problems associated with transnational crime. Of the 193 countries surveyed, only 50 responded, and from the data obtained through this effort the United Nations listed 18 categories of transnational crime as global threats (see Table 13.1).

Since this undertaking by the United Nations in 1990, an additional seven surveys on crime trends, spanning the time period of 1990 through 2009, have been sent to member countries, and the results have been analyzed in detail. The survey reports appear to have at least one significant common denominator: With the possible exception of aircraft hijacking, the rates for the remaining categories of crime listed in Table 13.1 seem to be increasing steadily (United Nations Crime Prevention and Criminal Justice Division, 2009).

As should be clear from the following table, the categories of crime that fall under the umbrella of transnational crime seem to overlap (e.g., organized crime and white collar crime). With the exception of terrorism, all of the categories of crime listed in Table 13.1 are directly linked to what police officials and researchers define as either organized or white collar crime. The issue is further complicated when we consider the

Table 13.1 Categories of Transnational Crime Identified by the United Nations	
Money laundering	Computer crime
Terrorism	Environmental crime
Theft of art and cultural objects	Trafficking in persons
Theft of intellectual property	Trade in human body parts
Illicit traffic in arms	Illicit drug trafficking
Aircraft hijacking	Fraudulent bankruptcy
Sea piracy	Infiltration of legitimate business
Land hijacking	Corruption and bribery of public officials
Insurance fraud	Other offenses committed by organized crime groups

fact that five of those categories of crime are frequently regarded as both organized and white collar crime. These include money laundering, insurance fraud, computer crime, environmental crime, and the bribery of public officials. We now turn our attention to a discussion of the similarities and differences between organized and white collar crime.

❖ Organized Crime

The FBI (2010b) defines **organized crime** as follows:

> Any group having some manner of a formalized structure and whose primary objective is to obtain money through illegal activities. Such groups maintain their position through the use of actual or threatened violence, corrupt public officials, graft, or extortion, and generally have a significant impact on the people in their locales, region, or the country as a whole. (p. 1)

This basic definition serves chiefly as a foundation to build upon. If it is to be understood in its proper context, organized crime—with all its complexities—requires a more sophisticated approach to its definition. Abadinsky (2010, pp. 2–5) offered a typology for distinguishing between organized crime or criminal organizations and other groups of criminals. Though there are other typologies, Abadinsky's (2010) makes a clear distinction between organized crime and terrorist groups, which is why this particular point of reference was chosen. The typology includes the simultaneous demonstration of the following eight characteristics or attributes:

1. *Non-ideological in nature.* Criminal organizations have no political or religious ideals or agenda to achieve. Their goals are money and power.

2. *Hierarchical.* The structural organization of the group is pyramid-like, having at least three permanent levels or tiers. Recently, however, many criminal organizations have transitioned from this top-down, bureaucratic structure to a smaller, cell-like structure for ease of operation and to mitigate intelligence gathering operations by law enforcement agencies.

3. *Limited/exclusive membership.* Criminal organizations significantly limit membership, which is usually based on race, ethnicity, or kinship and by sponsorship of an existing member. All new members start as apprentices or associate members and must prove themselves with regard to a show of respect to ranking members, a willingness to commit crimes, and a refusal to cooperate with law enforcement officials.

4. *Perpetuation.* The group shows the ability to stand the test of time. Regardless of the death or incarceration of members, there are new members and affiliates on hand to replenish those losses in order for the group to carry on.

5. *Use of violence and bribery.* When violence is required to achieve their criminal pursuits, members must be willing and able to engage in it. Bribery, if necessary, will also be used to gain protection from the authorities in order to maintain their criminal operations.

6. *Division of labor.* Large and sophisticated criminal organizations have specialized functions that designated members perform or are responsible for (i.e., political fixers, money launderers, killers, etc).

7. *Monopolistic.* This refers to the ability of criminal organizations to dominate or control certain illicit activities in a given geographical area or control one specific criminal enterprise or both.

8. *Governed by rules and regulations.* These criminal organizations are governed by a set of both informal and formal rules, the violation of which may result in the punishment of the offender, including death under certain circumstances.

A wide variety of crimes have been included under the term *organized crime.* They include, but are not limited to, the following:

Table 13.2 Crimes Commonly Associated With Organized Crime

Illicit gambling	Sea piracy	Murder	Kidnapping
Loan sharking	Theft of art and cultural objects	Distribution of obscene matter	Embezzlement from pension and welfare funds
Extortion	Insurance fraud	Unlawful procurement of citizenship	Reproduction or sale of citizenship papers
Money laundering	Computer crime	Forgery of or false use of a passport	Welfare fraud
Narcotics trafficking	Environmental crime	Unlawful reproduction of copyrighted materials	Interstate transportation of stolen motor vehicles or parts
Labor union and industrial racketeering	Manipulation of market economies	Sale of contraband cigarettes	Fraudulent sale of stocks and securities
Bribery of public officials	Fraudulent bankruptcy	Violations of the Currency and Foreign Transactions Reporting Act	Acts in violation of the Immigration and Nationality Act
Trafficking in persons (labor and sexual exploitation)	Mail fraud	Wire fraud	Sexual exploitation of children
Hobbs Act violations	Financial institution fraud	Sports bribery	Extortionate credit transactions

Source: Referenced in part from Title 18 USC Sec. 1962 Prohibited Activities.

The list of crimes cited in Table 13.2 is by no means an exhaustive list of unlawful acts associated with organized crime groups. However, the illicit activities identified represent a sizeable portion of the criminal activities undertaken by members of these groups.

Table 13.3 presents a matrix listing the vast majority of criminal organizations that exist and operate currently, all of which are engaged in the global phenomenon known as transnational crime. Many of these groups have been in existence for centuries, while some have emerged or have elevated themselves to this status in the past 50 years or so. In the matrix, the groups are identified by name, countries of origin, present countries of operation, major illegal activities, and known cooperative relationships between two or more of the groups.

Table 13.3	Types of Criminal Organizations by Countries of Origin and Operation, Associated Criminal Activities, and These Groups' Cooperative Efforts			
Name	**Country of origin**	**Countries of operation**	**Major crimes**	**Cooperative efforts**
Boryokudan, aka Yakuza	Japan	Japan, USA, Mexico, Canada, UK	Extortion, narcotics trafficking, manipulation of financial markets, money laundering, alien smuggling (labor/sex), bribery of public officials, murder	Mafia; Chinese triads; South, Central, and North American drug cartels; ROC groups
Chinese triads	China	China, USA, Canada, Malaysia, Singapore, Brazil, numerous other Asian countries	Narcotics trafficking, extortion, illegal gambling, money laundering, alien smuggling (labor/sex), bribery of public officials, murder	Mafia, Boryokudan, ROC groups, various Asian and North American drug cartels
Colombian drug cartels	Colombia	Colombia, Peru, Bolivia, USA, Canada, other South and Central American countries	Narcotics trafficking, money laundering, bribery of public officials, extortion, murder	Mexican drug cartels, Mafia, ROC groups
Gangs (meta/super gangs): Gangster Disciples, Latin Kings, Crips, Bloods, Mara Salvatrucha (aka MS-13)	USA	USA, Canada, Mexico, China, Japan, Russia, numerous other South and Central American countries	Narcotics trafficking, extortion, money laundering, forgery of immigration documents, alien smuggling (labor/sex), supply of enforcers for other criminal organizations, kidnappings, arms smuggling, corruption of public officials, murder	Mafia, OMGs, ROC groups, Mexican drug cartels, Colombian and other Central and South American drug cartels
Mafia, aka La Cosa Nostra	Italy	USA, Canada, most of the counties of Europe, Brazil, Argentina, China, Japan	Narcotics trafficking, money laundering, loan sharking, illicit gambling, alien smuggling (labor/sex), contraband cigarettes, labor	ROC groups, street gangs, OMGs, Chinese triads, Boryokudan

Name	Country of origin	Countries of operation	Major crimes	Cooperative efforts
			and industrial racketeering, murder, manipulation of the stocks and bonds industry, prostitution, bribery of public officials, distribution of obscene matter, computer fraud, mail fraud, wire fraud	North, South and Central American drug cartels
Mexican drug cartels	Mexico	Mexico, USA, Canada, numerous South and Central American counties	Narcotics trafficking, money laundering, violence against public officials, bribery of public officials, arms smuggling, kidnapping, murder	Street gangs, OMGs, major Central and South American drug cartels, Mafia, ROC groups
Outlaw motorcycle gangs (OMGs) (e.g., Hell's Angels, Outlaws, Banditos, Pagans)	USA	USA, Canada, Mexico, several European counties, Major Australian and Oceania countries, major countries of South America	Narcotics trafficking, arms and explosives smuggling, murder, extortion, money laundering, bribery of public officials, prostitution	Street gangs, Mafia, Mexican drug cartels, ROC groups
Nigerian organized crime groups	Nigeria	Nigeria, USA, Canada, Malaysia, Albania, UK, India, Pakistan, Thailand, China	Narcotics trafficking, money laundering, computer fraud, credit card fraud, counterfeiting, falsifying of immigration documents, bribery of public officials	Street gangs, Asian OC groups, Mafia, ROC groups.
Russian organized crime groups (ROC)	Former Soviet Union (FSU)	All states of the FSU, USA, Canada, UK, Italy, France, Germany, Spain, Poland, China, Japan, Malaysia, Singapore, major South and Central American countries	Narcotics trafficking, money laundering, computer fraud, murder, bribery and intimidation of public officials, alien smuggling (labor/sex), falsification of immigration documents, extortion, loan sharking, unlawful influencing of the banking industry in Russia, smuggling of arms, including nuclear materials	Mafia, street gangs, OMGs, Chinese triads, Boryokudan, Nigerian organized crime groups, North, South, and Central American and European-based drug cartels.

Sources: From *Organized Crime* (9th ed.), by H. Abadinsky, 2010, Belmont, CA: Wadsworth; *Organized Crime: World Perspectives*, by J. Albanese, D. Das, and A. Verma, 2003, Upper Saddle River, NJ: Prentice-Hall; International Association for the Study of Organized Crime, 2010, http://www.iasoc.net/#; *Organized Crime* (4th ed.), by M. Lyman and G. Potter, 2006, Upper Saddle River, NJ: Prentice Hall; *Octopus,* by C. Sterling, 1990, *Octopus.* New York: Simon & Schuster; Terrorism, Transnational Crime and Corruption Center, 2010, http://policy-traccc .gmu.edu/publications/publications.html

❖ PHOTO 13.2 The intricate body tattooing depicted is a tell-tale membership sign of Japan's most notorious transnational crime organization, Boryokudan, a.k.a. Yakuza.

The important fact to be gleaned from the previous information is not that each of these groups are transnational criminal organizations, but that they share common denominators, particularly regarding the specific crimes in which they engage. Members of each of these groups engage in the following identical criminal activities:

- Narcotics trafficking
- Money laundering
- Bribery of public officials
- Willingness to use violence, including murder
- Criminal partnerships or associations with other transnational organized crime groups

During an interview, one veteran and well respected FBI agent from the Chicago field office pointed to public corruption as the base of the insidious nature of organized crime.

It's been proven that it's not just the police, I mean the police are actually the lowest level of corruption; the highest would be the politicians because they control who gets named police chief . . . they name the judges . . . they control the courts. So, if you can, the politicians get all three; judicial corruption, political corruption, and they get key police officials, that's what organized crime is, that's why it's so evil. (Scaramella, 1998, p. 107)

The corruption of public officials in Russia, Mexico, Colombia, and many other countries is commonplace. Examine the following case in point from our own country.

☞ CASE IN POINT 13.1

Operation Greylord

It was a Friday, and a group of lawyers—some prosecutors, some defense attorneys—had gathered in a Loop hotel for a bachelor party. But the celebrating stopped when the television news broke this stunning story: For three years, the FBI had been running an undercover operation aimed at Cook County's court system. It featured at least one undercover operative and a listening device in a judge's chambers.

One lawyer in the room—Terrence Hake—was not surprised by the news. Disgusted with the corruption that permeated the Cook County court system, he had become the FBI's mole in its unprecedented investigation of judicial corruption. First as a prosecutor and later as a defense lawyer, Hake had burrowed into the dark side of justice, handing out bribes to fix cases concocted by the FBI. Four months after the Greylord investigation was revealed, the first indictments were announced, naming two judges, a former judge, three attorneys, two court clerks, and a police officer. "I believe this will be viewed as one of the most comprehensive, intricate and difficult undercover projects ever undertaken by a law-enforcement agency," U.S. Attorney Dan Webb said in announcing those charges.

The allegations ranged from fixing drunken-driving cases to more serious felony charges. One lawyer was caught on tape bragging that "even a murder case can be fixed if the judge is given something to hang his hat on." By the end of the decade, nearly 100 people had been indicted, and all but a handful were convicted. Of the 17 judges indicted, 15 were convicted. The tally of convictions included 50 lawyers, as well as court clerks, police officers, and sheriff's deputies.

Greylord was not the first federal investigation of public corruption in Chicago, but it was a watershed in its use of eavesdropping devices and a mole to obtain evidence instead of relying on wrongdoers to become government informants.

(Continued)

(Continued)

In the years that followed, federal authorities conducted additional sting operations aimed at corruption spurred by corrupt members of the Illinois legislature, judiciary, law enforcement community, and noted organized crime figures. See Operations "Incubator," "Silver Shovel," "Lantern," "Gambat," and "Safebet" for a bird's eye view of these corrupt alliances.

Source: From "Operation Greylord: A Federal Probe of Court Corruption Sets the Standard for Future Investigations," by M. Possley, 1983, *Chicago Tribune.* Available from http://www .chicagotribune.com/news/politics/chi-chicagodays-greylord-story,0,4025843.story. From *The Chicago Tribune,* © 1983 *The Chicago Tribune.* All rights reserved. Used by permission.

It should also be noted that many of these criminal organizations, primarily due to their links with one another, have become both a national and international security threat. For example, the breakup of the former Soviet Union in 1991 left the infrastructure of the region quite vulnerable to exploitation. One of the key elements of that infrastructure was the military and its stockpile of weapons, including an array of nuclear materials; since 1991, many of those nuclear materials have been stolen. According to the International Atomic Energy Agency (IAEA) (2006), between 1993 and 2005, there have been 160 ". . . confirmed incidents of illicit trafficking and other unauthorized activities involving nuclear and radioactive materials . . ." These incidents have occurred in 10 separate countries, including the United States, and many involved the acts of members of transnational crime organizations (IAEA, 2006).

To wrap up this section on organized crime and illustrate additional and potentially serious implications that these transnational alliances pose for the police, it may be worthwhile to reflect on some of the events following the terrorist attacks of September 11, 2001.

The U.S. Patriot Act, federal legislation designed to combat terrorism more effectively and proactively, was passed shortly after the 9/11 disaster. One of the more significant components of that legislation involved police agencies and pertained directly to the relaxing of restrictions on inter- and intra-agency sharing of valuable intelligence between law enforcement organizations at all levels of government. There is perhaps no greater obstacle to effective criminal investigation than the lack of intelligence sharing between agencies. This phenomenon sometimes occurs because of bureaucratic disclosure restrictions, on occasion so as to not compromise the integrity of an investigation, but more often than not because of petty jealousies or the fear of being upstaged by a different agency. Speaking to this very issue in a speech to the U.S. Conference of Mayors, FBI Director Robert Mueller III (2001) said, in part,

. . . that no one agency or entity at any level, whether it be federal, state or local, has the length or the breadth of talent and expertise. We must work together. Law enforcement, quite simply, is only as good as its relationships. . . . I have asked the special agents in charge in cities where we do not already have a joint terrorism task force to get one up and running quickly . . . they do break down stereotypes and communications barriers, more effectively coordinate leads, and help get the resources in the right places. In short, they are an excellent tool for melding us together in ways that make information sharing a non-issue. (pp. 13–14)

The comments made by Director Mueller are reminiscent of what many in policing have known for decades. For example, speaking at a conference on transnational crime just a few short years before the catastrophe of 9/11, a senior agent from the Bureau of Alcohol, Tobacco, and Firearms (ATF) stated the following regarding the Hell's Angels outlaw motorcycle gang (OMG):

> . . . the larger OMGs are better equipped, more organized, and more efficient than many of the police agencies that are investigating them. With respect to the Hell's Angels . . . every one of their chapters throughout the world meet once per month. The minutes from each of these chapter meetings are then distributed via sophisticated computer technology to all of the other chapters. Within a few short days, every chapter throughout the world is made aware of each other's activities. (Scaramella, 1997, p. 8)

That agent concluded his presentation to the audience (made up almost exclusively of police personnel) with the following question: "Can we, as a law enforcement community, make similar claims?" (as quoted in Scaramella, 1997). The silence from the audience was deafening.

Only time will tell if this reluctance to share information on the part of law enforcement can be changed.

The Costs of Organized Crime

Up to the mid 1980s, various presidential commissions were formed to address the issues of organized crime in great detail, including the costs associated with this form of crime, but they dealt almost exclusively with what is commonly referred to as *traditional organized crime* or the *Mafia*. In addition, these investigations focused on the Mafia's operations within our nation's borders.

According the President's Commission on Organized Crime (PCOOC) of 1986, the cost of Mafia-related crime to U.S. citizens from an economic perspective was estimated at $18.2 billion 1986 dollars. However, this cost estimate did not take into account the hidden costs associated with Mafia-related crime with regard to their infiltration of legitimate business and industry and did not include other transnational organized crime groups.

> Organized crime infiltration into legitimate business and labor unions has many impacts, not all of which are obvious and all of which are difficult to measure. The effects of organized crime on the legitimate economy show up in higher prices for consumers when competition is suppressed, low wages for workers when labor unions are controlled and low safety when corners are cut on construction projects or toxic waste is not disposed of properly. (PCOOC, 1986, pp. 431–432)

Not even one decade later, as more attention was focused on other transnational criminal organizations, the costs of organized crime changed dramatically. Sterling (1994) wrote about criminal organizations from the four corners of the world coming together to form what was referred to as the Pax-Mafiosa, a partnership of various transnational crime groups to end turf battles and form new alliances to create and establish a global monopoly over the illegal goods and services that they had provided for years. As Sterling (1994) so aptly stated:

> International organized crime, an imaginary menace for many in 1990, was a worldwide emergency by 1993. The big syndicates of East and West were pooling services and personnel, rapidly colonizing western Europe and the United States, running the drug traffic up to half a trillion dollars a year, laundering and reinvesting an estimated quarter of a trillion dollars in legitimate enterprise. (p. 14)

Additional costs of organized crime to society pertain to the vast proliferation of publicized scandals involving the corruption of politicians, judges, and law enforcement officials and their collusion with members of these criminal organizations. This may lead to a loss of faith on the part of the public in the criminal justice system and an overall disrespect for the law. These are the costs that may prove to be the most difficult to recover.

Next, let us examine the fundamentals of another form of crime conducted by transnational crime groups: white collar crime.

❖ White Collar Crime

A phrase coined by noted criminologist Edwin Sutherland during a speech to the American Sociological Society in 1939, **white collar crime** has evolved into a multibillion dollar per year criminal enterprise, the effects of which are felt around the world. Sutherland's definition of this rather new form of crime at that time was as follows: "Crimes committed by a person of respectability and high social status in the course of his occupation." (Sutherland, 1983, p. 7)

Since that time, the focus on white collar crime by criminologists, police officials, and prosecutorial bodies has ranged from and can be characterized as complete cessation to occasional interest and, only relatively recently (the past 10–15 years), as one of the criminal justice system's top priorities (Rosoff, Pontell, & Tillman, 2007). Today's focus on white collar crime is based on a more specific definition than the one espoused by Sutherland some 70 years ago. Moreover, because of these priority shifts by scholars and practitioners, numerous definitions have been posited, most of which are quite similar but with some points of distinction. To account for accepted variances between definitions, scholars from the White Collar Crime Center proposed the following definition: "White collar crimes are illegal or unethical acts that violate fiduciary responsibility of public trust by an individual or organization, usually during the course of legitimate occupational activity, by persons of high or respectable social status for personal or organizational gain." (Helmkamp, Ball, & Townsend, 1996, p. 351)

In similar fashion, noted white collar crime scholar Gilbert Geis (2002) spoke to the promulgation of different twists given to the definition of white collar crime from the early days of Sutherland to the present. The following comments speak clearly to his definitional notions of white collar crime: "I remain persuaded that Sutherland, however errantly, focused on a matter of singular practical and intellectual importance—the abuse of power by persons who are situated in high places where they are provided with the opportunity for such abuse" (p. 21).

Geis (2002) also agreed strongly with Braithwaite's (1985) earlier conclusion regarding the definition of white collar crime, namely that "... probably the most sensible way to proceed ... is to stick with Sutherland's definition." (p. 19)

The specific categories of crimes fitting such a definition are numerous, and most, if not all, of the following crimes are transnational in nature (Rosoff et al., 2007).

- *Crimes against the consumer:* Including, but not limited to, consumer fraud, telemarketing fraud, false advertising, price fixing, price gouging, and knockoff rip-offs.
- *Manufacture and sale of unsafe products:* These products include such items as motor vehicles, tools, foods, pharmaceutical products, and medical devices, among others.
- *Environmental crime:* The crimes include such unlawful practices as water pollution, air pollution, environmental racism (relegation of toxic dump sites to low-income communities), toxic terrorism (the unlawful disposal of toxic waste both inside and outside of our borders), and violations of the provisions of the Occupational Safety and Health Act (OSHA).
- *Institutional corruption:* Examples include, but are not limited to, corruption of the mass media (i.e., television and print media) and corruption relative to religious frauds (i.e., phony faith healers, embezzlement of funds by church leaders, and the televangelist scandals of the 1980s).
- *Securities, investment, insurance, and banking frauds:* These categories of white collar crime include such unlawful practices as insider trading, manipulation of the stock and bond industries, pension fund fraud, insurance fraud in its many forms, the fraud-induced collapse of both the savings and loan industry during the 1980s, and the more recent collapse of some of the largest banks in our country and the subsequent government buy out.
- *Crimes by the government:* These crimes are varied and range from our own government's practice in eugenics and the use of human beings as guinea pigs to violations of sovereignty and the abuse of power by governmental agencies.
- *Corruption of public officials:* Unfortunately, world history is replete with many such instances. These crimes include political corruption at all three branches of government, including those at the state and local levels. Unlawful acts such as bribery, unlawful campaign contributions, ghost pay rolling, influence pedaling, and the many forms of police misconduct are prime examples of this genre of white collar crime.
- *Medical crime:* These crimes include such things as fraudulent equipment sales, home care fraud, hospital frauds, Medicare and Medicaid fraud, and nursing home abuses.
- *Computer crime:* This form of crime is ever evolving and thus has become a significant crime problem of global proportions. Specific crimes include, but are not limited to, the use of computers to embezzle and commit other financial thefts, hacking, the intentional infusion of viruses into computer networks, espionage, unlawful gambling, distribution of obscene matter and child pornography, harassment, and cyberterrorism.

AROUND THE WORLD

What Does Environmental Crime Have in Common With Organized Crime?

Environmental crime is often transnational in nature and involves organized crime activities such as trafficking in natural resources, the illegal trade in wildlife, illegal, unregulated and unreported fishing and illegal exploitation of and trafficking in minerals and precious stones.

It is widely recognized that environmental crime is a rising challenge for developed and developing countries. The impact of illegal activities broadly covered by the term "environmental crime" goes well beyond the obvious effects on the environment and biodiversity. Crimes against the environment have serious social, development and economic consequences, particularly in least developed countries, and are a threat to basic human rights.

The transnational nature of environmental crimes, the established involvement of organized criminal groups and the failings of Government structures that often sustain these forms of criminality, make them highly relevant to the work of UNODC. Forest products, including timber, wildlife, and other forest biological resources, and hazardous waste are the object of international trafficking, often perpetrated by organized criminal groups that might also be engaged in the trafficking of other goods, often relying on failures in the criminal justice system.

In 2007, the Commission on Crime Prevention and Criminal Justice adopted its resolution 16/1 entitled "International cooperation in preventing and combating illicit international trafficking in forest products, including timber, wildlife and other forest biological resources." This resolution strongly encourages Member States to cooperate at bilateral, regional and international levels to prevent, combat and eradicate these forms of trafficking by applying the United Nations Convention against Transnational Organized Crime and the United Nations Convention against Corruption.

UNODC field offices have recently begun developing several projects concerning environmental crime in Moscow, Bangkok, Jakarta and Bogota. The projects have been set up in response to the needs of beneficiaries and have secured funding in a relatively short time, demonstrating the relevance of UNODC skills in the fight against the trafficking in natural resources.

In dealing with environmental crime, UNODC will continue to adopt a comprehensive and multidisciplinary response and will continue to develop profound expertise and strengthen its existing mandate.

Source: What Does Environmental Crime Have in Common With Organized Crime? By United Nations Office on Drugs and Crime, 2009, Available from http://www.unodc.org/unodc/en/frontpage/what-does-environmental-crime-have-in-common-with-organised-crime.html

The Costs of White Collar Crime

Attempts to estimate the various costs of white collar crime are somewhat difficult due to the manner in which these crimes are reported. For example, the Uniform Crime Report (UCR) and other official measures of crime do not include categories for many forms of white collar crime. Couple that with the fact that a significant portion of white collar crime goes unreported, and attempts to estimate the economic cost of these crimes becomes a difficult task. Nonetheless, as cited in Friedrichs (2007), "…estimates calculated by the FBI and the Association of Certified Fraud Examiners regarding the economic cost of white collar crime in 2006 were in the range of $300 to $600 billion" (p. 46). Even more staggering are the estimates pertaining to the global economic costs of white collar crime. As cited by McFayden (2010), the World Federation of United Nations Associations estimated the global costs of white collar crime in 2008 to be in excess of $10 trillion.

There are other costs associated with this form of criminality as well, such as the many adverse social and political costs. Regretfully, there are numerous examples that have significant global consequences. Social costs include such issues as increased feelings of cynicism among citizenries; a weakening of respect for the law, spawned by acts of public corruption involving judges, politicians, and law enforcement personnel; the loss of faith in various institutions when scandals come to light, such as religious frauds and criminal activity such as money laundering, by once respected "legitimate" financial institutions (Rosoff et al., 2007, pp. 578–80).

Finally, there are the political costs of white collar crime. Actions by government officials that can be characterized as violations of sovereignty have a profound impact on the reputations of governments worldwide and an accompanying decline in faith by their respective citizenries. As stated by Rosoff et al. (2007), bribery of national and foreign politicians by corporations and government officials from around the world

> . . . disrespects the principle of **national and international sovereignty**, which is the cornerstone of global order. For example, a single corporation—Lockheed—effectively toppled a government in Japan, nearly destroyed the Dutch monarchy, corrupted national elections in Germany, Portugal, and Brazil, and caused the arrest of a former Italian prime minister. (p. 387)

The information in this portion of the chapter has merely scratched the surface regarding the serious nature and consequences of this form of transnational crime (see You Decide 13.1 below). The reader is encouraged to explore the many aspects of white collar crime in further detail in the vast literature pertaining to this subject.

YOU DECIDE 13.1

Postponed Violence

Noted consumer advocate Ralph Nader coined the phrase *postponed violence* to dispel the myth that white collar crime is nonviolent and largely victimless in nature. He points to the severe injuries and even deaths caused by corporate greed.

(Continued)

(Continued)

Accounts from the related literature such as the "Love Canal" environmental incident, the Ford Motor Pinto vehicle case, the overall unsafe nature of working conditions for coal miners and other industrial and manufacturing industries, and a host of other similar incidences support this concept of postponed violence as a major consequence of these forms of white collar crime.

Another good example of this form of crime pertains to the asbestos industry and the fact that the manufacturers of the product knew from their own scientists that there was a link between prolonged exposure to asbestos and serious respiratory illness. However, they chose to keep that fact hidden from their workers and the public for fear of significant losses of profit. As these respiratory illnesses took many years to manifest themselves, the illnesses and subsequent deaths of thousands of people caused by the cover-ups years earlier were merely postponed.

Investigate the details of some of the other examples cited above and decide whether or not those responsible for postponed violence should be held criminally liable. Provide reasoning for your belief.

❖ Terrorism

No discussion of local policing would be complete without consideration of **terrorism**— a phenomenon that has plagued numerous societies throughout the world for years. Only in the last two decades or so have the effects of terrorist acts been felt in the United States of America. Even before the acts of terrorism on September 11, 2001 (9/11), we endured others of significance, such as the bombing of the federal building in Oklahoma City in 1995 and the first attack on the World Trade Center in 1993. Other incidences of terrorism have affected the United States in earlier years as well. The following table, courtesy of the Center for Defense Information (CDI), offers a detailed accounting of terrorist attacks against U.S. targets dating back more than 25 years.

Table 13.4 Terrorist Attacks Against U.S. Targets				
Date	Target	Means	Location	Casualties
09–11–01	Twin Towers, U.S. Pentagon	4 commercial jetliners	New York City/Washington DC	Approx. 5,000 dead
10–12–00	U.S. Navy Vessel (*USS Cole*)	Bomb	Aden, Yemen	17 dead; 39 injured
08–07–98	U.S. Embassies	Bombs	Nairobi, Kenya; Dar es Salaam, Tanzania	301 dead; 5077 injured
06–21–98	U.S. Embassy	Grenades	Beirut, Lebanon	None

Date	Target	Means	Location	Casualties
07–27–96	Olympic Games	Pipe bomb	Atlanta, Georgia	1 dead; 111 injured
06–25–96	U.S. Air Force Installation	Truck Bomb	Dhahran, Saudi Arabia	19 dead; 515 injured
11–13–95	U.S. Military Personnel	Car bomb	Riyadh, Saudi Arabia	7 dead
04–19–95	U.S. Federal Building	Truck bomb	Oklahoma City, OK	168 dead; 600+ injured
02–26–93	World Trade Center	Truck bomb	New York City	6 dead; 1042 injured
12–21–88	Pan-Am Jetliner	Bomb	Lockerbie, Scotland	270 dead
04–05–86	Discotheque (frequented by U.S. Military personnel)	Bomb	West Berlin, Germany	2 dead; 150 injured
04–02–86	TWA jetliner	Bomb	Athens, Greece (landing at airport)	4 dead
12–27–85	U.S. and Israeli Airport Check-in areas	2 simultaneous suicide bombings	Rome, Italy Vienna, Austria	20 dead Unknown injured
08–09–85	U.S. Military Base	Car bomb	Frankfurt, Germany	2 dead; 20 injured
06–19–85	Outdoor cafe	Machine gun	San Salvador, El Salvador	13 dead Unknown injured
06–14–85	TWA jetliner	Hijacking	Beirut, Lebanon	1 dead Unknown injured
04–12–85	Restaurant near U.S. Air Base	Bomb	Madrid, Spain	18 dead 82 injured
11–26–84	U.S. Embassy	Bomb	Bogota, Colombia	1 dead Unknown injured
10–23–83	U.S. Marine Barracks French Military Site	Simultaneous truck bomb(2)	Beirut, Lebanon	241 dead 58 dead Unknown injured
04–18–83	U.S. Embassy	Truck bomb	Beirut, Lebanon	63 dead 34 injured

Source: Adapted from *Chronology of Major Terrorist Attacks Against U.S. Targets,* by the Center for Defense Information, Washington DC. Retrieved from http://www.cdi.org/terrorism/chronology.html

Until the terrorist acts of 9/11, the American police community had not been very proactive with respect to counterterrorism activities, particularly at the state and local levels. For the most part, the burden of counterterrorism work had been placed squarely on the shoulders of federal law enforcement agencies. Now, however, it is clear that policing at all levels must assume some responsibility for and commitment to the containment of both domestic and international terrorism. This new priority has created a number of concerns for criminal justice administrators, ranging from budgetary deficiencies and training issues to investigative techniques and expanded police powers, which may be subject to constitutional abuse in the name of national defense.

The Proliferation of Terrorism

Before proceeding to a discussion of variables that have had an impact on the relatively recent growth in terrorism, we must first define the term *terrorism*, for which there are numerous definitions. The one relied upon most frequently before the acts of 9/11 was the definition espoused by the Federal Bureau of Investigation (FBI), as cited in Simonsen and Spindlove (2000): "Terrorism is the unlawful use of force or threat of violence against persons or property to intimidate or coerce a government, the civilian population, or any segment thereof, in furtherance of political or social objectives" (p. 19). Through the years, however, researchers and law enforcement officials have changed their definitions of terrorism in order to be more aligned with the current state of terrorism and related activities. Martin (2006) analyzed more recent definitions of terrorism promulgated by scholars and practitioners from the law enforcement community and combined the integral components of each to arrive at the following definition:

> Terrorism is a premeditated and unlawful act in which groups or agents of some principal engage in a threatened or actual use of force or violence against human or property targets. These groups or agents engage in this behavior intending the purposeful intimidation of governments or people to affect policy or behavior with an underlying political objective. (p. 48)

It should be noted that terrorism takes many forms, all of which are serious and some of which are not so obvious. In addition to bombings, which have become commonplace around the world, emergency service personnel also must be able to respond to biological, chemical, and technological (or cyberterrorism) attacks. Recent incidents where mail that was contaminated with the deadly anthrax virus (Hu, 2001) and the increased potential for "tampering with data and software in the virtual system [that] could have major repercussions in the physical world, involving such things as disruption of air traffic control systems and tampering with automated pharmaceutical or food production" (Williams, 1999, p. 18) are realities that now must be anticipated and investigated.

As noted earlier in the chapter, terrorism, as a criminal activity, was identified as the second most prevalent form of transnational crime by a United Nations report titled *Fourth United Nations Survey of Crime Trends and Operations of Criminal Justice Systems* (United Nations Crime Prevention and Criminal Justice Division, 2009).

The increase in terrorism is underscored by many factors, the most significant of which is globalization. As stated by Williams (1999),

> ...the threats to national and international security posed by transnational...terrorist groups...can be understood as a result of two processes—globalization (the emergence of a variety of systems or activities that are global rather than national or regional in scope and that are generally not controlled by states and the crisis of state authority—both of which contribute to a contraction of the domain of state authority. (p. 19)

Other factors directly related to globalization have also contributed to the rise in terrorism. They are as follows: the current unprecedented mobility of people, as it is estimated that there are currently over 100 million migrants worldwide; increased trade flows spurred by the lowering of tariffs, the creation of free trade agreements, and the relatively recent democratization of eastern Europe; the establishment of a global financial system, which has enabled countries and financial institutions throughout the world to exchange with one another on a 24-hour-per-day basis; and the rise of megacities, cities with a population of more than 8 million inhabitants, that are linked to one another by advanced telecommunication systems. According to Williams (1999), "Such cities are excellent incubators for...terrorist groups. They provide anonymity and encourage the kinds of survival skills and bonding mechanisms that underpin all successful criminal enterprises" (p. 34); *the growth of transnational networks* or "cellular structures adopted by many terrorist organizations...in which there is sufficient duplication and redundancy that the elimination of particular cells can have only a modest impact" (p. 39); and the *growth of global communication systems and/or telecommunication capabilities* that have created never-before-seen opportunities for cross-border contacts and the subsequent development of more sophisticated networks, which will more than likely improve the success of recruitment efforts on behalf of terrorist organizations (pp. 24–41).

Similarly, Shelley's (2001) overview of transnational crime victimization, terrorism included, points to several factors at work. First, she identified the illegal trade in nuclear materials, large scale arms smuggling, international narcotics trafficking as a way of financing other transnational crimes like terrorism, and illegal alien smuggling as "...exacting an even higher human cost in large numbers of source and destination countries." Second, the massive profits generated by transnational crime groups, estimated at "...thousands of millions of dollars," much of which is laundered through the world economic markets, place the security of these marketplaces at serious risk. Third, due to the huge profits generated by these crimes, the resultant public corruption places all governments and legal systems at great risk as well.

Many of these same issues emerged as central themes at an international criminal justice conference that focused on global changes in organized crime and terrorism. As stated by one conference speaker, an FBI agent, "Undoubtedly, terrorism is here to stay and it is the greatest threat to national security. Increased mobility, improved communication, and the potential use of weapons of mass destruction, such as biological threats, will be major challenges for investigators" (Levinson, 1999, p. 9).

One need only examine daily newspaper headlines to see the rapid expansion of terrorism. According to the Worldwide Incidents Tracking System (WITS), a subsidiary of the New York Times and a clearinghouse for various statistics related to terrorism, in the year 2009 there were 65,879 terrorist incidents that occurred in 130 countries throughout the world. These incidents claimed a total of 364,664 victims, including 95,907 deaths, 191,280 persons injured, and 77,477 persons held hostage (Worldwide Incidents Tracking Systems [WITS], 2010). What has been the response of the police community, and what are some of the recommendations for improvement?

❖ Homeland Security and the Police Response

Prior to 9/11, many in the police community predicted that acts of terrorism would proliferate if authorities did not begin to focus on the "front end" of the terrorist problem—in other words, if they did not focus on the situation from a "proactive and preventive organizational dynamics perspective" (McHugh, 1998, p. 57). The problem with the traditional American response to terrorism, according to McHugh (1998),

> [was] that the terrorists [were] always one attack ahead of the law enforcement and security professionals, and as a result of this advantage, [were] frequently successful. This advantage can be neutralized by reinforcing the government's counter-terrorist information collection and by integrating threat analysis and threat based security countermeasures tailored to interdiction operations. (pp. 57–58)

Shortly after 9/11, and in response to the warnings from the police community, former president George W. Bush and the U.S. Congress passed two key pieces of legislation that have forever changed the way the United States deals with terrorism.

Office of Homeland Security

When the **Office of Homeland Security** was formed in 2001, its the mission was

> ". . . to develop and coordinate the implementation of a comprehensive national strategy to secure the United States from terrorist threats or attacks . . . and . . . coordinate the executive branch's efforts to detect, prepare for, prevent, protect against, respond to, and recover from terrorist attacks within the United States." (White House, 2001)

The Department of Homeland Security (DHS) was then officially formed in March 2003 (Ward, Kiernan, & Marbrey, 2006, p. 58).

According to a 2001 report by the U.S. General Accounting Office (GAO), these executive-level mandates are to be accomplished by implementing a risk management approach to reduce the risk and mitigate the consequences of future terrorist attacks. This will be accomplished by conducting threat assessments "to evaluate the likelihood of terrorist activity against a given asset or location . . . [which] helps to establish and prioritize security program requirements, planning, and resource allocation" (p. 3); by conducting vulnerability assessments to identify and respond to "weaknesses in physical structures, personnel protection systems, processes, or other areas that may be exploited by terrorists" (p. 5); and by performing criticality assessments "designed to systematically identify and evaluate important assets and infrastructure in terms of various factors, such as the mission and significance of a target" (p. 6).

The DHS has broadened its scope over the past several years. Current legislation now includes specifically defined roles for the intelligence community and the U.S. Military; promotes and funds public-private partnerships, including "citizen ready" initiatives; provides recommendations and funding for improved critical infrastructure protection, including "the transportation and communications and information technology industries; and includes preparation for and responding to incidents involving weapons of mass destruction and natural disasters" (Ward et al., 2006). Readers are strongly advised to view the organizational chart of the DHS to get an understanding of the multiagency approach and other related complexities to gain some basic insights regarding our national strategy in our fight against terrorism. For access, refer to the following URL: http://www.dhs.gov/xlibrary/assets/DHS_OrgChart.pdf

The U.S. Patriot Act

The other piece of legislation passed into law and viewed as necessary by many in the law enforcement community to effectively conduct counterterrorism operations is known as the **U.S. Patriot Act**, which is an acronym for the Uniting and Strengthening of America by Providing the Appropriate Tools Required to Intercept and Obstruct Terrorism Act. This antiterrorism law was designed to dramatically expand federal law enforcement and intelligence-gathering authority. Specifically, this new law expands federal police powers in the following ways:

- The authorization of roving wiretaps or the need for just one court order to tap multiple phone numbers, including cell phones, fax machines, and pagers
- Allowing for the detention of non-U.S. citizens suspected of terrorist activity for up to seven days without formal charges
- Giving law enforcement officials greater subpoena power for e-mail records of suspected terrorists
- Relaxing of restrictions on information sharing between U.S. law enforcement and intelligence-gathering agencies
- Expanding current money laundering statutes by requiring more record keeping and account holder information
- Lengthening the statute of limitations for prosecuting acts of terrorism described as being "egregious" (Ward et al., 2006, pp. 241–258)

While this legislation has safeguards in place to prevent or significantly mitigate abuse of power by law enforcement agencies, the law is not without critics. Worries concerning potential constitutional abuses in the name of national security and patriotism are not without merit, particularly when viewed in light of past abuses by many U.S. police agencies.

It is interesting to note that during past national crises (i.e., wars and conflicts with other nations), Congress has almost always expanded the powers of federal law enforcement agencies, perhaps because the vast public relations campaigns that accompanied our nation's efforts allowed for easy passage of such legislation. Whatever the reason, what almost always followed, however, were law enforcement and intelligence-gathering operations that seemed to follow hidden agendas, many times violating the constitutional rights of U.S. citizens. For example, from 1953 to

1973, covering much of the Korean conflict and the Vietnam War, "... the Central Intelligence Agency intercepted, opened, and photographed more than 250,000 personal letters" (Rosoff et al., 2007, p. 396) ; collected the names (from arrest reports) of over 300,000 persons arrested for homosexual acts; and regularly monitored the activities of persons whom they identified as political dissidents, including keeping them under surveillance, burglarizing their homes, and eavesdropping on their telephone conversations.

In addition, from the period extending from World War I through the Vietnam War, the FBI—the most prestigious of all American law enforcement agencies—spied on people who opposed the draft or engaged in labor organizing efforts; conducted warrantless searches and wiretapped communications of persons suspected of communist activities; infiltrated the American Civil Liberties Union, numerous peace organizations, and various professional coalitions; and more or less targeted anyone who advocated for social change or reform (Rosoff et al., 2007, pp. 399–402).

Finally, in similar fashion, during the 1960s, military intelligence agencies collected and maintained information on "... the financial affairs, sex lives, and psychiatric histories of persons engaged in domestic unrest ..." (Rosoff et al., 2007, pp. 396-97) or those who sought to change existing government policies. If there is any credence to the adage that history tends to repeat itself, the most recent expansion of federal police powers is likely to become subject to abuse and deserves close attention by Congress and the courts.

Another area of great public concern regarding the new police response to terrorism is the issue of racial profiling or biased enforcement, discussed at length in Chapter 8. Because of the events that occurred on 9/11, should persons of Middle Eastern ancestry be targeted by various police initiatives? Clearly, the answer is no, and recently expanded police powers must be tempered by the responsible exercise of discretionary authority and that the actions of the law enforcement community should be closely monitored.

A more recent issue related to this concern about the potential abuse of power by law enforcement officials is the State of Arizona's 2010 passage of new legislation that authorizes state and local police officers, acting under the legal doctrine of reasonable suspicion, to detain and question persons suspected of being illegal immigrants. Many politicians and citizen groups claim the law is unconstitutional, and others feel the law was necessary due to the failure of federal officials to secure the state's borders. Almost immediately, litigation at the state and federal levels was initiated. No court decisions have been reached thus far ("Arizona Immigration," 2010).

Racketeer Influenced and Corrupt Organizations (RICO) Statute

While laws addressing the various crimes perpetrated by individual members of transnational criminal organizations are numerous, none of them reach the depth and breadth of the **RICO** statute. Enacted into law as part of the Organized Crime Control Act of 1970, this far reaching conspiracy statute addresses the criminal organization itself, in effect making it unlawful to belong to an organization that is involved in a pattern of racketeering, which is identified by a list of numerous federal and state crimes, identified in Table 13.2. New crimes are added to those lists on a consistent basis as the nature and type of transnational crimes evolve.

The goal of prosecutors using this statute is to demonstrate a pattern of crimes (racketeering) through an organization or enterprise. The statute defines an enterprise as ". . . any individual, partnership, corporation, association or other legal entity, and any union or group of individuals associated in fact, although not a legal entity" (18 U.S.C. Sections 1961–68). Thus, prosecutors no longer have the burden of proving separate conspiracies because RICO, for all intents and purposes, makes it a crime in and of itself to belong to an enterprise involved in a pattern of racketeering, even if said crimes constituting the pattern of racketeering are committed by other persons in the enterprise. This prosecutorial tool, which was designed to attack the leadership structures of these criminal organizations, has been quite effective. Prior to RICO, the leaders of these enterprises were insulated because the individual crimes were committed by lower ranking members, albeit via the direction of higher ranking members (Abadinsky, 2010). To fulfill the pattern requirement of RICO, prosecutors must prove the commission of at least two of the crimes cited in Table 13.2 within a 10 year time span.

There are also civil provisions in the statute that can be used by citizens, business entities, or federal prosecutors. These provisions have been used successfully by private citizens regarding issues pertaining to the sexual abuse of minors by clergy members of organized religious groups, antiabortion activists who resorted to acts of property damage to voice their protests, and many other groups accused of other civil offenses (Abadinsky, 2010).

RICO, however, is not without its critics. The major criticisms of the statute by attorneys familiar with this law are that its various provisions, especially those dealing with the definitions of racketeering, are unconstitutionally vague (Abadinsky, 2010). There are many other criticisms, but they are beyond the scope of this text. However, the use of RICO against criminal organizations and other entities has proven to be quite effective due to its far reach and significant penalties in terms of incarceration and asset seizures. As noted several times throughout this chapter, readers are encouraged to learn more about this statute by perusing pertinent websites as the issues surrounding this law are extremely complex and are consistently being modified through case law. In Table 13.5, we offer a list of broad categories of federal criminal statutes that are commonly used against members of transnational crime organizations.

First Responder Preparedness and the Role of the Public

It would be naive to believe, even with the creation of the Office of Homeland Security, the expansion of powers given to the police, and the public's heightened awareness, that we have seen the last of domestic terrorism. Perhaps the best we can hope for and focus on is preparedness for and mitigation of similar acts in the future. In this regard, there are a number of things that can be done to accomplish these objectives. Placing all of the responsibility for counterterrorism on the shoulders of the federal authorities is obviously unwise. While the federal government must assume the lead role in this endeavor, the nation's response to terrorism must be a concerted, multilevel effort on behalf of the police and other agencies. Accordingly, there are a variety of strategies and plans that have been implemented and performed at the state and local level. States and municipalities, for example, cooperate and must continue to cooperate with the various **joint task forces** sponsored by federal law enforcement organizations such as the FBI, ATF, ICE (which is a combination of agencies formerly

Table 13.5 Categories of Federal Criminal Statutes Associated With the Prosecution of Transnational Crime

TITLE 18 > PART I > CHAPTER 2	TITLE 18 > PART I > CHAPTER 31
CHAPTER 2—AIRCRAFT AND MOTOR VEHICLES TITLE 18 > PART I > CHAPTER 5	**CHAPTER 31—EMBEZZLEMENT AND THEFT** TITLE 18 > PART I > CHAPTER 37
CHAPTER 5—ARSON TITLE 18 > PART I > CHAPTER 9	**CHAPTER 37—ESPIONAGE AND CENSORSHIP** TITLE 18 > PART I > CHAPTER 39 > § 831
CHAPTER 9—BANKRUPTCY TITLE 18 > PART I > CHAPTER 10 > § 175	**§ 831. Prohibited transactions involving nuclear materials** TITLE 18 > PART I > CHAPTER 41
§ 175. Prohibitions with respect to biological weapons TITLE 18 > PART I > CHAPTER 11B > § 229	**CHAPTER 41—EXTORTION AND THREATS** TITLE 18 > PART I > CHAPTER 44
§ 229. Prohibited activities TITLE 18 > PART I > CHAPTER 19 > § 371	**CHAPTER 44—FIREARMS** TITLE 18 > PART I > CHAPTER 46
§ 371. Conspiracy to commit offense or to defraud United States TITLE 18 > PART I > CHAPTER 19 > § 373	**CHAPTER 46—FORFEITURE** TITLE 18 > PART I > CHAPTER 47
§ 373. Solicitation to commit a crime of violence TITLE 18 > PART I > CHAPTER 25	**CHAPTER 47—FRAUD AND FALSE STATEMENTS** TITLE 18 > PART I > CHAPTER 50
CHAPTER 25—COUNTERFEITING AND FORGERY TITLE 18 > PART I > CHAPTER 26 > § 521	**CHAPTER 50—GAMBLING** TITLE 18 > PART I > CHAPTER 51
§ 521. Criminal street gangs TITLE 18 > PART I > CHAPTER 27	**CHAPTER 51—HOMICIDE** TITLE 18 > PART I > CHAPTER 55
CHAPTER 27—CUSTOMS TITLE 18 > PART I > CHAPTER 57	**CHAPTER 55—KIDNAPPING** TITLE 18 > PART I > CHAPTER 97
CHAPTER 57—LABOR TITLE 18 > PART I > CHAPTER 61	**RAILROAD CARRIERS AND MASS TRANSPORTATION SYSTEMS ON LAND, ON WATER, OR THROUGH THE AIR** TITLE 18 > PART I > CHAPTER 103
CHAPTER 61—LOTTERIES TITLE 18 > PART I > CHAPTER 63	**CHAPTER 103—ROBBERY AND BURGLARY** TITLE 18 > PART I > CHAPTER 105

CHAPTER 63—MAIL FRAUD AND OTHER FRAUD OFFENSES TITLE 18 > PART I > CHAPTER 69	**CHAPTER 105—SABOTAGE** TITLE 18 > PART I > CHAPTER 110
CHAPTER 69—NATIONALITY AND CITIZENSHIP TITLE 18 > PART I > CHAPTER 71	**CHAPTER 110—SEXUAL EXPLOITATION AND OTHER ABUSE OF CHILDREN** TITLE 18 > PART I > CHAPTER 113
CHAPTER 71—OBSCENITY TITLE 18 > PART I > CHAPTER 75	**CHAPTER 113—STOLEN PROPERTY** TITLE 18 > PART I > CHAPTER 113A
CHAPTER 75—PASSPORTS AND VISAS TITLE 18 > PART I > CHAPTER 77	**CHAPTER 113A—TELEMARKETING FRAUD** TITLE 18 > PART I > CHAPTER 113B
CHAPTER 77—PEONAGE, SLAVERY, AND TRAFFICKING IN PERSONS TITLE 18 > PART I > CHAPTER 79	**CHAPTER 113B—TERRORISM** TITLE 18 > PART I > CHAPTER 114
CHAPTER 79—PERJURY TITLE 18 > PART I > CHAPTER 81	**CHAPTER 114—TRAFFICKING IN CONTRABAND CIGARETTES AND SMOKELESS TOBACCO** TITLE 18 > PART I > CHAPTER 117
CHAPTER 81—PIRACY AND PRIVATEERING TITLE 18 > PART I > CHAPTER 95	**CHAPTER 117—TRANSPORTATION FOR ILLEGAL SEXUAL ACTIVITY AND RELATED CRIMES**
CHAPTER 95—RACKETEERING TITLE 18 > PART I > CHAPTER 96	
CHAPTER 96—RACKETEER INFLUENCED AND CORRUPT ORGANIZATIONS TITLE 18 > PART I > CHAPTER 119	
CHAPTER 119—WIRE AND ELECTRONIC COMMUNICATIONS INTERCEPTION AND INTERCEPTION OF ORAL COMMUNICATIONS	

Source: 18 USC Part I Chapters 1–123.

* To access each of these chapters and more, readers are urged to refer to the following government website: http://www.gpoaccess.gov/uscode/browse.html

known as U.S. Immigration and U.S. Customs), DEA, and the U.S. State Department. Using this strategy, local police officers are assigned to the agencies cited previously and are officially sworn to enforce federal laws. The advantages are numerous, especially with regard to intelligence sharing, and the benefits in terms of preparedness are significant (Davies & Plotkin, 2005).

POLICE STORIES

While working as an investigator in the Intelligence Section for the Chicago Police Department's Organized Crime Division, I and other team members conducted a moving surveillance on a mob-connected bookmaker. Toward the end of one of those days, I saw some investigators from the Vice Control Division in the same area. (The Vice Control office was directly next to the Intelligence Section office in the same building.) When I inquired about what they were up to, they said they were following the same individual that we were. When I revealed that we were doing likewise, we agreed that the next day we would inform our supervisors of this wasted manpower and suggest either to have one unit stop or to conduct a joint investigation that would call for less manpower.

The following day when I arrived at the office, I informed my sergeant of what had happened the previous day and made my suggestions to him. He gave an approving nod and said that he would speak to the lieutenant who would then speak with the unit commander. A short time later the phone on my desk rang; it was the commander's secretary who told me in a hushed voice that the commander wanted to see me right away.

I entered the commander's office, almost expecting to be commended for my suggestion, but he stood up from behind his desk, his face turned beet red, and began screaming at me. He said "If I find out you gave any of our information to those assholes in Vice I'll have you transferred back to patrol tonight."

As I exited his office and made my way back to my desk, my tail between my legs, I could see and hear my sergeant and lieutenant laughing. They taught me a lesson regarding the spirit of intra-agency cooperation in the Chicago Police Department.

To this day, I still think about the absurdity of the situation. We had police officers from the same department and the same division duplicating their effort, and we were instructed not to share information nor cooperate with one another. The goal, at least from the point of view of the commander, was competition, not cooperation. His unit was not to be upstaged by another unit. It still boggles my mind whenever I think of that incident.

Focusing on the preparedness issue, Scaramella and Rodriguez (2004) set out to elicit and examine the attitudes, beliefs, and perceptions of police officers from the Chicago metropolitan area regarding various issues of **first responder** preparedness to an assortment of transnational crime issues, as well as preparedness for natural disasters.

Based on knowledge concerning the state of transnational crime, it seemed logical to assume that local police agencies would begin to provide at least basic training for their personnel to prepare them to respond to these crimes in an effective manner. This was the focus of the authors' research. The current state of police training, at least in the state of Illinois, paints a dismal picture. For example, the Illinois Law Enforcement Training and Standards Board (ILETSB), the regulatory body that oversees the training

❖ **PHOTO 13.3** The multi-agency disaster preparedness plans of various communities must be frequently practiced to be effective.

and certification of all state and local police officers in the state, currently mandates little or no basic training or continuing education in any of the crimes that have been identified as transnational in nature. The only exception is the limited amount of training directed at environmental crime and narcotics trafficking (Illinois Law Enforcement Training and Standards Board [ILETSB], 2003).

A written survey was developed and designed to elicit respondents' opinions regarding perceived preparedness to deal with transnational crime on a variety of different fronts. The variables of interest for the purposes of this chapter were directed at the following issues: whether or not respondents received any formal training in terrorism; whether or not respondents' respective agencies had a formal plan designed to address this issue; whether or not respondents were familiar with the plan and if they had practiced the plan in the past 12 months; respondents' perception regarding the degree of effectiveness of preparedness training they may have received; respondents' perception as to whether or not the plan(s) provide(s) adequate protection for their respective communities; respondents' perception regarding the necessary equipment for confronting various acts of terrorism and natural disasters; and their perception regarding overall preparedness to confront these issues.

The key findings from the sample population of 260 police officer respondents from the Chicago metropolitan area are noted below:

- 4% of the respondents reported receiving no inservice training with respect to terrorism.
- More than one third (36%) reported that their agency had no formal plan in response to terrorism threats.
- More than half (52%) of the respondents indicated that their agencies had no plans or that they had not read nor were familiar with those that existed.
- More than two thirds (67%) of respondents indicated that they had not practiced any plans in this regard.

- More than half (54%) of respondents were undecided or responded in some level of disagreement with the notion that training was adequate to ensure readiness to respond to these acts.
- The proportion of those that perceived plan inadequacy (34%) was nearly equal to the proportion that believed their existing plans were adequate (36%) to protect the public.
- 58% of respondents disagreed with the notion of equipment availability.
- 61% of respondents reported a negative perception of their preparedness.

For police administrators, the implications are clear. Merely having a plan to respond to transnational crime activities is not sufficient to protect the public from the devastating effects of transnational crime in all its forms. If officer perceptions are accurate, a comprehensive approach is necessary to adequately protect the public. Enhanced and comprehensive training from a variety of sources; dissemination of plan details to personnel beyond the perfunctory requirements found in departmental general orders; familiarizing officers with the available, sufficient equipment; and comprehensive practicing of existing plans are all necessary to maintain the level of readiness officers believe is required to protect the public (Scaramella & Rodriguez, 2004).

Smaller communities with limited budgets also must encourage their police departments, fire departments, social service agencies, health care professionals, and volunteer organizations to work together to increase their level of preparedness in response to the varied threats that acts of terrorism pose. A good example of this new spirit of cooperation was exemplified at a disaster planning conference sponsored by the Casualty Care Research Center. The Center lent their medical expertise to a variety of local emergency service personnel by helping them plan and prepare for emergency procedures following a possible chemical or biological attack (Seaton, 2001).

Another more grassroots approach to assisting in this regard lies within academia. Since 9/11, universities and other institutions of higher education are increasingly offering courses pertaining to terrorism; world politics; religion; war; race, ethnicity, gender, and class; and foreign policy (Simmons, 2001). It is important to note that all of these offerings have one central theme—making students begin to think globally in order to put world events into the proper perspective. As one professor stated, "We have a tendency to be very critical of the Taliban and bin Laden . . . and rightfully so. They did attack us . . . [but] we're remiss for not trying to get a little deeper and find out where they're coming from. They didn't attack us just because they hate Americans" (Simmons, 2001, p. 1D).

It is disturbing to think that it took the catastrophic events of 9/11 to persuade many in academia to incorporate internationally based course offerings into their curricula. For example, some months before the events of 9/11, a proposal was made to administrators at a regional university to form an academic institute designed to focus primarily on the international issues facing criminal justice communities, with terrorism being targeted as a central issue. University administrators accepted the proposal, but it was rejected by the state's chief governing authority because of its international emphasis, which was seen as outside the scope of a regional university. Since that time, the academic community appears to have reconsidered so that it's now difficult to find a college or university that does not either offer or mandate the study of international issues.

Another obvious component of the local response to terrorism should be to provide state and local emergency service personnel with meaningful continuing education and training activities. The content of such training, in addition to focusing on terrorism, should stress the topics of ethics, professionalism, and the judicious exercise of discretionary authority. These efforts should assist in mitigating potential abuses that may arise during the efforts of the police to combat terrorism successfully.

Public awareness is also an essential ingredient in the recipe for mitigating instances of terrorism. A good example of this heightened public awareness in the years following the 9/11 attack occurred in New York City. On May 1, 2010, in the crowded Times Square area of New York City, a car bomb was discovered when a T-shirt vendor saw something suspicious (smoke coming from an unoccupied SUV on 45th Street near 7th Avenue) and alerted police. The would-be car-bomber left an SUV loaded with propane and gas cans, fireworks, timing devices, and more than 100 pounds of fertilizer on the street, though luckily, the fertilizer the offender chose was not the type that explodes. Police evacuated the crowds from the vicinity of the vehicle, and the bomb squad disabled the device. Within two days, police investigators working for all levels of government identified and located the offender and placed him under arrest. It should be noted that in addition to professional police work, investigators were aided by video recordings from surveillance cameras in the nearby area and, ultimately, by the actions of an alert citizen who reported the suspicious vehicle to police (Esposito, James, & Schabner, 2010).

In addition to the local response by our nation's police, the United States has been very proactive in their attempt to train and better prepare local police from around the globe to effectively address transnational threats. The FBI set up training academies for, and assists personnel from other foreign training academies with, investigative methodologies and expertise that address transnational crime. These efforts continue with increasing frequency and significant successes. Examine the following efforts currently in force:

- *The Budapest International Law Enforcement Academy.* Modeled after their own training academy in Quantico, Virginia, this full-service FBI academy in Hungary strictly serves members of the international law enforcement community.
- *Iraqi Training Initiative.* This is part of a multinational plan to help Iraqi police deal effectively with transnational threats.
- *Middle Eastern Law Enforcement Training Center.* The result of a formal relationship between the FBI and the Dubai National Police, as well as other police agencies throughout the region.
- *Latin American Law Enforcement Executive Development Seminar.* The counterpart of the FBI's U.S.-based National Academy program, which offers state of the art leadership and administrative training to command staff from local police agencies.
- *Arabic Language Law Enforcement Executive Development Seminar.* Same strategy as the previous organization, but it serves the police communities from Middle Eastern and North African countries.
- *Plan Colombia: Anti-Kidnapping Initiative.* Provides effective training to Colombian law enforcement agencies for investigating crimes committed by transnational crime organizations with special emphasis on kidnapping and other crimes related to the illicit drug industry.
- *Pacific Training Initiative.* A program designed to specifically address terrorism and public corruption for command staff personnel from law enforcement agencies in the Pacific Rim and Asia.

- *Antiterrorism Assistance Program.* Focuses on strategies for an effective law enforcement response to acts of terrorism, particularly those that target U.S. citizens outside American borders.
- *International Counterproliferation Program.* In tandem with the U.S. Department of Defense, this initiative provides training designed to prevent the growth of transnational crime for the global law enforcement community. (FBI, 2010a)

❖ Chapter Summary

As stated in the beginning of the chapter, continuous advances in technology, the increased mobility of persons from one country to another, significant changes in the socioeconomic conditions of the global marketplace, and modified legal agreements and changing political relationships between the United States and other countries have combined to dramatically change the way in which the police community operates.

The factors cited, as well as other related ones, have given rise to a global crime phenomenon known as transnational crime. Inclusive in this broad category of crime are additional and complex forms of deviance such as organized and white collar crime. In all of its forms, the repercussions caused by transnational crime are devastating on a number of fronts. In addition to the human tragedies that have occurred throughout the world, costs to the global financial markets have been significant—estimated to be at least several trillion dollars annually. Moreover, the social and political costs associated with transnational crime are significant as well. These costs are felt in the form of an overall loss of faith or trust in governments by their respective citizenries and the many strained political relationships between leaders of many countries due to violations of national and international sovereignty.

Thankfully, the post-9/11 local police response to these new crime threats has changed significantly from being responsive to proactive in nature. Are we at the point where we should be? No, but we are certainly going in the right direction. For example, proactive police practices such as participation with federal law enforcement task forces, improved intra- and interagency cooperation regarding the sharing of pertinent information, and engaging in continuous planning and training regarding first responder preparedness have become a major goal of local law enforcement agencies. The issue of preparedness must also include input from emergency medical services personnel and academicians, via their curriculum offerings on international issues, and a continued focus on public awareness campaigns.

Recent legislation like the U.S. Patriot Act and other effective laws such as RICO must continue to be applied toward these global crime organizations, and agreements between countries on effective international laws and treaties must continue as well.

The final, and perhaps most significant, point to be made from the discussion in this chapter is that if we, as a nation, are to respond to terrorism effectively, we must do so justly, lawfully, and responsibly, and perhaps most important of all, we must be guided by the spirit of interagency and interdisciplinary cooperation and public awareness.

❖ Key Terms

transnational crime

organized crime

North American Free
   Trade Agreement (NAFTA)

Perestroika

Boryokudan

Triads

gangs (meta/super gangs)

mafia

outlaw motorcycle gangs

money laundering

white collar crime

postponed violence

institutional corruption

terrorism

Homeland Security

U.S. Patriot Act

RICO Statute

task force

first responder

❖ Discussion Questions

1. What major global issues have affected local police operations in the United States?

2. What particular international incidents have led to the vast expansion of transnational crime?

3. What did the United Nations Survey of other countries reveal about the different forms of transnational crime?

4. Based on Abadinsky's (2010) typology of criminal organizations, can terrorist groups be called a criminal organization? Why or why not?

5. Based on the characteristics of the various transnational groups listed throughout the chapter, what common attributes do they share?

6. Are any of the categories of white collar crime listed in the chapter transnational in nature? If yes, identify those categories.

7. What are some of the many economic, social, and political costs associated with white collar crime?

8. Do you agree with Nader's notion of postponed violence? Why or why not?

9. What global conditions gave rise to the frequency of acts of terrorism?

10. What are the major functions of the Department of Homeland Security?

11. Do the fundamental constructs of the U.S. Patriot Act and the RICO statute overlap? How so?

12. What are some of the various roles of local law enforcement with respect to terrorism?

13. What recommendations can you make for improved law enforcement and citizen responses to terrorism?

❖ Internet Exercises

1. Using the Web, identify at least three international organizations that are involved in the fight against transnational crime.

2. Use the Web to identify other key legislation that was part of the Organized Crime Control Act of 1970 (in addition to RICO) and that is effective against members of transnational criminal organizations.

3. Use the Web to find at least three incidences of what Nader called postponed violence with respect to white collar crime.

14

Private and Contract Police

❖ History and Background

As is the case with most major aspects of policing, private or contract policing came to the United States along with early settlers. The need to protect property and people led to the use of fortifications in some cases and the hiring of night watchmen. The slow development of public policing at local, state, and federal levels, along with increasing crime rates, eventually led to the emergence of private security forces in the middle 1800s, when Allan Pinkerton founded the Pinkerton agency. The agency conducted

❖ **PHOTO 14.1** Private police from the early days of the private security industry engaged in many duties now associated with public policing.

investigations and provided security for railroads, railroad yards, and other industrial concerns (Fischer, Halibozek, & Green, 2008). Members of the agency worked for the federal government collecting intelligence during President Lincoln's term, and the agency is credited with foiling a plot to assassinate President Lincoln.

At about the same time, Henry Wells and William Fargo established Wells Fargo and Company, which provided detective services and armed security personnel to guard freight shipments. A few years later, Washington Brink established Brinks, Incorporated, which provided services similar to those outlined but eventually expanded into armored-car and carrier services. During the same era, Edwin Holmes became the first to offer burglar alarm service, and American District Telegraph (ADT) also began installing and servicing alarm systems (Fischer et al., 2008).

In the early 1900s, William Burns, the head of the Bureau of Investigation, Secret Service (the forerunner of the Federal Bureau of Investigation), founded a detective agency under his own name. The William J. Burns Detective Agency was to become the second largest contract guard and investigative service in the United States (Pinkerton being the largest) until the end of the 20th century. The first fire control and detection system was developed during this period as well under the title of Baker Industries.

The Development of the Modern Security Era

Throughout the 20th century, protection of industrial business relied almost exclusively on the private agencies discussed previously. Few businesses hired their own security staffs. However, with the United States' entry into World War II, industrial firms started developing their own security systems.

The impetus for modern private security operations began with federal standards established by the Industrial Security Program, which were designed to protect the war industry and its secrets. This program eventually became the Defense Industrial Security Program, which, under the authority of the National Industrial Security Program, oversees private industry's need for access to classified information (Fischer et al., 2008).

In addition, soon after the end of the Korean War, security managers who handled security operations during both World War II and the Korean War formed the American Society for Industrial Security (ASIS). ASIS was the first professional security organization in the United States. Today, it has grown into a global representative for security interests. For most security professionals, 1955, the founding year for ASIS, signifies the beginning of modern security (Fischer et al., 2008).

For a variety of reasons, we have seen a considerable increase in the use of private and contract police services. Reflecting changing societal conditions, such services became common in hotels, hospitals, warehouses, and retail establishments. As the types of crimes committed against these businesses became increasingly sophisticated, security consulting and private investigations firms were established to deal with fraud, arson, and employee theft, among other crimes. In the 1960s and 1970s, loss prevention became a major focus for private security firms, and repositories of security information were developed and shared through various alliances, bureaus, or security institutes. Today, these alliances share information, sometimes by subscription or with membership only, by circulating "hot" lists and newsletters through electronic distributions. Some of the more prominent groups are the National Insurance Crime Bureau, the Jewelers Security Alliance, and the International Association of Arson Investigators (Fischer et al., 2008).

❖ Security Today

The increasing size of the private security force in the United States in the first decade of the 21st century is due, in part, to the growth of gated communities in which more affluent Americans pay for premium services through voluntary associations. At the same time, demands for security personnel are increasing due to the fear of crime and cutbacks in public services and due to an increased need for security related to the Internet and computer usage and the accompanying storage and transmission of highly sensitive data (Nalla, 2009). This growth in security personnel includes **in-house security personnel** (who typically conduct security activities within an organization), **contract security personnel** (security guards or officers hired by security firms and then contracted to another firm to secure and protect assets and personnel), and **hybrid systems** (in-house management personnel with contract officers). Hybrid security operations are rapidly becoming the norm in many categories of security, particularly industrial protection.

Terrorism and Modern Private Security Operations

On September 11, 2001, al-Qaeda terrorists hijacked four passenger jets and intentionally crashed two of them into the Twin Towers of the World Trade Center in New York City. Everyone on board was killed, as were many of those working in the buildings. Both towers collapsed, destroying nearby buildings and damaging others. The hijackers crashed a third airliner into the Pentagon, just outside Washington, DC. The fourth plane crashed into a field in rural Pennsylvania after some of its passengers and flight crew attempted to retake control of the plane, which the hijackers had redirected toward Washington, DC. There were no survivors from any of the flights. All told, 2,976 victims and 19 hijackers died in the attacks. The vast majority of casualties were civilians, including nationals from over 90 countries.

The United States responded to the attacks by launching a "War on Terrorism" and enacting the Patriot Act (discussed in Chapters 5 and 13). Many other countries also strengthened their antiterrorism legislation and expanded law enforcement powers. Based on the events of 9/11 as well as the nature of responses to several natural disasters, law enforcement officials and the newly created Department of Homeland Security determined that security officers are often first responders. Congress enacted several liability protections for providers of antiterrorism technologies in the Homeland Security Act of 2002. Thus, protecting against terrorism became an additional responsibility for many private security personnel (Zalud, 2009). In fact, Bennett (2009) argued that since 9/11 the private security industry has been draining the NYPD of "serious, smart and experienced officers the city needs the most in a crisis" (p. 1). Today, he concluded, the industry involves primarily former military and police personnel who provide "everything from diplomatic, convoy, embassy weapon storage and energy infrastructural security to gathering intelligence, conducting interrogations, patrolling borders on land, fighting pirates on sea and transporting goods and personnel by air" (p. 1).

Still, the response of the private sector to 9/11 has varied. Much of the private investment has been the direct result of federal regulations designed to protect the American public while in transit. Other federal mandates include protection of water and food supplies, as well as protection of power sources (gas, oil, and electric). ASIS International used the interest in increased professional security to work with Congress to pass industry standards included in the 2002 Intelligence Reform Act that was signed by President Bush in December of 2005. The Department of Justice now allows private security employers in all 50 states to access FBI criminal background information (ASIS International, 2006).

While the most visible changes in security have occurred in the country's airports, most of the increased protection is now under direct law enforcement control. Although airlines retain their security staffs, federal air marshals and the Transportation Security Administration have taken over tasks once performed by private security personnel. In other transportation venues, including trucks, buses, trains, and water transportation, private police continue to provide security for passengers.

Another major improvement in security operations occurred in the power industry. While the Nuclear Regulatory Commission (NRC) regulations required power companies to protect nuclear facilities, there were few security regulations governing other electric producing and transmitting stations. Today, the Federal Energy Regulation Commission (FERC) has developed security standards that all electric utilities must meet (Gips, 2002).

The oil and gas industries have been impacted by recent Department of Transportation, Office of Pipeline Safety standards. All pipelines are to be checked by operators to identify and address risks where a rupture would have the greatest impact on populations or the environment. Fear of terrorist attacks aimed at disrupting the flow of vital fuels and new government regulations have prompted companies operating pipelines to assess and, where necessary, step up security measures (Treat & Bartle, 2009).

Water utilities, whether private or municipal, have also been given new guidelines that have created an increased demand for security. The Public Security and Bioterrorism Act mandates that water systems serving communities of 100,000 or more must meet federal standards for protection. The cost of meeting these standards as reported to Congress is more than $276.8 billion over a 20-year period starting in 2003. In 2005, the Water Sentinel program, designed to establish early warning systems in major cities in the event of chemical or biological contamination of the water system, was initiated (Tieman, 2006).

Public spaces in private business areas have also been impacted in the aftermath of 9/11. Retail security, particularly in malls, has been intensified. A number of mall security managers now train security personnel to spot suicide bombers. The International Council of Shopping Centers has held antiterrorism classes since 2004 (Apuzzo, 2004). Similar concerns have also created interest in increasing security measures in civic and cultural city centers. For example, the Town Center Improvement District, Houston, Texas—which covers 1.5 square miles, employs approximately 15,000 people, and has over 1.5 million visitors each year—has included security measures such as mounted patrols and contract security services (Premo, 2002).

To prevent further attacks, the management at Yankee Stadium decided to have 1,500 police officers on alert following the 9/11 attack. They also employed jet fighters and sharpshooters. Bomb-sniffing dogs were used in the crowds, and all flights over the stadium were banned. While these measures seem extreme, the predictions of additional terrorist attacks at that time warranted such measures. Many major sports facilities have increased security measures with tightened restrictions on fans carrying in bags, coolers, and other items. Facilities are locked down between major events, and many facilities now monitor air intakes and water systems (Gips, 2003).

Similar changes have occurred at hotels, conference centers, museums, and hospitals. Even farmers have become involved with the growing concern over perceived agroterrorism. Fear of what would happen to the meat industry if disease were to infect the animal population has farmers and authorities watching our borders for possible introduction of infected animals. Two approaches have been implemented. The United States Department of Agriculture is working with Homeland Security to determine high risk plant pathogens as well as monitor our borders. The second initiative involves the education of farmers as the front line of defense. For example, the American Farm Bureau reports that it is now encouraging farmers to track who is on their property (Gips, 2003).

❖ Private and Contract Security Personnel

By the year 2000, private security expenditures exceeded $100 billion annually and the number of protective services employees in the total economy rose to 3.1 million (Hobijn & Sager, 2007 [Note that estimate differs from that provided by Gamiz in Chapter 1 and may be based upon different sources.]). It is important to note here that the number of private security personnel is roughly three times that of public law enforcement personnel.

The share of protective services employees in total employment has remained fairly constant at 2.3%. In the private sector, where roughly 80% of protective services employees are security guards, the share of workers employed in protective services occupations has also held steady, at 1.0% in both 2001 and 2005 (Bureau of Labor Statistics [BLS], 2009). Private security personnel can be divided into a number of arbitrary categories:

- Security managers
- Personal security (bodyguards)
- Private investigators and detectives

- Security consultants
- Security equipment and service sales personnel
- Industrial security guards
- Retail security officers
- Hospital security personnel
- Airline security officers
- Hotel security officers
- Campus security officers
- Bank security personnel
- Contract security officers
- Locksmiths
- Computer and intellectual property security personnel

Selected categories are described in more detail in the following sections.

POLICE STORIES

After 15 years of working as a police officer, I received an opportunity to work as the corporate Director of Security for a major newspaper in Chicago. In addition to their facility, which housed the corporate offices, they also had remote locations where specialized printing and production services were performed. In addition, many of the departments at all of the locations ran on a 24-hour per day basis.

The duties of the security operation were numerous and varied; they included, but were not limited to, access control for employees and visitors; roving security of the physical premises inside and outside; the investigation of issues pertaining to internal and external criminal conduct; enforcement of internal policies and regulations; disaster and evacuation planning; the monitoring of activities throughout the facility via the use of cameras, which tape recorded the activities occurring in strategic points in the building and outside perimeter; protective services when dignitaries visited the editors; and a host of other duties similar in nature.

My entire department consisted of contract security guards. The biggest problem I had, which was a constant source of anxiety, was the scheduling and overall conduct of these security officers. Entry-level guards are not paid well, and the benefits in terms of medical insurance and other such issues were meager at best—and sometimes nonexistent. In addition, the training requirements imposed by the state of Illinois were, and remain, very weak. The successful completion of 20 hours worth of instruction from a recognized vendor was all that was required, at least for unarmed personnel. Those who could carry firearms required an additional 20 hours of training.

The most problematic issues regarding these contract guards were a very high turnover rate, poor communication skills, sleeping or hiding on the job, and a lack of professionalism. However, they were compensated at a rate barely exceeding minimum wage. Thus, the old adage that "you get what you pay for" was most applicable. In the eyes of the corporate executive staff, though, that was no excuse for poor performance. I always told them, "You want FBI agents walking through your halls, but the pay sucks. If you want better guards, you need to pay more." That always ended these types of conversations.

The bottom line is that the private security industry, as it applies to entry-level guard services, is facing the same conundrum that public police found themselves in during the early days (i.e., minimum education and training standards, low pay, and an overall lack of professionalism). Until those who contract these services for their places of employment begin to pay a decent wage, the problems I have alluded to will persist. My personal opinion is that most facilities managers and other executives who make these decisions do so not for the protection of their employees and the public, but rather because case law requires the presence of security in order to mitigate their potential civil liability if and when you know what hits the fan.

Let me end this story with a pitiful but humorous event, at least at the time that it occurred. I made an unexpected visit to the newspaper late one evening and entered through the rear dock area, where there was a constant coming and going of trucks and vehicles of various service providers. The area beyond the docks is where the printing presses were located. When I got to the rear door, I entered with my access card; there before me, as well as anyone else working in the area, was our security officer with his feet up on the desk and sound asleep. I woke him and said in an excited voice, "Have you seen him? There was a call on the radio that a male dressed in Muslim attire, carrying a backpack with a long fuse protruding from it, was wandering around the press area." He attempted to compose himself and began searching this huge area for the man with a backpack with a fuse hanging out. I watched as he scurried about, asking one worker after another if they had seen such a man. It took him a good half-hour before he realized I sent him on a wild goose chase. When he returned to the office he said, "OK boss, you got me. I deserved that."

Thankfully, this was just a joke, but something like this actually could have occurred—and the person in charge of guarding against trespassers was asleep on the job.

❖ **Photo 14.2** Private security officers are found in virtually all large office complexes and buildings. Owners of these structures mitigate potential civil liability if someone was assaulted or otherwise injured on the premises by having security officers on scene. In addition, these security officers control access to the buildings in question and will detain anyone who may have committed a criminal offense on their property. The offenders are then turned over to the public police agencies.

Private Detectives and Investigators

Most **private detectives** and **investigators** have some college education even though there are no formal education requirements for most private detective and investigator jobs. In most states, they are required to be licensed. Although related experience is usually required, some people enter the occupation directly after graduation from college, generally with an associate's or bachelor's degree in criminal justice or police science.

According to the Bureau of Labor Statistics (BLS) (2009), the 2006 educational attainment for private detectives and investigators, in percent, was as follows:

Level of Education	Percent
High school graduate or equivalent	18
Some college, no degree	26
Associate's degree	8
Bachelor's degree	34
Master's degree	13
Professional degree or PhD	3

Corporate investigators generally have at least a bachelor's degree, and many have master's degrees in business administration or law or are CPAs. For computer forensics work, a computer science or accounting degree provides good background knowledge for investigating fraud.

On-the-job training, in which new investigators are put on cases and gain skills as they go, occurs frequently. Corporate investigators hired by large companies, however, may receive formal training in business practices, management structure, and various finance-related topics (BLS, 2009).

The majority of states require private detectives and investigators to be licensed, with requirements varying from state-to-state. Some states, such as Alabama, Alaska, Colorado, Idaho, Mississippi, Missouri, and South Dakota, have no licensing requirements; some states have few requirements; and still others have stringent regulations. Generally, detectives and investigators who carry handguns must meet additional requirements for a firearms permit (BLS, 2009).

Many investigators enter the field after serving in law enforcement, the military, government auditing and investigative positions, or federal intelligence jobs. Former law enforcement officers, military investigators, and government agents sometimes become private detectives or investigators in a second career. Most computer forensic investigators learn their trade while working for a law enforcement agency, either as a sworn officer or as a civilian computer forensic analyst.

Private detectives and investigators held about 52,000 jobs in 2006, with slightly less than one third being self-employed and another third in investigation and security services, including private detective agencies. The remainder worked in various jobs in department or other general merchandise stores, state and local government, legal services firms, employment services companies, insurance agencies, and credit mediation establishments, including banks and other depository institutions (BLS, 2009). As of May 2006, median annual earnings of salaried private detectives and investigators were $33,750 (BLS, 2009).

Security Guards and Gaming Surveillance Officers

Security guards, or **security officers**, patrol and inspect property to protect against fire, theft, vandalism, terrorism, and illegal activity. They use radio and telephone communications to call for assistance from police, fire, or emergency medical services as the situation dictates. Security guards write comprehensive reports outlining their observations and activities during their assigned shift. In addition, they may interview witnesses or victims, prepare case reports, and testify in court (BLS, 2009). Their specific tasks depend on whether they work in a static security position or on a mobile patrol. Guards assigned to static security positions stay at one location for a specified length of time; they become closely acquainted with the property and people associated with their station and often monitor alarms and closed-circuit TV cameras. Guards assigned to mobile patrol drive or walk from one location to another and conduct security checks within an assigned geographical zone. They may detain or arrest criminal violators, answer service calls concerning criminal activity or problems, and issue traffic violation warnings.

Security guards often work with undercover store detectives to prevent theft by customers or employees and help apprehend shoplifting suspects. Some patrol parking lots to deter car thefts and robberies. Others work in office buildings, banks, and hospitals, maintaining order and protecting customers, staff, and property. Still others work at air, sea, and rail terminals and other transportation facilities, protecting people, freight, property, and equipment. Security guards also work in public buildings such as museums, factories, laboratories, government buildings, data processing centers, and military bases, where they protect information, products, computer codes, and defense secrets and check the credentials of people and vehicles entering and leaving the premises. Working at universities, parks, and sports stadiums, security personnel perform crowd control, supervise parking and seating, and direct traffic (BLS, 2009).

Armored car guards protect money and valuables during transit, and they protect individuals responsible for making commercial bank deposits from theft or injury. They pick up money or other valuables from businesses and transport them to another location. **Gaming surveillance officers** act as security agents for casino managers and patrons. They observe casino operations for irregular activities, such as cheating or theft; monitor compliance to rules, regulations, and laws; and sometimes walk the casino floor (BLS, 2009).

There typically are no specific education requirements for security guards, but employers usually prefer to fill armed-guard positions with people who have at least a high school diploma. Gaming surveillance officers often need some education beyond high school. In most states, guards must be licensed. The amount of training guards receive varies. It is more rigorous for armed guards because their employers are legally responsible for any use of force, so armed guards receive formal training in areas such as weapons retention and laws covering the use of force. An increasing number of states are making ongoing training a legal requirement for retention of licensure (BLS, 2009).

Guards who are employed at establishments that place a heavy emphasis on security usually receive extensive formal training. For example, guards at nuclear power plants undergo several months of training before going on duty—and even then, they perform their tasks under close supervision for a significant period of time. They are taught to use firearms, administer first aid, operate alarm systems and electronic security equipment, and spot and deal with security problems.

❖ Licensure

A study completed in 2005 found that 43 states licensed or regulated the security industry. This is a significant increase from the 1990 figure, when only 25 states had any imposed training or licensure standards (Associated Criminal Justice and Security Consultants, LLC., 2005). In most states, to be licensed as a guard individuals must be at least 18 years old, pass a background check and drug test, and complete classroom training in such subjects as property rights, emergency procedures, and detention of suspected criminals. However, given the size of the private protective force in the United States, it is unfortunate that the average training provided to security personnel is 8 hours—compared to the national median training for police officers at 720 hours (Fischer et al., 2008).

Guards who carry weapons must be licensed by the appropriate government authority, and some receive further certification as special police officers, allowing them to make limited types of arrests while on duty. As an example, according to the Washington, DC Police Department, any private security employee who is armed must be licensed as a "special police" officer with arrest powers (Goldstein, 2007). Washington DC, at one time, had over 4,000 special police officers.

❖ Employment

Security guards and gaming surveillance officers held over 1 million jobs in 2006 (BLS, 2009). More than half of all jobs for security guards were in investigation and security services, including guard and armored car services. These organizations provide security on a contract basis, assigning their guards to buildings and other sites as needed. Most other security officers were employed directly by educational services, hospitals, food services and drinking places, traveler accommodations (hotels), department stores, manufacturing firms, lessors of real estate (residential and nonresidential buildings), and governments. Gaming surveillance officers work primarily in gambling industries; traveler accommodation, which includes casino hotels; and local government (BLS, 2009).

Executive Protection Services

Every year in the United States, hundreds of individuals fall victim to workplace crimes such as violence and stalking. Internationally, incidents of violence against Americans, including robbery, kidnapping, and terrorism, are increasing. In response to these threats, experienced **executive protection agents** use strategies based on U.S. Secret Service methods to ensure the safety of at-risk individuals. Meticulous planning, advance preparations, and coordinated close protection help keep potential targets safe. Among the targeted individuals are corporate executives, attorneys, wealthy families, sports celebrities, movie stars, national news and talk show personalities, political figures, presidential candidates, and civil rights leaders (Critical Intervention Services, 2009).

There are numerous other roles for security personnel in the United States. These, as mentioned earlier, include security managers or directors, security consultants, hospital security, airport and airline security, campus security, banking security, loss prevention, and alarm response and technology experts. All of these roles can be fulfilled more effectively if there is coordination and cooperation with public police.

❖ Public Police and Private Security

Today, private security industry employees far outnumber those employed in public policing. Private security companies in the United States number over 10,000, with estimated annual revenues exceeding $15 billion. Conservative employment estimates for the United States suggest that there are about

67,000 registered private investigators,

27,600 in-house store detectives,

371,300 security officers, and

95,800 managers and staff, representing in total well over 500,000 personnel (Nalla, 2009).

At the same time, the number of public police is declining in some areas around the country. For example, over the past 15 years, significant decreases in state police forces have occurred in Georgia (−10%), Michigan (−15%), Oregon (−31%), and South Carolina (−19%) (Copeland, 2009). Similarly, the "recession is altering local law enforcement in the U.S. by forcing some agencies to close precincts, merge with other departments or even shut down. Once largely spared from the deepest budget cuts, some police departments are struggling to provide basic services, police officials say" (Johnson, 2009, p. 1). Among the changes the public may observe are longer response times and reduced police presence in some areas. In response to police cutbacks, in many areas in the United States those living in townhouses, apartments, and condominiums have banded together to employ private protection agents. In numerous housing projects, largely independent police personnel are now responsible for security.

> In some low-income housing projects here [Los Angeles], the U. S. Department of Housing and Urban Development pays for security guards to protect residents from gang warfare. New York City uses private guards to police schools. Miami hires rent-a-cops to patrol its Metrorail system. . . . In Kansas City, MO, police want to contract private companies to pick up 22 jobs done by the department. Already they've replaced civilian officers at school crossings and may soon be hired to respond to security alarm calls. (Nasser, 1993, p. 9A)

In fact, "some cities are pushing for armed private security personnel to patrol the streets, perform arrests and transport civilians" (Bennett, 2009, p.1). Could it be that private security personnel can help fill the gap caused by reduced funding of public police, freeing valuable police resources to deal with serious criminal matters?

YOU DECIDE 14.1

In light of your reading and the discussion above:

1. Do you believe private security personnel are qualified to perform some of the tasks currently assigned to public police?

2. If yes, what tasks, specifically, would you include?

3. If not, what changes would have to occur to convince you that private security personnel could perform such tasks?

4. Do you believe private security personnel and public police officers working together would improve security in the United States? Why or why not?

Public and private police frequently perform similar services, such as patrol and protection of threatened individuals, though the former are community or society-oriented while the latter tend to be client oriented. Most private security personnel do not have police powers equivalent to those of public officers, but in some circumstances, private security personnel are granted such powers in specific areas on specific premises by statute. Contract personnel (typically uniformed), for example, tend to do policing more often than in-house personnel (see Case in Point 14.1), but there are circumstances and contexts in which in-house personnel, although not uniformed, conduct policing activities very similar to those of public police and contract personnel (Nalla, 2009). For example, Goldstein (2007) argued that private-sector security is "expanding into spheres—complex criminal investigation and patrols of downtown districts and residential neighborhoods—-that used to be the province of law enforcement agencies alone" (p. 1). And of course, in some cases private security personnel and public police officers are one and the same since public officers not infrequently moonlight in the private security field, and significant numbers of police officers retire and enter the private security field. Nonetheless, some believe private police tend to focus on the priorities of their employers and not the priority of public safety and individual rights (Goldstein, 2007).

☞ CASE IN POINT 14.1

Details of Shootout Between
Police Officer and Suspected Shooter

Army police officer Kimberly Munley arrived at the scene of Thursday's shooting about seven minutes after it began. She was outside the Soldier Readiness Center building when the shooter, who officials say is Maj. Nidal Malik Hasan, emerged from the building gun in hand, said Chuck Medley, the director of emergency services at Fort Hood. Hasan ran toward Munley, firing at her, Medley said. Munley returned fire with her pistol, hitting him.

Munley is a civilian police officer with the Department of the Army and serves as a SWAT team member and firearms instructor for the department, Medley said. Medley said the Army police department had been doing "active shooter training" as a precautionary measure since 2007.

"When you have an active shooter hurting people, our protocol is to move to the threat and eliminate it. That takes some courage and skill," he said. "If there was a person there to respond, Kim Munley is the one we would want to be there."

Some of Munley's training in how to respond to a mass shooting came from instructors from a Texas State University-San Marcos program called Advanced Law Enforcement Rapid Response Training.

The program, known as ALERRT, teaches police officers and first responders how to engage "active shooters," gunmen whose only intention is to kill.

(Continued)

(Continued)

"First responders have to be ready to engage the shooter, that's what she did," Nichols said of Munley. "She almost sacrificed her life to save others."

Patrol officers are taught the kind of tactics usually given only to SWAT and the military, including how to get past a barricaded door safely and how to work in low light. Part of the training simulates what it's like to be fired upon in combat—something many police officers never encounter until it's actually happening.

Source: Adapted from "Police officer credited with halting rampage called lifesaver . . . again: Officer has years of training, some from Texas State University Program," Mark Lisheron and Patrick George, November 7, 2009, statesman.com.

More than 30 years ago, the Task Force on Private Security indicated that public and private security efforts should be complementary, and indeed, public and private officers frequently interact cooperatively. However, according to Fischer et al. (2008), the relationship between the two groups is often uneasy for several reasons, including the following:

- Lack of mutual respect
- Lack of communication
- Lack of enforcement knowledge of private security personnel
- Perceived competition
- Lack of standards for private security personnel
- Perceived corruption of public officers
- Jurisdictional conflicts
- Confusion of identity and issues flowing from it, such as arming and training of private police
- Mutual image and communications problems
- Provision of services in overlapping areas
- Moonlighting policies for public police
- Differences in legal powers
- False alarm rates (pp. 60–61)

Furthermore, some warn that the constitutional safeguards that apply to police questioning and searches do not apply in the private sector (Goldstein, 2007).

In spite of all these potential problems, however, cooperation between the two types of police appears to be improving. In part, this is due to the fact that the federal government hires thousands of contract security officers who patrol federal buildings and provide security at military bases. And in cities across the United States, private security officers protect courthouses and other public facilities. Further, in many instances, private security personnel investigate thefts, fraud, drugs, and violence in the workplace (Fischer et al., 2008, p. 62). And as the threat of terrorism within the United States has grown, so has the need to utilize all forms of security to prevent and apprehend terrorists. Thus, Morabito and Greenberg (2005) believe law enforcement and private security must work collaboratively because neither possesses the necessary resources to prevent terrorism alone. Continued improvement in the relationship between public police and private/contract security personnel may depend upon the following:

- Upgrading private security, including statewide statutes requiring background checks, training, ethical codes, and licensing
- Increased knowledge of the value of private security functions on the part of the police
- Increased interaction on joint projects
- The possible transfer of some public police functions to the private sector (Fischer et al., 2008, p. 62)

Some progress has already occurred and is exemplified by partnerships such as the NYPD-Shield (Area Police/Private Security Liaison), Virginia Police and Private Security Alliance (VAPPSA), and Dallas/North Texas Regional Law Enforcement and Security Program (LEAPS)—all of which pursue mutually agreed upon goals in the various communities in question (Gunter & Kidwell, 2004). Operation Cooperation represents a major national initiative to encourage partnerships between public police and private security professionals. The driving force behind this effort is a passion among practitioners who see the great benefits to be gained from public–private teamwork (Anonymous, 2001). Most agree that partnerships offer a number of benefits to both sides.

- Creative problem solving
- Increased training opportunities
- Information, data, and intelligence gathering
- "Force multiplier" opportunities
- Access to the community through private sector communications technology
- Reduced recovery time following disasters (Morabito & Greenberg, 2005, p. vii)

Still, as Sherman (1990) indicated some time ago, one problem with the hiring of private security officers to protect private space and property is a "disinvestment in public safety and the increased investment in private safety [which] raises issues of class, equality, and the increasing gap between the rich and the poor" (p. 11). Nonetheless, privatization of certain police functions may help solve some of the problems that hinder law enforcement agencies' efforts to achieve their goals. Properly defined and managed partnerships with private security firms might well make the efforts of police officers more effective and rewarding (Youngs, 2004).

From the preceding discussion, it is clear that some cooperative and complimentary efforts are being made by both private and public police. But what can be done to improve the perceptions of the two areas toward each other and increase cooperation? The formation of joint task forces has already proven effective and should be encouraged to study responses to terrorism and major crime issues and to develop joint responses. Data files, in both the public and private sectors, should be more freely shared. Private security personnel are often not

❖ PHOTO **14.3** The complex public safety issues of the time require cooperation and coordination of planning between police, fire, and private security personnel. As mentioned throughout the chapter this has been one of the top priorities of the public safety sector since the 9/11 terrorist attacks.

granted access to information on criminal cases, even as a follow-up to cases they initially investigated.

It is likely that the private sector will continue to increase its presence in crime prevention activities. This should free public law enforcement to concentrate on violent crimes and respond rapidly to serious crimes.

Still, there are areas of concern and conflict that slow the growth of understanding and cooperation. Some companies do not report criminal offenses to the police in order to protect the company image. The company often cites lax charging policies, court proceedings that might be damaging to the organization, and a general feeling that the courts are not sympathetic to business losses (Fischer et al., 2008).

In 2004, the National Policy Summit project through the Department of Justice partnered with the International Association of Chiefs of Police, ASIS (American Society of Industrial Security), the National Association of Security Companies, and the International Security Management Association. The group produced five recommendations:

1. Leaders in law enforcement and private security should make a formal commitment to cooperate.

2. The federal government should fund research and training on relevant legislation, private security, and law enforcement cooperation.

3. The federal government should create an advisory council composed of law enforcement and private security professionals to oversee implementation issues related to partnerships.

4. Leaders at the federal, local law enforcement, and private security levels, along with relevant membership organizations should promote a cooperative agenda.

5. There should be local partnerships set to address the following:
   - Joint response to critical incidents
   - Coordinated infrastructure protection
   - Improved communications and data interoperability
   - Better information and intelligence sharing
   - Coordinated responses to workplace security issues (COPS, 2004).

Issues such as those already discussed are not unique to the United States but are global in nature, as Around the World indicates. Countries such as Australia, where the government regulates the security industry, and South Korea are also experiencing major growth in the private security industry and are focused on improving relationships between public and private police.

AROUND THE WORLD

Private Security in Australia: Trends and Key Characteristics

Data show that in Australia in 2006, there were 52,768 personnel employed full-time in the security industry, compared with 44,898 police. A decade previously, police outnumbered security. When comparing the characteristics of security to police personnel, both industries have similar ratios of male to female employees (approximately 76% to 24% respectively); however, security personnel frequently occupy an older age demographic than police, while police are more highly educated and paid. Available data indicates there are over 5,000 security and investigative businesses registered in Australia, and over 110,000 licenses issued mainly to individuals with five companies, which make up nearly half of the security industry market share. The private sector is expected to continue to grow, especially with the increase in electronic surveillance, monitoring, and cash-in-transit.

Source: "Private Security in Australia: Trends and Key Characteristics," by T. Prenzler, K. Earle, and R. Sarre, 2009, *Trends and Issues in Crime and Criminology, 374*, pp. 1–6.

Relations Between Police and Private Security Officers in South Korea

Similar to the experience of many developed and developing economies, South Korea has experienced a significant increase in the number of private security personnel employed in the last three decades relative to law enforcement officers.

(Continued)

(Continued)

Both law enforcement and private security officers are positive about their relationship with each other, and security officers are more optimistic about achieving improvements in those relationships. Both police officers and security professionals believe that the other group could do more to encourage a positive working relationship.

Source: Adapted from "Relations Between Police and Private Security Officers in South Korea," by M. K. Nalla and E. G. Hwang, 2006, *Policing, 29*(3), 482.

❖ Chapter Summary

During the past 20 years or so, there has been a vast proliferation in the number of private security personnel. This growth intensified after the 9/11 attacks, and private police now far outnumber public police officers. There are a number of reasons for this growth in the private security industry. Some examples include the inability of the police to respond to all of the requests for security-related services due to manpower shortages; the potential civil liability imposed by court decisions that mandate that owners of public venues such as office buildings, large retail stores, museums, sports arenas, and the like provide security for the safety of the public; and a need by the private sector for specialized services such as executive security, computer crime, various insurance frauds, security of gated communities, and financial crimes such as embezzlement and internal thefts. In addition, many in the private sector prefer to avoid the negative press that may occur when police agencies become involved.

Through the years, though (and to a degree even today), public police and private security personnel have not always worked well together. Probably the most significant reasons for this strained relationship center on four discrete, but related, issues. First, many police officers view security personnel as "police wannabees" who lack the capabilities and wherewithal to perform law enforcement related functions. Second, the majority of individuals who make up the private industry are uniformed guards one often sees at the public venues cited in the preceding paragraph. State-imposed training and education requirements for private security personnel are often meager in comparison to their public counterparts. Most are required to undergo only 20 to 30 hours of very basic training to obtain certification. The third issue, which accounts for part of this larger problem, is that the uniformed security guards are not perceived by many private citizens as being competent. In response to these and other issues, ASIS, the largest professional organization in the world representing the private security industry, is in the process of trying to increase training and education requirements and thus change these perceptions by the public. ASIS also attempts to promote better working relationships between the police and security personnel. Finally, the pay for most entry level guard work pales in comparison to the remuneration for police officers (interestingly enough, at the upper end of the scale, private security managers and private investigators of various kinds may earn considerably more than their public counterparts).

The private security industry is expected to continue to grow in the foreseeable future and to continue the movement toward professionalization in order to both increase effectiveness and improve the public's perception regarding the competence of security officers. It is important that public police and private security personnel coordinate their efforts and work together to combat both crime and catastrophic events.

❖ Key Terms

in-house security personnel

contract security personnel

hybrid systems

private detectives (investigators)

security officers

gaming surveillance officers

executive protection agents

❖ Discussion Questions

1. Discuss the extent of the growth of private security in the United States and some of the reasons for this growth.

2. What is the importance of licensing requirements for private detectives and investigators? What are some possible consequences of failure to license?

3. What is the impact of the events of 9/11 on the private security industry in the United States?

4. Relationships between private security personnel and public police are not always pleasant. Discuss some of the reasons for this state of affairs.

5. What, in your opinion, does the future hold with respect to cooperation and coordination between private and public police?

❖ Internet Exercises

1. Visit the Internet to determine the requirements for becoming a private detective or investigator in your state. Do these requirements seem reasonable to you? Why or why not?

2. Using the key words "police and private security partnerships," locate and discuss Internet articles dealing with such partnerships. Do such partnerships appear to be mutually beneficial to the partners? Why or why not?

15

The Future of Policing in the United States

CHAPTER LEARNING OBJECTIVES

- Identify the role(s) that the practice of community-oriented policing may play in the future of policing.
- Identify the role(s) the private security industry may play in the future and describe the likely effect on the public's relationship with and expectations of the police.
- Highlight the qualifications that will likely be needed for future police leaders.
- Describe the roles that education and training may play in the future of policing.
- Discuss the concept of technological advancement in the context of the future of policing.
- Identify and elaborate on what role(s) accreditation will play in the future of policing.
- Identify and elaborate on the likely role(s) to be played by police agencies with respect to terrorism in the future.
- Highlight and briefly comment on the inadequacies of the current police response to terrorism and discuss recommendations for an improved response.

❖ **Photo 15.1** The issues confronting police organizations in the coming years will likely have much to do with transnational crime issues.

Although it is risky to make projections for the future, it is clear that a vision of where one is going is an important part of getting there. The following discussion of the future of policing in the United States is based on an analysis of current trends, projected demographic changes, and, in some instances, pure speculation. As Crank (1995) noted with respect to defining the future of policing, "Any such effort is self-evidently preposterous, and therein lies the sheer delight of it. The notion that anyone can hope to predict the future of his or her own life for even the proximate moment, let alone the future of a social institution over the next eighteen years is pretentious" (p. 107). Consider Stephens (2005), who discovered that "even the most optimistic future-oriented thinkers in the field find it difficult to imagine how police will be able to cope with the emerging complexity of combating terrorism and Internet crime while simultaneously keeping a lid on conventional street crime and creating cohesive neighborhoods" (p. 53).

❖ The Changing Police Role

As we have shown, police strategies do not exist in a vacuum. Legislation, political attitudes, and local resources shape these strategies. Still, there is room for change in attitudes and resources, and change must be regarded as a critical ingredient in effective policing. New police strategies are being, and must be, adopted to meet the changing needs of communities over time. Future police organizations may or may not resemble today's police. For example, Stephens (2005) believes "the twenty-first century has put policing into a whole new milieu—one in which the causes of crime and disorder often lie outside the immediate community, demanding new and innovative approaches from police" (p. 52). Street crimes of the past often involved perpetrators and victims from the same general area. Thus, prevention included some form of surveillance, analyzing activity in the immediate area and taking action to head off problems (what many referred to as problem-oriented policing) (Stephens, 2005). However, in many areas various types of reported street crime have declined, and we have seen the development of terrorism and Internet crimes. In many instances "offenders are thousands of miles away while planning and even committing these crimes. Hackers and crackers halfway around the globe can shut down a community's Internet dependent monetary and energy system" (Stephens, 2005, p. 52).

As an example of the prevalence of Internet related crimes, the FBI (2005) recognized identity theft as one of the fastest growing crimes and dominant white collar crime problems of the 21st century. The numbers are expected to increase in the future as identity thieves become more sophisticated and as the techniques of theft are embraced by large criminal organizations. Similar trends were proposed by Thibault, Lynch, and McBride (2007, p. 464), who expect the following changes in police strategies:

- Deployment of community policing, including more authority for remote supervisors and human service and communications training for officers
- Proactive planning and intelligence to include planned and unplanned events, including critical incident and hot spot management and centralized rapid-response teams organized for instant deployment
- Greater dependence on private police, auxiliary police, and community volunteers; major corporation private police begin to have more public police powers
- Police executives will be more highly educated and professionalized and will move between major police departments.

Further insight was provided by Peak (2009, p. 434), who believes the police will undergo a metamorphosis in the future:

- Ethics will be woven into everything the police do, and a majority of police officers will be required to obtain a college degree.
- Major cities will no longer require that a police chief have prior police experience and instead will employ from private industry.
- The paramilitary style associated with police organizations will become obsolete and will be replaced with work teams.

We believe a number of demographic, economic, and workforce changes will affect the future of policing. For example, the U.S. population is expected to increase to 402 million by 2050 and to 572 million by 2101 (U.S. Census Bureau, 2000). The Hispanic population is predicted to approach 30% of the total population, while Asians and blacks will each constitute about 12% of the population. In the 21st century, problems related to race and ethnicity will be even more prevalent in the administration of justice. The current state of the criminal justice system represents a shift from the rehabilitative model of treating offenders to one of increased incarceration due in part to society's low level of tolerance for any type of offender. Those persons most affected during increased periods of protecting society from criminal elements are minorities, the poor, and the legally underrepresented.

In the future, elderly persons will present a significant challenge to health care, police, and local government organizations. Some implications of this trend for the police include increased calls for service for real and perceived victimizations, different types of crime, and a new potential class of perpetrators (senior citizens) (Jensen & Levin, 2007). Thus, the advice from Bennett (1993) is still applicable today:

> We cannot simply continue with business as usual. Since most agencies are not equipped with crystal balls, true progress comes from trying something new, seeing if it works, making changes and trying it again. If the organization and its leaders are afraid to fail, stagnation quickly sets in. (p. 86)

However, Braga and Weisburd (2006) do not anticipate a new wave of strategic police innovations in the near future:

> The current context of policing suggests that future innovations will be incremental in nature. The conditions of the 1980s and 1990s that created the pressure for innovation simply no longer exist. Indeed, the atmosphere is precisely the opposite of earlier decades. Crime is down and federal funds available for demonstration projects to spur innovation are very limited. (p. 347)

We are once again in the position of having to admit that the police cannot be all things to all people and that the police can be effective only if they have widespread community support. This is not at all surprising when we realize that municipal police emerged as a result of citizen needs. Those needs, however, change at a sometimes frightening pace, depending on economics, demographics, and social policies. To continue to meet the changing demands of citizens, police agencies at all levels must first have a realistic view of these needs and, second, invite citizen input as to how best to achieve them. In other words, according to Braga and Weisburd (2006), in the future, police will "continue to institutionalize the innovative practices" that have affected crime control and community benefits through "administrative adjustments and the development of supporting strategies to fit the problems of the neighborhoods they police" (p. 348).

Research and Planning As Police Functions

Alpert and Dunham (1992) stated the following:

> In a society such as ours, there are bound to be different priorities placed on the police by different people who live in different communities. In addition, police officers are not all the same, do not have similar opinions or expectations, do not perform at the same level, and do not operate with the same style. (p. 195)

How are the police to respond to these differing public priorities, in what ways will different types of officers respond, and what styles of policing are best suited to particular communities? These and other questions relating to areas such as terrorism and crime management, level of satisfaction with supervisors, amount of perceived stress among officers, civil and criminal liability of police personnel, and dozens of other areas can best be addressed through the implementation of proper research and planning techniques.

In the research area, projects may be as simple as surveying community residents to determine their priorities, fears, satisfaction with police services, and perceptions of police misconduct, or it can be as complex as attempting to measure the relationships among education, training, job performance, and supervisory evaluations. We might want to assess the impact of combined enforcement groups on drug trafficking or to develop a profile of a specific type of offender. We might want to examine the nature and extent of relationships among police agencies at the local, state, federal, and international levels. Or we might want to evaluate officer productivity in terms of certain criteria. All of these projects require a certain degree of expertise in research (and, for that matter, a good deal of planning).

Police administrators could, of course, contract for such projects, but the potential for miscommunication in "hired hand" research is considerable, and research funds and grants are not always available for projects when they need to be completed (Fitzgerald & Cox, 2002, pp. 18–20). Thus, greater reliance on in-house research and evaluation is desirable for a number of reasons. The conduct of in-house research requires that at least some staff members have the training and expertise necessary to design and implement scientific inquiries. The value and ease of conduct of such inquiries is increased considerably when an evaluation component is built into new initiatives from the start. According to Fitzgerald and Cox (2002), in order to understand the nature and current state of affairs in criminal justice, practitioners and students alike must be able to read and comprehend research reports and must know when and how to apply the results of such research. Many will also find it necessary or advantageous to conduct research themselves to do their jobs as effectively and efficiently as possible. It is quite true that any in-depth study of research methods and statistical analysis would take years, but it is equally true that a student can achieve a basic understanding in a relatively short period of time. Complicated research designs and sophisticated statistical procedures do not necessarily result in better or more useful research, and often, useful insights can be gained through relatively simple research designs and elementary statistical analyses.

Conducting such research, of course, requires considerable planning—both short and long range. For a variety of reasons, police administrators have regularly demonstrated their abilities to engage in the former, but rarely in the latter. This might have been true in part because of a public service mentality that characterized not only police chiefs, but also other chief executive officers in the public sector. This mentality was, for years, based on the premise that last year's budget plus 10% was a safe bet in most fiscal years. In the public sector, planning for no increases in funding, or for budgetary cutbacks, was unheard of, and the assumptions appeared to be (1) that evaluation of programs was beyond the responsibility of the public-sector executives and (2) that fiscal responsibility was less important than in the private sector because funds, especially for emergency services, would always be made available.

As we have seen, in the past several years, dramatic economic changes have occurred in the public sector. First, taxpayer revolts made it clear that zero-based budgeting and budget cutbacks were not only possible, but also likely alternatives to the automatic 10% increase. Second, the demand for accountability in the public sector increased. The need for full-time fire departments was questioned in some small communities; public safety officers who could perform both police and fire-fighting functions were hired in some areas; and police departments began to lose positions through attrition. Third, women and minorities were hired in greater numbers, and the issue of their performance on the job led to a number of evaluation studies. Fourth, the Kansas City Preventive Patrol Experiment (Kelling, Pate, Dieckman, & Brown, 1974) demonstrated the ability of police agencies to participate in the design and evaluation of responsible research. Fifth, the number of well-educated police officers (at all levels) increased, making possible the formation and utilization of research and planning units along with other specialized units. Sixth, as personal computers became available at reasonable cost, their capabilities were considerably improved, and police personnel became acquainted with and accustomed to their use in dozens of applications. (See chapter 12 for a more detailed discussion.) Finally, serious budgetary problems related to the increasing national debt have led to calls for cutbacks in federal, state, and local police (as well as other public) agencies. As a result, we must seek new strategies for doing more with less, and research plays a critical role in the search for such solutions.

All of the factors outlined above make it likely that research and planning will become increasingly important to and utilized by police administrators seeking to justify new programs and demonstrate the value of existing efforts.

❖ Changing the Police Image

In spite of the fact that specialization is likely to continue to characterize police in the 21st century, patrol officers will remain the backbone of policing at the local level as a result of their sheer numbers and the visibility and frequency of contact with the public. Police patrol will continue to be necessary in the future since there will be

❖ **PHOTO 15.2**   Police in Europe are shown utilizing the vast public surveillance systems they have throughout their cities. These technologies have proven useful in the prevention of many terrorist attacks.

random and planned acts of violence, domestic disputes, vehicular accidents, lost children, and numerous other situations referred to police services (Conser & Frissora, 2007). However these authors also believe patrol will experience changes in the areas of methods, equipment, communications, and caliber of police officers. One major change in future police patrol will be the removal of officers from being physically present while patrolling (Conser & Frissora, 2007). The authors propose that surveillance systems, public policing linkages, and partnerships with private police, among others, will permit changes in current methods of patrol.

Community and Problem-Oriented Policing

There is little doubt that the wave of the future in policing will include expanded involvement of civilians in police work as employees in police agencies; as members of advisory, planning, and direct support groups as critics and reviewers of police activities; and as sources of information to fight terrorism. The message is clear: The police cannot control crime or maintain order by themselves. The involvement of citizens other than police officers in crime prevention, apprehension of offenders, and order maintenance is absolutely essential. A partnership is required, but the partnership must be legitimate. In the past, police partnerships with other citizens meant the police allowing these citizens to be minimally involved in police activities in which the police served as the experts, in which citizen input was sought in certain areas but denied in others, and in which policy making remained the exclusive right of the police.

The recession that began in 2007 has affected the economic status of community and problem-oriented policing programs. Houde and Cox (2009) found that many local departments eliminated antidrug programs, purchases of squad cars, gang-prevention programs, and after-hour presentations to citizen groups concerning home security and other issues. Departments have informed the International Association of Chiefs of Police that officers are being laid off or taking furloughs, police positions are being left vacant, and in some cases entire departments are closing or consolidating ("Even Cops Losing," 2009). (See Case In Point 15.1 concerning the layoff of state police officers.)

☞ CASE IN POINT 15.1

The Illinois State Police plan to lay off more than 450 state troopers. At the same time they will close five district state police headquarters. Including retirements, the Illinois State Police will reduce sworn personnel by 600 or 30 percent from a force of approximately 2000 sworn state troopers.

The Acting Director said "districts were chosen for closing if other police agencies were available in the area or if crime rates in an area are relatively low."

Source: "State Police to Lay off More Than 450 Troopers," by Gatehouse News Service, 2010, *Journal Star*, p. B 5.

Even though there has been a debate over the relationship between crime and the economy in the past, many believe the recession will result in a rise in crime. Forty-four percent of the 233 police departments surveyed by the Police Executive Forum reported a rise in certain types of crime that were attributed to the United States' worst economic and financial crisis in decades (Colvin, 2009). For example, Community Oriented Policing Services (COPS) (2009) discovered that states with high foreclosure rates realized increases in vacant properties, which created opportunities for several types of crime including property theft, graffiti, and drug activity.

We believe the future will continue to involve increased efforts on behalf of the police to improve citizen cooperation in high-crime areas. In many cases, these areas were identified as high crime density locations or hot spots and then were assigned additional patrols and specialized units. However, the threat posed by economic crises means that many police departments will no longer have these options available to reduce crime and violence (Colvin, 2009). The reality is that most of the people living in such areas are not criminals but victims. They continue to be victims because the streets and dwellings do not belong to them, but to gangs and other less well organized but equally predatory criminals. Police will continue to provide patrol to these areas and to maintain a semblance of order, but the overwhelming evidence is that, by themselves, they have little impact on crime.

AROUND THE WORLD

President Hamid Karzai mandated that 5,000 additional policewomen be added to the Afghanistan force by 2014. "Currently there are under 1,000 women serving in the police; a negative public opinion, low pay, lack of support from male family members and the dangerous nature of the job make female recruitment a difficult process."

Currently, most women in Afghanistan must secure their patriarch's permission before joining the police force. Women police recruits who completed the eight-week training will be paid and unlike male trainees can return to homes with their families at night.

There are many positive aspects associated with the employment of women in the Afghan National Police. For example, "if an ANP female is questioning a female, she'll get more information than a male police officer. A woman will feel more comfortable speaking with another woman."

Sergeant Shohra Saheem was 14 years of age when she joined the police force. Today the minimum age to be a police officer is 18 years of age.

Source: "Afghan National Police Discuss, Plan Future," by NATO Training Mission Combined Security Transition Command, 2010. Available from http://www.ntm-a.com

Civilianization

In keeping with community-oriented policing efforts, increasing numbers of civilians are likely to continue to be involved in policing as employees of police agencies and as volunteers. This trend is beneficial in that it helps to break down barriers between the police and other citizens, often frees police officers to concentrate more of their time on matters for which they have been specifically trained, and fosters the belief that civilians play an important role in both order maintenance and law enforcement.

Accreditation

To an extent, the image of the police has changed as a result of the incorporation of high standards of performance and conduct by many departments through the process of accreditation. A growing number of state and local police agencies have demonstrated their desire to be considered among the best in the profession by undergoing the painstaking, lengthy process of accreditation by the Commission on Accreditation for Law Enforcement Agencies. Departments originally accredited have now been through the reaccreditation process.

Many other agencies are doing self-evaluations to determine whether to pursue accreditation. Even for those who decide not to apply for accreditation, there is, for the first time, a set of standards that allow police personnel to examine the extent to which they are operating according to the recognized standards of the profession. Some states have formed associations that help individual agencies prepare for accreditation, and this has fostered improved communications among agencies. In addition, accreditation now requires the use of community surveys on a regular basis, thereby enhancing the police–community partnership and the use of research techniques by police personnel. The trend toward accreditation and the accompanying benefits seems well established.

Lateral Entry

The concept of lateral entry, or movement from one geographic location to enter employment in another area, has existed for some time but is still resisted by some police agencies. Acceptance of the concept would allow police agencies to recruit personnel from other agencies for various supervisory as well as line positions and would allow officers from one department to apply for comparable positions in other departments. As it is, most police officers wishing to transfer from one area or department to another have to start as entry-level officers, even though they may have attained higher rank. While we are willing to accept lateral entry at the level of police chief, we have been far more hesitant to do so at other levels, limiting the pool of applicants for supervisory positions to those inside the department.

Although this strategy does protect insiders from competition from the outside, it is based on the assumption that there are always individuals qualified for promotion inside the department. This assumption, however, does not always hold true. Further, refusal to accept lateral entry at entry-level positions deprives police departments of the pool of already trained applicants seeking to leave their current positions or locations in search of better opportunities. There is little doubt that the benefits of lateral entry outweigh the objections raised against it, and more and more police administrators, city managers, and personnel directors are likely to recognize this fact.

Training

Police personnel will have increasing opportunities to participate in training offered by a variety of training institutes. All training is, or should be, interrelated. The special skills learned at training institutes need to be updated on a continuing basis and can be shared with others through inservice training by those who have attended the institutes. Such sharing is both cost effective and rewarding to those who have received the training and should be encouraged on a widespread basis. In the past, the effects of training have infrequently been properly assessed by police agencies because of the assumptions that the information provided is understandable and absorbed. Increasingly, routine evaluations, which include a pretest of attendees' knowledge of the material to be presented and a posttest of such knowledge, are being employed. This trend should continue because failure to evaluate training may lead to a waste of training resources. The content of police training, of course, varies with time, place, personnel involved, subject matter, and training goals. In general, however, it may be said that the content should be relevant to the needs of trainees, timely, well organized, and clearly presented. When these requirements are met, trainees can best appreciate the value of the training. It is imperative that the information conveyed in training sessions be current and accurate. The range of subjects that may be covered in training sessions is limited only by the imagination of planners and presenters.

A basic purpose of training is to keep police personnel up to date with respect to important changes in the profession. In a larger sense, however, the purposes of training depend on the way in which the role of the police is defined. As indicated throughout this book, in the 1960s and 1970s, crime fighting and law enforcement were emphasized, and to some extent, many officers still view these aspects of the police role as the most important part of police work. However, Vodde (2009) concluded that the traditional military model for police training, which served well in the past, has come under question. Birzer (2003, p. 29) supported this view and discovered that many police training programs are conducted in a very behavioral and militaristic environment. In other words, "the sophistication of today's culturally diverse, quick paced, ever-changing, technically advanced and globally influenced society" (Vodde, 2009, p. 17) demands a set of skills and competencies that are substantially different and more complex compared to the past.

Today we recognize that while law enforcement and crime fighting are critical parts of the police role, they are not the most important in terms of time spent or citizen satisfaction. The fact that today's police personnel spend the majority of their time negotiating settlements between spouses or lovers or neighbors and providing other services that have little or nothing to do with law enforcement will become increasingly apparent. Successful intervention into the daily lives of citizens requires such skills as well as cooperation on the part of the nonpolice citizens involved. Increasingly, then, communications skills (both verbal and nonverbal); human-, community-, and minority-relations skills; and problem solving skills are emerging as among the most important assets of a competent, effective police officer.

Realizing the limitations of the traditional methods for police training, Vodde (2009) proposed an andragogical instructional methodology for training future police officers. "**Andragogy** is based on the belief that adults learn differently from children, bases its practices on the needs, interests, readings, orientation, experience and motivation of adult learners (Vodde, 2009, p. 19). As an example, Birzer (2003) encouraged training academies to deviate from the mechanical, militaristic aspect of training and "inform police how to identify, respond to, and solve problems such as crime, drugs, fear of crime, and urban decay within neighborhoods they serve" (p. 32). He proposed a "greater emphasis on experiential techniques—techniques that tap into the experience of learners, such as group discussions, simulation exercises, problem-solving activities, case method and laboratory methods—over transmittal techniques" (Birzer, 2003, p. 33).

Education

One of the most popular proposals for improving the quality of policing has focused on better educated officers. In the United States in the 1970s and 1980s, the idea that a college-educated police officer is a better police officer spawned a federal program (LEAA) that provided millions of dollars annually in support of such education, a dramatic increase in the numbers of college programs related to policing, and a sharp increase in the number of police officers with at least some college education. The debate over the importance of police education continued, federal funding for such education diminished, and there were continuing concerns over the content and quality of police education. However, in 1994 the Omnibus Crime Bill began to provide funding to states for the Police Corps. The Police Corps was a federal program designed to address violent crime by increasing the number of patrol officers with advanced education and training. Typically, these officers served in low-income, high-crime urban areas or isolated rural areas (U.S. Department of Justice, 2000). Funding was discontinued in 2007, but it allowed officers to complete a baccalaureate degree and up to 24 weeks of academy training. As we previously discussed, enormous resources and funds have been devoted to providing college educations for police. Many of the current concerns surrounding police education result from our inability or unwillingness to decide what we want the police to accomplish in today's society. It is extremely difficult to develop courses and curricula for the police under these circumstances. Some believe that liberal arts courses provide the best background for police officers in a multiethnic, multicultural society; others are convinced that specialized courses in criminal justice are preferable; while still others question the value of college education for police officers.

POLICE STORIES

As I mentioned in one of my earlier police stories, I worked at a suburban Chicago police department prior to joining the Chicago Police Department. Now, going back to circa 1981, the agency applied for and received a grant to install Mobile Data Terminals (MDTs) in their squad cars. It also had computer-aided dispatch (CAD) capabilities. Looking back, this was ground breaking technology for the time, and the department was fortunate to get these computer devices.

I remember clearly that this was met with much resistance on the part of the troops. Even our supervisors, a generation older than most of the patrol officers, resisted using these "new fangled devices." It got to a point that required the upper administration to get involved by creating a general order mandating the use of the MDTs. The administration even had a meeting with us to try and explain the advantages and why we should make good use of this new technology. When Q & A time came around, I was one of the first officers to voice my disapproval with the new mandate. I stated with absolute confidence that "computers are a passing fad and they'll be obsolete in a couple of years."

Going forward, I was referred to as the department's "futurist." What can I say? I also am one of those guys that bought an eight-track stereo rather than a cassette player and a beta-max video recorder instead of a VHS recorder. Needless to say, I have never attempted to write about anything to do with the future.

There is a point to this story. Nobody has a crystal ball to look through to predict what we can expect in policing 5 or 10 years from now. All we can do is be good students of history and plan accordingly. The pace at which technology is evolving seems to be growing by the day; political, economic, and social conditions from around the world have impacted us in ways we never could have imagined in our wildest dreams just a decade or two earlier; the courts, through case law, are always modifying or sometimes completely changing the practices of the police; crime analysis and crime mapping capabilities are only recently starting to be used somewhat effectively to prevent and investigate crime; the field of forensics is becoming increasingly complex, causing paradigm shifts in related training and education; video surveillance is getting to a point where invasion of privacy crimes, long a rarely reported crime to police, will likely soon significantly increase the caseloads of investigators; and computer technology in general has generated and will continue to generate a new venue for criminals to ply their trades—all of which will require the field of policing to keep pace and prepare for as many eventualities as possible.

Police Leadership

As we have seen, the quality of leadership in police organizations has varied tremendously. Some carefully select entry-level personnel, carefully evaluate their potential for promotion, promote based on merit, and prepare those who are to be promoted by sending them to appropriate training or educational programs. Other police organizations do none of these things. Many, perhaps most, departments have a difficult time deciding what types of leaders or supervisors to appoint. Should leadership positions be filled by those with skills in communicating with and supervising personnel? Should they be filled by personnel with extensive street experience? Are policing skills or management skills more important? Answers to these questions are crucial in determining the criteria for promotion to leadership positions. However, there is little rigorous research concerning police leadership—"most of which is limited to case studies of how chiefs matter or try to matter in shaping the policies, practices and performance of their departments (Mastrofski, 2006, p. 24).

Private and Contract Security Personnel

For a variety of reasons, we are likely to see a considerable increase in the use of private and contract security personnel in the future. Policing in rural areas is becoming an increasingly expensive proposition as standards for police officers improve, as gangs and predatory criminals become more mobile and recognize that small-city and small-town police are ill prepared to deal with either swift hit-and-run crimes or more long-term invasions, and as the technology of policing becomes more sophisticated and more costly while the willingness and ability of taxpayers to fund public services diminishes. (See Chapter 14 for a more complete discussion of this subject.)

This trend indicates both a desire and a need for improved communication and cooperation between the police, private security, and business communities. However, Cetron and Davies (2008) predicted more territorial conflicts between police agencies and private security firms that are responsible for the needs of corporations and wealthy communities. They believe security will be one of the great growth industries over the next 20 years.

Technological Changes in Policing

No discussion of the future of policing would be complete without a brief look at the impact of advancing technology on the field. (See Chapter 12 for a more detailed examination of this topic.) The computerized innovations of the past decade have left us on the threshold of challenging and sometimes controversial possibilities. The advancements in technology vary widely between police agencies—some of whom are providing wireless access to law enforcement databases, mug shot files, agency communications, and scheduling and management tools and are testing voice recognition to simplify data processing along with speed report writing (Ruderman, 2008). (See Case In Point 15.2, which describes advances in the Washington DC Metropolitan Police Department.)

☞ **CASE IN POINT 15.2**

Chief Cathy L. Lanier recently upgraded the Washington DC Metropolitan Police Department (MPD). All police vehicles have computers, and MPD now uses closed-circuit television cameras, automated license plate readers, and shot spotter devices to detect and report firearm discharges.

The Chief discovered that the increased use of technology improved police efficiency and that response times have decreased while the number of calls has increased. Furthermore, MPD has established a listserv that allows residents to contact the police and a "text tip line," which have provided information related to homicide and school shootings.

MPD has also established a fusion center that collects crime and terror alerts. According to Chief Lanier, "If identified terror suspects attempted to enter the Capitol, their vehicles could be tracked with the Department's automated license plate readers."

Source: Adapted from "DC Police Chief Cathy Lanier Describes How Technology is Changing Police Work in the Capitol, By H. Kenyon, 2010, AFCEA International. Available online from http://www.afcea.org

---

Some believe the new technology in today's society is a double-edged sword— it will create new forms of crime and at the same time assist police in fighting crime.

❖ Clarifying the Police Role

The impact of the changes discussed in this chapter on the nature of the police role will be considerable. Although economic circumstances will fluctuate with the times, doing more is likely to remain the guiding principle for most police agencies. Police have always been expected to make efficient use of allocated resources, but this is extremely important given the budget crises many are facing. Beck and McCue (2009) believed that as police face new budget restraints and limitations the question to ask with more urgency is "Why just count crimes when you can anticipate, prevent and respond more effectively" (p. 1)? Next we will discuss predictive policing and how this emerging strategy could "effectively deploy resources in front of crime in order to do more with less and change outcomes" (Beck & McCue, 2009, p. 7).

Predictive Policing

Predictive policing involves using data and analysis to predict future police problems and to implement strategies to prevent or ameliorate those problems

(Casady, 2009). Casady (2009) found that the concept of predictive policing involved principles from "problem-oriented policing, information-led policing, hot-spot policing, community policing, situational crime prevention, evidence-based policing, and intelligence led policing" (p. 1).

> At the simplest level, this might mean using crime analysis to determine the likely patterns of drive-by shootings, then deploying the police officers to the areas and at the times these are most likely to occur in order to preempt the crime. At a more complex level, it might mean watching the trends in the spot copper price, and implementing strategies (such as legislation and scrap business monitoring) to reduce the marketability of stolen copper in advance of an anticipated spike in thefts. (Casady, 2009, p.1)

Predictive policing includes both strategic and tactical applications and employ forecasting techniques similar to those used by businesses to anticipate market conditions and industry trends over time (U. S. Department of Justice, 2009). Predictive policing models in the future may include the following:

- Statistical analysis to forecast CompStat-like performance
- Advanced models to determine the risk of offending or victimization of particular individuals or groups
- Advanced analytical tools including social network analysis tools and intelligent decision support systems related to relationships between suspects, victims, and others
- Geospatial tools to analyze trends in demographics, land use, income, and other sources to predict allocation of police resources
- Integrated sensor and information systems to protect critical public spaces
- Crime prediction models using a variety of input variables
- Forensic tools to detect and interdict criminal activity (U.S. Department of Justice, 2009)

Even small police agencies are using predictive policing. As an example, Erlanger Police Department (Kentucky) implemented software that monitors increases in injuries related to vehicle accidents on certain sections of roadway (Perlman, 2008). During specific hours, police can determine if a hazard is the cause of the increased accidents or assign radar enforcement to reduce the speed of traffic.

Let us briefly consider three examples of law enforcement's response to the terrorist problems: community policing, intelligence-led policing, and the enactment of laws.

The Role of Community Policing

Police officers assume an important role in the attempts to prevent terrorism. Docobo (2005) described the link between traditional crime and terrorism. In fact, most terrorist groups commit crimes including fraud, money laundering, drug-trafficking, and identity theft to provide the revenues needed to commit terrorist attacks.

❖ **Photo 15.3** It is predicted that the concept of gated communities will proliferate and residents will look to private security personnel for their communities' protective services more and more.

Police officers have the capability to "identify potential terrorists" who live and "operate in their jurisdictions" and who are involved in these crimes, "help to protect vulnerable targets", and "coordinate the first response to terror attacks" (Clarke & Newman, 2007, p. 9). COPS (2009) believed the partnership elements of community policing were the most useful in preventing terrorism. In other words, through community policing, police establish a dialogue with the community. "Just as street-level knowledge is important to breaking up narcotics activities in a neighborhood, community partnerships and trusting relationships will inspire the confidence of citizens to pass along information that can help to uncover terrorist individuals or cells" (COPS, 2009, p. 1). Because of the similarities between traditional crime and policing, departments that have instituted a community policing philosophy should make an easy transition to addressing terrorism and terrorism-related crimes (Docobo, 2005). For example, in New York City the Police Department tip line received a number of calls about a person's anti-American rhetoric. An investigation revealed the plans for an attack at the Herald Square subway station in 2004, near the time of the Republican National Convention (Kelling & Bratton, 2006).

Chapman and Scheider (2008) discovered that traumatic events such as terror attacks can cause organizations to fall back on more traditional methods of doing business and in some cases eliminate community policing. For example, there is some concern that the close association with the military and the terrorist oriented mission of the police will accelerate the militarization and isolation of the police, rather than bring them closer to the community partnerships that served as the source of legitimacy for community policing (Mastrofski, 2006). More specifically, since the attacks of September 11th, some have called for police to take a more active stance in counterterrorism activities, which emphasize intelligence gathering, covert investigations, information sharing, and immigrant enforcement (Ortiz, Hendricks, & Sugie, 2007). However, Ortiz, Hendricks, and Sugie (2007) believed a majority of police agencies have not shifted their core goals and priorities after September 11th to reflect homeland security policing.

Intelligence-Led Policing and Terrorism

Intelligence-led policing (ILP) is a management philosophy that ensures resource allocations are based on improved awareness of the operating environment (Barrett, 2006). According to Barrett (2006), ILP supports decision makers through data collection and intelligence analysis and is vital for the prevention, response to, and mitigation of terrorist attacks, crime incidents, and natural disasters. As an example, the New York Police Department has more than 1,000 police officers dedicated to counterterrorism, employs intelligence experts, has officers fluent in many foreign languages, constantly monitors news source and intelligence data, and has agents stationed overseas in terrorist hot spots (Finnegan, 2005).

Clarke and Newman (2007) believed a fatal flaw of intelligence-led policing is the "assumption that if the police simply collect as much information as they can, they will at some point identify suspicious activity" (p. 4) that will lead them to terrorist activity. The authors argue that behaviors and events labeled as suspicious leave open the opportunity for individuals to exercise prejudices and preconceptions, and in many cases, useless information is more common than useful information.

McGarrell, Freilich, and Chermak (2007) wondered if intelligence-led policing might be at a stage similar to that of community policing 15 to 20 years ago. "The concept is being endorsed by all the key law enforcement professional organizations and there are reports of promising practices ... but it remains a fairly nebulous concept and most agencies are just toying with implementation" (p. 154).

Terrorism Laws

Shortly after 9/11, and in response to the warnings from the law enforcement community, President George W. Bush and the U.S. Congress passed two key pieces of legislation that, if carried out as intended, should forever change the way the United States deals with terrorism. First, the **Department of Homeland Security** was formed, the mission of which is ... "to lead the unified national effort to secure the country and preserve our freedoms" (Department of Homeland Security, 2010, p. 1). While the Department was created to secure the country against those who seek to disrupt the American way of life, the mission also includes preparation for and response to all hazards and disasters (Department of Homeland Security, 2010).

The other piece of legislation passed into law and viewed as necessary by many in the law enforcement community to effectively conduct counterterrorism operations is known as the **Patriot Act**. The purpose of the Act is to deter and punish terrorist acts in the United States and around the world and to enhance law enforcement investigatory tools and other purposes (Financial Crimes Enforcement Center, 2010).

While these new laws are applauded by many, they are not without critics. Probably the most serious criticism is that the expansion of these police powers may be abused or not applied as Congress intended. Worries concerning potential constitutional abuses in the name of national security and patriotism are not without substance, particularly when viewed in light of past abuses by many U.S. law enforcement agencies. For example, consider the fact that in March of 2007 the U.S. Justice Department Inspector General found that the FBI lacked sufficient controls concerning agents obtaining administrative subpoenas, which do not require a judge's prior approval (Johnston & Lipton, 2007). Close supervision of those in the DHS and those operating under the provisions of the Patriot Act is a must if abuses are to be minimized.

YOU DECIDE 15.1

As police departments in many areas have succeeded in reducing various types of reported crime, they have begun looking to the future for "the thing that will take us to the next level." As we discussed in Chapter 15 many believe the future may involve some form of predictive policing. Predictive policing involves computer analysis of previous crime related information in order "to predict where and when crimes will occur."

For example, researchers are current attempting to "forecast the time and place of crimes using the same mathematical formulas that seismologists use to predict the distribution of aftershocks emanating from an earthquake." Additional research involves creating "computer simulations of criminals roving through city neighborhoods in order to better understand why they tend to cluster in certain areas and how they disperse when the police go looking for them."

Currently Los Angeles Police Department is considering the dynamics of implementing predictive policing at the command and patrol officer levels. For example, patrol officers on LAPD would utilize "mapping software on in-car computers and hand-held devices would show continuous updates on the probability of various crimes occurring in the vicinity, along with the addresses and background information about paroled ex-convicts living in the area."

Source: Adapted from "Predicting crime before it happens: Researchers offer a glimpse into the future of police work" by J. Rubin, September 5, 2010, *Houston Chronicle*. Available online at: http://infoweb.newsbank.com.ezproxy.wiu.edu/iw-search/we/InfoWeb

1. What are the privacy implications for the implementation of predictive policing?

2. How is predictive policing different from community policing, problem-oriented policing and other innovations that are current in place in many police departments?

❖ Chapter Summary

It is risky to forecast the future of policing in the United States. However, there are a number of issues that will more than likely impact the future of police agencies. These issues include, but are not limited to, the continued advance in technology; the future roles or duties of police related to global issues, such as transnational crime; adequate and effective continuing education and training; increased responsibilities for the private security industry; effective leadership capabilities; and an increased need for a holistic response to crime and disaster incidents, based upon the cooperative efforts of the public and private sectors.

In light of these important issues, police officials are well advised to concentrate on breaking down barriers between the police and the private security sectors; formulating response plans for acts of terrorism and other disasters, natural or otherwise; and perhaps most important of all, practicing those plans and continuing to modify them as circumstances warrant.

❖ Key Terms

andragogy

predictive policing

terrorism

intelligence-led policing

Department of Homeland Security

❖ Discussion Questions

1. What is the role of community policing in the future of American policing?

2. Discuss the current relationship between the private security industry and public policing. Is that relationship likely to change in the next few years? If so, in what ways? Explain.

3. What qualifications should we look for in tomorrow's police leaders?

4. Will the emphases on police education and training remain the same in the years to come? If not, what changes do you anticipate?

5. Discuss some technological changes that are likely to have a major impact on policing in the future.

6. What do you see as the future for accreditation? What do you see as the future for lateral entry?

7. Discuss the role of the municipal police in dealing with terrorism. What recommendations can you make as to how this role could best be fulfilled?

❖ Internet Exercises

1. Go to the Internet and find information about intelligence-led policing and predictive policing. What is the level of effectiveness of these innovations? How can we evaluate intelligence-led policing and predictive policing? Explain.

2. Using your favorite search engine, go online and search for information on new technologies to detect and prevent terrorism. Will the development of new technologies in the future alter the nature of terrorism? Explain.

Glossary

911 policing—allocation of police resources in a case-by-case fashion

Academy of Criminal Justice Sciences (ACJS)—one of the largest professional organizations in the world dedicated to the advancement of knowledge in the criminal justice profession

accountability—refers to the fact that the police are public employees and are therefore accountable to the public for their actions

accreditation—development of standards containing a clear statement of professional objectives

administrative and staff services division—consists of sworn and civilian personnel who often perform record keeping, communication, and research

affirmative action—programs that are intended to prevent discrimination in present hiring and promotion practices and are used to remedy past discrimination in hiring and promotion

Allocation Model for Police Personnel—a model involving several variables for estimating the number of required police personnel

andragogy—instructional methodology based on the belief that adults learn differently than children

areal policing—involves tailoring of police services to specific areas within broader police jurisdictions

arrest—occurs when an individual authorized to take a person into custody detains that person with the intention of making an arrest and when the person being arrested understands that the intention of the person making the arrest is detaining him for that purpose

artifacts—most visible forms of the organizational culture (sounds, behaviors, language)

assessment center—formal process that involves a series of exercises (simulation and role playing) designed to test how well a candidate would perform in a job

Automatic Number Plate Recognition (ANPR)—technology that uses optical character recognition to read the license plates on vehicles

Automatic Vehicle Location (AVL)—a means for automatically determining the geographic location of a vehicle and transmitting the information to a requester, most often through the use of GPS

Baby Boomer Generation—people born between 1946 and 1964

biased-enforcement—police practice that results from enforcement of the law based on any number of personal and occupational-based biases

bicycle patrol—a popular form of patrol because of the low cost and possible coverage compared to foot patrol

blue wall of silence—protective, supportive, and shared attitudes, values, understandings, and views of the world associated with the police society

body armor—a defense covering worn by police officers that is usually constructed of woven fibers that are sewn into a vest or soft clothing

bona fide occupational qualification—requirement that is necessary to the normal operation of an organization

Boryokudan—also known as the Yakuza; the criminal organization initially formed in Japan that has since developed into a transnational organized crime group

bribery—type of malfeasance that can take many forms but at its core involves police officers taking no enforcement action when they are normally required to do so, usually in exchange for monetary remuneration

broken windows policing—based on a theory that suggests that a reduction in minor crimes will lead to a decrease in violent ones

broken windows theory—theory stating that neighborhood social disorder causes a decline of the overall condition of the neighborhood, which leads to criminal activity

burnout—exhaustion and cynicism resulting from repeated exposure to high levels of stress

calmative agent—pharmaceutical or sedative drugs that produce a calming or tranquil state

CAPS: Chicago Alternative Policing Strategy—community-policing strategy in Chicago

CCTV—closed circuit television

cell phone—a portable phone that operates over a cellular network consisting of switching points and base stations

Christopher Commission—investigative body created by former Los Angeles Mayor Tom Bradley in 1991 in response to several high-profile media accounts of various acts of misconduct by LAPD members

civil law—defines and determines the rights of individuals to protect their persons and property

collective bargaining—negotiations between an employer and groups of employees to determine conditions of employment

Commission on Accreditation for Law Enforcement Agencies—established in 1979 (operational in 1983), conducts evaluations based on specific standards for law enforcement agencies and accredits agencies meeting the criteria

community-oriented policing—a philosophy based on the belief that law-abiding citizens should have input with respect to policing

community–police mediation program—a voluntary process in which community members and officers sit down in a neutral and confidential setting facilitated by a professional mediator to discuss their differences

community policing—a model of policing based upon establishing partnerships among police and other citizens in an attempt to improve quality of life through crime prevention, information sharing, and mutual understanding

community relations programs—programs sponsored by police agencies that attempt to improve police–community relations

community service officers (CSOs)—nonsworn employees who perform duties not requiring a sworn police officer

comparative approach—involves comparing the number of police officers between cities of similar characteristics or the ratio of police officers to population

CompStat—stands for computer statistics and is based on collecting and analyzing data from crime maps and other performance measures while holding police administrators accountable for their performance as measured by the data collected; a multifaceted system used to administer police operations based on a comprehensive, continuous analysis of results

Computer-Aided Dispatch (CAD)—a system in which dispatch is accomplished through the use of computers

conducted energy devices—devices such as a Taser that can induce involuntary muscle contractions that can temporarily incapacitate people

consent decree—agreement related to an employer achieving a balance in terms of race, ethnicity, and gender in the workforce

consent search—occurs when an individual voluntarily waives her Fourth Amendment rights and allows a police officer to search her person, belongings, vehicle, or home

contract security personnel—security guards or security officers hired by organizations from outside agencies to secure and protect assets and personnel

corruption of authority—the most widespread form of police misconduct; includes a wide variety of unauthorized material inducements or gratuities, ranging from discounted clothing and meals to free alcoholic beverages and commercial sex

crackdowns—increases in the number of police targeted toward a specific type of law violation

crime analysis—the systematic study of crime and disorder problems, including sociodemographic, spatial, and temporal factors

crime control model—allows for the arrest of individuals who are known to be factually guilty of committing a crime

crime mapping—a process of using a geographic information system to conduct spatial analysis of crime problems and other police issues

Crime Prevention Through Environmental Design (CPTED)—based on the premise that proper design and effective use of the built environment can lead to a reduction in the fear of crime and incidence of crime

criminal law—that body of law established to maintain peace and order to protect society from the injurious acts of individuals

critical incident—an event that has a stressful impact sufficient to overwhelm the effective coping skills of a person

CSI Effect—refers to the perception of scientific testing by television viewers

cynicism—in this context, involves a loss of faith in people or loss of enthusiasm for police work

density analysis mapping—mapping used to reveal areas with elevated crime activity, known as hot spots

deoxyribonucleic acid (DNA)—one of two types of molecules that encode genetic information

Department of Homeland Security–federal agency responsible for a unified national effort to secure the country and preserve freedom

deployment models—the assignment of police personnel to districts, zones, and areas

differential response policing—involves classifying calls by their seriousness to determine the appropriate police response

Digital Collection System Network (DCSNet)—connects FBI wiretapping rooms to switches controlled by traditional landline operators, internet-telephony providers, and cellular companies

directed energy devices—uses radiated energy to achieve the same effect as blunt force with a lower probability of injury

directed patrol—involves increasing police presence in a specified area

discrimination—treating people differently with respect to their employment because of their race, gender, religion, or national origin; involves behavior that, in its negative form, excludes all members of a certain group from some rights, opportunities, or privileges

double marginality—refers to the fact that black officers were not fully accepted by their white coworkers and were also distrusted by other blacks

Drug Abuse Resistance Education (DARE)—educational programs presented by police officers in cooperation with school authorities in an attempt to prevent abuse of drugs by youth

dual career ladder (DCL)—allows police officers to advance in salary without being promoted to a higher rank

due process model—requires that evidence of guilt presented in court be obtained according to legal guidelines

early intervention programs—administrative practice of identifying officers whose behavior is problematic, intervening to correct the problem behavior, and monitoring those who have received said intervention

education—the provision of familiarity with the theoretical concepts and principles underlying the training

Electronic Communications Privacy Act (ECPA)—wiretapping regulation that protects e-mail, pagers, and cell phone calls

Electronic Non-Radar Device (ENRADD)—a speed detection system using infrared beams to measure a car's speed as it passes through a 3-foot-long section of road using sensors placed on each side of the road to detect when a vehicle enters and exits the section

emotional abuse/psychological harassment—type of wrongdoing normally associated with the use of racial slurs and other negative descriptions of certain classes of citizens (e.g., gays, drug addicts, homeless persons, and protesters, to name the most common)

enforcer—believes in enforcing the law versus protection of individual rights

era of Homeland security—based on Homeland Security agents who are familiar with information technology, intelligence gathering, processing, disseminating, and technical skills involving knowledge of weapons of mass destruction, response to mass casualty events, and both antiterrorism and counterterrorism methodologies

ethos—fundamental spirit of a culture

equal protection clause—of the Fourteenth Amendment, applies to the police in that it prevents both the federal government and all states from denying the protection of the law to any group of persons by making arbitrary, unreasonable distinctions based on race, religion, gender, national origin, and so on

evidence-based policing—involves using the scientific method to support an informed decision making process

excessive use of force—also referred to as *police brutality,* this form of malfeasance pertains to situations in which officers overextend their legal authority by using excessive force to either effect an arrest of or to coerce information from individuals with whom they interact during the course of their duties

executive protection agents—private security personnel hired to protect executives, attorneys, wealthy families, sports celebrities, movie stars, and political figures among others

exigent circumstances—circumstances that may exist when the police are in hot pursuit of a fleeing felon, when there is a danger of imminent destruction of evidence, when a suspect is escaping, or when there is imminent danger to the officer or others

field associates—term used to describe the use of specially trained officers to obtain intelligence regarding corrupt police practices

field training—period of time immediately following successful recruit training. During this time new officers are paired with specially trained veterans and are evaluated regarding how they perform on the street, normally in the patrol division. Field training programs normally last anywhere from six weeks to six months.

Fifth Amendment—provides that no citizen is to be tried for a capital or "otherwise infamous crime without a presentment or indictment" by a grand jury (exception as relates to crimes committed during wartime and the military), or may be subject to trial for the same offense twice, or compelled to incriminate himself, or be deprived life, liberty, or property without of due process of law

fingerprint scanner—takes an image of the finger and determines whether the pattern of ridges and valleys in the image matches the pattern of ridges and valleys in prescanned images

First Amendment—states that Congress shall make no law prohibiting free exercise of religion or abridging the rights of free speech and peaceful assembly

first responder—in the context of law enforcement or emergency response preparedness, these are the individuals to provide the first line of defense (i.e., police officers, firefighters, emergency medical personnel, public utility personnel, etc.)

foot patrol—the original form of police patrol; is often employed today at parades, concerts, and sporting events

Foreign Intelligence Surveillance Act (FISA)—specifies that the purpose of electronic surveillance must be to obtain intelligence in the U.S. on foreign powers (such as enemy agents or spies) or individuals connected to international terrorist groups

forensic science—branch of science used in the resolution of legal disputes

Fourteenth Amendment—often referred to as the *due process* amendment because it provides that no state can deprive any person of life, liberty, or property without due process of law

Fourth Amendment—prohibits unreasonable searches and seizures of persons, houses, papers, and effects and requires that probable cause be demonstrated prior to the issuing of warrants

fruit of the poisonous tree doctrine—evidence found indirectly as a result of a constitutional violation

functional organization design—creation of positions and departments in an organization based on specialized activities

galvanic skin response—changes in electrical resistance in the skin over time

gaming surveillance officers—hired to act as security agents for casino managers and patrons

gangs (meta/super gangs)—these street gangs have assumed the characteristics of a criminal organization and include groups such as the Gangster Disciples, Latin Kings, Crips, Bloods, and MS-13, which are considered transnational crime groups

general adaptation syndrome—stages of stress experienced by a person after the exposure to stressors

Generation X—people born between 1964 and 1984

Generation Y—people born between the 1980s and the late 1990s

Geographic Information System (GIS)—computer programs that capture, analyze, store, and present spatial data and make it easy to visualize and interpret geographic information

Global Positioning System (GPS)—a U.S. space-based global navigation satellite system providing positioning, navigation, and timing services to users

good faith doctrine—involves searches conducted with a warrant and states that when a police officer acting in good faith obtains a warrant, conducts a search, and seizes evidence, that evidence will not be excluded from court proceedings even if the warrant is later invalidated

graffiti cameras—talking surveillance cameras

grass eaters—term coined by the Knapp Commission to refer to officers who engage in minor acts of corrupt practices (i.e., acceptance of gratuities, etc.) and passively accept the wrongdoings of other officers

hierarchies—organization structures that take the shape of a pyramid, with many employees at the bottom and few management personnel at the top

Homeland Security—Law enforcement agency of the U.S. Department of Justice whose mission is " . . . to develop and coordinate the implementation of a comprehensive national strategy to secure the United States from terrorist threats or attacks" (White House, 2001). The agency coordinates the executive branch's efforts to detect, prepare for, prevent, protect against, respond to, and recover from terrorist attacks within the United States.

Homeland Security Act and the Patriot Act—laws passed by the United States Congress that focus on terrorism prevention strategies and tactics

hot spots—geographic areas with clusters of criminal offenses occurring within a specified interval of time

human relations—refers to everything we do to, for, and with other people

hybrid systems—consist of in-house management personnel with contract officers

hyperstress—an overload resulting from too many complex demands for the time allotted

hypostress—low levels of mental or physical activity

idealist—value is placed on individual rights

Illinois Citizen and Law Enforcement Analysis and Reporting (I-CLEAR)—a computerized data warehouse designed to allow police officers to search for suspects based on nicknames, tattoos, country of origin, vehicle make and model, and other characteristics in partnership with the Illinois State Police and residents of Chicago

Immutable characteristics—characteristics determined at birth or characteristics individuals should not be asked to change

impasse—occurs when negotiations fail to lead to a compromise

Incident Command System—coordinates police personnel, allocates resources, and allows emergency responders to adopt and integrate organization structure; attempt to achieve effective coordination of police personnel while insuring appropriate allocation of resources and providing emergency responders an integrated organizational structure unhindered by jurisdictional boundaries

independent source doctrine—holds that illegally obtained evidence may be admitted if it was also obtained through an independent source not tainted by police misconduct

inevitable discovery doctrine—allows the admission of illegally obtained evidence if it would have been discovered lawfully in the normal course of events anyway

in-house security personnel—typically employees who conduct security activities within an organization

inservice training—also known as continuing professional education, the intent is to keep professionals up to date with continuous changes affecting their practice

institutional corruption—crimes affecting the organization of a society or culture, such as religion, the media, education, and so on

institutional discrimination—unfair testing procedures, hiring practices, job assignments, and educational requirements

Integrated Automated Fingerprint Identification System (IAFIS)—a national fingerprint and criminal history system maintained by the Federal Bureau of Investigation

intelligence-led or *intelligence-based policing*—a policing model that originated in Britain and that focuses on risk assessment and risk management. Involves identifying risks or patterns associated with groups, individuals, and locations in order to predict when and where crime is likely to occur; builds on community policing and problem-oriented policing and includes an information gathering process that allows police agencies to better understand their crime problems and take a measure of resources available to be able to decide on enforcement and prevention strategies

International Law Enforcement Educators and Trainers Association (ILEETA)—professional organization dedicated to serving the professional needs of its members. ILEETA

publishes three periodicals, periodically e-mails the *ILEETA e-Bulletin,* publishes an annual issue of *The ILEETA Chronicle,* and presents an annual international training conference and exposition (ILEETA, 2009).

Internet Protocol (IP) cameras—closed-circuit television (CCTV) cameras that use the Internet to transmit image data and control signals over an Ethernet link

intuitive approach—little more than an educated guess concerning the appropriate number of police personnel

job action—occurs when negotiations fail to lead to an agreement and can include blue flu, work slow down, and work speed ups

kickbacks—type of police corruption that refers to the practice of obtaining goods, services, or money for business referrals by police officers (e.g., attorneys, doctors, tow truck operators, auto body shops, and board-up service companies)

Kansas City preventative patrol experiment—one of the most comprehensive assessments of police patrol

Knapp Commission—investigative committee formed in 1972 by the city of New York in response to allegations of large-scale corruption amongst NYPD officers by one of their own. This form of investigation set the stage for many cities and states in the years that followed.

laser radars—ladars (LAser Detection And Ranging) or lidars (LIght Detection And Ranging) use laser light to determine speed

Law Enforcement Assistance Administration (LEAA)—during the 1960s and 1970s, provided a billion dollars each year to improve and strengthen criminal justice agencies

legalistic style—focus is on law enforcement and arrests

less-than-lethal force—force used by an officer that is not likely to result in serious bodily harm or death

lethal or deadly force—force that may result in great bodily harm or death

Lexow Commission—investigative committee formed in 1894 by the city of New York in response to allegations of large-scale corruption amongst NYPD officers. This form of investigation set the stage for many cities and states in the years that followed.

liability—legal responsibility for costs or damages

License Plate Recognition System (LPR)—reads license plates of parked and moving vehicles and compares them to vehicle databases

line personnel—performs actual police work and includes patrol officers and investigators

mafia—a criminal organization formed centuries ago in Italy that is known for conducting illegal activities in most of the countries of the world

malfeasance—any intentional act that is either based on illegality or disregard of the Law Enforcement Code of Ethics or departmental policy

management rights—rights reserved for management, which include determining the organization's mission, direction of employees, and so on

mandatory data collection—primarily in response to the racial profiling issues associated with the late 1990s and early 2000s, the federal government and each individual state mandated that law enforcement agencies maintain data regarding various demographic issues during police stops of vehicles (i.e., race of the driver and occupants of the vehicle stopped, reason or probable cause for the stop, whether or not any occupants or the vehicle was searched, justification for the search, length of detention, and whether or not any tickets were issues or arrests made)

matrix structure—involves multiple support systems and authority relationships often found in a drug task force

meat eaters—term coined by the Knapp Commission to describe officers who engaged widely in corrupt and unlawful practices during the performance of their duties

media relations policy—policy based on the public's right to know and the police department's obligation to keep the public informed

minority group—comprised of individuals who are accorded unequal treatment from dominant group members in the form of discrimination and who are relatively easy to identify because of their physical or cultural characteristics, which differ from those of the dominant group

Mobile Data Terminals (MDTs)—computers in patrol vehicles

Mollen Commission—created by former New York City Mayor Rudolph Giuliani in 1994 and headed by retired New York State Supreme Court Justice Milton Mollen, the charge of the committee was to investigate allegations of misconduct, analyze the effectiveness of anticorruption mechanisms within the department, and offer recommendations for improvement

money laundering—attempts to disguise the original source of monies, normally through illegal means, and infuse said monies into the legitimate marketplace

Multiple-Hurdle Procedure—battery of tests or hurdles that must be completed before a recruit can become a police officer

National Advisory Commission on Civil Disorders (1967)—another major effort to better understand styles of policing, police-community relations, and police selection and training

National Advisory Commission on Criminal Justice Standards and Goals (1973)—another attempt to better understand styles of policing, police community relations, and police selection and training

National Security Letters (NSL)—written demands from the FBI that compel Internet service providers, credit companies, financial institutions, and others to hand over confidential records about their customers (such as subscriber information, phone numbers, e-mail addresses, and websites visited)

night watch system—early policing system that required able-bodied males to donate their time to help protect cities

noble cause corruption—form of misconduct pertaining to various situations in which officers circumvent the law in order to serve what they perceive to be the greater good (e.g., manufacturing probable cause, perjury to gain a conviction in court, etc). This is also akin to the philosophy of "the ends justify the means."

nonfeasance—in the context of policing, this form of misconduct refers to the reluctance of honest, hard-working police officers to report misconduct committed by their peers. This reluctance on the part of honest officers has been identified as one of the factors perpetuating this issue and is normally the result of the influence of the police subculture

North American Free Trade Agreement (NAFTA)—agreement for free trade between the United States, Canada, and Mexico that became effective in 1994

occupational discrimination—discrimination that results, in part at least, from being a member of a particular work group

Office of the Police Corps and Law Enforcement Education—created by the U.S. Department of Justice (1999), the goal of this program was to weave a college education with state-of-the-art police training to produce highly qualified personnel who would be able to confront the demands and intricacies of 21st century policing. Unfortunately, funding for the program has been eliminated and the Police Corps is no longer awarding scholarships or providing training.

operations division—division of a police agency consisting of patrol and investigation

opportunistic theft—form of misconduct pertaining to police officers who steal money or other valuables when, for example, they are guarding a crime scene (as in the case of a burglary), or steal other such goods from unconscious, inebriated, or dead people

optimists—service oriented and value individual rights

order maintenance—police calls for service such as suspicious person complaints and loud music

organizational assumption—deeply held beliefs that guide behaviors in an organization

organizational socialization model—belief that police personality develops from work itself, which often includes exposure to violence, corruption, and danger

organizations—rational, efficient form of grouping people

organized crime—Any group having some manner of a formalized structure and whose primary objective is to obtain money through illegal activities. Such groups maintain their position through the use of actual or threatened violence, corrupt public officials, graft, or extortion, and they generally have a significant impact on the people in their locales, region, or the country as a whole (FBI, 2010b, p. 1).

outlaw motorcycle gangs—motorcycle gangs that have assumed the characteristics of a criminal organization and that operate on a transnational level; these gangs include the Hell's Angels, Banditos, Pagans, and Outlaws

Patrick Colquhoun—Superintending Magistrate of the Thames River Police, a forerunner of the Metropolitan police and author of works on metropolitan policing

Pendleton Act—extended civil service protection first to federal and later to state and local employees

Perestroika—formal policy implemented by Russian authorities following the collapse of the former Soviet Union. Its goal was to introduce a more democratic form of government and a free market economy for its citizens.

performance measures—indicators that assess the extent to which police patrol officers achieve the designated outcomes

photo radar—automatically detects a speeding violation and photographs or video records the driver, the vehicle, and the license plate, and records vehicle speed and typically the date, time, and location

physical restraints—a variety of products employed to physically restrain or impede the movement of a person

place design—geographical establishment of primary units in an organization, includes assignment of personnel to beats, zones, districts, and areas

plain view doctrine—holds that if a police officer sees an incriminating object in plain view during a legitimate stop, he may seize the object

police—derived from the Greek words *polis* and *politeuein,* which refer to being a citizen who participates in the affairs of a city or state

Police Accredited Training Online—innovative and inexpensive way to provide a myriad of inservice training opportunities to officers on a state-wide basis. This asynchronous, online training initiative was formed by a partnership between the Minnesota Chiefs of Police Association, the Minnesota Sheriff's Association, and the League of Minnesota Cities Insurance Trust.

Police Association for College Education (PACE)—formerly known as the American Police Foundation, PACE is a professional organization dedicated to the professionalization of law enforcement through higher education

Police Code of Conduct or Ethics—revised as of 2005, this code was formed and adopted by the International Association of Chiefs of Police, which sets forth standards of conduct for police officers on and off duty

police code of silence—also known as the *blue wall of silence,* it is a major tenet of the police subculture that promotes the tolerance of acts of misconduct by many officers

police–community relations—consists of both human and public relations

police corruption—various acts of police officers carried out in a manner that places their personal gain ahead of duty, resulting in the violation of police procedures, criminal law, or both

police discretion—the exercise of individual choices or judgments that police officers have concerning possible courses of action

police ethics—standards of conduct based on moral and professional principles that influence a variety of actions taken or not taken by police officers on and off duty

police paramilitary unit—highly specialized police unit such as a special response team

police personality—combination of characteristics and behaviors that are used to stereotype the police

police subculture—shared values, attitudes, and norms created within the occupational and organizational environment of policing; a set of informal norms, largely based on tradition and passed on from generation to generation, that greatly influence police behavior and the perception of the public by police. Certain of these subcultural forces have a significant influence on the use of discretion, in both positive and negative ways.

Police Training Officer (PTO) program—recently developed field training program that many researchers and police executives claim is effective at developing new officers entering the field with problem-solving skills rarely seen at the early stages of their career. The PTO program involves two primary training areas: substantive topics and core competencies, the details of which are identified in the chapter.

polygraph—a device that registers involuntary physical processes that is often used in an attempt to detect whether or not a suspect is telling the truth

POSDCORB—seven tasks performed by organization administrators

postponed violence—term coined by consumer activist Ralph Nader to describe the practice of intentionally exposing workers and consumers to harmful products that will adversely affect said workers and consumers years later

Post Traumatic Stress Disorder—emotional disturbance leading to a numbing of emotions, insomnia, and depression

predictive policing—a model that involves using data and analysis to predict future police problems and implement strategies to resolve problems

predispositional model—belief that policing attracts individuals who possess a certain type of personality

prejudice—unfavorable attitudes toward a group or individual not based on experience or fact; a feeling about a person or persons based on faulty generalizations

Presidential Commission on Law Enforcement and the Administration of Justice (1967)—represented a major effort to better understand styles of policing, police community relations, and police selection and training

private detectives (investigators)—detectives (investigators) who are not members of the police but are hired by individual clients or companies and often licensed by the state

privilege against self-incrimination—implies that no person can be compelled to incriminate herself—the suspect need not answer questions or disclose information that would support her own conviction

probable cause—exists when facts and circumstances within a police officer's knowledge, which are based upon reasonably trustworthy information, are sufficient to warrant a person of reasonable caution to believe that an offense has been or is being committed by the person being arrested

probationary period—length of time during which the performance of new officers, from the day they start recruit training, is evaluated. This period of time ranges from six months to two years, depending on the agency. It should also be noted that during this time period officers are "employees at will" and do not enjoy any of the employment protections afforded those officers who successfully completed their probationary periods.

problem-oriented policing—encourages officers to take a holistic approach, working with other citizens and other agency representatives to find long-term solutions to a variety of recurrent problems

profession—occupation often requiring some form of accreditation, certification, or licensing and usually including a code of ethics

professionalism—an end state that is largely based on ethical practice and other related characteristics such as good personal character, personal and organizational accountability, a commitment to higher education and continuous training, and intolerance for misconduct

protection of illegal activities—the most egregious of all forms of misconduct; involves police officers taking money or other valuables in exchange for their protection of criminal activities

protective coloration—refers to the facts that black police officers can often gather information that would be extremely difficult for white officers to gather; that having black police officers on the force may make charges of racial brutality against the police less likely; and that federal funding is partly dependent on equal employment opportunities and affirmative action programs

psychological harassment—harassment based on the use of racial slurs and other attempts to embarrass or humiliate members of the minority group

public information officer—personnel who represent the police department in all contacts with any form of media

public relations—from the police perspective, they include all of the activities in which police engage while attempting to develop or maintain a favorable public image

pulling levers policing—an innovation that focuses attention on a small number of chronic offenders responsible for a large share of the crime problems

qualified individual with a disability—interpreted to mean the job applicant must be able to perform the essential elements of the job with or without reasonable accommodation

quotas—commonly known as measures or standards of performance that are frequently based on the number of traffic tickets issued and arrests made by police officers. Many times, this method of evaluation may lead to biased-enforcement practices if left unmonitored.

racial profiling—the targeting of minority group members by police for traffic and other law enforcement practices, resulting from an improper and potentially unlawful use of discretion

Radio Detection and Ranging (RADAR) systems—use remote sensors that emit electromagnetic radio waves to determine vehicle speeds

random preventative patrol—method of performing police work that permits the officer to control their area

rank structure—chain of command that identifies who communicates with whom and identifies lines of authority

realists—focuses on neither law enforcement nor protection of individual rights

reasonable accommodation—refers to new construction or modification of existing facilities and work schedules, as long as the modification does not cause the agency undue hardship

reasonable suspicion—when based on objective facts and logical conclusions given a specific set of circumstances, may be used as the basis for stopping and frisking suspicious individuals

reasonableness—generally refers to what a reasonable person, in similar circumstances, based upon similar information, might conclude

reassurance policing—focuses on the signal crimes concept and using a formal method for identifying signals

recruit training—refers to the initial training successful police applicants are exposed to; topics such as criminal law, traffic code enforcement, arrest techniques, firearm training, self-defense tactics, vehicle searches, and a host of other similar topics are presented. Successful recruit training provides certification as a sworn police or peace officer.

red light cameras—record stop light violations at intersections

Reform movement (Reform Era)—involved radical reorganization of police agencies, including strong centralized administrative bureaucracy, hiring and promotion based upon merit, highly specialized units, application of science to crime through improved record keeping, fingerprinting, serology, and criminal investigation

Reno Model—field training programs based on this model focus more on instructing trainees in the development of both problem-solving abilities and adult learning techniques, referred to generally as the problem-based approach to learning.

responsiveness—refers to the provision of appropriate police services promptly and competently, with appropriate referrals in cases not within agency jurisdiction

RICO Statute—federal legislation enacted in 1970 that allows prosecutors to go after the organization, rather than individuals; defines racketeering in a broad manner and makes it a crime to belong to an organization involved in a pattern of racketeering

role ambiguity—confusion a person experiences related to expectations of others

role conflict—the result of inconsistent or incompatible expectations being communicated to a person

rotten apple hypothesis—long-standing belief of police executives who point to the "few spoiled apples in the barrel" as an explanation of any police misconduct that might occur

saturation patrol—involves adding patrol officers to a specific area in order to increase police visibility

search—occurs when an expectation of privacy that society is prepared to consider reasonable is infringed upon

Second Amendment—states that a well regulated Militia being necessary to the security of a Free State, the right of the people to keep and bear Arms shall not be infringed

security officers—privately hired to patrol and inspect property to protect against fire, theft, vandalism, terrorism, and illegal activity

seizure—of property occurs when there is some meaningful interference with an individual's possessory interests in that property

service style—searches for alternatives to arrest and the uses of formal sanctions

shakedowns—type of corruption that involves officers taking money or other valuables and personal services from offenders they have caught during the commission of a crime. Drug dealers, pimps, and motorists are among the favored targets for this practice.

sheriff—typically an elected official responsible for county law enforcement and, in many instances, the county jail

signal crimes—acts that breach either the criminal law or conventions of social order and in the process function as warning signals about the presence of a risk to security to people

simulation or work sample test—measures job skills of an applicant using samples of behavior under realistic job-like conditions

Sir Robert Peel—founder of modern territorial policing (London Metropolitan Police) in 1829 in London

situational crime prevention—focuses on reducing crime by reducing crime opportunities and increasing risk to the offenders

slippery slope—term coined during the Knapp Commission era that refers to the likelihood of officers who may start out by justifying minor transgressions, such as accepting gratuities, but may slowly progress toward justifying more serious forms of misconduct. This may be viewed as the possible transition from grass eater to meat eater.

solution-oriented policing—focuses on the fact that some community–police issues are best addressed through the development of unique approaches or thinking outside the box

span of control—ratio of supervisors to subordinates

status test—related to an applicant's citizenship, possession of or ability to obtain a driver's license, residency requirement, and age and education level

stereotypes—preconceived notions based on prior encounters, word of mouth/rumor/gossip, and information provided by the media

strategic management era—based on the practice of computer-generated crime data and a resulting convergence of police management, technology, strategy, and community involvement

stress—occurs when an event involves a constraint, opportunity, or excessive physical or psychological demand

symbolic assailants—involves a level of suspicion accorded by police to most citizen–police encounters

Taser—electroshock weapon that uses electrical current to disrupt voluntary control of muscles

task force—law enforcement strategy based on the promotion and use of interagency cooperation. These units are normally headed by a federal law enforcement agency with local police officers being detailed or assigned to work on the various task forces.

terrorism—the unlawful use of force or threat of force against persons or property to intimidate or coerce a government, a civilian population, or any part thereof in furtherance of political or social objectives; "The premeditated and unlawful act in which groups or agents of some principal engage in a threatened or actual use of force or violence against human or property targets. These groups or agents engage in this behavior intending the purposeful intimidation of governments or people to affect policy or behavior with an underlying political objective" (Martin, 2006, p.48).

terrorism-oriented policing—adds new duties to those already assumed by the police in an attempt to detect and prevent terrorist acts

third party policing—involves police attempts to convince organizations or non-offending persons to take some responsibility for preventing crime or reducing the crime problem

time design—an organizational design that involves assignment of personnel based on watches, tours, or shifts

totality of circumstances—requires that an officer has a particularized and objective basis for suspecting that a particular person is or has been involved in criminal activity; may be based upon a variety of objective observations, information from police reports, and consideration of modes or patterns of operation of certain kinds of offenders from which a police officer may draw inferences and makes deductions concerning the probability that the party in question is involved in criminal conduct

training—The provision of basic skills necessary to perform essential job functions

transnational crime—"Crime that takes place across national borders . . . [that] is poorly understood but has had profound consequences for the ordering of the world system" (Sheptycki, 2007, p. 391).

Triads—the criminal organization originally formed in China that has since developed into a transnational organized crime group

unfair labor practice—violation of certain protected rights by an employer or labor organization

unity of command—each member of the organization has an immediate supervisor

Use of Force Training Simulator (UFTS)—technology that employs computer-generated images (CGI) and speech technology that enables variability in characters and scenarios as well as character and scenario responses to user commands and conversation

U.S. Patriot Act—federal legislation enacted shortly after the 9/11 terrorism incidents that was designed to improve our national strategy and law enforcement response to terrorism

Visual Average Speed Computer And Recorder (VASCAR)—a semiautomated technique for determining the speed of a moving vehicle by recording the moment that a vehicle passes two fixed objects that are a known distance apart and the time the target vehicle takes to travel between them

warrant—an order in writing, issued by a judicial authority, authorizing a police officer to take specific actions

watchman style—focuses on an order maintenance style of policing

Westwood COACT (COmmunity ACTion) Mentors Program—sponsored by the Memphis Police Department, this program was created to promote positive behavior among at-risk children

white collar crime—"Illegal or unethical acts that violate the fiduciary responsibility of public trust by an individual or organization, usually during the course of legitimate occupational activity, by persons of high or respectable social status for personal or organizational gain" (Helmkamp et al., 1996, p. 351).

workload analysis—consists of an elaborate information system with defined levels of police performance for computing the number of appropriate police personnel

zero-tolerance arrest policies—policies normally reserved for high crime areas, usually found in geographic areas of low socioeconomic status and high minority population. When narcotics, gang crime, and vice enforcement are conducted in this fashion, allegations of unethical and otherwise inappropriate police behavior, justified or not, are sure to follow. Such policies are also notorious for increasing the probability of biased-enforcement practices.

References

Chapter 1

Alpert, G. P., & Dunham, R. G. (1997). *Policing urban America* (3rd ed.). Prospect Heights, IL: Waveland Press.

Barlow, D. E., & Barlow, M. H. (2000). *Policing in a multicultural society: An American story.* Prospect Heights, IL: Waveland Press.

Barlow, H. D. (2000). *Criminal justice in America.* Upper Saddle River, NJ: Prentice Hall.

Berg, B. L. (1992). *Law enforcement: An introduction to police in society.* Boston: Allyn and Bacon.

Bittner, E. (1974). Florence Nightingale in pursuit of Willie Sutton: A theory of the police. In J. Hubert (Ed.), *The potential for reform of criminal justice* (pp. 17–44). Beverly Hills, CA: Sage.

Bouza, A. V. (1990). *The police mystique.* New York: Plenum.

Braga, A. A., & Weisburd, D. (2007, May). *Police innovation and crime prevention: Lessons learned from police research over the past 20 years.* Paper presented at the National Institute of Justice Policing Research Workshop: Planning for the Future, Washington, DC.

Bureau of Justice Statistics. (2007, June). *Census of state and local law enforcement agencies, 2004* (NCJ 212749). Washington, DC: Author. Retrieved October 20, 2009, from bjs.ojp.usdoj.gov/content/pub/pdf/csllea04.pdf

Childs, G. (2009, March 5). Tool tracks city crime. *Journal Star,* pp. A1, A8.

Conser, J. A., & Russell, G. D. (2000). *Law enforcement in the United States.* Gaithersburg, MD: Aspen.

Crank, J. P., & Giacomazzi, A. L. (2007). Areal policing and public perceptions in a non-urban setting: One size fits one. *Policing, 30*(1), 108–131.

Davis, E. M. (1978). *Staff one: A perspective on effective police management.* Englewood Cliffs, NJ: Prentice Hall.

Dunham, R. G., & Alpert, G. P. (1997). *Critical issues in policing: Contemporary readings* (3rd ed.). Prospect Heights, IL: Waveland Press.

Federal Bureau of Investigation. (2009). Police employee data. *Crime in the United States, 2008.* Retrieved from http://www.fbi.gov/ucr/cius2008/police/index.html

Gaines, L. K., Kappeler, V. E., & Vaughn, J. B. (1999). *Policing in America* (3rd ed.). Cincinnati, OH: Anderson.

Gamiz, M., Jr. (2010, March 2). Private security industry grows as pay rate stays flat. *The Morning Call.* Retrieved on March 2, 2010, from www.mcall.com/business/local/outlook/all-security-030908%2C0%2C2413617.story

Goldstein, H. (1977). *Policing a free society.* Cambridge, MA: Ballinger.

Goldstein, H. (1979). Improving policing: A problem-oriented approach. *Crime and Delinquency, 25,* 236–258.

Gottstein, J. (2008, September). *Intelligence-based policing.* Retrieved July, 8, 2009, from www.hendonpub.com/resources/articlearchive/details.aspx?ID=207059

Green, D. (2003, January). Changes in policing. *Law & Order.* http://policechiefmagazine.org/magazine/

Innes, M. (2005). What's your problem? Signal crimes and citizen-focused problem solving. *Criminology & Public Policy, 4*(2), 187–201.

Jackson, D. (2000, October 22). Sordid ties tarnishing city police. *Chicago Tribune,* p. A1.

Johnson, D. R. (1981). *American law enforcement: A history.* St. Louis, MO: Forum Press.

Kelling, G. L., & Moore, M. H. (1988, Nov.). The evolving strategy of policing. *Perspectives on policing.* Washington, DC: U.S. Government Printing Office.

Lane, R. (1992). Urban police and crime. In M. Tonry & N. Morris (Eds.), *Modern policing* (pp. 1–50). Chicago: University of Chicago Press.

Langworthy, R. H., & Travis, L. F., III. (1999). *Policing in America: A balance of forces.* Englewood Cliffs, NJ: Prentice Hall.

Lee, M. (1971). *A history of the police in England.* Montclair, NJ: Patterson Smith.

Lyman, M. D. (1999). *The police: An introduction.* Upper Saddle River, NJ: Prentice Hall.

Meadows, R. J. (1998). Legal issues in policing. In R. Muraskin & A. R. Roberts (Eds.), *Visions for change: Crime and justice in the twenty-first century.* Upper Saddle River, NJ: Prentice Hall.

Miller, W. (2000, August). The good, the bad & the ugly: Policing America. [On-line], *History Today, 50*(8), 29–35. Retrieved from http://www.findarticles.com

Petersilia, J. (1993). Influence of research on policing. In R. G. Dunham & G. P. Alpert (Eds.).

Critical issues in policing: Contemporary readings. Prospect Heights, IL: Waveland.

Pierce, G., et al. (1987). *Evaluation of an experiment in proactive police intervention in the field of domestic violence using repeat call analysis.* Boston: The Boston Fenway Project.

Richardson, J. F. (1974). *Urban police in the United States.* Port Washington, NY: Kennikat Press.

Roberg, R., & Kuykendall, J. (1993). *Police in society.* Belmont, CA: Wadsworth.

Roberg, R., Novak, K., & Cordner, G. (2005). *Police & society* (3rd ed.). Los Angeles: Roxbury.

Sherman, L. W. (1978). *The quality of police education.* San Francisco: Jossey-Bass.

Skolnick, J. H., & Bayley, D. H. (1986). *The new blue line: Police innovation in six American cities.* New York: Free Press.

Sweatman, B., & Cross, A. (1989). The police in the United States. *C. J. International, 5*(1), 11–18.

Toch, H., & Grant, J. D. (1991). *Police as problem solvers.* New York: Plenum.

Walker, S. (1999). *The police in America.* Boston: McGraw-Hill

Weisburd, D., & Braga, A. (2006). *Police innovation: Contrasting perspectives.* New York: Cambridge University Press.

Chapter 2

Alpert, G. P., & Dunham, R. G. (1997). *Policing urban America* (3rd ed.). Prospect Heights, IL: Waveland.

Arlington Virginia Police Department. (2009). *Police officer exam process.* Retrieved from http://www.arlingtonva.us

Association of Test Publishers. (2000, Winter). Court upholds employer's right not to hire based on high test score. *Test Publisher, 2,* 1-4. Retrieved from http://www.testpublishers.org

Bartol, C. R., & Bartol, A. (2008). *Introduction to forensic psychology: Research and application.* Thousand Oaks, CA: Sage.

Baxley, N. (2000). Recruiting police officers in the new millennium. *Law and Order, 48, 371.*

Beck, J., & Wade, M. (2004). *Got game: How the gamer generation is reshaping business forever.* Boston: Harvard Business School Press.

Bell, D. (2004). *Race, racism and American law* (6th ed.). New York: Aspen Publishers.

Benner, A. W. (1989). Psychological screening of police applicants. In R. G. Dunham & G. P. Alpert (Eds.), *Critical issues in policing: Contemporary readings* (pp. 72–86). Prospect Heights, IL: Waveland.

Billikopf, G. (2006). Validating the selection process. University of California. Retrieved from http://www.cnr.berkeley.edu/ucce50/ag-labor/7labor/03.htm

Bouza, A. V. (1990). *The police mystique: An insider's look at cops, crime, and the criminal justice system.* New York: Plenum.

Brandon, H., & Lippman, B. (2000). Using the Web to improve recruitment. *Police Chief, 67,* 37–41.

Burns, J. A. (2009). *Supreme Court creates new risk for employers who use tests or other screening devices.* Employment Law Watch. Retrieved from http://www.employmentlawwatch.com/tags/ricci-v-destefano/

Cochrane, R. E., Teft, R. P., & Vandecreek, L. (2003). Psychological testing and the selection of police officers. *Criminal Justice and Behavior, 30*, 511–537.

Colbridge, T. D. (2000). The Americans with disabilities act. *FBI Law Enforcement Bulletin, 69*, 26–31.

Colbridge, T. D. (2001). The Americans with disabilities act: A practical guide for police departments. *FBI Law Enforcement Bulletin, 70*, 23–32.

Cosner, T. L., & Baumgart, W. C. (2000). An effective assessment center program: Essential components. *FBI Law Enforcement Bulletin, 69*, 1–5.

Cox, S. M., & Fitzgerald, J. D. (1996). *Police in community relations: Critical issues* (3rd ed.). Dubuque, IA: Brown & Benchmark.

Decicco, D. A. (2000). Police officer candidate assessment and selection. *FBI Law Enforcement Bulletin, 69*, 1–6.

Delord, R. G. (2006). Police unions and police reform. Paper presented at the annual conference on Police Reform From the Bottom Up. University of California Berkeley, Berkeley, California.

District of Columbia Fire and Emergency Medical Services Department. (2008). *Pregnancy policy. Bulletin 29*. Retrieved from http://fems.dc.gov/fems/lib/fems/pdf/bull._29_pregnancy_policy_.pdf

Eckberg, J. (2008). Successful effective interview with Claire Raines. *Generations at work*. Retrieved from http://www.generationsatwork.com/articles_motivate.php

Elk Grove Village. (2008). *Hiring information*. Retrieved from http://egv:illinois.gov/police/images/pdhiring2008.pdf

Epstein, R. A. (2009). *Ricci v. DeStefano*. Forbes.com. Retrieved from http://www.forbes.com/2009/06/29/ricci-destefano-new-haven-supreme-court-affirmative-action-opinion-column

Equal Employment Opportunity Commission. (2009). *Employers and other entities covered by eeo laws*. Retrieved from http://www.eeoc.gov/abouteeo/overview_coverage.html

Executive Office for Administration and Finance. (2009). *Regional assessment center initiative*. Retrieved from http://www. mass.gov

Falkenberg, S., Gaines, L. K., & Cox, T. C. (1990). The oral interview board: What does it measure? *Journal of Police Science and Administration, 17*, 32–39.

Federal Bureau of Investigation. (2009). *FBI police officer physical requirements*. Retrieved from http://www.fbijobs.gov/1261.asp

Find Law. (2002). *Race/color discrimination: Facts*. Retrieved from http://employment.findlaw.com/.../employment-employee-race-discrimination-facts.html

Frankel, B. (1992, November 19). Police chiefs worry about job security. *USA Today*, p. 10A.

Gaines, L. K., & Kappeler, V. E. (2008). *Policing in America* (6th ed.). Cincinnati, OH: Anderson Publishing.

Good, G. W., Maisel, S. C., & Kriska, S. D. (1998). Setting an uncorrected visual acuity standard for police officer applicants. *Journal of Applied Psychology, 83*, 817–824.

Gordon, N. J. (2008). Today's instrument for truth testing. *Police Chief Magazine, 75*, 1–9. Retrieved from http://www.policechiefmagazine.org

Hale, C. (2005). Assessment centers. *Law and Order, 53*, 22–24.

Harrison, B. (2007). Gamers, millennials and generation next: Implications for policing. *Police Chief Magazine, 74*, 1–6. Retrieved from http://policechiefmagazine.org/magazine/index.cfm?fuseaction=display_arch&article_id=13128&issue_id=12007

Holden, R. N., & Gammeltoft, L. L. (1991). Toonen v. Brown County: The legality of police vision standards. *American Journal of Police, 10*, 59–66.

Holloway, J. (2000). Oh, those oral board blues. *Women Police, 34*(3), 14.

Hubbard, G., Cromwell, R. K., & Sgro, T. (2004). Mission possible: Creating a new face for the FBI, *Police Chief Magazine, 71*, 1–5. Retrieved from http://policechiefmagazine.org/magazine/index.cfm?fuseaction=display_arch&article_id=1390&issue_id=12004

Humphrey, K. R., Decker, K. P., Goldberg, L., Pope, H. G., Gutman, J., & Green, G. (2008). Anabolic steroid use and abuse by police officers: Policy and prevention. *Police Chief Magazine, 75*, 1–10. Retrieved from http://policechiefmagazine.org

International Public Management Association for Human Resources. (2009). *Entry-level police tests.* Alexandria, VA: Author. Retrieved from http://www.ipma-hr.org

Israelsen-Hartley, S. (2008). Utah police aim to close generation gap. *PoliceOne.com News.* Retrieved from http://www.policeone.com/police-recruiting/articles/1760219-Utah-police-aim-to-close-generation-gap/

Johnson, K. (2009). Police agencies buried in resumes. *USA Today.* Retrieved from http://www.usatoday.com/news/nation/2009–03–11–copjobs_N.htm

Kroecker, T. (2000). Developing future leaders: Making the link to the promotional process. *Police Chief, 67,* 64–69.

Landy, F., & Conte, J. M. (2009). *Work in the 21st century: An introduction to industrial and organizational psychology* (3rd ed.). Hoboken, NJ: Wiley-Blackwell.

Landy, F., & Salas, E. (2005). *Employment discrimination litigation: Behavioral, quantitative, and legal perspectives.* Hoboken, NJ: John Wiley and Sons.

Lonsway, K. A. (2004). Failing grades: Physical agility tests in police selection. *Women Police, 38,* 7–11.

Los Angeles Police Department. (2009). *Qualifications.* Retrieved from http://www.joinlapd.com/qualifications.html

Love, K., & DeArmond, S. (2007). The validity of assessment center ratings and 16PF personality trait scores in police sergeant promotions: A case of incremental validity. *Public Personnel Management, 36*(1), 21.

Lundborn, J. R. (2002). Managing the generation yers—simply put. *Police and Security News.* Retrieved from http://www.policeandsecuritynews.com/julyaug02/genyers.htm

Marston, C. (2007). *Motivating the "what's in it for me" workforce: Manage across the generational divide and increase profits.* Hoboken, NJ: John Wiley and Sons.

McCafferty, F. L. (2003). The challenge of selecting tomorrow's police officers from generations x and y. *Journal of the American Academy of Psychiatry and the Law, 31,* 78–88.

McLaurin, M. (2005). How to run an assessment center. *Police Magazine.* Retrieved from http://www.policemag.com

Med-Tox Health Services. (2009). *Law enforcement physical agility testing.* Retrieved from http://www.med-tox.com/policetest.html

Meier, R. D., Farmer, R. E., & Maxwell, D. (1987). Psychological screening of police candidates: Current perspectives. *Journal of Police Science and Administration, 15,* 210–215.

Memphis Police Department. (2009). *Requirements.* Retrieved from http://mpdacademy.com/requirements.php

New York State Police Recruitment Center. (2009). *Height and weight standards.* Retrieved from http://www.nytrooper.com/height_weight.cfm

New Zealand Police. (2009). *Frequently asked questions.* Retrieved from www.newcops.co.nz

Ohio Association of Chiefs of Police. (2001). *Assessment center exercise menu.* Retrieved from www.oacp.org/advise/exercise.pdf

O'Leary, L. R. (1989). Assessment centers. In W. G. Bailey (Ed.), *The encyclopedia of police science* (pp. 28–30). New York: Garland.

Patti, P. (2009). Sixteen traits recruiters are looking for. *Police Link: The Nations Law Enforcement Community.* Retrieved from http://www.policelink.com/benefits/articles/7602

Pendergrass, V. E. (1987). Psychological assessment of police for entry-level selection. *Police Chief, 11,* 8–14.

Philadelphia Police Department. (2009). *Veteran's preference.* Retrieved from http://www.ppdonline.org/career/career_vets.php

Pincus, F. (2003). *Reverse discrimination: Dismantling the myth.* Boulder, CO: Lynne Rienner Publishers.

Piotrowski, T. (2007). *Police chief selection process: A study of selected Illinois police departments.* Unpublished master's thesis, Western Illinois University—Macomb.

Privacy Rights Clearinghouse. (2009). *Employment background checks: A jobseeker's guide.* Retrieved from http://www.privacyrights.org/fs/fs16-bck.htm

Raines, C. (2002). Managing millennials, *Generations at Work.* Retrieved from http://generationsatwork.com/articles/millenials.htm

Rafilson, F. M., & DeAngelis, T. (2008). *Master the police officer examination.* Georgetown, CT: ARCO Publishing.

Rhodes, R. A. (2002). Legal discrimination in four letters: BFOQ. *Connecticut Employment Law Letter.* Retrieved from http://www.halloran-sage.com

Ruiz, J., & Hummer, D. (2007). *Handbook of police administration*. Boca Raton, FL: CRC Press.

Sanders, D., & Stefaniak, A. (2008). To protect and serve: What generation y brings to law enforcement and how police agencies can benefit. *Police Perspectives*. University of Utah, Center for Public Policy & Administration. Retrieved from www.cppa.utah.edu/publications/work force.PP_To_Protect_and_Serve.pdf

San Diego Police Department. (2009). *Police recruit vision requirements*. Retrieved from http://www.sandiego.gov/police/recruiting/join/recvision.shtml

Santa Rosa Police Department. (2009). *Illegal drug use guidelines*. Retrieved from http://cisanta-rosa.ca.us/doclib/Documents/Drug-Standard.pdf

Schapiro, A. (2008). How community policing has changed what police departments are looking for in recruits. *Community Policing Dispatch, 1*, 1–2. Retrieved from http://www.cops.usdoj.gov/html/dispatch/october2008/nugget.htm

Tawney, M. (2008). Integrity testing: The selection tool of the future. *Law and Order, 56*, 34–39.

Thernstrom, A. (2009, July 1). The Supreme Court says no to quotas. *The Wall Street Journal*. p. A13.

U.S. Department of Commerce. (2010). *NOAA civil rights office*. Retrieved from http://www.eeo.noaa.gov/glossary.htm

U.S. Department of Justice. (2006). *Questions and answers: The American with disabilities act and hiring police officers*. Retrieved from http://www.ada.gov/copsq7a/.htm

U.S. Equal Employment Opportunity Commission. (2002). *Americans with disabilities act: Questions and answers*. Retrieved from http://www. ada.gov/q%26aeng02.htm

Winters, C. A. (1992). Socio-economic status, test bias, and the selection of police. *Police Journal, 65*, 125–135.

Wolpe, P. R., Foster, K. R., & Langleben, D. D. (2005). Emerging neurotechnologies for lie-detection: Promises and perils. *American Journal of Bioethics, 5*(2), 39–49.

Chapter 3

Aamodt, M., & Flink, W. (2001). Relationship between educational level and cadet performance in a police academy. *Applied HRM Research, 6*(1), 75–76.

Academy of Criminal Justice Sciences. (2009). *ACJS certification standards*. Retrieved from http://www.acjs.org/pubs/167_667_3517.cfm

Baeher, E. M., Furcon, J. E., & Froemel, E. (1968). *Psychological assessment of patrolman qualifications in relation to field performance*. Washington, DC: U.S. Government Printing Office.

Baro, A., & Burlingame, D. (1999, Spring). Law enforcement and higher education: Is there an impasse? *Journal of Criminal Justice Education, 10*, 57–73.

Barry, M., & Runyan, G. B. (1995). A review of distance learning studies in the U.S. military. *The American Journal of Distance Education, 9*, 37–56.

Birzer, M. L. (1999). Police training in the 21st century. *FBI Law Enforcement Bulletin, 68*, 16–19.

Bostrom, M. (October, 2005). The influence of higher education on police officer work habits. *The Police Chief, 72*(10), 18, 20–25.

Bracey, D. H. (1990a, August). *Future trends in police training*. Paper presented at the Third Annual

Sino-American Criminal Justice Institute, Taipei, Taiwan.

Bracey, D. H. (1990b). Preparing police leaders for the future. *Police Studies, 13*, 178–182.

Broderick, J. (1987). *Police in a time of change*. Prospect Heights, IL: Waveland.

Bruns, D. (2005, September). Patrol officers' opinions on the importance of a college degree. *Law and Order, 53*, 96–99.

Bumgarner, J. (2001). Evaluating law enforcement training. *Police Chief, 68*, 32–36.

Bunyard, S. R. (1991). Police higher training in England and Wales. *Crime & Justice International, 7*, 11–17.

Bureau of Justice Statistics. (2009). *State and local law enforcement training academies, 2006* (NCJ 222987). Washington, DC: Author. Retrieved from http://bjs.ojp.usdoj.gov/content/pub/pdf/slleta06.pdf

California Commission on Peace Officer Standards and Training. (2009). *Command college program*. Retrieved from http://www.post.ca.gov/Training/Command_College

Carlan, P. (2007). The criminal justice degree and policing: Conceptual development or occupational primer? *Policing: An International Journal of Police Strategies and Management, 20*(4), 608–619.

Carlan, P., & Byxbe, F. (2000). The promise of humanistic policing: Is higher education living up to societal expectation? *American Journal of Criminal Justice, 24*, 235–245.

Carter, D., & Sapp, A. (1992, January). College education and policing: Coming of age. *FBI Law Enforcement Bulletin, 61*, 8–14.

Cohen, B., & Chaiken, J. (1972). *Police background characteristics: Summary report.* Washington, DC: U.S. Government Printing Office.

Conners, T. D. (1998). *Distance learning for not-for-profit organizations.* New York: John Wiley & Son.

Cox, B., & Moore, R., Jr. (1992). Toward the twenty-first century: Law enforcement training now and then. *Journal of Contemporary Criminal Justice, 8*, 235–256.

Cunningham, S. (2006, August). The Florida research. *Police Chief, (73)*8, 20–22.

Daniels, E. (1982, September). The effect of a college degree on police absenteeism. *Police Chief, 49*, 70–71.

Davis v. City of Dallas, 777 F.2d 205 (5th Cir. 1985, certiorari denied to Supreme Court May 19, 1986).

del Carmen, R. V., & Walker J. T. (2000). *Briefs of leading cases in law enforcement* (4th ed.). Cincinnati, OH: Anderson.

Farrell, B., & Koch, L. (1995). Criminal justice, sociology, and academia. *American Sociologist, 26*, 52–61.

Frye, S. (1990). Mandatory continuing education for professional re-licensure: A comparative analysis of its impact in law and medicine. *Journal of Continuing Higher Education, 38*, 16–25.

Giannoni, M. (2002). *An ethnographic investigation of police education: Implications for professionalism and continuing criminal justice education.* Unpublished doctoral dissertation, Northern Illinois University.

Golden, T., & Seehafer, P. (2009, February). Delivering training material in a practical way. *FBI Law Enforcement Bulletin*, 21–24.

Graves, F. (1991). Trainers technique syndrome. *Police Chief, 58*, 62–63.

Griffin, G. (1980). *A study of relationships between level of college education and police patrolman's performance.* Saratoga, NY: Twenty One.

Hayeslip, D., Jr. (1989). Higher education and police performance revisited: The evidence examined through meta-analysis. *American Journal of Police, 8*, 49–59.

Hickman, M. (2005, January). *State and local law enforcement academies, 2002* (NCJ 204030). Washington, DC: Bureau of Justice Statistics. Retrieved from http://bjs.ojp.usdoj.gov/content/pub/pdf/slleta02.pdf

Holmes, G., Cole, E., & Hicks, L. (1992, November). Curriculum development: Relevancy and innovation. *Police Chief, 59*, 51–52.

Illinois Department of Financial and Professional Regulation. (2009). *Categories of regulation.* Chicago: Author. Retrieved from http://www.idfpr.com/dpr/default.asp

Ilsley, P., & Young, W. (1997). Transforming criminal justice education through continuing professional education. *Crime & Justice International, 13*, 5–6.

International Law Enforcement Educators and Trainers Association (ILEETA). (2009). Retrieved from http://www.ileeta.org

Jang, H. (2005). *In-service training* and distance learning. *TELEMASP Bulletin, 12*(4), 1–8.

Johnson, R. (1998, December). Citizen complaints: What the police should know. *FBI Law Enforcement Bulletin, 67*, 1–5.

Kappeler, V., Sapp, A., & Carter, D. (1992). Police officer higher education, citizen complaints and departmental rule violations. *American Journal of the Police, 11*, 37–54.

Kiley, W. (1998, October). The advanced criminal investigation course: An innovative approach to detective in-service training. *FBI Law Enforcement Bulletin, 67*, 16–18.

Krimmel, J., & Lindenmuth, P. (2001). Police chief performance and leadership styles. *Police Quarterly, 4*(4), 469–483.

Landahl, M. (2009). WANT TO GET AHEAD? Stop stalling and go get your degree. *Sheriff, 1*(1), 26–29.

Liming, D., & Wolf, M. (2008, Fall). Job outlook by education, 2006–16. *Occupational Outlook Quarterly, 52*(3).

Magers, J., & Klein, L. (2002). Police basic training: A comparative study of states' standards in the United States. *Illinois Law Enforcement Executive Forum, 2*(2), 103–113.

Maple, G. (1987). Continuing education for the health sciences. *Australian Journal of Adult Education, 27*, 22–27.

Marsh, H., & Grosskopf, E. (1991). The key factors in law enforcement training: Requirements, assessments and methods. *Police Chief, 58*, 64–66.

Massoni, M. (2009, February). Field training programs: Understanding adult learning styles. *FBI Law Enforcement Bulletin*, 1–5.

Mayo, L. (2006). Support for college degree requirements: The big picture. *Police Chief, 73*(8). Retrieved July 25, 2010, from http://www.policechiefmagazine.org/magazine/index.cfm?fuseaction=archivecontents&issue_id=82006

McCambell, M. S. (1986). *Field training for police officers: State of the art*. Washington, DC: National Institute of Justice.

Meagher, M. (1983, March). *Perceptions of the police patrol function: Does officer education make a difference?* Paper presented at Academy of Criminal Justice Sciences Meeting, San Antonio, TX.

Means, R. (2008). Evaluation and recognition systems. Law & *Order, 56*(7), 17–20.

Michals, J. E., & Higgins, J. M. (1997). Relationship between education level and performance ratings of campus police officers. *Journal of Police and Criminal Psychology, 12*(2), 15–18.

Narciso, D. (2001, July 24). New fund lets police division sell its own training programs. *Columbus Dispatch*, p. 2B.

National Advisory Commission on Criminal Justice Standards and Goals. (1973). *Report on the police*. Washington, DC: U.S. Government Printing Office.

National Law Enforcement and Corrections Technology Center. (2008). Imaging, speech technology boost simulation training. Washington, DC: U.S. Department of Justice.

Nelson, K. R. (2006). Police education for the 21st century. *FBI Law Enforcement Bulletin, 75*(7), 14–17.

Nelson, S. D. (1998). Distance learning and criminal justice education: Exploring the possibilities. *Journal of Criminal Justice Education, 9*(2), 333–342.

Nowicki, E. (1990a). Police training: A sense of priority. *Police, 14*, 4.

Nowicki, E. (1990b). New dogs, new tricks. *Police, 14*, 31–51.

Nowicki, E. (2006). Eight qualities of highly effective trainers. *Law & Order, 54*(7), 32–34.

Nowicki, E. (2008). Training meets competition. *Law & Order, 56*(3), 32–37.

Office of Justice Programs. (2004). *Department of Justice names new Police Corps director*. Washington DC: Department of Justice. Retrieved from http://www.ojp.usdoj.gov/archives/pressreleases/2004/OPC04089.htm

Office of Justice Programs. (2007). *Education in law enforcement: Beyond the college degree*. Washington, DC: National Institute of Justice. Retrieved from http://www.ojp.usdoj.gov/nij/speeches/police.htm

Oregon State Police. (2007). *Police corps*. Retrieved from http://www.oregon.gov/OSP/CJS/police_corps.shtml

Overton, W., & Black, J. (1994). Language as a weapon. *Police Chief, 65*, 46.

PATROL Minnesota. (2009). Police accredited training online. *League of Minnesota Cities Insurance Trust*. Retrieved from http://www.nexportsolutions.com/patrolminnesota/index.html

Phillips, L. (1987). Is mandatory continuing professional education working? *Mobius, 7*, 57–63.

Pitts, S., Glensor, R., & Peak, K. (2007). Police training officer (PTO) program: A contemporary approach to postacademy recruit training. *The Police Chief, 74*(8), 34–40.

Police Association for College Education. (2009). *Annotated bibliography on performance of officers with bachelor's degrees*. Retrieved from http://www.police-association.org/index.html

Polk, O., & Armstrong, D. (2001). Higher education and law enforcement career paths: Is the road to success paved by a degree? *Journal of Criminal Justice Education, 12*, 77–99.

Pritchett, G. L. (1993). Interpersonal communication: Improving law enforcement's image. *FBI Law Enforcement Bulletin, 62*, 22–26.

Rainey, H. G. (2003). *Understanding & managing public organizations* (3rd ed.). San Francisco: Jossey-Bass.

Reiss, A. J., Jr. (1971). *The police and the public*. New Haven, CT: Yale University Press.

Roberg, R., & Bonn, S. (2004). Higher education and policing: Where are we now? *Policing: An International Journal of Police Strategies and Management, 27*(4), 469–486.

Rockhill, K. (1983). Mandatory continuing education for professionals: Trends and issues. *Adult Education, 33,* 106–116.

Sapp, A. (1986, November). Education and training requirements in law enforcement: A national comparison. *Police Chief, 53,* 48–62.

Sapp, A., Carter, D., & Stephens, D. (1988). Higher education as a bona fide occupational qualification (BFOQ) for police: A blueprint. *American Journal of Police, 7,* 15–59.

Sapp, A., Carter, D., & Stephens, D. (1989). Police chiefs: CJ curricula inconsistent with contemporary police needs. *ACJS Today, 7,* 1, 5.

Scaramella, G. (1997). Professionalizing the police. *Crime & Justice International, 13,* 7–8.

Schwartz, M., & Yonkers, S. (1991). Officer satisfaction with police in-service training: An exploratory evaluation. *American Journal of Police, 10,* 49–63.

Scott, W. (1986). College educational requirements for entry level and promotion: A study. *Journal of Police and Criminal Psychology, 2,* 10–28.

Sherman, L. W., & Blumberg, M. (1981). Higher education and police use of force. *Journal of Criminal Justice, 9,* 317–331.

Smith, A., Locke, B., & Walker, W. (1968). Authoritarianism in police college students and non-police college students. *Journal of Criminal Law, Criminology, and Police Science, 59,* 440–443.

Stevens, D. (1999). College educated officers: Do they provide better police service? *Law & Order, 47,* 37–41.

Swanson, C., Territo, L., & Taylor, R. (1998). *Police administration: Structures, processes, and behavior* (4th ed.). Upper Saddle River, NJ: Prentice-Hall.

Travis, J. (1995, Feb. 10). *Education in law enforcement: Beyond the college degree.* Retrieved July 25, 2010, from http://www.ojp.usdoj.gov/nij/speeches/police.htm

United States Department of Justice. (1999). *State and local law enforcement statistics.* Washington DC: U.S. Government Printing Office. Retrieved from http://www.ojp.usdoj.gov/bjs/sandlle.htw#education

Vodde, R. F. (2009). *Andragogical instruction for effective police training.* New York: Cambria Press.

Walker, J. (2005). Law enforcement field training models: Is it time for a change? *Campus Law Enforcement Journal, 35*(5), 23–30.

Wilson, H. (1999). Post-secondary education of the police officer and its effect on the frequency of citizen complaints. *Journal of California Law Enforcement, 33,* 3–10.

Worden, R. (1990). A badge and a baccalaureate: Policies, hypotheses, and further evidence. *Justice Quarterly, 7,* 580–592.

Chapter 4

Adams, T. F. (2007). *Police field operations* (7th ed.). Upper Saddle River, NJ: Prentice-Hall.

Adcox, K. (2000). Doing bad things for good reasons. *Police Chief, 67,* 16–27.

Adorno, T. W., Frenkel-Brunswik, E., Levinson, D., & Sanford, N. (1950). *The authoritarian personality.* New York: Harper and Brothers.

Alpert, G. P., & Dunham, R. G. (1997). *Policing urban America* (3rd ed.). Prospect Heights, IL: Waveland.

Arter, M. (2008). Stress and deviance in policing. *Deviant Behavior, 29*(1), 43–69.

Barker, T., Hunter, R. D., & Rush, J. P. (1994). *Police systems & practices: An introduction.* Englewood Cliffs, NJ: Prentice Hall.

Bayley, D. H., & Bittner, E. (1989). Learning the skills of policing. *Law and Contemporary Problems, 47,* 35–59.

Benner, A. (1994). The challenge for police psychology in the twenty first century: Moving beyond efficient to effective. In M. Chapin, S. J. Brannen, M. I. Singer, & M. Walker. (2008). Training police leadership to recognize and address operational stress. *Police Quarterly, 11,* 338–351.

Bennett, R. R., & Schmitt, E. L. (2002). The effect of work environment on levels of police cynicism: A comparative study. *Police Quarterly, 5*(4), 493–522.

Berg, B. L. (1999). *Policing in modern society.* Burlington, MA: Butterworth-Heinemann.

Bittner, E. (1970). *The functions of the police in modern society.* Chevy Chase, MD: National Institute of Mental Health.

Blumberg, A. S., & Niederhoffer, E. (1985). The police family. In A. S. Blumberg & E. Neiderhoffer

(Eds.), *The ambivalent force: Perspectives on the police* (3rd ed., pp. 371–372). New York: Holt, Rinehart and Winston.

Borum, R., & Philpot, C. (1993). Therapy with law enforcement couples: Clinical management of the high-risk lifestyle. *American Journal of Family Therapy, 21,* 122–135.

Bouza, A. V. (1990). *The police mystique: An insider's look at cops, crime, and the criminal justice system.* New York: Plenum.

Broderick, J. J. (1987). Police in a time of change (2nd ed.). Prospect Heights, IL: Waveland. In K. J. Peak (2009). *Policing America: Challenges, and best practices* (6th ed.). Upper Saddle River, NJ: Pearson Prentice-Hall.

California sees drop in officers killed in line of duty. (2009, December 28). *Los Angeles Times.* Retrieved from http://latimesblogs.latimes.com

Carey, L. R. (1994). Community policing for the suburban department. *Police Chief, 61,* 24–26.

Carpenter, B., & Raza, S. (1987). Personality characteristics of police applicants: Comparisons across subgroups and other populations. *Journal of Police Science and Administration, 15,* 10–17.

Carter, D. L., & Radelet, L. A. (1999). *The police and the community* (6th ed.). Upper Saddle River, NJ: Prentice-Hall.

Chambers, L. (2008). An investigation of police officers bereaved by police suicides. Unpublished dissertation abstract, Walden University. Retrieved from http://proquest.umi.com

Champoux, J. E. (2006). *Organizational behavior* (3rd ed.). Cincinnati, OH: Thomson South-Western.

Cox, S. M., & Fitzgerald, J. D. (1996). *Police in community relations: Critical issues* (3rd ed.). Dubuque, IA: W. C. Brown.

Crank, J. P. (2004). *Understanding police culture* (2nd ed.). Cincinnati, OH: Anderson.

Crosby, A. E., & Sacks, J. J. (2002). Exposure to suicide: Incidence and association with suicidal ideation and behavior: United States, 1994. *Suicide and Threatening Behavior, 32,* 321–328. In Violanti, J. M., Fekedulegn, D., & Charles, M. E. (2009). *American Journal of Criminal Justice, 34,* 1, 41–57.

Cullen, F., Link, B., Travis, L. T., & Lemming, T. (1983). Paradox in policing: A note on perceptions of danger. *Journal of Police Science and Administration,* 11, 457–462. In Crank, J.P. (2004). *Understanding police culture* (2nd ed.). Cincinnati, OH: Anderson Publishing Company.

Dantzker, M. L. (2005). *Understanding today's police.* Monsey, NY: Criminal Justice Press.

Dorsey, R. R., & Giacopassi, D. J. (1987). Demographics and work-related correlates of police officer cynicism. In D. B. Kennedy, & R. J. Homant (Eds.), *Police and law enforcement* (pp. 173–188). New York: Ames Press.

Dowling, F. G., Moynihan, G., Genet, B., & Lewis, J. (2006). A peer-based assistance program for officers with the New York City Police Department: Report of the effects of September 11, 2001. *American Journal of Psychiatry, 163,* 151–153. In Gershon, R., Barocas, B., Canton, A., Li, X., & Vlahov, D. (2009). Mental, physical, and behavioral outcomes associated with perceived work stress in police officers. *Criminal Justice and Behavior, 36*(3), 275–289.

Dumont, L. F. (1999). Recognizing and surviving post shooting trauma. *Law and Order, 47*(4), 93–98.

Ellison, K. (2004). *Stress and the police officer.* Springfield, IL: Charles C. Thomas. In U.S. Department of Justice. (2005). Stress and stress management. Retrieved from http://fbilibrary.fbiacademy.edu

Flynn, R. S. (1997). *Stress reduction techniques for police officers* (NCJ 171561). National Criminal Justice Reference Service. Retrieved from http://www.ncjrs.gov

Frye, A. (2006, February 12th). Blue wall of silence perceived in police force. *Daily Bulletin.* Retrieved from http://www.dailybulletin.com

Gaines, L. K., Kappeler, V. E., & Vaughn, J. B. (2008). *Policing in America* (6th ed.). Cincinnati, OH: Anderson.

Garcia, L., Nesbary, D. K., & Gu, J. (2004). Perceptual variations of stressors among police officers during an era of decreasing crime. *Journal of Criminal Justice, 20*(1), 33–50.

Gershon, R., Barocas, B., Canton, A., Li, X., & Vlahov, D. (2009). Mental, physical, and behavioral outcomes associated with perceived work stress in police officers. *Criminal Justice and Behavior, 36*(3), 275–289.

Golembiewski, R. T., & Kim, B. S. (1991). Burnout in police work: Stressors, strain, and the phase model. *Police Studies, 14,* 74–80.

Goodman, A. M. (1990). A model for police officer burnout. *Journal of Business and Psychology, 5,* 1, 85–89. In McCarty, W. P. Zhao, J., & Garland, B. E. (2007). Occupational stress and burnout between male and female police officers: Are there any gender differences? *Policing, 30*(4), 672–679.

Gould, L. (2000). A longitudinal approach to the study of the police personality: Race/gender differences. *Journal of Police and Criminal Psychology, 15*(2), 41–51.

Graves, W. (1996). Police cynicism: Causes and cures. *FBI Law Enforcement Bulletin, 65,* 16–20.

Greenwood, J. K. (2009, December, 13). Police rookies, recruits believe doing job trumps danger. *Pittsburgh Tribune-Review* (Record number 657574). Retrieved February 8, 2010, from http://infoweb.newsbank.com

Hickman, M. J., Piquero, N. L., & Piquero, A. R. (2004). The validity of Neiderhoffer's cynicism scale. *Journal of Criminal Justice, 32*(1), 1–13.

Higginbotham, C. E. (2000). Organizational consultant program takes aim at officers' stress. *Police Chief, 67,* 104–106.

Inciardi, J. A. (1990). *Criminal justice* (3rd ed.). San Diego, CA: Harcourt Brace Jovanovich.

Johnson, A. L. (2007). *Organizational cynicism and occupational stress in police officers.* Unpublished dissertation abstract, Central Michigan University. Retrieved from http://www.proquest.com

Johnson, L. B., Todd, M., & Subramanian, G. (2005). Violence in police families: Work-family spillover. *Journal of Family Violence, 20*(1), 3–9.

Johnson, O. (2010). *Blue wall of silence: Perceptions of the influence of training on law enforcement suicide.* Dissertation Abstract, University of Phoenix. Retrieved from http://dissertation.com

Kappeler, V. E., Sluder, R., & Alpert, G. (1998). *Forces of deviance: Understanding the dark side of policing.* Prospect Heights, IL: Waveland. In Bennet, R. R., & Schmitt, E. L. (2002). The effect of work environment on levels of police cynicism: A comparative study. *Police Quarterly, 5*(4), 493–522.

Kirschman, E. (2000). *I love a cop: What police families need to know.* New York: The Guilford Press.

Klein, R. (2000). The extent of domestic violence within law enforcement: An empirical study. In L. B. Johnson, M. Todd, & G. Subramanian. (2005). Violence in police families. Work-family spillover. *Journal of Family Violence, 20,* 1, 3–9.

Kulbarsh, P. (2007). Critical incident stress. *Officer.com.* Retrieved from http://www.officer.com

Lind, S. L., & Otte, F. L. (2006). Management styles, mediating variables, and stress among HRD professionals. *Human Resource Development Quarterly, 5*(4), 301–316.

Lindsay, V., Taylor, W. B., & Shelley, K. (2008). Alcohol and the police: An empirical examination of a widely-held assumption. *Policing, 31*(4), 596–605.

Manning, P. K. (1977). *Police work: The social organization of policing.* Cambridge, MA: MIT Press.

More, H. W. (1998). *Special topics in policing* (2nd ed.). Cincinnati, OH: Anderson Publishing Company.

National Institute of Justice. (2000). On-the-job stress in policing (NCJ 180079). *National Institute of Justice Journal, 19*(24). Retrieved from http://www.ncjrs.gov/pdffiles1/jr000242d.pdf

National Institute of Justice. (2006). Police response to officer-involved shootings. *National Institute of Justice Journal, 53.* (NCJ 21226). Retrieved from http://www.ojp.usdoj.gov

National Law Enforcement Officers Memorial Fund. (2009a). *A tale of two trends: Overall fatalities fall, fatal shootings on the rise.* Retrieved from http://www.nleomf.org

National Law Enforcement Officers Memorial Fund. (2009b). *Facts and figures.* Retrieved from http://www.nleomf.org/facts/

Niederhoffer, A. (1967). *Behind the shield: The police in urban society.* Garden City, NY: Doubleday.

Nelson, D. E., & Quick, J. C. (2006). *Organizational behavior: Foundations, reality and challenges* (5th ed.). Florence, KY: Cengage Learning.

Number of cops fatally shot up 24 percent in 2009. (2009). *CBS News.* Retrieved from http://www.cbsnews.com

Paoline, E. A. (2003). Taking stock: Toward a richer understanding of police culture. *Journal of Criminal Justice, 31,* 199–214.

Paoline, E. A. (2004). Shedding light on police culture: An examination of officers' occupational attitudes. *Police Quarterly, 7*(2), 205–236.

Paoline, E. A., Myers, S., & Worden, R. (2000). Police culture, individualism, and community policing: Evidence from two police departments. *Justice Quarterly, 17,* 575–605.

Paton, D. (2006). Critical incident stress risk in police officers: Managing resilience and vulnerability. *Traumatology, 12,* 198–210.

Peak, K. J. (2009). *Policing America* (6th ed.). Upper Saddle River, NJ: Prentice-Hall.

Picanol, J. R. (2009). *Coping styles that have a negative influence on police marriages.* Unpublished doctoral dissertation, Carlos Albizu University. Retrieved from http://proquest.umi.com

Pollock, J. M. (2008). *Ethical dilemmas and decision making in criminal justice* (6th ed.). Florence, KY: Wadsworth Publishing.

Post, G. M. (1992). Police recruits: Training tomorrow's workforce. *FBI Law Enforcement Bulletin, 61,* 19–24.

Prabhu, S., & Turner, N. (2000). Rising to the challenge: Preventing police officer domestic violence. *Police Chief, 67*(11), 43–55.

Quinney, R. (1970). *The social reality of crime.* Boston: Little, Brown.

Regoli, R. M., & Poole, E. D. (1978). Specifying police cynicism. *Journal of Police Science and Administration, 6,* 98–104.

Reuss-Ianni, E. (1983). *Two cultures of policing.* New Brunswick, NJ: Transaction Books.

Ritter, J. (2007, February 9). Suicide rates jolt police culture. *USA Today,* p. 3A.

Roberg, R., Crank, J., & Kuykendall, J. (2000). *Police and society.* Los Angeles: Roxbury.

Rubinstein, J. (1973). *City police.* New York: Farrar, Straus and Giroux.

Scaramella, G., Shannon, E., & Giannoni, M. (2005). Rekindling police burnout: Implications for the motivation and retention of personnel. *Professional Issues in Criminal Justice, 1*(1), 1–15.

Selye, H. (1974). *Stress without distress.* Philadelphia, PA: Lippincott.

Siegel, L. (2009). *Introduction to criminal justice* (12th ed.). Florence, KY: Wadsworth-Cengage Learning.

Skolnick, J. (1966). *Justice without trial.* New York: John Wiley & Sons.

Skolnick, J. H., & Fyfe, J. J. (1993). *Above the law: Police and the excessive use of force.* New York: Free Press.

Sparrow, M. K., Moore, M. H., & Kennedy, D. M. (1992). *Beyond 911: A new era for policing.* New York: Basic Books.

Stevens, D. J. (1999). Police officer stress. *Law and Order, 47,* 77–81.

Storms, L. H., Penn, N. F., & Tenzell, J. H. (1990). Policemen's perception of real and ideal policemen. *Journal of Police Science and Administration, 17,* 40–43.

Sykes, R. E., & Brent, E. E. (1980). The regulation of interaction by police: A systems view of taking charge. Criminology, 18, 182–197. In Paoline, E. A. (2003). Taking stock: Toward a richer understanding of police culture. *Journal of Criminal Justice, 31,* 199–214.

Terrill, W., Paoline, E. A., & Manning, P. K. (2003). Police culture and coercion. *Criminology, 41*(4), 1003–1035.

Terry, W. C. (1989). Police stress: The empirical evidence. *Police Science and Administration, 9,* 61–75.

Torres, S., & Maggard, D. L. (2003). Preparing families for the hazards of police work. *Police Chief, 70*(10), 1–7.

Twersky-Glasner, A. (2005). Police personality: What is it and why are they like that? *Journal of Police and Criminal Psychology, 20*(1), 56–65.

University of Oklahoma Police. (2008). *Mission statement.* Retrieved from http://www.ou.edu/oupd/mission.htm

Van Maanen, J. (1978). The asshole. In J. VanMaanen & P. K. Manning (Eds.), *Policing: A view from the street* (pp. 221–238). Santa Monica, CA: Goodyear.

Violanti, J. M., & Marshall, J. R. (1983). The police stress process. *Journal of Police Science and Administration, 11,* 389–394.

Waters, J. A., & Ussery, W. (2007). Police stress: History, contributing factors, symptoms, and interventions. *Policing, 30*(2), 169–178.

Westley, W. (1970). *Violence and the police.* Cambridge, MA: MIT Press.

Whisenand, P. M. (2001). *Supervising police personnel* (4th ed.). Upper Saddle River, NJ: Prentice-Hall.

Yarmey, A. D. (1990). *Understanding police and police work: Psychosocial issues.* New York: New York University Press.

Zhao, J., He, N., & Lovrich, N. (2002). Predicting five dimensions of police officer stress: Looking more deeply into organizational settings for sources of police stress. *Police Quarterly, 5*(1), 43–62.

Chapter 5

Alliance to End Repression et al., v. City of Chicago, 356 F.3d 767 (7th Cir. 2004).

American Civil Liberties Union. (2005). *ACLU memo to interested persons regarding the conference report on the USA PATRIOT Improvement and Reauthorization Act of 2005*. Retrieved July 21, 1010, from http://www.aclu.org/cpredirect/22384

Arizona v. Gant 556 U.S. __(2009).

Barker, B., & Fowler, S. (2008). The FBI joint terrorism task force officer. *FBI Law Enforcement Bulletin, 77*(11), 12–17.

Berghuis v. Thompkins, 560 U. S. (2010).

Brinegar v. United States, 338 U. S. 160 (1949).

Chimel v. California 395 U.S.752, 762–63. (1969).

Conser, J. A., & Russell, G. D. (2000). *Law enforcement in the United States*. Gaithersburg, MD: Aspen Press.

Court looks at reach of Second Amendment. (2010, March 2). *Associated Press*. Retrieved from http://www.msnbc.msn.com/id/35671214

Cox, S. M. (1996). *Police: Practices, perspectives, problems*. Needham Heights, MA: Allyn & Bacon.

Cox, S. M., & McCamey, W. P. (2008). *Introduction to criminal justice: Exploring the network*. Thousand Oaks, CA: Sage.

Devanney, J., & Devanney, D. (2003, August 8). Homeland security and patriot acts. *Law and Order, 51*, 10–12.

Dowe, D. (2009). Everything you need to know about less-than-lethal options: Part 1. *Tactical Response, 7*(3), 38–43.

Escobedo v. Illinois 378 U.S. 478 (1964).

Federal Bureau of Investigation. (2006). *Terrorism 2002-2005*. Retrieved July 21, 2010, from http://www.fbi.gov/publications/terror/terrorism2002_2005.htm

Federal Law Enforcement Training Center. (2009). *Arizona v. Gant*. Retrieved from http://www.fletc.gov/training/programs/legal-division/the-informer/Arizona-vs-gant.pdf/view

Ferdico, J. N. (2002). *Criminal procedure for the criminal justice professional*. Belmont, CA: Wadsworth/Thomson.

Ferrechio, S. (2010, May 10). Holder wants changes in Miranda rule. *Washington Examiner*. Retrieved June 3, 2010, from http://www.washingtonexaminer.com/politics/Holder-wants-changes-in-Miranda-rule-93240504.html#ixzz0ppGpHshJ

Fischer, R. J., Halibozek, E., & Green, G. (2008). *Introduction to security* (8th ed.). Burlington, MA: Elsevier.

Garland, N. M. (2009). *Criminal law for the criminal justice professional* (2nd ed.). Boston: McGraw Hill.

Herring v. United States 555 U.S.__ (2009).

Illinois v. Gates 462 U.S. 213 (1983).

Illinois v. Rodriquez 497 U.S. 177 (1990).

Johnson, K. (2009, September 17). States revamp photo lineups used by police. *USA Today*, p. 3A.

Kappeler, V. E. (2001). *Critical issues in police civil liability (3rd ed.)*. Prospect Heights, IL: Waveland.

Legislative discussion opens on reducing police rights. (2005, June 27). *China Daily*. Retrieved from http://www.chinadaily.com.cn/english/doc/2005-06/27/content_455023.htm

Mapp v. Ohio 367 U.S. 643, 655 (1961).

McCormack, W. (2009). State and local law enforcement: Contributions to terrorism prevention. *FBI Law Enforcement Bulletin, 78*(3), 1–8.

McDonald v. Chicago pending (2010).

Means, R., & Seidel, G. (2009). Maintaining proportionality and managing force escalations. *Law & Order, 57*(2), 31–33.

Michigan v. Long 463 U.S. 1032, 103 (1983).

Miranda v. Arizona 384 U.S. 457–58 (1966).

Murray v. United States 487 U.S. 533, 539 (1988).

Ori, R. (2009, July 18). Polices say concealed carry law would deter criminals. *Journal Star*. Retrieved July 21, 2010, from http://www.pjstar.com/news/x1730895291/Police-say-concealed-carry-law-would-deter-criminals

Pittsburgh police trial on First Amendment delayed. (2009). *Philadelphia Inquirer*. Retrieved from http://www.philly.com/inquirer/loca/nj/20090909

Reid, S. T. (2009). *Criminal law: The essentials*. New York: Oxford University Press.

Savage, D. (2009, April 1). Who's policing the Fourth Amendment? *ABA Journal*. Retrieved from http://www.abajournal.com

Schneckloth v. Bustamonte 412 U.S. 218, 228 (1973).

Scott v. Harris 127 S. Ct. 1769, U. S. Sup. Ct., No. 05–1631 (2007).

Senter, J. (2009, February 7). ACLU taking Taser use to Supreme Court. *Santa Rosa Press Gazette*. Retrieved March 10, 2010, from http://www.srpressgazette.com/news/court-6101-supreme-aclu.html

Sheehan, D. C., Everly, G. S., & Langlieb, A. M. (2004, September). How agencies help law enforcement officers cope with major critical incidents. *FBI Bulletin, 73*(9), 1–12.

Skelton, D. T. (1998). *Contemporary criminal law.* Boston: Butterworth-Heinemann.

State v. Garland 482 A.2d 139, 144 (Me. 1984).

State v. Lewis 611 A.2d.69 (Me. 1992).

Tennessee v. Garner 471 U.S. 1, 11–12 (1985).

Terry v. Ohio 392 U.S. 1 (1968).

Thornton v. United States, 541 U.S. 615 (2004).

Townsend v. Sain 372 U.S. 293, 307–08 (1963).

United States v. Cortez 449 U.S. 411 (1981).

United States v. Gonzalez-Basulto, 898 F.2d 1011, 1012-13 5th Cir. (1990).

United States v. Hensley 469 U.S. 221 (1985).

United States v. Jacobsen 466 U.S. 109,113 (1984).

United States v. Leon 468 U.S. 897 (1984).

United States v. Simmons 567 F.2d 314, 320 (1977).

Weeks v. United States 232 U.S. 383 (1914).

Wilson v. Arkansas 514 U.S. 927, 934 (1995).

Winters, N., & Barros, R. (2009, April 22). Concealed weapons bill meets objections on campus. *Columbia Missourian.* Retrieved from http://www.columbiamissourian.com/stories/2009/04/22/concealed-weapons-bill-met-objections-campus

Wolf v. Colorado, 338 U.S. 25 (1949).

Zash. C. (2010, June 2). Miranda rights rule changes, must say want to be silent. *Digtriad.com* Retrieved June 3, 2010, from http://www.digtriad.com/news/local_state/article.aspx?storyid=143135

Chapter 6

Adams, T. F. (2007). *Police field operations* (7th ed.). Upper Saddle River, NJ: Prentice-Hall.

Alpert, G. P., & Dunham, R. G. (1997). *Policing urban America* (3rd ed.). Prospect Heights, IL: Waveland.

Anderson, G. (2008). *A patrol staffing study of the Aurora, Elgin, and Joliet, Illinois police departments utilizing the allocation model for police patrol.* Unpublished master's thesis, Western Illinois University—Macomb.

Bayley, D. H. (1994). *Police for the future.* New York: Oxford University Press.

Bayley, D. H. (1998). *What works in policing.* New York: Oxford University Press.

Braunstein, S. (2007). Adapting to change in law enforcement public information. *Police Chief Magazine, 74,* 42.

Broderick, J. (1977). *Police in a time of change.* Morristown, NJ: Gene Learning Press.

Brook, D. (2006, February 19th). The cracks in 'broken windows.' *The Boston Globe.* Retrieved from www.boston.com

Brooks, L. W. (1997). Police discretionary behavior: A study of style. In R. G. Dunham & G. P. Alpert (Eds.), *Critical issues in policing* (3rd ed.). Prospect Heights, IL: Waveland Press.

Brooks, L. W. (2001). Police discretionary behavior: A study of style. In R. G. Dunham & G. P. Alpert (Eds.), *Critical issues in policing* (4th ed.). Prospect Heights, IL: Waveland Press.

Bruce, C. (2009). Districting and resource allocation: A question of balance. *Geography & Public Safety, 1,* 1–3.

Caddy, B., & Cobb, P. (2004). Forensic science. In P. C. White (Ed.), *Crime scene to court: The essentials of forensic science.* Philadelphia, PA: Royal Society of Chemistry.

CALEA Online. (2009). *Accreditation works: Case number 59.* Retrieved from http://www.calea.org/Online/newsletter/No92/cn59.htm

Chicago Police Department. (1998a). *Information collection for automated mapping* (ICAM). Retrieved from http://w5.ci.chi.il.us/CAPS/ToDelete/NewTech/ICAM.html

Chicago Police Department. (1998b). *Mounted patrol unit.* Retrieved from http://www.ci.chi.il.us/communitypolicing/DistrictHome/Special Functions/Mounted.html

Cordner, G., & Scarborough, K. E. (2007). *Police administration* (6th ed.). Cincinnati, OH: Anderson.

Cordner, G., & Sheehan, R. (1999). *Police administration* (4th ed.). Cincinnati, OH: Anderson.

Cox, S. M., & Fitzgerald, J. M. (1996). *Police in community relations: Critical issues* (3rd ed.). Dubuque, IA: W. C. Brown.

Crank, J. P. (1998). *Understanding police culture.* Cincinnati, OH: Anderson.

Dantzker, M. L. (1999). *Police organization and management.* Boston: Butterworth-Heinemann.

Dempsey, J. S. (1999). *Policing* (2nd ed.). St. Paul, MN: West.

Dempsey, J. S. & Forst, L. S. (2009). *An introduction to policing* (5th ed.). Florence, KY: Delmar Cengage Learning.

Denver Police Department. (2000). *Air support unit.* Retrieved from http://www.denvergov.org/content/template2922.asp

Douglass, J. (2009). Tactical deployment: The next great paradigm shift in law enforcement. *Geography & Public Safety, 1,* 6–8.

Engel, R. (2003). *How police supervisory styles influence patrol officer behavior.* Rockville, MD: National Institute of Justice.

Famega, N., Frank, N., & Mazerolle, L. (2005). Managing police patrol time: The role of supervisor directives. *Justice Quarterly, 22,* 540–560.

Fantino, J. (2007). Forensic science: A fundamental perspective. *The Police Chief, 74*(11). Retrieved from http://policechiefmagazine.org

Federal Bureau of Investigation. (2009). *What we investigate.* Retrieved from http://www.fbi.gov/hq.htm

Finckenauer, J. O. (2007). *Effectively combating transnational organized crime.* National Institute of Justice. Retrieved July 29, 2010, from http://www.ojp.usdoj.gov/nij/topics/crime/transnational-organized-crime/effective-practices.htm

Gilbert, J. N. (2001). *Criminal investigation* (5th ed.). Upper Saddle River, NJ: Prentice-Hall.

Gilbert, J. N. (2009). *Criminal investigation* (8th ed.). Upper Saddle River, NJ: Prentice-Hall.

Golub, A., Johnson, B. D., Taylor, A., & Eterno, J. (2003). Quality of life policing: Do offenders get the message? *Policing: An International Journal of Police Strategy and Management, 26,* 690–707. In Good, J. (2006). Are we fixing broken windows? Paper presented at the annual meeting of the American Sociological Association, Montreal Convention Center, Montreal, Quebec, Canada.

Greene, J. R. (2006). *The encyclopedia of police science* (3rd ed.). Boca Raton, FL: CRC Press.

Greene, J. R., & Klockars, C. B. (1991). What police do. In C. B. Klockars & S. D. Mastrofski (Eds.), *Thinking about police: Contemporary readings* (2nd ed., pp. 273–284). New York: McGraw-Hill.

Greenwood, P. (1979). *The Rand criminal investigation study: Its findings and impacts to date.* Santa Monica, CA: Rand Corporation.

Greenwood, P. W., & Petersilia, J. (1975). *The criminal investigation process: Volume I. Summary and policy recommendations.* Santa Monica, CA: Rand.

Honolulu Police Department. (2009). *Powers, duties and functions.* Retrieved from www.honolulu.gov/csd/budget/23hpd.pdf

Illinois General Assembly. (2010). *Illinois compiled statutes, Article 11. Corporate powers and functions.* Retrieved from www.ilga.gov/legislation/ilcs/ilcs.asp?ActID=802&ChapterID=14

Illinois Police Accreditation Coalition. (2009). *Most wanted interpretation: Agency workload assessments.* Retrieved from http://www.i-pac.org/agency_workload_assessments.htm

Jurkanin, T., Hoover, L., Dowling, J., & Ahmad, J. (2001). *Enduring, surviving, and thriving as a law enforcement executive.* Springfield, IL: Charles C. Thomas.

Kelling, G., Pate, T., Dieckman, D., & Brown, C. (1974). *The Kansas City preventive patrol experiment: A summary report.* Washington, DC: Police Foundation. In Thistlewaite, A. B., & Wooldredge, J. D. (2010). *Forty studies that changed criminal justice.* Upper Saddle River, NJ: Pearson Education.

Kelling, G., & Wilson, J. Q. (1982, March). Broken windows. *The Atlantic Magazine.* Retrieved from http://www.theatlantic.com/magazine/archive/1982/03/broken-windows/4465/

LaGrange, R. L. (1998). *Policing American society* (2nd ed.). Chicago: Nelson-Hall.

Lamb, H., Weinberger, L. E., & DeCuir, W. J. (2002). The police and mental health. *Psychiatric Service, 53,* 1266–1271.

Levinson, D. (2002). *Encyclopedia of crime and punishment* (Vols. I–IV). Thousand Oaks, CA: Sage.

Longmont, CO Police Department. (2006). *Staffing study: Updated 2006.* Retrieved from http://www.ci.longmont.co.us

MacDonald, H. (2000). N.Y. press to NYPD: Drop dead: The police are too aggressive, except when they're not aggressive enough. *American Enterprise, 11,* 16–17.

MacDonald, H. (2001). The myth of racial profiling. *City Journal, 11,* 14–27.

Mark, R. (1977). *Policing a perplexed society.* London: Allen & Unwin.

McGreevy, P. (2006). Panel gives Bratton vote of confidence. *Los Angeles Times.* Retrieved from http://www.latimes.com/news/local/la-me-chief20dec20,1,7062859.story. In Shane, J. M. (2007). *What every chief executive should know: Using data to measure police performance.* Flushing, NY: Looseleaf.

Menton, C. (2008). Bicycle patrols: an underutilized resource. *Policing, 31,* 93.

Metro Nashville Police Department. (2000). *Bicycle patrol.* Retrieved from http://www.nashville.net/~police/citizen/bicycle_patrol.htm

Michigan Commission on Law Enforcement Standard. (2006). *Statewide job analysis of the patrol officer position.* Retrieved from http://www.michigan.gov/documents/mcoles/Detroit_Police_Department_185900_7.pdf

Miller, J., Davis, R. C., Henderson, J., Markovic, J., & Ortiz, C. W. (2004). *Public opinions of the police: The influence of friends, family, and news media* (Document number 205619). Washington, DC: U.S. Department of Justice.

Moore, M. (1992). Problem-solving and community policing. In G. Alpert & A. Piquero (Eds.), *Community policing* (2nd ed.). Prospect Heights, IL: Waveland.

Moore, M., Thacher, D., Dodge, A., & Moore, T. (2002). *Recognizing value in policing.* Washington, DC: Police Executive Forum.

Morley, E. M., & Jacobson, M. J. (2007). Building a successful public information program. *Police Chief Magazine, 74,* 1.

National Institute of Justice. (2009). *Statistics on the use of force.* Washington, DC: U.S. Department of Justice, Office of Justice Programs. Retrieved from http://www.ojp.usdoj.gov/nij/topics/law-enforcement/use-of-force/statistics.htm

New York Police Department. (2000). *Mission statement.* Retrieved from http://www.ci.nyc.ny.us/html/nypd/html/pct/psb_mission.html. Palmiotto, M. (2004). *Criminal investigation.* Lanham, MD: University Press of America.

Office of Neighborhood Involvement. (2009). *Community Foot Patrols.* Retrieved from http://www.portlandonline.com/oni/index.cfm?c=4143&a=26680

Palmiotto, M. (2004). *Criminal investigation.* Lanham, MD: University Press of America.

Parks, R. B., Mastrofski, S. D., Dejong, C., & Gray, M. K. (1999). How officers spend their time with the community. *Justice Quarterly, 16,* 484–518.

Pelfrey, W. (2000). Precipitating factors of paradigmatic shift in policing. In G. Alpert & A. Piquero (Eds.), *Community policing.* Prospect Heights, IL: Waveland.

Police Foundation. (2009). *The Kansas City preventive patrol experiment.* Retrieved from http://www.policefoundation.org/docs/kansas.html

Radosevich, F. (2008). Department expected to launch web site displaying names and faces. *The Peoria Journal Star,* A1.

Reaves, B. A. (2007). *Census of state and local law enforcement agencies, 2004* (NCJ 212749). Washington, DC: Bureau of Justice Statistics.

Reaves, B. A., & Hickman, M. J. (2004). *Law enforcement management and administrative statistics, 2000: Data for individual state and local agencies with 100 or more officers.* Washington, DC: U.S. Department of Justice.

Rich, T. F. (1996). *The Chicago police department's information collection for automated mapping (ICAM) program.* Washington, DC: National Institute of Justice. In Roberg, R., Novak, K., & Cordner, G. (2009). *Police and society* (4th ed.). New York, NY: Oxford University Press.

Roberg, R., Kuykendall, J., & Novak, K. (2002). *Police management* (3rd ed.). New York: Oxford University Press.

Roberg, R., Novak, K., & Cordner, G. (2005). *Police and society* (3rd ed.). Los Angeles: Roxbury Publishing. In Greene, J.R. (2006). *The encyclopedia of police science* (3rd ed.). Boca Raton, FL: CRC Publishing.

Roberg, R., Novak, K., & Cordner, G. (2009). *Police and society* (4th ed.). New York: Oxford University Press.

Roman, J., Reid, S., Reid, J., Chalfin, A., Adams, W., & Knight, C. (2009). Cost-effectiveness analysis of the use of DNA in the investigation of high-volume crimes. *The Urban Institute.* Retrieved from http://www.urban.org

Scaramella, E., & Newman, A. (1999). Community education and the media: A partnership for effective crime control. *Crime and Justice International, 15,* 9–10, 12.

Shane, J. M. (2007). *What every chief executive should know: Using data to measure police performance.* Flushing, NY: Looseleaf Law.

Shelton, D. E. (2008). The 'CSI effect': Does it really exist? *National Institute of Justice Journal.* Retrieved from http://www.ojp.usdoj.gov.nij.journals/259/csi-efect.htm

Staszak, D. (2001). Media trends and the public information officer. *FBI Law Enforcement Bulletin, 70,* 10–13.

Taslitz, A. E. (2006). *Reconstructing the fourth amendment.* New York: NYU Press.

Thibault, E. A., Lynch, L. M., & McBride, R. B. (2001). *Proactive police management* (5th ed.). Upper Saddle River, NJ: Prentice-Hall.

Virginia State Police. (2000). *Computer crimes.* Retrieved from http://www.vsp.state.va.us/bci_gid_cyber.htm

Waco Police Association. (2008). Justex survey outline. Retrieved from http://wacopa.org/user files/Justex%20Survey%20Outline.pdf

Walker, S. (2008). *The police in America* (3rd ed.). Boston: McGraw-Hill.

Webster, J.A. (1970). *Police task and time study.* In Famega, C. N., Frank, J., & Mazerolle, L. (2005). Managing police patrol time: The Role of supervisor directives. *Justice Quarterly, 22,* 540–560.

West Virginia State Police Forensic Laboratory. (2009). *Examinations and functions.* Retrieved from http://www.wvstatepolice.com/crime/crime.shtml

Wilson, J. (1968). *Varieties of police behavior: The management of law and order in eight communities.* Cambridge, MA: Harvard University Press.

Wilson, J. Q., & Kelling, G. L. (1999). Broken windows. In V. E. Kappeler (Ed.), *The police and society* (2nd ed., pp. 154–167). Prospect Heights, IL: Waveland.

Young, J. (2000). Community policing in Savannah, Georgia. In G. Alpert & A. Piquero (Eds.), *Community policing* (2nd ed., pp. 305–323). Prospect Heights, IL: Waveland.

Chapter 7

Barker, T., Hunter, R. D., & Rush, J. P. (1994). *Police systems and practices: An introduction.* Englewood Cliffs, NJ: Prentice-Hall.

Bayley, D. (1994). *Police for the future.* New York: Oxford University Press.

Bureau of Justice Assistance. (2004). *Police chiefs desk reference.* Washington, DC: Office of Justice Programs.

Bureau of Labor Statistics. (2010). Economic news release. United States Department of Labor. Washington, D.C. Retrieved from http://www.bls.gov/news.release/union2.nr0.htm

CALEA Online. (2009). *Law enforcement accreditation.* Retrieved from http://www.calea.org/Online/CALEA/Programs/LawEnforcement/lawenfstandards.htm

Caplow, T. (1983). *Managing an organization.* New York: Holt, Rinehart and Winston.

Carter, L., & Wilson, M. (2006). Measuring professionalism of police officers. *Police Chief Magazine.* Retrieved from http://www.policechiefmagazine.org/magazine/index.cfm

Chriss, J. (2007). *From generalist to specialist back to generalist: The shifting roles of police over time.* Paper presented at the annual meeting of the American Society of Criminology, Atlanta Marriott Marquis, Atlanta, GA. Retrieved from http://www.allacademic.com/meta/p174160_index.html

City of Santa Barbara and Santa Barbara Police Management Association. (2009). *Memorandum of understanding. July 1, 2008 through June 30,* *2010.* Retrieved from http://www.santabarbaraca.gov/documents/Salary_and_MOU/Memorandums_of_Understanding_(MOU)_Documents/2008-010%20Police%20Management%20Association%20MOU.pdf

Cornell University Law School. (2009). *Collective bargaining and labor arbitration: An overview.* Legal Information Institute. Retrieved from http://topics.law.cornell.edu/wex/collective_bargaining

Cox, S. M., & Fitzgerald, J. D. (1996). *Police in community relations: Critical issues* (3rd ed.). Madison, WI: Brown & Benchmark.

Cox, S. M., & McCamey, W. P. (2008). *Introduction to criminal justice: Exploring the network.* Durham, NC: Carolina Academic Press.

Dantzker, M. L. (1999). *Police organization and management.* Boston: Butterworth-Heinemann.

Dantzker, M. L. (2005). *Understanding police today.* Monsey, NY: Criminal Justice Press.

Delord, R.G., Sanders, J., Alley, M., Hoover, J., Huett, H., Cameron, P. D., Edwards, M. D., Dowling, J., & Hoover, L. (2006). *Police labor-management relations: Volume 1. Perspectives and practical solutions for implementing change, making reforms and handling crises for managers and union leaders.* Washington, DC: U.S. Department of Justice, Office of Community Oriented Policing Services. In Dempsey, J. S., & Forst, L. (2009). *Introduction to Policing,* 5th ed. Florence, KY: Delmar Cengage Learning.

Engelson, W. (1999). Leadership challenges in the information age. *Police Chief, 66,* 64–66.

Friedmann, R. R. (2006). University perspective: The policing profession in 2050. *Police Chief Magazine.* Retrieved from http://www.police chiefmagazine.org/magazine/index.cfm

Gaines, L. K., & Kappeler, V. E. (2008). *Policing in America* (6th ed.). Albany, NY: Lexis Nexis.

Gaines, L. K., Kappeler, V. E., & Vaughn, J. B. (1999). *Policing in America* (3rd ed.). Albany, NY: Lexis Nexis.

Gaines, L. K., Southerland, M. D., & Angell, J. E. (1991). *Police administration.* New York: McGraw-Hill.

Gaines, L. K., & Swanson, C. R. (1997). Empowering police officers: A tarnished silver bullet? In L. K. Gaines & G. W. Cordner (Eds.), *Policing perspectives: An anthology* (pp. 363–371). Los Angeles: Roxbury.

Greenwood, P. W., Chaiken, J., & Petersilia, J. R. (1977). *The criminal investigation process* (Chaps. 14, 15). Lexington, MA: D.C. Heath.

Gulick, L. (1937). Notes on the theory of organizations. In L. Gulick & L. Urwick (Eds.), *Papers on the science of administration* (pp. 3–13). New York: Institute of Public Administration.

Hellriegel, D., & Slocum, J. W. (2008). *Organizational behavior* (12th ed.). Cincinnati, OH: South-Western Cengage Learning.

Hellriegel, D., & Slocum, J. W. (2011). *Organizational behavior* (13th ed.). Cincinnati, OH: South-Western Cengage Learning.

Hodgson, J. F., & Orban, C. (2005). *Public policing in the 21st century: Issues and dilemmas in the United States and Canada.* Monsey, NY: Criminal Justice Press.

Holden, R. N. (2000). *Modern police management* (2nd ed.). Englewood Cliffs, NJ: Prentice-Hall.

Hoover, L. T., Dowling, J. L., & Blair, G. (2006). *Management and labor in community policing: Charting a course.* Washington, DC: U.S. Department of Justice.

Johnson, K. (2006, September 18). Police agencies find it hard to require degrees: Education standards tricky for short-handed departments. *USA Today,* p. A3.

Jones, M. (2008). A complexity science view of modern police administration. *Public Administration Quarterly, 32*(3), 433–458.

Kelling, G. L., Pate, T., Dieckman, D., & Brown, C. E. (1974). *The Kansas City preventive patrol experiment: A summary report.* Washington, DC: Police Foundation.

Kerilikowske, G. (2004). The end of community policing: Remembering the lessons learned. *FBI Law Enforcement Bulletin, 73*(4), 6–9.

King, W. R. (2005). Toward a better understanding of the hierarchical nature of police organizations: Conception and measurement. *Journal of Criminal Justice, 33,* 97–109.

Kostelac, C. A. (2006). *Civilianization in law enforcement organizations.* Paper presented at the annual meeting of the American Society of Criminology, Los Angeles Convention Center, Los Angeles, CA. Retrieved from http://www.allacademic.com/meta/p126524_index.html

LaGrange, R. L. (1998). *Policing American society* (2nd ed.). Chicago, IL: Nelson-Hall.

Lavery, K. (2008, August 25). Changing patrol operations. Why? One word: Survival. *Officer.com.* http://www.officer.com

Lee, J. (2007). *Has community policing run its course? Community policing implementation after 9/11.* Paper presented at the annual meeting of the American Society of Criminology, Atlanta Marriott Marquis, Atlanta, GA.

Maguire, E. R. (2003). *Organizational structure in American police agencies.* Albany, NY: State University Press.

Mastrofski, S. (2006). Community policing: A skeptical view. In D. Weisburg & A. A. Braga (Eds.), *Police innovation contrasting perspectives* (pp. 44–73). New York: Cambridge University Press.

Moore, D. T., & Morrow, J. G. (1987). Evaluation of the four/ten schedule in three Illinois Department of State Police districts. *Journal of Police Science and Administration, 15,* 105–109.

Moore, S. (2007). Coalition focuses on Iraqi police infrastructure, organization. *American Forces Press Service.* Retrieved August 2, 2010, from http://www.defenselink.mil/news/newsarticle.aspx?id=48345

Muzzatti, S. L. (2005). The police, the public, the post-liberal politics of fear: Paramilitary policing post-9/11. In J. F. Hodgson & C. Orban (Eds.), *Public policing in the 21st century: Issues and dilemmas in the U.S. and Canada* (pp. 107–125). Monsey, NY: Criminal Justice Press.

National Institute of Justice (2000). *Fighting crime with COPS and citizens.* Retrieved from http://www.ojp/usdoj.gov/nij/publications/cops/impact.html

New York Police Department. (2010). *Precincts.* Retrieved from http://home2.nyc.gov/html/nypd/html/home/precincts.shtml

Peak, K. J. (1997). *Policing America* (2nd ed.). Upper Saddle River, NJ: Prentice-Hall.

Peak, K. J. (2008). *Policing America* (6th ed.). Upper Saddle River, NJ: Prentice-Hall.

Rainguet, F. W., & Dodge, M. (2001). The problems of police chiefs: An examination of the issues in tenure and turnover. *Police Quarterly, 4,* 268–288.

Regoli, R. M., & Hewitt, J. P. (2007). *Exploring criminal justice* (2nd ed.). Sudbury, MA: Jones and Bartlett.

Reitz, M. (2007, July 16). Public access to public sector collective bargaining. *Evergreen Freedom Foundation.* Retrieved from http://www.effwa.org/main/article.php?article_id=2107

Robbins, S. P. (2005). *Organizational behavior* (11th ed.). Upper Saddle River, NJ: Pearson Prentice-Hall.

Roberg, R. R., Crank, J., & Kuykendall, J. (2000). *Police and society* (2nd ed.). Belmont, CA: Wadsworth.

Roberg, R. R., & Kuykendall, J. (1993). *Police management* (2nd ed.). Los Angeles: Roxbury.

Roberg, R. R., Novak, K., & Cordner, G. (2009). *Police and society* (4th ed.). New York: Oxford University Press.

Sapp, A. D. (1985). Police unionism as a developmental process. In A. S. Blumberg & E. Niederhoffer (Eds.), *The ambivalent force: Perspectives on the police* (3rd ed., pp. 412–419), New York: Holt, Rinehart and Winston.

Schroeder, D. J., & Lombardo, F. A. (2004). *Police sergeant exam.* Hauppauge, NY: Barrons Education Services.

Sherk, J. (2008). Mandatory public-safety collective bargaining could be made less onerous. *The Heritage Foundation.* Retrieved from http://www.policyarchive.org/bitstream/handle/10207/13660/wm_1923.pdf.sequence1

Skolnick, J. H., & Bayley, D. H. (1986). *The new blue line: Police innovation in six American cities.* New York: Free Press.

Sparrow, M. K., Moore, M. H., & Kennedy, D. M. (1990). *Beyond 911: A new era for policing.* New York: Basic Books.

Stenberg, C., & Austin, S. L. (2007). *Managing local government services: A practical guide.* Atlanta, GA: ICMA Press.

Stevens, D. J. (2008). *An introduction to American policing.* Sudbury, MA: Jones and Bartlett.

Sullivan, J. (2008, September 11). Tiny cameras going with Seattle cops out on the street. *Seattle Times,* p. B1.

Sawada, K. (2008). A model of adding relations in two levels to an organization structure of a complete binary tree. *International Journal of Innovative Computing, Information and Control, 4*(5), 1134–1140.

Swanson, C. R., Territo, L., & Taylor, R. W. (2001). *Police administration* (5th ed.). New York: Macmillan.

Swanson, C. R., Territo, L., & Taylor, R. W. (2007). *Police administration* (7th ed.). New York: Macmillan.

Thibault, E. A., Lynch, L. M., & McBride, R. B. (2007). *Proactive police management* (7th ed.). Englewood Cliffs, NJ: Prentice-Hall.

Toch, H., & Grant, J. D. (1991). *Police as problem solvers.* New York: Plenum.

Tucker, W., Jordan, J., & Deliums, R. (2007). *Police reform white paper.* Retrieved from http://www.oaklandnet.com/MayorsPress/PoliceReformWhitePaperv4.pdf

Turner, Y. C. (2000). Decentralizing the specialized unit functions in small police agencies. *Police Chief, 77,* 50–51.

U.S. Department of Labor. (2009). *What is an incident command system?* Washington, DC: Occupational Safety and Health Administration. Retrieved from http://www.osha.gov/SLTC/etools/ics/what_is_ics.html

Viverette, M. A. (2008). President's message: Prepare tomorrow's police leaders. *International Association of Chiefs of Police.* Retrieved from http://www.theiacp.org/Training/CPL/PresidentsMessage/tabid/156/Default.aspx

Vollmer, H. M., & Mills, D. L. (1966). *Professionalization.* Englewood Cliffs, NJ: Prentice-Hall.

Walker, S. (1999). *The police in America* (3rd ed.). Boston: McGraw-Hill.

Walker, S., & Katz, C. (2008). *The police in America* (6th ed.). Boston, MA: McGraw-Hill.

Whisenand, P. M. (2001). *Supervising police personnel* (4th ed.). Upper Saddle River, NJ: Prentice-Hall.

Wilson, S., Zhao, J., Ren, L., & Briggs, S. (2006). The influence of collective bargaining on large police agency salaries: 1990-2000. *American Journal of Criminal Justice, 31*(1), 1.

Chapter 8

Allen, J., Mhlanga, B., & Khan, E. (2006). Education, training and ethical dilemmas: Responses of criminal justice practitioners regarding professional and ethical issues. *Professional Issues in Criminal Justice, 1*(1), 3–28.

Anonymous. (2007). More than 100 police agencies enroll for U.S. training to spot illegal aliens. *Crime Control Digest, 41*(45), 1–2.

Arnold, T. (1997). A case study analysis of police ethics training in Illinois (Doctoral dissertation, Northern Illinois University, 1997), *Dissertation Abstracts International,* 58(12), Sec. A, 4522.

Barovick, H. (1998, June 15). DWB: driving while black. *Time.com,* 151(23). Retrieved from http://www.pathfinder.com/time/magazine/1998/dom/980615/nation_driving_while.html

Bills, J., Ching-Chung, K., Heringer, R., & Mankin, D. (2009). Peer-to-peer accountability. *FBI Law Enforcement Bulletin,* 78(8), 12–20.

Brooks, L. W. (1993). Police discretionary behavior: A study of style. In R. G. Dunham & G. P. Alpert (Eds.), *Critical issues in policing: Contemporary readings* (2nd ed., pp. 140–164). Prospect Heights, IL: Waveland.

Close, D., & Meier, N. (Eds.). (1995). *Morality in criminal justice: An introduction to ethics.* Belmont, CA: Wadsworth.

Cox, S. (1996). *Police: Practices, perspectives, problems.* Boston: Allyn & Bacon.

Cox, S. (2002, May 20). Personal interview with Cox. Macomb, IL. (1996). *Police: Practices, perspectives, problems.* Boston: Allyn & Bacon.

Cox, S., & McCamey, W. (2008). *Introduction to criminal justice: Exploring the network* (5th ed.). Durham, SC: Carolina Academic Press.

Delattre, E. (1996). *Character and cops* (3rd ed.). Washington, DC: AEI Press.

Delattre, E. (2002). *Character and cops* (5th ed). Washington, DC: AEI Press.

Del Pozo, B. (2005). One dogma of police ethics: Gratuities and the 'democratic ethos' of policing. *Criminal Justice Ethics,* 24(2), 25–46.

Dorn, D. (2001). *Police officer gratuity policies: An exploratory story.* Unpublished Master's Thesis, Western Illinois University—Macomb.

Gaines, L. K., Kappeler, V. E., & Vaughn, J. B. (1994). *Policing in America.* Cincinnati, OH: Anderson.

Harris, D. (1999). The stories, the statistics, and the law: Why "driving while black" matters. *Minnesota Law Review, 84,* 265–326. Retrieved from http://www.udayton.edu/race/03justice/dwb01.htm

Higgins, M. (2000, May 26). 1992 ticket-writing lesson helped Bloomingdale cops. *Chicago Tribune.* Retrieved from http://articles.chicagotribune.com/2000-05-26/news/0005260320_1_black-drivers-traffic-tickets-officers-and-motorists

International Association of Chiefs of Police. (2005, March 22). *Police code of conduct.* Alexandria, VA: Author. Retrieved from http://shr.elpasoco.com/NR/rdonlyres/7A3D02A5-E92B-4055-AF7E-90D92A3DF6D3/0/code_of_conduct.pdf

International Conference on Police Accountability and the Quality of Oversight: Global Trends in National Context. (2005). *Approaches to the Mexico City police force and its makeup* (Mexico). The Hague, Netherlands, October 19–21, 1–16. Retrieved from http://www.altus.org/pdf/m_mlk_en.pdf

Keoun, B. (2000, May 22). Video cameras in squad cars gain popularity among police [Electronic version]. *Chicago Tribune,* Sec. 2, p. 2.

Klockars, C., Ivkovic, S., & Haberfeld, M. (Eds.). (2004). *The contours of police integrity.* Thousand Oaks, CA: Sage.

Knapp Commission. (1972). *Report on police corruption.* New York: George Braziller.

Langworthy, R. H., & Travis, L. F. (1994). *Policing in America: A balance of forces.* New York: Macmillan.

Law Enforcement Employment Bulletin. (2008, September). *Ethical training: Don't neglect ethics as part of overall instruction.* 25(9), 1.

Lersch, K., Bazley, T., & Mieczkowski, T. (2006). Early intervention programs: An effective police accountability tool, or punishment of the productive? *Policing,* 29(1), 58–77.

Manning, P. (1978). The police: Mandate, strategies and appearances. In P. Manning & J. Van Maanen (Eds.), *Policing: A view from the street* (pp. 7–13). Santa Monica, CA: Goodyear.

Mueller, R., III. (2006, May 11). *Federal Bureau of Investigation, Major Executive Speeches.* Speech presented at City Club of San Diego, San Diego, CA. Retrieved from http://fbi.gov/pressrel/speeches/mueller051106.htm

National Institute of Justice. (2005, December). *Enhancing police integrity.* Washington, DC:

U.S. Department of Justice, Office of Justice Programs.

Newport, F. (1999, December 9). Racial profiling is seen as widespread, particularly among young black men. *Gallup News Service*. Retrieved from http://www.gallup.com/poll/3421/racial-profil ing-seen-widespread-particularly-among-young-black-men.aspx

Nickels, E. (2007, September/October). A note on the status of discretion in police research. *Journal of Criminal Justice, 35*(5), 570.

O'Malley, T. (1997, April). Managing for ethics: A mandate for administrators [Electronic version]. *FBI Law Enforcement Bulletin*.

Pendergraph, J. T. (2008). Law enforcement partnerships: A potent tool in fighting illegal immigration. *Sheriff, 60*(5), 75.

Reiss, A. J. (1992). Police organization in the twentieth century. In M. Tonry & N. Morris (Eds.), *Modern policing* (pp. 51–98). Chicago: University of Chicago Press.

Ricciardi, N., & Rabin, J. (2000, March 13). Report echoes Christopher panel's findings. *Los Angeles Times*, p. A5.

Scaramella, G. (2001, February). Attitudes of undergraduate criminal justice majors toward ethical issues in criminal justice. *Illinois Law Enforcement Executive Forum, 1*, 9–25.

Scaramella, G., Rodriguez, R., & Allen, J. (2009). A longitudinal analysis of four inquiries of ethical attitudes of criminal justice higher education students and police officers. *Contemporary Issues in Criminology and the Social Sciences, 4*(2), 1–20.

Schafer, J., & Martinelli, T. (2008). First-line supervisor's perceptions of police integrity: The measurement of police integrity revisited. *Policing, 31*(2), 306–323.

Schmalleger, F. (2008). *Criminal justice: A brief introduction* (7th ed.). Upper Saddle River, NJ: Pearson Prentice-Hall.

Stephens, N. (2006, November). Law enforcement ethics do not begin when you pin on the badge. *FBI Law Enforcement Bulletin, 75*(11), 22–23.

Trautman, N. (2002). Administrator misconduct. *Law and Order, 50*, 118–126.

Turano, R. (2001). *A comparative study of undergraduate criminal justice college students and DuPage county police officers involving ethical attitudes*. Unpublished Master's thesis, Western Illinois University.

U.S. Department of Justice. (2001). *Principles for promoting police integrity: Examples of promising police practices and policies*. Washington, DC: U.S. Government Printing Office.

U.S. Department of Justice. (2007). *Former Cedartown police officer pleads guilty to stealing money from Hispanic motorists during traffic stops*. Retrieved from http//Atlanta.fbi.gov/doj pressrel/pressre107/civil rights031207.htm

U.S. General Accounting Office. (1998). *Drug-related police corruption*. Washington, DC: U.S. Government Printing Office.

Walker, S. (2005). *The new world of police accountability*. Thousand Oaks, CA: Sage.

Zuidema, B., & Duff, H., Jr. (2009, March). Organizational ethics through effective leadership. *FBI Law Enforcement Bulletin, 78*(3), 8–11.

Chapter 9

4 Chicago officers admit barging into homes, theft. (2009, September 19). *Journal Star*, p. B2.

American Law and Legal Information Law Library. (2009). Wickersham commission. *Law Library*. Retrievable from http://law.jrank .org/pages/11309/Wickersham-Commission .html

Anonymous. (2008). Ex-Chicago police official arrested in torture cases. *Police Department Disciplinary Bulletin, 16*(12), 7–9.

Anonymous. (2009a). Big police scandal in a small town. *Police Department Disciplinary Bulletin, 17*(2), 4–7.

Anonymous. (2009b). Fifteen officers in Illinois are buzzed in FBI sting, *Police Department Disciplinary Bulletin, 17*(1), 3–5.

Barker, T., & Carter, D. L. (1986). *Police deviance*. Cincinnati: Pilgrimage.

Barker, T., & Roebuck, J. B. (1974). *An empirical typology of police corruption: A study in organizational deviance*. Springfield, IL: Charles C. Thomas.

Barker, T., & Wells, R. O. (1982, March). Public administrators' attitudes toward the definition and control of police deviance. *FBI Law Enforcement Bulletin, 51*, 8–16.

Bittner, E. (1970). *The functions of the police in modern society.* Chevy Chase, MD: National Institute of Mental Health Center for Studies of Crime and Delinquency.

Bouza, A. V. (1990). *The police mystique: An insider's look at cops, crime, and the criminal justice system.* New York: Plenum.

Bracey, D. H. (1989). Proactive measures against police corruption: Yesterday's solutions, today's problems. *Police Studies, 12,* 175–179.

CBS News/New York Times Poll. (2008, July 7–14). Retrieved from http://www.pollingreport.com/institut.htm

Chevigny, P. (1969). *Police power: Police abuses in New York City.* New York: Vintage Press.

Christopher Commission. (1991). *Report of the independent commission on the Los Angeles Police Department.* Los Angeles: The Commission.

Coleman, S. (2004). When police should say "No!" to gratuities. *Criminal Justice Ethics, 23*(1), 33–45.

Cooksey, O. E. (1991, September). Corruption: A continuing challenge for law enforcement. *FBI Law Enforcement Bulletin, 60,* 5–9.

Cox, S., & McCamey, W. (2008). *Introduction to criminal justice: Exploring the network.* Durham, NC: Carolina Academic Press.

Cox, S. (1996). *Police: Practices, perspectives, problems.* Boston: Allyn & Bacon.

Cray, E. (1972). *The enemy in the streets: Police malpractice in America.* Garden City, NY: Anchor Books.

Davis, R., Mateu-Gelabert, P., & Miller, J. (2005). Can effective policing also be respectful? Two examples in the south Bronx. *Police Quarterly, 8,* 229–247.

Defense of the Lexow Measures; Senator Pound writes a letter in reply to Charles Stewart Smith. (1895, March 29). *New York Times,* p. 2.

Delattre, E. (2002). *Character and cops* (4th ed.). Washington, DC: AEI Press.

DeLeon-Granados, W., & Wells, W. (1998). Do you want extra police coverage with those fries? An exploratory analysis of the relationship between patrol practices and the gratuity exchange principle. *Police Quarterly, 1,* 71–85.

Durose, M., Smith, E., & Langan, P. (2007, April). Contacts between the police and the public, 2005. *National Institute of Justice* (NCJ 215243). Retrieved from http://www.ojp.usdoj.gov//nij

Fitzgerald, G. (1989). *Commission of inquiry into possible illegal activities and associated police misconduct.* Brisbane, QLD: Government Printing Office.

Foley, M. (2000). *Police perjury: A factorial analysis.* National Institute of Justice (NCJ 181241). Doctoral dissertation, City University of New York.

Frankel, B. (1993a, September 30). "You'll be in the fold" by breaking law. *USA Today,* p. 1A.

Frankel, B. (1993b, October 7). For NYC cops, license for crime. *USA Today,* p. 3A.

Gallup Poll. (2009, June). *Major institutions.* Retrieved from http://www.pollingreport.com/crime.htm

Greene, J., Piquero, A., Hickman, M., & Lawton, B. (2004). *Police integrity and accountability in Philadelphia: Predicting and assessing police misconduct.* National Institute of Justice (NCJ 207823). Retrieved from http://www.ncjrs.gov/APP/Publications

Government Accounting Office. (1998, May). *Report to the Honorable Charles B. Rangel, House of Representatives, Law enforcement: Information on drug-related police corruption.* Washington, D.C.: USG-PO, 3.

Hacker, A. (1992). *Two nations: Black and white, separate, hostile, and unequal.* New York: Ballantine Books.

Harrison, B. (1999, August). Noble cause corruption and the police ethic. *FBI Law Enforcement Bulletin, 68,* 1–7.

Human Rights Watch. (1998). Shielded from justice: Police brutality and accountability in the United States. *Los Angeles: The Christopher Commission Report.* Retrieved January 20, 2001, from http://www.hrw.org/reports98/police/uspo73.htm

Hyatt, W. (2001). Parameters of police misconduct. In M. Palmiotto (Ed.), *Police misconduct,* 75–99. Upper Saddle River, NJ: Prentice-Hall.

Ivkovic, S. (2003). To serve and collect: Measuring police corruption. *Journal of Criminal Law and Criminology, 93*(2/3), 593.

Ivkovic, S. (2005). Police misbehavior: A cross-cultural study of corruption seriousness. *Policing, 28*(3), 546.

Ivkovic, S., & Shelley, T. (2008). The contours of police integrity across Eastern Europe: The case of Bosnia and Herzegovina and the Czech Republic. *International Criminal Justice Review, 18*(1), 59.

Johnson, D. R. (1981). *American law enforcement: A history.* St. Louis, MO: Forum Press.

Johnson, K. (2007, December 17). Milwaukee beating case busts officers' 'code of silence.' *USA Today.* Retrieved from http://www.usatoday.com/news/nation/2007-12-17-Copside_N.htm

Johnson, R. (1998, December). Citizen complaints: What the police should know. *FBI Law Enforcement Bulletin, 67,* 1–5.

Jones, J. (2005, November 10). *Confidence in local police drops to 10-year low.* The 2005 Gallup Public Opinion Poll.

Klockars, C. (1989). Police ethics. In W. G. Bailey (Ed.), *The encyclopedia of police science* (pp. 427–432). New York: Garland Press.

Klockars, C., Ivkovich, S., & Haberfeld, M. (2005, December). Enhancing police integrity. *National Institute of Justice, Research for Practice.* Retrieved from http://www.ojp.usdoj.gov//nij

Klockars, C., Ivkovich, S. K., Harver, W. E., & Haberfeld, M.R. (2000, May). *The measurement of police integrity. Research in Brief.* Washington, DC: National Institute of Justice, U.S. Government Printing Office.

Knapp Commission. (1973). *The Knapp Commission report on police corruption.* New York: George Braziller.

Lacayo, R. (1993, October 11). Cops and robbers. *Time,* pp. 43–44.

Lieberman, D. (2008, August 17). A closer eye on the police. [Letter to the Editor]. *The New York Times.* Retrieved from http://www.nytimes.com

Lurigio, A. J., Greenleaf, R. G., & Flexon, L. L. (2009). The effects of race on relationships with the *police:* A survey of African American and Latino youths in Chicago. *Western Criminology Review, 10*(1), 29–42.

Lynch, G. W. (1989). Police corruption from the United States perspective. *Police Studies, 12,* 165–170.

Main, F., Sadovi, C., & Sweeney, A. (2000, November 22). 4 cops charged with shakedowns. *Chicago Sun Times.* Retrieved from http://www.highbeam.com/doc/1P2-4568326.html

Manning, P. K. (1974). Police lying. *Urban Life, 3,* 283–306.

Marche, G. (2009, June). Integrity, culture, and scale: An empirical test of the big bad police agency. *Crime, Law and Social Change, 51*(5), 463.

Meese, E., & Ortmeier, P. (2003). *Leadership, ethics, and policing: Challenges for the 21st century.* Upper Saddle River, NJ: Prentice-Hall.

Mollen Commission. (1995). *Commission to fight corruption.* New York: Author.

National Advisory Commission on Civil Disorders. (1968). *Report.* Washington, DC: U.S. Government Printing Office.

National Institute of Justice. (1997). *Police integrity: Public service with honor.* Washington, DC: U.S. Government Printing Office.

National Institute of Justice. (1999). *Use of force by police: Overview of national and local data.* Washington DC: U.S. Government Printing Office.

National Institute of Justice. (2000). *Public attitudes toward abuse of authority: Findings from a national study.* Washington DC: U.S. Government Printing Office.

Packman, D. (2010, February 25). Conspiracy cops—Bad apples or bad barrels? *Injustice Everywhere.* Retrieved from http://www.injusticeeverywhere.com/?p=1904

Reiss, A. (1968). Police brutality . . . answers to key questions. In M. Lipsky (Ed.), *Police encounters* (pp. 10–19). Chicago: Aldine.

Reiss, A. (1971). *The police and the public.* New Haven, CT: Yale University Press.

Richardson, J. F. (1974). *Urban police in the United States.* Port Washington, NY: Kennikat Press.

Roberg, R. R., & Kuykendall, J. (1993). *Police in society.* Belmont, CA: Wadsworth.

Rosoff, S., Pontell, H., & Tillman, R. (2007). *Profit without honor: White collar crime and the looting of America* (4th ed.). Upper Saddle River, NJ: Prentice-Hall.

Rothwell, G., & Baldwin, J. (2006, September). Ethical climates and contextual predictors of whistle-blowing. *Review of Public Personnel Administration, 26,* 216–244.

Rubinstein, J. (1973). *City police.* New York: Farrar, Straus and Giroux.

Ruiz, J., & Bono, C. (2004). At what price a "freebie"? The real cost of police gratuities. *Criminal Justice Ethics, 23*(1), 44–55.

Seron, C., Pereira, J., & Kovath, J. (2004). Judging police misconduct: "Street-level" versus professional policing. *Law & Society Review, 38*(4), 665–710.

Skolnick, J. H. (1966). *Justice without trial.* New York: John Wiley.

Stoddard, E. R. (1968, June). The informal code of police deviance: A group approach to "blue-coat crime." *Journal of Criminal Law, Criminology and Police Science, 59,* 201–213.

Sykes, G. (1999). NYPD blues. *Ethics Corner, 6*(1). Southwestern Law Enforcement Institute, Center for Law Enforcement Ethics.

Tran, M. (1994, July 8). Corruption riddles New York police: Inquiry says drug dealing rogue cops acted like gangs. *The Gazette* (Montreal), p. A9.

Treaster, J. (1994, July 10). Mollen Panel says buck stops with top officers. *New York Times,* Sec. 1, p. 21, col. 2.

Trojanowicz, R. (1992). Preventing individual and systemic corruption. *Footprints, 4,* 1–3.

U.S. Department of Justice. (2001). *Principles for promoting police integrity: Examples of promising police practices and policies.* Washington, DC: U.S. Government Printing Office.

U.S. General Accounting Office. (1998). *Drug-related police corruption.* Washington, DC: U.S. Government Printing Office.

Walker, S. (2001). *Police accountability.* Belmont, CA: Wadsworth/Thomson Learning.

Walker, S., Spohn, C., & DeLone, M. (2006). *The color of justice: Race, ethnicity, and crime in America* (4th ed.). Belmont, CA: Wadsworth/Thompson Learning.

Weisburd, D., & Greenspan, R. (2000, May). Police attitudes toward abuse of authority: Findings from a national study. *Research in Brief, National Institute of Justice.* Washington, DC: U.S. Government Printing Office.

Zuidema, B., & Duff, H., Jr. (2009, March). Organizational ethics through effective leadership. *FBI Law Enforcement Bulletin,* pp. 8–11.

Chapter 10

ACLU (American Civil Liberties Union). (2004). Sanctioned bias: Racial profiling since 9/11. New York: Author. Retrieved from http://www.aclu.org/FilesPDFs/racial%20profiling%20report.pdf

Alex, N. (1969). *Black in blue.* New York: Appleton-Century-Crofts.

Alex, N. (1976). *New York cops talk back.* New York: Wiley.

Ancheta, A. N. (2006). *Race, rights and the Asian American experience* (2nd ed.). Chapel Hill, NC: Rutgers University Press.

Asian American Lawyers Association of Massachusetts. (2003, March). AALAM members discuss Asian gangs in Massachusetts. *The Newsletter of the Asian American Lawyers Association of Massachusetts, 18,* 1.

Astier, H. (2006, October 30). Suburban gangs defy French police. *BBC News.* Retrieved from http://news.bbc.co.uk/go/pr/fr/-/2/hi/europe/6096706.stm

Baldwin, J. (1962). *Nobody knows my name.* New York: Dell.

Balkin, J. (1988). Why policemen don't like policewomen. *Journal of Police Science and Administration, 16,* 29–37.

Barak, G., Flavin, J. M., & Leighton, P. S. (2001). *Class, race, gender and crime.* Los Angeles: Roxbury.

Barlow, D. E., & Barlow, M. H. (2000). *Police in a multicultural society: An American story.* Prospect Heights, IL: Waveland.

Bartol, C. R., Bergen, G. T., & Volckens, J. S. (1992). Women in small-town policing: Job performance and stress. *Criminal Justice and Behavior, 19,* 240–260.

Bartollas, C., & Hahn, L. S. (1999). *Policing in America.* Boston: Allyn & Bacon.

Basich, M. (2008). Region 9 extra: Female police officers must walk a fine line between fitting in and making their own way in law enforcement. *Women Police, 42*(3), 28–30.

Bazar, E. (2009, October 15). On fence over illegal immigration controls. *USA Today,* p. 3A.

Belkin, A., & McNichol, J. (2002). Pink and blue: Outcomes associated with the integration of open gay and lesbian personnel in the San Diego Police Department. *Police Quarterly, 3*(1), 63–95.

Bell, D. J. (1982). Policewomen—Myths and reality. *Journal of Police Science and Administration, 10,* 112–120.

Berger, J. (2006, May 1). Influx of Asians in New Jersey is not reflected in police ranks. *The New York Times.* Retrieved from http://www.nytimes.com

Bickham, T., & Rossett, A. (1993). Diversity training: Are we doing the right thing? *Police Chief, 60,* 43–47.

Block, P., & Anderson, D. (1974). *Policewomen on patrol: Final report.* Washington, DC: Urban Institute.

Bouza, A. (2001). *Police unbound: Corruption, abuse, and heroism by the boys in blue.* Amherst, NY: Prometheus Books.

Breci, M. G. (1997). Female officers on patrol: Public perceptions in the 1990s. *Journal of Crime & Justice, 20,* 153–166.

Brown, B. (2004). Community policing in diverse society. *Law Enforcement Executive Forum, 4*(5), 49–56.

Brown, R. A., & Frank, J. (2006). Race and officer decision making: Examining differences in arrest outcomes between black and white officers. *Justice Quarterly, 23,* 96–127.

Brunson, R. K., & Miller, J. (2006). Young black men and urban policing in the United States. *British Journal of Criminology, 46,* 613–640.

California Commission on Peace Officers Standards and Training. (2009). *Cultural diversity program.* Retrieved from http://www.post.ca.gov/training/diversity.asp

Campbell, D. J., Christman, B. D., & Feigelson, M. E. (2000). Improving the recruitment of women in policing: An investigation of women's attitudes and job preferences. *Police Chief, 67,* 18–28.

Carlan, P. E., & McMullan, E. C. (2009). A contemporary snapshot of policewomen attitudes. *Women & Criminal Justice, 19,* 60.

Carrick, G. (2000). Professional police traffic stops: Strategies to address racial profiling. *FBI Law Enforcement Bulletin, 69,* 8–10.

Carter, D. L., & Sapp, A. D. (1991). *Police education and minority recruitment: The impact of a college requirement.* Washington, DC: Police Executive Research Forum.

Charles, M. T. (1982). Women in policing—The physical aspect. *Journal of Police Science and Administration, 10,* 194–205.

Chavis, B. F., & Williams, J. D. (1993). Beyond the Rodney King story: NAACP report on police conduct and community relations. *NAACP News, 93,* 42.

Childers v. Dallas Police Department, 513 F.Supp. 134 (N.D. Tex. 1981), aff'd 669 F.2d 732 (5th Cir. 1982).

Clearwater Police Department. (2009). *The chronology of the Clearwater police department's Hispanic outreach programs.* Retrieved from http://www.clearwaterpolice.org/hispanic/chronology.asp

Clemmons, A., & Rosenthal, R. (2008). Mediating citizen complaints: The Denver program. *Police Chief, LXXV* (8). Retrieved from http://www.ncjrs.gov

Cohen, B. (2000). Are female cops a safety risk? One cop's answer. *Women Police, 34,* 3.

Cox, S. M. (1984). Race/ethnic relations and the police: Current and future issues. *American Journal of the Police, 3,* 169–183.

Cox, S. M., & Fitzgerald, J. D. (1996). *Police in community relations: Critical issues* (3rd ed.). New York: McGraw-Hill.

Cox, S. M., & Hazlett, M. H. (2001, July). Biased enforcement, racial profiling, and data collection: Addressing the issues. *Illinois Law Enforcement Executive Forum,* 91–99.

Cox, S. M., & McCamey, W. P. (2008), *Introduction to criminal justice: Exploring the network.* Durham, NC: Carolina Academic Press.

Daye, D. D. (1997). *A law enforcement sourcebook of Asian crime and cultures: Tactics and mind sets.* Boca Raton, FL: CRC Press.

Dorschner, J. (1987). The dark side of the force. In R. G. Dunham & G. P. Alpert (Eds.), *Critical issues in policing: Contemporary readings.* Prospect Heights, IL: Waveland.

Dulaney, M. (1996). *Black police in America.* In R. G. Dunham & G. P. Alpert (Eds.). (2010). *Critical issues in policing.* Long Grove, IL: Waveland Press.

Egerstrom, L. (2009, May 3). St. Paul police get $250,000 grant for work with Muslim/Somali communities. *Pioneer Press.* Retrieved from http://www.policegrantshelp.com/news/126873-St-Paul-police-get-250-000-grant-for-work-with-Muslim-Somali-Communities/

Eisenberg, A. C. (2007). Region 9 Extra: Seattle's first female officers on the beat. *Women Police 41*(3), 40–43.

Federal Bureau of Investigation. (2008, September). *Crime in the United States, 2007.* Retrieved from http://www.fbi.gov/ucr/cius2007/police/table_guide.html

Federal Bureau of Investigation. (2009, September). *Crime in the United States, 2008.* Retrieved from http://www.fbi.gov/ucr/cius2008/police/table_guide.html

Fields, G. (2000, March 30). Study: Police forces lack female officers. *USA Today,* p. 4A.

Fox, K., Nobles, M., & Piquero, A. (2009). Gender, crime victimization and fear of crime. *Security Journal 22*(1), 24–39.

Fry, L. (1983). A preliminary examination of the factors related to turnover of women in law enforcement. *Journal of Police Science and Administration, 11,* 149–155.

Fry, L. W., & Greenfield, S. (1980). An examination of attitudinal differences between policewomen and policemen. *Journal of Applied Psychology 65,* 123–126.

Fullbright, L. (2007, May, 17). *Minority population grows to 100 million—1 of 3 in U.S.* Retrieved from http://www.sfgate.com/cgi-bin/article.cgi?f=/c/a/2007/05/17/MNGA3PSJRK1.DTL&feed=rss.news

Gabor, T. (2001). Racial profiling: A complex issue made simple. *Journal of California Law Enforcement, 35,* 15–17.

Gay and Lesbian Liaison Unit. (2009). *About the gay and lesbian liaison unit.* Washington, DC: Author. Retrieved from http://www.gllu.org/resources/index.htm#pubs

Gold, M. E. (2000). The progress of women in policing. *Law & Order, 48,* 159–161.

Grown, M. C., & Carlson, R. D. (1993). Do male policemen accept women on patrol yet? Androgyny, public complaints, and dad. *Journal of Police and Criminal Psychology, 9,* 10–14.

Hacker, A. (1992). *Two nations: Black and white, separate, hostile, unequal.* New York: Ballantine Books.

Harlow, C. W. (2005, November). *Hate crimes reported by victims and police* (NCJ 209911). Washington, DC: Bureau of Justice Statistics. Retrieved April 15, 2010, from http://bjs.ojp.usdoj.gov/index.cfm?ty=pbdetail&iid=949

Harris, W. (1999). Recruiting women: Are we doing enough? *Police, 23,* 18–23.

Henderson, N. J., Ortiz, C. W., Sugie, N. F., & Miller, J. (2008, July). *Policing in Arab-American communities after September 11* (NCJ 221706). Washington, DC: U.S. Department of Justice. Retrieved April 10, 2010, from http://www.ncjrs.gov/app/publications/abstract.aspx?ID=243589

Hennessy, S. M. (1993, August). Achieving cultural competence. *Police Chief, 60,* 46–54.

Hennessy, S. M., Hendricks, C., & Hendricks, J. (2001). Cultural awareness and communication training: What works and what doesn't. *Police Chief, 68,* 15–19.

Hickman, B., & Reaves, B. (2006). *Local police Departments, 2003* (NCJ 210118). Washington, DC: U.S. Department of Justice. Retrieved from http://www.ojp.usdoj.gov/bjs/pubascii/lpd03.txt

Hickman, M. J. (2006, June). *Citizen complaints about police use of force. LEMAS.* Washington, DC: U.S. Department of Justice. Retrieved from http://www.ojp.usdoj.gov/bjs/pub/pdf/ccpuf.pdf

Hispanics and the criminal justice system. (2009, April 7). *State News Service.* Retrieved from http://www.lexisnexis.com

Homant, R. J. (1989). Citizen attitudes and complaints. In W. G. Bailey (Ed.), *The encyclopedia of police science* (pp. 54–63). New York: Garland Press.

Homant, R. J., & Kennedy, D. B. (1985). Police perceptions of spouse abuse—A comparison of male and female officers. *Journal of Criminal Justice, 13,* 29–47.

Hoover, L. T. (2001, July). Police response to racial profiling: You can't win (NCJ 207424). *Illinois Law Enforcement Executive Forum,* 1–13.

Horne, P. (1980). *Women in law enforcement.* Springfield, IL: Charles Thomas.

House, C. H. (1993). The changing role of women in law enforcement. *Police Chief, 60,* 139–144.

Jackson, C., & Wallach, I. (1973). Perceptions of the police in a black community. In J. R. Snibbe & H. M. Snibbe (Eds.), *The urban police in transition* (pp. 382–403). Springfield, IL: Charles C. Thomas.

Jacobs, J. B., & Cohen, J. (1978). The impact of racial integration on the police. *Journal of Police Science and Administration, 6,* 179–183.

Jurik, N., Miller, S., & Forest, K. (2003). Diversity in blue: Lesbian and gay police officers in a masculine occupation. *Men and Masculinities, 5*(4), 355–385.

Jurkanin, T. J. (2001, July). Editorial. *Illinois Law Enforcement Executive Forum,* i.

Kane, E. (2001, July 15). In 2001 America, whites can't believe blacks treated unfairly. *Milwaukee Journal Sentinel,* p. B3.

Kanter, R. (1977). *Men and women of the corporation.* New York: Basic Books.

Kennedy, J. M. (1988, October 1). Latino FBI agents bias victims: Judge. *Journal Star,* p. A2.

Kerber, K. W., Andes, S. M., & Mittler, M. B. (1977). Citizen attitudes regarding the competence of female officers. *Journal of Police Science and Administration, 5,* 337–347.

Koenig, E. J. (1978). An overview of attitudes toward women in law enforcement. *Public Administration Review, 38,* 267–275.

Kranda, A. H. (1998). Women in policing: The importance of mentoring. *Police Chief, 65,* 54–56.

Kuykendall, J., & Burns, D. (1980). The black police officer: An historical perspective. *Journal of Contemporary Criminal Justice, 1,* 103–113.

Leinen, S. (1984). *Black police, white society.* New York: University Press.

Leinwald, D. (2009, October 3). Police try to uphold 'need to know' rule. *USA Today,* p. 3A.

Lin, T. (1987). *Chinese-American police officers in New York City.* Unpublished master's thesis, Western Illinois University—Macomb.

Linn, E., & Price, B. R. (1985). The evolving role of women in American policing. In A. S. Blumberg & E. Niederhoffer (Eds.), *The ambivalent force: Perspectives on the police* (3rd ed., pp. 69–80). New York: Holt, Rinehart and Winston.

Lott, J. R., Jr. (2000). Does a helping hand put others at risk? Affirmative action, police departments, and crime. *Economic Inquiry, 38,* 239–277.

Lurigio, A., Greenleaf, R., & Flexon, J. (2009). The effects of race on relationships with the police: A survey of African American and Latino youths in Chicago. *Western Criminology Review 10*(1), 29–41.

Lydersen, K. (2009, October 4). Shooting by police ignites racial tensions in Illinois town. *Washington Post.* Retrieved from http://www.washingtonpost.com/wp-dyn/content/article/2009/10/03/AR2009100302144.html

MacDonald, H. (2001). The myth of racial profiling. *City Journal, 11,* 14–27.

Margolis, R. (1971). *Who will wear the badge? A study of minority recruitment efforts in protective services.* Washington, DC: U.S. Government Printing Office.

Martin, S. E. (1993). Female officers on the move? A status report on women in policing. In R. G. Dunham & G. P. Alpert (Eds.), *Critical issues in policing: Contemporary issues* (pp. 312–329). Prospect Heights, IL: Waveland.

Martin, S. E., & Jurik, N. C. (2006). *Doing justice, doing gender: Women in legal and criminal justice occupations* (2nd ed.). Thousand Oaks, CA: Sage Publications.

Maxson, C., Hennigan, K., & Sloane, D. C. (2003, June). *Factors that influence public opinion of the police* (NIJ 197925). Retrieved on April 15, 2010, from http://www.ncjrs.gov/txtfiles1/nij/197925.txt

McCarty, W. P., Zhao, J., & Garland, B. E. (2007). Occupational stress and burnout between male and female police officers: Are there any gender differences? *Policing, 30*(4), 672.

McDowell, J. (1992, February 17). Are women better cops? *Time,* pp. 70–72.

McGeorge, J., & Wolfe, J. A. (1976). Comparison of attitudes between men and women police officers—A preliminary analysis. *Criminal Justice Review, 1,* 21–33.

McKeever, J., & Kranda, A. (2000, Summer). Recruitment and retention of qualified police personnel: A best practices guide. *Big Ideas for Smaller Departments, 1*(3), 14.

Minckler, D. (2008, May 14). *U.S. minority population continues to grow.* America.gov. Retrieved from http://www.america.gov/st/diversityenglish/2008/May/20080513175840zjsredna0.1815607html

Mors, T. M. (2005). The police/media relationship: Lessening the anxiety. *Law Enforcement Executive Forum, 5*(5), 51–54.

Moskos, P. C. (2008). Two shades of blue: Black and white in the blue brotherhood. *Law Enforcement Executive Forum, 5,* 57–86.

Mroz, J. (2008, April 6). Female police chiefs, a novelty no more. *New York Times.* Retrieved from http://www.nytimes.com/2008/04/06/nyregion/nyregionspecial2/06Rpolice.html

National Advisory Commission on Civil Disorders (Kerner Commission). (1968). *Report.* Washington, DC: U.S. Government Printing Office.

National Center for Women and Policing. (2001). *Recruiting & retaining women: A self-assessment guide for law enforcement.* Los Angeles: National Center for Women & Policing.

Navarro, M. (2009, February 10). For Hipanics, extra barriers can complicate college more. *The New York Times.* Section A, p. 14.

Nolte, L. W. (1979). *Fundamentals of public relations: Professional guidelines, concepts, and integrations.* New York: Pergamon.

O'Brien, J. T. (1978). Public attitudes toward the police. *Journal of Police Science and Administration, 6,* 303–310.

Palmiotto, M. J. (2000). *Community policing: A policing strategy for the 21st century.* Gaithersburg, MD: Aspen.

Pogrebin, M., Dodge, M., & Chatman, H. (2000). Reflections of African-American women on their careers in urban policing. Their experiences of racial and sexual discrimination. *International Journal of the Sociology of Law, 28,* 311–326.

Police continue to use excessive force against Hispanics [Editorial]. (2007, May 4). *La Prensa San Diego.* Retrieved from www.laprensa-sandiego.org/archieve/2007/may04–07/police .htm

Polisar, J., & Milgram, D. (1998). Strategies that work. *Police Chief, 65,* 42–52.

Poole, E. D., & Pogrebin, M. R. (1988). Factors affecting the decision to remain in policing: A study of women officers. *Journal of Police Science and Administration, 16,* 49–55.

Poteyeva, M., & Sun, I. Y. (2009), Gender differences in police officers' attitudes: Assessing current empirical evidence. *Journal of Criminal Justice, 37*(5), 512.

President's Commission on Law Enforcement and the Administration of Justice. (1967). *Task force report: The administration of justice.* Washington, DC: U.S. Government Printing Office.

Rabe-Hemp, C. E. (2008a). Female officers and the ethic of care: Does officer gender impact police behavior? *Journal of Criminal Justice. 36*(5), 426.

Rabe-Hemp, C. E. (2008b). Survival in an "all boys club": Policewomen and their fight for acceptance. *Policing 31*(2), 251.

Reuters. (2008, February 12). *Whites to become minority in U.S. by 2050.* Retrieved from http:// www.reuters.com/article/topNews/idUSN1110 177520080212?rpc=64

Reiss, A. J. (1968, July/August). Police brutality—Answers to key questions. *Trans-action, 5,* 15–16.

Reiss, A. J. (1970). *The police and the public.* New Haven, CT: Yale University Press.

Robbin, L. (2009, July 23). Officer defends arrest of Harvard professor. *New York Times.* Retrieved from http://www.nytimes.com/2009/07/24/us/ 24cambridge.html

Schaefer, R. T. (2000). *Racial and ethnic groups* (8th ed.). Upper Saddle River, NJ: Prentice-Hall.

Scott, E. L. (1993). Cultural awareness training. *Police Chief, 60,* 26–28.

Scoville, D. (2008). The blue mosaic. *Police. 32,* 42.

Seattle Police Department. (2009, November 6). SPD community outreach programs: Demographic advisory councils. *Seattle.gov.* Retrieved from

http://www.seattle.gov/police/programs/advisory/ default.htm

Sherman, L. J. (1975). Evaluation of policewomen on patrol in a suburban police department. *Journal of Police Science and Administration, 3,* 434–438.

Shusta, R. M., Levine, D. R., Harris, P. R., & Wong, H. Z. (1995). *Multicultural law enforcement: Strategies for peacekeeping in a diverse society.* Englewood Cliffs, NJ: Prentice-Hall.

Somvadee, C., & Morash, M. (2008). Dynamics of sexual harassment for policewomen working alongside men. *Policing, 31*(3), 485.

Sullivan, P. S. (1989). Minority officers: Current issues. In R. Dunham & G. Alpert (Eds.), *Critical issues in policing: Contemporary readings.* Prospect Heights, IL: Waveland.

Surette, R. (1992). *Media, crime & justice: Images and realities.* Pacific Grove, CA: Brooks/Cole.

Swan, R. D. (1988). The history of American women police. *Women Police, 22,* 10–13.

Sykes, G. (1978). *Criminology.* New York: Harcourt Brace Jovanovich.

Thornton, K., McKinnie, R. L., & Stetz, M. (1999, August 29). Treatment of minorities harsher, officers admit. *Union-Tribune.* Retrieved from http://www-psy.ucsd.edu/~eebbesen/psych 16298/162PolicePrejdice.html

Torres, S., & Vogel, R. E. (2001). Pre- and post-test differences between Vietnamese and Latino residents involved in a community policing experiment: Reducing fear of crime and improving attitudes towards the police. *Policing, 24,* 40–55.

U.S. Census Bureau. (2006). *Hispanics in the U.S.* Retrieved from http://www.census.gov/popula-tion/www/socdemo/hispanic/files/Internet_ Hispanic_in_US_2006.pdf

Walker, S. (2001). *Police accountability: The role of citizen oversight.* Belmont, CA: Wadsworth.

Walker, S., Spohn, C., & DeLone, M. (1995). *The color of justice: Race, ethnicity, and crime in America.* Belmont, CA: Wadsworth.

Weaver, G. (1992). Law enforcement in a culturally diverse society. *FBI Law Enforcement Bulletin, 61,* 1–9.

Weitzer, R., & Tuch, S. A. (2004, June). *Rethinking minority attitudes toward the police—Final technical report* (NCJ 207145). Washington, DC: U.S. Department of Justice. Retrieved on April 15, 2010, from http://www.ncjrs.gov/pdffiles1/nij/ grants/207145.pdf

Weitzer, R., & Tuch, S. A. (2008). Police–community relations in a majority-black city. *Journal of Research in Crime and Delinquency, 20*(10). Retrieved from http://www.skogan.org/files/Police_Community_Relations_in_Majority _Black_City.JRCD_2008.pdf

Wexler, J. G., & Logan, D. D. (1983). Sources of stress among women police officers. *Journal of Police Science and Administration, 11,* 46–53.

Williams, L. (1988, February 14). Police officers tell of strains of living as a "Black in Blue." *New York Times,* pp. 1, 26.

Wooditch, A. C., & Ruiz, J. M. (2009). Out of the closet and into the blue: An inquiry into biases in policing. *Police Forum, 18*(2). Retrieved from http://www.sulross.edu/policeforum/docs/archives/Volume_18_Number_2.pdf

Chapter 11

Barlow, D. E., & Barlow, M. H. (2000). *Policing in multicultural society: An American story.* Prospect Heights, IL: Waveland.

Boba, R. (2009). *Crime analysis with crime mapping.* Thousand Oaks, CA: Sage.

Braga, A. A. & Weisburd, D. L. (2007). *Police innovation and crime prevention: Lessons learned from police research over the past 20 years.* Paper presented at the National Institute of Justice Policing Research Workshop: Planning for the Future, Washington, DC, November 28–29, 2006. Retrieved from http://ncjrs.gov/pdf files1/nij/grants/218585.pdf

Braga, A. A. (2008a). *Crime prevention research review no. 2: Police enforcement strategies to prevent crime in hot spot areas.* Washington, DC: U.S. Department of Justice Office of Community Oriented Policing Services.

Braga, A. A. (2008b). Pulling levers focused deterrence strategies and the prevention of gun homicide. *Journal of Criminal Justice, 36,* 332.

Breci, M. G. (1997). The transition to community policing: The department's role in upgrading officers' skills. *Policing, 20,* 766–776.

Brown, B. (2004). Community policing in a diverse society. *Law Enforcement Executive Forum, 4*(5), 49–56.

Buerger, M. E., & Mazerolle, L. G. (1998). Third-party policing: A theoretical analysis of an emerging trend. *Justice Quarterly, 15,* 301–328.

Bureau of Justice Statistics. (1999). State and local law enforcement statistics. Retrieved from http://www.nrc.uscg.mil/insum2005/facilityfire1.html

Burgreen, B., & McPherson, N. (1992). Neighborhood policing without a budget increase. *The Police Chief, 59,* 31–33.

Cardarelli, A. P., McDevitt, J., & Baum, K. (1998). The rhetoric and reality of community policing in small and medium-sized cities and towns. *Policing, 21,* 397–415.

Carey, L. R. (1994). Community policing for the suburban department. *Police Chief, 61,* 24–26.

Cherney, A. (2008). Harnessing the crime control capacities of third parties. *Policing 31*(4), 631.

COPS Office. (2008, July 28). CHRP announcement toolkit. Retrieved August 6, 2010, from http://www.cops.usdoj.gov/Default.asp?Item= 2208

Cornish, D. B., & Clarke, R. V. (2003). Opportunities, precipitators and criminal decisions: A reply to Wortley's critique of situational crime prevention. *Crime Prevention Studies, 16,* 41–96.

Cox, J. F. (1992). Small departments and community policing. *FBI Law Enforcement Bulletin, 61,* 1–4.

Culf, A. (2008, June 22). Police praised as German hooligans are detained. *Guardian News and Media.* Retrieved from http://www.guardian.co .uk/football/2006/jun/22/worldcup2006.sport5

Dolan, H. P. (1994). Community policing: Coping with internal backlash. *The Police Chief, 61,* 28–32.

Eck, J. E., & Spelman, W. (1988). *Problem-solving: Problem-oriented policing in Newport News.* Washington, DC: National Institute of Justice.

Garner, R. (2004). Solution-oriented policing: Application in practice. *Law Enforcement Executive Forum, 4*(5), 43–47.

Glasser, J. (2000). The case of the missing cops. *U.S. News & World Report, 129,* p. 22.

Goldstein, H. (1979). Improving policing: A problem oriented approach. *Crime and Delinquency, 25,* 236–258.

Goldstein, H. (1990). *Problem-oriented policing.* New York: McGraw-Hill.

Greene, J. R. (2006). *The encyclopedia of police science* (3rd ed.). Boca Raton, FL: CRC Press.

Harcourt, B. E., & Thacher, D. E. (2005, October 17). Is broken windows policing broken? *Legal Affairs*. Retrieved from http://www.legalaffairs.org/webexclusive/debateclub_brokenwindows1005.msp

Hartnett, S. M., & Skogan, W. G. (1999, April). Community policing: Chicago's experience (NCJ 177464). *National Institute of Justice Journal*, 2–11.

Hatler, R. W. (1990, October). Operation CLEAN: Reclaiming City Neighborhoods. *FBI Law Enforcement Bulletin, 59*, 23–25.

Hickman, M. J., & Reeves, B. A. (2001). *Community policing in local police departments, 1997 and 1999*. Washington, DC: Bureau of Justice Statistics.

Holt, T. J., Blevins, K. R., & Kuhns, J. B. (2008). Examining the displacement practices of johns with on-line data. *Journal of Criminal Justice, 36*, 522–528.

Institute for Pure and Applied Mathematics. (2007). *Crime hot spots: Behavioral, computational and mathematical models*. Retrieved from http://www.ipam.ucla.edu/programs/chs2007/

Jensen, C. J. (2006). Consuming and applying research evidence-based policing. *The Police Chief, 73*, 2–5.

Jesilow, P., Meyer, J., Parsons, D., & Tegler, W. (1998). Evaluating problem-oriented policing: A quasi-experiment. *Policing, 21*, 449–464.

Kane, R. J. (2000). Permanent beat assignments in association with community policing: Assessing the impact on police officers' field activity. *Justice Quarterly, 17*, 259–278.

Kobolt, J. R., & Tucker, K. A. (2004). The fourth era of American policing: Strategic management. *Law Enforcement Executive Forum, 4*(5), 61–69.

Liederbach, J., Fritsch, E. J., Carter, D. L., & Bannister, A. (2008). Exploring the limits of collaboration in community policing: A direct comparison of police and citizen views. *Policing, 31*(2), 271–291.

Louisiana Department of State Civil Service. (2007). *Dual career ladder*. Baton Rouge, LA: Author. Retrieved from http://www.civilservice.louisiana.gov/HRHandbook/Classification/DualCareerLadder.asp

Lurigo, A. J., & Rosenbaum, D. P. (1994). The impact of community policing on police personnel: A review of the literature. In D. P. Rosenbaum (Ed.), *The challenge of community policing: Testing the promises* (pp. 147–163). Thousand Oaks, CA: Sage.

Mazerolle, L., & Ransley, J. (2006). *Governance, risk and crime control*. New York: Cambridge University Press.

McDonald, P. P. (2002). *Managing police operations*. Belmont, CA: Wadsworth/Thomson.

McGarrell, E. F., Chermak, S., & Weiss, A. (2002). *Reducing firearms violence through directed patrol: Final report on the evaluation of the Indianapolis Police Department's directed patrol project*. Washington, DC: U.S. Department of Justice.

McGarrell, E. F., & Freilich, J. D. (2007). Intelligence-led policing as a framework for responding to terrorism. *Journal of Criminal Justice, 23*, 142–148.

Meares, T. L. (2006). Third-party policing: A critical view. In D. Weisburd & A. Braga (Eds.), *Police innovation: Contrasting perspectives*. New York: Cambridge University Press.

Memphis Police Department. (2009). *Leaders of tomorrow*. Retrieved from http://www.memphispolice.org

Mitchell, M., & Casey, J. (2007). *Police leadership and management*. Annandale, Australia: Federation Press.

National Institute of Crime Prevention. (2009). *Crime prevention through environmental design*. Retrieved from http://www.cptedtraining.net

National Response Team. (2000). *Incident command system/unified command (ICS/UC): Technical assistance document*. Retrieved from http://www.nrt.org/Production/NRT/NRTWeb.nsf/AllAttachmentsByTitle/SA-52ICSUCTA/$File/ICSUCTA.pdf?OpenElement

National Response Team. (2005).

Offer, C. (1993). C-OP fads and emperors without clothes. *Law Enforcement News, 19*, 8.

Oliver, W. M. (2006). The Era of Homeland Security: September 11, 2001 to . . . *Journal of California Law Enforcement, 40*(3), 19–30.

Oliver, W. M., & Bartgis, E. (1998). Community policing: A conceptual frame work. *Policing, 21*, 490–509.

Palmiotto, M. J. (2000). *Police misconduct: A reader for the 21st century*. Upper Saddle River, NJ: Prentice-Hall.

Pisani, A. L. (1992). Dissecting community policing—Part 1. *Law Enforcement News, 18*, 13.

Philadelphia Police Department. (2009). *Compstat process*. Retrieved from http://www.ppdonline.org/hq_compstat.php

Ratcliffe, J. H., & Guidetti, R. (2008). State police investigative structure and the adoption of intelligence-led policing. *Policing, 31,* 109–119.

Reed, C. (2008). The community policing umbrella. *FBI Law Enforcement Bulletin, 77*(11), 22–25.

Sacramento Police Department. (2009). File online reports now. Retrieved from http://www.sacpd .org/reports/fileonline/filenow

Sadd, S., & Grinc, R. M. (2000). Implementation challenges in community policing. In R. W. Glensor, M. E. Correia, & J. K. Peak (Eds.), *Policing communities: Understanding crime and solving problems* (pp. 97–116). Los Angeles: Roxbury.

Sadovi, C. (2009, April 2). Chicago police plan curfew crackdown. *Chicago Breaking News.* Retrieved August 6, 2010, from http://www.chicagobreaking news.com/2009/04/curfew-chicago-police-crack down-students-killed.html

Scrivner, E. (2004). The impact of September 11 on community policing. In L. Fridell & M. A. Wycoff (Eds.), *Community policing: The past, present, and future.* Washington, DC: Police Executive Research Forum.

Sherman, L. (1998). *Evidence-based policing. Ideas in American policing.* Washington, DC: Police Foundation. Retrieved from http://www.police-foundation.org/pdf/sherman.pdf

Sherman, L., Shaw, J. W., & Rogan, D. P. (1995). The Kansas City gun experiment. Washington, DC: National Institute of Justice. In McGarrell, E., Chermak, S. & Weiss, A. (2002). *Reducing firearms violence through directed police patrol: Final report on the evaluation of the Indianapolis Police Department's directed patrol project.* Washington, D.C: U. S. Department of Justice.

Silverman, E. (2006). Compstat's innovation. In D.L. Weisburd & A. Braga (Eds.), *Police innovation: Contrasting perspectives.* Cambridge, UK: Cambridge University Press.

Skogan, W. (1992). *Impact of policing on social disorder: Summary of findings.* Washington, DC: U.S. Department of Justice, Office of Justice Programs.

Skogan, W., & Frydl, K. (2004). *Fairness and effectiveness in policing: The evidence.* Washington, DC: The National Academies Press.

Skolnick, J. H., & Bayley, D. H. (1986). *The new blue line: Police innovation in six American cities.* New York: Free Press.

Sousa, W., & Kelling, G. (2006). Of "broken windows," criminology, and criminal justice. In D. L. Weisburd & A. Braga (Eds.), *Police innovation: Contrasting perspectives* (pp. 77–97), Cambridge, UK: Cambridge University Press.

Stevens, D. J. (2001). *Case studies in community policing.* Upper Saddle River, NJ: Prentice-Hall.

Stevens, D. J. (2008). *An introduction to American policing.* Sudbury, MA: Jones and Bartlett.

Tafoya, W. L. (2000). The current and future state of community policing. In R. W. Glensor, M. E. Correia, & K. J. Peak (Eds.), *Policing communities: Understanding crime and solving problems* (pp. 304–314). Los Angeles: Roxbury.

Toch, H., & Grant, J. D. (1991). *Police as problem solvers.* Newark: Plenum.

Trojanowicz, R. C. (1990). Community policing is not police-community relations. *FBI Law Enforcement Bulletin, 59,* 6–11.

Trojanowicz, R. C., & Bucqueroux, B. (1992). Preventing individual and systemic corruption. *Footprints, 4,* 1–3.

Trojanowicz, R. C., Kappeler, V. E., Gaines, L. K., & Bucqueroux, B. (1998). *Community policing: A contemporary perspective* (2nd ed.). Cincinnati, OH: Anderson.

Vance, N., & Trani, B. (2008, Fall). Situational prevention and the reduction of white collar crime. *Journal of Leadership Accountability and Ethics,* 9–13.

Walker, S. (2008). *The police in America* (3rd ed.). Boston: McGraw-Hill.

Walters, P. M. (1993). Community-oriented policing: A blend of strategies. *FBI Law Enforcement Bulletin, 62,* 20–23.

Weis, J. (2008, November 15). *CAPS youth sports program announced.* Retrieved from http://www .abclocal.go.com/wls/story?section=news/local &id=6508022

Weisburd, D., & Braga, A. (2006). Hot spots policing as a model for police innovation. In D. Weisburd & A. Braga (Eds.). *Police innovation: Contrasting perspectives* (pp. 225–244). New York: Cambridge University Press.

Welsh, B. C. (2006). Evidence-based policing for crime prevention. In D. Weisburд & A. Braga (Eds.), *Police innovation: Contrasting perspectives* (pp. 305–321). New York: Cambridge University Press.

Wilber, D. (2003, September 2). Baltimore is among cities beefing up intelligence. *Baltimore Sun.* Retrieved from http://www.baltimoresun.com

Williams, H. (2003). *Foreword.* In Willis, L., Mastrofski, S., & Weisburd, D. (2003). Compstat in practice: An in-depth analysis of three cities. Washington, D.C.: Police Foundation. Retrieved from http://www.policefoundation.org/pdf/compstatinpractice.pdf

Wilson, J., Hiromoto, T. F., Tita, G., & Riley, J. (2004). *Homicide in San Diego: A case study analysis* (WR-142-OJP). Santa Monica, CA: Rand.

Wilson, J., & Kelling, G. (1982). Broken windows: The police and neighborhood safety. *Atlantic Monthly, 24*(9), 29–38.

Zanfardino, K. (2009). *Steps to creating dual-career ladders at your company.* Retrieved from http://www.hrtools.com/insights/kelley_zanfardino/steps_to_creating_dual_career_ladders_at_your_company

Zhao, J., Thurman, Q. C., & Lovrich, N. P. (2000). Community-oriented policing across the U.S. In R. W. Glensor, M. E. Correia, & K. J. Peak (Eds.), *Policing communities: Understanding crime and solving problems* (pp. 229–238). Los Angeles: Roxbury.

Chapter 12

Achanta, A. (2006, May). *Non-linear acoustic concealed weapons detector.* Blacksburg, VA: Luna Innovations. Retrieved May 19, 2010, from http://www.stormingmedia.us/05/0520/A052054.html?searchTerms=Non-linear~acoustic~concealed~weapons~detector

Bair, S. (2009). New trends in advanced crime and intelligence analysis: Understanding the utility and capability of ATAC in law enforcement. *Crime Mapping News 8*(1), 6–9.

Boba, R. (2001). *Introductory guide to crime analysis and mapping.* Washington, DC: Community Oriented Policing Services. Retrieved from http://www.policefoundationorg/pdf.introguide.pdf

Boba, R. (2009). *Crime analysis with crime mapping.* Thousand Oaks, CA: Sage.

Bonsor, K. (2010). *How the future force warrior will work.* Retrieved from http://science.howstuffworks.com/ffw.htm/

Brickhouse Security. (2010). *Portable voice lie detector.* Retrieved March 22, 2010, from http://www.brickhousesecurity.com/portable-lie-detector.html

Chan, J. B. L. (2001). The technological game: How information technology is transforming police practice. *Criminology and Criminal Justice, 1*(2), 139–159.

Chansanchai, A. (2008, April 16). *No lie: Polygraph exams go portable. Shrinking technology means professional examiners can easily come to you.* Retrieved March 22, 2010, from http://www.msnbc.msn.com/id/24114951/ns/technology_and_science-tech_and_gadgets/

City of Baltimore. (2010). *Baltimore citistat.* Retrieved from http://www.baltimorecity.gov

Connect802. (n.d.). *Understanding wireless IP cameras.* Retrieved May 19, 2010, from http://www.connect802.com/camera_facts.htm

Daubert v. Merrell Dow Pharmaceuticals, Inc., 43 F. 3d 1311—Court of Appeals, 9th Circuit (1995).

Deedman, B. (2008, April 9). *New anti-terror weapon: Hand-held lie detector.* Retrieved March 21, 2010, from http:// www.msnbc.msn.com/id/23926278/

DeLorenzi, D., Shane, J. M., Amendola, K. L. (2006). The compstat process: Managing performance on the pathway to leadership. *The Police Chief, 73*(9), 1–6. Retrieved from http://policechiefmagazine.org

DuBois, J., Skogan, W., Hartnett, S., Bump, N., & Morris, D. (2007, August). *CLEAR and I-CLEAR: A report on new information technology in Chicago and Illinois.* Evanston, IL: Illinois Criminal Justice Authority. Retrieved March 20, 2010, from http://www.icjia.org/public/pdf/ResearchReports/CLEAR%20and%20ICLEAR%20report%20Aug%202007.pdf

Farrell, M. (2010, March 1). Obama signs Patriot Act extension without reforms. *The Christian Science Monitor.* Retrieved May 20, 2010, from http://www.csmonitor.com/USA/Politics/2010/0301/Obama-signs-Patriot-Act-extension-without-reforms

Federal Bureau of Investigation. (2008, March 13). *Integrated automated fingerprint identification system or IAFIS.* Retrieved March 22, 2010, from http://www.fbi.gov/hq/cjisd/iafis.htm

Firman, J. R. (2006). Deconstructing compstat to clarify its intent. *Criminology and Public Policy, 2*(3), 457–460.

Geoghegan, S. (2006). Compstat revolutionizes contemporary policing. *Law and Order, 54*(4), 42–46.

Hand germs as evidence. (2010, March 19). Retrieved March 23, 2010, from http://www.silobreaker.com/hand-germs-as-evidence-5_2263305544666185766 [url doesn't work]

Harris, T. (n.d.). How fingerprint scanners work. *HowStuffWorks.com.* Retrieved March 23, 2010, from http://www.computer.howstuffworks.com/fingerprint-scanner.htm

Harris, T. (2001, May 8). How wiretapping works. *HowStuffWorks.com.* Retrieved May 20, 2010, from http://people.howstuffworks.com/wiretapping.htm

Harris, T. (2008). How body armor works. *HowStuffWorks.com.* Retrieved from http://science.howstuffworks.com/body-armor.htm

Hart, S. V. (2007*). Less-than-lethal weapons.* Washington, DC: U.S. Department of Justice. Retrieved from http://www.ojp.usdoj.gov/nij/speeches/aviation.htm

Helfand, L. (2010, February 11). Clearwater police use computer language program Rosetta Stone to enhance communication. *St Petersburg Times.* Retrieved March 20, 2010, from http://www.tampabay.com/news/publicsafety/article1072347.ece

Hughes, T. (2010, March 4). Police partner with license plate readers. *USA Today,* p. 3A.

Human Genome Project Information. (2009, June 16). *DNA forensics.* Washington, DC: U.S. Department of Energy, Office of Science. Retrieved March 23, 2010, from http://www.ornl.gov/sci/techresources/Human_Genome/elsi/forensics.shtml

International Association of Chiefs of Police [IACP]. (2005). *In-car camera report.* Alexandria, VA: IACP Research Center Directorate. Retrieved March 20, 2010, from http://www.theiacp.org/PublicationsGuides/Projects/InCarCameraTechnicalAssistance/2005IACPIncarCameraReport/tabid/340/Default.aspx

International Biosciences. (2010). *DNA tests: Impact on death row.* Retrieved March 23, 2010, from http://www.ibdna.com/regions/UK/EN/?page=impactOnDeathRow

Jussila, J. (2001). Future police operations and non-lethal weapons. *Medicine, Conflict and Survival, 17*(3), 248–259.

Kaye, D. H. (2001). Bioethical objections to DNA databases for law enforcement: Questions and answers. *Seton Hall Law Review, 31*(4), 936–948.

Lakoski, J. M., Murray, W. B., & Kenny, J. M. (2000). *The advantages and limitations of calmatives for use as a non-lethal technique.* University Park, PA: Pennsylvania State University. In Weiss, J.D.

(2008). Calming down: Could sedative drugs be a less-lethal option? National Institute of Justice. Washington, D.C.: U.S. Department of Justice. Retrieved from http://www.ojp.usdoj.gov/nij/journals/261/calmatives.htm

Maghan, J., O'Reilly, G. W., & Chong Ho Shon, P. (2002). Technology, policing, and implications of in-car videos. *Police Quarterly, 5*(1), 25–42.

May, J. (2007, June). Deconstructing Daubert: Rule 702 and non-scientific evidence. *Champion Magazine,* 18.

Michigan State Police. (2010). *Speed measurement devices.* Retrieved March 30, 2010, from http://www.michigan.gov/msp/0,1607,7–123–1593_47093_25802–16134—,00.html

Moser, P. (2008, January 19). *The vital role of forensic science: Forensics has led to increased conviction rates.* Retrieved March 22, 2010, from http://forensicscience.suite101.com/article.cfm/the_role_of_forensic_science#ixzz0iveRxHD1

Most Wanted Criminal and Fugitive Database Websites. (n.d.). Retrieved May 19, 2010, from http://www.indexoftheweb.com/Information/WantedCriminalDatabases.htm

National Human Genome Research Institute. (2009). *DNA microchip technology.* Retrieved March 23, 2010, from http://www.genome.gov/10000205

National Institute of Justice. (2008a). *Body armor.* Washington, DC: U.S. Department of Justice. Retrieved from http://www.ojp.usdoj.gov/nij/topics/technology/body-armor/welcome.htm

National Institute of Justice. (2008b). *Types of less-lethal devices.* Washington, DC: U.S. Department of Justice. Retrieved from http://www.ojp.usdoj.gov/nij/topics/technology/less-lethal/types.htm

National Institute of Justice. (2009a). *MAPS: Automobiles and traffic safety.* Washington, DC: U.S. Department of Justice. Retrieved from http://www.ojp.usdoj.gov/nij/maps/traffic-safety-projects.htm

National Institute of Justice. (2009b). *MAPS: Geospatial tools.* Washington, DC: U.S. Department of Justice. Retrieved from http://www.ojp.usdoj.gov/nij/maps/tools.htm

NetworkCameraReviews.com. (2009).*What is an IP camera?* Retrieved May 19, 2010, from http://www.networkcamerareviews.com

Niederberger, M. (2008, September 29). Police device finds speeders without radar. *Pittsburgh Post-Gazette.* Retrieved March 30, 2010, from http://www.policeone.com/police-products/traffic-enforcement/articles/1738131-Police-device-finds-speeders-without-radar/

Nordland, R. (2008, December 18). The evil solution. *Newsweek.* Retrieved May 19, 2010, from http://www.newsweek.com/id/175980/page/3

Nunn, S. (2001). Police information technology: Assessing the effects of computerization on urban police functions. *Public Administration Review, 61*(2), 221–234.

Officer.com. (2010). *Talon net gun system.* Retrieved from http://www.directory.officer.com

O'Neill, R. (2004, December 13). Police given computer spy powers. *The Sydney Morning Herald.* Retrieved from http://www.smh.comau/news/National/Police-given-computer-spy-powers/2004/12/12/1102786954590.html

Philadelphia Police Department. (2010a). *CompStat process.* Retrieved from www.policeone.com/.../articles/1995855-Pa-police-to-watch-schools-with-help-of-laptops

Philadelphia Police Department. (2010b). *Technology: Mobile data terminals.* Retrieved March 16, 2010, from http://www.ppdonline.org/ops/ops_tech_mdt.php [url doesn't work]

Paterra, P. (2010). Pa. police to watch schools with help of laptops: The video feeds are to be used only in emergencies. *PoliceOne.com.* Retrieved from http://www.policeone.com/police-technology/mobile-computers/articles/1995855-Pa-police-to-watch-schools-with-help-of-laptops/

RadarGuns.com. (2010). *Laser Radar: Lidar, Ladar Facts.* Retrieved March 30, 2010, from http://www.RadarGuns.com

San Francisco Police Department. (2010). *SFPD CompStat.* Retrieved from http://sf-police.org

Santiago, K. (2009, June 22). Cell phone tracking software helps police, emergency workers. *The Star-Ledger.* Retrieved March 23, 2010, from http://www.nj.com/news/index.ssf/2009/06/cell_phone_tracking_software_h.html

Sawicki, D. S. (2009). Police traffic radar handbook: A comprehensive guide to speed measuring systems. *CopRadar.com.* Retrieved March 29, 2010, from http://www.CopRadar.com

Schultz, P. D. (2008). The future is here: Technology in police departments. *The Police Chief, 75*(6), 19–27.

Seaskate, Inc. (1998). *The evolution and development of police technology: A technical report prepared for The National Committee on Criminal Justice Technology.* Washington, DC: National Institute of Justice. Retrieved May 19, 2010, from http://www.police-technology.net/id59.html

Singel, R. (2007, August 28). Inside DCSNet, the FBI's nationwide eavesdropping network: Surveillance system lets FBI play back recordings as they are captured, like TiVo. *ABC News.* Retrieved April 2, 2010, from http://www.abcnews.go.com/Technology/story?id=3535528&page=1

Spielman, F. (2004, October 27). Computers bringing police files to cop cars in Chicago: "Squad cars of the future." *The Associated Press.* Retrieved March 20, 2010, from http://www.police-grantshelp.com/news/93093-Computers-Bringing-Police-Files-to-Cop-Cars-in

Tompkins, D. (2006). Body armor safety initiative: To protect and serve . . . better. *NIJ Journal,* 254. Retrieved from http://www.ojp.usdoj.gov/nij/journals/254/body_armor_html

Traffic Safety Systems, Inc. (2010, March 30). *VAS-CAR-plus® home page.* Richmond, VA: Author. Retrieved March 30, 2010, from http://www.vascarplus.com

United States v. Finley, 2007 U.S. App. LEXIS 1806 (5th Cir. 2007)

University of Maryland. (2010). *Implementing and institutionalizing compstat in Maryland.* Retrieved from http://www.compstat.umd.edu/faq.php

White, B. (2009, June, 3). New programs put crime stats on the map. *Wall Street Journal,* p. D1.

White, M., & Wiles, T. (2009). Jacksonville sheriff's office: Mapping with text analysis. *Crime Mapping News, 8*(1), 1–5.

Wild, N. (2003, March). Handheld concealed weapons detector development. *JAYCOR.* Retrieved May 19, 2010, from http://www.stormingmedia.us/keywords/infrared_detection.html

Willis, J. J., Mastrofski, S. D., & Weisburd, D. (2003). *Compstat in practice: An in-depth analysis of three cities.* Washington, DC: Police Foundation. Retrieved from http://www.policefoundation.org/pdf/compstatinpractice.pdf

Wilson, L., & Spencer, W. (2001). The impact of kyllo: Don't discard those thermal imaging devices. *The Police Chief, 68*(6), 10–12.

Worsley School. (2001). *Fingerprints.* Retrieved March 23, 2010, from http://www.worsleyschool.net/science/files/finger/prints.html

Zakhary, Y. A. (2007). Ballistic body armor: A chief's refresher course. *The Police Chief 74*(12), 1–7. Retrieved from http://policechiefmagazine.org

Zetter, K. (2009, May 19). FBI use of Patriot Act authority increased dramatically in 2008. *Wired.* Retrieved May 20, 2010, from http://www.wired.com/threatlevel/2009/05/fbi-use-of-patriot-act-authority-increased-dramatically-in-2008/

Chapter 13

Abadinsky, H. (2010). *Organized Crime* (9th ed.). Belmont, CA: Wadsworth.

Albanese, J., Das, D., & Verma, A. (2003). *Organized crime: World perspectives*. Upper Saddle River, NJ: Prentice-Hall.

Arizona immigration law faces new challenges. (2010, April 26). *CBS News*. Retrieved from http://www.cbsnews.com/stories/2010/04/27/national/main6436027.shtml

Braithwaite, J. (1985). White collar crime. In R. Turner & J. Short (Eds.), *Annual review of sociology* (Vol. 11, pp. 1–25).

Center for Defense Information. (n.d.). *Chronology of major terrorist attacks against U.S. targets*. Retrieved May, 30, 2010, from http://www.cdi.org/terrorism/chronology.html

Davies, H., & Plotkin, M. (2005). *Protecting your community from terrorism: The strategies for local law enforcement series Vol. 5: Partnerships to Promote Homeland Security, Police Executive Research Forum*. Washington, DC: U.S. Department of Justice, Office of Community Oriented Policing Services.

Esposito, R., James, M., & Schabner, D. (2010, May 2). COPS: Times Square Car Bomber Got the Wrong Fertilizer. *ABC World News*. Retrieved from http://abcnews.go.com/WN/times-square-bomb-scare-york-authorities-probe-evidence/story?id=10532755&page=1

Federal Bureau of Investigation. (2010a). *International training*. Washington, DC: Author. Retrieved from http://www.fbi.gov/hq/td/academy/itp/itp.htm

Federal Bureau of Investigation. (2010b). *Organized crime*. Washington, DC: Author. http://www.fbi.gov/hq/cid/orgcrime/glossary.htm

Friedrichs, D. (2007). *Trusted criminals: White collar crime in contemporary society* (3rd ed.). Belmont, CA: Thompson Higher Education.

Geis, G. (2002). White collar crime: What is it? In D. Shichor, L. Gaines, & R. Ball (Eds.), *Readings in white collar crime* (pp. 7–25). Prospect Heights, IL: Waveland Press.

Helmkamp, J., Ball, J., & Townsend, K. (1996). *Definitional dilemma: Can and should there be a universal definition of white collar crime?* Morgantown, WV: National White Collar Crime Center.

Hu, W. (2001, November 14). A nation challenged: The suburbs; small towns find their ingenuity tested by terrorist threat. *New York Times*, p. B6.

Illinois Law Enforcement Training and Standards Board. (2003). *Basic law enforcement recruit training curriculum*. Springfield, IL: Printed by the authority of the state of Illinois.

International Association for the Study of Organized Crime. (2010). *Home page*. Retrieved February 11, 2010, from http://www.iasoc.net/#

International Atomic Energy Agency. (2006, August 21). *Trafficking in nuclear and radioactive material in 2005: I.A.E.A. releases latest illicit trafficking database statistics*. Retrieved from http://www.iaea.org/NewsCenter/News/2006/traffickingstats2005.html

Levinson, A. (1999). Twenty-first century crime goes global. *Crime & Justice International, 15*, 9–10, 33.

Lyman, M., & Potter, G. (2006). *Organized crime* (4th ed.). Upper Saddle River, NJ: Prentice Hall.

Martin, G. (2006). *Understanding terrorism* (2nd ed.). Thousand Oaks, CA: Sage.

McFayden, E., Jr. (2010, January 3). Global implications of white collar crime. *Social Science Research Network*, Available at SSRN: http://ssrn.com/abstract=1530685

McHugh, S. (1998). Intelligence, terrorism, and the new world disorder. In C. Moors & R. Ward (Eds.), *Terrorism and the new world disorder* (pp. 57–59). Chicago: Office of International Criminal Justice.

Mueller, R., III. (2001, December). Responding to terrorism. *FBI Law Enforcement Bulletin, 70*, 12–14.

Possley, M. (1983, August 5). Operation greylord: A federal probe of court corruption sets the standard for future investigations. *Chicago Tribune*. Retrieved from http://www.chicagotribune.com/news/politics/chi-chicagodays-greylord-story,0,4025843.story

President's Commission on Organized Crime. (1986). *The impact: Organized crime today*. Washington, DC: U.S. Government Printing Office.

Racketeer Influenced and Corrupt Organizations ("RICO") Act, 18 U.S.C. §§ 1961–68

Rosoff, S., Pontell, H., & Tillman, R. (2007). *Profit without honor: White collar crime and the looting of America* (4th ed.). Upper Saddle River, NJ: Prentice-Hall.

Scaramella, G. (1997). Cooperative efforts between criminal organizations. *Crime & Justice International, 13*(10), 8–9.

Scaramella, G. (1998). *Containing organized crime: Implications for continuing criminal justice education.* Unpublished doctoral dissertation, Northern Illinois University.

Scaramella, G., & Rodriguez, R., (2004). Local law enforcement and transnational crime preparedness. *Illinois Law Enforcement Executive Forum, 4*(4), 169–181.

Seaton, R. (2001, November 28). Federal research center is helping: County workers prepare for disaster. *St. Louis Post-Dispatch*, p. 2.

Shelley, L. (2001, August 6). Crime victimizes both society and democracy. *Global Issues: Arresting Transnational Crime*, p. 2. Retrieved August 10, 2003, from http://usinfo.state.gov/journals/itgic/0801/ijge/gj06.htm

Sheptycki, J. (2007). Criminology and the transnational condition: A contribution to international political sociology. *International Political Sociology, 1*(4), 391.

Simmons, K. (2001, December 11). Plotting a new course: Sept. 11 prompts some state colleges to tailor studies of world issues. *Atlanta Journal and Constitution*, p. 1D.

Simonsen, C., & Spindlove, J. (2000). *Terrorism today: The past, the players, the future.* Upper Saddle River, NJ: Prentice-Hall.

Sterling, C. (1990). *Octopus.* New York: Simon & Schuster.

Sterling, C. (1994). *Thieves' world.* New York: Simon & Schuster.

Sutherland, E. (1983). *White collar crime: The uncut version.* New Haven, CT: Yale University Press.

Terrorism, Transnational Crime and Corruption Center. (2010). *Publications page.* Retrieved March 17, 2010, from http://policy-traccc.gmu.edu/publications/publications.html

United Nations Crime Prevention and Criminal Justice Division (2009). *United Nations Surveys on Crime Trends and the Operations of Criminal Justice Systems (CTS).* Retrieved from http://www.unodc.org/unodc/en/data-and-analysis/United-Nations-Surveys-on-Crime-Trends-and-the-Operations-of-Criminal-Justice-Systems.html

United Nations Office on Drugs and Crime. (2009, January). *What does environmental crime have in common with organized crime?* Retrieved from http://www.unodc.org/unodc/en/frontpage/what-does-environmental-crime-have-in-common-with-organised-crime.html

United States Criminal Code. *Crimes and Criminal Procedure, Title 18, Part I.* Retrieved from http://www.law.cornell.edu/uscode/18/usc_sup_01_18.html

U.S. General Accounting Office. (2001). *Homeland security: Key elements of a risk management approach.* Washington, DC: U.S. Government Printing Office.

Ward, R., Kiernan, K., & Marbrey, D. (2006). *Homeland security: An introduction.* Southington, CT: Anderson Publishing.

White House. (2001, October 8). *President establishes Office of Homeland Security.* Retrieved January 8, 2002, from http://www.whitehouse.gov/news/releases/2001/10/ 20011008.html

Williams, P. (1999). Getting rich and getting even: Transnational threats in the twenty-first century. In S. Einstein & M. Amir (Eds.), *Organized crime: Uncertainties and dilemmas* (pp. 19–63). Chicago: Office of International Criminal Justice.

Worldwide Incidents Tracking System. (2010). *Terrorist attacks grouped by country for the year 2009.* Retrieved May 1, 2010, from https://wits.nctc.gov/FederalDiscoverWITS/index.do?t=Reports&Rcv=Incident&N=0

Chapter 14

Anonymous. (2001). Operation cooperation. *Sheriff, 53*(1), 42–45.

Apuzzo, M. (2004, November 29). Mall security gets terrorism training: Gripping a bag tightly defined as hallmark of terrorism. *Associated Press.* Retrieved April 23, 2010, from http://www.prisonplanet.com

ASIS International. (2006, February 7). *Press Release: Workplace security legislation supported by ASIS International—Implemented by Department of Justice.* Alexandria, VA: Author. Retrieved April 23, 2010, from http://www.asisonline.org

Associated Criminal Justice and Security Consultants, LLC. (2005, June). *Evaluation of basic training programs in law enforcement, security and corrections.* Unpublished research paper.

Bennett, J. R. (2009, May 18). Police: Going private. *ISN Security Watch.* Retrieved from http://www .isn.ethz.ch/isn/Current-Affairs/Security-Watch/ Detail/?lng=en&id=100297

Bureau of Labor Statistics. (2009). *Occupational outlook handbook, 2008–09 edition: Private detectives and investigators.* Washington, DC: U.S. Department of Labor. Retrieved from http:// www.bls.gov/oco/ocos157.htm

Copeland, L. (2009, November 16). State police forces shrink: Shortages leave areas unpatrolled. *USA Today,* p. 1A.

COPS. (2004). *National policy summit: Building private security/public policing partnerships.* Washington, DC: U.S. Department of Justice. Retrieved April 22, 2010, from http://www.copsusdoj.gov/

Critical Intervention Services. (2009). *Threat management services/Executive protection.* Retrieved from http://www.cisworldservices.org/execu tiveprotection.html

Cunningham, W., & Taylor, T. (1985). *Private security and police in America: The Hallcrest report,* Portland, OR: Chancellor Press.

Fischer, R., Halibozek, E., & Green, G. (2008). *Introduction to security* (8th ed.). Boston: Butterworth-Heinemann.

Gips, M. A. (2002, June). They secure the body electric. *Security Management,* 77–81.

Gips, M. A. (2003, February 1). Survey assesses sports facility security (News and Trends). *The Free Library.* Retrieved April 23, 2010, from http://www .thefreelibrary.com/Survey assesses sports facility security. (News and Trends).-a097873063

Goldstein, A. (2007, January 2). The private arm of the law. *The Washington Post.* Retrieved from http://www.washingtonpost.com

Gunter, W., & Kidwell, J. (2004, June). Law enforcement and private security liaison: Partnerships for cooperation. *International Foundation for Protection Officers.* Retrieved from http://www.ifpo.org/arti clebank/lawprivateliaison.html

Hobijn, B., & Sager, E. (2007). What has homeland security cost? An assessment: 2001–2005. *Current Issues in economics and finance, 13*(2). Retrieved from http://www.newyorkfed.org/ research/current_issues/ci13–2/ci13–2.html

Johnson, K. (2009, May 17). Economy limiting services of local police. *USA Today.* Retrieved from http://www.usatoday.com/news/nation/2009– 05–17-police-closure_N.htm

Morabito, A., & Greenberg, S. (2005). *Engaging the private sector to promote homeland security: Law enforcement-private security partnerships.* Rockville, MD: Bureau of Justice Assistance Clearinghouse.

Nalla, M. K. (2009). *Police: Private police and industrial security—Scope of security work, nature of security work, legal authority, public vis-à-vis private police.* Retrieved from http://law .jrank.org/pages/1691/Police-Private-Police- Industrial-Security.html

Nalla, M. K., & Hwang, E. G. (2006). Relations between police and private security officers in South Korea. *Policing, 29*(3), 482.

Nasser, H. F. (1993, June 15). Stop the anti-white hatred and violence. *Cincinnati Post,* p. 9A.

Premo, R. (2002, April). City center solutions. *Security Management,* 85–92.

Prenzler, T., Earle, K., & Sarre, R. (2009). Private security in Australia: Trends and key characteristics. *Trends and Issues in Crime and Criminology, 374.*

Sherman, L. T. (1990). LEN interview: Lawrence Sherman. *Law Enforcement News, 16,* 9–12.

Tieman, M. (2006, May 3). Safe drinking water act: Implementation and issues. *Congressional Research Service.* Retrieved April 23, 2010, from http://www.policyarchive.org

Treat, R., & Bartle, A. (2009). New regulations drive expanded SCADA curriculum. *Pipeline & Gas Journal 236*(9). Retrieved April 23, 2010, from http://www.pipelineandgasjournal.com

Youngs, A. (2004). The future of public/private partnerships. *FBI Law Enforcement Bulletin, 73*(1), 7–12.

Zalud, B. (2009). Officers face more complex threats. *Security, 42*(2), 48–52.

Chapter 15

Alpert, G. P., & Dunham, R. G. (1992). *Policing urban America* (2nd ed.). Prospect Heights, IL: Waveland.

Alpert, G. P., & Dunham, R. G. (1997). *Policing urban America* (3rd ed.). Prospect Heights, IL: Waveland.

Barrett, M. (2006). The need for intelligence-led policing. *Domestic Preparedness.* Retrieved from www.domesticpreparedness.com

Beck, C., & McCue, C. (2009). Predictive policing: What can we learn from Wal-mart and Amazon about fighting crime in a recession. *The Police Chief, 76*(11), 20–29.

Bennett, C. W. (1993). The last taboo of community policing. *Police Chief, 60,* 86.

Birzer, M. L. (2003). The theory of andragogy applied to police training. *Policing: An International Journal of Police Strategies and Management, 26*(1), 29–42.

Braga, A. A., & Weisburd, D. (2006). Conclusion: Police innovation and the future of policing. In D. Weisburd & A. A. Braga (Eds.), *Police innovation: Contrasting perspectives.* New York: Cambridge University Press.

Brown, S. (2010). *Afghan national police discuss, plan future.* NATO Training Mission.

Combined Security Transition Command. Retrieved from http://www/ntm-a.com

Casady, T. (2009, November 24). Predictive policing. *The Chief's Corner.* Retrieved from http://lpd304.blogspot.com/2009/11/predictive-policing.html

Cetron, M. J., & Davies, O. (2008). 55 trends now shaping the future of policing. The *Proteus Trends Series, 1*(1), 1–200.

Chapman, R., & Scheider, M. C. (2008). *Community policing: Now more than ever.* Washington, DC: U.S. Department of Justice, Office of Community Oriented Policing Services. Retrieved from http://www.cops.usdoj.gov

Clarke, R. V., & Newman, G. R. (2007). Police and the prevention of terrorism. *Policing, 1*(1), 9–20.

Colvin, R. (2009, January 27). U.S. recession fuels crime rise, police chiefs say. *Reuters.* Retrieved from http://www.reuters.com

Community Oriented Policing Services. (2009). Mortgage crisis is affecting local property crime. *Community Policing Dispatch, 2*(2), 1–3. Retrieved from http://cops.usdoj.gov/html

Conser, J. A., & Frissora, G. G. (2007). The patrol function in the future—One vision. In J. Shafer (Ed.), *Policing 2020: Exploring the future of crime, community and policing* (pp. 173–208). Washington, D.C: U.S. Department of Justice, FBI, Police Futurist International

Crank, J. (1995). The community-policing movement of the early twenty-first century. In J. Klofas & S. Stojkovic (Eds.), *Crime and justice in the year 2010* (pp. 107–125). Belmont, CA: Wadsworth.

Department of Homeland Security. (2010). *Strategic plan.* Retrieved from http://www.dhs.gov/xabout/strategicplan/

Docobo, J. (2005). Community policing as the primary prevention strategy for homeland security at the local law enforcement level. *Homeland Security Affairs, 1*(1), 23–30.

Even cops losing their jobs in recession. (2009). *Associated Press.* Retrieved from http://www.msnbc.msn.com/id/31530751/ns/us_news-life/

Federal Bureau of Investigation. (2005). *Congressional testimony. Senate Judiciary Committee.* Washington, DC: U.S. Department of Justice. Retrieved from www.fbi.gov

Financial Crimes Enforcement Center. (2010). *US patriot act.* Washington, DC: U.S. Department of Justice. Retrieved from http://www.fincen.gov

Finnegan, W. (2005, July 25). The terrorism beat: How is the NYPD defending the city? *New Yorker, 81*(21), 58–71. In Clarke, R. V. & Newman, G. R. (2007). Police and the prevention of terrorism. *Policing, 1*(1), 9–20.

Fitzgerald, J. D., & Cox, S. M. (2002). *Research methods and statistics in criminal justice: An introduction* (4th ed.). Belmont, CA: Wadsworth./Thompson Learning.

Gatehouse News Service. (2010, March 24). State police to lay off more than 450 troopers. *Journal Star*, p. B 5.

Houde, G., & Cox, B. (2009, April 22). Police feel sting of recession: Departments pare programs, purchases to keep cops on streets. *Chicago Tribune.* Retrieved from http://www.policeone.com/pc_print.asp?vid=1813441

Jensen, C. J., & Levin, B. H. (2007). The world of 2020: Demographic shifts, cultural change, and social challenge. In J. A. Shafer (Ed.), *Policing 2020: Exploring the future of crime, community and policing* (pp.31–70). Washington, DC: U.S. Department of Justice, FBI, Police Futurists International.

Johnston, D., & Lipton, E. (2007, March 9). FBI criticized over use of Patriot Act. *The New York Times.* Retrieved from http://www.nytimes.com

Kelling, G. L., & Bratton, W. J. (2006). Policing terrorism. *Civic Bulletin, 43.* In Community Oriented Policing Services (2008). Community partnerships: A key ingredient in an effective homeland security approach. *Community Policing Dispatch, 1*(2), 1–3.

Kelling, G. L., Pate, T., Dieckman, D., & Brown, C. E. (1974). *The Kansas City preventive patrol experiment: A summary report.* Washington, DC: The Police Foundation.

Kenyon, H. (2010). DC police chief Cathy Lanier describes how technology is changing police work in the Capitol. *AFCEA International.* Retrieved from http://www.afcear.org

Lipman, I. A. (2010). The time for urgency is now. *Security Management, 54*(2), 2–7.

Martin, J. (2010, February 16). Tiny cameras seen as future in police work. *USA Today.* Retrieved from http://www.usatoday.com

Mastrofski, S. (2006). Community policing: a skeptical view. In D. Weisburd & A. A. Braga (Eds.), *Police innovation: Contrasting perspectives* (pp. 44–76). New York, NY: Cambridge University Press.

McGarrell, E. F., Freilich, J. D., & Chermak, S. (2007). Intelligence-led policing as a framework for responding to terrorism. *Journal of Contemporary Criminal Justice, 23.* Retrieved from http://ccj.sagepub.com/cgi/content/abstract/23/2/142

Ortiz, C. W., Hendricks, N. J., & Sugie, N. F. (2007). Policing terrorism: The response of local police agencies to homeland security concerns. *Criminal Justice Studies: A Critical Journal of Crime, Law and Society, 20*(2), 91–109.

Peak, K. J. (2009). *Policing America: Challenges, and best practices.* Upper Saddle River, NJ: Pearson Prentice-Hall.

Perlman, E. (2008). Policing by the odds. *Governing.* Retrieved from http://www.governing.com

Ruderman, J. (2008). Looking toward agencies of the future: Standard technology for one department may be a vision of the future. *Officer.com.* Retrieved from http://www.officer.com

Simonsen, C., & Spindlove, J. (2000). *Terrorism today: The past, the players, the future.* Upper Saddle River, NJ: Prentice-Hall.

Stephens, G. (2005). Policing the future: Law enforcement's new challenges. *The Futurist, 39*(2), 51–58.

Thibault, E. A., Lynch, L. M., & McBride, R. B. (2007). *Proactive police management* (7th ed.). Upper Saddle River, NJ: Pearson Education.

U.S. Census Bureau. (2000). Population projections of the total resident population by quarter. Washington, DC: Statistical Information Staff, Population Division. Retrieved from http://www.census.gov/population/projections/nation/summary/np-t2.txt

U.S. Department of Justice. (2000). *Office of the police corps and law enforcement education.* Washington, DC: Author. Retrieved from http://www.ojp.usdoj.gov/opclee

U.S. Department of Justice. (2009). *Solicitation: Predictive policing demonstration and evaluation program.* Washington, DC: Author. Retrieved from http://www.ncjrs.gov/pdffiles1/nij/s1000877.pdf

U.S. General Accounting Office. (2001). *Homeland security: Key elements of a risk management approach.* Washington, DC: U.S. Government Printing Office.

Vodde, R. F. (2009). *Andragogical instruction for effective police training.* Amherst, NY: Cambria Press.

Photo Credits

Photo 1.1a © Bettmann/CORBIS

Photo 1.1b © iStockphoto.com/David Lentz

Photo 1.2 © Bettmann/CORBIS

Photo 1.3 © J. Gerard Sidaner/Photo Researchers, Inc.

Photo 2.1 © TANNEN MAURY/epa/Corbis

Photo 2.2 © J. Gerard Sidaner/Photo Researchers, Inc.

Photo 2.3 © iStockphoto.com/vm

Photo 3.1a © iStockphoto.com/Sebastien Cote

Photo 3.1b © iStockphoto.com/Lisa F. Young

Photo 3.2 © Spencer Grant/Photo Researchers, Inc.

Photo 3.3 © Steve Liss/Time Life Pictures/Getty Images

Photo 4.1 © Guy Cali/Corbis

Photo 4.2 © iStockphoto.com/Frances Twitty

Photo 4.3 © iStockphoto.com/tillsonburg

Photo 5.1 © iStockphoto.com/Song Speckels

Photo 5.2 © Gusto/Photo Researchers, Inc.

Photo 5.3 © David R. Frazier/Photo Researchers, Inc.

Photo 6.1 © iStockphoto.com/Lisa F. Young

Photo 6.2 © iStockphoto.com/Nancy Louie

Photo 6.3 © Gene Blevins/LA Daily News/Corbis

Photo 7.1 © Spencer Grant/Photo Researchers, Inc.

Photo 8.1 © iStockphoto.com/Nicholas Belton

Photo 8.2 © Larry W. Smith/Stringer/Getty Images News/Getty Images

Photo 8.3 © iStockphoto.com/Deborah Cheramie

Photo 9.1 © Gene Scaramella

Photo 9.2 © Steve Starr/CORBIS

Photo 9.3 © iStockphoto.com/Joey Boylan

Photo 10.1 © Spencer Grant/Photo Researchers, Inc.

Photo 10.2 © Bettmann/CORBIS

Photo 10.3 Courtesy of the Skokie, Illinois Police Department

Photo 11.1 © iStockphoto.com/Brett Hillyard

Photo 11.2 © George Steinmetz/Corbis

Photo 11.3 © New York Daily News Archive/Contributor/New York Daily News/Getty Images

Photo 12.3 Courtesy of the U.S. Air Force, http://www.kirtland.af.mil/

Photo 13.1 © iStockphoto.com/Terraxplorer

Photo 13.2 © Horace Bristol/CORBIS

Photo 13.3 © HO/Reuters/Corbis

Photo 14.1 © Bettmann/CORBIS

Photo 14.2 © Brian Donnelly/Corbis

Photo 14.3 © Ramin Talaie/Corbis

Photo 15.1 © iStockphoto.com/Jonathan Parry

Photo 15.2 © Christopher Pillitz/Reportage/Getty Images

Photo 15.3 © David Butow/CORBIS SABA

Index

About the Authors

Gene L. Scaramella currently serves as the Dean of Academic Programs at Ellis University and is proud to have served as a police officer in the Chicago metropolitan area for more than 15 years. His areas of academic foci include organized and white collar crime, research methodologies, and policing. He can be reached by e-mail at GScaramella@ellis.edu

Steven M. Cox earned his BS in psychology, MA in sociology, and PhD in sociology at the University of Illinois in Urbana/Champaign. Dr. Cox was a member of the Law Enforcement and Justice Administration faculty at Western Illinois University from 1975 to 2007. For the past 40 years, he has served as trainer and consultant to numerous criminal justice agencies in the United States and abroad and has worked with several universities in the area of course development. In addition, Dr. Cox has authored or co-authored numerous books and articles.

William P. McCamey has been a professor in the School of Law Enforcement and Justice Administration since 1982. Dr. McCamey earned a BS and MA in Law Enforcement Administration and a PhD in Higher Education Administration at the University of Iowa in Iowa City. His primary areas of teaching include criminal justice management, policing, and online fire administration courses for the National Fire Academy. Dr. McCamey has served as a criminal investigator and police trainer and has co-authored two other books and numerous journal articles.